COUNTRYSIDE LAW IN SCOTLAND

Edited by

Jeremy Rowan-Robinson

*Professor of Planning and Environmental Law, University of Aberdeen
Consultant in Planning and Environmental Law,
Paull & Williamsons, Solicitors*

and

Donna W. McKenzie Skene

Senior Lecturer in Law, University of Aberdeen

T&T CLARK
EDINBURGH
2000

T&T CLARK LTD
59 GEORGE STREET
EDINBURGH EH2 2LQ
SCOTLAND

First published 2000

ISBN 0 567 00538 0

British Library Cataloguing-in-Publication Data.
A catalogue record for this book is available from the British Library.

—

Typeset by Waverley Typesetters, Galashiels
Printed and bound in MPG Books, Bodmin

PREFACE

There is said to be an ancient Chinese curse "may you live in interesting times", and for those involved in the use, development and management of Scotland's countryside, these are undoubtedly interesting times. Within its wider plans for land reform generally, the Scottish Executive is bringing forward a trilogy of reforms having particular relevance to rural areas: rural communities are to have a stronger role in land management decisions that affect them; Scotland is to have its first national park; and there is to be a general right of access to the countryside. Other changes are also in the pipe-line: in particular, the arrangements for safeguarding sites of nature conservation and landscape importance are under review.

This is, therefore, an exciting time to bring forward a book looking at countryside law in Scotland. Although it is a time of change, the changes will take some time to carry through, and a primary purpose of this book is to provide a context for them and for the continuing discussions surrounding them. Furthermore, notwithstanding the significance of these reforms, much of the law relating to the countryside will remain unchanged. In view of the current interest in this area, this seems an appropriate point in time to gather together the various strands that make up our countryside law.

In one sense, of course, there is no such thing as countryside law: there is no separate body of law relating specifically to the countryside as opposed, for example, to the town. What is meant here by countryside law, however, is the law relating to the principal rural land uses. Inevitably, given the range of activity carried on in the countryside, there will be some rural land uses which are not covered, but we have tried to be as comprehensive as possible and to cover the most important areas as we saw them. Furthermore, because of the range of subjects covered, the book may seem, at first glance, to lack an obvious coherence, but again this is perhaps inevitable given the subject-matter, and we hope that the first two chapters provide an overall context for the remainder.

We embarked on this book with the intention that it should be of interest and use to a number of different audiences including the legal profession, those involved in the use, development and management of the countryside, those engaged in policy formulation and students of relevant disciplines. The contributors accordingly aimed to make the text sufficiently detailed to be of use to the legal profession while providing sufficient in terms of context, policy and observation to be of interest and use to a non-legal audience, and we hope and believe that they have struck an appropriate balance in this respect.

The pace of change in the areas to which we have already drawn attention made it particularly difficult to determine at which date to state the law, and in the end we selected 1 July 1999. Inevitably, there have been some changes since then. It was possible to take account of some of these in the individual chapters. There are other changes to which reference should be made. First, with regard to Chapter 7 "Forestry", it should be noted that the Environmental Impact Assessment (Forestry) (Scotland) Regulations 1999 (SSI 1999/43) have replaced the 1998 Regulations. The new Regulations have essentially the same structure and effect as the 1998 Regulations but there are some important differences. Most significantly, the 1999 Regulations apply not only to afforestation but also to deforestation, that is conversion from woodland to another land use. The Regulations also include thresholds below which projects will only exceptionally be regarded as having significant effects on the environment and thus requiring a formal assessment. The thresholds vary according to the sort of project and whether it is in a sensitive area, such as an SSSI or a European site, and in several cases the threshold is set at zero. Second, the new Rural Development Regulation (EC 12/57/1999 OJ L160/80) is in place reflecting the recent reforms to the Common Agricultural Policy. At the time of writing the precise implications of the Regulation are unclear. Third, the Water Industry Act 1999 was brought into effect, so far as it applies to Scotland, on November 1, 1999. The Act gives effect to the recommendations of the review of the Scottish industry carried out in 1997. It establishes a Water Industry Commissioner for Scotland who has the general function of promoting the interests of customers of water and sewerage authorities. The Commissioner replaces the Water and Sewerage Customer Council established under the Local Government etc. (Scotland) Act 1994. The Act also establishes a Water Industry Consultative Committee for each of the water and sewerage authorities.

In bringing this book together we have been fortunate in the support and encouragement we have received from many people and we are pleased to be able to acknowledge this. We are particularly grateful to Dr Ian Jardine, John Thompson and Peter Pitkin of Scottish Natural Heritage; to Christopher Bond, Martin Ritchie and Morris Fraser of the Scottish Executive Rural Affairs Department; to Ian Mitchell of the Scottish Executive Development Department; to Neil Davidson and Martyn Cox of the Crown Estate; to the staff in the Taylor Law Library at Aberdeen University, particularly Valerie Stevenson, Liz Mackie and Alison Steed; and to David Fletcher and Dr Carole Dalgleish of T & T Clark. We are also indebted to our families and friends for their patience.

Jeremy Rowan-Robinson
Donna McKenzie Skene

School of Law
University of Aberdeen

CONTENTS

THE AUTHORS

Douglas Cusine holds a law degree from the University of Glasgow. He is a solicitor and at the time of writing was Professor of Conveyancing and Professional Practice of Law at the University of Aberdeen and a member of the Council of the Law Society of Scotland. He is now Sheriff of Grampian, Highland and Islands at Peterhead.

Hew Dalrymple is a partner in the Private Client Department of Brodies WS, Edinburgh, specialising in all aspects of rural property law and private client work including agriculture, minerals and taxation. He studied law at the University of Edinburgh and joined Brodies WS as an apprentice in 1975 becoming a partner in 1980.

Sharon Fitzgerald is a solicitor working for Masons and is based in their Glasgow office. She works in the firm's Projects Team which is involved with PFI projects in relation to various areas including water, health and education. She has a PhD from the University of Strathclyde.

Derek Flyn was a Sheriff Clerk from 1962–72 including three years at Portree. He then took an LLB degree at the University of Dundee before entering practice as a solicitor with Macleod and MacCallum in Inverness where he specialises in crofting law. In 1990 he co-authored with D.J. MacCuish the first textbook on the subject for more than 50 years. He is the vice-chairman of the Crofting Law Group and President (1999–2000) of the Scottish Law Agents Society, the largest voluntary organisation in Scotland.

Christopher Hardie holds an LLB (Hons) degree from the University of Dundee. He was admitted as a solicitor in 1979 and joined Brodies WS in 1991 where he is an associate specialising in rural property law. He is also a keen fisherman.

Sheonagh Hill holds an LLB (Hons) degree and a Diploma in Legal Practice from the University of Edinburgh. She is currently an associate with Brodies WS specialising in agricultural matters, principally quotas and European subsidies.

Kathryn Last holds the degrees of LLB (Hons) and PhD from the University of Sheffield. Formerly a lecturer at the University of Durham, she is currently a lecturer at the University of Dundee where she specialises in nature conservation law, cultural heritage law and English law of property and trusts.

Donna McKenzie Skene holds an LLB (Hons) degree and Diploma in Legal Practice from the University of Aberdeen. Having qualified as a solicitor, she practised in Aberdeen and Peterhead, specialising in civil court work, until 1992, when she returned to the University of Aberdeen to take up a lectureship in law. Now a senior lecturer in law, her main research interests are in the fields of insolvency law and countryside law. Recent publications in the area of countryside law include "Civil Liability for Injury and Damage Arising from Access to the Countryside" (with Jeremy Rowan-Robinson and Anne-Michelle Sanders), 1997 SLPQ 214, 274; "Self Help and Access to the Countryside" (with Jeremy Rowan-Robinson), 1998 JR 299; and "Stewardship: From Rhetoric to Reality" (with Jeremy Rowan-Robinson, Roderick Paisley and Douglas Cusine), 1999 ELR 151. "Environmental Regulation and the Role of the Common Law: A Scottish Perspective" (with Jeremy Rowan-Robinson) is due to be published in *Environmental Protection and the Common Law*, eds J. Lowry and R. Edmunds, later this year.

Adele Nicol holds an LLB degree and a Diploma in Legal Practice from the University of Aberdeen. She is an associate at Brodies WS specialising in all aspects of rural property law.

Christina Philp holds a BSc (Hons) degree in Ecology from the University of Sheffield and an LLM in Environmental Law and Management from the University of Wales, Aberystwyth. She is currently in the Law School at the University of Aberdeen researching the implementation of the Habitats Directive for her PhD.

Colin Reid is Professor of Environmental Law at the University of Dundee, where he has taught since 1991 after beginning his academic career at the University of Aberdeen. He has written widely on environmental law issues, notably on nature conservation and forestry, as well as on matters of public law. He was a founder member of the UK Environmental Law Association, established and convenes an environmental law section within the leading association of academic lawyers, and serves on several editorial boards.

Jack H.B. Robertson holds a BSc degree in Marine Resource Management and an LLM in Environmental Law from the University of Aberdeen. He was previously a fisheries scientist at the Scottish Office Agriculture, Environment and Fisheries Department where his responsibilities included the formulation of regulations for European and UK fisheries technical measures. He is currently undertaking research for a book on the conservation and legal regimes for global marine fisheries.

Andrea Ross holds an LLB degree from Osgoode Hall Law School in Toronto and worked as a solicitor in Ontario before graduating from the University of Aberdeen with an LLM in Environmental Law. She is currently a lecturer with the Department of Law at the University of Dundee specialising in the public law aspects of environmental law.

Jeremy Rowan-Robinson is Professor of Planning and Environmental Law in the Aberdeen University Law School and a Consultant in Planning and Environmental Law with Paull and Williamsons, Solicitors. He holds an MA from the University of Kent and an LLM from the University of Aberdeen. He is a Solicitor of the Supreme Court of England and Wales and a Legal Associate of the Royal Town Planning Institute. He practised in local government as a solicitor for 10 years initially in London and then with the Lake District Special Planning Board. He moved to Aberdeen University in 1978 and was, for a while, Head of the Department of Land Economy. His main research interests have been in the fields of planning, compulsory purchase and compensation, environmental and countryside law, and he is author or co-author of seven books and numerous articles in these areas. He is a member of the main board of Scottish Natural Heritage and chairman of the Access Forum.

Carolyn Shelbourn holds an LLB (Hons) degree and Master of Jurisprudence degree from the University of Birmingham. She is a lecturer at the University of Sheffield where she currently teaches environmental law, planning law, and heritage and conservation law. Her research interests include the protection of the historic built environment and of archaeological sites and finds, and issues of art and law. She is an Associate Member of the Institute of Historic Building Conservation and a member of the Institute of Art and Law.

Maria de la Torre took a law degree at the Universidad Complutense (Madrid) and is a member of the Law Society of Madrid. After completing an LLM in environmental law at the University of Aberdeen she worked as a researcher and teaching assistant in environmental law in the Department of Land Economy and in the Law School at the University. She subsequently secured an ESRC studentship and is currently researching the role of the law in habitat protection for her PhD.

TABLE OF CASES

TABLE OF STATUTES

TABLE OF
STATUTORY INSTRUMENTS

TABLE OF
INTERNATIONAL LEGISLATION

EUROPEAN DIRECTIVES

TABLE OF
CIRCULARS, PANs AND NPPGs

CHAPTER 1

INTRODUCTION

Jeremy Rowan-Robinson
Donna McKenzie Skene

Scotland's countryside is one of its greatest assets. The outstanding and diverse land and seascapes, the variety of habitats and the wealth of species are a major attraction for visitors and are of substantial economic value. They are also important for those who live and work in Scotland. The countryside exerts a strong cultural influence and contributes significantly to the quality of life. It is an important workplace. It is the focus of a variety of resource-based industries such as agriculture and forestry, mining and quarrying and conventional and alternative energy sources. The countryside is a major recreational asset, both for organised sport such as hunting, shooting and fishing, and for more informal recreation such as walking, mountaineering, canoeing, sailing, skiing, cycling and riding. It is also home for a small but growing proportion of the population (1.5 million in 1996), whether those who commute to the major urban areas, those who live and work in the less populated intermediate areas and those who make up the small and sometimes scattered communities of the more remote rural areas.

This book is about the law governing the use, development and management of the Scottish countryside. It looks at the principal public sector agencies exercising powers and duties with regard to the countryside; explains the law relating to activities such as agriculture, forestry, crofting and land development; examines how the law works to protect landscapes, species, habitats and archaeological sites; draws attention to the principal environmental controls; describes the law applying to organised sports such as hunting, shooting and fishing; considers the application of the law to informal recreation on land and water; and assesses developments in the law with regard to the coastal zone. Its concern, therefore, is with rural Scotland, the land outwith urban areas, and not just with the "open country" as defined in section 10(2) of the Countryside (Scotland) Act 1967.[1]

The law is an important means of delivering government policy objectives for rural Scotland. In this introductory chapter we look in general terms at these

---

[1] As amended by the Countryside (Scotland) Act 1981, s. 2.

1

policy objectives and at some of the proposals for change. More specific policies for particular land uses are touched on in the appropriate chapters. The law provides a framework within which these general and specific policy objectives can be achieved. It sets out to shape behaviour between individuals and between individuals and the state. Much of this chapter is given over to consideration of the way in which the law works, or could work, to achieve these objectives.

Responsibility for Scottish countryside matters has been devolved to a very large extent following the coming into force of the Scotland Act 1998 (see Chapter 2). Although much of the current legislation refers to the Secretary of State for Scotland and much of the policy documentation refers to the Scottish Office, reference should now be made to the Scottish Executive. The Scottish Executive comprises the First Minister and such Ministers as the First Minister may appoint, together with the Lord Advocate and the Solicitor General for Scotland (section 44(1)). The members of the Scottish Executive are collectively referred to as "the Scottish Ministers" (section 44(2)). In day-to-day practice, interest is likely to focus on the Scottish Minister having particular responsibility for a countryside matter (referred to in this book simply as "the appropriate Minister" or "the Minister") and the appropriate constituent department of the Scottish Executive. Scottish countryside matters fall to quite a large extent within the remits of the Scottish Executive Rural Affairs Department and the Scottish Executive Development Department.

Policy for the countryside

In *Towards a Development Strategy for Rural Scotland* the Government states that "the overall aim of all our policies for rural Scotland is to foster and enable the sustainable development of rural communities".[2] Two of the terms employed in this statement require further consideration. These are "sustainable development" and "rural communities".

Sustainable development

"Sustainable development" is a term which is appearing increasingly in policy statements and which is beginning to appear in legislation.[3] As it lies at the heart of government policies for rural Scotland, and as the law provides a means of delivering these policies, it is a term which deserves attention. Sustainable development is a very generalised concept and, as such, gives rise to definitional problems. The generality of the term means that different and sometimes competing interests can embrace it with confidence. It is a term which might be said to have "Humpty Dumptyish" qualities. "When *I* use a word", Humpty Dumpty said in *Through the Looking Glass* in rather a scornful tone, "it means just what I choose it to mean—neither more nor less".

---

[2] *Towards a Development Strategy for Rural Scotland: The Framework* (Scottish Office, 1998), p. 2.
[3] See the Natural Heritage (Scotland) Act 1991, s. 1(1) which requires Scottish Natural Heritage (SNH) to have regard to the desirability of securing that anything done, whether by SNH or any other person, in relation to the natural heritage of Scotland is undertaken in a manner which is "sustainable"; and the Environment Act 1995, s. 31(3) which requires the Scottish Environment Protection Agency (SEPA) to have regard to guidance issued by the Minister with regard to the contribution which SEPA can make towards achieving sustainable development.

The most widely cited definition of the term was provided in the Bruntland Report[4]:

"development that meets the needs of the present without compromising the ability of future generations to meet their own needs".

The concept was endorsed at the UN Conference on Environment and Development at Rio de Janeiro in 1992 and is central to the Fifth Action Programme on the Environment adopted by the European Commission in 1992. The concept offers the prospect of a beneficial relationship between environmental resource conservation and economic development.[5] However, there is no doubt that the concept requires considerable refinement if it is to guide policy formulation and decision-making in the countryside. Pearce *et al.* draw a distinction between weak and strong sustainable development.[6] In this discussion, we do not use the terms "weak" and "strong" in any pejorative sense, but as an indication of the policy approach. Both definitions require the passing on to the next generation of an aggregate capital stock no less than the one that exists now. The distinction between them is that weak sustainable development is indifferent to the form in which we pass on the capital stock. As has been observed, with weak sustainable development:

"all forms of capital may be substituted for each other so that environmental capital may be traded for economic or other goals of society. Strong sustainable development, on the other hand, accepts that there are limits to the extent to which environmental capital may be substituted by man-made capital. On this approach, certain environmental assets may be defined as 'critical natural capital' in the sense that they are critical to our well-being and survival. Strong sustainable development involves the protection of critical natural capital".[7]

In *Towards a Development Strategy for Rural Scotland* sustainable development is defined as "development that is planned with appropriate regard for its longer term consequences, for example in relation to the environment, but can lead to further opportunities and a higher quality of life for rural people". The paper goes on to say that this means action on three fronts: economic, social and environmental. It is not entirely clear but the approach seems to bear the hallmarks of weak sustainable development in which environmental capital may be substituted for economic or social goals of society. Certain environmental capital, for example Sites of Special Scientific Interest, may be protected but they are not sacrosanct. This approach would seem to be reinforced by the recent report of

---

[4] *Our Common Future* (World Commission on Environment and Development), 1987.

[5] P. Healey and T. Shaw, "Planners, plans and sustainable development" (1993) 27 *Regional Studies* 769.

[6] D. Pearce, R. Turner, T. O'Riordan, N. Adger, G. Atkinson, I. Brisson, K. Brown, R. Durborg, S. Frank-Hauser, A. Jordan, D. Maddison, D. Moran and J. Powell, *Blue Print 3* (Earthscan, 1993). See too M. Jacobs, *The Green Economy* (Pluto, 1991); A. Blowers, "The environment—political problem with no solution" (1990) 61 *Town and Country Planning* 132; and J. Rowan-Robinson, A. Ross and W. Walton, "Sustainable development and the development control process" (1995) 66(3) *Town Planning Review* 269.

[7] J. Rowan-Robinson *et al.*, op. cit.

the Land Reform Policy Group, *Recommendations for Action* (see below).[8] This states that the objective of land reform is "to remove the land-based barriers to the sustainable development of rural communities". It goes on to say that in practice sustainable development will consist of development which is planned with appropriate regard for local communities, local employment and the environment. Again, it is not altogether clear but the statement and the remainder of the report seem to sit more comfortably with weak rather than strong sustainable development. Indeed, it would seem to be a particularly weak expression of the term in that it appears to have lost sight of inter-generational equity.

An attempt to refine the concept in a stronger form is to be found in *Sustainable Development and the Natural Heritage*.[9] This policy paper gives guidance on Scottish Natural Heritage's (SNH) approach to discharging its duty under section 1(1) of the Natural Heritage (Scotland) Act 1991 to "have regard to the desirability of securing that anything done, whether by SNH or any other person, in relation to the natural heritage of Scotland is undertaken in a manner which is sustainable" (see Chapter 2). The paper states, among other things, that non-renewable resources should be used wisely and sparingly, at a rate which does not restrict the options of future generations and that renewable resources should be used within the limits of their capacity for regeneration. In situations of great complexity or uncertainty we should act in a precautionary manner.

Perhaps the important point which emerges from the employment of "sustainable development", whether strong or weak, at the heart of government policy for rural communities is that it emphasises the need for an holistic approach to policy formulation and decision-making which, in terms of rural land use and management, values all aspects of the countryside. In the meantime, the Government has commissioned research to refine the application of the concept to different policy areas.[10]

Rural communities

The second term used in the statement of policy which requires consideration is "rural communities". The term is problematic for two reasons. First of all, it appears to oppose urban and rural, town and country, and to imply that there are two distinct societies with distinct interests. The very title of this book, *Countryside Law in Scotland*, may suggest that there is one law for people in the country and another for those in towns. The policy statement emphasises that this apparent opposition between town and country is not intended. It is not the purpose of government policy to set rural Scotland apart; it is more a question of adjusting policies and mechanisms of delivery to take account of rural conditions. There is a precedent for such an approach. The Select Committee on Scottish Affairs in its influential report on *Land Resource Use in Scotland*[11] distinguished urban from rural land use but emphasised that this was for convenience only and that the inevitable closeness and the importance of the inter-relation between

---

  [8] (Scottish Office, 1999).
  [9] (Scottish Natural Heritage, 1993).
  [10] *Towards a Development Strategy for Rural Scotland* (Scottish Office, 1998).
  [11] Session 1971–72 (HMSO, 1972).

town and country should be recognised. There are, however, distinctive rural conditions. Obvious distinctions include the pattern of the rural economy, the density and distribution of the population, the problems of service provision and the incidence of important natural resources. All of these conditions require responses which may differ in form and degree from those appropriate in urban areas; and these responses are reflected in the law which we have gathered together in this book.

Second, the term raises the question "what is a community?". The recent focus of interest on community ownership (see below) might suggest, for example, that it applies to the more remote rural settlements. Of course, it includes such communities; but the term goes much further than that, as the recent report of the Land Reform Policy Group recognises. In promoting increased involvement in the way land is owned and used, the Group recognises that what is meant by "community" will depend on the context:

> "In some cases it will be right to define this quite narrowly, in terms of those who live and/or work on the land in question. In other cases, it should also include all those whose livelihoods are affected by the management of an area of land. In other circumstances the issue is community involvement in wider decision-making, where the right definition may be in terms of the local rural partnership or community council. Broader communities of interest also exist, for example those with a specific conservation interest, and those visiting the area."[12]

This diversity of community is reflected in this book. It is concerned with the law as it applies to landowners, tenant farmers and crofters, to those promoting the development of land, to those engaged in hunting, shooting and fishing, to those concerned with the protection of species and habitats, and to those taking access to land and water.

Reform of countryside policy

There is, of course, nothing static about countryside policy. It is constantly evolving. So too is the law. What is unusual at the time of writing is the pace of change. Proposals for the reform of the law relating to access to the countryside and of the regime for protecting Sites of Special Scientific Interest are discussed in the appropriate chapters. There are, however, two other important reforms which do not fit neatly into other chapters and which are, therefore, mentioned now. These are the recommendations of the Land Reform Policy Group for land reform and the recommendations of Scottish Natural Heritage with regard to the establishment of national parks.

Land reform

In 1997, the then Secretary of State for Scotland set up the Land Reform Policy Group (LRPG) under the chairmanship of Lord Sewell. The remit of the Group was:

---

[12] *Recommendations for Action* (Scottish Office, 1999), para. 1.3.

"To identify and assess proposals for land reform in rural Scotland, taking account of their cost, legislative and administrative implications and their likely impact on the social and economic development of rural communities and on the natural heritage."

The Group has been working concurrently with the Scottish Law Commission which has put forward detailed proposals for the abolition of the feudal system[13] and for the reform of the law relating to real burdens.[14] The LRPG issued two consultation papers, *Identifying the Problems* and *Identifying the Solutions*, before submitting its report, *Recommendations for Action*, in January 1999. Even before it had reported, the Secretary of State for Scotland, in the Fifth John McEwen Memorial Lecture on Land Tenure in Scotland,[15] committed himself to taking forward the process of land reform: "we can now move forward from talking about land reform to doing something about it. At last it is time for action not just words".

In line with the Government's development strategy for rural areas (see above), the LRPG proposed that the central objective of land reform should be to remove the land-based barriers to the sustainable development of rural communities. To achieve this the Group proposed two broad principles: (1) increased diversity in the way in which land is owned and used; and (2) increased community involvement in the way land is owned and used, so that local people are not excluded from decisions which affect their lives and the lives of their communities. Its specific agenda for legislation included:

- power for duly constituted community bodies to have a community right to buy land in rural areas of special importance as and when it changes hands and at a price to be set by a government-appointed valuer;
- a period of time for the community to assess whether it wants to buy such land when it comes to be sold;
- a new compulsory purchase power for Scottish Ministers to help deter evasion of these proposals. The sort of situation which the Group appeared to have in mind was where the beneficial ownership of land was transferred for value in cases where the community should have been given the opportunity to purchase it.

Further non-legislative action to achieve the objective was also identified. This included:

- the preparation of a code of good practice for rural landownership, compliance with which should wherever possible become a condition of public assistance;
- the preparation of a code of good practice on rural land use setting out standards for land uses such as agriculture, forestry, sporting and conservation as appropriate;

---

[13] *Report on Abolition of the Feudal System*, Scot. Law Com. No. 168 (1999).
[14] *Discussion Paper on Real Burdens*, No. 106 (1998).
[15] September 4, 1999 (unpublished).

- a requirement for all public bodies with rural landholdings to involve local communities in the formulation and implementation of plans for the management of the land;
- encouragement to public bodies to use compulsory purchase powers as a last resort when this will assist implementation of local plans or other strategies;
- the establishment of a Scottish Land Fund to support community action.[16]

The items on the LRPG agenda for legislation referred to above have now been adopted by the Scottish Executive in a White Paper published in July 1999.[17] The Scottish Landowners' Federation is resisting strongly the proposed power to acquire land at a price to be set by a government-appointed valuer. However, it is by no means completely opposed to reform. Indeed, it has produced its own "draft code of practice for responsible land management".[18] This acknowledges that there are responsibilities associated with the ownership and management of land, recognises that there is a community interest and a wider public interest in how land is managed, and accepts that land should be managed with proper regard for nature and nature's processes. Compliance with the code is seen as a way of improving the quality of land management and raising public confidence in stewardship of the countryside.

National Parks

One of the most striking features of countryside policy in Scotland has been the absence until now of National Parks. This seems likely to change with enabling legislation coming forward in the first session of the Scottish Parliament. The legislation will mark the culmination of a debate which began with the report of the Addison Committee in 1931.[19] The Committee examined the case for National Parks and concluded that, with the exception of the Cairngorms, parks on the North American model were not feasible in Britain. It confirmed the need for new measures to protect the countryside and promoted two kinds of park: the first to make better provision for recreation near where people live; and the second to protect scenery and wildlife. The proposals foundered in the depression of the 1930s.

The end of the Second World War saw the revival of the countryside movement. In 1945 the Dower Report recommended the establishment of a series of National Parks in England and Wales and this was reflected in due course in the National Parks and Access to the Countryside Act 1949. In the same year the National Parks Survey Committee, under the chairmanship of Sir Douglas Ramsay, made a similar recommendation for Scotland[20] and these recommen-

---

[16] Highlands and Islands Enterprise has now established a Land Purchase Fund to complement the work of its Community Land Unit. The Government is contributing £1 million annually to the fund over the next three years. Scottish Enterprise is to follow this lead.

[17] Scottish Executive, *Land Reform Proposals for Legislation* (HMSO).

[18] January 1999.

[19] For a full description of the debate about National Parks in Scotland see G.E. Cherry, *Environmental Planning 1939–1969*, Vol. II (*National Parks and Recreation in the Countryside*) (HMSO, 1975); and D. Mackay, *Scotland's Rural Land Use Agencies* (Scottish Cultural Press, 1995), Chap. 9.

[20] Cmd. 6631 (1945).

dations were developed in the report of the Scottish National Parks Committee under the same chairmanship in 1947.[21] Five parks were proposed in:

- Loch Lomond and the Trossachs;
- Ben Nevis, Glen Coe and the Black Mount;
- Glen Affric, Glen Cannich and Strath Farrar;
- the Cairngorms; and
- Torridon, Loch Maree; and Loch Broom.

Ramsay laid considerable emphasis on a role for state ownership of land in the parks and favoured freedom of access to open moorland. However, the proposals ran into opposition from powerful landowning interests and this, combined with a lack of consensus over the effect of visitor pressures, lukewarm support from the local authorities and the relatively weak amenity and access lobby, was sufficient to frustrate any further progress. Instead, the five Ramsay areas were designated as National Park Direction Areas in 1951, a safeguarding arrangement giving the Secretary of State oversight of planning decisions in the area.

There the matter rested until resurrected by the Select Committee on Land Resource Use in 1972 during the hearing of evidence from the Countryside Commission for Scotland (CCS). CCS recognised that more effective arrangements were required for safeguarding landscape quality and for promoting informal recreation. In 1974 the Commission published *A Park System for Scotland*. This proposed a hierarchical park system with a top tier of "Special Parks" comprising areas of outstanding scenery which were under heavy recreational and other pressures. The term "National Park" was studiously avoided; it was said to be incompatible with the classification used by the World Conservation Union. These areas were identified as Loch Lomond and the Trossachs, the Cairngorms, and Ben Nevis and Glen Coe. A lower level of "Recreational Parks" was also proposed and it was acknowledged that some designation was required for other areas of national scenic quality which were not under such pressure. The proposal for Special Parks was rejected by the Government. Recreational Parks were eventually given effect through the provisions for "Regional Parks" in the Countryside (Scotland) Act 1981 (see Chapter 3). Work on a further land-scape designation was carried forward and in 1978 CCS published *Scotland's Scenic Heritage* which identified 40 areas of national scenic quality. These were subsequently designated as National Scenic Areas,[22] a designation which carried certain planning consequences (see Chapter 3). The National Park Direction Areas were cancelled.

National Parks were subsequently restored to the agenda for CCS in 1989 by Lord James Douglas Hamilton, then Minister for Home Affairs and the Environment at the Scottish Office. He requested CCS to "study management arrangements for popular mountain areas such as the Cairngorms, taking into consideration the case for arrangements on national park lines in Scotland". The outcome was the report *The Mountain Areas of Scotland*, published by CCS in

---

[21] Cmd. 7235 (1947).
[22] SDD Circulars 20/1980 and 9/87.

1990. The report concluded that there were four areas which required special management arrangements because of their high heritage value and that they should be designated National Parks. The areas were:

- the Cairngorms;
- Loch Lomond;
- Ben Nevis, Glen Coe and the Black Mount;
- Wester Ross.

However, after an extensive consultation exercise the Government decided not to take the proposals any further at that time. It concluded that the Commission had failed to establish sufficient local commitment for the concept in the areas to be designated; nor had it demonstrated how the structures proposed would resolve the problems identified.[23]

Nothing further happened until 1997 when Lord Sewell, then Minister for Agriculture, Fisheries and the Environment at the Scottish Office, stated that there was an important gap in Scotland's present designation system for the care of a few large areas which were of national importance for their outstanding natural heritage and for the opportunities they provided for enjoyment by the public. National Park designation would be the best way forward for Loch Lomond and the Trossachs, he said, quite probably also for the Cairngorms, and possibly for a few other areas as well. Scottish Natural Heritage was asked to advise on how National Parks could best operate.

Following consultation on the matter, SNH responded in February 1999 with *National Parks for Scotland*.[24] The report advanced the following statement of purposes:

> "National Parks in Scotland are areas of outstanding natural heritage of special importance to the nation where management in perpetuity will:
>
> - safeguard and enrich the biodiversity, natural beauty and amenity, the natural systems which support these qualities, and the cultural heritage of the area;
> - promote the sustainable use of its natural resources;
> - promote the social well-being and economic prosperity of its local communities; and
> - provide for and enrich the enjoyment and understanding by the public of its natural and cultural values.
>
> These purposes should be pursued in ways which are mutually supportive. The resolution in the event of any conflict between them shall be guided by a precautionary approach in favour of the long-term conservation of the natural resources" (para. 3.5).

When compared with the objectives of National Parks in England and Wales, the statement is unusual in putting the social well-being and economic prosperity of

---

[23] D. Mackay, *Scotland's Rural Land Use Agencies* (Scottish Cultural Press, 1995), p. 166.
[24] Scottish Natural Heritage's Advice to Government, January 1999.

the local communities alongside the other purposes. However, mindful of the fate of the report on *The Mountain Areas of Scotland* in 1990 and having regard to the emphasis on community development in government policy discussed above, this would seem to be realistic. The statement also recognises that these purposes may not always be compatible and, as in England and Wales, gives priority to the long-term conservation of natural resources in the event of irreconcilable conflict. The report sees the development and implementation of a National Park plan as essential for the achievement of National Park purposes (para. 3.15). The establishment of a new National Park body for each park is recommended but it is suggested that the appropriate distribution of functions (including the difficult matter of planning functions) between the new body and other existing bodies, particularly local authorities, is something that should vary from park to park (para. 4.2). The report also suggests that, while an independent authority would probably be the best approach in most circumstances, the structure of the National Park body is something that could be tailored to the specific needs of each area (para. 4.26). Specific proposals are put forward with regard to the powers, structure and geographic area of National Parks for Loch Lomond and the Trossachs and for the Cairngorms. No specific proposals are made for other areas given the present lack of overwhelming support; but the report recommends that the designation of further areas should be kept under review (para. 7.3).

In a speech in February 1999, the then Secretary of State for Scotland announced that he was accepting SNH's advice as the basis on which to prepare proposals for legislation by the Scottish Parliament. Enabling legislation is to be brought forward at an early date.

Mechanisms for achieving policy goals

So far in this chapter we have been considering government policy for the Scottish countryside and proposals for reform. However, as this is a book on Scottish countryside law, our main interest is in the way in which the law works to deliver these policy goals, including the way in which it impacts on existing rights of landowners at common law. The individual chapters explain in detail how the law works in the context of particular areas of countryside policy. In the remainder of this chapter we propose to look in a general way at the sort of legal mechanisms that can be employed to achieve policy goals.

There are, of course, different ways in which the Government may intervene to achieve its purposes. The LRPG first consultation paper identified a number of options. These included public acquisition, legal barriers to adverse activity (ie regulation), financial penalties, financial incentives, and other more miscellaneous forms of intervention. These options can be further refined to incorporate a change in the nature of landownership itself and to separate designation from regulation. These options are now considered in turn[25]; but it is important to note that in practice two or more of the options may work in combination to achieve a particular purpose.

---

[25] For a detailed discussion of the different options for intervention in a rural context see D. McKenzie Skene, J. Rowan-Robinson, R. Paisley and D. Cusine, "Stewardship: From Rhetoric to Reality", 1999 *Edinburgh Law Review* 151.

Altering the nature of landownership

At the present time, most land in Scotland, urban or rural, is held under a system of tenure that is feudal in origin. The person normally referred to as the owner of land is the vassal, the holder of the *dominium utile*. The vassal comes at the bottom of the chain of feudal relationships which has the Crown as ultimate superior and any number of mid-superiors between the Crown and the vassal. A key element of the Government's land reform programme is the abolition of the feudal system[26] and a Bill to achieve this is to be brought forward in the first session of the Scottish Parliament. In effect, proprietors will become absolute owners of their land.

Notwithstanding the draft code of practice prepared by the Scottish Landowners' Federation referred to above, landownership in Scotland is generally perceived to be about rights rather than responsibilities. Gordon identifies two substantive rights which are implied in the ownership of land.[27] First of all, there is the right to the exclusive use of the land. This goes to the heart of the current debate about public access to the countryside because the corollary of the right is that, subject to limited exceptions, other people have no right to use the land and may be excluded by the owner on the basis that their actions constitute either encroachment or trespass (see Chapters 12 and 14).[28] Second, a landowner has the right to use and enjoy the land, including the right to grant the use and enjoyment to someone else. This means that, subject to what is said below, choices about the use, development and management of land rest with the landowner. Although particular landowners may have regard to the wider public interest when formulating proposals and making decisions, the important point is that the decision rests with them. These rights will not change with the abolition of the feudal system; indeed, it may be perceived to enhance them. Not surprisingly, these substantive rights underpin the discussion in a number of the chapters of this book.

The statement that landownership is about rights rather than responsibilities must, however, be seen in its wider context. These rights are subject, at present, to any rights retained by the Crown as feudal superior and also to the rights of the Crown as sovereign (see below). They may also be qualified by any real burdens that attach to the land and by any subordinate or third party rights that may have been created. In addition, they are qualified by the extent to which the Government has seen fit to intervene to regulate activity through legislation and, as we shall see in the individual chapters of this book, such intervention has been quite extensive.

One way of achieving public policy goals would be to qualify the essential nature of landownership so that ownership would be about responsibilities as well as rights. This has been the subject of discussion in the context of stewardship.[29] There have been suggestions that the public interest in the use, development and management of land could be secured through the imposition of a

---

[26] LRPG, *Recommendations for Action* (Scottish Office, 1999), para. 2.2.

[27] W.M. Gordon, *Land Law* (Scottish Universities Law Institute, 1989), para. 13.03.

[28] This right will be qualified by the general right of public access to all land which the Government is committed to introducing (*Land Reform: Proposals for Legislation* (Scottish Executive, July 1999), part 7; and see Chap. 14).

[29] See D. McKenzie Skene *et al.*, op. cit., n. 25.

stewardship obligation. Wightman[30] and Callender,[31] for example, both call for a redefinition of private rights of ownership so as to provide a proper balance between public and private interests.[32] Incorporating a stewardship obligation into the essential nature of landownership would, it is argued,[33] switch the focus of attention away from who owns land to how land is managed: "[t]he obligation would come with the land itself irrespective of the nature or proclivities of the owner".[34]

This could be achieved by augmenting the role of the Crown, thus making a single change at the top of the system which would affect all those further down the chain. The Crown is referred to here in its capacity as the executive government and not as the monarch in her individual capacity. The role of the Crown could be augmented by adjusting its role as landowner holding the paramount feudal infeftment. However, this is unrealistic in view of the imminent demise of the feudal system. The alternative would be to augment the role of the Crown in its capacity as sovereign. The sovereign capacity of the Crown is apparent in a number of significant cases, including public rights of way, public rights of recreation, whitefishing and navigation in respect of the foreshore and seabed.[35] These public rights are held by the Crown not as its exclusive property but in trust for the general public as beneficiaries.[36] The Crown's responsibility in respect of these existing public rights has emerged as a result of centuries of development of the common law but could be expanded by statute to encompass a stewardship obligation or some general public interest obligation in the use, development and management of land.

The nature of any such obligation would require careful consideration, as would the method of enforcement.[37] So too would the question of compensation. In the UK there is no constitutional safeguard such as exists in many countries providing for full compensation for expropriation. Here the question whether a particular restriction on rights amounts to a compensatable event is a policy decision, the outcome of which will be reflected in legislation. There is, however, a well-established judicial presumption in interpreting such legislation that an intention to take away the property of a subject without full compensation is not to be imputed to the legislature in the absence of clear wording.[38] However, the alteration in the nature of ownership consequent on the introduction of a stewardship or other general obligation would be not so much an expropriation as regulation. Although the picture is not entirely consistent,[39] the general position

---

[30] A. Wightman, *Who Owns Scotland* (Canongate, 1996), p. 208.

[31] R. Callender, *How Scotland is Owned* (Canongate, 1998), p. 37.

[32] See too the press release by the World Wide Fund for Nature of April 30, 1998 and the response of Scottish Natural Heritage to the LRPG first and second consultation papers.

[33] D. McKenzie Skene *et al.*, op. cit., n. 25.

[34] Ibid.

[35] W.M. Gordon, op. cit., n. 27, paras 24–105 to 24–154 and 27–05 to 27–07.

[36] Ibid, para. 24–106.

[37] See D. McKenzie Skene *et al.*, op. cit., n. 25.

[38] *Burmah Oil Co. (Burma Trading) Ltd* v *Lord Advocate* 1964 SC (HL) 117; 1964 SLT 218; *Tiverton and North Devon Railway Co.* v *Loosemore* (1884) 9 App Cas 480, HL; *Attorney General* v *Horner* (1884) 14 QBD 245; *Cannon Brewery Co. Ltd* v *Gas Light and Coke Co.* [1904] AC 331, HL; *Colonial Sugar Refining Co. Ltd* v *Melbourne Harbour Trust Commissioners* [1927] AC 343, PC; *Bond* v *Nottingham Corporation* [1940] 1 Ch 429.

[39] See J. Rowan-Robinson and A. Ross, "Compensation for Environmental Protection in Britain: a Legislative Lottery", 1993 5(2) *Journal of Environmental Law* 245.

is that the mere regulation of property rights does not qualify for compensation in the absence of a specific provision to that effect.[40] The European Convention on Human Rights, which would also need to be considered, appears to draw the same distinction between expropriation (compensable) and regulation (not compensable).[41]

Acquisition of the right of ownership or a lesser right

The second way in which government could intervene to secure public policy goals would be through the acquisition of land or the acquisition of some lesser right. A number of the public bodies exercising powers and duties in relation to the countryside already have power to acquire land. For example, Scottish Natural Heritage (SNH) has power to acquire land either by agreement[42] or compulsorily[43] and in Chapter 11 it is suggested that there are certain limited circumstances in which SNH may be required now to exercise these powers.

In the late 1960s the former Highlands and Islands Development Board contemplated invoking its compulsory powers to intervene in cases where poor estate management affected the well-being of local communities, only to be advised that its powers were insufficient.[44] An attempt in the late 1970s to acquire more effective powers to intervene in the land market came to nothing.[45] Now the climate has changed. The LRPG report *Recommendations for Action* advocates the granting of compulsory powers to Ministers to support the community acquisition of land, and this has been taken up in the recent White Paper *Land Reform: Proposals for Legislation*[46] (see above). The LRPG report also recommends explicit support for the use of compulsory powers as a last resort by public bodies to assist the implementation of local plans and other strategies.

An alternative to land acquisition by public bodies would be for such bodies to support the acquisition of land by others who would hold it in the public interest. Highlands and Islands Enterprise and SNH, for example, both supported the recent acquisition by the local community of the Knoydart Estate. Other means of supporting the community acquisition of land were referred to earlier in this chapter during the discussion of land reform. The Government is proposing legislation to assist local communities to enter the land market by conferring a right to buy land in certain circumstances at a price to be set by a government-appointed valuer as and when an owner chooses to dispose of it. And it is not just local communities whose objectives as landowners may coincide up to a point with public policy. Both Wightman[47] and the LRPG note a recent marked increase in land ownership in Scotland by voluntary conservation bodies

---

[40] *France Fenwick & Co.* v *The King* [1927] 1 KB 458; *Belfast Corporation* v *OD Cars Ltd* [1960] AC 490; *Westminster Bank Ltd* v *Minister of Housing and Local Government* [1971] AC 508.

[41] See Arts 1 and 8.

[42] Natural Heritage (Scotland) Act 1991, s. 2(1).

[43] National Parks and Access to the Countryside Act 1949, s. 17, and Natural Heritage (Scotland) Act 1991, s. 5.

[44] M.G. Lloyd and D.M. Shucksmith, "Economic development and land policies in the Highlands and Islands of Scotland" (1985) 2 *Land Use Policy* 114.

[45] Ibid; and see "Proposals for changes in the Highlands and Islands Development (Scotland) Act 1965 to allow more effective powers over rural land use" (HIDB, 1978).

[46] (Scottish Executive, July 1999), paras 5.1–5.7.

[47] A. Wightman, op. cit., n. 30, Chap. 12.

(see Chapter 11) whose conservation objectives share some common ground with those pursued by government.

It will sometimes be possible to achieve public interest goals through the creation of a right which falls short of ownership. The LRPG, for example, recommends that land ownership should in appropriate cases be subject to "conditionality".[48] This proposal is not enlarged on although it is linked to the Scottish Law Commission's proposals for the reform of real burdens.[49] A number of models of "conditionality" already exist which allow for the control of activity on land in the wider public interest. For example, section 49A of the Countryside (Scotland) Act 1967 enables SNH or a planning authority to enter into an agreement with a landowner to provide for the doing of "whatever in the opinion of the parties may be necessary to secure the conservation and enhancement or to foster the understanding and enjoyment of the natural heritage of Scotland". If recorded, these agreements are enforceable against successors in title. Other examples of statutory agreements are given in Chapters 4 and 11.

Another example is paragraph 7 of the Schedule to the National Trust for Scotland Confirmation Act 1938. This enables the Trust to enter into agreements with persons having an interest capable of binding land with a view to "restricting the planning, development or use of the land". Such agreements may bind the land permanently for a specified period and, if recorded, may be enforced by the Trust against successors in title. The conditions restricting the planning, development or use of the land are to be in conformity with the purposes for which the Trust was established, which include the promotion, for the benefit of the nation, of the preservation of lands and buildings in Scotland of historic or national interest or natural beauty and of access to them by the public. Considerable use has been made of such agreements by the Trust and thousands of hectares of the countryside and miles of coastline are protected in this way.

The Scottish Law Commission Discussion Paper on *Real Burdens*[50] proposes that the range of existing statutory agreements might be replaced, or at least supplemented, by a general provision allowing categories of public bodies to enter into "conservation burdens". The difficulty with this proposal and, indeed, with the existing statutory agreements, is that they rely on the voluntary approach to achieve public purposes. If the landowner cannot be persuaded to enter into an agreement, the public interest will not be secured. This has been recognised and in some instances provision is made for compulsorily creating a right which falls short of acquisition where negotiation fails. For example, if a planning authority is unable to negotiate an access agreement or a public path creation agreement, it may make an access or public path creation order; and if a utility is unable to negotiate a wayleave for its apparatus, it may promote a compulsory "servitude" (see Chapter 18). Although the powers available to the utilities seem to work well enough, there has been very limited experience with the use of such powers in the context of access to the countryside. Not only are there procedural and resource disincentives but the fear is that the compulsion is likely to be anathema to the sort of partnership approach that these arrangements necessitate (see Chapters 13 and 14).

---

[48] *Recommendations for Action*, p. 33.
[49] *Discussion Paper on Real Burdens*, No. 106 (1998).
[50] Ibid, paras 2.56–2.60.

Designation

The purpose of designation is to flag up areas which have been singled out as special in some way. As will be clear from the chapters which follow, designation is widely employed in the Scottish countryside. Natural resource management, in particular, relies heavily on designation.[51] Such designations include:

- Special Areas of Conservation;
- Special Protection Areas for Birds;
- National Nature Reserves;
- Local Nature Reserves;
- Marine Nature Reserves;
- Sites of Special Scientific Interest;
- Ramsar Sites;
- World Heritage Sites;
- National Scenic Areas;
- Natural Heritage Areas;
- Areas of Great Landscape Value;
- Environmentally Sensitive Areas;
- Forest Parks;
- Nitrate-Sensitive Areas;
- Nitrate-Vulnerable Zones;
- National Heritage Property;
- Regional Parks;
- Country Parks.

As we mentioned earlier, National Parks may shortly be added to this list; in addition, planning authorities in their development plans operate an informal zoning arrangement of which Green Belts provide an example.

The consequences of designation vary. Ramsar Sites and World Heritage Sites, for example, are non-statutory designations and have no legislative significance (Chapter 11). Generally, however, designation will be linked to one or other of the legal instruments described in this chapter. Environmentally Sensitive Areas and Nitrate-Sensitive Areas, for example, are linked to financial incentives (Chapter 4). Owners and occupiers may receive payments for agreeing to carry on farming operations in an environmentally benign way. Nature Reserves and Country Parks are areas to which regulation through byelaws may be applied. The designation of an area as a Site of Special Scientific Interest invokes a limited form of regulation through the requirement to give prior notification of a proposal to carry on certain operations and may also trigger a financial incentive (Chapter 11); it also carries some development control significance. The classification of an area as National Heritage Property opens the door to inheritance tax relief, a

---

[51] See generally *Natural Heritage Designations in Scotland* (Scottish Office, 1998).

financial incentive (Chapter 11). Green Belts are designated in a planning authority's development plan. The designation itself has no statutory significance but will have an important influence on the regulation of development in such areas. National Scenic Areas were designated by the Scottish Office and are principally a development control designation (Chapter 3); they also trigger limited procedural safeguards. National Parks, like Regional Parks, will be areas which, because of their characteristics, are subject to particular objectives. A special management structure is introduced in such areas to achieve those objectives. The designation of an area as a Special Area of Conservation or a Special Protection Area for Birds will trigger the rigorous control of activity through the Conservation (Natural Habitats etc.) Regulations 1994 (Chapter 11).

Confusingly, it is not uncommon to find a site which is subject to multiple designations. A site may, for example, be a candidate Special Area of Conservation, a Special Protection Area for Birds, a Nature Reserve, a Site of Special Scientific Interest and a National Scenic Area. The boundaries may not be identical, but there could be substantial overlap.

Regulation

Regulation might be regarded as the conventional means of seeking to control the use, development and management of land in the public interest. Such an approach has the advantage that the characteristics of regulation are well known and there is general acceptance that the Government must intervene in the wider public interest to regulate activity from time to time. The ownership and occupation of land in the countryside is already subject to a certain amount of regulation, although not to the same extent as in urban areas.

Regulation can be made to apply to all land or just to land falling within certain categories identified, for example, through a designation scheme. Some systems of regulation are triggered by lists, for example the lists of protected species drawn up under Part I of the Wildlife and Countryside Act 1981 (see Chapters 8 and 10) or the list of buildings of architectural or historic interest or the schedule of ancient monuments (see Chapter 16). Most systems of regulation, whether or not they are linked to a designation or a list, operate through a requirement to obtain a permit. Activity is proscribed in the absence of the permit. This sort of approach is very much at the heart of planning (Chapter 3) and pollution control (Chapter 4). It is essentially a preventive approach to environmental protection. An application for a permit will have to be accompanied by sufficient information to enable the regulator to assess the likely impact of what is proposed. In some cases, the information requirement can be extensive, such as when a development proposal has to be accompanied by an environmental statement (see Chapter 3). The permit itself, if granted, will often be subject to conditions designed to control the way in which the activity is carried on. Sanctions will be provided for in the legislation in the event of a breach of control.

A disadvantage of regulation is that it can create a climate of confrontation rather than co-operation. It is for this reason that the European Union Fifth Action Programme on the Environment advocates a broadening of the range of instruments employed to secure environmental protection. The Programme notes that "whereas previous environmental measures tended to be prescriptive in character with an emphasis on the 'thou shalt not' approach, the new strategy leans more towards a 'let's work together' approach".[52]

Financial penalties

With one exception, financial penalties are not currently employed as instruments for securing public interest goals in the countryside[53]; indeed quite the reverse. Reliance is placed instead on financial incentives to bring about behavioural change (see below).

The exception is the landfill tax introduced by the Finance Act 1996. This may be said to apply to the countryside only in the sense that many landfills are located outside or on the edge of the towns and cities. The principal objective of the tax is to reduce the amount of waste disposed of to landfill. To achieve this a tax is paid by the operator of a landfill, levied on the weight and composition of the waste disposed of in this way. The cost is passed on to the producers of the waste in the form of increased charges for disposal.

Increasing interest is beginning to be shown at both European and domestic levels in financial penalties as a means of achieving policy goals. There have been proposals for a Green Belt tax to be levied on developers building on green field sites,[54] a tax on pesticides is under consideration (see Chapter 4) and draft legislation for an aggregates tax to compensate for some of the landscape implications of mineral workings has been published by H.M. Customs and Excise.[55] The aggregates tax will be introduced if the Quarry Producers Association fails to come up with a satisfactory package of voluntary measures to mitigate the impact of quarrying on the countryside.[56] Any tax regime, as with the landfill tax, would need to be clearly and comprehensively provided for in legislation.

A paper on *Economic Instruments for Water Pollution*, published jointly by the Scottish Office, the Department of the Environment, Transport and the Regions, the Welsh Office and the Department of the Environment for Northern Ireland in 1997, points out the advantage of financial penalties when compared with conventional regulation. Such penalties "make clear to polluters the wider cost of their polluting activities. In short, they aim to demonstrate the 'price' of environmental damage and make polluters pay accordingly. Polluters then have a choice between paying that price or taking action to reduce their pollution".[57] The paper gives the example of product charges which could, for example, be used to increase the cost to farmers of using fertilisers and pesticides. This in turn would reduce their level of use and thus the level of pollution from these sources.

It has been suggested that one difficulty in using financial penalties to protect and enhance the public interest in land is the need to put a price on those interests.[58] Although economists have made considerable advances in the use of

---

[52] *Towards Sustainability*, COM(92)23 (1993).

[53] It should be noted that permit procedures are increasingly passing on the cost of operating the procedures to applicants through an application fee and this is sometimes put forward as an example of "the polluter pays" and might be classed as a form of financial penalty.

[54] *The Independent*, January 20, 1998.

[55] www.hmce.gov.uk.

[56] *Scottish Environment News*, May 1999.

[57] Executive summary, para. 8.

[58] D. McKenzie Skene *et al.*, op. cit., n. 25.

pricing mechanisms, their application to the landscape and to aspects of the public interest such as nature conservation remain controversial, and some aspects of the natural heritage may be considered so sacrosanct that no price should be put on it.

Financial incentives

Financial incentives are used extensively to secure the management of land in the countryside in the wider public interest. Indeed, so extensive are these provisions that it is reasonable to suggest that there is a real danger of confusion between the agricultural support schemes, the agri-environment schemes and schemes directed at habitat protection. Rodgers and Bishop observe that the number of grant schemes aimed at encouraging environmentally beneficial land management has proliferated in the last 15 years and that they are administered by a variety of government agencies.[59] Indeed, where land is covered by more than one designation, they note that it is possible for incentives to be available simultaneously under several different schemes. They found that this can give rise to particular difficulties where negotiations under the different schemes are confidential. The commonest problem they encountered was where an agreement for an Environmentally Sensitive Area had been concluded with one government agency, the details of which were confidential and unknown to another government agency negotiating an agreement for a Site of Special Scientific Interest on the same land with the same landowner.

The role of the law with financial incentives is concerned with setting up the legislative framework within which the incentives are paid and with securing that the benefits, for which payment is made, are delivered. These incentives take various forms. For example, in Chapter 4 reference is made to payments made to farmers in Environmentally Sensitive Areas and under the Countryside Premium Scheme for having regard in the conduct of their farming operations to the natural heritage; in Chapter 5 the various subsidies to promote agricultural production are described; in Chapter 7 the operation of the woodland grant scheme is considered; and in Chapter 11 the payments for profits forgone by owners and occupiers in Sites of Special Scientific Interest are discussed; mention is also made of the relief from inheritance tax which is available in respect of National Heritage Property.

The mechanism commonly employed to secure that, in return for the payment, the benefits are delivered is the management agreement. Such agreements impose legally binding obligations. They are used in Environmentally Sensitive Areas, under the Countryside Premium Scheme, in Sites of Special Scientific Interest and for National Heritage Property. Such agreements generally have a statutory basis; and, if entered into with a person capable of binding the land and subsequently recorded in the Register of Sasines or the Land Register for Scotland, they can be enforced not only against the original contracting party but against successors in title.

The use of agreements to secure public benefits contrasts with systems of regulation.[60] Regulation involves an open, objective permit process quite often

---

[59] C. Rodgers and J. Bishop, *Management Agreements for Promoting Nature Conservation* (RICS, 1998).
[60] See A. Ross and J. Rowan-Robinson, "Behind Closed Doors: The Use of Agreements in the UK to Protect the Environment" (1999) 1(2) *Environmental Law Review* 82.

involving public notice, access to information and an opportunity for public participation. It is a process to which the well-established principles of administrative law apply. Agreements, on the other hand, involve an essentially private contractual process, a "behind the scenes" negotiation from which the public are likely to be excluded. The opportunties for access to information and public participation will be limited. There are no generally established procedural safeguards; there are no appeal mechanisms except, in some cases, with regard to the level of payment; and it is uncertain how far, if at all, such agreements are open to judicial review

However, the benefits of using financial incentives coupled with agreements to achieve behavioural change and to create a favourable climate for co-operation in promoting the public interest should not be underestimated. It relies, though, on the willingness of owners and occupiers to recognise and promote the public interest. While some will be genuinely interested in doing so and others will be persuaded by the financial benefits, co-operation has not always been forthcoming and the resource implications of negotiating co-operation can be considerable.[61] There have also been reservations about a system which, with regard to Sites of Special Scientific Interest, rewards someone simply for agreeing not to damage the natural heritage and the Government's recent consultation paper on this issue advocates, *inter alia*, a move towards a more conventional system of regulation.[62] The LRPG also in effect expressed reservations about continuing to rely so heavily on the voluntary approach as a way of achieving the good management of land. It suggests that this form of control could be strengthened by extending the cross-compliance mechanisms which already exist in a number of cases to ensure that, in all cases where grants and subsidies are paid, public assistance is conditional on compliance with a code of good practice on rural land use.[63]

Codes of practice and other mechanisms

Although normally having no legal force,[64] codes of practice deserve mention in the context of mechanisms for achieving public policy goals because they are increasingly being used to complement legislative provisions. For example, they are used quite widely to promote environmentally sound agricultural practice. As we mentioned earlier during the discussion of land reform, the LRPG has recommended the introduction of two codes of practice.[65] The first is a code of good practice for rural landownership dealing with such matters as relations with local communities. It is proposed that compliance with the code should, where appropriate, become a condition of public assistance. The second, to which we have just referred, is a code of good practice on rural land use setting out standards for land uses such as agriculture, forestry, sporting and conservation.

---

[61] L. Livingstone, J. Rowan-Robinson and R. Cunningham, *Management agreements for nature conservation* (Department of Land Economy Occasional Paper, Aberdeen University, 1990).

[62] *People and Nature* (Scottish Office, 1998).

[63] *Recommendations for action* (Scottish Office, 1999), s. 7.

[64] Exceptionally, regulators will have to, in certain circumstances, act in accordance with guidance produced by the Minister in connection with the contaminated land regime introduced by Part IIA of the Environmental Protection Act 1990 (as amended by the Environment Act 1995)—when the regime eventually takes effect.

[65] *Recommendations for action* (Scottish Office, 1999), s. 7.

Again, it is proposed that compliance with the code should become a condition of public assistance.

A further example is provided in the report submitted to the Government by Scottish Natural Heritage on *Access to the Countryside for Open-Air Recreation* (1999). This recommends that the proposed general right of access to land for informal recreation and passage should be supported by a new Scottish Countryside Code. The report recommends that the code should have a clear foundation in secondary legislation and should be "the reference point for the definition of responsible behaviour by all parties" (para. 25). In other words, the implications of the general right contained in primary legislation will be unpacked in the code of practice.

Codes of practice are both useful and convenient. Their advantage is that they are flexible, those whose behaviour is to be regulated can be involved in drafting and implementation, they are written in everyday language and they are readily adjusted to meet changing conditions and to reflect experience in practice. Their disadvantage is a lack of status; they are for guidance and are not normally binding.

Consultation is another mechanism which is employed to bring particular public interests into the decision-making process. A number of public bodies exercise functions which may have an impact on other areas of the public interest in relation to the countryside and a requirement to consult with the bodies responsible for those other areas is a common device. For example, planning authorities, the Capital Taxes Office, the Forestry Authority and the Scottish Executive Rural Affairs Department are all required to consult with Scottish Natural Heritage in defined circumstances. Consultation will generally be built in to some other instrument for achieving policy goals, for example regulation and financial incentives. It is employed as a mechanism for tackling the problem of fragmentation in the discharge of countryside functions (see Chapter 2). However, it is implicit in consultation that the matter consulted about is only one of a number of factors to be taken into account by the consulting body. The position of the consultee can, however, be strengthened by requiring a reference to the appropriate Minister in the event of a disagreement between the consulting and the consulted body.

Finally, statements of intent deserve mention. Considerable interest is being shown at domestic and European levels in the use of such statements, sometimes referred to as voluntary agreements, as a means of introducing control into a new area with a minimum of effort. Typically the Government will negotiate with the appropriate representative body for a sector of industry and agree environmental targets to be achieved. The outcome of the negotiation will be reflected in an agreement, in effect a statement of intent. The representative body will then be responsible for ensuring that those targets are achieved by its membership. Several such agreements are currently in operation.[66] The Concordat on Access[67] entered into by Scottish Natural Heritage, landowning interests and

---

[66] For example, the Department of the Environment has entered into an agreement with the appropriate trade association representing the aerosol, foam and fire extinguishing equipment industries to control the use of greenhouse gases in the manufacture and operation of such equipment.

[67] *Scotland's Hills and Mountains: a Concordat on Access* (1996).

a number of the leading recreational bodies is an example of a statement of intent in a rural context. Still at draft stage is the statement of intent by the Quarry Producers Association. The Association has been asked to put together a voluntary package of measures to mitigate the external impact of quarrying activities.[68]

Statements of intent avoid the need for legislation and, apart from the initial negotiation and subsequent monitoring, require no input of public resources. They place on the target group the onus of demonstrating that the voluntary approach can work. It would seem to be implicit in the approach that a failure to deliver the targets could be followed by a more formal means of intervention. The Quarry Producers Association, for example, has been threatened with an aggregates tax if it cannot establish a voluntary agreement.[69]

This discussion of the range of instruments which can be employed to achieve public policy goals for the countryside is intended to set the context for the chapters which follow. These chapters examine in detail the law relating to particular aspects of the use, development and management of the countryside and, with the exception of financial penalties, all of the instruments which have been described will be encountered. Before embarking on this examination of the law, however, it is appropriate to introduce the principal public sector bodies with responsibilities for countryside functions. This is the purpose of Chapter 2.

---

[68] *Scottish Environment News*, May 1999.
[69] Ibid.

CHAPTER 2

THE INSTITUTIONAL FRAMEWORK

Andrea Ross

Introduction

In Chapter 1 reference was made to landowners' right to the use and enjoyment of their land. Mention was also made of the public interest in the use, development and management of Scotland's countryside and of the constraint which public interest can place on the owners' right. Quite a lot of this book is devoted to an explanation of the way in which the public interest, whether in safeguarding the natural heritage, protecting ancient monuments, preventing pollution or promoting access, is secured.

The purpose of this chapter is to introduce the bodies principally responsible for promoting public policy and securing the public interest goals in the countryside. Its focus is on the structure and organisation of these bodies and on their functions. For some of the bodies, the manner in which these functions are discharged and the mechanisms which are employed to discharge them (see Chapter 1) are detailed in later chapters.

Historically in rural Scotland the promotion of public policy goals has evolved in a piecemeal fashion. Some of these goals, particularly those focused on dominant rural land uses such as agriculture and forestry, have been pursued through central government departments. Others, such as planning control, have been the responsibility of local government. Others still, such as environmental protection, nature conservation, the promotion of recreation, water supply, deer management and, to quite a large extent, economic development, have been given in large measure to non-departmental public bodies (NDPBs). As Mackay observes, the number and variety of distinctive agencies with a finger in the pie of rural land use in Scotland is remarkable[1] and this deserves some comment.

There is, of course, nothing very new about the setting-up of specialist bodies to carry out specialist functions. The use of NDPBs to perform public functions is often justified on two grounds. First of all, NDPBs can focus on their tasks free from the sort of day-to-day political control to which government departments

---

[1] D. Mackay, *Scotland's Rural Land Use Agencies* (Scottish Cultural Press, 1995), p. 8.

and the Scottish Executive are subject. NDPBs have been described as government "at arm's length".[2] This allows for a relatively single-minded approach to the discharge of functions. Secondly, the system of appointing rather than electing members to these bodies enables a measure of expertise to be brought to the discharge of what is quite often a fairly specialist task—whether it is safeguarding the nature conservation interest, overseeing the management of Scotland's deer herd or setting standards for the control of pollution. Harlow and Rawlings summarise the advantages of using such bodies:

> "Independence from, or an arm's length relationship with, government is said to facilitate the continuity of, and flexibility or responsiveness in, policy formulation and implementation, as also a disinterested expertise; in addition, that is, to helping to deflect criticism or political responsibility and reducing government overload. The specialist, multifunctional agency fits well the model of regulation as sustained and focused control."[3]

The advantage of expertise is reinforced in some instances by a legislative requirement to draw membership from people with knowledge of the work that the agency is to discharge. For example, the Forestry Act 1967 provides that the Forestry Commissioners must include at least three having special knowledge and experience of forestry, at least one with scientific attainments and technical knowledge of forestry and one with special knowledge and experience of the timber trade.[4] And in making appointments to Scottish Natural Heritage, the Minister is to have regard to the desirability of ensuring that the membership of SNH contains at any time, so far as is practicable, persons of knowledge or experience relevant to the principal areas of activity of SNH.[5]

Reliance on NDPBs, however, is not without criticism. There are issues of institutional legitimacy or accountability.[6] They have been described as undemocratic, powerful bodies who make important decisions without any need to account. Harlow and Rawlings note that "semi-autonomy undermines the doctrine of ministerial responsibility by blurring the division of responsibilities between Ministers and the chief executives of agencies".[7] A further criticism is the opportunities for patronage. This criticism has been partly addressed following recommendations made by the Nolan Committee on Standards in Public Life in its First Report.[8] The Conservative Government in December 1995 appointed an independent Commissioner for Public Appointments to monitor, regulate and approve departmental appointment procedures to executive non-departmental public bodies. The Commissioner has issued guidance to government departments and to the Scottish Executive which includes a requirement to announce appointments through press notices and other suitable means. Details of appointments are made available to the public.[9]

---

[2] See A. Davies, *What's Wrong with Quangos?* (Outer Circle Policy Unit, 1979), p. 3.
[3] C. Harlow and R. Rawlings, *Law and Administration* (Butterworths, 2nd edn, 1997), p. 308.
[4] Forestry Act 1967, s. 2(2).
[5] Natural Heritage (Scotland) Act 1991, Sched. 1, para. 4.
[6] See generally, Davies, op. cit., n. 2.
[7] Harlow and Rawlings, op. cit., n. 3, p. 21
[8] Nolan Committee on Standards in Public Life, First Report, Cm. 2850-1.
[9] Public Appointments Unit Home Page http://www.open.gov.uk/pau/pauhome.htm.

There is a further problem in relying heavily on special bodies to discharge special tasks and that is the risk of fragmentation. The Select Committee on Scottish Affairs in its report on Land Resource Use in Scotland in 1972[10] observed that:

"We were impressed by the quality and high purpose of the many organisations and individuals who submitted evidence to us. Within the spheres of their special land use interests they were excellent, but always the main matter with which we were concerned kept recurring—how far was the optimum land use being furthered through institutions that were predominantly separate and sectional in their standpoint and whether greater advantage might not accrue from lessening the separateness? That optimum land use was not being achieved in many spheres seemed clear to us; the separate standpoint of the farmer and the forester is an example that could be duplicated many times where we thought and think that the marrying of interests would produce a better and longer lasting advantage to the nation. It seemed to us that our problem was to find a way of lessening separateness."[11]

The Government, in its response to the Select Committee report, acknowledged the problem and the need for improvement and committed itself to promoting closer liaison between the various agencies.[12] A Standing Committee on Rural Land Use was established to help deliver this closer liaison. It achieved no more than limited success. Problems of fragmentation or "separateness" continued to emerge. In 1986 a very public row broke out between the Nature Conservancy Council on the one hand and the Forestry Commission and the Highlands and Islands Development Board on the other over proposals for afforestation in the Flow Country, a large peat covered area comprising 45 per cent of the land of the counties of Caithness and Sutherland. The question at issue was how much forestry was appropriate in this area characterised by a variety of habitats. The details of the row are beyond the scope of this chapter and are described elsewhere.[13] The matter was eventually resolved through negotiation. There is little doubt, however, that it was an important factor in the decision to break up the Nature Conservancy Council as a UK body and establish a separate Nature Conservancy Council for Scotland and, subsequently, Scottish Natural Heritage.

A further well-publicised example of fragmentation occurred at about the same time when an application for forestry grant in respect of 640 hectares of land at the Glenlochay Estate was refused on nature conservation grounds.[14] The Nature Conservancy Council found itself liable to the landowner for compensation in respect of the frustrated scheme amounting to around £700,000, a sum which took into account the grant to which the landowner would otherwise have received. The case highlighted the absurdity of the interrelation

---

[10] Select Committee on Scottish Affairs, *Land Resource Use in Scotland*, Vol. 1, Session 1971–72, para. 445.

[11] Ibid, para. 445.

[12] Cmnd. 5428 (1973).

[13] Mackay, op. cit., n. 1, pp. 114–116.

[14] Ibid, pp. 116–117.

between the grant and compensation regimes operating at that time which effectively placed landowners in a "win, win" situation.[15] The same point had been picked up by the House of Commons Select Committee on the Environment in 1985:

> "By the offer of capital grants and the working of the price support mechanism farmers are, in effect, actively encouraged by MAFF policy to damage the environment. DOE, NCC or a local planning authority then enter the arena and have to fight against that pressure by compensating them . . . The illogicality of one part of government (MAFF) offering financial inducement to someone to do something which another part of government (DOE and related bodies) then has to pay him not to is clear."[16]

The problems of fragmentation are being tackled in several ways. At a general level, fragmentation is being challenged by the drive to promote sustainable development at all levels of state action. Sustainable development requires a more holistic view which, in terms of rural land use and management, values all aspects of the countryside: environmental, economic and social, for the benefit of this generation and future generations. This is emphasised in *No Small Change— Sustainable Development in Scotland*, published by the Scottish Office in 1997, which provides that: "It is not enough to take account of environment alone, we need to think about social and community aspects and we need to maintain a strong economy. That is the kernel of sustainable development."[17]

More specifically, fragmentation is being tackled through some measure of integration, through greater strategic guidance from the centre, through the introduction of balancing obligations, through greater cross-compliance and through increased consultation. These are considered briefly in turn.

First of all, an attempt to promote greater integration in the pursuit of public policy goals, while still retaining the benefits of specialist bodies operating at arm's length from central government, may be seen in the amalgamation of the Countryside Commission for Scotland with the Nature Conservancy Council for Scotland in 1991 to form Scottish Natural Heritage (SNH).[18] SNH brings together responsibilities for nature conservation, countryside recreation and, to a lesser extent, landscape protection. The bringing together of the functions of the river purification boards, Her Majesty's Industrial Pollution Inspectorate, the Hazardous Waste Inspectorate, with the waste regulation and local air pollution control functions of local authorities under the umbrella of the Scottish Environmental Protection Agency (SEPA) is a further example of this move towards integration and towards a "one-stop shop" for pollution control.[19]

---

[15] J. Rowan-Robinson, "Heads I win, tails you lose: Cameron v Nature Conservancy Council" (1991) 34 *Scottish Planning Law and Practice*, pp. 10–13.

[16] House of Commons Committee on the Environment, First Report, *Operation and Effectiveness of Part II of the Wildlife and Countryside Act 1985*, HMSO, Vol. 1, Chap. 3, para. 45.

[17] Scottish Office, 1997. See also *A Better Quality of Life: A strategy for sustainable development for the UK*, Cm. 4345 (1999); European Community, *Towards Sustainability*, Fifth Action Programme on the Environment, 1992, COM (92)23, OJ C485; *This Common Inheritance*, Cm. 1200 (1990); and the annual reports for most of the countryside bodies listed below which all essentially call for sustainable development to play a part in the policy making of all areas.

[18] Natural Heritage (Scotland) Act 1991, s. 1.

[19] Environment Act 1995, s. 20.

A second means of tackling the problems of fragmentation has been through the publication of more in the way of strategic guidance from the centre. The intention is that this guidance will be implemented on a day-to-day basis by the local authorities and the NDPBs involved in rural land use and management. For example, the Scottish Office policy paper *Towards a Development Strategy for Rural Scotland* (1998) identifies the key principles that should underpin the formulation and development of a rural strategy and sets out a framework within which these principles can be delivered; the National Planning Policy Guideline 15 "Rural Development" issued by the Scottish Office Development Department in 1999 explains how these principles should be interpreted by local authorities in exercising their development planning and development control functions. Strategic guidance, directed at tackling the problem of fragmentation, may also emerge at the local level. By way of example, structure plans prepared by planning authorities are expected to contain indicative forestry strategies which will guide decisions by the Forestry Authority on planting grant applications (see Chapter 7).

Thirdly, countryside agencies are increasingly being subjected to a "balancing obligation"; in other words, they are required to have regard to other interests when exercising their own functions. For example, under section 32 of the Environment Act 1995 SEPA, when exercising its functions, is to have regard to the desirability of conserving and enhancing the natural heritage of Scotland and of protecting and conserving buildings, sites and objects of archaeological, architectural, engineering or historic interest; it must have regard to the social and economic needs of any area; and it must have regard to the desirability of preserving public access to the countryside. Under section 3(1) of the Natural Heritage (Scotland) Act 1991 SNH is obliged when exercising its functions to have regard to the interests of agriculture, fisheries and forestry, the need for social and economic development, the need to conserve the cultural heritage, and the interests of owners and occupiers and local communities. Under section 1(3A) of the Forestry Act 1967[20] the Forestry Commission, when exercising its functions, must endeavour to balance the objectives of afforestation with the conservation and enhancement of natural beauty and the conservation of flora, fauna and geological or physiographical features of special interest. And the Deer Commission is required under the Deer (Scotland) Act 1996, when exercising its functions, to have regard to the impact of Scotland's deer herd on the natural heritage and must consider the needs of agriculture and forestry and the interests of owners and occupiers. Furthermore, a general balancing obligation was introduced in section 66 of the Countryside (Scotland) Act 1967 which imposes on every Minister, government department and public body in the exercise of their statutory functions relating to land an obligation to have regard to the desirability of conserving the natural heritage of Scotland.

The requirement simply "to have regard to" in these balancing obligations is, of course, a weak expression of the desire for better integration. It is not an obligation that is readily enforceable; it would be difficult to show that an agency had failed to discharge the requirement. Nonetheless, the obligation is intended to promote a greater awareness by agencies of the other interests that may be

---

[20] Added by the Wildlife and Countryside (Amendment) Act 1985, s. 4.

affected by their decisions and is a step towards breaking down the narrow, sectoral approach which tended to characterise decision-making in the 1960s and 1970s.

Fourthly, better integration can be promoted by expressly bringing other interests in as a factor in decision-making. The best example of this is to be found in Article 6 of the Treaty of Rome which in its amended form provides that "[e]nvironmental protection requirements must be integrated into the definition and implementation of Community policies and activities referred to Article 5 in particular with a view to promoting sustainable development". Although this approach to integration does not exist at the domestic level, it should be noted that environmental and other considerations are increasingly entering into initial decisions over grant aid. For example, planting grant applications are now considered by the Forestry Authority under the woodland grant scheme not only on their silvicultural merits but also in the light of landscape, environmental, social and recreational considerations (see Chapter 7); and the Minister is under a duty to consider conservation objectives when making certain farm capital grants.[21]

Finally, a consultation requirement will go some way towards ensuring that other interests are at least considered in the decision-making process. For example, a planning authority is required to consult with SNH, SEPA and the water authorities when their interests may be affected by a development proposal.[22] The Forestry Commission must consult with SNH and with the appropriate planning authority over woodland grant scheme applications (see Chapter 7). And SEPA must consult with SNH before carrying out or authorising certain works in Sites of Special Scientific Interest.[23]

The nature of the countryside bodies in Scotland

The bodies involved in countryside management in Scotland are diverse in terms of character, organisation and powers. Some bodies are international, others national, others local. Some bodies are democratically elected, while others are appointed. Some control not only their own purse strings but those of other agencies. Still other bodies have charitable status. Indeed, the management of the Scottish countryside is spread among bodies which range from the European Community and Whitehall through the Scottish Executive and NDPBs, such as SNH and the Deer Commission, to charities such as the National Trust for Scotland and the Royal Society for the Protection of Birds. A convenient, if somewhat arbitrary, distinction may be drawn for the purposes of this chapter between government, in one form or another, on the one hand and NDPBs on the other. In the first group are the European Community, central government and the Scottish Executive, local government, Historic Scotland, the Crown Estate Commissioners and the Forestry Commission. In the second group are Scottish Natural Heritage, the Scottish Environmental Protection Agency, the Water Authorities, the Deer Commission, Scottish Enterprise, Highland and Islands Enterprise and the local enterprise companies, and the Crofters Commission. For

---

[21] C. Rodgers, *Agricultural Law* (Butterworths, 2nd edn, 1998), para. 2.06.

[22] The Town and Country Planning (General Development Procedure) (Scotland) Order 1992, reg. 15.

[23] Environment Act 1995, s. 35(4).

convenience the National Trust for Scotland and the Cairngorms Partnership are also considered with this group. These bodies are now considered in turn.

Government bodies

European Community: European Community law has a substantial impact on most of the activities which occur in the UK countryside. The Common Agricultural Policy and its subsequent reforms have significantly affected the farming industry. The Common Fisheries Policy has also had a significant impact on rural fishing communities in Scotland. The Birds and Habitats Directives have introduced significant added protection for certain designated habitats (see Chapter 11). And, as a manifestation of the preventative approach, the Directive on environmental assessment, as amended, requires that an increasing number of proposals for land use change and development must be accompanied by an environmental statement when they are submitted for approval (see Chapter 3). It seems likely that the requirement for such assessment will be extended in due course from projects to plans and programmes. An awareness of Community law is essential given its influence in countryside matters in Scotland. The substantive content of the relevant laws are described in the appropriate chapters in this book. This section simply offers a brief outline of the basic framework of Community involvement in countryside matters.

The UK has been a member of the European Community since 1972.[24] As a Member State the UK is subject to the laws of the European Community. The powers and competence of the Community depend on the treaties which create it. The European Community was initially focused on creation of the single European market. It was under these original provisions that the Common Agricultural Policy was developed *inter alia* to increase agricultural productivity, rationalise development of agricultural production, ensure a fair standard of living for the agricultural community, stabilise markets, assure the availability of supplies and ensure supplies reach consumers at reasonable prices.[25] In its original form, there was no mention of environmental matters in the treaty establishing the European Community (the "EC Treaty"). However, this did not prevent the EC from taking an interest in environmental matters and a range of environmental measures were introduced relying on Article 100 which provides for the harmonisation of laws affecting the establishment of the common market and Article 235 which allows measures to be taken where necessary for the attainment of the Community's objectives and where the Treaty has not provided the specific powers. Furthermore, starting in 1972 the Community's institutions have been involved in the preparation of a series of Action Programmes for the environment: the first in November 1973 (OJ C112), the second in May 1977 (OJ C139), the third in February 1983 (OJ C46), the fourth in 1987 (OJ C328/1) and the fifth in May 1993 (OJ C138) which runs until 2000. The programmes are agreed, not only by the Community, but also by the representatives of the Governments of the Member States meeting in Council. The earlier programmes focused on environmental clean-up measures, the reduction of pollution and the improvement of certain aspects of the environment. The second and third programmes also focused on the longer term, stressing the preventative aspects

---

[24] European Communities Act 1972.
[25] European Communities Treaty, Title II—Agriculture.

of policy to improve overall environmental quality. The fifth action programme advocates sustainable development and a broadening of mechanisms to safeguard the environment to include economic instruments.

In 1987 the Treaty was amended to include environmental objectives and a new title on the Environment was added which conferred on the Community powers relating to the environment.[26] The Community is expressly empowered now to take action with the objectives of preserving, protecting and improving the environment, contributing towards the protection of human health and ensuring the prudent and rational utilisation of natural resources.[27] These provisions have subsequently been amended by the Treaty on European Union and by the Amsterdam Treaty.[28] A great deal of environmental law has emerged from the Community including laws relating to noise, waste management, air and water quality, species and habitat protection and integrated pollution control.

While EC policies on agriculture and nature conservation have at times been in conflict, there is no doubt that there is now an emphasis on the integration and co-ordination of policy.[29] For example, as mentioned earlier, amended Article 6 of the Treaty provides generally that "environmental protection requirements must be integrated into the definition and implementation of Community policies and activities referred to Article 5 in particular with a view to promoting sustainable development". More specifically, the Agri-environment Regulation[30] establishes a Community aid programme to promote *inter alia* the use of farming practices which reduce the polluting effects of agriculture, the development of ways of using agricultural land which are compatible with protection and improvement of the environment, the countryside, the landscape, natural resources, the soil and genetic diversity, long-term set-aside for environmental reasons and land management for public access and leisure activities.[31]

Community law comes in the form of regulations, directives and decisions from the European Court of Justice. Regulations automatically become part of the domestic law of the Member States and must be followed and enforced in the same way as other laws within the national legal system. Directives are addressed to the Member States which are required to take whatever measures are necessary to ensure that the objectives set out in the directive are implemented within their own national legal systems within a specified period. Therefore, where the national law does not already provide for the requirements of the directive, new national law should be introduced, and in the UK this can be achieved by

---

[26] European Communities Treaty, Arts 174–176.

[27] Ibid, Art. 174.

[28] The latter renumbered the provisions in the Treaty of European Union and the Treaty establishing the European Community. The numbers given in this chapter are the new numbers.

[29] Nicholas Schoon reported for *The Independent* on June 18, 1993 that hundreds of thousands of skylark nests and chicks were ploughed into the ground because of EC rules for taking farmland out of production. The rules allowed farmers to plough set aside land in May in order to remove weeds before they produce seeds and this ploughing in happened before many of the chicks left their nests. More generally see C. Rodgers, "Environmental Gain, Set Aside and the Implementation of EU Agricultural Reform in the United Kingdom" in *Nature Conservation and Countryside Law* (University of Wales Press, C. Rodgers (ed.), 1996), Chap. 5.

[30] Part of the 1992 Reform of the Common Agricultural Policy, EC Reg. 2078/92 OJ L215/85.

[31] Rodgers, op. cit., n. 29.

delegated legislation under the European Communities Act 1972.[32] Any implementing measures are to be interpreted so far as possible to ensure that the terms of the directive are in fact completely satisfied.

If a directive has not been fully or properly implemented, the European Commission (frequently acting on a complaint from an individual) can take steps to ensure that the defaulting state fulfils its obligations to give effect to the directive, a process which can lead ultimately to an action before the European Court of Justice.

A directive which has not been implemented by the due date may also have direct effect. This means that an individual can rely on its terms as if they were part of the national law in any dealing with a branch of the defaulting state (but not in actions against individuals). Direct effect is of limited use for most environmental directives which are generally designed to protect the environment rather than confer rights on individuals. Furthermore, direct effect is only available when the relevant provisions are sufficiently precise and unconditional for it to be clear exactly what the legal position would have been had the directive been properly implemented.[33]

An individual who has suffered harm as a direct result of a Member State failing to implement a directive may also be entitled to claim compensation from the state.[34] However, where a directive gives a Member State a large amount of discretion, it is unlikely that any individual will be able to demonstrate a sufficiently direct loss to benefit from the potential for compensation.

The European Community has enacted laws which impact on many aspects of life in rural Scotland and given its supremacy over domestic laws it cannot be ignored.

The Scottish Parliament, the "appropriate Minister" and the Scottish Executive: As a result of the Scotland Act 1998, many functions relating to the countryside previously exercised by the Secretary of State for Scotland through the Scottish Office have now been devolved and are exercised by the Scottish Executive. As explained in Chapter 1, the members of the Scottish Executive are collectively referred to as "the Scottish Ministers" (s. 44(2)). In day-to-day practice, particular countryside matters will be the responsibility of a particular Scottish Minister (referred to in this book simply as "the appropriate Minister" or "the Minister"). The Act divides legislative competence by reserving certain matters to the Westminster Parliament, such as foreign policy, defence and broadcasting, and stating that all remaining matters are to be devolved to the Scottish Parliament.

---

[32] For example, the Conservation (Natural Habitats etc.) Regulations 1994 (SI 1994/2716) were made under the 1972 Act to bring UK habitat protection in line with EC Directive 92/43 on the conservation of natural habitats of wild fauna and flora.

[33] Whether a directive should be given direct effect is a matter which the domestic courts have not found easy to determine. For conflicting decisions on whether the EC Directive 85/337 on the assessment of the effects of certain public and private projects on the environment was of direct effect see *Twyford Parish Council* v *Secretary of State for Transport* (1990) 4 JEL 273 where it was held that the requirement to carry out an environmental assessment was directly effective in relation to projects covered by Annex I and *Wychavon District Council* v *Secretary of State for the Environment* [1994] JEL 351 where it was held that none of the provisions in the Directive have direct effect. For more information see L. Kramer, "The Implementation of Community Environmental Directives with Member States: Some Implications of the Direct Effect Doctrine" [1991] 3 JEL 39.

[34] *Francovich* v *Italy* (cases c6 and 9.90) [1991] ECR 1–5357.

As a result, the Act contains no specific list of devolved matters. That said, it is clear from the list of reserved matters and from the Government White Paper *Scotland's Parliament*[35] that most matters pertaining to the Scottish countryside will be the responsibility of the Scottish Parliament and its Executive, including planning, environmental concerns, nature conservation, agriculture, forestry, fishing and recreation. Some key exceptions are transport, energy and aspects of sea fishing.

The Scottish Parliament is responsible for implementing Community law as it pertains to devolved matters.[36] It is outside the competence of the Scottish Parliament to introduce laws which are contrary to EC law[37] and the Secretary of State for Scotland (a UK Minister) may intervene to prevent the passage of a Bill which he believes will or may be contrary to EC law or beyond the legislative competence of the Scottish Parliament.[38] Furthermore, the UK Parliament has the power to vary any law of the Scottish Parliament which it has reason to believe is beyond the legislative competence of that Parliament including being contrary to EC law.[39] Central government remains answerable to the European Court of Justice for any alleged failure to fully implement EC legislation or any breaches thereof. As a result the UK Parliament is still able to legislate for Scotland, even in devolved matters if necessary, and one area where it might do so would be to pass legislation to implement EC law if this had not been done. That said, the Scottish Executive, like other bodies with public functions, is responsible for implementing EC legislation and may be answerable in domestic courts.[40]

To a large extent most of the functions previously exercised by the Scottish Office are now devolved to the Scottish Parliament and the Scottish Executive. The influence which the Scottish Executive has over countryside matters is extensive and can be exercised through several different mechanisms. First of all, following devolution, representation at EC level for countryside matters is reserved to Westminster. However, it is proposed that internal arrangements be developed which will enable the Scottish Executive to participate in negotiations on devolved matters where Scotland has a substantial interest.[41] The Executive therefore has an opportunity to be involved in the negotiation and agreement of relevant EC legislative and policy initiatives.

A second means of exerting influence over what happens in the countryside is through the power to initiate primary and secondary legislation within its sphere of competence. For example, it seems likely that one of the matters which will occupy the attention of the Scottish Parliament fairly early in its life is whether to implement the recommendations from the Land Reform Policy Group on rural land reform[42] and from SNH to legislate with regard to National Parks and for a general right of access.[43]

---

[35] Cm. 3658 (1997).
[36] Scotland Act 1998, Sched. 5, para. 6.
[37] Scotland Act 1998, ss 28(2)(d) and 53(2).
[38] Scotland Act 1998, s. 33.
[39] Scotland Act 1998, s. 92.
[40] See, eg, *Francovich* v *Italy* (cases c6 and 9/90) [1991] ECR 1–5357.
[41] Scotland Act 1998, Sched. 5, para. 6.
[42] Land Reform Policy Group, *Recommendations for Action* (Scottish Office, 1999).
[43] *National Parks for Scotland: Scottish Natural Heritage's Advice to Government* (SNH, 1999).

Third, the Scottish Executive, like the Scottish Office before it, will develop its own policies and guidance relating to the countryside. The expectation is that such policies and guidance will be followed by local authorities, NDPBs and others engaged in day-to-day decisions about the use, development and management of the countryside. This guidance may be general, such as the National Planning Policy Guidelines on the National Heritage and on Rural Development. Sometimes, however, this form of intervention can be quite detailed. The Scottish Office, for example, set out detailed guidance in Circular 6/1995 on the implementation of the Habitats Directive[44] and in Planning Advice Note 39 on the siting and design of farm and forestry buildings.

Fourth, Government can and does exert considerable control of the use, development and management of land through designation. Over the years the Scottish countryside has become much designated. If we include designations by local government and by NDPBs, there are National, Local and Marine Nature Reserves, Special Protection Areas and candidate Special Areas of Conservation, Ramsar Sites, Sites of Special Scientific Interest, Heritage Coasts, Special Scenic Areas and Areas of Great Landscape Value, Environmentally Sensitive Areas, Regional Parks, Country Parks, Conservation Areas, Green Belts and Nitrate-Vulnerable Zones. National Parks are to be added to this list. The proliferation of designations is undoubtedly confusing. Each designation carries its own significance. Some, such as Green Belts, carry no statutory consequences but are, nonetheless, very important in decisions about land use and development. Others, such as Special Areas of Conservation, have direct and important statutory consequences for what can happen in the designated area.

Fifth, the appropriate Minister exercises quite wide appellate functions. As the final arbiter on matters of merit, the Minister exercises considerable control over the substance of actions and decisions. For example, the Minister approves structure plans, determines planning appeals, makes nature conservation orders and special nature conservation orders and confirms access orders and compulsory purchase orders.

Finally, the Scottish Executive has significant influence, not just over particular actions and decisions of other countryside agencies, but over their general approach to the discharge of their functions. The amount of influence exerted is largely determined by the actual institutional relationship between the Executive and the particular agency. For example, Historic Scotland, and the Scottish Fisheries Agency which monitors Scottish fisheries and enforces fisheries regulations, are both next steps agencies. Next steps agencies are executive agencies which are somewhat detached from the Executive. Day-to-day operational control is left with the Chief Executive of the Agency while the appropriate Minister retains responsibility for overall policy decisions. However, these agencies are actually part of the Executive and are not separate legal personalities. The Executive has less direct influence over NDPBs such as Scottish Natural Heritage, the Scottish Environmental Protection Agency, the Crofters' Commission and the Deer Commission, all of which are separate legal entities. However, in practice the Executive still exercises significant influence over these bodies

---

[44] Directive 92/43 on the conservation of natural habitats and of wild fauna and flora.

through control over the appointment of the chairperson and members and the approval of their budgets. Furthermore, annual reports and accounts must be presented to the appropriate Minister. A significant amount of power is also exerted over democratically elected local authorities which are becoming more and more financially dependent on the grant they receive from the Scottish Executive.

In all these ways, the Scottish Executive (and the Scottish Office before it) is well placed to ensure that local authorities and other countryside agencies carry on their functions in line with national policy. That said, the Executive does not generally interfere with their day-to-day work.

Historic Scotland: Historic Scotland is a next steps agency within the Scottish Executive which deals with the Minister's responsibilities for the built heritage.[45]

Its functions include advising the Minister on scheduling monuments of national importance (see Chapter 16), listing buildings of special architectural or historic interest (see Chapter 3) and responding to applications for consent to change. It also assists owners and others with maintenance and repair. In 1996–97, £12.4 million was awarded in historic building repair grants to 145 projects, levering another £15 million from private owners.[46] Historic Scotland also manages an estate of 330 properties which are in the care of the Scottish Executive. The estate includes Edinburgh Castle, Skara Brae and the Stanley Mills in Perthshire.[47] Historic Scotland is the largest operator of paid tourist attractions in Scotland. The Agency also ensures archaeological surveys and excavations are carried out at sites threatened by natural or development hazards and researches issues and develops skills relating to the built heritage. For example, it recently sponsored the University of Edinburgh and the Fire Protection Association to research the effects of fire on historic buildings and the benefits of water sprinkler systems.[48]

The Crown Estate Commissioners: The Crown Estate is the property of the Sovereign "in right of the Crown".[49] In Scotland, the Crown Estate owns a substantial holding including commercial property in Edinburgh and Glasgow, around 100,000 acres of agricultural land, half of the foreshore and almost all of the seabed out to the 12-mile territorial limit. Until the reign of George III, the Sovereign received the rent and profits from the Estate. However, since 1760, the entire surplus revenue, after deducting management costs, has been passed on by the Sovereign to the Exchequer every year as part of the arrangement for the provision of the Civil List.

The Crown Estate was established in its present form by the Crown Estate Act 1961 which provides that the Estate be managed by a Board of Commissioners who have a duty to "maintain and enhance the value of the estate and the return obtained from it, but with due regard to the requirements of good management".

---

[45] See generally Historic Scotland's website at http://www.historic-scotland.gov.uk.
[46] Historic Scotland Annual Report and Accounts 1996–97 and Corporate Plan 1997–2000, p. 3.
[47] Corporate Plan 1997–2000, p. 6.
[48] Corporate Plan 1997–2000, p. 4.
[49] Crown Estate *Commissioners' Report for the year ended 31st March, 1998*; Crown Estate website entitled "About the Crown Estate" at http://www.crownestate.co.uk.

At present, there are no specific environmental or conservation duties imposed on the Crown Estate Commissioners although this has been proposed. They are, however, bound by the general balancing duties applicable to all public bodies[50] and are involved in conservation efforts such as under the Firths Initiative which brings together public and private bodies and individuals with an interest in the sustainable management and use of firths.

The Estate has to remain an estate in land with only such cash or gilt-edged investments as are required for the discharge of the Commissioners' functions. The Commissioners have no power to borrow. There are eight Commissioners who are appointed by the Sovereign based on their wide knowledge and experience of matters directly relevant to the management of all aspects of the Crown Estate. A number of firms of Chartered Surveyors are appointed as managing agents to carry out the direct management of the Estates and to provide professional advice.

The Crown Estate Commissioners have a large impact on the Scottish countryside. The Estate manages over 100,000 acres of countryside in Scotland. At its largest estate, Glenlivet, the Commissioners have considered ways of broadening the economic base of this remote Highland community. The result has been the successful integration of tourist facilities such as footpaths, cycle paths and bridle ways which complement and support existing as well as new business while also delivering wider public benefits. As owners of approximately half of the foreshore and almost all of the seabed around the coastline of Scotland, it is the Crown Estate's role to issue consents for any activity which makes use of the resource. Everything from seaweed collection to nine major port developments is covered. The main form of consent comes in the form of leases for fish farming developments. These are only granted after consultation with organisations concerned with matters such as economic development, the environment, water quality, navigation and local interests.

The Crown Estate, in exercising it powers with regard to fish farming, is faced with a potential conflict of roles. The Commissioners are required to regulate the fish farming industry by, for example, requiring environmental assessments to be carried out for farming operations; yet at the same time it is the Crown Estate which serves to gain added revenue from the lease of the fish farming rights. The Crown Estate itself appears from its literature to be uncomfortable about the potential conflict. In its response to the Government's proposals for land reform in Scotland, the Crown Estate noted that any quasi-planning or regulatory functions should be undertaken by central or local government and not by the Crown Estate. It acknowledged the concern surrounding its role as owner and regulator in regard to fish farming and called for a formal statutory regime that would meet demands for democratic accountability. It also welcomed the current proposals to extend planning controls to incorporate offshore fish farming,[51] and the interim arrangements which are now in place for handling marine fish farm applications on the west coast, the Western Isles and part of Orkney.

---

[50] Countryside (Scotland) Act 1967, s. 66.
[51] Crown Estate response to the Land Reform Policy Group consultation paper *Identifying problems* (1998) at http://www.crownestate.co.uk/news/landreform.shtml.

The Forestry Commission: The Forestry Commission was established after the First World War to promote the interests of forestry in the UK following fears about the UK's dependency on foreign timber. It is the government department responsible for Forestry (see Chapter 7).[52] It is subject to the direction of the Forestry Ministers who include one of the Ministers attached to the Scottish Executive. The Commission implements government policy within a legislative framework.[53] However, it differs from other departments in that legal control is not with the responsible Ministers but with the Commissioners who are appointed by the Crown from the various interests associated with forestry.[54]

The original aim of the Forestry Commission was to promote the interests of forestry through the development of afforestation and the production and supply of timber and other forest products. As already mentioned, this aim is now tempered by a balancing obligation which requires the Commission, in carrying out its statutory functions, to endeavour to achieve a reasonable balance between (a) the development of afforestation, the management of forests and the production and supply of timber, and (b) the conservation and enhancement of natural beauty and the conservation of flora, fauna and geological or physiographical features of special interest.[55] More recently, other policy aims have been added which include the promotion of biodiversity, public access and education, woodland recreation and community participation.[56]

The Forestry Commission has a dual role. It is the owner of vast amounts of forest and is responsible for the management of its own estate. At the same time, it is responsible for regulating the private forestry industry in the UK. Following concern about the potential conflict of roles, the organisation of the Commission was changed to separate these functions. First of all, Forest Enterprise was set up as an executive agency to manage the large areas of woodland held in public ownership. In recent years Forest Enterprise has increased public access to its woodlands through the waymarking of walks and the laying out of orienteering, horse and bike trails. Secondly, the Forestry Authority was set up with responsibility for implementing the Government's forestry policy, including setting standards for the industry, the control of tree felling, the administration of the payment of grants for approved planting, restocking and management schemes, providing advice to private owners and monitoring the performance of private sector forestry and that of the Forest Enterprise. These two aspects of its role are examined in more detail in Chapter 7.

Local authorities: Since 1995, a unitary system of local government comprising of 32 democratically elected all-purpose councils has been in place in Scotland.[57] Local authorities are multi-function bodies and many of these functions are relevant to the countryside. These include planning, coastal protection, local roads and transportation, economic development, education, waste disposal, council

---

[52] For general information about the Forestry Commission see website at http://www. forestry. gov.uk.

[53] In particular the Forestry Act 1967, as amended.

[54] eg, the timber trade, forestry science and conservation.

[55] Forestry Act 1967, s. 1(3A), inserted by the Wildlife and Countryside (Amendment) Act 1985, s. 4.

[56] See *Sustainable Forestry—the UK Programme*, Cmnd. 2429 (1994).

[57] Set up under the Local Government etc. (Scotland) Act 1994, ss 1 and 2.

housing, cemeteries, the regulation of noise pollution and public nuisance, public health, the designation of local nature reserves, the provision of country parks and other recreational facilities and the negotiation and management of public access to the countryside. Although responsible for the day-to-day discharge of these functions, authorities are subject to considerable control by the Scottish Executive (see above) and must consult from time to time with other countryside agencies.

Councils tend to delegate many of their functions to committees and the committees are supported by a departmental structure of full-time officials. Many authorities have organised themselves into areas for the discharge of their day-to-day functions, a sort of local devolution, and this can be particularly helpful in rural Scotland.

Authorities in rural areas are often faced with the need to balance landscape and nature conservation interests against economic development in determining land use. They also face difficult decisions in allocating limited budgets to meet the competing demands of their different functions.

Non-departmental public bodies (NDPBs)

As explained earlier in this chapter, NDPBs are public bodies which are not part of central government, the Scottish Executive or a local authority and which have their own legal personality. A distinction is often drawn between advisory and executive NDPBs; but those involved in the management of the Scottish countryside, such as SEPA, SNH and Highland and Islands Enterprise, while exercising some advisory functions, are also executive agencies with their own staff, budget and important regulatory and administrative functions.

The following non-departmental public bodies are examined below: Scottish Natural Heritage, the Scottish Environmental Protection Agency, the Water Authorities, the Deer Commission, Scottish Enterprise, Highland and Islands Enterprise and the LECs, the Crofters' Commission, the National Trust for Scotland and the Cairngorm Partnership.

Scottish Natural Heritage: Scottish Natural Heritage ("SNH") was created in 1991 under the Natural Heritage (Scotland) Act 1991. It is the result of a merger between the agency responsible for nature conservation in Scotland, the Nature Conservancy Council for Scotland and the agency responsible for public access and recreation in Scotland, the Countryside Commission for Scotland. The aim of this merger was to provide the opportunity for an integrated approach to be taken in all conservation and countryside matters. At the same time as the merger, there was a transfer of ministerial control for nature conservation from the Department of the Environment to the Scottish Office in recognition of the fact that the issues and pressures affecting conservation in Scotland differ in important respects from those which affect England.[58] It was hoped that a more locally based body would help to improve relations between those responsible for promoting conservation and the local communities.

SNH has two general aims[59]: to secure the conservation and enhancement of, and to foster understanding and facilitate the enjoyment of, the natural heritage

---

[58] Post-devolution SNH is accountable to the "appropriate Minister" of the Scottish Executive.

[59] Natural Heritage (Scotland) Act 1991, s. 1(1). See also the SNH website at http://www.snh. org.uk.

of Scotland. "Natural heritage" is defined to include the flora and fauna of Scotland, its geological and physiographical features and its natural beauty and amenity.[60] SNH is further charged with ensuring that anything done, either by itself or by any other person, in relation to the natural heritage is undertaken in a manner which is sustainable.[61] SNH was the first agency in the UK to be given a mandate which includes the promotion of sustainability. The legislation, however, stops short of defining the term. SNH accordingly developed its own definition in a policy paper entitled *Sustainable Development and the Natural Heritage: The SNH Approach* (1993). This states that in promoting sustainability SNH will be guided by the ethical principles of intergenerational equity, international equity, societal equity and inter-species equity. The paper goes on to set out guidelines for sustainability which guide SNH's own action and its advice to others. For example, the paper advocates that renewable resources should be used within the limits of their capacity for regeneration, that non-renewable resources should be used wisely and sparingly and at a rate which does not restrict the options of future generations and that in situations of great complexity or uncertainty we should act in a precautionary manner.

As already indicated, SNH must also balance nature conservation with other interests such as agriculture, forestry, the cultural heritage, economic development and the interests of owners and occupiers and local communities.[62]

The agency is run by a Board appointed by the appropriate Minister and consisting of between eight and twelve members, one of whom is the chairman. Reference was made earlier to the requirement in appointing members to have regard to the desirability of bringing in persons of knowledge or experience relevant to SNH's principle areas of activity.[63] SNH operates a devolved structure so far as possible. It is organised into three areas with area boards for the discharge of its day-to-day functions. Each area comprises a number of local offices. The organisation is shown on Map 1.

An important general function of SNH is advising the appropriate Minister on the development and implementation of policies for or affecting the natural heritage.[64] Recent examples include policy advice to Ministers on national parks, access to the countryside and important landscapes and responding to proposals for rural land reform and for changes to the regime of SSSIs. Rather more specifically, SNH has responsibility for promoting biodiversity, securing the wise management of special natural heritage sites, promoting public enjoyment of the natural heritage, particularly access to the countryside, facilitating the integrated management of the Cairngorms and Loch Lomond and the Trossachs, improving environmental education, licensing certain activities with regard to species, commissioning or supporting research on natural heritage matters and acting as consultee on such matters as planning applications, applications for woodland grant and inheritance tax relief.

Scottish Natural Heritage, the Nature Conservancy Council for England and the Countryside Council for Wales all belong to the Joint Nature Conservation

---

[60] Natural Heritage (Scotland) Act 1991, s. 1(3).
[61] Natural Heritage (Scotland) Act 1991, s. 1(1).
[62] Natural Heritage (Scotland) Act 1991, s. 3(1).
[63] Natural Heritage (Scotland) Act 1991, Sched. 1, para. 4.
[64] Natural Heritage (Scotland) Act 1991, s. 2(1)(a).

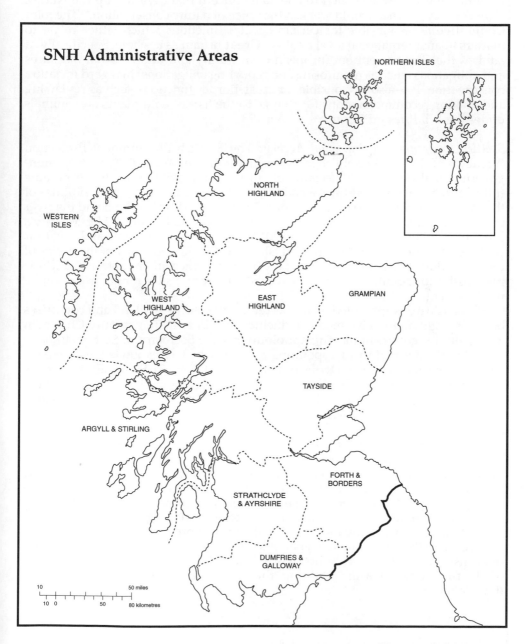

SNH Administrative Areas

NORTHERN ISLES

NORTH HIGHLAND

WESTERN ISLES

WEST HIGHLAND

EAST HIGHLAND

GRAMPIAN

TAYSIDE

ARGYLL & STIRLING

FORTH & BORDERS

STRATHCLYDE & AYRSHIRE

DUMFRIES & GALLOWAY

10   50 miles

10   0   50   80 kilometres

Map 1

Committee which was created to alleviate concern that dividing up the Nature Conservancy Council would weaken the voice of nature conservation.[65] The Joint Committee is responsible for certain special functions which either relate to matters at an international level or affect Great Britain as a whole. Specifically, it advises the Government on European Community and international measures and obligations (such as monitoring and reporting obligations) in regard to nature conservation. It is also responsible for cross-border functions such as reviewing and making recommendations for change to the lists of wild plants and animals under the Wildlife and Countryside Act 1981.[66]

Scottish Environmental Protection Agency: The Scottish Environment Protection Agency ("SEPA") was established by the Environment Act 1995.[67] SEPA is a non-governmental public body accountable to the appropriate Minister. It became fully operational on April 1, 1996 and took over the duties and responsibilities of the following bodies: the seven river purification boards in Scotland and the river purification functions undertaken by the three islands Councils; Her Majesty's Industrial Pollution Inspectorate (HMIPI); the waste regulation and local air pollution functions of the District and Islands Councils and many of the duties of the Hazardous Waste Inspectorate of the Scottish Office. In broad terms, SEPA is responsible for pollution control whereas SNH is responsible for natural resource management.

SEPA's Board is appointed by the Secretary of State for Scotland and comprises between eight and twelve members including a Chairman, a deputy Chairman and Chief Executive. In making appointments the Secretary of State is to have regard to the desirability of appointing persons who have knowledge or experience in some matter relevant to the functions of SEPA.[68] Like SNH, SEPA operates so far as possible in a devolved manner. It operates through three regional offices each with a Regional Board. Each region comprises a number of local offices which allow for the provision of services at a local level. These provide a "one-stop" approach for all SEPA's services. The devolved arrangement is shown on Map 2.

SEPA is obliged to have regard to guidance issued by the appropriate Minister with respect to the aims and objectives considered appropriate for SEPA to pursue in the performance of its functions.[69] Unlike the Environment Agency for England and Wales, the 1995 Act sets out no overall aim for SEPA. Instead, this is to be found in the guidance issued by the Minister. The guidance states that SEPA's overall aim should be the provision of an efficient and integrated environmental protection system in Scotland which will both improve the environment and contribute to the Government's goal of sustainable development. The guidance must also indicate the contribution which SEPA should make by the performance of its functions towards attaining the objective of achieving sustainable development.[70]

---

[65] Environmental Protection Act 1990, s. 128(4).
[66] Wildlife and Countryside Act 1981, ss 22(3) and 24(1).
[67] s. 20(1).
[68] 1995 Act, s. 20(2) and Sched. 6, para. 4.
[69] 1995 Act, s. 31(1).
[70] 1995 Act, s. 31(2). This contrasts with SNH (above) which has been left to work out its own role with regard to sustainability.

SEPA Offices

STIRLING ●   SEPA office location

▪▪▪▪▪▪▪   SEPA regional boundary

⌒⌒⌒⌒   SEPA local boundary

Glasgow ●   Other major city or town

KIRKWALL

LERWICK

Durness

THURSO

Wick

STORNOWAY

Ullapool

Dornoch

DINGWALL

ELGIN

Banff

FRASERBURGH

Portree

Inverness

Peterhead

Kyle of Lochalsh

Aviemore

NORTH REGION

ABERDEEN

Mallaig

Stonehaven

FORT WILLIAM

Montrose

EAST REGION

Dundee

ARBROATH

Oban

PERTH

St. Andrews

GLENROTHES

LOCHGILPHEAD

STIRLING

NORTH
GLASGOW

Falkirk

Edinburgh

Glasgow

RICCARTON

Berwick upon Tweed

EAST KILBRIDE

Kilmarnock

Campbeltown

AYR

GALASHIELS

WEST REGION

DUMFRIES

Stranraer

NEWTON STEWART

10   50 miles

10   0   50   80 kilometres

Map 2

The guidance sets out seven strategic objectives for SEPA including working with all sectors of society (including regulated organisations) to develop approaches which deliver environmental requirements and goals, without imposing excessive costs (in relation to benefits gained) on regulated organisations and society as a whole.[71]

Like SNH, SEPA has very explicit balancing obligations. Section 32 of the 1995 Act provides that, in formulating or considering any proposals relating to any of its functions, SEPA is to have regard to the desirability of conserving and enhancing the natural heritage of Scotland and protecting and conserving buildings, sites and objects of archaeological, architectural, engineering or historic interest. The agency is also to have regard to the social and economic needs of any area of Scotland, particularly the needs of rural areas. Furthermore, SEPA must have regard to the desirability of preserving for the public any freedom of access (including access for recreational purposes) to areas of forest, woodland, mountains, moor, bog, cliff, foreshore, loch or reservoir and other places of natural beauty. It must also have regard to the desirability of maintaining the availability to the public of any facility for visiting or inspecting any building, site or object of archaeological, architectural, engineering or historic interest. SEPA must take into account any effects which proposals would have on all of the above. In discharging its functions, SEPA is also obliged to have regard to any code of practice approved by the Secretary of State which promotes desirable practices or gives practical guidance to SEPA in regard to these environmental and recreational duties.[72]

SEPA has responsibility for the day-to-day running of most of the pollution control regimes in Scotland. These include integrated pollution control, air pollution control, waste management, water pollution, hazardous waste and radioactive waste. This is a huge undertaking. In 1997/98, in regard to water quality alone, SEPA processed 1,114 applications for licences, undertook 17,047 inspections and took 1,774 samples.[73] SEPA maintains a number of public registers including those for the water, integrated pollution control and radioactive substances regimes. SEPA is also charged with advising the Minister on environmental protection and pollution control matters, assisting in the development of relevant policy such as the National Waste Strategy, conducting and funding relevant research and educating the public on environmental matters. It will also have responsibility for enforcement of the provisions relating to such contaminated land as may be designated as a special site—once these come into force.[74]

In deciding whether to exercise any of its powers and in deciding the manner in which to exercise any of its powers, SEPA must take into account the likely costs and benefits of the exercise or non-exercise of power or its exercise in the manner in question.[75] This cost/benefit assessment does not arise if it is unreasonable for it to be undertaken in view of the nature or purpose of the

---

[71] *Management Statement for Scottish Environmental Protection Agency* (Scottish Office, 1996).
[72] Environment Act 1995, s. 36.
[73] Scottish Environment Protection Agency Annual Report for 1997–98 (SEPA, 1998), p. 56.
[74] Environmental Protection Act 1990, Pt IIA (particularly s. 78A(9)) added by s. 57 of the Environment Act 1995.
[75] Environment Act 1995, s. 39(1).

power or in the circumstances of the particular case. The guidance issued by the Minister (above) gives some indication of what this obligation means in practice.

The Water Authorities: In England and Wales, responsibility for water supply and sewerage was privatised in 1992. Privatisation was strongly resisted in Scotland. While a reorganisation did occur with effect from April 1, 1996 under the Local Government etc. (Scotland) Act 1994, and responsibility for water supply and sewerage was transferred from the local authorities to three new water authorities, control stayed in public hands. These authorities are, respectively, the East of Scotland, the West of Scotland and the North of Scotland Water Authorities. The three water authority areas are shown on Map 3. The authorities are corporate bodies whose members are appointed by the appropriate Minister. Each authority has a chief executive and between seven and eleven members drawn from persons having knowledge or experience relevant to the functions they are to discharge. In order to ensure the representation of consumers' interests under the new system, a Scottish Water and Sewerage Customers Council has been established.

In terms of sewerage, the principal legislation is the Sewerage (Scotland) Act 1968. The water authorities are under a duty to provide and maintain such public sewers as may be necessary for effectually draining their area of domestic sewage, surface water and trade effluent. They must also make such provision as may be necessary, generally through sewage treatment works, for effectually dealing with the contents of their sewers.[76] The authorities must take their public sewers to such point as will enable the owners of premises to connect up their drains or private sewers at a reasonable cost.[77] These duties, however, do not require the authority to do anything which is not practicable at reasonable cost.[78] Disputes over reasonable cost are to be determined by the Minister. Owners and occupiers of premises are entitled, subject to obtaining the consent of the authority, to connect their drains and private sewers to the public sewer and to discharge domestic sewage and surface water from those premises into the public sewer.[79] The authorities are now also under a duty to empty septic tanks where this is reasonably practicable and are able to charge for this service.[80] The discharge of trade effluent into public sewers is subject to a separate consent procedure but is commonly dealt with by way of an agreement which will make provision for the quantity and quality of the effluent and for reimbursement of the authorities' costs.[81] The authorities are responsible for the disposal of the contents of the sewer system which may involve a discharge into the water system requiring a consent from SEPA.[82]

The principal legislation with regard to water supply is the Water (Scotland) Act 1980. It is the duty of the water authorities to supply wholesome water to every part of their limits of supply where a supply of water is required for

---

[76] Sewerage (Scotland) Act 1968, s. 1(1).
[77] Sewerage (Scotland) Act 1968, s. 1(2).
[78] Sewerage (Scotland) Act 1968, s. 1(3).
[79] Sewerage (Scotland) Act 1968, s. 12.
[80] Sewerage (Scotland) Act 1968, s. 10, substituted by s. 102 of the Local Government etc. (Scotland) Act 1994.
[81] Sewerage (Scotland) Act 1968, Pt II.
[82] See ss 30F, 30H and 34 of the Control of Pollution Act 1974, as amended.

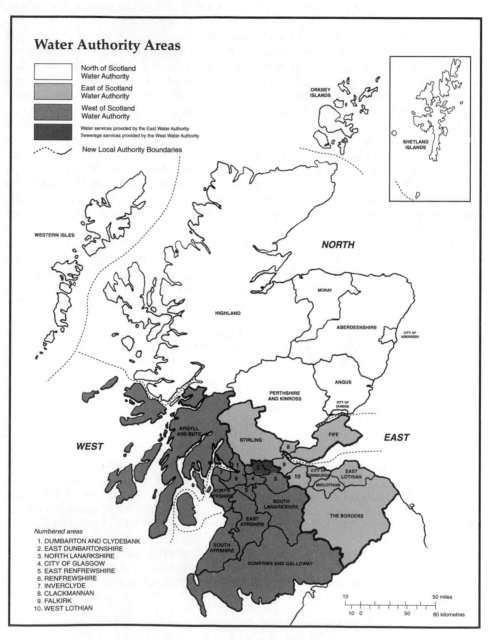

Water Authority Areas

North of Scotland
Water Authority

East of Scotland
Water Authority

West of Scotland
Water Authority

Water services provided by the East Water Authority
Sewerage services provided by the West Water Authority

- - - New Local Authority Boundaries

ORKNEY
ISLANDS

SHETLAND
ISLANDS

WESTERN ISLES

NORTH

MORAY

HIGHLAND

ABERDEENSHIRE

CITY OF
ABERDEEN

ANGUS

PERTHSHIRE
AND KINROSS

CITY OF
DUNDEE

ARGYLL
AND BUTE

STIRLING

FIFE

EAST

WEST

8

1

2

9

6

4

3

10

CITY OF
EDINBURGH

EAST
LOTHIAN

5

MIDLOTHIAN

NORTH
AYRSHIRE

SOUTH
LANARKSHIRE

THE BORDERS

EAST
AYRSHIRE

SOUTH
AYRSHIRE

DUMFRIES AND GALLOWAY

Numbered areas
1. DUMBARTON AND CLYDEBANK
2. EAST DUNBARTONSHIRE
3. NORTH LANARKSHIRE
4. CITY OF GLASGOW
5. EAST RENFREWSHIRE
6. RENFREWSHIRE
7. INVERCLYDE
8. CLACKMANNAN
9. FALKIRK
10. WEST LOTHIAN

10   50 miles

10 0   50   80 kilometres

Map 3

domestic purposes and can be provided at a reasonable cost.[83] The supply of water for non-domestic purposes is subject to the ability of authorities to meet their domestic commitments and is subject also to agreement on terms and conditions including reimbursement of cost.[84] The duty to supply wholesome water is refined by provisions which implement EC water directives regarding fitness of water for human consumption.[85] Water for food production must also meet certain standards under the Food Safety Act 1990. In order to fulfil these obligations the water authorities have extensive powers to construct reservoirs and pipelines and to secure supplies of wholesome water. Powers are available through byelaws and regulations to prevent the contamination or pollution of water which may contribute to an authority's water supply.[86] Authorities may enter into agreements with regard to land drainage for the more effectual collecting, conveying or preserving of the purity of their water supplies.[87]

Water authorities have a balancing duty, in so far as it is consistent with their other duties. They must further the conservation and enhancement of natural beauty and the conservation of flora and fauna and of geological or physiographical features of special interest; they must have regard to the desirability of preserving for the public any freedom of access to the countryside; and they must have regard to the desirability of protecting and conserving buildings, sites and objects of archaeological, architectural or historic interest and of maintaining access to them for the public.[88]

The Deer Commission: The first Red Deer Commission was established under the Deer (Scotland) Act 1959 following tensions between those concerned about an increased incidence of damage to agriculture by deer and a public outcry against organised poaching. Its general functions were to further the conservation and control of red deer in Scotland and to keep under review all matters relating to red deer. In 1996, following fresh concerns regarding the effect of the increasing deer population on the natural heritage, especially native woodland, the Deer Commission for Scotland was established as the successor to the Red Deer Commission.[89] Its powers cover all species of deer (see Chapter 8). In exercising its functions, it is to take into account, as may be appropriate in the circumstances, the size and density for the deer population and its impact on the natural heritage, the needs of agriculture and forestry and the interests of owners and occupiers of the land.[90]

Under the Deer (Scotland) Act 1996, the appropriate Minister is to appoint the Deer Commission from persons who appear to him to have experience of deer management, agriculture (including crofting), forestry and the natural heritage.[91] Organisations representing these interests have the opportunity to suggest names to the Secretary of State. It is for the Minister to determine which organisations

---

84 Water (Scotland) Act 1980, s. 6(1).
84 Water (Scotland) Act 1980, s. 9.
85 Water Act 1989, Sched. 22 and Water (Scotland) Act 1980, ss 76A–76L.
86 Water (Scotland) Act 1980, ss 70–76.
87 Water (Scotland) Act 1980, s. 68.
88 Local Government etc. (Scotland) Act 1994, s. 65(2). See too s. 73.
89 Deer (Amendment) (Scotland) Act 1996, s. 1 and the Deer (Scotland) Act 1996, s. 1.
90 Deer (Scotland) Act 1996, s. 1(2).
91 Deer (Scotland) Act 1996, s. 1(5).

appear to represent these interests. One-third of the Commission is to be drawn from names suggested by organisations representing deer management.[92]

The functions of the Commission are outlined in Chapter 8. In summary it advises the Minister and landowners on all deer-related matters[93] and is responsible generally for promoting the sustainable management of Scotland's deer herd.

Scottish Enterprise, Highlands and Islands Enterprise and the LECs: Scottish Enterprise and Highlands and Islands Enterprise took over responsibilities of the former Scottish Development Agency and the Highlands and Islands Development Board respectively as of April 1991.[94] Both also took on the remit of the training agency for their areas.

Their main function is to promote economic development and training, both directly and through the network of Local Enterprise Companies (LECs) which they supervise and fund. Each LEC is effectively an independent company charged with the task of promoting economic development and training within specified areas. LECs are involved with property development, urban regeneration, land renewal and environmental improvements. Each LEC has to produce a business plan for its areas setting priorities for new property development and environmental improvement. For example, Western Isles Enterprise invested £2.9 million and attracted a further £5.8 million in private sector investment that went towards supporting projects such as the Harris Tweed industry and the expansion of the auction markets on Lewis and Harris as well as training and apprenticeship programmes in the Western Isles.[95]

Crofters Commission: The Crofters Commission was established in 1955 to serve the interests of the crofting community throughout the Highlands and Islands.[96] The Crofters (Scotland) Act 1993 enables the appropriate Minister to appoint Commissioners to represent the crofting areas. At present the Commission has seven Commissioners, one being the part-time Chairman. Each Commissioner is responsible for a particular area to ensure that all crofters are equally represented.[97]

The functions of the Commission are explained in Chapter 6. In summary, they are to reorganise, develop and regulate crofting; to keep matters relating to crofting under review; to collaborate with any person in the carrying out of measures for the economic development and social improvement of the crofting counties; and to advise the appropriate Minister on crofting matters.[98]

In carrying out its functions, the Commission is to have regard to local circumstances and conditions.[99] This limited balancing obligation does allow the

---

[92] Deer (Scotland) Act 1996, s. 1(6).
[93] Deer (Scotland) Act 1996, s. 2(1).
[94] Enterprise and New Towns (Scotland) Act 1990.
[95] See generally the Scottish Enterprise website at http://www.scotent.co.uk and the Highlands and Islands Enterprise website at http://www.hie.co.uk.
[96] The Crofters (Scotland) Act 1955, s. 1. See now the Crofters (Scotland) Act 1993, s. 1.
[97] The areas are Shetland and Orkney; Caithness and Sutherland; East Inverness, East Ross-shire and East Sutherland; West Ross-shire, South and West Inverness; Lewis and Harris; Skye and the Small Isles; and Argyll, the Argyll Islands, the Uists and Barra.
[98] Crofters (Scotland) Act 1993, ss 1(2) and 2.
[99] Crofters (Scotland) Act 1993, s. 1(3).

Commission to consider the local environment including nature conservation as well as other (non-crofting) aspects of the local economy.

More specifically, the Commission is responsible for the regulation of changes in tenancy, re-letting of vacant crofts, apportionment of land used by crofters together (so that one or more may obtain the exclusive use of the land) and the regulation of the management and use of common grazings. The Commission also administers the Crofting Counties Agricultural Grants (Scotland) Scheme on behalf of the Scottish Executive which provides a wide range of agricultural grants to crofters and others. The Commission runs several schemes such as the croft entrant scheme which is designed to encourage inactive crofters to release crofts to young people in areas with fragile population structures. It also maintains a Register of Crofts (see Chapter 6).[100]

In carrying out some of its functions, the Commission undertakes the role of arbiter, balancing the different interests of individuals and the community. The Commission also acts as a tribunal hearing proposals for, among other things, the control of re-letting, assignation and sub-letting of crofts, the apportionment of common grazings and the decrofting of land.[101]

For example, under the Transfer of Crofting Estates (Scotland) Act 1997, a Crofting Trust or other body approved by the appropriate Minister may acquire the Minister's interest as owner of a crofting property and take over its day-to-day management and ensure that the property acquired may be used, developed and exploited in accordance with local needs and priorities (see Chapter 6). The Commission must be consulted prior to such an acquisition and in responding to the consultation must have regard to the general interests of the local crofting community and the views of the wider community and all the affected tenants must also be considered.[102]

The Commission has the assistance of a panel of assessors in carrying out its functions. There are approximately 100 assessors who are appointed by the Commission mainly on nomination of committees appointed by the crofters themselves to manage crofting at local or township level. The functions of the assessors are to provide an objective assessment of localised crofting matters or issues to the Commission and to inform townships in their areas of Commission policies and initiatives.[103]

National Trust For Scotland: The National Trust for Scotland ("NTS") was incorporated under a private Act of Parliament in 1935.[104] Its purpose is to promote the permanent preservation and, where necessary, the restoration of Scottish buildings, places and articles of national importance including their architectural, artistic, antiquarian or historical value. The purpose extends to landscapes of natural beauty along with their animal and plant life, where appropriate. The Trust is also to encourage and facilitate public access to and enjoyment of such places.

---

[100] Crofters (Scotland) Act 1993, s. 41.
[101] Crofters (Scotland) Act 1993, ss 8, 24, 27 and 48. See also the Transfer of Crofting Estates (Scotland) Act 1997.
[102] Transfer of Crofting Estates (Scotland) Act 1997, s. 2(2).
[103] Crofters (Scotland) Act, s. 2(2).
[104] National Trust of Scotland Order Confirmation Act 1935.

The NTS enjoys all the privileges of a charity. All gifts and bequests to the Trust are exempt from tax and it can accept deeds of covenant in respect of membership subscriptions. In 1996 the Trust had 228,000 members, took in £1.8 million from legacies and another £1.9 million in donations[105] making it the largest and most influential conservation body in Scotland. It is governed by a Council consisting of a president, up to six vice-presidents, up to 50 members elected by the membership of the NTS and up to the same number of members from other British and Scottish societies and organisations relevant to the work of the Trust.[106] The Council appoints an Executive Committee to supervise and accept responsibility for the management of the Trust within the policies laid down by the Council.

The NTS has wide powers to carry out its stated aims. It can own land, make byelaws, manage property owned by others and work with others to promote a greater understanding of conservation. Around 185,000 acres of countryside are in the Trust's care including farmland, forest, islands and gardens.[107] Certain land held by the NTS is inalienable and must continue to be used for the Trust's purposes.[108] There is provision for the NTS to lease inalienable property in cases where it is clear that this will be of benefit to the public. It may also enter into conservation agreements with the owner of any property which is considered to be worthy of preservation in the national interest whereby conditions are imposed restricting planning development and use. Often public access requirements are imposed on many of the properties. There are over 600 agreements which protect in excess of 56,000 acres including 84 miles of coastline.[109]

Cairngorm Partnership: The Cairngorm Partnership was set up by the Secretary of State for Scotland in 1994[110] to prepare and implement a management strategy for the Cairngorms area. This was to be a framework to guide and encourage the use and management of land and other relevant activities in a manner compatible with both environmental care and the need to promote the social and economic well-being of the area.

The Partnership was incorporated in March 1995 as a company limited by guarantee and has charitable status. The Partnership Board is made up of 20 representatives from the relevant local authorities, local communities, land managers, the business and tourism community, environmental and conservation interests, recreation, and agriculture and forestry interests. The Partnership has no real power of its own. It is reliant on the powers that its Partners bring to the table in terms of grant-giving and advisory and regulatory powers, and must

---

[105] The National Trust for Scotland 66th Annual Report, 1995/96, pp. 2 and 5.

[106] Such as the Scottish Landowners' Federation, SNH, the National Farmers' Union of Scotland and the Mountaineering Council of Scotland.

[107] For example, in 1996 the Trust purchased the estate next to Ben Lawers, Morenish and in June 1995 it acquired the Mar Lodge Estate with the assistance of a private donation and grant aid from the Heritage Lottery Fund.

[108] The Trust's Council has the power to declare Trust property inalienable under the National Trust for Scotland Order Confirmation Act 1935. The Council uses this power when it decides that a property should be preserved for the benefit of the nation.

[109] National Trust for Scotland, "Who we are and what we do: an introduction for newer members" (1997).

[110] This was a response to the recommendation of the Cairngorm Working Party in its Report: *Common Sense and Sustainability: a partnership for the Cairngorms*, 1992.

rely on the co-operation of existing agencies to deliver the programmes identified in the Management Strategy. One of the tasks of the partnership is to secure the effective use of such powers and make the best use of available resources. Funding from the partnership comes from the Scottish Executive and is channelled through Scottish Natural Heritage.

A draft Management Strategy was published in August 1996 and was followed by an extensive period of consultation with all partners. The Final Strategy entitled *Managing the Cairngorms* was published in 1997 and sets out a series of strategic objectives to be delivered by harnessing all the interest both local and national. It provides a detailed prospectus for the next steps of action required to meet the real needs of the area.

As a co-operative venture, the Partnership has not been able to address some of the larger issues which have arisen in recent years, notably the debate about the development of a funicular railway to replace the ageing main chairlift facilities at the Cairngorm ski area. There has also been continued debate about meeting conservation objectives through private land management following the changes to the ownership of important properties at the heart of the mountain massif. The Government has now responded positively to calls for the area to be designated as one of Scotland's two national parks (the other proposal is for the Loch Lomond area). It is argued that a national parks authority created by statute would provide "a clearer and stronger basis to move from a crucial phase of planning and debate to the delivery of the Partnership strategy. A statutory National Park Body with clear duties and powers and lines of accountability offers the prospect of continuity which the current voluntary arrangements do not".[111]

---

[111] *National Parks for Scotland: Scottish Natural Heritage's Advice to Government*, 1999, para. 6.6.

CHAPTER 3

DEVELOPMENT IN THE COUNTRYSIDE

Jeremy Rowan-Robinson

Introduction

It is sometimes suggested that planning law has little impact on rural land use and development. Like many generalisations, that statement is correct up to a point. As we shall see, the *use* of land for agriculture and forestry is not "development" within the meaning of the planning legislation and is not therefore subject to planning control; and certain agricultural and forestry *operations*, although falling within the definition of "development", are the subject of a general planning permission so that the level of control that can be exercised by a planning authority is limited (see below). However, the statement should not be relied on beyond that. Other activities in the countryside may be subject to planning control. These include housing, hotels, mineral working and other rural industry, leisure, recreational and tourism developments and some estate management activity. It should also be noted that certain agricultural and forestry operations fall outwith the terms of the general planning permission and are therefore subject to control by the planning authority. Furthermore, the report of the Land Reform Policy Group *Recommendations for Action* (1999) questions whether planning control might in the future be extended to agriculture and forestry.[1]

Although planning authority control over rural land use and development is subject to limitations, the control when it applies can be more restrictive than is the case in urban areas. This is because quite large areas of the countryside are the subject of safeguarding policies and development in such areas is confined to that which meets an essential local need. Stringent safeguarding policies apply, for example, in Green Belts, National Scenic Areas, Areas of Great Landscape Value and Sites of Special Scientific Interest; and generally restrictive planning policies apply in much of the rest of the Scottish countryside. "There are extensive areas", states National Planning Policy Guideline (NPPG) 15, *Rural Development*, "where conservation and protection of environmental quality remain the primary concerns . . . In certain areas, protection of prime quality agricultural land may

---

[1] Annex B.

51

also be a concern."[2] The purpose of these restrictions is partly to conserve important natural resources, partly to secure a rational distribution of infrastructure and partly to retain the countryside as a pleasant rural environment for the benefit of all. In some areas, such as parts of West Lothian, small-scale development has been seen as the key to upgrading areas of limited landscape value; and in some of the more remote rural areas of Scotland, the role of development in sustaining rural communities may outweigh restrictions on development. NPPG 15 states that new housing will continue to be required in remote areas to sustain economic activity and the viability of small village communities (para. 22).

This chapter explains the way in which planning control works. Its focus is on what is usually referred to as "mainstream planning control", the process of development control set out in Parts III and VI of the principal planning Act, the Town and Country Planning (Scotland) Act 1997 (referred to in this chapter as "the 1997 Act"). It follows the process, as it were, from gynaecology (the definition of development) through to pathology (the enforcement of planning control).

However, the planning legislation provides for a number of other control systems which operate alongside mainstream planning control. These other controls apply to buildings included in the list of buildings of architectural and historic interest prepared by the appropriate Minister, to areas designated by planning authorities as conservation areas, to trees which planning authorities have subjected to tree preservation orders, to the display of advertisements, to mineral working, to the bringing onto land of hazardous substances and to the tidying-up of waste land. Some of these controls are additional to mainstream planning control, some are a substitute for it, and some regulate activities which fall outwith planning control. Space precludes any discussion of these other controls.[3]

Mainstream planning control is a well-established and sophisticated system of regulation. It is essentially a preventive approach to the problems of land development. A permit, a grant of planning permission, is required for the development of land. Application is made to the planning authority, the local authority for the area. Subject to what is said below about structure plans, each of the 32 local authorities exercises all planning functions in its area. The permit process is an opportunity to identify and take account of the land use problems which may arise from the development. The process is open and members of the public and others have an opportunity to make representations about a planning application. In determining an application, the planning authority must have regard to the response to consultations, to any representations, to relevant planning policy and to other material considerations. As we shall see, policy plays a very important role in planning control. National planning policy emanates from the Scottish Executive Development Department and regional and local planning policy emanates from the local authorities. A planning permission may be conditional and there is provision to extend the scope of

---

[2] Scottish Office Development Department (1999), para. 26.
[3] See generally the *Scottish Planning Encyclopedia* (W. Green/Sweet & Maxwell, the Hon. Lord Gill (ed.)); N. Collar, *Planning* (W. Green/Sweet & Maxwell, 2nd edn, 1999); A. McAllister and R. McMaster, *Scottish Planning Law* (Butterworths, 2nd edn, 1999); and E. Young and J. Rowan-Robinson, *Scottish Planning Law and Procedure* (W. Hodge & Co. Ltd, 1985).

control through a linked agreement, a sort of private contract between the owner of the development site and the planning authority which has as its objective the restriction or regulation of the development or use of the land. The applicant may appeal to the appropriate Minister against an adverse decision on the application. The planning authority has at its disposal an array of mechanisms for tackling unauthorised development or development which proceeds in breach of a condition. The process is now examined under four headings: the requirement to submit a planning application, application procedure, decision-making and enforcement.

The requirement to submit a planning application

The definition of development

Planning permission is required for the "development" of land.[4] It seems that the reference to land is to land above the low-water mark of tidal waters.[5] The definition of development is very much the key to development control. If an activity falls outwith the definition, it falls outwith planning control. The first question to ask therefore is whether an activity constitutes development.

Development is defined in section 26 of the 1997 Act. The definition is very wide-ranging. Section 26(1) states that "development" means "the carrying out of building, engineering, mining or other operations in, on, over or under land, or the making of any material change in the use of any buildings or other land". A "building operation" is defined to include the demolition or rebuilding of buildings, the carrying out of structural alterations or additions to buildings or the undertaking of other operations normally carried on by a builder.[6]

The definition is therefore in two parts: the carrying out of an operation of some sort or the making of a material change of use. It is only necessary for an activity to fall within one of the parts for planning permission to be required. Sometimes, however, an activity will comprise both an operation and a material change of use: for example, the building of a new house on a greenfield site.

Operations: Generally, determining whether an activity constitutes an operation requiring planning permission is relatively straightforward. The construction of a new building, the rebuilding or extension of an existing building, the putting up of an enclosure and the laying out of an access road will all constitute development. Section 26(2) goes on to provide that certain operations are not to be taken to involve development. These include the carrying out of works for the maintenance, improvement or other alteration of a building which affect only the interior or which do not materially affect the external appearance of the building.[7]

For some time it was uncertain whether demolition of a building constituted development. This has now been clarified by expressly including demolition within the definition of a building operation (see above). However, section

---

[4] Town and Country Planning (Scotland) Act 1997, s. 28(1).
[5] *Argyll and Bute District Council* v *Secretary of State for Scotland* 1976 SC 248; 1977 SLT 33.
[6] Town and Country Planning (Scotland) Act 1997, s. 26(4).
[7] 1997 Act, s. 26(2)(a).

26(2)(g) of the 1997 Act goes on to provide that the demolition of any description of a building specified in a direction given by the Minister is not to be taken as involving development. The Town and Country Planning (Demolition which is not Development) (Scotland) Direction 1995 provides that the demolition of any building *other than* a dwelling-house or flat,[8] or the demolition of a listed building, a building which is a scheduled ancient monument, a building in a conservation area, or a building not exceeding 50 cubic metres (measured externally), is not to be taken to involve development. Nor is the demolition of the whole or any part of a gate, fence, wall or other means of enclosure.

Section 26(6) expressly provides that the placing or assembly of a tank in inland waters for the purposes of fish farming is to be treated as the carrying out of an engineering operation over the land covered with water.[9]

Material change of use: Determining whether an activity constitutes a material change of use can be more difficult. The position is straightforward with a change in kind, for example, from an agricultural use to a residential use. The determination can be more difficult where what is involved is a change to a similar use, for example from a flat for a large single family to a flat in multiple occupation by students or a change which involves the introduction of an ancillary use or the intensification of an existing use. It is only if a change of use is "material" that the requirement to obtain planning permission is triggered. Materiality is to be construed in planning terms.[10] In other words, the change must give rise to planning considerations of substance or, as was said in *Glasgow District Council* v *Secretary of State for Scotland*,[11] must lead to a change in the character of the use of the land. Beyond that very general guidance, the question whether a change is material is very much a question of fact and degree.

Where several activities are carried on within the same planning unit, there may be a single primary use to which all other uses are ancillary. For example, a farm may have a small sales area selling produce grown on the farm. Although retailing is not an agricultural use, it is ancillary to the agricultural use and the use of the planning unit, the farm, is for agriculture. A change from one purpose ancillary to the primary (agricultural) use to another purpose ancillary to that use will not usually amount to development. Nor will the introduction of a new ancillary use. However, where an ancillary use develops to such an extent that it becomes a separate use in its own right, for example if the farmer starts buying in produce to sell from the retail outlet on the farm, then planning permission will be required.

Determining the planning unit against which to judge the materiality of a change will not always be easy. This is generally, but not always, taken as the

---

[8] Although the demolition of a house or flat comprises development, in some cases that development will have the benefit of a general planning permission by virtue of the Town and Country Planning (General Permitted Development) (Scotland) Order 1992 (SI 1992/223), Sched. 1, Pt 23 (see below).

[9] "Fish farming" is defined as the breeding, rearing or keeping of fish or shellfish (including any kind of crustacean or mollusc); "inland waters" are defined as waters which do not form part of the sea or of any creek, bay or estuary or of any river as far as the tide flows; and "tank" is defined to include any cage and any other structure for use in fish farming (s. 26(6)).

[10] *Devonshire County Council* v *Allens Caravans (Estates) Ltd* (1962) 61 LGR 57.

[11] 1997 SCLR 417.

unit of occupation.[12] For example, where a barn on a farm is occupied for the purposes of storing plant and machinery used on the farm, the unit of occupation and thus the planning unit is the farm as a whole. Where, however, that barn becomes redundant to farm purposes and is leased off for the storage of plant and machinery used by a building contractor, it is no longer occupied as part of the farm but in its own right. There has been a change in the planning unit[13] and a consequent change in the use of the barn from an agricultural to a storage use and, thus, a material change of use.

Section 26(2) gives some assistance in determining whether a change of use is material by providing that the introduction of certain uses are not to be taken to involve development.[14] This applies, first of all, to the use of any buildings or other land within the curtilage of a dwelling for any purpose incidental to the enjoyment of the dwelling.[15] Second, the use of any land for the purposes of agriculture[16] or forestry[17] (including afforestation) and the use for any of those purposes of any building occupied together with land so used is not to be taken to involve development.[18] This exemption owes much to the need to promote domestic food production in the aftermath of the Second World War. Such uses were also regarded as environmentally benign. The advent of food surpluses and experience of the environmental effects of modern agricultural methods may lead to a review of this exemption. The third exemption is a change from one use to another within the same class of use specified in an order made by the Minister.[19] The current order is the Town and Country Planning (Use Classes) (Scotland) Order 1997 ("the UCO").[20] The Schedule to the Order lists 11 different classes of use. For example, the heading for Class 1 is "shops" and the Order lists within that Class 11 different types of shop. By virtue of section 26(2)(f) of the 1997 Act and Article 3 of the Order, a change from one type of shop to another type of shop on the list is exempt from planning control. Other classes include financial, professional and other services (Class 2), food and drink (Class 3), business (Class 4) and general industrial (Class 5). A change between classes is not covered by the exemption and is likely to constitute development. The Order is a deregulatory mechanism which removes from planning control changes of use which are unlikely to give rise to planning considerations.

Permitted development

Having determined that an activity falls within the definition of development, the second question to ask is whether an application for planning permission is required. There are a number of situations in which it is not. Of these, the most

---

[12] *Burdle* v *Secretary of State for the Environment* [1972] 1 WLR 1207.
[13] *G. Percy Trentham Ltd* v *Gloucestershire County Council* [1966] 1 WLR 506.
[14] s. 26(3) declares for the avoidance of doubt that certain uses involve a material change of use.
[15] s. 26(2)(d).
[16] "Agriculture" is defined in the 1997 Act, s. 277.
[17] In *Farleyer Estate* v *Secretary of State for Scotland* 1992 SC 202 it was held that a use of land for the purposes of forestry included the felling of trees and the extraction and storage of the timber on land at some distance (some 1,500 metres) from the forest where it was cut.
[18] s. 26(2)(e).
[19] s. 26(2)(f).
[20] SI 1997/3061.

important is where the activity has the benefit of a general planning permission granted by a development order. Article 3 of the Town and Country Planning (General Permitted Development) (Scotland) Order 1992[21] ("the GPDO") grants planning permission for the 69 classes of development listed in Schedule 1. These classes are grouped together into Parts. Where the permitted development would be likely to have a significant effect on a proposed or designated European site, as defined in Directive 92/43 on the conservation of natural habitats and of wild fauna and flora, it is subject to the prior approval of the planning authority.[22] Development otherwise covered by any of the 69 classes is not permitted if it should be the subject of an environmental assessment under the terms of the Environmental Assessment (Scotland) Regulations 1999.[23] The permission granted for the 69 classes of development is subject to tolerances and conditions.

The permission granted by the GPDO may be withdrawn by the Minister or by a planning authority by way of a direction made under Article 4 of the Order. Subject to limited exceptions, a direction by the planning authority requires the approval of the Minister (Art. 4(3)). A direction takes effect from the date on which public notice is given of its making or approval (Art. 4(5)). The effect of a direction is that planning permission will be required for the development in question from the planning authority in the normal way. If, however, permission is refused or is conditioned more onerously than would have been the case under the GPDO, an entitlement to compensation may arise.[24]

Like the UCO, the GPDO is also a deregulatory mechanism. It removes from the jurisdiction of the planning authority certain categories of development which either are relatively minor and can be allowed to go ahead subject to certain tolerances and conditions or are being carried on by bodies discharging functions in which there is a strong public interest dimension. In the former category come development within the curtilage of a dwelling-house, sundry minor operations, certain changes of use between one class of the Use Classes Order and another, temporary buildings and uses, agricultural and forestry buildings and operations, industrial and warehouse development and mineral exploration. In the latter category comes development by local authorities, repairs to services, development by statutory undertakers, aviation development, development by the Coal Authority and telecommunications development. As this is a book about countryside law, the permitted development rights for temporary uses of land, for caravans and for agricultural and forestry operations, which are most relevant in a countryside context, deserve a fuller explanation.

Part 4, Class 15—Temporary uses: Class 15 permits the use of land (other than a building or land within the curtilage of a building) for any purpose, except as a caravan site or an open-air market, on not more than 28 days in total in any calendar year. The erection or placing of moveable structures on the land for the purpose of that use is also permitted. The scope of this permission is considerable

---

[21] SI 1992/223.
[22] See Art. 3(1) of the GPDO and regs 60–63 of the Conservation (Natural Habitats etc.) Regulations 1994 (SI 1994/2716).
[23] Scottish SI 1999/1.
[24] 1997 Act, s. 77.

and may be used by farmers, for example to permit camping on their land in the summer. The 28 days do not need to be consecutive.

Part 5, Class 16—Caravan sites: The use of land as a caravan site is excluded from the permission granted by Class 15. It is covered instead by Class 16 which permits the use of land (other than a building) as a caravan site in the circumstances set out in paragraphs 2–10 of Schedule 1 to the Caravan Sites and Control of Development Act 1960. These circumstances include use by agricultural and forestry workers, use by a person travelling with a caravan for not more than two nights, the use of holdings of five acres or more in certain circumstances, and sites occupied and supervised by or approved by exempt organisations. Development required by the conditions of a caravan site licence granted under the 1960 Act is also permitted.

Part 6, Classes 18–21—Agricultural buildings and operations: Class 18 permits the carrying out on agricultural land comprised in an agricultural unit of:

- works for the erection, extension or alteration of a building;
- the formation, alteration or maintenance of private ways; or
- any excavation or engineering operations

requisite for the purposes of agriculture within that unit. "Agricultural land" is defined as land which, before the development permitted by the Order is carried out, is land in use for agriculture and which is so used for the purposes of a trade or business.[25] The definition excludes any dwelling-house or garden or any land used for the purposes of fish farming. An "agricultural unit" means agricultural land which is occupied as a unit for the purposes of agriculture other than fish farming.[26] "The purposes of agriculture" include fertilising land used for the purposes of agriculture and the maintenance, improvement or alteration of any buildings, structures or works occupied or used for such purposes on land so used. "Agriculture" is not defined in the GPDO and it is necessary to refer back to the definition in section 277(1) of the 1997 Act.

Development is not permitted by Class 18 if it would be carried out on agricultural land less than 0.4 hectares in area,[27] if it would consist of or include the erection, extension or alteration of a dwelling or if a building, structure or works not designed for the purposes of agriculture would be provided on the land. There is a limitation on the ground area[28] that may be covered by certain categories of development permitted by this Class including any new or extended building. There are also height limits. The permission does not apply to development within 25 metres of the metalled portion of a trunk or classified road. There is also a *cordon sanitaire* prescribed for development involving buildings or structures used for the intensive rearing of certain animals or for the storage of sewage sludge or slurry. The permission does not apply if the development is to be within 400 metres of the curtilage of an occupied building other than an agricultural building.

---

[25] See the interpretation paragraph for Classes 18–21.
[26] Ibid.
[27] For the calculation of the area see Class 18, para. (5)(a).
[28] For the calculation of the ground area see Class 18, para. (5)(b).

The permission granted by Class 18 is conditional.[29] Furthermore, development comprising the erection of a building or the significant extension or alteration of a building[30] is subject to a prior notification requirement.[31] A person wishing to exercise the permission must first seek a determination from the planning authority as to whether the siting, design and external appearance of the building is to be subject to their prior approval. Where prior approval is required, the development must be carried out in accordance with the approved details. The prior approval requirement enables the planning authority to control the impact of the development on the landscape but not the principle of development.

Class 19 permits the winning and working of minerals located within an agricultural unit for the agricultural purposes being carried on in that unit. Class 20 permits the carrying out of works required for the improvement or maintenance of watercourses or for land drainage. Class 21 permits the winning and working of peat by any person for the domestic requirements of that person.

Part 7, Class 22—Forestry buildings and operations: Class 22 permits the carrying out on land used for the purposes of forestry, including afforestation, of development reasonably necessary for those purposes consisting of:

- works for the erection, extension or alteration of a building;
- the formation, alteration or maintenance of private ways;
- operations on that land, or on land held or occupied with that land, to obtain the materials required for the formation, alteration or maintenance of such ways;
- other operations (not including engineering or mining operations).

The permission does not cover the provision or alteration of a dwelling; nor does it cover buildings or works above a certain height or development within 25 metres of the metalled portion of a trunk or classified road.

Development consisting of the erection of a building or the significant extension or alteration[32] of a building is subject to a prior notification requirement in the same way as agricultural buildings permitted by Class 18 (see above). As with Class 18 buildings, this enables the planning authority to control the impact of the development on the landscape but not the principle of development.

Application procedure

If an activity constitutes development and is not permitted by the GPDO, planning permission is required from the planning authority before it can be commenced. The procedure to be followed in making and determining an

---

[29] Class 18, para. 3.

[30] It should be noted that development comprising the significant extension or alteration of a building may only be carried out once in respect of that building (Class 18, para. (4)(b)). For the definition of significant extension and alteration see the interpretation paragraph for Classes 18–21.

[31] Ibid, para. 4.

[32] For the meaning of significant extension or alteration see the interpretation paragraph for Class 22.

application is set out in the Town and Country Planning (General Development Procedure) (Scotland) Order 1992.[33]

Outline and full applications

An application for planning permission is made on a form obtained from the planning authority. The application will describe the development to which it relates and be accompanied by a location plan and such other plans and drawings as are necessary. It must be accompanied by the appropriate ownership and neighbour notification certificates (see below) and by the appropriate fee.

An application for planning permission for an operation may be submitted in outline to test the principle of the development.[34] Such an application will be accompanied by a location plan but the preparation of detailed drawings will be postponed until the principle has been determined. There may be little point, for example, in going to the expense of preparing detailed plans for a development in the Green Belt until it is clear that the planning authority is prepared to accept the principle of the development. The planning authority may notify the applicant that the application cannot be entertained unless details of all or any of the reserved matters are supplied.[35] Where outline planning permission is granted, the subsequent approval of the planning authority will be required to such reserved matters as may be specified by the authority in the consent. The outline permission establishes the principle of the development and the planning authority cannot resile from that when determining the application for approval of reserved matters. It will be a condition of an outline consent that an application for approval of any matter reserved in the outline must be made within three years of the date of the consent.[36] An application made after that date is to be treated as not made in accordance with the terms of the outline consent.[37]

Environmental assessment

Certain applications must be accompanied by an environmental statement. The requirement is set out in the Environmental Assessment (Scotland) Regulations 1999[38] which implement EC Directive 85/337[39] on the assessment of the effects of certain public and private projects on the environment.

Article 2 of the Directive, as amended, requires that public or private projects likely to have significant effects on the environment by virtue, *inter alia*, of their size or location are made the subject of an assessment with regard to their effects. The Directive lists certain projects which, if they meet prescribed thresholds, are to be subject to a mandatory assessment (Annex 1). The list is replicated in Schedule 1 to the Regulations. These are the projects with the greatest potential for environmental impact. They include crude oil refineries, thermal power stations, integrated chemical installations, waste disposal installations, waste

---

[33] SI 1992/224.

[34] 1997 Act, s. 59, and 1992 Regulations, reg. 4.

[35] 1992 Regulations, reg. 4(3). For the definition of "reserved matters" see reg. 2.

[36] The time-limit is adjusted where an earlier application for approval has been refused or where an appeal has been lodged against a refusal (s. 59(2)(a)).

[37] 1997 Act, s. 60(4)(b).

[38] Scottish SI 1999/1.

[39] As amended by Directive 97/11.

water treatment plants, dams, installations for the intensive rearing of pigs or poultry, quarries and open-cast mining. The Directive also lists other categories of development (Annex II) which are to be subject to an assessment where Member States consider their characteristics so require. The list of Annex II projects is replicated in Schedule 2 to the Regulations. The projects are grouped into categories which include agriculture and aquaculture, the extractive industries, the energy industry, infrastructure projects and tourism and leisure. Thresholds and criteria for these projects are prescribed in Schedule 2. Regulation 3(2) provides that a planning authority (or the Minister or a reporter on a call-in or on an appeal) must not grant planning permission for a Schedule 1 or 2 project unless it has first taken into account environmental information in respect of the proposed development.

Determining whether an application falls within Schedule 2 to the Regulations may not be straightforward. To assist the determination, certain thresholds and criteria are set out in the Regulations. The determination should be informed by the selection criteria for screening Schedule 2 developments set out in Schedule 3. These criteria focus on the characteristics of the development, its location and the characteristics of its potential impact on the environment. The determination at the end of the day is an exercise of discretion: the question to be asked is whether the project is likely to have a significant effect on the environment. An applicant who is uncertain about whether an environmental statement should be provided may request a ruling from the planning authority and reasons must be given for a decision to require the provision of a statement. If the applicant disagrees with the ruling, a direction may be sought from the Minister (reg. 5(6)). In *R. v Swale Borough Council, ex p. RSPB*[40] Simon Brown J. held that the decision whether development was or was not within the scheduled descriptions of development for the purposes of the Regulations was a matter for the planning authority subject only to *Wednesbury* unreasonableness.[41] In other words, questions of classification for the purposes of the Schedules are essentially matters of fact and degree rather than law.

There is no statutory format for an environmental statement but it must deal with the matters set out in Schedule 4 to the Regulations (reg. 2(1)). These include a description of the development, an outline of the main alternatives studied, a description of the aspects of the environment likely to be significantly affected by the development, the measures to be taken to mitigate these effects and a non-technical summary of all of this. If requested the planning authority must give an opinion of the information which the developer is obliged to provide.

The authority has power to call for the provision of additional information (reg. 19(1)). Public notice must be given of the submission of the statement (reg. 13(5)) and it is to be made available to the public. The authority must consult with certain bodies about the information in the statement including Scottish Natural Heritage (SNH), the Scottish Environment Protection Agency (SEPA) and the appropriate water authority (reg. 14(1)).

At the end of the day, the Directive and the Regulations simply require that the environmental information comprising the statement and the response to it must

---

[40] [1991] 1 PLR 6.
[41] See *Associated Provincial Picture Houses Ltd* v *Wednesbury Corporation* [1948] 1 KB 223.

be taken into consideration. It seems that provided the objectives of the Directive are in substance achieved in a particular case, a court may decline to quash the planning decision notwithstanding a failure to comply with the Regulations.[42] Nonetheless, if there is a substantive failure, the decision is likely to be quashed.[43] The planning authority are already required to give reasons for refusing planning permission. The Regulations require that reasons must also be given for granting consent in cases where an environmental statement is provided (reg. 21(1)).

Publicity

As mentioned above, development control is an open process. Although the applicant does not have to own the land which is the subject of the application, notice of the application must be given to the owner and the application must be accompanied by the appropriate certificate.[44] Any agricultural tenant must be notified. The 1992 Regulations also require neighbours to be notified[45] and the application must be accompanied by the appropriate certificate to this effect. With applications for development in the countryside there will quite often be no neighbours, within the meaning of the requirement, to be notified. Public notice must be given of certain proposals falling within the list of "bad neighbour" developments.[46] These include the introduction of operations or uses which will alter the character of an area of established amenity, bring crowds into a generally quiet area or introduce significant change into a homogenous area. The planning authority must supply community councils with a weekly list of applications received and must respond to requests from the councils for information about particular applications.[47] Applications must also be lodged in a register which must be available for inspection by the public at all reasonable hours.[48]

Consultation

In addition to the publicity requirements described above, the planning authority may be required to consult other public bodies about an application. The consultation requirement is set out in regulation 15 of the 1992 Regulations. For example, SNH must be consulted where the development may affect a site of special scientific interest. SEPA must be consulted about certain categories of development which may give rise to pollution. District salmon fishery boards must be consulted about fish farms. And the appropriate water authority must be consulted about developments which are likely to require a material addition to, or a material change in, the services provided by that authority.

The planning authority is not obliged to follow the advice given in response to the consultation exercise.[49] However, the Minister must be notified in certain

---

[42] *Berkeley* v *Secretary of State for the Environment* [1998] 3 PLR 39.

[43] *R.* v *Rochdale Metropolitan Borough Council, ex p. Milne*, Queen's Bench Division, unreported, May 1999.

[44] 1997 Act, s. 35, and 1992 Regulations, reg. 8.

[45] The requirements are set out in reg. 9. The definition of "neighbour" for the purposes of the notification exercise is complex and is set out in reg. 2.

[46] The list is set out in the Town and Country Planning (General Permitted Development) (Scotland) Order 1992, Sched. 2.

[47] 1992 Regulations, regs 11(9) and 15(1)(n).

[48] 1997 Act, s. 36, and 1992 Regulations, regs 10 and 11 and Sched. 5.

[49] See, however, the discussion of the implications of the Habitats Directive (below).

cases where the planning authority is minded to grant planning permission against the advice of a consultee.[50] The circumstances in which notification must occur include a development which would involve a change of use of 10 hectares or more of class 1, 2 or 3.1 agricultural land and either the development would be contrary to an adopted or approved local plan or there is no such local plan or an official from the Scottish Executive Rural Affairs Department has advised against granting permission; and development which SNH has advised will adversely affect a national scenic area[51] or certain sites of nature conservation importance. The purpose of notification is to enable consideration to be given to the issuing of a direction to the planning authority to refer the application to the Minister for a decision.[52]

Decision-making

The essential characteristic of the decision-making process for planning applications is that it is a system of discretionary development control operating within a framework of indicative policy guidance. The important role of policy in decision-making distinguishes planning from many other systems of regulation; but other factors such as the response to publicity and consultations and other material considerations must be taken into account.

Planning policy

A planning authority, like any other public body making a decision, is subject to the general principles of administrative law and must have regard to all relevant considerations, must not be influenced by irrelevant considerations and must not reach a decision which no authority, properly advised, would have reached.[53] Relevant policy is clearly something which must be taken into account in reaching a decision and failure to do so could open the decision to challenge in the courts. Planning policy may be formulated at the national level by the Scottish Executive Development Department or at the local or regional level by the planning authority or by that authority working in conjunction with an adjoining planning authority or authorities (see below). The requirement to have regard to relevant policy is reinforced with regard to local policy by statutory provisions.[54] These are examined below.

However, important as policy clearly is, it must not be of such a nature that it prevents an authority from considering an application on its own merits.[55] Nor is there any requirement that an authority should "slavishly adhere" to policy.[56] The policy (whether national or local) is for guidance and the authority may depart from it if there is good reason for doing so and providing any procedural requirements (below) are observed.

---

[50] See the Town and Country Planning (Notification of Applications) (Scotland) Direction 1997, annexed to Circular 4/1997.
[51] This is provided for in the Town and Country Planning (Notification of Applications) (National Scenic Areas) (Scotland) Direction 1987 (annexed to SDD Circular 9/1987).
[52] 1997 Act, s. 46.
[53] *Associated Provincial Picture Houses Ltd* v *Wednesbury Corporation* [1948] 1 KB 223.
[54] 1997 Act, s. 37(2). See too s. 25.
[55] *Stringer* v *Minister of Housing and Local Government* [1970] 1 WLR 1281.
[56] *Simpson* v *Edinburgh Corporation* 1960 SC 313; 1961 SLT 17.

National policy

Unlike the position with local policy, there is no obligation on the Minister to prepare national planning policy guidance. The Select Committee on Land Resource Use in Scotland recommended in 1972 that a national structure plan, a sort of national land use plan, should be prepared for Scotland as a whole.[57] The Government, in its response to the report, considered that the preparation of a rigid national plan would be impracticable, but accepted the need for more central guidance and undertook to build up "a set of guidelines on those aspects of land use which should be examined for Scotland as a whole".[58] The first such guidance emerged in 1974 with the "Coastal Planning Guidelines" (since replaced). These were a response to the disputes which had arisen over the location of oil rig construction yards around Scotland's coastline. The guidelines identified preferred development zones and preferred conservation zones. Other guidelines, called "national planning guidelines", were issued over the next decade which sought to identify natural resources having national significance and to safeguard them from or for development. Subsequently, the objective of the series was modified. The purpose of the guidelines is now to provide statements of government policy on nationally important land use and other planning matters, supported where appropriate by a locational framework, and the guidance has been revised and reissued under the title "national planning policy guidelines" (NPPGs). The NPPGs are statements of national policy which are expected to be applied by planning authorities in their local policies and in day-to-day development control decisions.

A number of the NPPGs have particular relevance to the countryside. These include NPPG 4 (*Mineral Working*), NPPG 6 (*Renewable Energy*), NPPG 11 (*Sport, Physical Recreation and Open Space*), NPPG 12 (*Skiing Development*), NPPG 13 (*Coastal Planning*), NPPG 14 (*Natural Heritage*) and NPPG 15 (*Rural Development*).

Other national policy guidance takes the form of circulars, which contain advice on policy implementation through legislative or procedural change, and planning advice notes (PANs) which provide advice on good practice and other relevant information. Recent PANs of particular relevance to countryside planning include PAN 36 (*Siting and Design of Houses in the Countryside*), PAN 39 (*Farm and Forestry Buildings*), PAN 42 (*Archaeology: The Planning Process and Scheduled Monument Procedures*), PAN 43 (*Golf Courses and Associated Developments*), PAN 44 (*Fitting New Housing into the Landscape*), PAN 45 (*Renewable Energy Technologies*), PAN 50 (*Controlling the Environmental Effect of Surface Mineral Workings*) and PAN 51 (*Planning and Environmental Protection*).

Local and regional policy

Planning authorities are required to prepare and keep up to date a development plan for their area. The plan is in two tiers: the structure plan and the local plan.

The structure plan: The structure plan is not map-based but will contain a key diagram. It is a written statement formulating the authority's policy and general

---

[57] *Land Resource Use in Scotland*, Vol. 1, Report of Proceedings (House of Commons Paper 511–I, Session 1971–72, HMSO, 1972).

[58] *Land Resource Use in Scotland: The Government's Observations on the Report of the Select Committee on Scottish Affairs*, Cmnd. 5428 (1973).

proposals in respect of the development and other use of land in its area. The plan focuses on key strategic land use issues for the area and must include measures for the conservation of natural beauty and amenity of the land, the improvement of the physical environment and the management of traffic.[59] Although a planning authority exercises no direct control over afforestation, in areas where a significant amount of tree planting can be expected, planning authorities are encouraged to prepare indicative forestry strategies[60] and to incorporate these into the structure plan (see Chapter 7). The strategy will provide guidance to potential investors, establish a framework for responses to consultations about planting grant applications and furnish material to be taken into account by the Forestry Commission and others when considering applications for grant.

The Minister has designated "structure plan areas" in respect of which authorities are to prepare and keep under review structure plans.[61] Some of these cover the area of more than one planning authority. In such cases the authorities must work together to produce and keep under review a joint structure plan.

The planning authority must give adequate publicity to the matters which they propose to include in the plan or in any alteration or replacement of the plan and allow an opportunity for representations, and such representations must be taken into account. The plan must be submitted to the Minister for approval and the Minister has power to arrange for an examination in public of selected key issues in the plan before reaching a decision with regard to approval. No such examination has been convened for some years now.

An important function of the structure plan is to provide a framework or context for the preparation of the local plan.

The local plan: Planning authorities are under a duty to prepare a local plan or plans covering all parts of their area and must keep the plan(s) under review.[62] The local plan comprises a written statement formulating the authority's proposals for the development and other use of land in their area including such measures as the authority thinks fit for the conservation of the natural beauty and amenity of land, the improvement of the physical environment and the management of traffic.[63] Unlike the structure plan, the local plan is map-based and the maps will clearly have an important bearing on development control decisions.

As with the structure plan, an authority engaged in preparing or replacing a local plan must give adequate publicity to the proposals and provide the public with an opportunity to make representations.[64] An expedited procedure may be used for alterations to the plan where the authority consider this appropriate.[65]

---

[59] 1997 Act, s. 7(1)(a).

[60] See SODD Circular 9/1999; and see Chap. 7.

[61] Designation of Structure Plan Areas (Scotland) Order 1995 (SI 1995/3002). Section 6(2) of the 1997 Act provides that where as the result of the making of the order, the area to be covered by a structure plan is different from the area for the structure plan for the time being in force, the authority must prepare a fresh structure plan for the new area.

[62] 1997 Act, ss 11(1) and 13(1).

[63] 1997 Act, s. 11(3).

[64] 1997 Act, s. 12.

[65] 1997 Act, s. 12(6).

Local plans do not require the Minister's approval (although the Minister may call in the plan for approval) and are generally adopted by the authority. Before doing so, the plan must be formally placed on deposit and an opportunity allowed for objection. An objector is entitled to be heard in support of an objection.[66] The planning authority must consider all objections before reaching a decision with regard to adoption of the plan. An authority may not adopt any plan or proposals which do not conform to an approved structure plan for the area.[67]

The status of the development plan: Section 37(2) of the 1997 Act provides that, when determining a planning application, the planning authority *must* have regard to the development plan so far as material to the application. This section must now be read in conjunction with section 25 which provides that, when in making a determination regard is to be had to the development plan, the determination shall be made in accordance with the plan unless material considerations indicate otherwise. In *City of Edinburgh Council* v *Secretary of State for Scotland*[68] Lord Clyde, giving judgment for the House of Lords, said that:

"[i]f it is thought to be useful to talk of presumptions in this field, it can be said that there is now a presumption that the development plan is to govern the decision on an application for permission".

He went on to say:

"By virtue of [section 25] if the application accords with the development plan and there are no material considerations indicating that it should be refused, permission should be granted. If the application does not accord with the development plan it will be refused unless there are material considerations indicating that it should be granted ... Thus the priority given to the development plan is not a mere mechanical preference for it. There remains a valuable element of flexibility. If there are material considerations indicating that it should not be followed then a decision contrary to its provisions can properly be given."

The weight to be accorded to the development plan and to other considerations in any particular case remains a matter for the decision-maker.

Departure procedure: As indicated above, the development plan is not binding; it is for guidance. However, as it will usually have been subject to the disciplines of public participation and merit testing, it is desirable that planning authorities should not be allowed to set it aside when determining a planning application without any procedural safeguards. There are three such safeguards. First of all, where the Minister has approved a structure or local plan, the Minister must be notified of any proposal which the authority is minded to approve which would amount to a significant departure from it. This provides an opportunity to

---

[66] 1997 Act, s. 15(2).
[67] 1997 Act, s. 17(3).
[68] 1997 SCLR 1112. See too NPPG 1, para. 44.

consider calling in the decision from the authority. Second, as the public had an opportunity to have a say in the plan, any proposed departure from it must be advertised and any response must be taken into account.[69] Third, in order to promote confidence in the decision-making process, authorities are encouraged to consider whether it might be appropriate to give all those who make representations about a departure application the opportunity of a hearing before a decision is taken.[70] Applicants should also have an opportunity to be heard in such cases.

Material considerations

Section 37(2) provides that in determining an application, regard must be had not only to the development plan but also to any other material considerations. This emphasises the discretionary nature of the development control process. Failure to have regard to a material consideration when making a decision could open the decision to challenge in the courts.[71]

Deciding what is encompassed by the term "material considerations" is not easy. In *Stringer* v *Minister of Housing and Local Government*[72] Cooke J. held that a material consideration was one relating to the use and development of land which was material in the circumstances. In *Tesco Stores Ltd* v *Secretary of State for the Environment*[73] Lord Keith observed that a material consideration meant a relevant consideration and that a consideration was material provided it had at least a tenuous relation to the subject-matter of the application. He went on to say that the weight to be attached to a material consideration was a matter for the decision-maker and the courts would not disturb the weighting in the absence of *Wednesbury* unreasonableness.

The compatibility of uses, the preservation of an existing use, the risk that a planning permission will establish an undesirable precedent and the question whether a better alternative site exists have all been accepted as material considerations in particular cases. In *Brighton Borough Council* v *Secretary of State for the Environment*[74] planning permission was refused for residential development on an unused part of playing fields attached to a school. The school building was listed because of its special architectural or historic interest and occupied a prominent place in a Conservation Area. The inspector conducting the inquiry into the appeal took account of the fact that the building's future would be assured if capital could be realised from the proposed development. The inspector's decision to grant planning permission was challenged on the ground that he had had regard to an irrelevant consideration—the financial circumstances of the school. It was held that safeguarding the future of the listed building was a planning consideration and the inspector was entitled to take account of the financial consequences for the building of granting the permission. In *Gateshead Metropolitan Borough Council* v *Secretary of State for the Environment*[75] it was argued

---

[69] The Town and Country Planning (Development Contrary to Development Plans) (Scotland) Direction 1996 (Annex B to PAN 41).
[70] PAN 41 (*Development Plan Departures*).
[71] See *Aberdeen District Council* v *Secretary of State for Scotland* 1993 SLT 1325.
[72] [1970] 1 WLR 1281.
[73] [1995] 1 WLR 759.
[74] (1980) 39 P&CR 46.
[75] [1994] 1 PLR 85.

that an inspector, in granting planning permission for a clinical waste incinerator, had failed to have regard to a material consideration, namely the potential pollution from the incinerator. The Court of Appeal held that the potential polluting effect of the development was a material consideration. So, too, was the existence of another system of regulation to control that pollution. Both these matters had been taken into account by the inspector. It was for the decision-maker to decide how much weight to attach to these considerations.

The Birds and Habitats Directives

When considering a planning application for development in the countryside, a planning authority may have to have regard to the effects of the Birds and Habitats Directives (see Chapter 11). Their effect can be significant.

Directive 79/409 on the conservation of wild birds ("the Birds Directive") requires Member States *inter alia* to take special measures to conserve the habitats of certain particularly rare species and migratory species of birds. As part of these special measures, States must classify the most suitable areas for these species as special protection areas for birds (SPAs). The Birds Directive has been amended by Directive 92/43 on the conservation of natural habitats and of wild flora and fauna ("the Habitats Directive"). This requires Member States to contribute towards establishing a coherent Community-wide network of special areas of conservation (SACs) called "Natura 2000". These will comprise sites hosting certain natural habitat types and sites comprising the habitats of certain rare species. All SPAs will form part of the Natura 2000 network.

The Habitats Directive has been given effect through the Conservation (Natural Habitats etc.) Regulations 1994.[76] It should be noted that the Government has decided that the Regulations should apply to proposed and classified SPAs and to candidate SACs.[77] In other words, they apply now to potential as well as actual sites.

Regulation 48 requires the planning authority to assess the implications of a development proposal affecting a SPA or SAC in the light of the site's conservation objectives. This process will be assisted by an environmental assessment which will normally be required in such cases. The authority may only grant planning permission for the development after having ascertained that it will not adversely affect the integrity of the site.[78] This significantly reduces the planning authority's discretion in such cases. Exceptionally, regulation 49 provides that a project which will adversely affect the integrity of a SPA or SAC and for which there is no alternative, may be granted permission for imperative reasons of overriding public interest. These might include economic or social considerations. However, where the site is one hosting a priority natural habitat type and/or a priority species (identified in the Habitats Directive) the only recognised overriding interests are those of human health, public safety, major benefits to the

---

[76] SI 1994/2716.

[77] See SOEnvD Circular 6/1995.

[78] In *WWF-UK Ltd and Another* v *Secretary of State for Scotland and Others* (OH), October 27, 1998 (unreported), Lord Nimmo Smith held that this could not be interpreted as demanding an absolute guarantee that the site will not be adversely affected. It was permissible to have regard to conditions on the planning permission and to any related planning agreement designed to prevent harmful consequences arising.

environment or other imperative reasons of overriding public interest accepted by the Commission. Where permission is given in such cases, the Government must ensure that the overall coherence of the Natura 2000 programme is protected by taking any necessary compensatory measures.

Landscape considerations

Compared with sites of nature conservation interest, listed buildings, ancient monuments and sites of archaeological interest, landscape considerations receive remarkably little recognition, at present, in legislation. This may seem surprising given the high quality of Scotland's landscape. As SNH observe, "[t]he beauty of our country is of great importance to the people of Scotland. It is part of our quality of life, part of our national identity, and of no small economic importance as the main attraction for our many visitors. In all these ways it is a great national asset".[79] Such considerations may, nonetheless, be an important material consideration when determining a planning application.

The need for some form of landscape designation can be traced back to the post-war debate about National Parks for Scotland. The Ramsay Committee recommended the introduction of five National Parks in Scotland (see Chapter 1).[80] This proposal foundered. Instead, the five areas were designated as "National Park Direction areas". The objective was to provide a mechanism for safeguarding the most valued landscapes. All planning applications in these five areas had to be notified to the Secretary of State who could consider whether to call them in for his own decision. Under section 9 of the Countryside (Scotland) Act 1967, the Secretary of State also had power to designate areas in which all planning applications within stated categories had to be notified to the Countryside Commission for Scotland (CCS). CCS would advise the planning authority with regard to the impact of the proposed development. In the event of a dispute, the matter would be referred to the Secretary of State who could call in the application. In addition to these nationally designated areas, planning authorities were encouraged to identify in their development plans Areas of Great Landscape Value within which special development control policies might apply.[81] These local designations are still relevant today. It seems that, in addition to Areas of Great Landscape Value, there is a range of other local landscape designations. Any such local designation may be a material consideration in a development control decision.

The position regarding national landscape designations is more complex. In 1974 CCS published a report entitled *A Park System for Scotland*. The report singled out three areas of outstanding landscape which were subject to particular pressures and recommended a management regime involving "Special Parks". This recommendation was the forerunner of the legislation on "Regional Parks" in Scotland (see Chapter 14). The report also recognised that, to secure better protection, some designation was required for other landscapes which were not under such pressures but which were "considered to be of unsurpassed attractiveness which must be conserved as part of our national heritage". This recommendation was followed by an extensive survey, the outcome of which was reported in *Scotland's Scenic Heritage*, published by CCS in 1978. This

---

[79] SNH, *National Scenic Areas: A Consultation Paper* (January 1999), Foreword.
[80] Scottish National Parks Survey Committee, Cmnd. 6631 (1945).
[81] SDD Circular 2/1962.

identified 40 areas considered to be of national scenic significance, the attractiveness of which should be conserved as part of the national heritage. SDD Circular 20/1980[82] gave effect to this recommendation by designating these areas as "National Scenic Areas" (see map).

Planning authorities were required to promote policies in their development plans to safeguard landscape quality in these areas. A limited number of categories of development were identified which were to be referred to CCS for comment. Where there was a difference of view between CCS and the planning authority about how to deal with such a development, it would be referred to the Secretary of State who could decide whether to call it in for his own decision. The National Park Direction Areas were extinguished.[83] Subsequently, National Scenic Areas (NSAs) received statutory recognition in section 262C of the Town and Country Planning (Scotland) Act 1972.[84] This provided that in such areas special attention was to be paid to the desirability of preserving or enhancing the character or appearance of an NSA in the exercise of any powers under the Planning Act (section 262C(4)). Section 262C was subsequently amended by the Natural Heritage (Scotland) Act 1991. This established Scottish Natural Heritage (SNH) in place of CCS. The effect of the amendment was to repeal the power to designate NSAs,[85] preserve the designation of NSA for the areas already so designated (unless and until subsequently cancelled by direction in any particular case) and provide in new cases for the designation instead of "Natural Heritage Areas" (NHAs).[86] To merit designation, the area must be considered by SNH to be of outstanding value to the natural heritage and SNH must believe that special protection measures are appropriate to it.[87] Section 262C(4) (above) (now section 264 of the 1997 Act) is applied to NHAs. No such areas have been designated although the Cairngorms Partnership was established to test the applicability of the designation to that area.[88] With the current commitment to national parks (see Chapter 1) it is thought unlikely that the designation will now ever be invoked.[89] In the meantime, SNH, at the Government's request, is reviewing the NSA regime.[90]

The important point to emerge from this rather complex review is that there are in place in Scotland at the present time 40 NSAs which have an important influence on development control decisions.[91] NPPG 14 *Natural Heritage* states that planning authorities should "take particular care to ensure that new development in or adjacent to a NSA does not detract from the quality and character of the landscape. They should also ensure that the scale, siting and design of such development are appropriate and that the design and landscaping are of a high standard" (para. 26).

---

[82] Subsequently amended by SDD Circular 9/1987.
[83] The Town and Country Planning (Notification of Applications) (Scotland) Direction 1980.
[84] Inserted by Sched. 11, para. 38 to the Housing and Planning Act 1986.
[85] Natural Heritage (Scotland) Act 1991, s. 27 and Sched. 11.
[86] Natural Heritage (Scotland) Act 1991, s. 6
[87] Natural Heritage (Scotland) Act 1991, s. 6(1).
[88] NPPG 14 *Natural Heritage*, para. 34.
[89] Ibid.
[90] SNH, *National Scenic Areas: A Consultation Paper* (January 1999).
[91] See generally SDD Circulars 20/1980 and 9/1987.

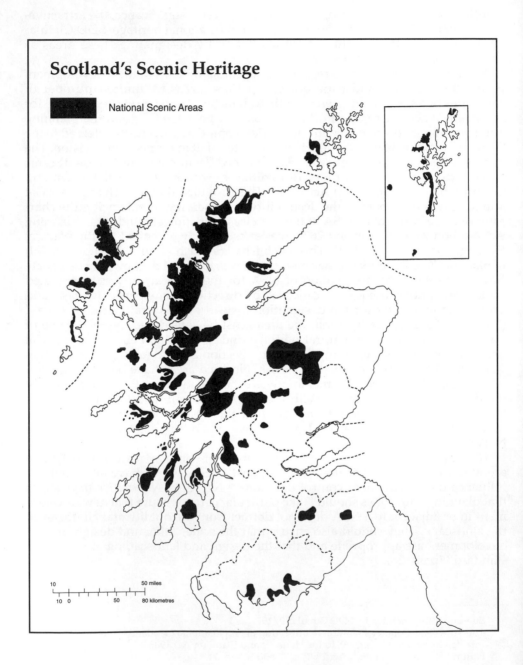

Scotland's Scenic Heritage

National Scenic Areas

Certain special procedures apply in NSAs. First of all, the general planning permission granted by the GPDO (above) has been withdrawn for certain categories of development affecting an NSA. The Town and Country Planning (Restriction of Permitted Development) (National Scenic Areas) Direction 1987[92] provides that a specific grant of planning permission will be required for the erection of agricultural or forestry buildings or structures over 12 metres high, the construction of vehicle tracks for agriculture of forestry purposes except forestry tracks which are part of an approved afforestation scheme and all local road works outside present road boundaries costing more than £100,000.

Secondly, the Town and Country Planning (Notification of Applications) (National Scenic Areas) (Scotland) Direction 1987[93] provides that where a planning authority proposes to grant planning permission for any development falling within a class set out in Schedule 1 of the Direction, it shall consult with SNH. Where SNH advises against granting planning permission or recommends conditions which the authority does not propose to impose, the application must be notified to the Minister who has an opportunity to call it in for a decision. The classes of development listed in Schedule 1 include those for which the general planning permission has been withdrawn but also others. The classes are proposals for five or more houses, chalets or flats (subject to a limited exception), sites for five or more mobile dwellings or caravans, all non-residential developments requiring more than 0.5 hectares of land, all buildings and structures over 12 metres high, all vehicle tracks except those forming part of an approved afforestation scheme, and all local road works outside present road boundaries costing more than £100,000.

Conditions[94]

Planning authorities have wide powers to impose conditions on a grant of planning permission. Section 37(1) provides that they may impose "such conditions as they think fit". Section 41(1) goes on to provide that, without prejudice to the generality of section 37(1), such conditions may regulate land under the applicant's control, whether or not it is land in respect of which the application is made, and may require the carrying out of works on such land. Although the power to impose conditions is expressed in broad terms, it has not been interpreted in this way by the courts. In *Newbury District Council v Secretary of State for the Environment*[95] Viscount Dilhorne said that "conditions imposed must be for a planning purpose and not for any ulterior one, and that they must fairly and reasonably relate to the development permitted. Also they must not be so unreasonable that no reasonable planning authority could have imposed them". In addition to these tests, conditions may also be void for uncertainty.[96]

The application of these tests can be difficult in practice. For example, it is often said that planning is concerned with the use of land and not with the users. However, in *Fawcett Properties Ltd v Buckingham County Council*[97] a condition

---

[92] Ibid.
[93] Annexed to SDD Circular 9/1987.
[94] See generally the Hon. Lord Osborne, "Planning Conditions" in *Scottish Planning Encyclopaedia* (the Hon. Lord Gill (ed.); W. Green/Sweet & Maxwell).
[95] [1981] AC 578.
[96] *Fawcett Properties Ltd v Buckingham County Council* [1961] AC 636.
[97] [1961] AC 636.

providing that the occupation of a pair of cottages should be limited to persons employed in agriculture or forestry was upheld. Underlying the condition was a clear planning purpose: the preservation of the Green Belt. In *Birnie* v *Banff County Council*[98] a condition was held to be *ultra vires* in that it required the carrying out of work, in that case the construction of an access, on land which was not under the applicant's control. The condition was therefore unreasonable. However, it will sometimes be the case that the land required for the provision of necessary infrastructure—for example upgrading the local road network—will be beyond the applicant's control. A refusal of planning permission in such cases may be an unduly negative response. One way round the difficulty is to use a suspensive condition. This is a negatively worded condition which makes the commencement or occupation of the development contingent on the happening of an event such as the upgrading of the road network. Such a condition is competent even if there is no reasonable prospect of the contingency being fulfilled.[99]

Helpful advice on the use of conditions is set out in Circular 4/1998.

Agreements

Section 75 of the 1997 Act enables a planning authority to enter into an agreement with any person having an interest in land for the purpose of restricting or regulating the development or use of the land. Such agreements may contain incidental financial provisions. If recorded, the agreements will be enforceable by the planning authority against singular successors.

Planning agreements are used quite commonly to strengthen the position of planning authorities in the development control process. A planning authority will indicate a willingness to grant planning permission subject to completion of an agreement. Agreements offer certain advantages to planning authorities. They can be used to impose obligations which go beyond those that can be achieved through conditions. Agreements can be used, for example, to secure the provision of infrastructure on land beyond the control of the applicant; and they can impose financial obligations, for example a payment in lieu of car parking, designed to address a problem raised by a development. Agreements also open the door to alternative methods of enforcement. Although the reforms introduced by the Planning and Compensation Act 1991 have addressed some of the problems being experienced with the enforcement regime in the Planning Act, planning authorities find the prospect of access to the sheriff court a reassurance. Furthermore, agreements leave control in the hands of the planning authority. There is no appeal against an agreement; it would be a contradiction in terms. This means that there is no risk of obligations contained in an agreement being overturned by the Minister on appeal.

Agreements have been used quite extensively in the countryside.[100] They have been used to control the occupancy of new houses in the countryside, to tie a new house to an economic unit, be it a farm, an hotel or a caravan site, to secure access and recreational benefits for the local community, to improve the country-

---

[98] 1954 SLT (Sh Ct) 90.

[99] *Grampian Regional Council* v *City of Aberdeen District Council* 1984 SLT 197; *British Railways Board* v *Secretary of State for the Environment* [1994] JPL 32.

[100] See generally J. Rowan-Robinson and R. Durman, *Section 50 Agreements* (Scottish Office, 1992).

side through amenity tree planting and the promotion of nature conservation, to control the number of boats in a marina, to limit the impact of mineral working and to secure restoration on completion, and to ensure the effective management of visitors to recreational facilities in the interests of nature conservation.

Although the use of agreements is a convenient way in which a planning authority can strengthen their position, there are legal limits to their use.[101] Agreements must serve a planning purpose and must not be unreasonable in the administrative law sense.[102] Furthermore, as the obligations in the agreement will influence the decision on the related planning application, then, in order to satisfy the requirements of section 37(2), they must either have been heralded in the development plan or must satisfy the test for a "material consideration". In other words, there must be at least a tenuous relationship between the obligations in the agreement and the subject-matter of the application.[103]

Appeals

If planning permission is refused or onerously conditioned, the applicant may appeal to the Minister (s. 47). The Minister is the final arbiter on matters of planning merit. In fact in almost all cases the decisions on appeals are delegated to "appointed persons", generally referred to as reporters, to determine. The reporters are drawn from the Inquiry Reporters' Unit

An appeal must be lodged within six months of the decision. The great majority of appeals (93 per cent) are disposed of by way of written submissions.[104] This involves an exchange of correspondence on the issues. If either the appellant or the planning authority so require or the Minister so decides, the appeal must be disposed of by way of a hearing, generally in the form of a public inquiry. The inquiry procedure takes longer, is more formal and is more expensive for the parties; but it allows for a more thorough testing of the evidence. The less formal hearing is not employed very much as an alternative to the inquiry in Scotland.

Procedural rules apply to both written submissions and inquiries. The former are governed by the Town and Country Planning (Appeals) (Written Submissions Procedure) (Scotland) Regulations 1990[105] and guidance on the operation of the Regulations is given in Circulars 26/1984 and 7/1990. The latter are governed by the Town and Country Planning (Inquiries Procedure) (Scotland) Rules 1997,[106] as amended,[107] for non-delegated cases; and the Town and Country Planning Appeals (Determination by Appointed Person) (Inquiries Procedure) (Scotland) Rules 1997,[108] as amended,[109] for delegated cases. The Minister or a reporter may

---

[101] See generally J. Rowan-Robinson and E. Young, *Planning by Agreement in Scotland* (W. Green/ The Planning Exchange, 1989).

[102] *Good* v *Epping Forest District Council* [1994] 1 WLR 376.

[103] *Tesco Stores Ltd* v *Secretary of State for the Environment* [1995] 1 WLR 759. See too the policy advice on the use of planning agreements set out in SODD Circular 12/1996.

[104] Inquiry Reporters' Unit, *Review of the Year 1996–97*, Table A2.

[105] SI 1990/507.

[106] SI 1997/796.

[107] By the Town and Country Planning (Inquiries Procedure) (Scotland) Amendment Rules 1998 (SI 1998/2311).

[108] SI 1997/750.

[109] By the Town and Country Planning Appeals (Determination by Appointed Persons) (Inquiries Procedure) (Scotland) Amendment Rules 1998 (SI 1998/2312).

deal with an appeal as though the application had been made to them in the first place. The parties to an appeal are expected to bear their own expenses, although an application may be made to the Minister for an award of expenses where a party has behaved unreasonably.[110]

Enforcement

There is little point in having a sophisticated system of development control unless there are effective means of enforcement. For many years, the arrangements for enforcement were regarded as the weakest link in the process.[111] These arrangements were strengthened by the Planning and Compensation Act 1991 following the recommendations in the Carnwath Report.[112] They are now contained in Part VI of the 1997 Act. The initial objective of the regime in Part VI is to secure compliance.[113] Only when that fails can the criminal law be invoked.

A breach of planning control occurs when development is carried out without planning permission or when there is a failure to comply with a condition subject to which planning permission has been granted.[114] A breach of planning control comprising the carrying out of an operation is immune from enforcement action at the end of four years from the substantial completion of the operation. A breach of control comprising the change of use of a building to a single dwelling is also immune after four years. All other breaches of control become immune after 10 years.[115]

A planning authority may commence formal enforcement action with the service of a planning contravention notice.[116] The purpose of the notice is to seek information about the activity being carried out on the land and to open a dialogue with the person responsible with a view to securing compliance. Where it appears to the authority that there has been a breach of planning control, they may serve an enforcement notice. This will describe the breach of control, specify the steps to be taken to comply with the notice and allow a period of time for compliance.[117] The recipient of the notice may appeal to the Minister[118] and this will operate to suspend the effect of the notice (except for activities covered by a stop notice)[119] until the appeal is determined.[120] Failure to comply with an

---

[110] Guidance on the circumstances in which an award of expenses may be made is set out in Circular 6/1990.

[111] J. Rowan-Robinson and E. Young, "Enforcement—The weakest link in the Scottish Planning Control System" (1987) 8 *Urban Law and Policy* 255.

[112] R. Carnwath, *Enforcing Planning Control* (HMSO, 1989).

[113] For guidance on the operation of the enforcement process see SODD Circular 4/1999 and PAN 54.

[114] 1997 Act, s. 123(1).

[115] 1997 Act, s. 124.

[116] 1997 Act, s. 125.

[117] 1997 Act, ss 127–128.

[118] 1997 Act, s. 130.

[119] 1997 Act, s. 140. A stop notice, as the term implies, requires the recipient to stop the activities listed in the notice until either the related enforcement notice takes effect and the time for compliance has passed or the related enforcement notice is quashed on appeal. Service of a stop notice will sometimes give rise to a compensation liability on the part of the planning authority.

[120] 1997 Act, s. 131(3).

enforcement notice, once it has taken effect and the time for compliance has passed, is a criminal offence.[121] In addition to invoking the criminal law, or alternatively, the planning authority may take direct action to remedy the default and recover the cost.[122]

Where the breach of control is a failure to comply with any condition, the authority may choose to serve a breach of condition notice.[123] The notice specifies the condition or conditions which have been breached and states what needs to be done to remedy the position and allows a period for compliance. The advantage of the procedure to the planning authority is that there is no right of appeal[124] and failure to comply is a criminal offence.[125] The 1997 Act also makes it clear that a planning authority may seek interdict to prevent any actual or apprehended breach of planning control.[126]

Challenge in the Court of Session[127]

Any person aggrieved by a decision of the Minister, for example on a planning appeal, may seek to question the validity of the decision by way of an application to the Court of Session under section 239 of the 1997 Act. Any such application must be made within six weeks of the date on which the decision was taken. The application may be made on the ground that the action is not within the powers of the Act or that any of the relevant requirements have not been complied with. The initial decision of the planning authority is not open to challenge under section 239. Although such decision may be susceptible to a petition for judicial review, it should be noted that there is a general principle that any statutory remedy must first be exhausted.[128] In other words, it may be necessary to appeal first to the Minister and then, if unsuccessful, apply to the Court of Session under section 239.

---

[121] 1997 Act, s. 136.

[122] 1997 Act, s. 135.

[123] 1997 Act, s. 145.

[124] The reason for this is that the condition could have been appealed when it was first imposed.

[125] 1997 Act, s. 145(9).

[126] 1997 Act, s. 146. For a review of the way in which the enforcement mechanisms are working in practice see School of Planning and Housing, Edinburgh College of Art/Heriot Watt University and Brodies, *Review of Planning Enforcement* (HMSO, 1998).

[127] See generally the Hon. Lord Reid, "Judicial Review" in *Scottish Planning Encyclopaedia* (the Hon. Lord Gill (ed.), W. Green/Sweet & Maxwell).

[128] C.T. Reid, "Failure to Exhaust Statutory Remedies", 1984 JR 185.

CHAPTER 4

ENVIRONMENTAL CONTROLS

Jeremy Rowan-Robinson

Introduction

Notwithstanding the title, the purpose of this chapter is not to provide a comprehensive description of the law relating to environmental protection. This is partly because many of the systems of environmental regulation, such as integrated pollution control, air pollution control, statutory nuisance and the new regime for tackling contaminated land, have an essentially urban focus and are adequately described elsewhere[1]; and partly because some of the environmental protection regimes that apply to the countryside are discussed in other chapters of this book. Planning control, for example, is dealt with in Chapter 3 and the law relating to the protection of habitats is described in Chapter 11.

Much of this chapter is concerned with the effects of farming on the environment. Its focus is on measures which have protection of the environment as an important objective. In this respect, it should be emphasised that landscape and biodiversity interests cannot be adequately safeguarded simply by restrictions designed to prevent things from happening. They require positive management action. The protection regimes relating to these interests have, therefore, come increasingly to consist of a combination of regulatory measures (such as pollution controls and planning restrictions) and incentives designed to promote appropriate management.

A distinction is made for the purposes of this chapter between commodity payments which are essentially a means of influencing production and which are dealt with in Chapter 5 and the payments made to farmers in Environmentally Sensitive Areas and under the Countryside Premium Scheme which are a means of promoting positive conservation measures and which are described in this chapter. However, this distinction is convenient rather than precise. Some agricultural subsidies, for example, are now subject to an element of environmental conditionality, a form of cross-compliance; nor does the distinction apply readily

---

[1] See C.T. Reid (ed.), *Environmental Law in Scotland* (W. Green/Sweet & Maxwell, 2nd edn, 1997); C. Smith, N. Collar and M. Poustie, *Pollution Control: The Law in Scotland* (T & T Clark, 1997).

to set-aside. Setting aside land from agriculture is primarily a means of controlling production and is referred to in Chapter 5. However, since 1992 the scheme has acquired an environmental emphasis and it is considered appropriate to deal with this aspect of it briefly in this chapter.

The first part of this chapter brings together several initiatives which are grouped under the broad heading of natural resource management. To this extent it has something in common with Chapter 3, which deals, among other things, with landscape protection, and with Chapter 11 which deals with the protection of habitats. However, unlike the regimes discussed in those chapters, the initiatives described in the first part of this chapter are truly voluntary; they *impose* no requirements of any sort on landowners unless landowners choose to sign up to them. This may be contrasted with the regime governing land designated as a site of special scientific interest where there is a statutory requirement to give prior notice of an intention to carry out certain activities (see Chapter 11). The second part of this chapter is concerned with pollution control and particularly, but not exclusively, with the measures taken to prevent water pollution.

Natural resource management[2]

The EC agri-environment programme

As we shall see later in this book, protection of the natural heritage relies quite heavily on specific conservation provisions directed at particular species or habitats (see Chapters 10 and 11). However, it is increasingly being recognised that these specific provisions must be supplemented, in Rodgers' words, "with broader measures creating a framework within which *sustainable* conservation of the character of the rural environment, and its important features, can be achieved".[3] A start on this framework was made with EC Regulation 797/85 on "Improving the Efficiency of Agricultural Structures" and with the Agriculture Act 1986 which provides for the designation of Environmentally Sensitive Areas (below) and was carried forward with the 1992 reforms to the Common Agricultural Policy (CAP). The objectives of CAP are described in Chapter 5. The reforms were directed primarily at tackling the problems of overproduction. The beginnings of this broader framework may be seen in particular in the Agri-Environment Regulation which was a part of the 1992 reforms.[4] The objective of the Regulation was to promote the use of farming practices "which are compatible with protection and improvement of the environment, the countryside, the landscape, natural resources, the soil and genetic diversity".[5] Hawke and Kovaleva comment that "the Regulation is central to important opportunities for Member States to design and implement agri-environmental schemes which differ from production-based initiatives such as set-aside by virtue of the fact that the former measures proceed on the exclusive basis of

---

[2] For a detailed discussion of the initiatives described in this section see N. Hawke and N. Kovaleva, *Agri-Environmental Law and Policy* (Cavendish Publishing Ltd, 1998), Chaps 4 and 5.

[3] C. Rodgers, "Environmental Gain, Set-aside and the Implementation of EU Agricultural Reform in the United Kingdom" in *Nature Conservation and Countryside Law* (C. Rodgers (ed.), University of Wales Press, 1996), p. 111.

[4] EC Regulation 2078/92, OJ L215/85, July 30, 1992.

[5] EC Regulation 2078/92, Art. 1.

direct payments to farmers for environmental measures in agriculture".[6] The Regulation provided co-financing for a number of agri-environment measures which Member States were given power to adopt. This objective has been implemented in Scotland through such initiatives as extension of the Environmentally Sensitive Area Scheme and the introduction of the Countryside Premium Scheme. These initiatives are considered in more detail below.

The broader framework is also evident in the use of the technique of cross-compliance (see Chapter 2) whereby public subsidies for agriculture are increasingly being subject to some form of environmental conditionality. In the past, access by farmers to subsidies from one government body has sometimes had the effect of inflating payments made to them by another government body for agreeing to adopt less intensive farming practices. "Conservation policy and agricultural price support policy", observes Rodgers, "are . . . often pulling in opposite directions",[7] an example of the problems of the fragmented approach to the management of the countryside discussed in Chapter 2. Since 1992 a pre-condition of access to some agricultural subsidies has been an undertaking to avoid environmentally damaging practices.

Agenda 2000, published by the European Commission in 1997,[8] proposed the further reform of CAP. Amongst other things, a coherent and comprehensive rural development policy with a more prominent role for agri-environmental measures was advocated which, if adopted, might have gone some way towards further advancing the development of the framework referred to above. The agreement on reform reached in March 1999 makes some progress towards further integration of environmental objectives into agricultural policy, although less than had originally been proposed. There is to be a new Rural Development Regulation which will bring together the agri-environment programme along with Less Favoured Areas, forestry, structural adjustment and wider rural development measures. Although the rhetoric emphasises the importance of agri-environment measures, there is, however, to be no significant switch of resources by the EU away from market support and compensation payments to rural development. Securing environmental benefits will, therefore, continue to rely on the existing measures which are described below and in Chapter 5.

Environmentally Sensitive Areas

Environmentally Sensitive Areas (ESAs) are designated and administered by the Scottish Executive acting through what is now the Scottish Executive Rural Affairs Department. Their origin lies in Article 19(1) of EC Regulation 797/85 on "Improving the Efficiency of Agricultural Structures".[9] Under the Regulation Member States were authorised, with the benefit of co-financing, to establish national schemes for the introduction or continued use in areas recognised for their ecological importance of agricultural production practices compatible with the requirements of conserving natural habitats while ensuring adequate income for farmers. The Regulation was implemented in the UK through the Agriculture Act 1986, section 18, which made provision for the designation of ESAs. The ESA

---

[6] N. Hawke and N. Kovaleva, op. cit., n. 2, p. 91.
[7] C. Rodgers, op. cit., n. 3, p. 113.
[8] *Agenda 2000 For a Stronger and Wider Union*, Com (97) 2000 final, July 15, 1997.
[9] Later modified by EC Regulation 1760/87.

scheme was subsequently incorporated as part of the UK response to the EC Agri-environment Regulation with more generous co-funding.[10]

The objective of the designation is to help conserve areas of high landscape, wildlife or historic value which are vulnerable to changes in farming practices. Certain farming systems by their nature provide habitats for wildlife or maintain attractive landscapes. Ten such areas have been designated so far in Scotland covering 1.4 million hectares. They are areas where traditional agricultural practices have been an important factor in establishing or maintaining the natural heritage value of the land. These are:

> Breadalbane;
>
> Loch Lomond;
>
> the machairs of the Uists, Benbecula, Barra and Vatersay;
>
> the Stewartry area of Dumfries and Galloway;
>
> Whitelaw and Eildon;
>
> the Argyll Islands;
>
> the Shetland Islands;
>
> the Cairngorm Straths;
>
> the Central Southern Uplands;
>
> the Western Southern Uplands.

Some of the areas encompassed by the designations are extensive; the two ESAs in the Southern Uplands, for example, cover over half a million hectares. Designation is by statutory instrument. The scheme is entirely voluntary. Although the take-up rate has been reasonable, there is concern that the ceilings imposed on payments in Scotland are still too low to attract applicants with large farms and high turnovers.

Farmers and crofters who participate in the scheme enter into an agreement covering all their land. They undertake to continue or to adopt specific farming methods which will help to protect and enhance the conservation value of their land, for example, reducing stocking levels. Early agreements were for five years; this has now been changed to 10 years with a review after five years. In return for the undertaking, farmers and crofters receive annual flat rate payments for the period of the agreement for each hectare of land. Additional standard payments are made for works carried out under a Farm Conservation Plan. The scheme was amended in 1994 to offer incentives to provide new opportunities for public access for informal recreation.

The Government has signalled an intention to merge the ESA and Countryside Premium Schemes, probably during the year 2000 (see below).

Countryside Premium Scheme

The Countryside Premium Scheme (CPS) was introduced by the Government under the Agri-environment Programme to give recognition to environmentally-friendly farming practices outwith ESAs. Like ESAs, the scheme benefits from

---

[10] EC 2078/92. See too the Agriculture Act (Amendment) Regulations 1994 (SI 1994/249).

co-funding. It came into operation in 1997 and applies only to Scotland.[11] It absorbed the Habitat Improvement Scheme which had been launched in 1994 under the Agri-Environment Programme and which had been targeted in part at land which had benefited from environmental improvements under the first set-aside scheme (below). It is currently administered by the Scottish Executive acting through the Scottish Executive Rural Affairs Department. It provides payments to encourage farmers, crofters and common grazing committees to go beyond normal good agricultural practice. The objective is to promote the adoption of environmentally friendly farming practices, the management of particular habitats and features in the interests of conservation and the undertaking of capital works required to support conservation management.

As with ESAs, the scheme is entirely voluntary. An application to participate in the scheme must be accompanied by a conservation audit and, in appropriate cases, by a moorland management plan.[12] The audit is an inventory of all the habitats and features on the agricultural unit which is the subject of the application together with an assessment of their current conservation interest. Financial support is available to assist in the preparation of the audit and plan.

The application will indicate which of the conservation options listed in the guide[13] the applicant intends to pursue. These options are:

- the management of grassland for birds;
- the management of species-rich grassland;
- the creation of species-rich grassland;
- the management of wetland;
- the creation of wetland;
- the management of water margins;
- the management of floodplains;
- the management of coastal heath;
- the management of moorland—stock disposal;
- the management of moorland—muirburn;
- the creation of grass margins or beetlebanks;
- the creation of conservation headlands;
- extensive cropping;
- the management of cropped machair;
- the creation of extended hedge;
- the management of scrub;
- the management of archaeological sites;
- the provision of access.

---

[11] See the Countryside Premium Scheme (Scotland) Regulations 1997 (SI 1997/330). Although the Countryside Premium Scheme is unique to Scotland, other country-wide schemes operate south of the border: Countryside Stewardship in England and Tir Gofal in Wales.
[12] See *Countryside Premium Scheme*, the Scottish Office Agriculture, Environment and Fisheries Department, 1998.
[13] *Countryside Premium Scheme*, Appendix 1.

For each option, the guide lists the management requirements. Unlike ESAs, the scheme is discretionary in the sense that there is no obligation on the Scottish Executive to accept an application; indeed, less than half the applications were accepted in the first year of the scheme. Applications are considered in the light of a priority ranking system. The priorities vary from area to area. Successful applicants undertake to follow the rules of the scheme and to observe general environmental conditions initially for five years but with scope for extension for a further five years. Annual payments are made for managing agreed habitats and features in the interests of conservation and for stock disposal. The payments are intended to compensate for loss of output and income resulting from the management of the land for conservation.

In June 1998 the Scottish Office announced plans to merge the ESA and CPS components of the Agri-environment Programme to provide an all-Scotland conservation management scheme. The existing schemes will continue until merger, probably in the year 2000.

Set-aside

Although the set-aside regime is concerned principally with controlling production rather than with promoting conservation, it has, as we mentioned earlier, an environmental dimension. It is convenient to deal with the regime at this point because this dimension is about natural resource management.

The set-aside scheme was first introduced by the European Commission in 1988 as a means of tackling surpluses. Its objective was to reduce the amount of land farmed for cereals and other crops.[14] The scheme was implemented in the UK through the Set-Aside Regulations 1988[15] and the Set-Aside (Amendment) Regulations 1990.[16] It was a voluntary scheme whereby farmers (owners or tenants) took arable land out of production for a period of five years in return for payments, part co-funded, intended to compensate for the loss resulting from not growing cereals.

The scheme was amended in 1992 as a part of the package of CAP reforms. The scheme is administered by the Scottish Executive acting through the Scottish Executive Rural Affairs Department. In order to qualify for cropping area payments for specified crops under the Arable Area Payments Main Scheme,[17] farmers are required to set-aside a minimum percentage of their arable land. The percentage may be varied annually in the light of market conditions (currently 10 per cent). Additional land may be entered into the scheme voluntarily. Strict rules determine what can, and cannot, be done on the set-aside land (see Chapter 5). As before, compensation is paid for the land set aside.

Although the primary objective of the scheme is the reduction of surpluses, set-aside, as we have already indicated, has always had an environmental dimension. Indeed, it is claimed that set-aside was one of the first areas in which environmental considerations were integrated into agricultural support.[18] How-

---

[14] EC Regulation 1272/88, April 27, 1988.

[15] SI 1988/1352.

[16] SI 1990/1716. For a discussion of the original set-aside provision see A. Lennon, "Set-aside of Agricultural Land: Policy, Practice and Problems" in *Agriculture, Conservation and Land Use* (W. Howarth and C. Rodgers (eds), University of Wales Press, 1993), Chap. 2.

[17] No set-aside requirement arises under the Simplified Scheme which applies to small farms.

[18] *Biodiversity: The UK Action Plan*, Cm. 2428 (1994), p. 97.

ever, it has been suggested that the environmental impact of the original scheme was minimal.[19] This changed with the introduction of the Arable Area Payments Scheme as a central feature of the reformed CAP in 1992.[20] Rodgers notes that "a greater emphasis on environmental protection, and the introduction of cross-compliance measures to guarantee environmental management of set-aside land, are central features of the new scheme".[21] There are two main forms of set-aside but a number of requirements are common to both: environmental features on or adjoining set-aside land must be safeguarded, a green cover must be established and maintained and there are restrictions on the use of fertiliser, manure, herbicides, fungicides and insecticides. With non-rotational set-aside, where land is taken out of agricultural use for a period of years, there are four management options from which farmers may choose in preparing management plans. All offer clear environmental gains. These are the grassland option, natural regeneration, the wild bird cover option and the field margins option. Non-rotational set-aside land can also be used to grow certain non-food crops under contract with a processor, although this option is less likely to bring direct benefits to the environment. Rotational set-aside, however, is the norm. With this form of set-aside, land is taken out of production for seven months on a rotational basis. This enables the land to be maintained in good agricultural condition. Although the common requirements (above) apply, it has been argued that this form of set-aside is driven by economic rather than environmental considerations and that the environmental benefits are inevitably transient.[22]

During the recent negotiations over the reform of CAP (above), a proposal was made to abandon the set-aside scheme for arable land from the year 2002. However, under the final agreement compulsory set-aside will continue at 10 per cent until at least 2006 and voluntary set-aside will be retained.

Pollution control

Discharges into controlled waters

The principal means of controlling water pollution is through a permit procedure operated by the Scottish Environment Protection Agency (SEPA) under Part II of the Control of Pollution Act 1974.[23] Section 30F of the 1974 Act[24] provides that it is an offence, in the absence of a permit from SEPA, to discharge noxious, poisonous or polluting matter into controlled waters. "Controlled waters" are defined in section 30A as relevant territorial waters, coastal waters, inland freshwater and groundwater.

Section 30C provides for the classification of the quality of the various descriptions of controlled water. With a view to maintaining and improving the quality of controlled waters, the Minister may set water quality objectives and

---

[19] C. Rodgers, op. cit., n. 3, Chap. 5.

[20] See EC Regulations 1765/92, OJ L181, July 1, 1992; EC Regulation 762/94, OJ L90, April 7, 1994; EC Regulation 231/94, OJ L30, February 3, 1994; and the Arable Area Payments Regulations 1995 (SI 1995/1738).

[21] C. Rodgers, op. cit., n. 3, p. 116.

[22] Ibid, pp. 123–124.

[23] As amended by s. 168 of and Sched. 23 to the Water Act 1989 and s. 106 of and Scheds 16 and 22 to the Environment Act 1995.

[24] Inserted by s. 106 of and Sched. 16 to the Environment Act 1995.

the Minister and SEPA must discharge their functions so as to achieve these objectives (s. 30D(1)).

Section 30F creates five principal offences with regard to the entry of effluent into controlled waters. These are:

(1) causing or knowingly permitting any poisonous, noxious or polluting matter or any solid waste matters to enter controlled waters (s. 30F(1));

(2) causing or knowingly permitting any matter, other than trade or sewage effluent, to enter controlled waters by being discharged from a drain or sewer in contravention of a prohibition imposed under section 30G of the Act (s. 30F(2));

(3) causing or knowingly permitting any trade or sewage effluent to be discharged into controlled waters or from land through a pipe into the sea outside the seaward limit of controlled waters (s. 30F(3));

(4) causing or knowingly permitting any trade or sewage effluent to be discharged in contravention of a prohibition under section 30G of the Act from a building or fixed plant onto land or into the water of a loch or pond which is not inland freshwater (s. 30F(4));

(5) causing or knowingly permitting any matter to enter any inland freshwater so as to impede the proper flow in a manner leading to, or likely to lead to, a substantial aggravation of pollution due to other causes or the consequences of such pollution (s. 30F(5)).

It is also an offence to contravene a condition of a discharge consent.

The provisions in section 30G for expressly prohibiting discharges enable certain section 30F offences to be focused only on those types of discharge most in need of control. Certain defences are provided for in section 30I. There is, for example, no offence under section 30F if the discharge is made in accordance with a consent given under the Act (below), or in accordance with an integrated pollution control authorisation under Part I of the Environmental Protection Act 1990 or a waste management licence granted under Part II of the 1990 Act or a licence granted under Part II of the Food and Environment Protection Act 1985. On summary conviction for an offence under section 30F a penalty of up to three months' imprisonment or a fine of up to £20,000 or both may be imposed. On conviction on indictment a penalty of up to two years' imprisonment or a fine or both may be imposed.

Section 34 deals with applications to SEPA for a consent to discharge effluent into controlled waters. Applications must be accompanied by full information and must be notified to other relevant public bodies and be the subject of public advertisement. SEPA may dispense with the publicity requirement if the discharge is thought likely to have no appreciable effect (s. 36(4)). SEPA has four months in which to reach a decision. It may grant consent, grant consent subject to conditions or refuse consent. The Agency may impose such conditions as it thinks fit. Without prejudice to the generality of the power, it may impose conditions dealing with the place of discharge, the quality and quantity of the discharge, the steps to be taken for the treatment of or for minimising the polluting effects of the discharge, the provision of facilities for taking samples, the provision and maintenance of monitoring information and the keeping of records and the making of returns (s. 34(4)). There is a right of appeal to the

Minister against a refusal of permission or the imposition of conditions (s. 39). In the event of an infringement, or the likelihood of an infringement of any such condition, SEPA may serve an enforcement notice specifying the default, requiring steps to be taken to put it right and stipulating the time for compliance (s. 49A). Failure to comply with an enforcement notice is an offence. Alternatively, if SEPA is of the opinion that prosecution would afford an ineffectual remedy, it may institute civil proceedings to secure compliance (s. 49A(4)). Furthermore, SEPA has power to serve a notice requiring works to be undertaken to remedy or forestall the pollution of controlled water and to execute such works in default and recover the costs (ss 46A–46D). Failure to comply with a works notice is an offence. SEPA must maintain a public register of applications, consents, conditions, enforcement notices and convictions (s. 41).[25]

SEPA has power to review consents from time to time and this may lead to variation or revocation of a consent to discharge (ss 38 and 38A).

Groundwater

A combination of growing concern about the consequences of sheep dip residues and pesticide wastes on groundwater quality together with the threat of legal action by the European Commission over the failure properly to implement the EC Directive on Groundwater Protection[26] led to the introduction of the Groundwater Regulations 1998.[27] The Regulations took effect from April 1, 1999, and apply throughout Great Britain. SEPA is primarily responsible for their implementation in Scotland. There is provision for the Minister to approve codes of practice containing guidance on how to meet the requirements of the Regulations (reg. 21).

The Regulations introduce a new permit procedure for certain activity, including agricultural activity, likely to have adverse consequences for groundwater quality. A distinction is made between List I and List II substances as defined in the Schedule to the Regulations. Discharges of the former are regarded as hazardous; discharges of the latter have the potential to cause groundwater pollution. The direct discharge of List I substances to groundwater is prohibited (reg. 4(1)). The disposal of such substances in such a way that it might give rise to an indirect discharge to groundwater must be the subject of a prior investigation (reg. 4(2)). No authorisation may be given for the disposal if the investigation reveals that there would be an indirect discharge of a List I substance to groundwater. The direct or indirect discharge of a List II substance must be the subject of prior investigation and any authorisation must include conditions which require all necessary technical precautions to be observed so as to prevent groundwater pollution (reg. 5(2)). The approach of the Regulations is essentially preventative. No authorisation is required for activities which are already subject to a discharge consent under the Control of Pollution Act 1974 (see above), which are subject to an authorisation under the integrated pollution control regime in Part I of the Environmental Protection Act 1990 or for which a waste management licence is required under Part II of the 1990 Act (see below). Nor is an authorisation required for a discharge of a List I or II substance in a quantity

---

[25] See the Control of Pollution (Registers) (Scotland) Regulations 1993 (SI 1993/1155).
[26] Directive 80/68, OJ L20, January 21, 1980.
[27] SI 1998/2746.

and concentration so small as to obviate any present or future danger of deterioration in the quality of the receiving groundwater (reg. 2(1)(c)).

A "prior investigation" is to include an examination of the hydrogeological conditions of the area concerned, of the possible purifying powers of the soil and subsoil, and of the risk of pollution of the quality of the groundwater from the discharge. The investigation must also establish whether the discharge of substances into groundwater is a satisfactory solution from the point of view of the environment (reg. 7).

An authorisation may be for a limited period (reg. 11(1)) and must contain appropriate conditions to safeguard groundwater quality (regs 9 and 10). SEPA is required to monitor compliance with conditions and the effect of discharges on groundwater (reg. 11(3)); and the terms of authorisations are to be reviewed at least once every four years. There is a right of appeal from a decision by SEPA to the Minister (reg. 20). Authorisations and monitoring information must be entered by SEPA in the public register maintained under section 41 of the Control of Pollution Act 1974.

SEPA may serve a notice to prohibit or control activity which might lead to an indirect discharge of a List I substance or which might lead to the pollution of groundwater from the indirect discharge of a List II substance (reg. 19(1)).

Nitrate sensitive areas[28]

Section 31B of the Control of Pollution Act 1974[29] provides for the designation by the Minister of nitrate sensitive areas (NSAs). The provision offers a means of tackling the problem of diffuse water pollution resulting from the leaching of nitrates into controlled waters. NSAs are also intended to be essentially a "preventive" mechanism; the provision was initially introduced as a response to the EC Drinking Water Directive[30] and the (then) proposed Nitrates Directive.[31] The corresponding provision south of the border was invoked in 1990 to designate 10 "pilot" NSAs for a period of five years.[32] A further 22 NSAs were designated south of the border in 1994[33] and the 10 initial NSAs were relaunched in 1995. The enlargement of the scheme owed much to the opportunities presented by the Agri-environment Regulation (above).[34] No NSAs have been designated in Scotland.

NSAs have operated in practice on a voluntary basis[35] with regulation being effected through a management agreement. Hawke and Kovaleva observe that "this voluntary scheme required farmers to change their husbandry according to a range of options and offers a wide range of payment rates to compensate for those changes which go substantially beyond good agricultural practice, for

---

[28] For a full discussion of the development of policy and practice on control of nitrates see J. Blackhurst and M. Payne, *Agricultural Pollution* (Sweet & Maxwell, 1997), pp. 81–102; also N. Hawke and N. Kovaleva, op. cit., n. 2, Chap. 8.

[29] Added by the Water Act 1989, Sched. 23.

[30] 80/778 (the proposed Nitrates Directive).

[31] Which became Directive 91/676.

[32] The Nitrate Sensitive Areas (Designation) Order 1990 (SI 1990/1013).

[33] The Nitrate Sensitive Areas Regulations 1994 (SI 1994/1729).

[34] Regulation EEC/2078/92.

[35] Although there is provision in the legislation for mandatory requirements.

example in requiring a change from intensive cropping to extensive grassland".[36] Agreements run for five years and are binding on successors in title.

Nitrate vulnerable zones

In 1996 the Government, in response to the requirements of the Nitrates Directive, made provision for the designation of Nitrate Vulnerable Zones (NVZs). The Nitrates Directive requires drinking water sources with a concentration of nitrate exceeding a prescribed level to be classed as polluted and for the areas of land which drain into these waters and which contribute to the pollution[37] to be designated as NVZs. In such zones an action programme must be prepared and implemented to reduce nitrate levels. The programme will lead to restrictions on farming practices, for example control over the application of manure. Rodgers comments that "the use of flexible action programmes, rather than prescriptive regulation, is intended to ensure that regulation is tailored to the agricultural conditions obtaining in each nitrate vulnerable zone, and can change and adapt as need arises".[38] An NVZ differs from an NSA in that the restrictions imposed by a programme are mandatory and no payments are made. Payments are made in NSAs, it seems, to persuade farmers to take voluntary measures which go substantially beyond good agricultural practice.[39] However, capital grants may be available in NVZs, for example to adapt manure storage and handling facilities.

Provision for the designation of NVZs in Scotland was made in the Protection of Water Against Nitrate Pollution (Scotland) Regulations 1996.[40] To date just one NVZ has been designated in Scotland: at Balmalcolm in Fife.[41] At the time of writing, the Scottish Executive have announced that a second NVZ is to be designated covering the Ythan catchment area in Aberdeenshire. SEPA have, however, suggested that a broader interpretation, leading to the designation of more NVZs, may be required to meet the requirements of the Nitrates Directive.[42]

Silage, sludge and slurry

Silage, slurry and fuel oil: A further example of the preventive approach in tackling the problems of diffuse water pollution from agricultural activity is provided by the Control of Pollution (Silage, Slurry and Agricultural Fuel Oil) (Scotland) Regulations 1991 made under section 31A of the Control of Pollution Act 1974.[43] The Regulations set minimum standards for the construction and siting of silage, slurry and fuel oil installations so as to protect vulnerable waters. Any crop which is being made into silage must either be kept in a silo, the construction and siting

---

[36] N. Hawke and N. Kovaleva, op. cit., n. 25, p. 171.

[37] On the question of contributing to pollution see *R. v Secretary of State for the Environment and Ministry of Agriculture, Fisheries and Food, ex p. Stanley and Others* Case C–293/97, April 29, 1999.

[38] C. Rodgers, *Agricultural Law* (Butterworths, 2nd edn, 1998), para. 14.41.

[39] "Government response to the consultation on the designation of Nitrate Vulnerable Zones in England and Wales" (Ministry of Agriculture, Fisheries and Food, 1995).

[40] SI 1996/1564; and see the Action Programme for Nitrate Vulnerable Zones (Scotland) Regulations 1998 (SI 1998/2927).

[41] SI 1996/888. As regards the action programme see the Action Programme for Nitrate Vulnerable Zones (Scotland) Regulations 1998 (SI 1998/2927).

[42] Ibid.

[43] SI 1991/346 as amended by SI 1996/973.

of which conforms to the requirements of the Regulations, be compressed into impermeable bales stored at least 10 metres from any inland or coastal waters (reg. 2) or be in the form of bulk bagged silage contained in bags which conform to a specified standard and which are stored at least 10 metres from any inland or coastal waters (reg. 6). Slurry must be kept in a reception pit or tank which conforms to specified standards with regard to construction and siting (reg. 3 and Sched. 2); and agricultural fuel oil in excess of 1,250 litres must be stored in above-ground tanks or fuel dumps conforming to prescribed standards with regard to siting and design (reg. 4 and Sched. 3). Contravention of the Regulations is an offence (reg. 11).

The Regulations are administered by SEPA who must be given prior notice of the construction and bringing into use of such installations (reg. 10). A Code of Good Practice for the Prevention of Environmental Pollution from Agricultural Activity has been issued to give advice and to promote best practice.[44]

Sludge: With the prohibition from December 1998 on the dumping of sewage sludge at sea, increasing interest has been shown in the spreading of sludge on land. The amount of sludge for disposal is also increasing as a result of improved treatment standards resulting from implementation of Directive 91/271 on urban waste water treatment. Although the application of sewage sludge to farmland has beneficial effects, it also carries environmental risks. Sewage sludge can contain quantities of heavy metal which may damage soil fertility and be detrimental to humans, flora and fauna. It can also cause nitrate to leach into water supplies and give rise to odour problems. The problem was addressed in the Directive on the use of sewage sludge on agricultural land[45] which has been implemented in Great Britain through the Sludge (Use in Agriculture) Regulations 1989.[46] The Regulations prohibit the use of sewage sludge on agricultural land unless certain requirements are fulfilled and no person is to supply sludge for such use if he has reason to believe that the requirements will not be observed (reg. 3). The sludge producer (generally the water authority) is to maintain records of the sludge supplied for the purposes of agriculture (reg. 6). The sludge and the soil to which it is to be applied must first be tested in accordance with the Regulations and limits are imposed on the concentration in the soil and the rate of addition to the land of certain chemicals (reg. 3). Untreated sludge must be worked into the soil (reg. 4). Where sludge or septic tank sludge has been used on agricultural land, certain activities are temporarily prohibited on that land (reg. 4). Contravention of the Regulations is a criminal offence (reg. 9).

A recent review by SEPA of the spreading of waste on land, including sewage sludge, has recommended a tightening up of standards and the preparation by owners and occupiers of land management plans.[47]

---

[44] The Water (Prevention of Pollution) (Code of Practice) (Scotland) Order 1992 (SI 1992/395).

[45] Directive 86/278, OJ L181, July 4, 1986.

[46] SI 1989/263 as amended by SI 1996/593 and SI 1996/973. Given the specific controls over the use of sludge on agricultural land, such use is not subject to the regulation of waste under the Environmental Protection Act 1990, Pt II.

[47] "SEPA pushes for tighter controls on land spreading of waste" (1998) 286 ENDS, p. 36.

Pesticides[48]

Pesticides are quite widely employed in agriculture but, unless handled with appropriate care, can cause injury to species, damage to habitats and pollution of water. The Food and Environment Protection Act 1985, Pt III, as amended by the Pesticides Act 1998, makes provision for regulating the use of pesticides.[49] Regulation operates at several levels. First of all, the Control of Pesticides Regulations 1986,[50] which apply in Great Britain, prohibit the advertisement, sale, supply, storage or use of any pesticide unless that pesticide has been approved by the appropriate Ministers. As regards the use of a pesticide, any conditions governing the use must be observed. Second, the Pesticides (Maximum Residue Levels in Crops, Food and Feedings Stuffs) Regulations 1994,[51] which apply also in Great Britain, specify, as the title suggests, the maximum levels of pesticide residues which may be left in crops, food and feeding stuffs. Third, in so far as the use of pesticides may affect water quality, note should be taken of the controls referred to above with regard to groundwater and nitrate vulnerable zones. Fourth, an Organic Aid Scheme was introduced in 1994 under the agri-environment programme which, in part, is intended to minimise reliance on pesticides by providing financial assistance to farmers to convert land to organic production. Finally, and also with a view to minimising reliance on pesticides, consideration is being given to the introduction of a tax.[52]

Muirburn and the burning of crop residues

The burning of heath and moorland, generally referred to as "making muirburn", and the burning of stubble and other crop residues after harvesting are accepted land management practices. However, these activities can cause a nuisance in the form of air pollution, may damage habitats and can, in some cases, create a traffic hazard.

Making muirburn is controlled under the Hill Farming Act 1946.[53] This provides that it is unlawful to make muirburn on moorland and upland areas between April 16 and September 30 in any year (s. 23(1)). Exceptionally, a proprietor of land, or a tenant with the authority of the proprietor or his factor, may make muirburn up to April 30, or on land above 450 metres[54] up to May 15. Furthermore, the Minister may in any year by direction extend the period to May 1, or on land above 450 metres[55] to May 16 (s. 23(3)). Contravention of this

---

[48] See generally J. Blackhurst and M. Payne, op. cit., n. 28, pp. 104–106; and N. Hawke and N. Kovaleva, op. cit., n. 2, Chap. 11.

[49] See also the Control of Pesticides Regulations 1986 (SI 1986/1510); and the Pesticides (Maximum Residue Levels in Food) Regulations 1988 (SI 1988/1378).

[50] SI 1986/1510 as amended by SI 1997/188.

[51] SI 1994/1985 as amended by SI 1996/1487, SI 1997/567 and SI 1998/2922. The 1994 Regulations were made under s. 2(2) of the European Communities Act 1972. See too the Plant Protection Products Regulations 1995 (SI 1995/887).

[52] "Water pollution charges dropped but pesticides tax draws closer" (1999) 290 ENDS, p. 21.

[53] As amended by the Wildlife and Countryside Act 1981, s. 72(2) and (3). See too the Code of Practice on Straw and Stubble Burning and Muirburn prepared jointly by the National Farmers Union of Scotland and the former Scottish Office Agriculture, Environment and Fisheries Department; and the code on muirburn issued by Scottish Natural Heritage.

[54] As substituted by the Agriculture (Adaptation of Enactments) (Scotland) Regulations 1977 (SI 1977/2007).

[55] Ibid.

provision is an offence (s. 23(4)). There is also a prohibition on making muirburn between one hour after sunset and one hour before sunrise (s. 25(a)); and it is an offence not to give notice to neighbours and not to have adequate staff and equipment to control the burning operations so as to prevent damage to adjoining land (s. 25(a) and (b)). Lack of due care during the burning process resulting in damage to adjoining land is also an offence (s. 25(d)) and could lead to a claim for damages at common law.[56]

The burning of straw, stubble and other crop residues is governed by section 152 of the Environmental Protection Act 1990. This gives the Minister power to make regulations prohibiting or restricting the burning of crop residues on agricultural land by persons engaged in agriculture. Such regulations may make different provision for different areas and circumstances and may provide for exemptions. They may also make a breach of control an offence. Regulations have been made for England and Wales[57] but not for Scotland. There is, however, a Code of Practice on Straw and Stubble Burning and Muirburn in operation prepared jointly by the National Farmers Union of Scotland and the former Scottish Office Agriculture, Environment and Fisheries Department.

Waste management

Many rural activities generate waste. Because of difficulties inherent in waste disposal, the Government is attempting to tackle the problem at source by reducing waste and promoting recycling. However, these are likely to be long-term solutions. In the meantime, steps have been taken to upgrade the level of control over the production, management and disposal of waste on land.

These controls are contained in Part II of the Environmental Protection Act 1990 and are administered by SEPA. Central to the controls is the definition of "waste". The definition is derived from the EC Waste Framework Directive[58]; indeed, the term formerly applied in the legislation was "Directive Waste".[59] Waste is now defined as "any substance or object in the categories set out in Schedule 2B to this Act[60] which the holder discards or intends or is required to discard".[61] The categories of waste listed in Schedule 2B are wide-ranging. The list begins with a reference to "production or consumption residues not otherwise specified below" and concludes with reference to "any materials, substances or products which are not contained in the above categories". It should be noted that waste from premises used for agriculture is excluded from the definition of controlled waste.[62]

Section 33(1) of the 1990 Act prohibits:

(1) the deposit of controlled waste, or knowingly causing or permitting the deposit of controlled waste in or on any land unless a waste management licence authorising the deposit is in force;

---

[56] *Mackintosh* v *Mackintosh* (1864) 2 M 1357.

[57] The Crop Residues (Burning) Regulations 1993 (SI 1993/1366).

[58] EC Directive 75/442, as amended by Directive 91/156.

[59] Waste Management Licensing Regulations 1994 (SI 1994/1056), reg. 1(3). See now s. 75 of the 1990 Act as substituted by the Environment Act 1995, Sched. 22, para. 88(2) and (4).

[60] The reference is to the 1990 Act, Sched. 2B, added by the Environment Act 1995, Sched. 22, para. 95.

[61] See further on this Scottish Office Environment Department Circular 10/94.

[62] s. 75(7).

(2) the treatment, keeping or disposal of controlled waste, or knowingly causing or permitting the treatment, keeping or disposal of waste, in or on any land or by means of any mobile plant except in accordance with a waste management licence;

(3) the treatment, keeping or disposal of controlled waste in a manner likely to cause pollution of the environment or harm to human health.[63]

"Controlled waste" is defined as household, industrial or commercial waste (s. 75(4)). This definition has now been amended to provide that waste which is not Directive waste shall not be treated as controlled waste.[64] In view of the breadth of the definition of "waste", it is not surprising that quite a long list of activities which are thought unlikely to give rise to environmental problems have been exempted from the requirement for a licence. These are set out in Schedule 3 to the Waste Management Licensing Regulations 1994.

Section 34 imposes a general duty of care on any person who imports, produces, carries, keeps, treats or disposes of controlled waste to take all such measures as are reasonable in the circumstances:

(1) to prevent the contravention of section 33;

(2) to prevent the escape of waste from his control or that of any other person;

(3) to secure the transfer of waste with an adequate written description of the waste and only to an authorised person.

Failure to comply with the duty of care is a criminal offence (s. 34(6)). A Code of Practice has been published giving practical guidance on how to discharge the duty imposed by section 34.[65]

Sections 35–40 of the 1990 Act make provision for the granting, variation, suspension and revocation, transfer and surrender of waste management licences. These provisions are amplified by the 1994 Regulations.[66] There are two types of licence: the site licence granted to the occupier of the land and a mobile plant licence which is granted to the operator of the plant. If planning permission is required for the use of land for which the waste management licence is required, the latter will not be issued until a planning permission or a certificate of lawful use or development is in place (s. 36(2)). A licence may be refused if the applicant is not a "fit and proper person"[67] or if the refusal is necessary to prevent pollution of the environment, harm to human health or serious detriment to the amenities of the locality (s. 36(3)). There is a wide power to impose such terms and conditions on the grant of a licence as appears to the Agency to be appropriate (s. 35(3)). There is a right of appeal to the Minister against the refusal of a licence or against the imposition of conditions. An appeal may also be made against the

---

[63] s. 33(6) provides that it is an offence to contravene the provisions of subs. (1). There is a due diligence defence (s. 33(7)).

[64] Waste Management Licensing Regulations 1994, reg. 24.

[65] Revised 1996.

[66] See too Scottish Office Environment Department Circular 10/94.

[67] Defined in s. 74 to cover technical competence, financial substance and freedom from conviction for a relevant offence.

subsequent modification of conditions, against the suspension or revocation of a licence and against a refusal to permit a transfer (s. 43).

Separate controls apply to the carriers of waste. It is an offence under section 1(1) of the Control of Pollution (Amendment) Act 1989 to carry controlled waste unless the carrier is registered with SEPA.[68] Waste may, however, be carried from one place to another within the same premises without a requirement to register. Registration may be refused if the applicant is not considered a fit person to carry waste.

Additional controls apply to what is referred to as "special waste". This is waste which, because of its hazardous nature, requires particular care. The controls are to be found in the Special Waste Regulations 1996[69] made under section 62 of the Environmental Protection Act 1990. The Regulations give effect to the Hazardous Waste Directive[70] and to Council Decision 94/904 which provides a list of hazardous wastes. Special waste is defined in the Regulations as:

(1) any controlled waste which is on the list of hazardous wastes in Part I of Schedule 2 to the Regulations[71] and which displays any of the hazardous properties listed in Part II of Schedule 2;

(2) any waste which is not on the list but which displays any of a more limited range of properties listed in Part II of the Schedule;

(3) a waste prescription. This refers only to medicine.

The regulations impose more rigorous control over the movement of special waste. The consignment note must be more detailed than for the ordinary controlled waste and must be coded for ease of identification. Furthermore, prior notice of the movement of special waste must be given to SEPA. Special waste may only be disposed of to a landfill site which is licensed to accept such waste and a record showing the location of the deposit must be made. There are restrictions on the mixing of different categories of waste.

---

[68] See the Controlled Waste (Registration of Carriers and Seizure of Vehicles) Regulations 1991 (SI 1991/1624).

[69] SI 1996/9727. See too the Special Waste (Amendment) Regulations 1996 (SI 1996/2019).

[70] 91/689.

[71] The list replicates the list in the EC Council Decision.

CHAPTER 5

AGRICULTURE

Hew Dalrymple
Sheonagh Hill

Introduction

The statutory definition of "agriculture" encompasses horticulture, fruit growing, seed growing, dairy farming and livestock breeding and keeping, the use of land as grazing land, meadow land, osier land, market gardens and nursery grounds and the use of land for woodlands where that use is ancillary to the farming of land for agricultural purposes.[1] It is therefore a very diverse land use and it has a major impact on the countryside in terms of landscape, nature conservation and employment. Much of the countryside as we know it today owes its appearance to the demands of agricultural husbandry.

However, unlike most other land uses, agriculture is largely free from planning control.[2] The explanation for this lies in the post-war emphasis on domestic food production and a belief at that time that agriculture was environmentally benign. With the passage of time, both parts of this explanation have required re-examination and agriculture is now the subject of extensive government intervention. The regulation of the environmental consequences of agriculture generally is considered in other chapters,[3] while this chapter focuses largely on the extensive intervention which has occurred in agriculture, particularly as a result of the European Union Common Agricultural Policy (hereafter "the CAP") to guide and control food production. This focus seems appropriate given the consequences of food production for the way in which the countryside is used and managed.

In Chapter 1, reference was made to the different ways in which government can intervene in the market to achieve public policy goals. What is singular about agriculture is the heavy reliance on economic incentives, and particularly subsidies, as a means of guiding and controlling food production. Much of this

---

[1] See Agriculture (Scotland) Act 1948, s. 86(3); Agricultural Holdings (Scotland) Act 1991, s. 85(1). The same definition is utilised in a variety of subordinate legislation.

[2] Planning control is discussed in Chap. 3, to which further reference should be made.

[3] See in particular Chaps 4 and 11.

93

chapter is therefore devoted to an explanation of the regulations which govern the payment of subsidy.

Agricultural law, however, is not simply about land use and about what can be produced and how much. It is about the people involved and in particular about the relationship between landlord and tenant. Land tenure, security of tenure, succession to agricultural holdings and dispute resolution have developed over the years into a specialist body of law. These aspects of the law cannot be ignored in this chapter, but it is impossible in the space available to do them justice. They are therefore dealt with in summary form and readers seeking more information on these matters are referred to one or other of the comprehensive up-to-date texts which are available.[4]

This chapter begins with an outline of the law relating to agricultural leases. There then follows a brief introduction to the CAP, followed by more detailed consideration of the regulations governing milk quota, arable crops and livestock premiums and quotas. The chapter concludes with a brief consideration of the changes which are anticipated in the future.

The CAP and the subsidies payable under the CAP as described in this chapter are also applicable to crofters and should be borne in mind when considering Chapter 6.

Use and occupation of agricultural land

In principle, owners and occupiers of agricultural land are required to manage the land in accordance with the rules of good estate management and to farm in accordance with the rules of good husbandry respectively, in both cases taking into account the character and situation of the land and other circumstances including, in the case of the occupier, the standard of management of the owner.[5] The rules of good estate management and good husbandry will therefore vary according to where the land is situated and the farming customs of that area: the demands of a hill sheep farm in Sutherland, for example, are very different to those of an arable farm in East Lothian. The principle derives from the common law and a series of agricultural statutes have been passed during this century with its preservation in mind, although it was first given definition in the Agriculture (Scotland) Act 1948 (hereafter "the 1948 Act").[6]

Many of the earlier statutes have since been repealed in whole or in part in response to the needs of a developing society. Following the Second World War, in the interests of promoting at least partial self-sufficiency, government sought to confer some degree of security of tenure on agricultural tenants as a matter of public policy. Owner-occupied farms, while subject to the whole panoply of the CAP, are only partly affected by certain provisions of the agricultural holdings legislation; but as soon as any form of tenancy is created the whole force of these statutes is brought to bear. In 1991, an attempt was made to consolidate much of the agricultural holdings legislation, but this was only partly successful. The Agricultural Holdings (Scotland) Act 1991 (hereafter "the 1991

---

[4] The Hon. Lord Gill, *The Law of Agricultural Holdings in Scotland* (3rd edn, W. Green, 1997); Sir Crispin Agnew of Lochnaw, *Agricultural Law in Scotland* (Butterworths, 1996).

[5] Agriculture (Scotland) Act 1948, s. 26 and Scheds 5 (owners) and 6 (occupiers).

[6] Ibid.

Act") repealed, restated and replaced much of the earlier legislation relating to landlord and tenant and is now the main statute regulating the relationship of landlord and tenant in the context of agricultural holdings. "Agricultural holding" is defined by section 1(1) of the 1991 Act as "the aggregate of the agricultural land comprised in a lease, not being a lease under which the land is let to the tenant during his continuance in any office, appointment or employment held under the landlord". Accordingly, where an occupier of agricultural land occupies under a lease from a landlord and pays a market rent, the relationship between the parties is defined and largely determined by the 1991 Act.

In broad terms, where there is a valid lease of agricultural land, a secure agricultural tenancy will exist.[7] The lease need not be in writing, but both landlord and tenant have certain rights to demand a written lease where none exists and to have the terms of any lease varied if they are at odds with the statutory provisions.[8]

While it is contrary to law to contract out of the security of tenure provision,[9] so that the courts have power to ignore artificial schemes to avoid security of tenure, there are various alternative means of managing the land open to a landowner which do not result in a secure tenancy being created. In brief, these include:

(i) a lease of agricultural land for less than a year with the approval in writing of the appropriate Minister under section 2(1) of the 1991 Act;

(ii) a grazing let for less than 365 days where a lease is entered into for mowing or grazing during a specified period of the year; and

(iii) some form of joint venture or share farming arrangement which is not tantamount to a lease.[10]

Longer-term arrangements entered into between a landowner and another party where the landowner intends to "profit" from the arrangement run the risk of being challenged as a sham, which could result in a court conferring security of tenure upon that other party.[11] The most popular method of seeking to avoid security of tenure in recent years has been through the use of a limited partnership. Limited partnerships are governed by the Limited Partnerships Act 1907 (hereafter "the 1907 Act"). They are used in the context of agricultural tenancies in order to provide a mechanism for terminating such a tenancy on a predetermined date or on the occurrence of a predetermined event. The tenant farmer will enter into a limited partnership under the 1907 Act with the landlord or a nominee of the landlord, who normally injects some capital into the business: the tenant will be the general partner, while the landlord or his nominee will be the limited partner. The landlord then grants a lease of the farm to the limited partnership. The lease will be terminated automatically on termination of the partnership, thereby avoiding security of tenure. Limited partnerships are registered in the Register of Limited Partnerships at Companies House, and the

---

[7] This is the effect of the 1991 Act.
[8] 1991 Act, s. 4.
[9] *Johnson* v *Moreton* [1980] AC 37; *Gisbourne* v *Burton* [1988] 3 WLR 921.
[10] For a detailed description, see Agnew, op. cit., n. 4, Chap. 4.
[11] *Gisbourne* v *Burton* [1988] 3 WLR 921; *Featherstone* v *Staples* [1986] 1 WLR 861.

effect of such registration is that the limited partner, ie the landlord or his nominee, is shielded from any liability for the debts of the partnership, while the general partner, ie the tenant, is liable for the debts of the partnership.[12] The tenant will be responsible for day-to-day running of the partnership: the limited partner is not entitled to take part in the day-to-day running of the partnership, otherwise he will become liable for its debts,[13] and nor will he participate in the profits of the partnership. The effectiveness of using limited partnerships as a means of avoiding security of tenure has been questioned from time to time, but the recent case of *MacFarlane* v *Falfield Investments Ltd*[14] has lent judicial support to the argument for the effectiveness of using limited partnership tenancies as a means of avoiding the security of tenure provisions in the agricultural holdings legislation in holding that there was nothing wrong with using this mechanism in order to avoid creating security of tenure.

Disputes between landlord and tenant

It is always open to the landlord and tenant to agree matters between them in the case of a dispute. Certain sections of the 1991 Act specify arbitration as a means of resolving disputes, but section 60(1) of that Act goes further than this in providing that "any question or difference" between the parties arising out of the tenancy or in connection with the holding is to be referred to arbitration except where otherwise provided in the 1991 Act. Space does not permit a detailed examination of the relevant provisions but in summary, and depending upon the circumstances, the parties may either choose their own arbiter, have an arbiter appointed by the appropriate Minister or refer the matter to the Scottish Land Court.

An arbiter might therefore be appointed to determine a whole range of issues including, for example, waygoing claims on termination of a lease, rent levels and stock valuation.

The Scottish Land Court was established by the Small Landholders (Scotland) Act 1911 and has a very important role in relation to agricultural matters. The 1991 Act states that reference must be made to the Scottish Land Court in a variety of cases, for example, to determine any disagreement between the landlord and tenant arising out of the findings of a record of condition of the fixed equipment on an agricultural holding prepared at the commencement of or during the subsistence of a lease.[15] In certain circumstances where a landlord has served a notice to quit on the tenant of an agricultural holding, the consent of the Land Court is required before the notice to quit can be upheld.[16]

The sheriff court and the Court of Session have jurisdiction in relation to certain matters, such as the removal of a tenant for non-payment of rent over a period of six months.[17] In fact, the ordinary courts retain wide jurisdiction in agricultural matters except where they are excluded by statute or jurisdiction is specifically conferred upon an arbiter or the Land Court. The sheriff court or the Court of Session may be called upon to consider appeals against decisions on points

---

[12] 1907 Act, ss 4(2) and 5.
[13] 1907 Act, s. 6.
[14] 1997 SCLR 894.
[15] 1991 Act, s. 8.
[16] 1991 Act, s. 22.
[17] 1991 Act, s. 22(2)(d).

of law and to rule on claims for damages following upon unlawful occupation of a holding. They have jurisdiction under both common law and statute.

Succession to agricultural tenancies

Although the validity of any bequest of the tenant's interest in an agricultural lease is a matter for the ordinary courts to decide, there are detailed procedural rules in the 1991 Act regulating succession to agricultural tenancies on both intestacy and testate succession.[18] The 1991 Act also stipulates which class of relative or beneficiary is entitled to succeed to the tenancy. The procedures which must be followed for notifying or contesting a claim are specific, complex and time-sensitive. A detailed consideration of the relevant provisions is beyond the scope of this chapter.[19]

The Common Agricultural Policy

The CAP has been established mainly under the provisions of Articles 38–47 of the Treaty of Rome. In terms of Article 39 of the Treaty of Rome, it has five principal objectives:

    (i) to increase agricultural productivity;

    (ii) to ensure a fair standard of living for the agricultural community;

    (iii) to stabilise markets;

    (iv) to ensure the availability of supplies; and

    (v) to ensure that such supplies reach consumers at reasonable prices.[20]

In terms of Article 40 of the Treaty of Rome, these objectives are to be achieved through a common organisation of agricultural markets, which may take one of three forms: common rules on competition, compulsory co-ordination of the various national market organisations or a European market organisation. The last of these has been the method most often utilised in practice, with the development of "common markets" in relation to particular agricultural products, for example milk, cereals, beef and veal.

The background against which the CAP was conceived was the immediate aftermath of the Second World War and food shortages both during and after the war. The CAP had the same motivation as the Agricultural Holdings Acts, that is, to provide an incentive to farmers to produce enough food to make their country self-sufficient, or as near self-sufficient as possible, in food.

It is readily apparent that the objectives of the CAP as set out above are mutually incompatible: for example, increasing the wages of employees in agriculture cannot readily be balanced with a cheap food policy. For many years, the way in which the CAP sought to reconcile these incompatibilities was to fix an intervention or base price below which the price of the agricultural commodity in question should not be allowed to fall. If the price of the commodity in the market did fall below the intervention price, the community would step in, using

---

[18] 1991 Act, ss 11 and 12.
[19] See Gill, op. cit., n. 4, Chaps 33 and 34.
[20] Treaty of Rome, Art. 39.

taxpayers' money, to buy the commodity for storage until the market price rose. If the market price did not rise, the product would be either destroyed or exported outwith the Common Market area.

The disadvantage of these intervention arrangements was that if a producer had the guarantee of a purchaser at the intervention price, he would continue to produce whether or not there was a real market for his product. The aim of increasing agricultural productivity, coupled with the intervention arrangements, meant that the volume of agricultural produce continued to increase as farmers had the guarantee of an intervention purchaser. This over-supply drove market prices down further and, as a result, more of the commodity was subject to intervention. This resulted in the infamous milk lakes, beef mountains and other surpluses of the 1970s onwards. As a result of these increasing surpluses, a number of important reforms were introduced with a view to reducing and controlling production.

The following sections deal in turn with the most important "common markets", namely those in milk, arable crops and livestock.

Milk

The Common Market in milk was established in 1968.[21] In 1977, a scheme to reduce production of milk by paying farmers to leave the sector temporarily was introduced.[22] The scheme required those producers to give up milk production and not allow their land to be used for dairying for a period of five years. In exchange, they received cash compensation and their dairy herd was either slaughtered immediately or exported outwith the Common Market. The scheme was, however, temporary in nature, lasting for a five-year period only. It was insufficient to reduce milk production to a level considered satisfactory and another means of restricting production was required.

With effect from April 1, 1984, therefore, milk quotas were introduced in an attempt to resolve the problem of surplus milk in the European Community.[23] Initially, the quota scheme was to operate for a period of five years, but it has been amended and extended on a number of occasions and was overhauled and consolidated in 1992.[24] It operates by allocating to each individual milk producer a quota for the amount of milk which he can produce, and punishes him by imposition of a fine, or super levy, if he exceeds the level of his quota. The amount of the super levy is calculated to exceed the price which he would actually achieve by selling his milk and therefore makes it uneconomic to overproduce.

Quota generally

The milk quota year runs from April 1 to March 31 the following year.[25] Quota is allocated to producers, a producer being a natural or legal person or a group of natural or legal persons farming a holding located within the geographical

---

[21] See EEC Council Regulation 804/68. This has been considerably amended over the years.

[22] EEC Council Regulation 1078/77.

[23] EEC Council Regulation 856/84; EEC Council Regulation 857/84. See also EEC Commission Regulation 1371/84, as amended, which sets out the detailed implementing rules. The Dairy Produce Quota Regulations 1997 (SI 1997/733), as amended, are the latest UK implementing legislation.

[24] EC Council Regulation 3950/92, which has itself been further amended over the years.

[25] EC Council Regulation 3950/92, Art. 1; Dairy Produce Quota Regulations 1997, reg. 2.

territory of the community and selling milk directly to customers or supplying it to a purchaser.[26] Each producer's quota is, however, tied to a farm or holding, which is defined as the amalgamation of all units used by that producer for the production of milk within the European Community.[27]

There are two types of quota: "direct sales quota", which relates to the sale of milk products direct to the public, and "wholesale quota". Each holder of wholesale quota must be registered with a milk purchaser and have a contract with that purchaser, although it is possible to change purchasers subject to the terms of the contract with the purchaser. When quota was first allocated in the United Kingdom on April 1, 1984, the allocation of wholesale quota to individual producers was based on their production in 1983, while the allocation of direct sales quota was based on production in 1981.[28]

All quota is tagged with a butter fat percentage which measures the amount of fat in the milk produced.[29] If the butter fat percentage of the milk actually produced is higher or lower than the butter fat percentage attached to the quota, the actual litreage of milk produced will be adjusted, upwards where the butter fat percentage exceeds the percentage with which the quota is tagged and downwards where the butter fat percentage is lower than that with which the quota is tagged.[30]

There is a national reserve of quota rights, which comprises such wholesale and direct sales quota as is not for the time being allocated to any person and includes quota which has been withdrawn under the relevant legislation.[31] Allocations to producers from the national reserve are made in accordance with the European legislation and the Dairy Produce Quota Regulations 1997.[32]

Milk quota in the UK is administered by the Intervention Board for Agricultural Produce[33] (hereafter "the Intervention Board") which, *inter alia*, maintains the various registers relating to quota provided for in the legislation and has important functions in relation to the transfer and leasing of quota.

Transfer and leasing of quota

Transfer of quota: Initially, milk quota could only be transferred with the holding to which it was attached, and this is still the basic principle,[34] although a number of devices may be utilised to get round this restriction and there are now certain limited exceptions to it: these are discussed further below.

Whenever a holding is sold, leased or transferred by inheritance, or is the subject of a transaction having a comparable legal effect, all or part of the corresponding quota must be transferred to the buyer, tenant, heir, or other appropriate person according to the procedures laid down by the Member State.[35] The relevant

[26] EC Council Regulation 3950/92, Art. 9(c); Dairy Produce Quota Regulations 1997, reg. 2.
[27] EC Council Regulation 3950/92, Art. 9(d); Dairy Produce Quota Regulations 1997, reg. 2.
[28] See *Stair Memorial Encyclopaedia of the Laws of Scotland* (hereafter "*Stair Memorial Encyclopaedia*"), Vol. 1, para. 926.
[29] EC Council Regulation 3950/92, Art. 11.
[30] EC Council Regulation 536/93, Art. 2.
[31] See Dairy Produce Quota Regulations 1997, reg. 12(1).
[32] Dairy Produce Quota Regulations 1997, reg. 12(2).
[33] Dairy Produce Quota Regulations 1997, reg. 21.
[34] EC Council Regulation 3950/92, Art. 7.
[35] Ibid.

procedures in the UK are set out in the Dairy Produce Quota Regulations 1997, which make provision for an apportionment of quota to be made when a relevant transfer of part of a holding is made. In such a case, the amount of the quota to be transferred is ascertained on the basis of the areas used for dairy production.[36] These may be determined by agreement between the parties themselves or, in the event of their being unable to agree, by an arbiter appointed by the Intervention Board.[37] Where the parties agree the areas used for milk production between themselves, they are free to look at areas currently used for dairy production; if an arbiter is appointed by the Intervention Board, he will look at areas used for dairy production in the last five years.[38] Areas used for dairy production have been held to include not only land used for current milk production but land which, taking into account the annual cycle of agriculture, is used to support the dairy herd and provide for future milk production: it therefore includes land used for dairy cows and heifers, the milking parlour and land used for dairy or dual-purpose bulls bred to enter the dairy herd rather than for sale.[39] The Intervention Board can reopen agreed apportionments[40]: in practice, it is unlikely to do so where a quota of less than 20,000 litres has been allocated to a hectare. Where no transfer has yet taken place, it is possible to get a prospective apportionment of quota in advance.[41]

In order to effect a transfer of quota, there must be both a transfer of all or part of the holding and a change of occupation, and where there is such a transfer and change of occupation, reregistration of the quota will be required.[42] Sales and leases of land and transfers on death will generally involve changes in occupation and therefore be sufficient to transfer the quota to the incoming purchaser/tenant/executor/beneficiaries. Other types of transaction which may have a similar effect include, for example, business reorganisations, or the calling-up of a standard security where possession is actually entered into with a view to recovering the loan.[43] Certain types of transaction are specifically stated not to effect a transfer of quota: in Scotland, these are the grant of a licence to occupy land, the grant of a lease under which all or part of a holding is occupied for less than eight months and the termination of any such licence or lease.[44] In the case of tenancies of more than eight months where the land is used throughout for dairying and the tenant does not use additional land for dairying, the milk quota would revert to the landlord at the termination of the tenancy. Where there is a transfer of a holding or part of a holding, the prescribed form and other evidence

---

[36] Ibid and Dairy Produce Quota Regulations 1997, reg. 7.
[37] See EC Council Regulation 3950/92, Art. 7 and the Dairy Produce Quota Regulations 1997, regs 7 and 8.
[38] Dairy Produce Quota Regulations 1997, reg. 8 and Sched. 3, para. 2.
[39] *Puncknowle Farms Ltd* v *Kane* [1985] 3 All ER 790.
[40] Dairy Produce Quota Regulations 1997, reg. 10.
[41] Dairy Produce Quota Regulations 1997, regs 7(4) and 9.
[42] Dairy Produce Quota Regulations 1997, reg. 7.
[43] See *Harries* v *Barclays Bank plc* (1997) EG 145. This case was an English case involving an English mortgage, but it is thought that the position would be the same with respect to a Scottish standard security, since the determining factor is the entry into possession. The security holder after entering into possession is in the same position as the borrower; he may therefore sell or lease the quota as discussed further below.
[44] Dairy Produce Quota Regulations 1997, reg. 7.

of the transfer must be submitted to the Intervention Board within 28 days of the change of occupation.[45] It should be noted that where a tenant was in occupation of a holding at April 1, 1984, on termination of the tenancy of that holding the landlord is obliged to pay compensation to the tenant for milk quota allocated in excess of that which would have been allocated had the tenant not carried out improvements to the holding and for quota which the tenant has purchased since April 1, 1984.[46]

As the demand for quota has grown and a market in quota has become established, the pre-requisite of a land transfer for a transfer of a quota has been gradually eroded, and as noted above, a number of devices may be utilised to get round this restriction and there are now certain limited exceptions to it.

The principal device for circumventing the requirement for a land transfer is the grant of a grazing let. This must be for at least eight months since, as noted above, a lease for less than eight months will not operate to transfer quota. In order to achieve the transfer of quota, the grazing tenant must be another milk producer, and must take the land out of milk production for the duration of the grazing let. On the commencement of the grazing let, the quota is transferred to the tenant and thereafter attaches to his quota holding and not to the holding of his landlord. When the grazing let expires, as the land has not been used for milk production, the quota remains attached to the tenant's quota holding and does not revert to the landlord.

From 1987 onwards, it has been possible to lease out milk quota for the quota year.[47] Initially, the quota holder had to retain a minimum litreage in his own name; however, it is now competent to lease out all or part of the quota holder's unused quota which is registered as permanently held by him. Leases must be notified to the Intervention Board by December 31 in the relevant quota year.[48]

Quota can be transferred without the land where the transfer is necessary to improve the structure of the business of the transferor and the transferee.[49] This procedure has been little used, first because of the availability of the grazing let route and secondly because of various undertakings that require to be given by the transferor and the transferee. These undertakings are to protect the principle that transfers without land are only to take place where there is a permanent change in the business of the two parties and to guard against any suggestion of trading in quota, and therefore the transferor must undertake not to transfer any quota either permanently or temporarily in the current and subsequent quota year and the transferee must undertake not to transfer out quota in the same period.[50]

There are a number of general restrictions on the transferring and leasing of quota:

---

[45] Dairy Produce Quota Regulations 1997, reg. 7.
[46] Agriculture Act 1986, s. 14 and Sched. 2.
[47] See now EC Council Regulation 3950/92, Art. 6; Dairy Produce Quota Regulations 1997, reg. 13.
[48] Ibid.
[49] EC Council Regulation 3950/92, Art. 8; Dairy Produce Quota Regulations 1997, reg. 11.
[50] Dairy Produce Quota Regulations 1997, reg. 11.

(i) quota within a Scottish Island area cannot be transferred or leased out-with it: these areas are "ring fenced" for this purpose.[51] Outwith these areas, however, quota can be transferred freely within the United Kingdom;

(ii) quota cannot be leased out where the party leasing out the quota has already leased in quota for that quota year[52];

(iii) quota which has been converted from wholesale to direct sale or vice versa in the current quota year cannot be leased out[53];

(iv) any quota which was acquired by transfer without land arrangements during the quota year of the transfer and the succeeding quota year cannot be leased out[54];

(v) the consent of the landlord of the holding and of any secured creditor to a transfer or lease of quota will be required.

Arable crops

The common market in cereals was established in 1967.[55] In 1992, as part of a series of reforms to the CAP generally, the Arable Area Payment Scheme (here-after "AAPS") was introduced.[56] The objectives of this reform were the reduction of grain surpluses, the bringing of EEC prices closer to world market prices to enable surpluses to be exported outwith the EEC with reduced or no export sub-sidies and the reduction of expenditure on the CAP. Reform was three-pronged: supply control, reduction in prices and compensation.

The AAPS comprises a harmonised system of arable area payments (hereafter "AAPs") for producers growing specified arable crops. The payments are designed to compensate such producers for the loss of income caused by the reduction in the institutional prices for such crops. Applications for compensation are made by the farmer under the Integrated Administration and Control System (hereafter "IACS"), also introduced in 1992.[57] A farmer for this purpose is an individual agricultural producer, whether a natural or a legal person or a group of natural or legal persons, whatever legal status is granted to the group and its members by national law, whose holding is within community territory.[58] All

---

[51] Dairy Produce Quota Regulations 1997, regs 7(4) (transfers) and 13(4) (leases). The three "ring-fenced" areas are (i) the islands of Shetland; (ii) the islands of Orkney; and (iii) the islands of Islay, Jura, Gigha, Bute, Arran, Great Cumbrae and Little Cumbrae and the Kintyre Peninsula south of Tarbert: Dairy Produce Quota Regulations 1997, reg. 2.

[52] Dairy Produce Quota Regulations 1997, reg. 11(2).

[53] Dairy Produce Quota Regulations 1997, reg. 16(4).

[54] Dairy Produce Quota Regulations 1997, reg. 11.

[55] EEC Council Regulation 120/67. This had been preceded by a transitional scheme established in 1962 under EEC Council Regulation 19 of April 4, 1962.

[56] EC Council Regulation 1765/92; see also EC Commission Regulations 2293/92, 2294/92, 2295/92, 2780/92, 334/93, 762/94 and 1586/97, which set out the detailed implementing rules. The Arable Area Payment Regulations 1996 (SI 1996/3142), as amended, are the latest UK implementing legislation.

[57] EC Council Regulation 3508/92; see also EC Commission Regulations 3887/92 and 3888/92, which set out the detailed implementing rules. The Integrated Administration and Control System Regulations 1993 (SI 1993/1317), as amended, are the relevant UK implementing legislation.

[58] EC Council Regulation 3508/92; Arable Area Payment Regulations 1996, reg. 2.

farms in the UK farmed as one unit by one business should therefore be the subject of a single application. The Scottish Executive Rural Affairs Department, by whom the AAPS is administered in Scotland, will consider the economic structure and organisation of each business by which an application is made and its operation and commercial management in order to ascertain whether or not it is a separate business in respect of which a separate application is justified.

There is a main scheme and a simplified scheme and claims for compensation may be made under either. Under the main scheme, AAPs are paid at different rates, fixed annually, for cereals, oil seeds and proteins. Under the simplified scheme, which applies only to small producers, that is, producers who make a claim for compensatory payments in relation to an area of land below a specified limit,[59] all AAPs are paid at the cereals rate whatever crop is actually sown.[60]

AAPs are paid to producers on four conditions:

(i) they have grown qualifying crops;

(ii) the crops have been grown on qualifying land;

(iii) any set-aside requirement has been met; and

(iv) the regional base areas have not been exceeded.

These are now considered in turn.

Qualifying crops

Qualifying crops include almost all cereals, oil seed and protein crops, field beans, peas and linseed, but potatoes, sugar beet, vining peas and herbage seeds are excluded from the Scheme.[61] All crops must generally be sown by May 15 to qualify for subsidy payments[62]: a later sowing date will only be allowed in exceptional circumstances.[63]

Qualifying land

In order to be eligible for AAPs, the land concerned must not have been under permanent pasture or used for permanent crop, or have been in forestry or in non-agricultural use, on December 31, 1991.[64]

Set-aside

To qualify for AAPs under the main scheme, a producer has to "set aside", that is, take out of production, a certain percentage of his land from the first Monday in January each year.[65] During the ensuing 12 months, the set-aside land cannot be used for any purposes connected with food production and the producer must

---

[59] EC Council Regulation 1765/92, Art. 8.

[60] Ibid.

[61] EC Council Regulation 1765/92, Art. 1 and Annex 1 as amended. See further Scottish Office Explanatory Booklet "The Integrated Administration and Control System" (1998).

[62] EC Council Regulation 1765/92, Art. 10.

[63] See EC Commission Regulation 3887/92, Arts 8 and 11.

[64] EC Council Regulation 1765/92, Art. 9.

[65] EC Council Regulation 1765/92, Art. 2.

comply with certain management requirements.[66] Compensation for the obligation to set aside is paid as if the areas set aside were sown with cereals.[67] The set-aside requirement must be met from land which has been farmed by the producer for at least two years preceding the start of the set-aside period,[68] and must either have been cultivated for cereals in the base year (1991–92) with the intention of producing a harvestable crop or have been previously set aside under the AAPS or the five-year set-aside scheme which preceded it.

Various types of set-aside have been allowed under the scheme in the past, including rotational set-aside, flexible set-aside, voluntary set-aside, additional voluntary set-aside, transferred set-aside and penalty set-aside. Detailed rules apply to each type, but consideration of these is beyond the scope of this chapter.

As an alternative to growing nothing on set-aside land, it is possible to grow certain "non-food" crops.[69] The rules are very strict and if the producer does not comply with these he will lose his AAPs and may incur further penalties.

There is no set-aside requirement under the simplified scheme.[70]

Regional base areas

Compensatory payments are granted for the area which is down to arable crops or subject to set-aside and which does not exceed a regional base area established under the European legislation.[71] If in any year the total area for which relevant claims are made exceeds the regional base area, all claims relative to that region will be reduced proportionately and the set-aside obligation for those participating in the main scheme will be increased for the following year.[72]

Administration of the AAPS

As noted above, the AAPS in Scotland is now administered by the Scottish Executive Rural Affairs Department. Payment of the relevant subsidies is to be made by December 31 in the marketing year concerned,[73] although payments for oil seeds are made in at least two parts. To claim AAPs, each producer must submit an IACS form by May 15 in each year.[74] This requires the producer to give details of the use to which the land is being put on a field-by-field basis and identifies the fields by reference to Ordnance Survey-based plans.[75] This form also requires to be submitted where applying for Sheep Annual Premium, Hill Livestock Compensatory Allowance, Suckler Cow Premium or Beef Special Premium, all of which are discussed further below.

---

[66] EC Commission Regulation 762/94, Art. 2. The current management requirements for set-aside land are contained in Sched. 2 to the Arable Area Payment Regulations 1996 as amended.

[67] EC Council Regulation 1765/92, Art. 7.

[68] EC Commission Regulation 762/94, Art. 3.

[69] EC Council Regulation 1765/92, Art. 7(4); see also EC Commission Regulation 334/93, which sets out the detailed implementing rules.

[70] EC Council Regulation 1765/92, Art. 8.

[71] EC Council Regulation 1765/92, Art. 2.

[72] Ibid.

[73] EC Council Regulation 1765/92, Art. 10.

[74] EC Council Regulation 3508/92, Art. 6. The May 15 deadline is a derogation from the requirements of this Regulation which is available to the UK, and may therefore be changed in future years.

[75] See generally EC Commission Regulation 3887/92.

Livestock

The livestock sector can conveniently be subdivided into (i) cattle and (ii) sheep. This section will consider first the specific schemes applying to all cattle and sheep, and thereafter the Hill Livestock Compensatory Allowances Scheme which applies to cattle and sheep in specified areas.

Cattle

The common organisation of the market in beef and veal was established in 1969.[76] Until the introduction of the 1992 reforms, the system was based on price support mechanisms aimed at keeping prices within the Community at an agreed level. In 1992, this system was reformed, and two beef premiums were introduced: Beef Special Premium and Suckler Cow Premium.[77] Suckler Cow Premium Rights are subject to a quota.[78]

There are a number of features common to both of these schemes. For the purposes of both schemes, a producer is defined as an individual farmer, whether an individual, partnership or company, whose holding is located within the Community territory and who is engaged in rearing bovine animals.[79] Holding is defined as meaning all production units managed by the producer and located within the territory of a single Member State[80]: this would be the UK and not Scotland. Under both schemes, the producer must, in broad terms, establish that his holding is not over-stocked: the stocking density rules are discussed further below. This concept is central to the Community's attempts to reward extensive and environmentally friendly farming methods and payment of premiums can be withdrawn or repayment of premiums already paid demanded if a producer over-grazes or uses unsuitable supplementary feeding methods.[81]

Producers claiming Beef Special Premium and/or Suckler Cow Premium must submit an IACS form.[82] As noted above, eligibility for premium payments is subject to stocking density rules.[83] The only exception to the application of the stocking density rules is where the producer claims subsidy on so few animals that the total livestock units (discussed below) claimed on the holding does not exceed 15.[84] To calculate the stocking density, it is necessary to identify the livestock units to be applied to animals on the holding and the forage area for the holding.[85] Livestock units are calculated by taking into account all male bovine

---

[76] See EEC Council Regulation 805/68. This has been amended many times over the years.

[77] See EC Council Regulation 2066/92, which extensively amended EEC Council Regulation 805/68. See also EC Commission Regulation 3886/92, as amended, which sets out the detailed implementing rules. The Suckler Cow Premium Regulations 1993 (SI 1993/1441), as amended and the Beef Special Premium Regulations 1996 (SI 1996/3241) are the latest UK implementing legislation.

[78] EEC Council Regulation 805/68 as amended; EC Commission Regulation 3886/92, as amended; Sheep Annual Premium and Suckler Cow Premium Quota Regulations 1997 (SI 1997/2844).

[79] EEC Council Regulation 805/68, Art. 4a; Suckler Cow Premium Regulations 1993, reg. 2 and Beef Special Premium Regulations 1996, reg. 2.

[80] Ibid.

[81] Suckler Cow Premium Regulations 1993, regs 3A and 3B and Beef Special Premium Regulations 1996, regs 11 and 12.

[82] Discussed in the preceding section.

[83] EEC Regulation 805/68, Art. 4g.

[84] Ibid.

[85] Ibid.

animals, suckler cows, sheep and goats for which premium applications have been submitted and the notional number of dairy cows required to fulfil the producer's milk quota.[86] Livestock on the holding for which no subsidy is claimed are ignored for the purpose of calculating livestock units at present but this is likely to change in the foreseeable future.[87] The forage area is the area of the holding which is available throughout the calendar year for rearing bovine animals, sheep and goats.[88] It does not include buildings, woods, paths or ponds, nor does it include land for which any area aid is claimed under the AAPS (including set-aside), any areas used for other crops benefiting from Community aid or land used for permanent crops or horticultural crops.[89] If the number of livestock units per hectare of forage area is less than two, the producer will qualify for Beef Special Premium and Suckler Cow Premium; if the number of livestock units per hectare of forage exceeds two, Beef Special Premium and Suckler Cow Premium will only be paid up to the level of two units per hectare. Additional premiums per premium granted (extensification premiums) are payable where the number of livestock units is less than 1.4 per hectare.[90] The particular features of each individual premium will now be considered.

Beef Special Premium: Each producer can claim this on up to 90 male cattle in certain specified age brackets in any year.[91] The relevant age brackets, calculated with reference to the start of the appropriate retention period (discussed further below), are from 10 to 21 months in the case of uncastrated cattle and 10 months and over 22 months respectively in the case of uncastrated cattle.[92] The animals must be retained for a two-month retention period from the date of lodging the application.[93] If the number of claims for Beef Special Premium exceed the regional ceiling, the payments will be scaled back proportionately.[94]

Suckler Cow Premium and Suckler Cow Premium quota[95]: A suckler cow is defined as a cow belonging to a meat breed or born of a cross with a meat breed and belonging to a herd intended for rearing calves for meat production or an in-calf heifer meeting the same criteria which replaces the suckler cow.[96]

Suckler Cow Premium is payable to producers keeping suckler cows on their holdings.[97] The main change effected by the 1992 reforms was the introduction of

---

[86] Ibid. Milk quota is discussed above. For the method of calculation of the number of dairy cows needed to fulfil a producer's milk quota, see EC Commission Regulation 3886/92, Art. 42.

[87] EEC Regulation 805/68, Art. 4g.

[88] Ibid.

[89] Ibid.

[90] EEC Regulation 805/68, Art. 4h.

[91] EEC Regulation 805/68, Art. 4b.

[92] Ibid.

[93] EC Commission Regulation 3886/92, Art. 4.

[94] EEC Regulation 805/68, Art. 4b; EC Commission Regulation 3886/92, Art. 5.

[95] See generally EEC Regulation 805/68, EC Commission Regulation 3886/92, the Suckler Cow Premium Regulations 1993, as amended and the Sheep Annual Premium and Suckler Cow Premium Quota Regulations 1997.

[96] EEC Council Regulation 805/68, Art. 4a. For the definition of meat breed, see EC Commission Regulation 3886/92, Art. 22.

[97] EEC Council Regulation 805/68, Art. 4d.

individual quotas for premium rights at producer levels.[98] Dairy farmers are not entitled to claim Suckler Cow Premium unless they are direct sellers or their milk quota is less than the specified limit.[99]

The grant of Suckler Cow Premium is conditional upon the producer complying with a retention period of six months immediately following the day on which the application for Suckler Cow Premium was lodged.[100] During the retention period, the producer must maintain a number of suckler cows at least equal to the number for which the premium has been requested on the holding for the six-month period.[101] The application period for Suckler Cow Premium begins on July 1 and runs until December 6 each year.[102]

Suckler Cow Premium quotas were allocated according to the number of animals for which premium was received in 1992.[103] Unlike Sheep Annual Premium quota, discussed below, Suckler Cow Premium quota was allocated to the partnership rather than to individual partners. Provisions were made for producers who did not receive premium rights in 1992 or received a lesser number than they would otherwise have done due to natural circumstances.[104]

Each Member State was required to set up a national reserve of between 1 per cent and 3 per cent of the total number of animals for which Suckler Cow Premium was granted in the reference year.[105] This national reserve is augmented by quota rights going into the national reserve via the siphon, that is, the automatic surrender of 15 per cent of quota where quota is transferred without the holding to which it relates,[106] and quota rights withdrawn for non-use.[107] The national reserve is divided into six divisions, each corresponding with a "sensitive zone" as defined in the Sheep Annual Premium and Suckler Cow Premium Quota Regulations 1997.[108] A wide range of producers can apply to the national reserve in any year for an award of Suckler Cow Premium rights and there is a hierarchy of applications.[109] In addition, each Member State was required to set up an additional reserve of 1 per cent of the total number of animals for which Suckler Cow Premium was granted in the less favoured areas of the Member State, to be assigned exclusively to producers in such areas.[110]

Ninety per cent of quota rights must be used each and every year otherwise the unused quota will be withdrawn without compensation and transferred to

---

[98] EEC Council Regulation 805/68, Art. 4d.

[99] Ibid.

[100] Ibid and EC Commission Regulation 3886/92, Art. 23.

[101] Ibid.

[102] Suckler Cow Premium Regulations 1993, reg. 3.

[103] EEC Council Regulation 805/68, Art. 4d.

[104] EC Commission Regulation 3886/92, Art. 38.

[105] EEC Council Regulation 805/68, Art. 4f.

[106] Ibid; Sheep Annual Premium and Suckler Cow Premium Quota Regulations 1997, reg. 5.

[107] See further below.

[108] Sheep Annual Premium and Suckler Cow Premium Quota Regulations 1997, reg. 9. The sensitive zones are specified in Sched. 1.

[109] See EEC Council Regulation 805/68, Art. 4f; Sheep Annual Premium and Suckler Cow Premium Quota Regulations 1997, reg. 11.

[110] EEC Council Regulation 805/68, Art. 4f. For the purposes of this provision, "producer" in a less favoured area is defined in EC Commission Regulation 3886/92, Art. 31 as a producer whose holding is in the areas defined pursuant to Art. 3 of Council Directive 75/268 or one to which certain other conditions apply.

the national reserve.[111] To use his quota rights, a producer must either claim Suckler Cow Premium on the number of eligible cows up to the amount of his quota rights or lease all or part of his quota rights to another producer; the lessee of the quota rights does not have to claim against these rights, but the quota holder will be treated as having used them.

A producer is free to transfer or lease Suckler Cow Premium rights either with or without land.[112] If, however, he transfers all or part of the Suckler Cow Premium quota rights to other producers without transferring his holding, as noted above, there is a siphon to the national reserve of 15 per cent. To avoid the siphon, all of the holding must be transferred with all of the quota. If the holding is sold in lots, all recipients must receive quota or the siphon will apply. The sale of land without quota does not, however, trigger the siphon; thus, where a lotted sale is proposed, lots which are not to receive quota should be sold off first. The siphon does not apply in the case of leases, but there is a limit on the frequency and volume of leasing that a producer may undertake. Over a five-year period starting in the year in which the producer first leases his quota rights, a producer must use all his quota himself in at least two consecutive years.[113] If he fails to do so, his quota effectively becomes unleasable.[114] There is an exception from this requirement for producers participating in Community extensification programmes.[115]

The lease or transfer of Suckler Cow Premium quota rights is only effective after both parties have notified the Quota Management Section of the Scottish Executive Rural Affairs Department.[116] Where the recipient of the quota being leased or transferred submits an application for premium within the application period, the deadline for notification is the date upon which he does so; where no such application is submitted, it is the end of the application period specified in regulation 3(1) of the Suckler Cow Premium Regulations 1993.[117] Quota can now therefore effectively be transferred until December 6 provided that (i) the recipient has not claimed premium for the marketing year prior to the date of transfer and (ii) the transferor/lessor of the quota has not claimed; if the transferor or lessor has claimed, his retention period will be running and his claims for premium would be invalidated.

Suckler Cow Premium quota is "ring-fenced" to avoid Suckler Cow Premium quota rights being moved away from regions where beef production is especially important to local communities.[118] The Sheep Annual Premium and Suckler Cow Premium Quota Regulations 1997 establish six "sensitive zones", and there are limitations on transfer and leasing of quota between these zones.[119] The ring fences

---

[111] EC Commission Regulation 3886/92, Art. 33 as amended. There are some exceptions for producers in extensification schemes.

[112] EEC Council Regulation 805/68, Art. 4e.

[113] EC Commission Regulation 3886/92, Art. 34.

[114] Ibid.

[115] Ibid.

[116] EC Commission Regulation 3886/92, Art. 34(2); Sheep Annual Premium and Suckler Cow Premium Quota Regulations 1997, reg. 4.

[117] Sheep Annual Premium and Suckler Cow Premium Quota Regulations 1997, reg. 4.

[118] As per the requirement in EEC Council Regulation 805/68, Art. 4e.

[119] Sheep Annual Premium and Suckler Cow Premium Quota Regulations 1997, reg. 8. The sensitive zones are specified in Sched. 1.

apply not only to quota movements but also to producers, so that if a producer moves outwith his ring fence area it will not normally be possible for him to move his quota rights with him. Quota is designated according to the location of the majority of the producer's holding.[120] Care should therefore be taken when enlarging holdings across ring fence boundaries: if this results in a redesignation of the holding, the producer may require to sell his quota from the original ring fence area and purchase or lease quota corresponding to the new ring fence area.

Sheep

The common market in sheep meat and goat meat was not established until 1980,[121] but it too has been subject to extensive reforms. Currently, provision is made for the payment of a Sheep Annual Premium which, like Suckler Cow Premium, discussed above, is subject to a quota.[122]

Sheep Annual Premium

The purpose of the Sheep Annual Premium scheme is to compensate sheep meat producers when the market price of sheep meat in the UK falls below the reference price fixed for the UK under the European Community legislation. The premium payable to the producer represents the difference between the market price and the reference price,[123] and as such, the level of the premium fluctuates from year to year. A producer is defined as an individual farmer, whether a natural or a legal person, who, on a permanent basis, assumes the risk or organises the rearing of at least 10 ewes within the territory of a single Member State[124]: this would be the UK and not Scotland. Unlike Suckler Cow Premium quota, Sheep Annual Premium quota is allocated to the individual members of producer groups, including partnerships.[125]

A producer must submit an application for Sheep Annual Premium on eligible ewes during the application period, which runs from December 4 in the preceding calendar year to February 4 in the claim year.[126] Eligible ewes are those which have had a lamb or are at least one year old at the expiry of the relevant retention period.[127] The producer must retain the eligible ewes in respect of which an application has been made on the holding for a minimum retention period[128]; this is currently 100 days, running from February 5 to May 14 in leap years and to May 15 in non-leap years.

---

[120] Sheep Annual Premium and Suckler Cow Premium Quota Regulations 1997, reg. 3.

[121] See EEC Council Regulation 1837/80. This has been amended extensively over succeeding years.

[122] See now EC Council Regulation 2467/98, which is a consolidating measure, and EC Commission Regulation 3567/92, as amended, which sets out the detailed implementing rules. See also the Sheep Annual Premium Regulations 1992 (SI 1992/2677), as amended, and the Sheep Annual Premium and Suckler Cow Premium Quota Regulations 1997.

[123] EC Council Regulation 2467/98, Art. 5.

[124] EEC Council Regulation 3493/90, Art. 1, as amended; Sheep Annual Premium Regulations 1992, reg. 2.

[125] EC Council Regulation 2467/98, Art. 5.

[126] Sheep Annual Premium Regulations 1992, reg. 3(2).

[127] Scottish Executive Rural Affairs Department Sheep Annual Premium Scheme Explanatory Note.

[128] EC Council Regulation 2467/98, Art. 5.

Sheep Annual Premium quota

The 1992 reforms limited a producer's right to claim Sheep Annual Premium by the imposition of individual quotas based on the number of claims made in 1991. In 1993 and 1994, headage limits applied, but these were abolished from 1995 onwards, and the premium claim is now limited to the number of quota rights held. The provisions are very similar, in some cases identical, to those applying to Suckler Cow Premium quota.

As in the case of Suckler Cow Premium, each Member State was required to set up a national reserve of Sheep Annual Premium rights[129] which is augmented by a siphon of 15 per cent of quota on transfers of quota without a transfer of the holding[130] and quota withdrawn from non-use.[131] The provisions relating to the siphon and to the non-use of Sheep Annual Premium quota are essentially identical to those for Suckler Cow Premium quota, discussed above. Again, as in the case of Suckler Cow Premium, the national reserve is divided into six divisions, each corresponding with a "sensitive zone" as defined in the Sheep Annual Premium and Suckler Cow Premium Quota Regulations 1997.[132] A wide range of producers can apply to the national reserve in any year for an award of Sheep Annual Premium rights and there is a hierarchy of applications[133]; each Member State was also required to set up an additional reserve for less favoured areas of the Member State, to be assigned exclusively to producers in such areas.[134] Because of difficulties with the establishment of the national reserve, special additional transfer and leasing periods have been available in the past to producers receiving quota from the national reserve or producers who applied but were unsuccessful in such applications.

Special provisions apply to producer groups/partnerships for Sheep Annual Premium quota. The ratio of the individual members' quota rights to the group/partnership total should match the individual members' interest in the group/partnership otherwise it will be necessary to restructure the manner of holding of the quota. Such restructuring by transfer of quota may attract the application of the siphon unless the transfer of quota is between members of the group/partnership[135]; in such circumstances, the siphon may not apply, but for the following three years there should be no further transfers between the parties. With partnerships, it is important that the ratio in which the quota is held by the individual partners corresponds to the formula set out in the partnership agreement for the distribution of capital at termination of the partnership.

As in the case of Suckler Cow Premium quota, a producer is able to transfer or lease his Sheep Annual Premium quota rights with or without land.[136] If, however, he transfers all or part of his quota rights without transferring his holding, as

---

[129] EC Council Regulation 2467/98, Art. 7.
[130] EC Council Regulation 2467/98, Art. 6(4)(b). There are limited exceptions for certain transfers between members of groups of producers: this is discussed further below.
[131] See EC Commission Regulation 3567/92, Art. 6.
[132] Sheep Annual Premium and Suckler Cow Premium Quota Regulations 1997, reg. 9. The sensitive zones are specified in Sched. 1.
[133] See EC Council Regulation 2467/98, Art. 7; Sheep Annual Premium and Suckler Cow Premium Quota Regulations 1997, reg. 11.
[134] EC Council Regulation 2467/98, Art. 7.
[135] See EC Council Regulation 2467/98, Art. 6(4)(b).
[136] EC Council Regulation 2467/98, Art. 6.

noted above, there is a siphon to the national reserve of 15 per cent,[137] and to avoid the siphon, all of the holding must be transferred with all of the quota. If the holding is sold in lots, all recipients of the holding must receive quota. As with Suckler Cow Premium quota, however, there are ways in which the siphon can be avoided in lotted sales (see above). The siphon does not apply to leases of Sheep Annual Premium quota rights, but there is a limit on the frequency and volume of leasing that a producer may undertake. Over a five-year period starting in the year in which the producer first leases his quota rights, a producer must use all his quota himself in at least two consecutive years.[138] If he fails to do so, his quota effectively becomes unleasable.[139] There is an exception from this requirement for producers participating in Community extensification programmes.[140]

No transfer or lease of quota is effective until it has been notified to the Quota Management Section of the Scottish Executive Rural Affairs Department by both parties to the transaction.[141] Where the recipient of the quota being leased or transferred submits an application for premium within the application period, the deadline for notification is the date upon which he does so; where no such application is submitted, it is the end of the application period specified in regulation 3(2) of the Sheep Annual Premium Regulations 1992.[142] Quota can now therefore effectively be transferred until February 4, provided that (i) the recipient has not claimed premium for the marketing year prior to the date of submission of notification of the transfer/lease, and (ii) the transferor/lessor has not claimed premium.

Like Suckler Cow Premium quota, Sheep Annual Premium quota rights are "ring fenced" to avoid quota rights moving from areas where sheep production is especially important to the local economy.[143] As noted above, the Sheep Annual Premium and Suckler Cow Premium Quota Regulations 1997 establish six "sensitive zones", and there are limitations on transfer and leasing of quota between these zones.[144] What is said above in relation to Suckler Cow Premium quota in this respect applies equally here.

Hill Livestock Compensatory Allowances

EEC Directive 75/268 makes provision for the designation of areas as "less favoured" because of disadvantages and constraints on agricultural production in those areas and allows Member States to pay compensatory allowances to farmers in such less favoured areas (hereafter "LFAs") to offset the natural handicaps with which farming in those areas is associated. A number of areas in Scotland have been designated as LFAs, and the provision for payment of compensatory allowances in such areas has been implemented in the UK as a

---

[137] EC Council Regulation 2467/98, Art. 6.
[138] EC Commission Regulation 3567/92, Art. 7.
[139] Ibid.
[140] Ibid.
[141] EC Commission Regulation 3886/92, Art. 34(2); Sheep Annual Premium and Suckler Cow Premium Quota Regulations 1997, reg. 4.
[142] Sheep Annual Premium and Suckler Cow Premium Quota Regulations 1997, reg. 4.
[143] As required by EC Council Regulation 2467/98, Art. 6.
[144] Sheep Annual Premium and Suckler Cow Premium Quota Regulations 1997, reg. 8. The sensitive zones are specified in Sched. 1.

whole by the Hill Livestock Compensatory Allowances Regulations 1996[145] as amended. These provide for payment of Hill Livestock Compensatory Allowances (hereafter "HLCAs") in relation to sheep and suckler cows retained by a producer for a specified period on eligible land. The retention period for sheep corresponds to the retention period applicable to Sheep Annual Premium, while that for cattle corresponds to the retention period for Suckler Cow Premium, both of which are discussed above.[146] Eligible land is land of not less than three hectares which is either disadvantaged or severely disadvantaged within the meaning given to those terms by the regulations.[147] The application period for HLCA in relation to sheep is identical to that for Sheep Annual Premium and in relation to cattle is identical to that for Suckler Cow Premium, both of which are discussed above.[148] However, while a claim for HLCA for cattle relates to the same year as the Suckler Cow Premium claim, a claim for HLCA for sheep relates to the previous year.

The stocking density rules discussed above in relation to Beef Special Premium and Suckler Cow Premium are also relevant to claims for HLCA: HLCA payments are subject to a cap of 1.4 livestock units per hectare of eligible land.[149] There is provision for the reduction or withholding of HLCA payments where there is overgrazing or where the claimant has used unsuitable supplementary feeding methods.[150]

Current and future issues

With the promulgation of the European Commission's Agenda 2000 proposals and the impending Uruguay Round of GATT negotiations, substantial changes can be expected to the subsidy regime in the near future. In the dairy sector, it is anticipated that prices will be reduced and a premium payment for dairy cattle introduced by way of compensation. However, following discussions in March 1999, these changes will be delayed until 2003. In the arable sector, it is anticipated that the subsidy payment for cereals, oil seeds and non-textile linseed will remain at the current level while protein crops will receive an additional direct payment over and above the standard payment for arable crops. It is also anticipated that set-aside will be retained while its normal default rate will be fixed at 10 per cent under expected conditions. Compensation per hectare of set-aside will be set at the same level as for cereals. In the beef sector, it is anticipated that the effective market support level will be reduced, although the level of premium payments may be increased.

All of this must be seen in the context of depressed agricultural markets, shrinking farm incomes and arguments between EU Member States over the funding of the European Union when the current CAP Budget is in the region of ECU 40 billion per annum.

---

[145] SI 1996/1500.
[146] Hill Livestock Compensatory Allowances Regulations 1996, reg. 2(2).
[147] Hill Livestock Compensatory Allowances Regulations 1996, reg. 2(1).
[148] Hill Livestock Compensatory Allowances Regulations 1996, reg. 8.
[149] Hill Livestock Compensatory Allowances Regulations 1996, regs 4(1)(d) and 5(1)(e).
[150] Hill Livestock Compensatory Allowances Regulations 1996, regs 4(3), 5(3) and 7.

Farm incomes have been under increasing pressure in recent times, partly due to the strength of sterling against competing currencies and a loss of export markets. Methods of food production are subject to close scrutiny by government and environmental agencies and farmers are being encouraged to find ways of supporting themselves other than in the production of food, while labouring under ever-increasing amounts of paperwork.

The advent of the Scottish Parliament also has implications for agriculture in Scotland. At the simplest level, the functions formerly exercised by the Scottish Office Agriculture, Environment and Fisheries Department are now being undertaken by the Scottish Executive Rural Affairs Department. It is anticipated, however, that the UK Agriculture Minister will still take the lead in negotiations relative to the CAP, with his Scottish counterpart taking the lead only in matters of prime interest to Scottish farmers.

The whole future of agriculture is also to a significant extent tied up with the issue of land reform, discussed in Chapter 1. The Land Reform Policy Group (hereafter "the LRPG") has recommended, *inter alia*, possible reforms to the Agricultural Holdings regime to introduce limited duration tenancies (akin to the Farm Business Tenancy regime currently applicable in England), to simplify arbitration procedures and to offer tenants wider opportunities for diversification[151] and there is a strong possibility that these reforms will be introduced in due course by the new Scottish Parliament. A tenant's right to buy, akin to that available to crofters,[152] was also canvassed as part of the possible reforms but rejected by the LRPG; questions such as whether a tenant should have a right to buy his land and, if so, whether there would be a market in tenanted land are, however, still under active consideration.

Some believe that all agricultural support systems should be removed and a free market allowed to operate so that prices can find their own level. There is much concern about whether, under the present systems, both the farmer and the consumer are getting a raw deal because of the power of the large supermarkets and the middle-men. On the assumption that domestic production of food will still be required in some shape or form in the next century, farmers will continue to play an important role in the Scottish countryside and the demands of agriculture will continue to have an important effect on the Scottish countryside. The exact form and shape of future agriculture remains, however, a matter of conjecture.

---

[151] Land Reform Policy Group: Recommendations for Action (January 1999).
[152] q.v. Chap. 6.

CHAPTER 6

CROFTING

Derek Flyn

Introduction

"Crofting is best described as a way of life. It is often equated with part-time agriculture. This is only partly true; agriculture links crofters with the land and crofting agriculture impacts significantly on rural economies. But crofting is more. It defines the economy, environment, culture, language and heritage for many rural communities."[1]

Crofting is, however, purely a creature of statute. The factors leading to the introduction of crofting tenure into Scots law, discussed further below, are complex, and nothing prepares you for crofting law itself. Although the terminology used is recognisably that of landlord and tenant and the general principles of Scots law apply, in many ways it is the law of a different land; perhaps this is hardly surprising, for it is intended to serve the needs of inhabitants of inaccessible and distant places. Crofting law is, notwithstanding a relatively recent consolidation of the relevant legislation,[2] a complex area, and this chapter does not attempt to give a detailed description of the law.[3] Rather, it gives a flavour of what crofting is and the main features of the law which make it what it is. It should be noted at the outset that this chapter is concerned only with crofting law, and not the law relating to smallholdings, which is a separate although related area.

Crofting law has promoted protection for the crofting way of life; but to explain why individuals and communities who have such a way of life should be so protected requires a brief examination of the major reasons for this protection. Most of the north and west half of Scotland is fundamentally different from other parts of the United Kingdom due mainly to its geological structure and remote

---

[1] Crofters Commission, Annual Report 1997–98, p. 4.
[2] See the Crofters (Scotland) Act 1993 (hereafter "the 1993 Act").
[3] For a detailed description of the law, see especially *Stair Memorial Encyclopaedia of the Laws of Scotland* (Butterworths/Law Society of Scotland, Edinburgh, 1987), Vol. 1 and 1998 Cumulative Supplement, and Donald J. MacCuish and Derek Flyn, *Crofting Law* (Butterworths/Law Society of Scotland, Edinburgh, 1990).

position. This area has long been known as "the crofting counties", although in common parlance that term has become synonymous with the Highlands and Islands. Although the two areas are almost identical, the former includes the Black Isle and Easter Ross, hardly highland in character, whilst the latter could sensibly include Arran and parts of Perthshire and Aberdeenshire.[4] In any case, "crofts" and "crofters" are vague, non-indigenous terms which have had different meanings in different parts of the country at various times.

The land which is now subject to crofting law as being either crofts or crofters' grazings is often uncertain or unclear, having been identified historically either as land occupied by existing tenants with the necessary statutory qualifications or land settled with new tenants by government action. There are only 17,710 recorded crofters' holdings and the large bulk of the population within the crofting counties does not live within any definable crofting community. Why then does crofting today command such a high profile, with its own unique statutory provision, the paternalistic supervision of the Crofters Commission, a Land Court with a specialised jurisdiction and the apparent goodwill of the population?

In order to answer this question, it is necessary to consider the historical background to the current law. Although there are many issues involved, few have dominated a nation's history so much and for so long as the Highland Clearances.[5] Following the Battle of Culloden, in order to put an end to further rebellion, the old clan system was terminated and feudal landownership imposed. Lands, formerly held in runrig, or organised by tacksmen with sub-tenants or by groups of small tenants, were simply cleared to make way for more profitable uses, such as sheep farming. The original occupiers of the land were provided with no protection against the legality of the rights obtained by the landowners and exercised by their local agents. Despite the debate among historians about causes and faults,[6] this is perhaps best explained as a result of a failure by government to make proper provision for the rights of the existing population at a time of transition. The legacy of that failure remains unresolved to this day, reflecting the abiding folk memory of both the perceived injustice and the harshness of the effective Hanoverian reprisals.

Recognition of rights

The first remedy for this problem was to recognise that those who remained on the land had rights. A general belief held by the people that occupation of land gave them an inalienable right to that land meant that title deeds were neither sought nor respected. Unrest developed into agitation at various locations after the Clearances. Illegal activity came to a head during the 1870s and 1880s and this provided sufficient momentum to affect central government.[7] Public attention was focused on the grievances of tenants in 1883 by the sittings of the peripatetic

---

[4] J.P. Day, *Public Administration in the Highlands and Islands of Scotland* (LUP, London, 1918), p. 11. For the purposes of the current legislation, the crofting counties are defined as the former counties of Argyll, Caithness, Inverness, Orkney, Ross and Cromarty, Sutherland and Zetland: 1993 Act, s. 61(1).

[5] James Grassie, *Highland Experiment* (AUP, Aberdeen, 1983), p. 69.

[6] See Ewen A. Cameron, *Land for the People* (Tuckwell Press, East Linton, 1996), pp. 1–9.

[7] See I.M. Macphail, *The Crofters War* (Acair, Stornoway, 1989).

Napier Commission, whose report was submitted expeditiously but without unanimity.[8] The diversity of conditions it had encountered could not be reflected in a short general account. However, the basic causes for complaint among tenants were identified as: (i) the size of holdings; (ii) the desire for security of tenure; (iii) the lack of compensation for tenants' improvements at waygo; (iv) high rents which did not reflect the value of the land; and (v) the continuing loss of land for sporting purposes.

As a matter of public expediency, and to prevent further disturbance, something had to be done. By extending the franchise, the Representation of the People Act 1884 enabled Scotsmen generally, and tenants in particular, to have political impact, and legislation soon followed. The Scottish Office was established in 1885;[9] the Crofters Holdings (Scotland) Act 1886 (hereafter "the 1886 Act") was passed on June 25 of that year[10] and was promptly followed by further statutes which together were designed to protect the bulk of the remaining occupiers of holdings in the crofting parishes. In essence, holdings which met prescribed statutory qualifications qualified for certain statutory protections, and a new type of tenancy, the crofting tenancy, was created which has been described as being, from the landowner's point of view, in almost every detail a material interference with freedom of contract and ownership.[11]

In place of ongoing troubles, therefore, a unique and unusual framework was provided which replaced the previous precarious relationship between the landowner and his tenantry. As the locations of the holdings in question were generally far removed from legal services, the framework was made simple, with standard statutory conditions of tenure and manifest protection for crofters, and its introduction was enhanced by the provision of a knowledgeable and specialised tribunal. This was the first Crofters Commission, which set about visiting all parts of the Highlands and Islands responding to applications within its jurisdiction, recognising those tenants who qualified as crofters and identifying those parishes in the crofting counties in which its writ would ultimately run.[12]

In whatever way it is viewed, and it has recently been subjected to much scrutiny, the significance of the 1886 Act is difficult to exaggerate. It not only halted the risk of further "clearances", but also acted as a watershed which has given shape to the subsequent history of the land and its people. But the protection of crofters did not come without complaints, and the inflexibility of crofting tenure has also received more general criticism, for it can perpetuate the conservatism of aged residents and exclude the younger members of its communities from its benefits. In fact, for most, the 1886 Act represented welcome and unambiguous gains for the crofters at the expense of their landlords, whilst not a few saw it simply as the recognition of historically valid rights and the beginning of a movement to correct long-standing wrongs.

---

[8] Report of the Commissioners of Inquiry into the Conditions of the Crofters and Cottars in the Highlands and Islands of Scotland, C. 3980 (1884).

[9] The Secretary for Scotland Act 1885.

[10] See James Hunter, *The Making of the Crofting Community* (John Donald, Edinburgh, 1976), pp. 161 *et seq.*

[11] John Rankine, *The Law of Leases in Scotland* (3rd edn, Edinburgh, 1916), p. 607.

[12] The duties of the first Crofters Commission, like the present one, were confined to the crofting counties, ie the then counties of Argyll, Caithness, Inverness, Ross and Cromarty, Sutherland, Orkney and Zetland.

The three basic tenets of crofting law remain now as they were when they were introduced in 1886. They are: (i) security of tenure, subject to compliance with standard conditions of tenancy[13]; (ii) the right to a fair rent for the duration of the tenancy[14]; and (iii) compensation for any permanent improvements provided by the tenant or his predecessors in the tenancy and left by him on termination of the tenancy.[15]

Land settlement

The second remedy was to settle people on the land. The rapid development of the deer forest system in the late nineteenth century had aroused a great deal of animosity and more than a third of the land in the crofting counties was sterilised in this manner, mostly remaining so until the First World War. Although it was said that substantial sums of money were thus invested in the crofting counties, it had little multiplier effect, and sportsmen were tacitly helping to perpetuate the underdevelopment and overcrowding of Highland communities.

To deal with those who were excluded from the 1886 Act and who were denied access to the land, a further Royal Commission on the Highlands and Islands was appointed in 1892. Its report led to the Congested Districts (Scotland) Act 1897, which set up a Congested Districts Board to administer a government fund for the improvement of such districts in the crofting parishes. The Congested Districts Board worked with the first Crofters Commission to promote land settlement, frequently on land which had earlier been cleared of crofters.

The value of the work of the first Crofters Commission was recognised in the Small Landholders (Scotland) Act 1911 (hereafter "the 1911 Act"). The 1911 Act effectively extended the existing Crofters Acts to the whole of Scotland, although it, together with the series of Acts which followed it,[16] actually replaced "crofters" with "landholders" and "statutory small tenants", who were defined with reference to different qualifications and who received different levels of protection. The 1911 Act also established the Scottish Land Court, which superseded and took over the remaining judicial functions of the first Crofters Commission, while the Board of Agriculture for Scotland replaced the Congested Districts Board. Following the First World War, further land agitation and intense demand within the crofting counties encouraged further state-aided land settlement schemes.

Notwithstanding these efforts, however, existing holdings were not always satisfactorily worked, and statutory attempts to require the occupancy and cultivation of crofts by their tenants were thwarted by judicial interpretation and never revisited by Parliament. In particular, the 1911 Act introduced a statutory condition requiring the landholder to "cultivate" his holding, but the term was broadly defined by the 1911 Act and the Land Court broadened it further to include simply growing a crop of grass for sale and allowing the tenant to use it by putting stock on to graze, hardly an onerous level of cultivation. The statutory requirement that the tenant should be resident on or close by his holding

---

[13] See now s. 5(1) of and Sched. 2 to the 1993 Act.
[14] See now s. 6 of the 1993 Act.
[15] See now ss 30–36 of the 1993 Act.
[16] The Land Settlement (Scotland) Act 1919 and the Small Landholders and Agricultural Holdings (Scotland) Act 1931.

was initially construed by lawyers to be a requirement intended to last throughout the period of the tenancy but in 1917 the Court of Session unexpectedly held that residency was not a continuing requirement[17] and this legal essential was lost, a decision from which it is arguable that the system has never recovered.[18] The land invested with statutory protection was thereafter identified not by its occupant or by its use but by way of historical investigations; it was no longer the holder of the land who was to be protected but the land itself, provided that it could be shown to be a protected holding.[19]

Special code for crofters

Following the recommendations of the Taylor Commission in 1954,[20] the crofting counties were once again provided with their own special code in the form of the Crofters (Scotland) Act 1955 (hereafter "the 1955 Act"), which introduced substantial changes in the crofting counties while leaving intact the existing small landholder provisions for the rest of Scotland. Under the 1955 Act, the Scottish Land Court remained but a new Crofters Commission was established with the functions of reorganising, developing and regulating crofting, of promoting the interests of crofters and of keeping under review matters relating to crofting.[21]

Since its establishment, the Commission has proposed and pursued its policies both within the existing framework and by legislative change. Many detailed and radical proposals have been put forward, but they have often met with limited success, usually against a background of misunderstanding or resistance and, often, ultimate rejection by crofters themselves. One such idea was the economically attractive one of enlarging holdings by way of amalgamation into more viable units, but the possibility of reorganising the ancient boundaries of holdings and grazings to provide more attractive crofts has, in the past, frequently failed for lack of support. Happily, small units have generally survived along with their part-time tenants, who are now recognised as perhaps the most valuable and persistent members of the crofting communities, and recent examples indicate that with care and co-operation some useful reorganisation can be accomplished.[22] Statutory powers to enforce the sub-letting of crofts not adequately used were introduced in 1961, but were met with such an adverse reaction that they have never been invoked.[23]

Some changes took a long time. As early as 1963, the Commission noted that non-agricultural development was inhibited by legal and financial difficulties

---

[17] *Rogerson* v *Viscount Chilton* 1917 SC 453.

[18] For the current provisions relating to absentee crofters, see s. 22 of the 1993 Act.

[19] The question of whether a particular holding is a croft or not is often one of the most difficult: for a detailed discussion, see texts cited at n. 3 above; Sir Crispin Agnew of Lochnaw, "When is a croft not a croft?" (1991) JLSS 115 and J.H.S. Stewart, "What is a Croft?" in *Introduction to Crofting Law*, April 22, 1997, The Law Society of Scotland Update Series.

[20] Report of the Commission of Enquiry into Crofting Conditions, Cmnd. 9091 (1954).

[21] See now the 1993 Act. The current provisions are discussed further below.

[22] For the current statutory provisions relating to reorganisation schemes, see ss 38 and 39 of the 1993 Act.

[23] Special provisions for compulsory sub-letting first appeared in the Crofters (Scotland) Act 1961, s. 12. They were retained following consolidation of the legislation as s. 28 of the 1993 Act, but have yet to be brought into operation.

arising from the nature of crofting tenure.[24] Because crofters were tenants, they could not offer their land in security for commercial loans, and if their landlords chose to facilitate an enterprise on their land, the compensation received by the crofters for the land thereby taken from them was assessed only at an agricultural level, taking no account of the development value. The pressure of industrial and speculative development, such as housing, fish farming and afforestation, led to calls for every crofter to have the right to buy his land. By 1969 the Crofters Commission considered the case for the wholesale conversion of crofting tenure into owner-occupation to be overwhelming,[25] for it was predicted that if there was a piecemeal change, the mixture of tenants and owner-occupiers would complicate the administration of agricultural grants and subsidies. However, reaction to the proposals was such that the Crofting Reform (Scotland) Act 1976 (hereafter "the 1976 Act") was introduced with purchase provisions which meant that such a mixture was inevitable.

The 1976 Act provided impetus for major changes in the crofters' position. The dual-ownership character of the crofter-landlord relationship was at last openly acknowledged, enabling the crofter to share in the value of any land taken from him for development.[26] He was also given an unchallengeable right to an affordable conveyance of the site of his dwelling-house and garden ground and to seek an owner's title to his croft land at a price fixed at 15 times the fair rent, and failure to agree with his landlord on any terms or conditions was sufficient to permit the crofter to seek a purchase order from the user-friendly Land Court.[27]

The Scottish Land Court

A purely judicial body, the Scottish Land Court was established in 1912[28] as the successor to the first Crofters Commission with a jurisdiction extended to cover the whole of Scotland in specified matters. It succeeded to a considerable body of case law and to a method of working unlike any other court. It is based in Edinburgh, but is peripatetic and both expert and user-friendly.

With its own recent consolidating statute,[29] the Court is composed of not more than seven persons appointed by Her Majesty on the recommendation of the First Minister, one of whom may be appointed as chairman.[30] At present, including the chairman, there are four members of the Court. Only the chairman has to be legally qualified but he must be of senior rank and on appointment takes office as though appointed a judge of the Court of Session.[31] The other members of Court are appointed after advertisement, generally from experienced agriculturalists. One member must be able to speak Gaelic.[32] The Principal Clerk

---

[24] Crofters Commission, Annual Report, 1963, p. 28 and see James Hunter, *The Claim of Crofting— The Scottish Highlands and Islands, 1930–1990* (Mainstream, Edinburgh, 1991), pp. 129 *et seq.*

[25] See D.J. MacCuish, "The Case for Converting Crofting Tenure to Ownership" 1969–70 TGSI 89.

[26] For the current statutory provisions, see s. 37 of the 1993 Act.

[27] For the current statutory provisions, see s. 12 of the 1993 Act.

[28] Small Landholders (Scotland) Act 1911, s. 3.

[29] Scottish Land Court Act 1993.

[30] Scottish Land Court Act 1993, s. 1(2). The First Minister must consult with the Lord President of the Court of Session before making a recommendation as to the appointment of the Chairman: Scottish Land Court Act 1993, s. 1(2A).

[31] Scottish Land Court Act 1993, s. 1(3).

[32] Scottish Land Court Act 1993, s. 1(5).

of Court is appointed by the relevant Minister[33] and the Court may have one or more additional solicitors as legal assessors along with such other staff as required.[34]

The Land Court has power to frame and issue its own rules.[35] In addition it prescribes and makes available its own forms of application which are available from the Court's offices along with the current scale of fees.[36] The Land Court's method of working endears itself to litigants. Not only does it have specialised knowledge, but it has power to delegate cases to any one or two members of the Court with or without the assistance of one or more land valuers, assessors or other skilled persons,[37] and both the full Court and any such Divisional Court may sit locally and are thereby able to inspect the *locus* of the dispute and to hear the evidence of witnesses on their home ground. Historically, applications to the Land Court have been received directly from lay persons and its involvement in resolving disputes is generally welcomed by the rural communities it serves.

A determination or order of the Court must be in writing[38] and, where required, may be enforced as if it were the decree of the sheriff having jurisdiction in that area.[39] The decisions of the Land Court are final on all questions of fact but on questions of law there is an appeal by special case to the Court of Session.[40]

Despite its name, the Scottish Land Court does not have general jurisdiction on all land matters.[41] It does, however, have an affinity with the Lands Tribunal for Scotland and at present they share both premises[42] and chairman,[43] and together these bodies have a significant role in resolving land disputes at a time when law reform points towards a need for confident resolution of such disputes.

The Crofters Commission

As noted above, the present Crofters Commission was set up in 1955 and it is located in Inverness.[44] Its purpose was to take over those duties of the Land Court which were essentially administrative in character. It may have up to nine members appointed by the relevant Minister, one of whom is appointed as chairman,[45] and at present has seven part-time members including the chairman. The members must include persons with knowledge of crofting conditions and at least one Gaelic speaker.[46]

---

[33] Scottish Land Court Act 1993, s. 1(8) and Sched. 1, para. 7.
[34] Scottish Land Court Act 1993, s. 1(8) and Sched. 1, para. 8.
[35] Scottish Land Court Act 1993, s. 1(8) and Sched. 1, paras 8 and 14. For the Scottish Land Court Rules, see *Parliament House Book* at L616/1. See also K.H.R. Graham, *Scottish Land Court—Practice and Procedure* (Butterworths, Edinburgh, 1993).
[36] Scottish Land Court Act 1993, s. 1(8) and Sched. 1, para. 8.
[37] Scottish Land Court Act 1993, s. 1(8) and Sched. 1, para. 6. Where such a delegation is made, which is common, the court so sitting is known as a Divisional Court.
[38] Scottish Land Court Act 1993, s. 1(8) and Sched. 1, para. 13(4).
[39] Scottish Land Court Act 1993, s. 1(8) and Sched. 1, para. 16.
[40] Scottish Land Court Act 1993, s. 1(6) and (7).
[41] For the jurisdiction of the Scottish Land Court, see Scottish Land Court Act 1993, s. 1(6).
[42] 1 Grosvenor Crescent, Edinburgh EH12 5ER.
[43] Currently the Hon. Lord McGhie.
[44] Its head office is at 4/6 Castle Wynd, Inverness IV2 3EQ.
[45] 1993 Act, s. 1(4).
[46] 1993 Act, s. 1(5).

The general functions of the Commission are reorganising, developing and regulating crofting in the crofting counties, promoting the interests of crofters, keeping under review matters relating to crofting and such other functions as may be conferred on them.[47] In exercising these functions, the Commission is required: (i) to keep under review all matters relating to crofts and crofting conditions and to make any relevant recommendations; (ii) to collaborate with other bodies or persons in carrying out any measures for the economic development and social improvement of the crofting counties; (iii) to advise the relevant Minister on crofting matters; and (iv) to exercise the statutory powers conferred on it.[48] The Commission is required, *inter alia*, to compile and maintain a Register of Crofts[49] and has powers to monitor the actual occupancy of crofts[50] and to approve the transfer of any tenancy away from the family of an existing or deceased crofter.[51] It also has an important role in relation to decrofting.[52] The Commission may appoint a panel of persons resident in the crofting counties to act as assessors for the purpose of assisting it in the local execution of their functions when required.[53]

The Register of Crofts

Since 1955, the Crofters Commission has been under an obligation to compile and maintain a Register of Crofts which is the principal source of statistical information on crofting.[54] It is not an easy task. The 1911 Act required a register of smallholdings to be compiled by the Board of Agriculture but that was never accomplished. The register should contain the name, location, rent and extent of every croft and the name of the tenant and landlord of each croft.[55] It may also include other matters relating to each croft as the Crofters Commission may decide with the approval of the appropriate Minister.[56]

Despite offering a valuable service to landlords, crofters, solicitors and others dealing with the crofting status of land, the register is notoriously incomplete and inaccurate and is frequently out of date. No steps have yet been taken to make it map-based despite recent improvements to land registration techniques. The fact that the Crofters Commission cannot certify the boundaries of any croft is a matter of surprise to many crofters and of the utmost concern to the legal profession, who are frequently called upon to investigate not only ownership but occupancy rights. The Land Court considers the register to be merely "an administrative tool".[57] The random nature of crofters' holdings and the inaccuracies of the register means there is a background of uncertainty to the current mixture of tenancy and owner-occupancy and formal and informal arrangements

---

[47] 1993 Act, s. 1(2).
[48] 1993 Act, s. 2(1).
[49] 1993 Act, s. 41(1).
[50] 1993 Act, s. 40.
[51] 1993 Act, s. 8.
[52] 1993 Act, ss 20–25.
[53] 1993 Act, s. 1(2).
[54] See now 1993 Act, s. 41.
[55] Ibid.
[56] Ibid.
[57] *Elder* v *Manson* 1964 SLT (Land Ct) 15.

regarding the day-to-day use of crofts. That a holding has been registered as a croft does not in itself prove crofting status.[58]

Many of the landlord's normal functions have now been usurped by the Crofters Commission's powers, and the position of the crofting landlord has therefore, at times, appeared anachronistic and trivial. The low level of fair rents coupled with the crofters' right to buy means that the landlord's interest is frequently less than valuable. Any reserved sporting rights may seem desirable and foreshore and mineral rights can be retained for future use, but the crofters' rights as tenants to occupy the land, which can last for generations,[59] is a peculiar right akin to a right of property and is in many ways more substantial than the landlords' titular ownership.

The crofters' refusal to take title to their lands and their desire to retain their tenant status are matters which external observers find inexplicable. Despite the introduction of the right to purchase, less than one-fifth of the 17,710 registered crofts are held in owner-occupancy[60] and the vast majority of the occupiers of crofts resolutely remain tenants of relatively inactive, if not necessarily benign, landlords.

Neither have recent opportunities for change revealed any great demand for ownership of common lands by their occupiers. This is true even where appropriate encouragement has been offered to the crofting communities and despite the widespread public support shown for the Assynt Crofters Trust and others who have already taken this path.

Crofting Trusts Advisory Service

The Crofting Trusts Advisory Service (hereafter "CTAS") was set up on January 22, 1996, by representatives of two crofting land trusts (Assynt in Sutherland and Borve in Skye), the Crofters Commission, Highland and Islands Enterprise and legal and management experts. It offers objective help and advice aimed at helping crofting townships through the challenge of community land ownership and is designed to help communities assess the benefit of community land ownership, identify the legal, financial and human implications, and enable local people to create a simple structure to manage lands to suit community needs.

The service is based on a three-stage process. Communities can seek initial advice from Advisors, who are members of the existing crofting trusts. If a community believes there may be benefits from community land ownership, it can then apply to CTAS for funding towards a feasibility study. If the study demonstrates benefits to the community, CTAS will help towards transferring the land to community ownership and the setting up of a suitable management structure, although it will not provide funding for the purchase of land.[61]

---

[58] *Elder* v *Manson* 1964 SLT (Land Ct) 15.

[59] For the current provisions relating to succession to crofts, see ss 10 and 11 of the 1993 Act.

[60] Register of Crofts Statistics, Crofters Commission, Annual Report 1997–98, p. 40.

[61] A guide detailing its services is available from CTAS, Castle Wynd, Inverness ((01463) 718953).

Conclusion

It has long been argued that crofting, as a system of tenure designed to meet the social and economic conditions of another age, has become an anachronism and a barrier to progress.[62] Opportunities for change have been hard-won even where resistance has been minimal,[63] although occasionally they have been provided by fortuitous judicial interpretation.[64] Any legislative willingness to take note of anomalies in crofting law has tended to have patchy results. The warning on land certificates regarding the rights of crofters and cottars, which are, in this context, overriding interests, has a hollow ring because the Land Register is not due to affect Argyllshire until 2002 nor the rest of the crofting counties until a year later.

Despite this, recent discussions on land law reform in Scotland have often focused on crofting because the protection afforded to croft land has patently ensured its accessibility to the indigenous population. The Land Reform Policy Group has acknowledged this to be so and a quarter of its recommendations relate directly to crofting. These recommendations include proposals for new legislation:

- to give all crofting communities a right to acquire their croft land;
- to allow the creation of new crofts;
- to allow the extension of crofting tenure to new areas;
- to devolve regulatory decisions to local bodies;
- to tighten control over decrofting, curtail control of sub-division and simplify letting and sub-letting;
- to remove the link between crofting grants and agricultural production; and
- to clarify the law on crofter forestry.[65]

In addition, the Group urged the Crofters Commission to act to encourage more community management of croft land and to tackle the problem of absenteeism.

Crofting law has also recently become more accessible for scrutiny: as noted above, the Crofters (Scotland) Act 1993 consolidated the existing legislation, although to some extent it has retained the problems and ambiguities inherent in the previous legislation. The Transfer of Crofting Estates (Scotland) Act 1997 provided for the transfer of crofting estates still in the ownership of the Secretary of State for Scotland to crofting trusts and for financial assistance in establishing such bodies, but there has been insufficient progress as yet to ascertain whether this will lead to more widespread community land ownership.

Once again it is being recognised that access to land and information about land is vital to sustainable rural communities.[66] With sympathetic treatment,

---

[62] See, eg, D.J. MacCuish, "The Case for Converting Crofting Tenure to Ownership", op. cit., n. 19 above.

[63] eg, in the case of the Crofter Forestry (Scotland) Act 1991.

[64] eg, in the case of *Whitbread* v *Macdonald* 1992 SLT 1144.

[65] Land Reform Policy Group, Recommendations for Action, s. 6 (January 1999).

[66] See ibid.

crofting communities have shown themselves approachable and capable of dealing with complicated local matters such as environmental issues. Since its formation in 1985, the Scottish Crofters Union, as the first modern representative body of these communities, has proved itself an able and active lobbyist on their behalf.

CHAPTER 7

FORESTRY

Colin Reid

Introduction

Forestry is a significant and very visible aspect of the way in which the Scottish countryside is used. Appropriately sited, designed and managed woodlands offer great benefits in terms of landscape, biodiversity and recreational and commercial opportunities. Badly sited, designed and managed plantations can blight landscapes, destroy valuable habitat, exclude visitors and damage water quality and flow, whilst bringing little commercial return. Current forestry policy is intended to ensure that the multiple benefits which forestry can bring are in fact realised.[1]

By the end of the nineteenth century the woodlands which had probably once covered about 85 per cent of Scotland had been reduced to extend to only about 5 per cent of the country. There had been some earlier recognition of the problems caused by excessive felling,[2] but it was after the First World War that the appreciation of the need for home-produced timber led to effective action to promote an expansion of forestry.[3] Initially for strategic reasons and then for commercial ones, policy was directed to expanding the area of productive woodland and these aims have been achieved to the extent that the area of Scotland under trees has now trebled, with very nearly half of the woodland in Britain being north of the border. The major role in this enterprise has been taken by the Forestry Commission. The Commission was created in 1919[4] and has contributed both through developing its own plantations on Crown land or land acquired for this purpose and through encouragement to private landowners to develop forestry on their land.

---

[1] See generally, C.T. Reid, "Forestry, the Law and the Environment" in C.P. Rodgers, *Nature Conservation and Countryside Law* (Cardiff, 1996).
[2] Many Acts of the Scottish Parliament dealt with protecting forests (eg APS II 343 c. 8 (1535), III 145 c. 22 (1579), IV 373 c. 6 (1607)), in one case noting that the wood of Scotland is "uterlie destroyit" (APS II 242 c.15 (1503)). The Scottish Parliament also noted the potential for exploiting the forests of the Highlands (APS IV 408 (1609)).
[3] See generally, M. Anderson, *A History of Scottish Forestry* (London, 1967).
[4] Forestry Act 1919.

127

The policy of expanding forestry production, with many plantations in the hands of the Forestry Commission, continued until the 1980s. During that decade, growing environmental concerns and political views insisting on a reduced role for the public sector led to major changes in forestry policy and in the way in which the Forestry Commission is organised and operates. The move away from timber production as the sole aim of forestry policy was confirmed by the emphasis given to sustainable forestry at the "Earth Summit" at Rio de Janeiro in 1992[5] and British forestry policy is now committed to achieving a range of benefits.

Current forestry policy has two main aims: the sustainable management of existing woods and forests, and the steady expansion of tree cover to increase the many, diverse benefits that forests provide. These aims were set out in the *Forestry Policy for Great Britain* announced in 1991,[6] and have been reaffirmed several times since in a series of documents developing the way in which these aims are to be achieved.[7] The transformation in policy is perhaps most clearly seen in the terms of the grant schemes to support private landowners. The Forestry Grant Scheme which operated until 1988 required that timber production be the primary aim of any project, whereas the Woodland Grant Scheme which replaced it places timber production as only one of a number of aims, the others being: improving the landscape, providing wildlife habitats, offering opportunities for recreation and sport, improving the economy of rural areas and providing a use of land in place of agriculture. It is an indication of the extent to which forestry has been regulated by administrative rather than legal means that the steps to implement this change of policy, and equally significant changes in how the Forestry Commission is organised, have been achieved with very little legislative intervention.

Forestry Commission

Responsibility for forestry matters in Great Britain[8] is in the hands of the Forestry Commission. This is a statutory body, governed under the Forestry Act 1967, which has the legal status and functions of a government department. The Commissioners are Crown appointments, in large part drawn from those with knowledge or experience of the industry,[9] and they have reported to the Forestry Ministers, namely the Secretary of State for Scotland (who was the lead Minister), the Secretary of State for Wales and the Minister of Agriculture, Fisheries and Food.

---

[5] Statement of Principles for a Global Consensus on the Management, Conservation and Sustainable Development of all Types of Forests, 1992 (Rio de Janeiro) (1992) 31 ILM 881; General Guidelines for the Sustainable Management of Forests in Europe, 1993 (Helsinki), printed as Annex B to *Sustainable Forestry: the UK Programme*, Cm. 2429 (1994).

[6] (Forestry Commission, 1991).

[7] *Sustainable Forestry: the UK Programme*, Cm. 2429 (1994); *Our Forests—The Way Ahead*, Cm. 2644 (1994); *The UK Forestry Standard: The Government's Approach to Sustainable Forestry* (Forestry Commission, 1998); see also *Forests for Scotland: Consultation towards a Scottish Forestry Strategy* (Forestry Commission, 1999).

[8] Essentially parallel mechanisms operate in Northern Ireland under the Department of Agriculture for Northern Ireland.

[9] Forestry Act 1967, s. 2.

Forestry is a devolved matter under the Scotland Act 1998,[10] and clearly this creates scope for divergence in forestry policy within Great Britain. The Forestry Commission has a National Office for Scotland which is in effect the "forestry department" in Scotland, answerable to the Scottish Executive.[11] The Commission is a "cross-border public body" under the 1998 Act[12] and as such reports to both the Scottish and Westminster Parliaments. Under the 1967 Act, the Commissioners are obliged to have National Committees for Scotland, England and Wales; so far these have not played a major role in the Commission's work and indeed have not met in recent years, but they may come to play a more significant role.[13] As a result of devolution, the powers stated in the Forestry Act 1967 as being in the hands of the Secretary of State are exercised by the relevant Scottish Minister.[14]

The changes in forestry policy away from regarding timber production as the sole aim to be pursued were reflected at a comparatively early stage by a "balancing duty"[15] being imposed on the Commission. The duty of the Commission to promote the interests of forestry,[16] is now tempered by a further duty. In carrying out its statutory functions, the Commission is required to:

"endeavour to achieve a reasonable balance between

(a) the development of afforestation, the management of forests and the production and supply of timber, and

(b) the conservation and enhancement of natural beauty and the conservation of flora, fauna and geological or physiographical features of special interest".[17]

This provision, which was introduced in 1985, was a reflection of existing trends rather than an attempt to force the Commission to change direction, and ensures that the Commission is free to take environmental considerations into account when exercising its many powers.

The structure of the Commission has been substantially altered over the last decade. The two main elements are the Forestry Authority, which is responsible for the regulatory aspects of its role, and Forest Enterprise, which manages the

---

[10] It is likewise one of the areas within which powers are devolved under the Government of Wales Act 1998; National Assembly for Wales (Transfer of Functions) Order 1999 (SI 1999/672), Sched. 1.

[11] A few aspects of the Commission's activities fall outwith the devolved matters and for these the existing link to the Secretary of State remains.

[12] Scotland Act 1998, s. 88. Scotland Act 1998 (Cross-Border Public Authorities) (Specification) Order 1999 (SI 1999/1319).

[13] Forestry Act 1967, s. 2(3); no meetings of the national committees were held in the periods covered by the *Forestry Commission Annual Reports for 1994–95, 1995–96* and *1996–97*; 1994–95 HC 749, p. 73, 1996–97 HC 3, p. 81, 1997–98 HC 250, p. 63.

[14] In order to give effect to the devolution arrangements, the Forestry Act 1967 has been amended in many places by the Scotland Act 1998 (Cross-Border Public Authorities) (Adaptation of Functions etc.) Order 1999 (SI 1999/1747).

[15] C.T. Reid, *Nature Conservation Law* (Edinburgh, 1994), pp. 41–45.

[16] Forestry Act 1967, s. 1(2)

[17] Forestry Act 1967, s. 1(3A), inserted by Wildlife and Countryside (Amendment) Act 1985, s. 4.

plantations in public hands.[18] The divide between these two branches was part of a general move to ensure that within government there was a clear separation between those elements which have operational tasks and those which have a regulatory role in the same area. This division also reflected the views of the Conservative Government which had been contemplating not only the separate management on more commercial lines of the publicly owned woodlands but even their privatisation.[19] The distinction became even clearer when Forest Enterprise became an executive agency in 1996, with its organisation, functions and relationship with the Forestry Commission set out in a framework document.[20]

The Forestry Authority is organised on the basis of National Offices for Scotland, England and Wales, with a structure of conservancies within these. There are six conservancies in Scotland: Highland, Grampian, Perth, Strathclyde, South-West Scotland, and Lothian and Borders. Forest Enterprise has two regions in Scotland, North and South, which are in turn divided into forest districts (10 in Scotland (North) and six in Scotland (South)).

Forest Enterprise owns just over 40 per cent of the woodland in Scotland.[21] Technically the land is not owned by Forest Enterprise or by the Forestry Commission, but is Crown land "placed at their disposal"[22] by the Government, and there are powers to acquire land for forestry and related purposes, by compulsory purchase if necessary.[23] The proportion of the country's woodlands in public hands has fallen as a result of the implementation of Conservative Government policy during the 1980s and early 1990s. This policy called for new forestry projects to be undertaken by the private rather than the public sector, and for the sale of publicly owned plantations. The Labour Government announced a moratorium on further sales of forestry land when it took office in 1997, and the policy of sales has now been formally abandoned.[24] Although not subject to the full scope of the Forestry Authority's controls, Forest Enterprise has to submit forest design plans for approval by the Authority[25] and has performance measures which include environmental considerations.

In addition to the means of controlling planting and felling discussed in detail below, the Forestry Commission has powers in relation to plant health,[26] pest control,[27] the provision of recreational facilities[28] and the making of byelaws

---

[18] There is also a small central secretariat, an Administration and Finance division and Forest Research, which deals with forestry- and tree-related research and surveys and was established as an agency of the Commission in 1997.

[19] C.T. Reid, "The Changing Pattern of Environmental Regulation: British Forestry and the Environmental Agenda" (1997) 9 JEL 23 at 33–35.

[20] *Forest Enterprise Framework Document* (Forestry Commission, 1996).

[21] 503,000 hectares of a total of 1,189,000 hectares of woodland in Scotland; *Forestry Commission: Facts and Figures 1996–97* (Forestry Commission, 1997).

[22] Forestry Act 1967, s. 3.

[23] Forestry Act 1967, ss 39–40 and Countryside (Scotland) Act 1967, s. 59.

[24] Written Answer by Lord Sewel, July 30, 1998 (HL Deb, Vol. 592, col. WA 246).

[25] *Forestry Commission Annual Report for 1993–94* (1993–94 HC 661), p. 20; these plans are included alongside private grant applications in the public register and are available for public inspection.

[26] Primarily under the Plant Health (Forestry) (Great Britain) Order 1993 (SI 1993/1283), as amended.

[27] Forestry Act 1967, s. 7 (see below).

[28] Countryside (Scotland) Act 1967, s. 58 (see below).

governing visitors to Forestry Commission land,[29] as well as powers of entry to support its functions.[30]

Planting controls

Until very recently there were no formal controls on the planting of trees, and even today only a very small proportion of planting is subject to direct regulation. The use of land for forestry purposes expressly falls outwith the definition of "development" for the purposes of the town and country planning legislation and therefore requires no planning permission.[31] The terms of this exception cover not only the actual planting, growing and felling of trees, but also associated operations, even at some distance from where the trees are growing.[32] Some further forestry-related operations are also authorised in planning terms as "permitted development".[33]

With the recent and very limited exception of some environmentally sensitive proposals (discussed below), there is no need for any formal permission to be obtained before tree planting takes place. Landowners are free to plant as many trees of whatever species they wish without being subject to any direct legal control. Instead, control is exercised by means of the grant schemes. Forestry developments are not usually commercially viable without an element of public financial support. In the past this came through a combination of tax relief and grant aid, but in 1988 the system was changed as a result of fears that the tax relief was encouraging some plantations to proceed for short-term financial reasons, without any consideration of their long-term future and by-passing the scrutiny given when applications for grant aid are considered. Tax relief was removed,[34] and all of the public support now comes through the grant schemes.

Although the grant schemes do not take statutory form,[35] their importance in practice has been recognised by the courts' willingness to subject to judicial review decisions on the award of grants.[36] As noted above, the terms of these grant schemes have been altered over the years to reflect the changes in forestry policy, and timber production is only one of the factors to be considered in the determination of applications.

Individual applications will be considered in the light of the Indicative Forestry Strategies which are contained in structure plans within the planning system.[37]

---

[29] Forestry Act 1967, s. 46 (see below).

[30] Forestry Act 1967, s. 48.

[31] Town and Country Planning (Scotland) Act 1997, s. 26(2)(e).

[32] *Farleyer Estate* v *Secretary of State for Scotland* 1992 SLT 476.

[33] Town and Country Planning (General Permitted Development) (Scotland) Order 1992 (SI 1992/223), Sched. 1, Pt 7; Chap. 3.

[34] Finance Act 1988, s. 65 and Sched. 6; commercial woodlands now operate outwith the income tax system, with no tax due on the income but no relief on the costs of establishing young trees.

[35] There is legislation conferring a general power for grants to be paid (Forestry Act 1979, s. 1) and some schemes, particularly those linked to agricultural policy and associated with European Community measures, do take statutory form, eg the Farm Woodland Premium Scheme Regulations 1997 (SI 1997/829).

[36] *Kincardine and Deeside District Council* v *Forestry Commissioners* 1992 SLT 1180; *Swan* v *Secretary of State for Scotland* 1998 SCLR 763.

[37] SODD Circular 9/99; for a critical review of practice throughout Great Britain see *Forestry Plan Scan, 96: A Review of Indicative Forestry Strategies* (1996, RSPB).

These strategies should indicate preferred areas where the expansion of forestry may be suitable, those areas where there is potential for forestry but also constraining interests, and sensitive areas where there are serious constraints on forestry development. The procedure for preparing structure plans should ensure an element of public participation in the process,[38] and the gradual increase in opportunities for the public to become informed about proposals for new planting and to make representations is another way in which the control of forestry has been transformed in the fairly recent past.

When a grant application is received, it is considered by the Forestry Authority not only for its silvicultural merits but also in the light of landscape, environmental, social and recreational considerations, and may be revised accordingly. The application will then be put on the public register, available at conservancy offices and on the Internet.[39] Any member of the public can ask for further details of the application and is given the opportunity to make representations. Applications are also notified to local authorities and other public bodies, for example Scottish Natural Heritage, and they too have the opportunity to comment. The application may again be revised in the light of representations, and the aim is to find a final plan acceptable to all sides.

If objections cannot be resolved, the matter may be referred to a Regional Advisory Committee. There are three such Committees in Scotland[40] and their membership has been extended to enable those members statutorily drawn from the forestry and timber industry to be balanced by members with interests and experience in environmental and recreational matters.[41] The aim is still to seek consensus and produce a proposal acceptable to all parties. Applications being considered by the Committees are advertised and members of the public can be invited to participate. The reports of the Committees, which need not be unanimous, are published. The final say on any application rests with the Minister.

The one situation where formal consent is required before planting can take place is governed by the Environmental Assessment (Forestry) Regulations 1998.[42] These Regulations represent the Government's second attempt to implement the terms of the EC Directive on environmental assessment[43] in relation to forestry. "Initial afforestation where this may lead to adverse ecological effects" appears in Annex II of the Directive which lists those categories of project where an environmental assessment is required when the characteristics of an individual project are such that it may have a significant effect on the environment. The Directive refers to the assessment being carried out "before consent is given" to the project.[44] In the absence of direct controls on forestry planting the decision was taken in the 1980s to add the environmental assessment procedure to the consideration of applications for grant support.

---

[38] See Chap. 3.
[39] At http://www.forestry.gov.uk.
[40] For the Highland and Grampian, Perth and Strathclyde, and South-West Scotland and Lothian and Borders conservancies.
[41] Forestry Act 1967, s. 38(3), amended by Forestry Act 1991, s. 1.
[42] SI 1998/1731 (hereafter "1998 Regulations").
[43] Directive 85/337.
[44] Directive 85/337, Art. 2.

Accordingly, the Environmental Assessment (Afforestation) Regulations 1988[45] required that grant applications for projects which were likely to have significant environmental effects were subject to a formal environmental assessment process. Since major planting is not commercially viable without grant support, this approach was considered by the Government to be adequate to ensure that all relevant afforestation projects would in fact be subject to environmental assessment. However, since the assessment was linked to the award of the grant, not to the giving of any official consent, and since trees could still lawfully be planted, on as large a scale and in as inappropriate a location as the landowner chose, without any need for official approval this clearly did not amount to full implementation of the Directive.[46] The 1988 Regulations have now been revoked and a different approach adopted.

Under the Environmental Assessment (Forestry) Regulations 1998 formal consent must be obtained for "initial afforestation where this may lead to adverse ecological effects" and for certain operations affecting forest roads,[47] in both cases where the project "is likely to have a significant effect on the environment".[48] Each element of the definition could be subject to argument: What effects are "significant"? For how many years must the land have been bare of trees before planting counts as "initial" aforestation? Over what time-scale and with reference to what indicators are ecological changes "adverse"? Some experience has been gained through the application of the same definition under the 1988 Regulations, but views may differ over whether a particular project falls within the definition, as shown in *Swan* v *Secretary of State for Scotland*.[49] The consent scheme is essentially similar to the procedure for obtaining planning permission where an environmental assessment is required.

The proposer may seek from the Forestry Commission (in practice such matters are dealt with by the Forestry Authority) an opinion whether a project falls within the relevant definition.[50] Whether the project is likely to have significant environmental effects will depend on the scale of the project and whether its location affects any sensitive areas, particularly those subject to some designation for their conservation value, for example SSSIs. If the Commission states that the project does fall within the Regulations, the proposer can seek a direction from the Minister confirming or overturning that decision.[51] If the project does not fall within the definition, then no formal approval is required before planting or other work can go ahead.

---

[45] SI 1988/1207. These Regulations were made after the deadline for implementation of the Directive, a crucial point in *Kincardine and Deeside District Council* v *Forestry Commissioners* 1992 SLT 1180.

[46] The adequacy of the Government's approach in the 1988 Regulations was initially one of the issues at stake in *Swan* v *Secretary of State for Scotland*, but in the light of the introduction of the 1998 Regulations, this point was not pursued at the substantive hearing ((1999) 73 SPEL 65; the decision on preliminary issues is reported at 1998 SCLR 763).

[47] Construction of roads or obtaining materials for their formation or maintenance; such operations are permitted development under para. 1(b) and (c) of Class 22 of Sched. 1 to the Town and Country Planning (General Permitted Development) (Scotland) Order 1992 (SI 1992/223).

[48] 1998 Regulations, regs 1(1) and 3.

[49] (1999) 73 SPEL 65.

[50] 1998 Regulations, reg. 4.

[51] 1998 Regulations, reg. 6.

Where the proposal does fall within the Regulations, the application for consent must be accompanied by an environmental statement prepared by the proposer.[52] The application must be advertised and members of the public given the opportunity to submit representations, and the Commission must consult with Scottish Natural Heritage, the local authority and any other public authority which appears to have an interest in the application, for example the Deer Commission for Scotland.[53] Grants of consent may be conditional and must include conditions that the work will commence within a set period (not more than five years) and that no work will be carried out after a set period (not more than 10 years).[54] There is a right of appeal to the Minister in the event of an application being refused or granted subject to any conditions other than the specification of the maximum time-limits noted above,[55] and any person aggrieved by a grant of consent can apply to the courts to have the consent quashed.[56]

The Forestry Commission has the power to issue enforcement notices where it appears that work is being carried out without consent or in breach of the conditions in a consent.[57] There is a right of appeal to the Minister against an enforcement notice and although the appeal suspends any positive obligations required by the notice (eg to restore the land or to apply for consent), any requirement to discontinue work remains in effect.[58] Breach of an enforcement notice is a criminal offence, punishable with an unlimited fine, and where an offence is committed by a body corporate, any director, manager or similar officer of the company (or a partner where a partnership commits the offence) may be personally liable if the offence is attributable to their own consent, connivance or neglect.[59] The Forestry Commission has powers of entry where it is reasonably suspected that work is taking place without consent or in breach of a condition, and where remedial action specified in an enforcement notice has not been taken, the Commission may undertake the work itself, recovering expenses from the defaulter.[60]

The introduction of the 1998 Regulations marks a major shift in policy, since previously the introduction of any formal approval procedure had been very strongly resisted by government. The vast majority of new planting will fall outwith the terms of the Regulations, but it remains to be seen whether this new consent procedure will remain an exceptional requirement existing purely to meet the terms of the EC Directive or will be the first step towards a more general consent requirement for forestry planting.[61]

---

[52] 1998 Regulations, reg. 7; the Commission can require the proposer to provide further information (reg. 8).

[53] 1998 Regulations, reg. 9.

[54] 1998 Regulations, regs 11 and 14.

[55] 1998 Regulations, reg. 13.

[56] 1998 Regulations, reg. 15.

[57] 1998 Regulations, reg. 16.

[58] 1998 Regulations, reg. 17.

[59] 1998 Regulations, reg. 18.

[60] 1998 Regulations, reg. 19.

[61] A willingness to contemplate further formal controls over forestry operations is indicated by the suggestion in the Government's papers on Land Reform that planning controls might be extended to at least some forestry operations currently outwith their scope; Land Reform Policy Group, *Identifying the Solutions* (Scottish Office, 1998) at 54 and *Recommendations for Action* (Scottish Office, 1999) at 35.

Felling controls

In contrast to the position in relation to planting, felling is subject to a formal licensing scheme. Under Part II of the Forestry Act 1967 the felling of trees is a criminal offence unless a felling licence from the Forestry Commission has been obtained or one of the exceptions applies.[62] No licence is required for topping or lopping, felling trees in gardens, orchards, churchyards or public open spaces, or felling to prevent danger or to prevent or abate a nuisance. The trimming and layering of hedges is also free from control, and in Scotland there is no equivalent of the protection for hedgerows provided in England by the Environment Act 1995 and associated Regulations.[63] Felling of trees smaller than eight centimetres in diameter[64] (15 centimetres in underwood or coppice) is also exempt, and the occupier of woodland is permitted to fell trees of no more than 10 centimetres in diameter as thinnings and also up to five cubic metres of wood in any quarter, provided that not more than two cubic metres are sold. Other exceptions apply for felling by statutory undertakers, in the interests of air safety or as a result of Dutch Elm disease, or where felling is immediately required for development authorised under the town and country planning system.[65] The further exception for felling in accordance with a plan of operations agreed with the Forestry Commission under one of the grant schemes is now restricted to plans agreed before April 1998.[66]

Applications for felling licences are advertised through the public register in the same way as grant applications. Licences may be granted subject to conditions and an aggrieved applicant can apply to the Minister to refer the matter to a special reference committee, who will hold a hearing before advising the Minister to confirm, overturn or modify the Commission's decision.[67] A similar procedure applies if a licence is refused, but only when a licence for the same land has been refused more than three years previously. If a licence is refused, the applicant is entitled to compensation.[68] The sum is based on the depreciation in the value of the trees attributable to the deterioration in the quality of their timber as a result of the felling being refused. In practice this provision is redundant as permission is unlikely to be refused for trees so far past their prime that their value is diminishing in this way.

Licences may be granted subject to conditions and in all but exceptional circumstances will include a restocking condition, requiring the land to be replanted after the felling has taken place.[69] In keeping with current policy, the details of the replanting scheme are likely to produce a greater diversity of age and species than in the mature plantations currently being felled. If a restocking condition is not complied with, the Commission can serve a notice requiring the

---

[62] Forestry Act 1967, s. 9.

[63] Environment Act 1995, s. 97; Hedgerows Regulations 1997 (SI 1997/1160).

[64] All diameters are measured over the bark at 1.3 metres above ground level (Forestry Act 1967, s. 9(6)); all of the measurements in these provisions were rendered metric by the Forestry Act 1979, s. 2 and Sched. 1.

[65] Forestry Act 1967, s. 9; Forestry (Exceptions from Restriction on Felling) Regulations 1979 (SI 1979/792) (as amended).

[66] Forestry (Exceptions from Restrictions of Felling) (Amendment) Regulations 1998 (SI 1998/603).

[67] Forestry Act 1967, s. 16.

[68] Forestry Act 1967, s. 11.

[69] Forestry Act 1967, s. 12.

default to be made good within a set time.[70] There is a right of appeal to the Minister, who refers the case to a special reference committee; the notice is suspended during this review. In the absence of a reasonable excuse, the failure to comply with the terms of a notice is a criminal offence and the Commission is given the power to enter the land and carry out the work itself, recovering the costs from the defaulter.

As noted above, felling without a licence is a criminal offence, and several prosecutions take place each year.[71] A person convicted of this offence is subject to a fine, either at level 4 on the standard scale or twice the value of the trees when they were felled, whichever is the higher. In *Campbell* v *Webster*,[72] a fine of £5,500 was imposed, representing half of the value of the trees felled, as opposed to the statutory maximum at the time of £1,000. Following a conviction, the Forestry Commission can serve a restocking notice requiring the land concerned, or other land as agreed, to be planted with trees.[73]

The Forestry Commission also has the power to direct the felling of trees where this is considered expedient in the interests of good forestry or for promoting adequate reserves of growing timber.[74] The felling must be to prevent the deterioration of the timber or to improve the growth of other trees, and a direction must be carried out within the period specified, which must be at least two years. There are various exceptions and rights to call for a review of the direction or for the Commission to purchase the trees or an interest in the land affected. This power is not used in practice.

In addition to the felling controls in the Forestry Act, some provisions in the town and country planning legislation may also be relevant.[75] In conservation areas, notice must be given to the planning authority before any uprooting, felling, cutting or lopping is carried out. The purpose of this is to give the authority the opportunity to consider whether a tree preservation order should be made, and the operations can go ahead only when the authority has given consent or six weeks have passed.[76]

Tree preservation orders can protect areas of woodland as well as individual trees or groups of trees.[77] Orders are made by the planning authority[78] "in the interests of amenity" and prohibit the felling of the trees specified unless the express consent of the planning authority has been given. Before an order can come into effect it must be advertised and notice given to the owners and occupiers of the land, the Keeper of the Registers of Scotland and the Forestry Commission (unless the Commission has agreed with the planning authority to

---

[70] Forestry Act 1967, ss 24–26.

[71] In Great Britain, there were 33 prosecutions in 1996–97: *Forestry Commission Annual Report for 1996–97* (1997–98 HC 250), p. 9.

[72] 1992 SCCR 167.

[73] Forestry Act 1967, ss 17A–17C; in 1996–97, 16 restocking notices were made in Great Britain (*Forestry Commission Annual Report for 1996–97* (1997–98 HC 250), p. 9).

[74] Forestry Act 1967, ss 18–23.

[75] C.T. Reid, *Nature Conservation Law* (Edinburgh, 1994), pp. 218–230.

[76] Town and Country Planning (Scotland) Act 1997, s. 172; the tacit consent given by an authority's failure to take other steps lasts for two years from the date of the notice.

[77] Town and Country Planning (Scotland) Act 1997, ss 160–171.

[78] The Minister has a default power to take action where an authority does not: Town and Country Planning (Scotland) Act 1997, s. 164.

waive this requirement). Representations can be made to the authority and a local inquiry held if necessary, and if the authority decides to confirm the order, the order must again be advertised and notified.[79] There is, however, the power to make provisional orders which take immediate effect but lapse after six months unless confirmed.[80] If a forestry grant has been made for the woodland, the Commission must consent before an order can be made.[81]

Consent to carry out activities restricted by the order is applied for in the same way as planning permission, and may be granted subject to conditions, including replanting conditions. A replanting condition must be imposed in relation to woodland covered by an order unless the consent was granted for the purposes of development which has planning permission, or the Minister approves the planning authority's waiver of this requirement. The applicant has a right of appeal to the Minister against a refusal of consent or the imposition of conditions. For woodland, the legislation states that consent *shall* be given so far as it accords with the principles of good forestry, except where the planning authority considers refusal necessary in the interests of amenity in order to maintain the special character of the woodland or the woodland character of the area.[82] There is a right to compensation for any loss or damage suffered as a result of a refusal of consent or the imposition of conditions, unless the authority has certified that its decision is in the interests of good forestry.[83]

Any person who cuts down, uproots, or wilfully damages or destroys a tree in breach of a tree preservation order is guilty of a criminal offence.[84] There is an exception for action which is urgently necessary in the interests of safety or necessary to prevent or abate a nuisance, provided that notice is given to the planning authority as soon as may be after the necessity has arisen, and for some work by statutory undertakers.[85] There is no limit to the fine which can be imposed for breach of a tree preservation order,[86] and the court is expressly directed to have regard to any financial benefit which might accrue as the result of the offence, for example the realisation of the development potential of land.[87] There is also a requirement to replace the trees on or near the affected land or on other land as agreed by the authority.[88] This binds the owners of the land for the time being, regardless of whether they had any responsibility for the breach, and the planning authority can enter the land and carry out the planting itself, recovering the cost from the owners, if the requirement is not fulfilled.

---

[79] Town and Country Planning (Tree Preservation Order and Trees in Conservation Areas) (Scotland) Regulations 1975 (SI 1975/1204), as amended by Town and Country Planning (Tree Preservation Order and Trees in Conservation Areas) (Scotland) Amendment Regulations 1981 (SI 1981/1385) and 1984 (SI 1984/329), regs 5–10.

[80] Town and Country Planning (Scotland) Act 1997, s. 163.

[81] Town and Country Planning (Scotland) Act 1997, s. 162.

[82] Town and Country Planning (Tree Preservation Order and Trees in Conservation Areas) (Scotland) Regulations 1975 (SI 1975/1204), Sched., para. 5(1).

[83] Town and Country Planning (Scotland) Act 1997, s. 165; Town and Country Planning (Tree Preservation Order and Trees in Conservation Areas) (Scotland) Regulations 1975, Sched., para. 9.

[84] Town and Country Planning (Scotland) Act 1997, s. 171.

[85] Town and Country Planning (Scotland) Act 1997, s. 160(6); 1975 Regulations, Sched. 2.

[86] The maximum fine in summary proceedings is £20,000.

[87] Town and Country Planning (Scotland) Act 1997, s. 171.

[88] Town and Country Planning (Scotland) Act 1997, ss 168–170

Where felling requires both a felling licence and consent under a tree pre-servation order, the matter is initially dealt with under the forestry legislation. The Forestry Commission may refer the matter to the planning authority, which must be notified if the Commission is minded to grant a licence.[89] If the authority has objections which cannot be resolved through the forestry procedures, the case is referred to the Minister for final determination and is dealt with under the planning legislation. The fact that the matter is dealt with through the forestry procedures first means that there is no real opportunity to claim compensation in the event of a licence being refused,[90] and now that the forestry policy takes amenity and environmental matters into account, there will be very few cases which are not resolved at that stage.

Biodiversity

The Forestry Commission has no specific role in nature conservation other than its general obligation to seek a reasonable balance between the development of forestry and the conservation of natural beauty and of flora and fauna. Indeed, the only specific powers in relation to wildlife contained in the forestry legislation authorise the Commission to undertake pest control activities.[91] Nevertheless, woodlands are particularly important in terms of biodiversity.

In legal terms, sizeable areas of woodland are covered by one or more of the statutory designations designed for nature conservation purposes. The owners and occupiers, whether Forest Enterprise or private owners, must therefore comply with the relevant rules affecting their management of the land.[92] Where afforestation is proposed for land which is of high conservation value, then an environmental assessment and the consent of the Forestry Commission are likely to be required under the new rules discussed above.[93]

More significantly, perhaps, forestry policy now takes account of conservation issues. The earlier drive for maximised timber production led to dense, single-species, single-age plantations of non-native conifer species harvested by clear-felling across large areas. All of these features are damaging to biodiversity. Policy now takes conservation matters into account. In order to attract support, proposals must usually include some species diversity, must include measures to limit the impact on natural features such as watercourses, and must be based on creating a mixed age profile. Woodlands based on native species offer greater biodiversity, and the Caledonian Pine Forest is a rare habitat recognised under the EC Habitats and Species Directive.[94] Special grant support is given to promote natural regeneration and to expand the area of such native woodland, and grant aid is also available at a higher rate for broadleaved species which in general (although not in all parts of Scotland) offer habitat for a wider range of wildlife. Woodland Improvement Grants are specifically available to enhance

---

[89] Forestry Act 1967, s. 15.

[90] Apart from the improbable circumstances of a claim for a loss in value of trees themselves, discussed above.

[91] Forestry Act 1967, s. 7 (see below).

[92] See Chap. 11.

[93] Environmental Assessment (Forestry) Regulations 1998 (SI 1998/1731).

[94] Directive 92/43; see Chap. 11.

the biodiversity of woodlands.[95] The Forestry Commission also plays a leading role in several of the specific plans developed by the Steering Group on Biodiversity.[96]

Although not used in practice, the Forestry Commission does have some pest control powers in order to protect trees.[97] The Commissioners may act where they are satisfied that trees are being or are likely to be damaged by rabbits, hares or other vermin, including squirrels, owing to the failure of the occupier of land to take adequate steps to destroy the animals or prevent their causing damage.[98] The owner and occupier of the land must be given a reasonable opportunity to take the requisite action before the Commissioners can take steps themselves, but the costs of any action can be recovered from the occupier.

Access and recreation

The opportunities presented by woodlands for recreation are among the multiple benefits expressly recognised in current forestry policy. On private land, the provision of such opportunities is encouraged by the grant schemes.[99] The Forestry Commission has been active for many years in promoting the recreational use of its woodlands, both for informal access and through the provision of specific facilities. The Commissioners have the power to provide recreational facilities on the land at their disposal, including accommodation, display centres and places to provide refreshments,[100] and land can be acquired for this purpose.[101] The employment of rangers to assist visitors is also authorised.[102]

Woodlands are heavily used for informal recreation. The general policy of the Forestry Commission is to allow "freedom to roam" throughout the woodlands managed by Forest Enterprise, except where safety requirements prevent this.[103] On such land the activities of visitors are controlled both by the general rights of Forest Enterprise as occupier of the land and through byelaws. The Forestry Commission Byelaws 1982[104] lay down the rules of conduct for those visiting

---

[95] Written Answer by Secretary of State for Scotland, April 25, 1996, HC Deb., Vol. 276, col. WA 218 (reprinted as Appendix 6 to *Forestry Commission Annual Report for 1996–97*, 1997–98 HC 250).

[96] *Biodiversity: The UK Steering Group Report* (HMSO, London, 1995); *Forestry Commission Annual Report for 1996–97* (1997–98 HC 250), pp. 23–25.

[97] Forestry Act 1967, s. 7

[98] The protection of woodland is one of the grounds for taking action against deer under the Deer (Scotland) Act 1996 (see Chap. 8).

[99] *Forestry Commission Annual Report for 1996–97* (1997–98 HC 250), p. 27.

[100] The 1995–96 Annual Report recorded that among the recreational facilities provided in Scotland there were 159 picnic places, 336 forest walks and nature trails, 115 cycle trails, 36 horse trails, 17 orienteering and wayfaring courses, 12 visitor centres, 14 wildlife hides, 270 car parks, 60 forest cabins and eight camping sites (*Forestry Commission Annual Report for 1995–96* (1996–97 HC 3) at 105 (Table 12)).

[101] Countryside (Scotland) Act 1967, ss 58–59; the Commissioners can authorise Scottish Natural Heritage to act on their behalf in these matters.

[102] Countryside (Scotland) Act 1967, s. 65, as amended by the Countryside (Scotland) Act 1981, Sched. 1, para. 4(a).

[103] If the land is leased rather than owned by the Forestry Commission, the terms of the lease may impose restrictions on public access, but this is a real issue only in parts of England rather than in Scotland.

[104] SI 1982/648.

Forestry Commission land, and breach of the byelaws is a criminal offence punishable at level 2 on the standard scale.[105]

Byelaw 5 lists 31 forms of conduct which are prohibited, covering restrictions on access, prevention of damage or disturbance to wildlife, prohibitions on commercial use of the land and the avoidance of disturbance to other visitors. Among the detailed provisions, it is an offence: to enter any area where a notice prohibiting entry is displayed, to enter any building unless a notice gives express or implied permission to enter, to leave open or obstruct any gate, to light any fire, to damage any Forestry Commission property, to disturb archaeological remains, to use a metal detector, to set up any tent, to graze animals, to ride or lead a horse except where specifically permitted, to allow a dog to worry any bird or animal or to fail to keep the dog on a leash when requested by a Commission officer, to hire any vehicle, to sell anything, to disturb, catch or injure any bird, fish, reptile or animal or to catch butterflies, moths or dragonflies for a collection, to carry or use any gun, bow or other missile weapon, to operate any aircraft, boat or raft, or models thereof, to play any sport, music or instrument so as to create danger or disturbance to other lawful visitors, to leave any litter, and wilfully to evade any charges or tolls levied for the use of car parks or forest roads. In relation to traffic, no vehicles other than prams and wheelchairs are allowed on Commission land except to park at the side of a highway during daylight hours or to use designated car parks. Any motor vehicles must have efficient silencers and nobody is allowed to drive as a learner driver.[106] In all cases the written authority of the Commissioners renders lawful conduct which is otherwise prohibited.[107]

The issue of access to woodlands was a matter of great concern when government policy was to sell the woodlands managed by Forest Enterprise. There was a real fear that private owners would be less generous in their approach to public access and that land which was sold would be lost for recreational use. In addition to the loss of the woodlands themselves as a recreational asset, other areas of land might also have been affected if access were restricted through the belts of trees which often stand between valley floors (which offer transport links) and the high hills. In response to these fears the Forestry Commission developed procedures which created a presumption against land which was generally available for access being sold unless access agreements could be made. For all sales, local authorities were to be offered the opportunity to enter a statutory management agreement, binding on future owners of the land and securing continued access, before the land was put on the market.[108] These procedures were not regarded as particularly successful and were subject to several revisions. Now that the policy of selling Forestry Commission land has been abandoned, there is no immediate threat of access being restricted in this way.

---

[105] Forestry Act 1967, s. 46.
[106] Forestry Commission Byelaws 1982, byelaws 6–7.
[107] Forestry Commission Byelaws 1982, byelaw 3(3).
[108] C.T. Reid, "Forestry, the Law and the Environment" in C.P. Rodgers, *Nature Conservation and Countryside Law* (Cardiff, 1996), at 157–159.

Conclusion

The law plays a remarkably small role in determining the way in which forestry in Scotland operates. The relevant legislation provides a very broad framework within which it is possible for quite different policies to be pursued. In recent years the few legal changes which have taken place have been directed to ensuring greater regard for environmental considerations in forestry matters,[109] but these legislative changes are only a small part of the way in which both the policies and organisation of the Forestry Commission have been transformed.

The previous policy of seeking commercial timber production, almost regardless of considerations of landscape, nature conservation and amenity, has been abandoned. Present policy is intended to seek the multiple benefits which forestry can bring and encourages new planting which through its location and design will achieve these diverse benefits.[110] The mature plantations which we see today—dense, single-aged, geometrically shaped plantations of single species of non-native conifers—are the product of the previous policy. Much new planting already reveals greater diversity. However, since trees grow slowly and there is a large legacy of planting based on older priorities, it will be many years before we can judge how successful the new policy is in achieving in practice the many benefits which it seeks.

---

[109] Notably the duty on the Commissioners to have regard to environmental matters (Forestry Act 1967, s. 1(3A), added by the Wildlife and Countryside (Amendment) Act 1985, s. 4) and the recent introduction of formal consents for certain afforestation projects (Environmental Assessment (Forestry) Regulations 1998), both discussed above.

[110] Indeed there has been concern that in pursuing these broader aims too little was being done to ensure adequate supplies of commercial timber for the future: *Our Forests—The Way Ahead: Enterprise, Environment and Access*, Cm. 2644 (1994), at pp. 10–11.

CHAPTER 8

HUNTING AND SHOOTING

Adele Nicol

Introduction

The laws regulating hunting and shooting and the protection of wild animals in Scotland date back many centuries. Their intention and purpose have varied throughout the years depending on whether the animal being pursued is viewed as essential for the provision of food and pelt, a quarry for the purpose of sport or an endangered species worthy of protection, or, even, indeed, all three. For example, rabbits were introduced into Scotland in the twelfth century for their fur and the royal warrens in the reign of Alexander II[1] were protected by statute with a penalty of death for poachers and confiscation of property. Nowadays, whilst the rabbit, along with other wild animals generally falling under the heading of "game", is afforded certain protection, most farmers would consider it a pest rather than an animal worthy of such elevated status.

A wild animal which is hunted for sport and capable of being eaten is defined in law as game.[2] In Scotland, and certainly in remote parts, the emphasis prior to approximately 1800 was on the value of the animal for food rather than sport. Royal hunting preserves or forests existed from early days and statutory protection for deer calves existed from as early as 1474.[3] However, it was in the middle to late eighteenth century that the concept of hunting other game animals for sport began to take hold. Bird shooting in the 1800s was already a popular sport in England. Greater intensification of farming methods and industrial development resulted in a reduction in England of habitats suitable for game. An improved transport system and the introduction of rail travel by the 1840s made Scotland and the Highlands more accessible. Scottish sport was also relatively cheap. The Scottish Highlands and their economy were still suffering the economic and social effects of the clearances. Prior to the 1800s it would be fair to say that the capture of game in Scotland was a matter of necessity rather than of

---

[1] 1214–49.
[2] Game (Scotland) Act 1772.
[3] Deer and Rabbits Act 1474.

sport. However, the sporting element is now a valuable incident of land owner-ship[4] and the control of how and when such rights may be exercised is now the subject of a variety of legislation.

The law in this field is a complex mix of statute and common law and it is impossible in a work of this nature to convey anything other than a flavour of the huge volume of rules and regulations which apply[5]; in this chapter, the most important aspects of the law in relation to the hunting and shooting of game are outlined under seven headings:

    (i) the right to hunt and shoot game;

   (ii) restraints on the exercise of sporting rights;

  (iii) firearms control;

  (iv) protection against trespassers and poachers;

   (v) the relationship of landowners, shooting tenants and agricultural tenants;

  (vi) deer and the Deer Commission;

 (vii) hunting.

These are now considered in turn.

The right to hunt and shoot game

There is no comprehensive definition of "game" in the various statutes which deal with wild animals and game. Some species may be game for one statute but not for another. Generally, "game" means capercailzie, grouse, ptarmigan, pheasant, partridge, quail, snipe, woodcock, wild duck, deer, hares and rabbits.[6] In the past, bustards and plover were recognised as legitimate quarry, but this is no longer the case.

All wild animals and birds are legally *res nullius*.[7] This is a principle derived from Roman law and essentially means that such animals and birds, being wild, have no owner and therefore become the property of anyone who catches them. Under the above principle, game species belong to the person who catches them. However, every landowner has the right to exclusive use of his own land which includes the right to hunt the game on his land and to prevent all un-authorised persons entering his land to pursue and take game. The right to hunt and capture wild animals and birds cannot be owned separately from the land,[8] unlike salmon fishings which can be owned separately from the riverbed and adjoining land.[9] A landowner can grant "sporting leases" and will frequently do so. In addition, although a lease to an agricultural tenant will generally reserve the sporting rights to the landlord, an agricultural tenant has certain rights to

---

  [4] *Birbeck v Ross* (1865) 4 M 272.

  [5] For a detailed analysis the reader should refer to the excellent Stanley Scott Robinson, *The Law of Game, Salmon and Freshwater Fishing in Scotland* (Butterworths, 1989) (hereafter referred to as "Scott Robinson") and the *Stair Memorial Encyclopaedia of the Laws of Scotland* (hereafter referred to as "*Stair Memorial Encyclopaedia*"), Vols 2, 10 and 11.

  [6] Game (Scotland) Act 1772; Night Poaching Act 1828; Game Act 1831.

  [7] Stair, *Inst.*, II.i.5; *Wilson v Dykes* (1872) 10 M 444.

  [8] *Becket v Bisset* 1921 2 SLT 33.

  [9] In relation to salmon fishings, see further Chap. 9.

capture and take certain animals if this is necessary to protect his crop.[10] Both of these issues are dealt with more fully below. In any case, however, the rights of the landowner, sporting tenant and agricultural tenant to take game are constrained by legislation regulating both the method and the time of capture.

Restraints on the exercise of sporting rights

The right to hunt and shoot is subject to a number of restraints. First, close seasons are prescribed during which the right to hunt and shoot cannot be exercised. Second, certain activities associated with hunting and shooting are controlled through licensing regimes. Third, in an effort to avoid unnecessary suffering to animals and birds, there are restrictions on the means which may be employed to capture and kill game. Finally, a number of restrictions apply specifically to the hunting and killing of rabbits and hares. These restraints are now considered in turn.

Close seasons

The earliest statute still in force with regard to close seasons is the Game (Scotland) Act 1772. That Act makes it a criminal offence to destroy, carry, buy or have in one's possession:

(i) any muir fowl or ptarmigan between December 10 and the following August 12;

(ii) any heath fowl between December 10 and the following August 20;

(iii) any partridge between February 1 and September 1; and

(iv) any pheasant between February 1 and October 1.

The corresponding open seasons are given in the Schedule at the end of this chapter. Under Scots law, the shooting of game on Sundays is not prohibited provided it is not done within the close seasons.

There is no close season for catching or killing hares or rabbits, only for the selling of hares.[11] Anyone who has the right to kill hares by virtue of being the owner or occupier of the land on which they are killed may exercise the right himself or authorise another person in writing to do so. Hares may not be sold, however, during March, April, May, June and July, although this restriction does not apply to foreign hares imported into this country.[12]

The close seasons for deer are dealt with below.

Licensing

There are two activities which are controlled through licensing: killing of game and dealing in game.

These are considered in turn.[13]

---

[10] *Jack* v *Nairne* (1887) 14 R (J) 20; 1 White 350.

[11] Hares Preservation Act 1892, s. 2.

[12] Hares Preservation Act 1892, ss 2 and 4.

[13] Reference should also be made to the discussion in Chap. 10 of the licensing provisions under Pt I of the Wildlife and Countryside Act 1981 and the Badgers (Protection) Act 1992 respectively.

Licences to kill: In terms of the Game Licences Act 1860, anyone wishing to hunt game or to assist anyone else to do so, or who uses a dog, net, gun or other instrument to catch or kill game must have a game licence.[14] It is an offence to carry out any of these activities without a licence and the offence can be prosecuted summarily and is punishable by a fine.[15] There are some exceptions, namely:

(i) the catching of woodcock or snipe by nets or springs;

(ii) the catching or destroying of rabbits on enclosed land by the landowner or tenant personally, or under their direction or with their permission;

(iii) the hunting or killing of hares with hounds;

(iv) the hunting or killing of hares by a landowner or occupier of enclosed land on his own land; and

(v) the hunting or killing of deer on enclosed land by the owner or occupier of such land personally or with their authority.[16]

There are also certain further exceptions for members of the Royal Family and their servants. The game licence of anyone convicted of any offence under the Game (Scotland) Act 1832 is automatically null and void.[17] The Game Licences Act 1860 does not define game, but in practice the definition given in the Night Poaching Act 1828 is used, ie including hares, pheasants, partridges, grouse, heath or moor game, black game or rabbits.[18] Licences can be obtained from the Post Office and need to be renewed annually.

Licences to deal: Anyone dealing in game must obtain a game dealer's licence which is issued by the local authority of the area as part of its general licensing powers. A trader in game needs a game dealer's licence from the local authority under the Game Act 1831[19] and also a game licence under the 1860 Act,[20] which levies a duty payable to the local authority. These licences require to be renewed annually and should be displayed in the business premises. Anyone selling game to a game dealer should have a licence to kill game under the 1831 Act.[21] It is an offence for any person who has not obtained either a licence to deal in game or a licence to kill game to sell game and it is also an offence for anyone who is legally entitled to sell game by virtue of holding a licence to kill it to sell such game to any person who is not a licensed dealer in game.[22] Under the Ground Game Act 1880, which deals only with ground game (ie hares and rabbits), the occupier of land, as an incidental right to his occupation or ownership of the land, has the right to catch and kill ground game on that land either personally or by

---

[14] Game Licences Act 1860, s. 4, as amended.

[15] Ibid; the fine is a fine not exceeding level 2 on the standard scale.

[16] Game Licences Act 1860, s. 5.

[17] Game Licences Act 1860, s. 11.

[18] Night Poaching Act 1828, s. 13.

[19] Game Act 1831, s. 18.

[20] Game Licences Act 1860, s. 14.

[21] Game Act 1831, s. 17.

[22] Game Act 1831, s. 25, as amended. The penalty is a fine not exceeding level 1 on the standard scale.

authorising other persons in writing so to do.[23] Only the occupier and one other person authorised by him in writing may kill ground game by firearms and such persons are exempt from the requirements to hold a licence to kill and sell such ground game.[24] Dealing in venison is dealt with specifically in the Deer (Scotland) Act 1996 and is discussed further below.

Restrictions on methods of capture

Under the Wildlife and Countryside Act 1981, certain methods of capturing and killing wild birds are prohibited. These are discussed in detail in Chapter 10 and are therefore only summarised here. A wild bird for the purposes of the Wildlife and Countryside Act 1981 does not generally include poultry or game birds,[25] but for the purpose of these particular provisions, game birds (meaning partridge, pheasant, grouse (or moor game), black (or heath) game and ptarmigan) are included.[26]

The prohibited methods are:

  (i) any spring, trap, gin, snare, hook, line or any electrical device and poisonous or stupefying substances;

 (ii) nets or baited board and bird lime or similar substance;

(iii) bows or crossbows;

 (iv) any explosive other than ammunition for a firearm;

  (v) any automatic or semi-automatic weapon;

 (vi) any shotgun the barrel of which has an internal diameter at the muzzle of more than one and three-quarters of an inch;

(vii) any device for illuminating a target or any sighting device for night shooting or any form of artificial lighting or any mirror or dazzling device;

(viii) any smoke or gas not falling within heads (i) and (ii);

 (ix) any chemical weapon agent;

  (x) the use as a decoy of any sound recording or any live bird or other animal which is tethered or secured by means of braces or a similar device or which is blind, maimed or injured;

 (xi) the use of any mechanically propelled vehicle in the immediate pursuit of a wild bird for the purpose of catching or killing it.[27]

There are certain exceptions provided a licence is obtained from the Minister and the act is done in accordance with the terms of the licence. Such a licence may be obtained for scientific or conservation purposes or similar activities or where it is necessary to preserve public health or public or air safety or to prevent the spread of disease or serious damage to livestock, foodstuffs, crops, fruit and vegetables,

---

[23] Ground Game Act 1880, s. 1.
[24] Ground Game Act 1880, s. 4, as amended.
[25] See Wildlife and Countryside Act 1981, s. 27.
[26] Ibid.
[27] Wildlife and Countryside Act 1981, s. 5.

growing timber or fisheries. Again, the arrangements for licensing are discussed in further detail in Chapter 10, to which reference should be made.

Section 11 of the Wildlife and Countryside Act 1981 contains similar restrictions on the methods of catching and killing wild animals, which include all game animals. These are also discussed in detail in Chapter 10, to which reference should be made.

In addition, the Wildlife and Countryside Act 1981 makes the following an offence:

(i) the use of any self-locking snare capable of causing injury to wild animals coming in contact with it;

(ii) failing without good reason to inspect at least daily any snare or trap set which is likely to injure any wild animal.[28]

Prohibitions in the Agriculture (Scotland) Act 1948

It is generally an offence to use a firearm for the purpose of killing rabbits and hares between the first hour after sunset and the first hour after sunrise,[29] but this does not apply to the owner of shooting rights on any land or to the occupier of any land.[30]

The use of any spring trap other than an approved trap is an offence[31]; and it is also an offence to fail to inspect any approved spring trap set for the purposes of catching rabbits or hares, or to arrange inspection by some competent person, at least once every day. The placing of a spring trap anywhere other than in a rabbit hole for the purpose of trapping hares and rabbits is prohibited.[32]

The deliberate use of a rabbit affected by myxomatosis to spread the disease amongst uninfected rabbits is also prohibited.[33]

Firearms control

Anyone intending to shoot game must hold a firearms certificate or shotgun certificate. Effective and comprehensive control on firearms was first introduced in the Firearms Act 1920. Prior to that, the Gun Licence Act 1870 merely required users of firearms to pay a licence fee and to hold a licence to use a gun of any description, but that Act did not apply to carrying or using a gun in a house or the area around it and a licence was not considered necessary if a householder only used the gun for the protection of his own home. It gradually became clear, however, that there was a growing international trade in arms and an increase in the possession of firearms, particularly following the First World War. Various legislation was passed seeking to impose increasing controls culminating in the passing of the Firearms Acts 1968–97. The 1968 Act was amended and the categories of prohibited weapons extended by the Firearms (Amendment) Act 1988 following the Hungerford incident in 1987. Further reforms were given effect

---

28 Wildlife and Countryside Act 1981, s. 11(3).
29 Agriculture (Scotland) Act 1948, s. 50(1)(a).
30 Wildlife and Countryside Act 1981, s. 12 and Sched. 7, para. 2(1).
31 Agriculture (Scotland) Act 1948, s. 50(1)(b).
32 Agriculture (Scotland) Act 1948, s. 50A(1) and (2).
33 Pests Act 1954, s. 12.

to by the Firearms (Amendment) Act 1997 following upon the public inquiry into the shootings at Dunblane Primary School.

The Firearms Acts 1968–97[34] impose restrictions on the possession, purchase, sale and transfer of weapons and ammunition. The legislation deals with four categories of weapons and ammunition, being:

(i) prohibited weapons and ammunition;

(ii) other arms and ammunition requiring firearm certificates;

(iii) shotguns; and

(iv) air weapons.[35]

The law relating to prohibited weapons and ammunition is beyond the scope of this chapter. Authorisation for the possession of such weapons is given by the appropriate Minister[36] and is not normally given to private individuals. Prohibited weapons would not be available by any legal means to a sportsman.

Anyone wishing to acquire, possess or use a firearm or ammunition, other than certain shotguns and air weapons, must obtain a firearms certificate from the Chief Officer of Police in the area in which he resides.[37] Possession without a firearms certificate is an offence punishable on summary conviction by imprisonment for a term not exceeding six months or a fine or both and on indictment by imprisonment for a term not exceeding five years or a fine or both.[38] A firearm is defined for the purposes of the Firearms Acts 1968–1997 as:

(i) any lethal barrelled weapon of any description from which any shot, bullet or other missile can be discharged; or

(ii) any prohibited weapon whether it is a lethal barrelled weapon or not; or

(iii) any component part of a lethal barrelled weapon or prohibited weapon; or

(iv) any accessory to a lethal barrelled weapon or prohibited weapon designed to diminish the noise or flash upon firing; or

(v) any imitation firearm which has the appearance of being and is so constructed or adapted as to be readily convertible into a certain type of firearm.[39]

It should be noted that possession of a firearm without a firearms certificate is a strict liability offence and the Crown does not have to prove that the accused knew he had a firearm, that is, it is no defence that the accused honestly believed that the item in his possession did not fall within the definition of a firearm if in fact it did so.[40]

---

[34] These are: the Firearms Act 1968, the Firearms Act 1982, the Firearms (Amendment) Act 1988 and the Firearms (Amendment) Act 1997.

[35] Firearms Act 1968, s. 5.

[36] Ibid, as amended.

[37] Firearms Act 1968, s. 26.

[38] Firearms Act 1968, s. 1.

[39] Firearms Act 1968, s. 57.

[40] *Smith* v *H.M. Advocate* 1996 SCCR 49; 1996 SLT 1338.

For the purposes of the Firearms Acts, "shotgun" is defined as a smooth-bore gun not being an air gun which (i) has a barrel not less than 24 inches in length and does not have any barrel with a bore exceeding two inches in diameter; (ii) is not a revolver gun; and (iii) either has no magazine or has a non-detachable magazine incapable of holding more than two cartridges.[41] The possession of a shotgun as defined requires a shotgun certificate, although a firearms certificate is not required.[42] A shotgun certificate must also be obtained from the Chief Officer of Police for the area in which the applicant resides.[43] This requirement applies to all shotguns which do not fall within the definition of firearms for which a firearms certificate would be required. It is, therefore, not the case that the greater includes the lesser, and anyone intending shooting or hunting using a rifle and shotgun will require both certificates. A shotgun certificate is not required if the shotgun has been borrowed from the occupier of private premises and is only used on those premises in the occupier's presence.[44]

Both shotgun and firearms certificates are valid for a period of five years or such other period as may be specified unless previously revoked or cancelled.[45] Applications for such certificates require to be made in the prescribed form.

An application for a firearms certificate will be granted provided the Chief Constable is satisfied that the applicant is fit to be entrusted with a firearm and is not a person prohibited by the Firearms Act from possessing a firearm, that the applicant has a good reason for having a firearm in his possession and that in all the circumstances the applicant can be permitted to have a firearm or ammunition in his possession without danger to the public safety or to the peace.[46] Similar provisions exist for the grant of the shotgun certificate.[47] There is a right of appeal to the sheriff in the event of a refusal.[48]

Protection against trespass and poachers

So far this chapter has focused on the law relating to the exercise of shooting rights. Landowners and others entitled to exercise such rights will be concerned to ensure that their rights are protected from infringement by unauthorised persons. The use of interdict and self-help by a landowner against a trespasser generally is discussed in Chapter 12, to which further reference should be made. Specific protection is afforded by the Game (Scotland) Act 1832 and the Night Poaching Acts of 1828 and 1848.

The Game (Scotland) Act 1832 is often referred to as the Day Trespass Act. This Act does not itself define game, but generally the definition in the Night Poaching Act 1828, discussed further below, is accepted, that is, hares, pheasants, partridges, grouse, heath or moor game and black game.[49] The courts have also

---

[41] Firearms Act 1968, s. 1(3)(a)(i)–(iii), as amended.
[42] Firearms Act 1968, s. 2(1).
[43] Firearms Act 1968, s. 28.
[44] Firearms Act 1968, s. 11(5).
[45] Firearms Act 1968, s. 26(3).
[46] Firearms Act 1968, s. 27(1) and (3).
[47] Firearms Act 1968, s. 28(2)(a).
[48] Firearms Act 1968, s. 44, as substituted by the Firearms (Amendment) Act 1997.
[49] Night Poaching Act 1828, s. 13.

held capercailzie to be game under this Act[50] but not deer.[51] This Act makes it an offence for any person to trespass on land without leave of the owner or the proprietor in search of game, woodcock, snipe, wild ducks or rabbits.[52] Merely being found in possession of game does not necessarily mean that someone has committed an offence under the Act; there has to be evidence that the accused is not only in possession of game but that he was on land unlawfully pursuing game or rabbits.[53] There is an interesting distinction between the Night Poaching Acts, discussed below, and the Day Trespass Act so far as tenant farmers are concerned. The offence under the latter is being on the land *without the consent of the owner*, but the tenant has, of course, every right to be on the land and therefore commits no offence. If the tenant kills game during the day his landlord has other remedies, for example interdict, a claim for loss or a claim for breach of the tenant's lease where, as is likely, the sporting rights have been reserved to the landlord. Under the Night Poaching Acts, however, the agricultural tenant does actually commit an offence if he is catching game on the tenancy land without any right to do so, that is, without right under his agricultural lease or any separate sporting lease or permission or otherwise.[54] Daytime starts at the beginning of the last hour before sunrise and ends at the end of the first hour after sunset.[55]

To commit an offence of statutory trespass under the Day Trespass Act the trespass need not have been physically committed by the accused himself: the offence is committed if the accused remained outside the land but sent his dog on to land to hunt game or rabbits.[56] Anyone trespassing in daytime in pursuit of game may be requested by the landowner or his gamekeeper or other employee to leave the land and to provide his name and address.[57] Failure to provide this information or failure to leave allows the landowner or his gamekeeper or other employee to apprehend the trespasser.[58] The prosecution of a trespasser under this Act is at the instance of the landowner, the occupier or the procurator fiscal and will be dealt with on summary procedure.[59] There is no offence committed under the Act by any person hunting or coursing upon land with hounds and in pursuit of any hare or fox already started upon other land on which such person was entitled to hunt or course.[60] Any trespasser found on land with game in his possession must, if requested to do so, hand over the game to the person who legally has the right to kill the game on that land or the occupier of that land or the gamekeeper of either such person[61]: this will normally be either the landowner, his shooting tenant or the gamekeeper of either of them.

The Night Poaching Acts 1828 and 1844 make it an offence unlawfully, that is with no right or permission to be there, to take or destroy any game (which

---

[50] *Colquhoun's Trs* v *Lee* 1957 SLT (Sh Ct) 50; 73 Sh Ct Rep 165.
[51] *Ferguson* v *McPhail* 1987 SCCR 52.
[52] Game (Scotland) Act 1832, s. 1, as amended.
[53] *Jameson* v *Barty* (1893) 1 Adam 91.
[54] Night Poaching Act 1828; *Smith* v *Young* (1856) 2 Irv 402.
[55] Game (Scotland) Act 1832; *Robertson* v *Adamson* (1860) 3 Irv 607.
[56] *Stoddart* v *Stevenson* (1880) 7 R (J) 11.
[57] Game (Scotland) Act 1832, s. 2, as amended.
[58] Ibid.
[59] Ibid.
[60] Game (Scotland) Act 1832, ss 1 and 2.
[61] Game (Scotland) Act 1832, s. 5.

includes hares, pheasants, partridges, grouse, heath or moor game, black game or rabbits) on any land, whether open or enclosed, or on any public road, or by night to enter on any land with any gun or other instrument for the purpose of taking or destroying game.[62] It is also an offence to be in the company of anyone who has a net for these purposes.[63] There are therefore two separate offences, one of catching game illegally at night and the separate one of entering at night on land with a gun, net or other instrument for the purpose of catching game. Night means the period between the end of the first hour after sunset and the beginning of the last hour before sunrise calculated by the reference to the time of sunset or sunrise at the locality where the offence occurs.[64]

Anyone found committing an offence under the Night Poaching Acts may be apprehended by the owner or occupier of the land or the gamekeeper or servant of such a person, and if he escapes may be apprehended at any other place to which he may escape, and then delivered to the custody of the police.[65] Prosecutions under the Night Poaching Acts are brought in the sheriff court at the instance of the procurator fiscal.

The relationship of landowners, shooting tenants and agricultural tenants

The relationship between landowners, shooting tenants and agricultural tenants is complex. The position of landowners and shooting tenants is considered first, followed by a brief outline of the relationship between landowners and agricultural tenants.

Shooting leases

It is now generally accepted in Scots law that a lease of shooting or sporting rights is a valid lease. This has not always been so and until the case of *Leith* v *Leith*[66] in 1862 it was thought that a shooting lease was not a lease in the proper sense but merely a licence or personal agreement and would not be binding on the landlord if he sold his property during the currency of the shooting lease. The issue is still not completely beyond doubt, since the *Leith* case, which was decided by the Full Bench of the Inner House of the Court of Session, has not been tested in the House of Lords. However, the principle was upheld in *Stewart* v *Bulloch*,[67] and it must be doubtful whether a shooting lease ceases to be valid against a new owner, particularly if the lease is a long lease (ie more than 20 years) registered in the Register of Sasines or the Land Register.[68] Shooting rights cannot, however, unlike salmon fishings, be sold separately from the land over which they are exercised.[69]

An agricultural lease will not include shooting rights unless it specifically says so and in most cases the landowner will want to reserve the shooting rights either

---

[62] Night Poaching Act 1828, s. 1.
[63] *H.M. Advocate* v *Granger* (1863) Irv 432.
[64] Night Poaching Act 1828, s. 12.
[65] Night Poaching Act 1828, s. 2, as amended.
[66] (1862) 24 D 1059.
[67] (1881) 8 R 381.
[68] *Palmer's Trs* v *Brown* 1989 SLT 128.
[69] Salmon fishings are discussed in Chap. 9.

for himself or to let separately to a sporting tenant. The agricultural tenant does, however, have certain rights laid down by statute to protect his crop from marauding deer and vermin and to secure control of game where damage to crops is being caused.

A shooting lease has a high degree of *delectus personae*, ie the tenant is the person specifically chosen by the landlord, and the right cannot be assigned to any other person.[70] A shooting lease is not, therefore, assignable by the tenant unless this is expressly provided for. Generally, the landowner will want to exercise control over who is exercising the sporting rights on his land.

The right to kill game will generally include the right to kill hares and rabbits, but if there is an agricultural tenant on the land, his rights to kill ground game will not be affected: the agricultural tenant has a concurrent right with the sporting tenant to kill hares and rabbits under the Ground Game Act 1880.[71] The sporting lease will generally have a clause obliging the shooting tenant to relieve the landlord of claims by the agricultural tenant for damage to crops by game or otherwise through the operation of the lease. The agricultural tenant will not claim directly against the sporting tenant but against the landlord, who will then be indemnified by the sporting tenant.

The lease will also generally provide that the sporting tenant has to carry his own public liability insurance and must indemnify the landlord from all claims which may arise as a result of the sporting rights being exercised. The level of public liability insurance required by the landlord is likely to be high, perhaps as high as £1 million or more, to guard against a possible award of damages in the event of a claim for damage or injury. The shooting lease may grant the sporting tenant exclusive shooting rights or specify some other arrangement and the landlord may retain concurrent rights.

The landlord and the agricultural tenant

Generally, an agricultural lease will not include the sporting rights. These rights may be exercised by the landlord himself or may be leased by the landlord to a sporting tenant. Where the agricultural tenant does not have the sporting rights, he should not attempt to catch game himself. If he does so, he commits an offence under the Night Poaching Acts if the act is carried out at night.[72] Curiously, as discussed above, there is no offence under the Day Trespass Act if the act is carried out during the day, although at both times he will be in breach of the terms of his lease. The tenant and his family and employees must not be put in danger by the activities of the landlord or the sporting tenant. The tenant may protect his crops by killing rabbits unless the right has been reserved to the landlord.[73] If the tenant has the right to kill rabbits he cannot recover damages from his landlord for the landlord's failure to do so. A tenant can erect scarecrows but is not allowed to fire blank cartridges in order to protect his crop.[74] The tenant is entitled to damages from the landlord or the sporting tenant if damage is caused

---

[70] *Earl of Fife* v *Wilson* (1864) 3 M 323.
[71] Ground Game Act 1880, s. 1.
[72] Night Poaching Act 1828; *Smith* v *Young* (1856) 2 Irv 402.
[73] *Inglis* v *Moir's Tutors and Gunnis* (1871) 10 M 204; *Wood* v *Paton* (1874) 1 R 868; *Gowans* v *Spottiswoode* (1914) 31 Sh Ct Rep 30.
[74] *Wymess* v *Gullard* (1847) 10 D 204.

to his land or crops due to their actions[75]; and if the agricultural tenant can show that during his lease there has been obvious visible increase in the game stock which is attributable to the acts of the landlord he may also have a claim for damage resulting to the crop.[76]

The tenant has a statutory right to compensation for damage done by game where the right to hunt and kill such game is not vested in the tenant.[77] For this purpose, game means deer, pheasants, partridges, grouse and black game[78]; ground game, ie hares and rabbits, is excluded because the tenant is permitted under the Ground Game Act 1880 to protect himself against damage by such ground game.

Deer and the Deer Commission

The laws relating to the control and preservation of deer deserve special mention. Somewhat surprisingly, deer are not and have never been considered "royal animals", ie animals which the Crown has the prerogative of hunting. Deer are therefore legally wild animals and the general principle that wild animals are *res nullius,* discussed above, applies. In other words, they become the property of the person who legally captures them on his own land or on land on which he is otherwise permitted to shoot. This, of course, does not apply to deer farms where the deer are owned as stock.

In terms of the Deer (Scotland) Act 1996, the appropriate Minister is obliged in respect of the female of every species of deer, and is able in relation to the male of any species of deer, to fix by order a period in each year during which no person is permitted to capture, kill or injure any deer of the sex and species named in the order.[79] The close seasons during which deer may not be shot or killed are as follows:

   (i) red deer stag: October 21 to the following June 30;
  (ii) red deer hind: February 16 to October 20;
 (iii) fallow deer stag: May 1 to July 31;
 (iv) fallow deer hind: February 16 to October 20;
  (v) roe deer stag: October 21 to the following March 31;
 (vi) roe deer hind: April 1 to October 20;
 (vii) sika deer stag: October 21 to the following June 30;
(viii) sika deer hind: February 16 to October 20;
 (ix) red and sika hybrid stag: October 21 to the following June 30;
  (x) red and sika hybrid hind: February 16 to October 20.[80]

The close seasons do not apply to commercial breeders and farmers of deer.

---

[75] *Hilton* v *Green* (1862) 2 F & F 821.
[76] *Morton* v *Graham* (1867) 6 M 71; *Kydd* v *Byrne, Byrne and Johnson* (1875) 3 R 255; *Cadzow* v *Locklard* (1876) 3 R 666.
[77] Agricultural Holdings (Scotland) Act 1991, s. 52(1).
[78] Agricultural Holdings (Scotland) Act 1991, s. 52(5).
[79] Deer (Scotland) Act 1996, s. 5(1).
[80] See Deer (Scotland) Act 1996, s. 48(5) and Sched. 6 in relation to red deer and the Deer (Close Seasons) (Scotland) Order 1984 (SI 1984/76) in relation to the other deer specified; no new order has been made under the Deer (Scotland) Act 1996 as yet.

An occupier of agricultural land or forestry land may kill deer on his own land at any time but only if there is a serious risk of damage to crops or trees.[81]

Night shooting of deer is generally prohibited at all times,[82] unless (i) by a member of staff of the Deer Commission; or (ii) to prevent suffering of an injured or diseased animal or of an orphaned kid; or (iii) to prevent crop damage by marauding deer, but then only by the occupier of the land in person.[83]

The Deer Commission may authorise the killing of deer if the deer are on agricultural land or woodland and causing serious damage to forestry or agricultural production and it is necessary to kill the deer to prevent further damage.[84]

It is an offence to kill or injure deer on land without legal right or permission and to remove the carcass of any deer from any land without permission from the person having such legal right.[85]

It is illegal in Scotland by virtue of the Deer (Scotland) Act 1996 to kill or injure deer by any means other than shooting, and the firearms and ammunition used must comply with the statutory requirements of the Firearms Acts.

Persons authorised by the Deer Commission do not require a licence to kill game.[86] Dealing in venison does, however, require a licence, which is granted by the local authority,[87] and dealers are required to keep certain records relating to their dealings in venison.[88] These provisions are reinforced by a number of offences.[89]

The Deer (Scotland) Act 1996 established the Deer Commission for Scotland as the successor to the Red Deer Commission. The Commission's functions are set out in section 1 of that Act, and are to further the conservation, control and sustainable management of deer in Scotland, to keep under review all matters relating to deer and such other functions as may be conferred on them. The Commission carries out its functions in accordance with general directions given by the appropriate Minister,[90] and in doing so, it has a duty to take account of the size and density of the deer population and its impact on the natural heritage, the needs of agriculture and forestry and the interests of owners and occupiers of land.[91]

The Deer Commission is appointed by the appropriate Minister after consultation with organisations representing persons concerned with deer management, agriculture, forestry and woodland management and natural heritage.[92] Its remit includes the following:

(i) to advise the appropriate Minister on deer-related matters including the fixing of close seasons;

---

[81] Deer (Scotland) Act 1996, s. 26.
[82] Deer (Scotland) Act 1996, s. 18(1).
[83] Deer (Scotland) Act 1996, ss 14, 25 and 26.
[84] Deer (Scotland) Act 1996, ss 18(2) and 37(1) and (2).
[85] Deer (Scotland) Act 1996, s. 17(1)–(4).
[86] Deer (Scotland) Act 1996, s. 38. Licences to kill game are discussed above.
[87] Deer (Scotland) Act 1996, s. 33.
[88] Deer (Scotland) Act 1996, ss 34 and 35.
[89] See Deer (Scotland) Act 1996, s. 36.
[90] Deer (Scotland) Act 1996, s. 1(3).
[91] Deer (Scotland) Act 1996, s. 1(2).
[92] Deer (Scotland) Act 1996, s. 1(6).

(ii) to issue guidance or advice to any person or organisation, for example, the Forestry Commission;

(iii) to conduct research relating to conservation, control and sustainable management of deer;

(iv) to institute control schemes for the extermination or reduction of deer where they have caused damage to woodland, agricultural production, the natural heritage, livestock or where they pose a danger to public safety, whether by voluntary agreement with landowners or by compulsory control scheme which requires the confirmation of the Minister;

(v) to undertake emergency measures to prevent damage by deer including authorising the killing of marauding deer; authorising the killing of deer during the close season; authorising the taking or killing of deer at night.[93]

The Commission may also require landowners to make returns showing the number of deer of each species and sex killed on their land.[94] It may appoint panels for different localities, subject to the approval of the Minister, and may exercise its powers through the local panels. It also sets target population figures for the deer herd in Scotland and carries out voluntary culls in agreement with landowners. It has not yet been necessary for the Commission to use its statutory powers to put a compulsory control scheme in place.

Hunting

Hunting with hounds for foxes is, at the time of writing, still legal in Scotland although it is not a practice which is widespread and it is generally confined to parts of the Borders, Dumfriesshire and Ayrshire.

A hunt has no right to enter upon private land except with the consent of the owner. The Master of the Hunt will try to anticipate the route of the hunt and to obtain consent; however, if the fox enters on land where consent has not been obtained the hunt has no right to follow. The hunt will be liable to make good any damage caused to crops or fences by its activities.

There has recently been much debate on the issue of hunting foxes with hounds, and it is likely that legislation for the purpose of banning such activity will be introduced to the Scottish Parliament in the coming session.

The hunting of otters has never been a widespread practice in Scotland and is now illegal by virtue of the fact that the otter is a protected species in terms of the Wildlife and Countryside Act 1981.[95]

---

[93] See Deer (Scotland) Act 1996, ss 2, 3, 5, 7, 8, 10, 11, 18 and 37.

[94] Deer (Scotland) Act 1996, s. 40.

[95] Wildlife and Countryside Act 1981, s. 1 and Sched. 5.

Schedule

SHOOTING SEASONS—Open Season

Pheasant	October 1 to the following February 1[1]
Partridge	September 1 to the following February 1[1]
Grouse and Ptarmigan	August 12 to December 10[1]
Black Game	August 20 to December 10[1]
Hare and Rabbit	There is no close season, and therefore no corresponding open season, but hares may not be offered for sale from March to July inclusive[2]
Common Snipe	August 12 to the following January 31[3]
Capercailzie	October 1 to the following January 31[3]
Woodcock	September 1 to the following January 31[3]
Duck and Geese	Inland: September 1 to the following January 31[4] Foreshore: September 1 to the following February 20[4]

[1] Game (Scotland) Act 1772, s. 1.
[2] Hares (Scotland) Act 1848.
[3] Wildlife and Countryside Act 1981, s. 2(4).
[4] Wildlife and Countryside Act 1981, s. 24(4).

CHAPTER 9

FISHING

Christopher Hardie

Introduction

Rather surprisingly, there is no statutory definition of fishing, perhaps because the meaning is obvious. However, the right to capture and kill fish, by whatever method, is a valuable asset, and the law impinges on such activity in a variety of ways. It is the purpose of this chapter to explain how the law does so.

From the earliest times salmon and trout, as well as deer and other game,[1] have been regarded as valuable assets and have been closely protected by statute in the interests of the Crown and of landowners who were entitled to exercise the rights to fish for salmon and trout to the exclusion of all others. As with all wild animals,[2] fish in their natural habitat are *res nullius*, that is, they do not belong to anyone,[3] although as will be seen below, appropriate permission to fish for wild fish will almost always be required. In contrast, fish which are kept in ponds or underwater cages, or in artificial enclosed waterways (commonly known as stanks) for the purposes of stocking or fish farming are considered the property of the landowner or fish farmer, and the taking of such fish may constitute theft. This chapter is primarily concerned with the law relating to freshwater fishing for wild salmon, trout and other freshwater fish; fish-farming and sea fisheries are discussed further in Chapter 17, to which reference should be made.

The law may conveniently be considered under the following headings:

    (i)   who owns, and who may exercise, the right to fish for wild fish;

   (ii) the method and time of capture, including the lawful means of catching fish and the season when they may be caught;

  (iii) the extent of, and rights incidental to, the right to fish;

---

[1] For deer and other game, see Chap. 8.
[2] See Chap. 8.
[3] *Stair Memorial Encyclopaedia of the Laws of Scotland* (hereafter "*Stair Memorial Encyclopaedia*"), Vol. 18.

(iv) the relationship of the right to fish with other rights which may com-
pete or otherwise interact with the right to fish, for example, the rights
of landowners and of those who use the water for navigational or
recreational purposes.

The law relating to salmon, sea trout and brown trout and other freshwater fish
will be considered separately. It is appropriate, however, to consider briefly first
the background of the development of statutory regulation, against which the
current law must be set, and the current issues affecting fishing.

Development of statutory regulation

There are currently a large number of statutes regulating salmon, trout and freshwater fishing in Scotland.[4] In some cases, these relate to specific rivers or waterways, for example the River Tweed, the Solway Firth and the Lake of Menteith.
The Border Esk, which runs along the border between Scotland and England, is
outwith the scope of this chapter as it is regulated under English Salmon Fisheries
Acts.

The development of statutory regulation in relation to the specific rights of
fishing for salmon, trout and other freshwater fish is more fully explained below
in the sections relating to each category of fish. For ease of reference, however, it
is appropriate to set out here the main Acts which will be referred to in this
chapter. These are:

    (i) the Solway Act 1804 ("the 1804 Act");

    (ii) the Tweed Fisheries Act 1857 ("the 1857 Act");

    (iii) the Tweed Fisheries Amendment Act 1859 ("the 1859 Act");

    (iv) the Salmon Fisheries (Scotland) Act 1862 ("the 1862 Act");

    (v) the Salmon Fisheries (Scotland) Act 1868 ("the 1868 Act");

    (vi) the Freshwater Fish (Scotland) Act 1902 ("the 1902 Act");

    (vii) the Trout (Scotland) Act 1933 ("the 1933 Act");

    (viii) the Salmon and Freshwater Fisheries (Protection) (Scotland) Act 1951
("the 1951 Act");

    (ix) the Tweed Fisheries Act 1969 ("the 1969 Act");

    (x) the Freshwater and Salmon Fisheries (Scotland) Act 1976 ("the 1976
Act");

    (xi) the Salmon Act 1986 ("the 1986 Act").

Current issues

The exercise of fishing rights is clearly dependent on sufficient stocks of fish
being available. In relation to salmon in particular, in some rivers the number of
salmon caught at certain times of the year has been so poor in recent times that

---

[4] The Scottish Law Commission is currently undertaking a project which may result in consolidation of the appropriate legislation.

the owners of the fishings have implemented a "catch and release policy", and the Scottish Salmon Strategy Task Force reported in 1997 recommending wide-ranging steps designed to preserve, enhance and, if possible, increase the numbers of salmon. This is discussed further below.

If National Parks are introduced in Scotland as currently proposed,[5] this may have an effect on certain waterways, for example Loch Lomond.

Salmon

Definitions

The 1986 Act defines salmon as meaning "all migratory fish of the species *salmo salar* and *salmo trutta* and commonly known as salmon and sea trout respectively or any part of any such fish".[6] The 1951 Act has the same definition, except that it uses the word "includes" rather than "means". Sea trout are considered separately below. The 1862 Act, now repealed, had a wider definition.

It is appropriate at this point to explain the life cycle of salmon. Salmon spawn in rivers and streams in the autumn and winter, burying their eggs in gravel nests or "redds" where there is a good flow of water both above and through the gravel. The eggs hatch the following spring. The newly hatched salmon are known as alevins and remain in the gravel for several weeks. They then emerge from the gravel as fry. Once they have grown larger, they are known as parr. After one, two or three, or occasionally as long as four or five, years as parr, the salmon become silvery and migrate downstream towards the sea and are known as smolts. As smolts, they migrate to the sea in order to feed in the rich feeding grounds there. Fish which return to fresh water after only one winter at sea are known as grilse. Those which remain longer at sea before returning to fresh water are known as adult salmon or simply salmon. Salmon return to fresh water, normally the same river from which they departed, in order to spawn.[7] Most salmon die after they have spawned, but those which survive return downstream to the sea: during their return downstream, they are known as kelts. Some salmon fail to spawn, and during their prolonged stay in the river beyond the normal breeding season, they are known as baggots. Those kelts lucky enough to return to the sea will once more feed, build up their strength and return to the river to spawn. A similar life cycle applies to sea trout.[8]

At all stages in the life cycle, wild salmon which remain in their natural habitat are *res nullius*.[9] Farmed salmon kept in cages belong to the fish farm operator and the unauthorised taking of such fish constitutes theft. As noted above, this chapter is not generally concerned with farmed fish. A farmed salmon which escapes and returns to its natural habitat, however, is treated in the same way as a wild salmon for the purposes of fishing for and capturing it. The effect of escaped farmed salmon on wild stocks is currently an issue of concern.

---

[5] See further below.

[6] 1951 Act, s. 24(1); 1986 Act, s. 40(1).

[7] Despite the fact that many are caught by rod and line, most salmon do not feed in the river at this time.

[8] Sea trout are discussed further below.

[9] See above.

The right to fish for salmon

As noted above, salmon themselves are *res nullius*, but the right to fish for salmon in both inland and territorial waters is vested in the Crown,[10] although it may be, and in many cases has been, conveyed to others. Unlike the right to fish for trout, which is an incident of the right of ownership of the land adjacent to the water concerned,[11] the right to fish for salmon is a separate tenement in land and may therefore be owned separately from the land itself. All proprietors of salmon fishings in Scotland apart from those in Orkney and Shetland derive their rights directly or indirectly from the Crown.[12] An example of a direct Crown grant of salmon fishings would be a specific conveyance by the Crown of the right to fish for salmon in specified waters. A right of salmon fishing may be acquired by prescription provided the title is habile, that is, capable of supporting such a right.

It follows from the fact that all salmon fishings are vested in the Crown or those who derive right from the Crown that there is no public right to fish for salmon.[13] Members of the public who wish to fish for salmon must therefore obtain the appropriate permission from the owner of the salmon fishings. Leases of salmon fishings are common and, because salmon fishings are a separate tenement in land as noted above, they may be let separately from the land.[14] Leases of salmon fishings are binding on the successors of the owner of the salmon fishings.[15] In the absence of express stipulation in the lease, sub-tenants and assignees are probably excluded. However, leases in favour of angling associations and such like are quite common and these will generally provide for the tenant to issue daily or weekly permits to members of the public.

Method and time of capture of salmon

The capture of fish requires to be carried out by lawful means. Within inland waters, the permitted methods are rod and line and net and coble, although any right of fishing for salmon in existence on May 10, 1951 may continue to be exercised and this includes such methods as fishing by cruive (a type of trap the use of which is now virtually extinct) and privileged fixed engines (a method of fishing in the Solway Firth).[16] Within a salmon fishery district[17] but outside estuary

---

[10] Stair, *Inst*, II.i.5 and II.iii.69; Erskine, *Inst*, II.i.6 and 10 and II.vi.15 and 17; Bell's *Principles*, ss 646, 671, 745, 1112; see also Rankine, *The Law of Land-ownership in Scotland* (4th edn), p. 304. The Crown's rights relate to the fishings, not the fish themselves; there does not appear to be any authority for treating salmon as "royal fish" (unlike, for example, sturgeon, which are royal fish).

[11] See further below.

[12] In Orkney and Shetland, the position is governed by udal law, which derives from ancient Norse law: *Lord Advocate v Balfour* 1907 SC 1360; 45 SLR 372. Accordingly, salmon fishings in Orkney and Shetland belong to the landowner adjacent to the water concerned.

[13] Public rights of fishing generally are discussed in Chap. 17.

[14] *Stephen v Lord Advocate* (1878) 6 R 282. See also Gordon, *Scottish Land Law*, para. 19–121.

[15] Cf. leases of trout and other freshwater fishings which, until the provisions of the 1976 Act came into force, were personal to the grantee and could not bind the landowner's successors: such leases are discussed further below.

[16] 1951 Act, s. 2. "Inland waters" includes all rivers above estuary limits and their tributary streams and all waters, watercourses and lochs whether natural or artificial which drain into the sea: 1951 Act, s. 24(1).

[17] Salmon fishery districts are discussed further below.

limits, the permitted methods are rod and line, net and coble, bag net, fly net or other stake net.[18] The meaning of rod and line, net and coble, bag net, fly net and other stake net is set out in the legislation.[19]

The capture of salmon must also take place at permitted times. There are annual and weekly close times during which the capture of salmon is prohibited[20]: for example, fishing for salmon on a Sunday is prohibited.[21] The legislation creates a number of statutory offences relating to both annual and weekly close times.[22] Close times are discussed in more detail below.

The extent of the right to fish and rights incidental to salmon fishings

With respect to the extent of the right, the owner of exclusive salmon fishing rights in a river may fish anywhere on the river and from both banks. Where more than one person has a right to fish in a particular stretch of river, the extent of their respective rights will generally be set out in the titles to the fishings or fixed by prescription where the title to the fishings is acquired by that method; where this is not the case, each proprietor may fish from his own bank or wade out or row his boat as far as the extent of his property up to the *medium filum* (the mid-line) of the river and cast into his neighbour's waters as far as he can from there.[23] Where the fishings are in a loch, the exclusive owner of the fishings may fish anywhere in the loch or from any of the banks; if, however, the owner of the fishings owns only a portion of the bank, he may fish anywhere on the loch by boat and from his own bank, but he may need permission to fish from any bank belonging to his neighbour.[24] The inter-relationship of the rights of neighbouring fishing proprietors is discussed further below.

The right to salmon fishing includes the lesser right of brown trout fishing.[25] If the proprietor of the salmon fishings is not the same as the owner of the land adjacent to the waters to which the salmon fishings relate, his rights to fish for brown trout will not be exclusive, because the owner of the land also has an implied right to fish for brown trout.[26] Accordingly, where different persons hold the right to fish for salmon and trout in the same waters, the landowner must exercise his right of trout fishing in a manner which will not interfere with the superior right of salmon fishing[27]; at the same time, however, the salmon fishings

---

[18] 1951 Act, s. 2(1A).

[19] For rod and line, see 1951 Act, s. 24(1) as amended; for the remainder, see the Salmon (Definition of Methods of Net Fishing and Construction of Nets) (Scotland) Regulations 1992 (SI 1992/1974), as amended.

[20] For the annual close times, see the 1986 Act, s. 6; for the weekly close times, see the 1951 Act, s. 13.

[21] 1951 Act, s. 13, as amended. These are discussed in greater detail below.

[22] For offences relating to the annual close times, see the 1868 Act, ss 15, 21, 22 and 23; these offences do not apply in the Tweed District, for which reference must be made to the 1859 Act. For offences relating to the weekly close times, see the 1951 Act, s. 13 and the 1868 Act, s. 24; of these offences, those in the 1951 Act apply to the Tweed District while that in the 1868 Act does not. Offences in relation to close times, *inter alia*, are discussed further below.

[23] *Fotheringham* v *Passmore* 1986 SC (HL) 96.

[24] With respect to access for the purposes of exercising a right to salmon fishing, see further below.

[25] *Stair Memorial Encyclopaedia*, Vol. 11, para. 5; see also Scott Robinson, *The Law of Game, Salmon and Freshwater Fishing in Scotland*, p. 229.

[26] See further below.

[27] *Mackenzie* v *Rose* (1830) 8 S 816; *Lord Somerville* v *Smith* (1859) 22 D 279.

should not be exercised in such a way as to prejudice the landowner's right of trout fishing to the extent that the salmon fishermen should not deliberately set out to fish for brown trout in such a manner as is oppressive to the normal enjoyment of the landowner's right to fish for brown trout.[28]

With respect to the rights incidental to salmon fishings, the right to salmon fishing includes such ancillary rights as are necessary for its beneficial enjoyment[29] and the owner of the salmon fishings is entitled to do anything necessary for the exercise of his right provided that he pays due regard to the rights of the bank owners.[30] The most important of the ancillary rights is probably that of access to the fishings: where the owner of salmon fishings does not own the land adjacent to the waters in which he has the right to fish, he has an implied right of access across land to reach those waters, although it must be exercised in such a manner as is least burdensome to the owner of the land, which will usually mean pedestrian access only.[31] Other ancillary rights are the right to draw nets onto the banks or beach, to fix posts and to moor boats[32]; there is probably no right, however, to erect a fishing hut without express permission of the landowner.[33] It has been held that a person owning salmon fishings and the land adjacent to them was entitled not only to repair the bank of the river in which his fishings were situated but to raise it higher in order to strengthen it notwithstanding that it had the incidental effect of improving his fishings.[34]

Relationship of the right of salmon fishing with other rights

This section considers the interaction of the right of salmon fishing with the rights of others either generally or in relation to particular operations.

Landownership: As noted above, the right to salmon fishing is entirely separate from the ownership of land. Consequently, the owner of land on either or both sides of a salmon river may not own the salmon fishings and the owner of salmon fishings may not own any land adjacent to the waters in which he has the right to fish. Indeed, it is quite common for the owner of salmon fishings to own no land adjacent to his fishings, but as noted above, he can have access to the water through land belonging to other landowners and will be entitled to fish from either side of the water.

Obstructions: The erection of artificial obstructions in a river to the prejudice of salmon fishings may be objected to by the proprietor of those fishings whether they are above or below the fishings.[35] Any such obstruction must, however, be material. The construction and alteration of dams, lades, etc, is regulated under

---

[28] *Campbell* v *Muir* 1908 SC 387.

[29] *Stair Memorial Encyclopaedia*, Vol. 11, para. 8; Gordon, op. cit., n. 14, para. 8–76.

[30] See *Berry* v *Wilson* (1841) 4 D 139.

[31] *Miller* v *Blair* (1825) 4 S 214 (NE 217); *Lord Advocate* v *Sharp* (1878) 6 R 108; *Middletweed* v *Murray* 1989 SLT 11.

[32] See cases cited ibid.

[33] *Mackinnon* v *Ellis* (1878) 5 R 832.

[34] *Duke of Sutherland* v *Ross* (1878) 5 R (HL) 137.

[35] *Colquhoun* v *Duke of Montrose* (1804) Mor 14283.

statute,[36] although construction of certain Hydro-Electricity installations are exempt from the relevant controls.[37] However, in terms of the Electricity Act 1989, certain obligations are imposed in relation to the preservation of, *inter alia*, fisheries in Scotland.[38]

Pollution: Proprietors of salmon fishings have rights against those who discharge pollutants into the water in the same way as other users of the water and may bring an appropriate action at common law if the fishings are harmed by such pollution.[39] It is not necessary for the proprietor to show that the pollution occurred within his own fishings; it is sufficient if, for example, spawning beds in another part of the river are harmed by pollution there.[40] There are also statutory controls on water pollution: these are discussed further in Chapter 4, to which reference should be made.

Abstraction of water: A riparian proprietor is not entitled to abstract water so as to alter the quality of the water or the strength of the current to the prejudice of salmon fishings.[41] Landowners have the right to draw water for domestic or agricultural use and to provide water for cattle, and may use or allow others to use waterways for recreational purposes but not, it is thought, to the material prejudice of salmon fishing rights owned by others.[42]

Navigation: The right of salmon fishing is inferior to the public right of navigation, and so the right of salmon fishing must not be exercised in such a way as to interfere with it,[43] although the right of navigation is not so absolute that it may be exercised oppressively. The inter-relation of the two rights was discussed at length in the case of *Will's Trs v Cairngorm Canoeing and Sailing School Ltd*.[44] The pursuers owned both banks of the River Spey at Knockando, the riverbed and the salmon fishings in that stretch of the river. The salmon fishings were described as being among the best in Scotland and were of great value. The defenders operated a training school for canoeing and sailing. The Court of Session held that there had been established a public right of navigation in that part of the river, but of a strictly limited character in respect of the recreational use of the river for the purpose of canoeing by members of the public who could obtain access to its waters. However, on appeal to the House of Lords, it was held that the Spey was subject to a public right of navigation and not to some more limited right and that use for recreation was as effective as use for transporting goods or other commercial purposes in proving such a right of navigation. It was further

---

[36] See the Salmon (Fish Passes and Screens) (Scotland) Regulations 1994 (SI 1994/2524). These Regulations are in effect for most of the works specified therein, but are not yet in effect for some others. They will, however, come into effect for such works on January 1, 2000.

[37] Salmon (Fish Passes and Screens) (Scotland) Regulations 1994, reg. 4.

[38] Electricity Act 1989, s. 38 and Sched. 9.

[39] See, eg, *Countess of Seafield v Kemp* (1899) 1 F 402.

[40] *Moncrieff v Perth Police Commissioners* (1886) 13 R 921.

[41] *Young & Co. v Bankier Distillery Co.* (1893) 20 R (HL) 76; *Ross v Powrie and Pitcaithley* (1891) 19 R 314; *Moncrieffe v Perth Police Commissioners*, ibid.

[42] See Gordon, op. cit., n. 14, paras 7–21 and 7–23.

[43] *Will's Trs v Cairngorm Canoeing and Sailing School Ltd* 1976 SC (HL) 30.

[44] Ibid.

held that where there was a public right of navigation, evidence as to damage to, or disturbance of, the fish was irrelevant.

Neighbouring fishing proprietors: The proprietor of salmon fishings is entitled to object to the use of illegal methods of fishing by anyone in another proprietor's fishings to the prejudice of his own, but not to the use of legal methods.[45] Consequently, a proprietor of salmon fishings who is prejudiced by the netting of salmon in the sea cannot object where such a method is legal. A landowner who owns one bank of the river and the salmon fishings in the whole of the river is probably not entitled to fish from the opposite bank without the permission of its owner. As noted above, if salmon fishings are owned up to the *medium filum* (the mid-line) of the river, each proprietor may fish from his own bank or wade out or row his boat as far as the *medium filum* and cast out into his neighbour's waters as far as he can from there.[46] What often happens in practice, however, is that the owners agree that salmon fishing rights over the whole width of the river are exercised on alternate days. If the owners cannot agree, the court may be asked to determine the rights of the parties in the circumstances. The inter-relation of salmon fishing and brown trout fishing have already been discussed above.

Statutory regulation

From as early as the fourteenth century, salmon fisheries have been subject to statutory regulation and numerous statutes passed by the original Scottish Parliament reflected a practical appreciation of the importance and commercial value of Scottish salmon fisheries.[47] The objectives of the legislation were, first, to ensure that salmon had unimpeded access to their natural spawning grounds; second, to allow the unimpeded return to the sea of smolts and kelts; and, third, to prohibit the killing of salmon out of season. Much of the old legisla-tion has now been repealed and replaced with modern legislation, principally in the form of the 1986 Act, although in essence it retains, with some additions, the basic format of administration of salmon fisheries established by the previous legislation. The main aspects of the modern regulatory regime may now be examined.

District Salmon Fisheries Boards: With one exception, the administration of salmon fisheries in Scotland is carried out by reference to salmon fishery districts, which are administered by District Salmon Fisheries Boards.[48] District Salmon Fisheries

---

[45] See Gordon, above, n. 14, para. 8–83; *Mackenzie v Gilchrist* (1829) 7 S 297.

[46] *Fotheringham v Passmore* 1986 SC (HL) 96.

[47] For a review of these statutes, see *Kintore Forbes* (1826) 4 S 641; see also *Anderson v Anderson* (1867) 6 M 117 at 119.

[48] The exception is the River Tweed. The Tweed is not a salmon fishery district except as otherwise provided in the 1986 Act (see 1986 Act, s. 1(5)) and the administration of salmon fisheries is carried out by the River Tweed Council on behalf of the River Tweed Commissioners: 1969 Act, s. 6(1). The powers and duties of the commissioners, which are vested in the Council and are set out mainly in the 1857 Act, are much the same as those of District Salmon Fishery Boards described below: for a more detailed description, see *Stair Memorial Encyclopaedia*, Vol. 11, para. 41. As noted above, the River Esk is regulated under the English Salmon Fisheries Acts and is not therefore included here. The current salmon fishery districts are based on those established under previous legislation.

Boards in their current form were set up under the 1986 Act which was passed, *inter alia*, to make fresh provision for the local administration of salmon fisheries. A District Salmon Fisheries Board under the 1986 Act takes the form of an association of the proprietors of the salmon fishings in the district, who elect a committee which becomes the Board. The Board comprises elected representatives of "upper" and "lower" proprietors qualified by entry of their fishings on the Valuation Roll, co-opted representatives of salmon anglers and tenant netsmen, and a Chairman, who is also elected. The purpose of District Salmon Fisheries Boards is to protect or improve salmon fisheries within their district,[49] and Boards have powers to do such acts, execute such works and incur such expenses as they think expedient for the protection or improvement of fisheries within their district, the increase of salmon or the stocking of the waters within their district with salmon.[50] Boards have financial powers, including the power to levy fishery assessments and to authorise expenditure, including expenditure for the purpose of acquiring heritable property, which has allowed Boards to purchase the fishing rights of lower proprietors in order to stop netting.[51] The general powers of the Boards provide for the increase of salmon and the stocking of waters with salmon fry.[52] The Board may apply to the Minister for variation of the annual close times and for specification of baits and lures for rod and line fishing[53] and they may appoint water bailiffs[54] who have statutory powers. The position of the Boards may be contrasted with that of Angling Associations, which perform similar functions but have no statutory powers or authority: any bailiffs or others appointed by such Angling Associations, for example, have no statutory powers of search, seizure or arrest such as those held by bailiffs appointed by District Salmon Fisheries Boards.

Criminal law: Almost all of the provisions of the statutes regulating salmon fishing rely on the criminal law for enforcement. Criminal penalties may include forfeiture of fish illegally caught and of equipment, vehicles and boats illegally used. As well as the specific statutory penalties, common law crimes such as theft may be relevant, and may allow for greater sentences where appropriate, for example where there has been serious poaching. The specific statutory provisions are built on the principles of conservation and protection, and accordingly provide for close times when fishing is not allowed: these provisions are also enforced by criminal penalties and are discussed further below. The principal statutory offences are:

    (i) It is an offence to take salmon without legal right or written permission.[55]

---

49 1986 Act, s. 14(1).
50 1986 Act, s. 16.
51 1986 Act, s. 15. In relation to fisheries assessments, see *Cormack* v *Crown Estate Commissioners* 1985 SLT (HL) 426, a case under the 1868 Act.
52 1986 Act, s. 16(1).
53 1986 Act, ss 6(4)(a) and 8(2)(a).
54 1986 Act, s. 16(3)(b).
55 1951 Act, s. 1, as amended.

(ii) It is an offence to fish for or take salmon in any inland water other than by rod and line or net and coble, subject to certain minor exceptions.[56]

(iii) It is an offence to use any explosive substance or to put any poison or other noxious substance in or near waters for the purpose of taking or destroying fish, or to use any electrical device for these purposes.[57]

(iv) It is an offence for any person other than a water bailiff, a police constable, a person authorised by the Minister or the District Salmon Fisheries Board or the owner or an agent of the owner of the salmon fishings to take any dead salmon or sea trout from any waters.[58]

(v) It is an offence to possess salmon or any instrument, explosive, poison or other noxious substance which could be used to take salmon or trout in circumstances affording reasonable grounds for suspicion that possession of it has been obtained as a result of, or for the purposes of, committing certain offences relating to illegal fishing.[59] It is also an offence to be in possession of salmon where it is believed, or there are circumstances in which it would be reasonable to suspect, that a relevant offence had at any time been committed in relation to the salmon.[60] The effect of this is that there is a completed offence whenever a person is found in possession of a salmon and he believes that a relevant offence has been committed in relation to it or there are surrounding circumstances from which it would be reasonable to suspect this. Surrounding circumstances giving rise to suspicion of a relevant offence could include the sale of the fish at well below market price or in what have come to be known as "back door deals", or marks on the fish indicating foul hooking or the use of other illegal instruments or types of net.

(vi) It is an offence to attempt to commit, or to do any act preparatory to the commission of, an offence.[61]

(vii) It is an offence to wilfully take, fish for or have in possession an unclean or unseasonable salmon.[62] An unclean salmon is one which has spawned, ie a kelt,[63] which is notable for its poor condition and elongated appearance; it has been held that a salmon which is very near to spawning is not unclean,[64] but in the case of *Brady* v *Barbour (No. 2)*,[65] it was held that a salmon which was near to spawning could be considered unseasonable. Baggots are also unseasonable salmon.[66]

---

[56] 1951 Act, s. 2(1). Methods of capture of salmon are discussed further above.
[57] 1951 Act, s. 4.
[58] 1951 Act, s. 6.
[59] 1951 Act, s. 7. A conviction may be obtained on the evidence of one witness.
[60] 1951 Act, s. 7A.
[61] 1951 Act, s. 8.
[62] 1868 Act, s. 20, as amended.
[63] *Nixon* v *White* 1958 SLT (Sh Ct) 38.
[64] Ibid.
[65] 1995 SLT 520; see also D. MacLeod, "The Unseasonable Salmon", 1995 JLSS 106.
[66] See Scott Robinson, op. cit., n. 25, at p. 148.

It may be difficult to distinguish a fish very near to spawning or a baggot from a fresh fish, and the evidence of an experienced local fisherman is generally relied on in this respect. The offence is independent of the close times,[67] but it is a defence to show that the fish in question was/were caught accidentally and immediately returned to the water with the least possible injury.[68]

Where two or more persons acting together do any act which would constitute an offence under section 1 or 2 of the 1951 Act, each such person is guilty of the offence and liable to the appropriate fine or imprisonment.[69] Furthermore, as noted above, on conviction of certain offences, the court may order forfeiture of any fish illegally caught and any equipment, vehicles and boats used in the commission of the offence.[70] Certain acts which would otherwise be illegal are permitted if done for scientific or other specified purposes and after receipt of the appropriate written permission, or where they are exempted by the Minister.[71] Fish farms are excepted from many of the provisions.[72]

Close times: As noted above, there are annual and weekly close times. With respect to the annual close times, in the River Tweed, the annual close time for nets is 153 days from September 14 to the following February 15; fishing by rod and line with an artificial fly only is permitted within that time for the periods from September 15 to November 30 and from February 1–14.[73] In relation to other salmon fisheries, the annual close time is a minimum period of 168 days, and in relation to each salmon fishery district is either specified in a designation order made under section 6 of the 1986 Act or, where no such order has been made, is that which was in force prior to January 7, 1987 in relation to the old district which had the same coastal limits as the salmon fishery district in question.[74] The annual close time may, subject to the 168-day limit, be varied by order on application of the District Salmon Fisheries Board.[75] In general, the annual close time is during the winter months at the turn of the year, when most salmon in the rivers at that time have reached the spawning redds. It is an offence to fish for or take salmon during the annual close time,[76] and there are a variety of other offences which may be committed in connection with the annual close time.[77]

With respect to the weekly close time, this extends from 6 p.m. on Friday to 6 a.m. on Monday.[78] Within that period, fishing by rod and line is permitted during Friday, Saturday and Monday, but no fishing is permitted on Sunday.[79] Fishing

---

[67] These are discussed further below.
[68] 1868 Act, s. 20.
[69] 1951 Act, s. 3.
[70] See the 1868 Act, ss 15, 18, 20, 21 and 23 and the 1951 Act, ss 1 and 19.
[71] See the 1951 Act, s. 9, as amended, and the 1986 Act, ss 27 and 28.
[72] As noted above, fish farms are not included within the scope of this chapter.
[73] 1859 Act, s. 6.
[74] 1986 Act, s. 6.
[75] Ibid.
[76] In relation to the Tweed, see the 1859 Act, s. 6; for other salmon fisheries, see the 1868 Act, s. 15.
[77] In relation to the Tweed, see, eg, the 1859 Act, s. 11; for other salmon fisheries, see, eg, the 1986 Act, ss 21, 22, 23 and 41 and the 1976 Act, s. 6 and Sched. 2.
[78] 1951 Act, s. 13, as amended.
[79] Ibid.

for or taking salmon on a Sunday, or fishing for or taking salmon on any other day during the weekly close period other than by rod and line is an offence.[80] These provisions apply equally to the Tweed as to other salmon fisheries.[81]

Protection orders: Protection orders are orders made under the 1976 Act by statutory instrument in relation to specified rivers and waterways and are designed to preserve, enhance and improve the stock of freshwater fish other than salmon within the waters affected by the order. A number of the principal salmon rivers are affected by protection orders, including the Tweed, the Spey and the Tay and their associated tributaries. Protection orders provide an effective procedure for protection of certain freshwater fisheries against the depredations of poachers and others having no legal right to fish in the waters, and although they are designed to protect freshwater fish other than salmon, they have a beneficial effect on salmon fishings also. This is because in practical terms, all persons wishing to fish for any type of fish in the area affected by the order must have written permission to do so and the protection order may prescribe any charges which may be imposed for fishing; permitted methods of fishing and tackle; the maximum number of fish that may be caught; the maximum permitted number of rods; the minimum permitted size of fish which may be taken; the number of persons permitted to fish who are not either owners, lessees or other occupiers having a right to fish in the waters or members of any club which is such an owner, occupier or lessee; and any other relevant matter. Protection orders are discussed further below in relation to freshwater fishing.

Current issues affecting salmon

Reference has already been made to the decline in numbers of salmon caught by rod and line. This, together with the rapid decline of the numbers of sea trout in certain west coast rivers in Scotland, prompted the appointment of the Scottish Salmon Strategy Task Force (hereafter "the Task Force") which produced its report on January 23, 1997. The aim of the Task Force was to make recommendations to maintain and improve wild salmon fisheries for the economic and social benefit of Scotland by increasing salmon abundance and conserving the diversity of salmon populations. In relation to the administration of salmon fisheries, it recommended that 20 new salmon fishery areas should be designated to replace the existing salmon fishery districts, each with an Area Fishery Board, and that each Area Fishery Board should have a number of nominated representatives who would put forward views relating to activities such as agriculture, forestry, hydro-electric power generation, fish farming and recreation as appropriate to local circumstances. It also recommended that Area Fishery Boards should receive grant aid to ensure that they could obtain any necessary professional and scientific management expertise. In relation to the management and regulation of fisheries, it recommended that fisheries should be progressively restricted to locations as close as possible to the rivers of origin of the wild fish; the ban on drift netting for salmon in Scottish waters should be maintained and

---

[80] Ibid. See also the 1868 Act, s. 24 which makes it an offence to fail to comply with weekly close time byelaws in relation to fixed nets.

[81] The offence contained in the 1868 Act, s. 24, described ibid, does not, however, apply to the Tweed.

all net fisheries outside estuary limits and net and coble fisheries above head of tide should be registered, only those so registered being permitted to continue operating. In relation to conservation, it recommended that tight control should be maintained over sources of pollution, and that the Forestry Authority should consult Area Fisheries Boards on all applications for planting, re-planting and felling, since forestry operations near rivers, particularly spawning redds, have proved to be particularly damaging. In relation to fish farming, it recommended that fish farmers should continue to adopt husbandry techniques reducing levels of disease, and that levels of sea lice infestation on salmon in fish farms should be reduced. Many believe that the proliferation of sea lice is the main cause of the reduction in numbers of sea trout in west coast rivers. The recommendations of the Task Force are currently under consideration.

The other major issue currently affecting salmon is the possible introduction of National Parks in Scotland. A Consultation Paper was produced in 1998[82] and the response in favour of the introduction of National Parks in Scotland was overwhelming. Legislation by the Scottish Parliament is likely to be forthcoming in the near future, and there will obviously be implications for fisheries situated within the boundaries of such National Parks. One area proposed as a National Park is Loch Lomond and the Trossachs. Salmon, sea trout, brown trout and other freshwater fish are all found in Loch Lomond. A recent study by scientists at Glasgow University[83] has found that the use of power boats on Loch Lomond has increased considerably and that as a result, pollution levels from spilled fuel has created problems for other water users, including those for whom the loch is a source of supply of drinking water. The study also concluded that the relative numbers of fishing boats, wind surfers and canoes have significantly decreased while the use of speed boats and jet skis has significantly increased. In relation to Loch Lomond, therefore, and in relation to any other proposed National Parks where fishing rights are relevant, the regulation of fishing rights and the way they interact with these other water users is a matter which may require attention in the proposed new legislation.

Sea trout

Definition

A sea trout is a migratory brown trout. For most legal and practical purposes, it falls within the definition of salmon.[84] In the case of *Lord Advocate* v *Balfour*,[85] Lord Johnston was "inclined to think" that sea trout were included in the definition of salmon.[86] What is certain is that they have in common with salmon the characteristics of breeding in fresh water and migrating to the sea. The 1862 Act included sea trout in the definition of salmon[87] and likewise the 1986 Act

---

[82] National Parks in Scotland, September 1998.
[83] "The Impact of Boat Engine Emissions on the Water Quality of Loch Lomond" by Mark Bannan and Colin Adams.
[84] Discussed above.
[85] 1907 SC 1360.
[86] Ibid at 1363.
[87] 1862 Act, s. 2.

defines salmon as meaning "all migratory fish of the species *salmo salar* and *salmo trutta* and commonly known as salmon and sea trout respectively or any part of such fish",[88] while the 1951 Act has a similar definition, except that it uses the word "includes" rather than "means".

The life cycle of sea trout is similar to that of salmon, but the migration of sea trout to the sea is over a much shorter distance than that of salmon. Sea trout which return to their native river to spawn during the same year they migrate are known as finnock and are generally smaller than those which stay at sea for a longer period. Like salmon, they may return to the sea after spawning and, although many do not survive, they can, like salmon, return to fresh water for spawning during several successive seasons.

The right to fish for sea trout

As the definition of salmon includes for most purposes sea trout and other migratory fish, the right to fish for sea trout is governed by the same rules as for salmon, discussed above.

Method and time of capture for sea trout

As the statutory definition of salmon includes for most purposes sea trout and other migratory fish, the statutory rules governing the method and time of capture for sea trout are the same as for salmon, described above. It must be noted, however, that the tackle and tactics used for catching sea trout can be similar to that used for catching brown trout.[89] Where the same fishing method can be used equally for catching brown trout, sea trout and grilse, therefore, it may be difficult to prove that a person equipped for fishing for brown trout and having the permission of the landowner to do so was really fishing for sea trout or grilse. Clearly, however, a person who catches sea trout or salmon when fishing for brown trout and who does not have a legal right or written permission to do so should return the same immediately to the water unharmed, otherwise they will not only infringe the rights of the salmon fishing proprietor but may commit a criminal offence.[90]

The extent of the right to fish and rights incidental to the right of sea trout fishing

As the definition of salmon includes for most purposes sea trout and other migratory fish, it is thought that the extent of the right to fish and the rights incidental to sea trout fishing are the same as in relation to salmon fishing, described above. Rights of access to water may be particularly important for sea trout fishing which, when fishing is by rod and line, is commonly done at night.

Relationship of the right of sea trout fishing with other rights

The position here is believed to be broadly the same as in relation to the right of salmon fishing, described above.

---

[88] 1986 Act, s. 40(1).

[89] See below.

[90] Criminal offences in relation to salmon are discussed above; since the statutory definition of salmon includes sea trout, as discussed, they apply equally to sea trout.

Statutory regulation

As the statutory definition of salmon includes for most purposes sea trout and other migratory fish, the statutory regulation of sea trout fishing is in all material respects the same as that for salmon fishing, described above.

Current issues affecting sea trout

The principal issue affecting sea trout is maintenance of sea trout numbers, but the problems of sea trout in this respect differ somewhat from those of salmon.[91] In particular, the stocks of sea trout in the west coast rivers in Scotland have in recent years been very badly affected. Various reasons have been given for this, including over-fishing of sand eels, believed to be a major food source for sea trout while at sea; proliferation of sea lice attracted to moored sea cages in which farmed salmon are reared which then attack wild fish; climatic change involving a rise in sea temperature; drift netting on the high seas and an increase in the number of common seals, cormorants and other natural predators. A combination of these factors may be relevant and research is continuing.

Brown trout and other freshwater fish

Definition

Freshwater fish normally found in Scottish waters include brown trout, char,[92] pike, grayling, perch and numerous other lesser known species. Rainbow trout are also found, although they are not natural to Scottish waters but were introduced some time ago from America; they are nonetheless prolific and, although occurring in rivers and streams, are usually reared in hatcheries for stocking ponds, stanks and other artificial waterways for sporting purposes. Only brown trout and rainbow trout are sought after for human consumption and are consequently referred to, like salmon and sea trout, as game fish, other freshwater fish generally being referred to as coarse fish. Rainbow trout do not spawn in still water and have only rarely been found to spawn in Scottish river systems. Brown trout, however, spawn like salmon in the autumn and winter months and the eggs develop over the winter. They do not, however, migrate from their native river, although they may travel considerable distances up and down the river system. Freshwater fish are defined in the 1951 and 1976 Acts as "fish living in fresh water including trout, eels and the fry of eels but exclusive of salmon and of any kind of fish which migrate between the open sea and tidal waters".[93] The 1951 Act defines trout as "non-migratory trout of the species *salmo trutta* living in fresh waters or estuaries",[94] while the 1902 Act refers to the common trout *salmo fario*[95] and the 1933 Act defines trout as "trout other than rainbow trout or migratory trout known as sea trout, bull

---

[91] The position of salmon in this respect is discussed above.

[92] Found in some Highland lochs.

[93] 1951 Act, s. 24(1); 1976 Act, s. 9(1), which refers back to the definition of freshwater fish in the 1951 Act.

[94] 1951 Act, s. 24(1).

[95] 1902 Act, s. 1.

trout or by any other local name".[96] *Salmo trutta* and *salmo fario* are not different species of fish: the name simply reflects changing scientific nomenclature.[97]

Trout and other freshwater fish are, like all wild animals, *res nullius*, that is, they belong to no one until they are captured. Trout or other fish enclosed in a fishpond, stank or other artificial waterway, however, are the property of the person with the right thereto[98] and the taking of such fish would constitute theft. Whether the unauthorised removal of fish from a river or stream which has been artificially stocked would constitute theft does not yet appear to have been decided.[99]

The right to fish for brown trout and other freshwater fish

As noted above, wild trout and other freshwater fish belong to no one until they are captured. The legal right to take such trout or other fish, however, belongs to the proprietor of the land which is adjacent to the river, stream or loch in which the fish are found. The right of trout fishing, unlike the right of salmon fishing, is not a separate estate in land, but is "an incident to the right of property".[100] It follows from this fact that in relation to private waters, only the proprietor of the land adjacent to the relevant waters or those authorised by him have the right to fish for such fish; there is no public right to fish for such fish in private waters and even where members of the public have a right of access to or along the bank or banks of such waters, they do not have the right to fish for and catch trout.[101] The protection of the landowner's right, however, except where the water is subject to a protection order (discussed further below), depends on the law of trespass: in other words, the only remedy open to the landowner against unauthorised fisherman is to take the appropriate civil action for trespass.[102] It was confirmed in the case of *Arthur v Aird*[103] that no one has any right to trespass on the lands of another for the purpose of fishing; no one, even if he is lawfully on the bank of a river or loch, has a (public) right to fish therein; and members of the public, having neither title nor right, cannot establish a right to fish by usage for however long a period. In practice, however, it may be difficult to stop unauthorised fishermen.[104] There is a public right to fish for brown trout in the tidal reaches of a river or sea loch[105]; the tide must ebb and flow at the point at which the right is claimed,[106] but since brown trout are non-migratory, it is perhaps doubtful whether they would be found in such waters. An agricultural tenant does not, in the absence of express provision, have the right to fish for

---

[96] 1933 Act, s. 3.

[97] See *Stair Memorial Encyclopaedia*, Vol. 11, para. 47.

[98] *Copland v Maxwell* (1871) 9 M (HL) 1.

[99] Lord Jauncey, *Fishing in Scotland—The Law for the Angler* takes the view that it would constitute theft.

[100] *Maxwell v Copland* (1868) 7 M 142, per Lord Neaves at 149.

[101] *Ferguson v Shirreff* (1844) 6 D 1363; see also *Lennox v Keith* 1993 GWD 30–1913, OH.

[102] See further Chap. 12.

[103] 1907 SC 1170.

[104] For a discussion of the difficulties with the law of trespass in the context of access, where the issues are not dissimilar, see Chap. 12.

[105] See *Bowie v Marquis of Ailsa* (1887) 14 R 649; *Grant v Henry* (1894) 21 R 358; *Nicol v Blaikie* (1859) 22 D 335.

[106] *Bowie v Marquis of Ailsa* (1887) 14 R 649.

trout or other freshwater fish within the boundaries of his farm even although he has the right to use the waters concerned for normal agricultural purposes.

Although the right to trout fishing or other freshwater fishing is not a separate estate in the land, it is now possible to create a lease of such fishings which will be binding on future owners of the land. Such a lease must, in order to be so binding, be in writing, for a consideration and for a period of not less than one year.[107]

Method and time of capture of trout and other freshwater fish

With regard to the method of capturing trout and other freshwater fish, in inland waters, the only legal method of fishing for trout is by rod and line, except that netting is permitted in a pond where all the proprietors are agreed and a proprietor or occupier having a right of freshwater fishing may take any freshwater fish other than trout by means of a net or trap.[108]

With regard to the time of capture of such fish, there is an annual close time for trout which runs from October 7 to March 15 in the following year.[109] Fishing for or taking such fish during the annual close time is an offence,[110] and there are certain other offences which may be committed in connection with the annual close time.[111] There is no weekly close time.

The extent of the right to fish and rights incidental to the right of trout and other freshwater fishing

With respect to the extent of the right to fish, as noted above, the right to fish for brown trout is not a separate estate in land and cannot be owned separately from heritage; it is an incident of property and although the right can be leased, the proprietor cannot otherwise be deprived of his rights of brown trout fishing on any waters passing through or adjacent to his land. Where waters run between the lands of different proprietors, each has the right to fish from his own bank, and probably to wade out or row his boat as far as the *medium filum* and cast out into his neighbour's waters as far as he can from there.[112] Where a loch is surrounded entirely by the land of one proprietor, he will have exclusive rights to fish for brown trout in the whole loch (unless the salmon fishings in the loch are owned separately, since the right of salmon fishing includes a right of brown trout fishing) and may fish anywhere from the banks or over the whole loch; where it is surrounded by the land of more than one proprietor, the presumption is that each has a common right of fishing in the entire loch,[113] and all proprietors have a right to sail and fish over the whole loch. The court may intervene, however, if the fishing rights of one proprietor are being exercised to the detriment of others. As discussed above in relation to salmon fishing, the right of salmon fishing includes a right of brown trout fishing, but this does not deprive the

---

[107] 1976 Act, s. 4.

[108] 1951 Act, s. 2(2).

[109] 1902 Act, s. 1, as amended, which applies to common trout, *salmo fario* (otherwise known as brown trout or *salmo trutta* which are different names for the same species).

[110] Ibid. There are certain limited defences provided in the section.

[111] See the 1933 Act, s. 2.

[112] *Fotheringham* v *Passmore* 1986 SC (HL) 96, discussed above in relation to salmon fishings: the same approach is likely to apply in relation to trout fishings.

[113] *Macdonald* v *Farquharson* (1836) 15 S 259.

landowner of his implied right to fish for brown trout, although the right of trout fishing is the inferior right and must therefore be exercised in such a way as not to interfere with the superior right of salmon fishing.

With respect to the rights incidental to the right of trout and other freshwater fishing, this does not generally arise since the right to fish is an incident of the landowner's own property and therefore questions such as access do not generally arise. It should be noted, however, that in respect of waters which cannot be wholly fished without recourse to a boat, a right to fish from a boat is implied.

Relationship of the right to fish for trout and other freshwater fish with other rights

The issue of the relationship of the right to fish for trout and other freshwater fish with other rights does not generally arise, since the right is an incident of the landowner's own property and there is limited interaction between the right and other rights. The interaction of the right to fish for trout and other freshwater fish with rights of salmon fishing and neighbouring fishing proprietors generally has already been described.[114]

Statutory regulation

There is considerably less statutory regulation of trout and other freshwater fishing than there is in relation to salmon and sea trout. The principal provisions are found in the 1902, 1933, 1951 and 1976 Acts. The main aspects of the regulatory regime, such as it is, may now be examined.

Criminal law: Like the statutory provisions relating to salmon and sea trout fishing, many of those relating to trout and other freshwater fishing rely on the criminal law for enforcement, and indeed a number of the offences relating to trout and other freshwater fishing are the same as or similar to those relating to salmon and sea trout fishing. The principal statutory offences are:

(i) It is an offence to fish for or take freshwater fish in any inland water other than by rod and line, subject to certain exceptions.[115]

(ii) It is an offence to use any explosive substance or to put any poison or other noxious substance in or near waters for the purpose of taking or destroying fish, or to use any electrical device for these purposes.[116]

(iii) It is an offence to possess non-migratory trout or any instrument, explosive, poison or other noxious substance which could be used to take salmon or trout in circumstances affording reasonable grounds for suspicion that possession of it has been obtained as a result of, or for the purposes of, committing certain offences relating to illegal fishing.[117]

(iv) It is an offence to fish for or take trout during the annual close time.[118]

---

[114] See preceding paragraph and, in relation to salmon fishing, further above.

[115] 1951 Act, s. 2(2). Methods of capture of trout and other freshwater fish are discussed further above.

[116] 1951 Act, s. 4.

[117] 1951 Act, s. 7. A conviction may be obtained on the evidence of one witness.

[118] Ibid. There are certain limited defences provided in the section. Those times are discussed further above.

Where two or more persons acting together do any act which would constitute an offence under section 2 of the 1951 Act, each such person is guilty of the offence and liable to the appropriate fine or imprisonment.[119] Furthermore, on conviction of certain offences, the court may order forfeiture of any fish illegally caught and any equipment, vehicles and boats used in the commission of the offence.[120] Certain acts which would otherwise be illegal are permitted if done for scientific or other specified purposes and after receipt of the appropriate written permission, or where they are exempted by the Minister.[121] Fish farms are excepted from many of the provisions.[122]

There are also a number of offences connected with protection orders under the 1976 Act, which are discussed further below.

Close times: Close times are discussed above in relation to method and time of capture.

Protection orders: As noted above in relation to salmon fisheries, protection orders are orders made under the 1976 Act by statutory instrument in relation to specified rivers and waterways and are designed to preserve, enhance and improve the stock of freshwater fish other than salmon within the waters affected by the order. Where a protection order is in force, in practical terms, all persons wishing to fish for any type of fish in the area affected by the order must have written permission to do so and the protection order may make provision for a variety of matters.[123] Protection orders are reinforced by the criminal law: where a protection order is in force, for example, it is an offence to fish for or take fish in the waters covered by the order without legal right or written permission from the person having such right[124] and it is also an offence to contravene any prohibition in the order, to attempt to commit such an offence or to do any act preparatory to the commission of such an offence.[125]

Current issues affecting brown trout and other freshwater fish

The maintenance of the population of brown trout and other freshwater fish is currently an important issue. In areas where brown trout have become scarce, stocks can be replenished by fry produced from eggs reared in hatcheries under strict supervision. The maintenance of clean water is important in maintaining and enhancing the population of brown trout and other freshwater fish. Other environmental factors which specifically affect migratory fish, such as coastal netting and the availability of food resources in the seas, are not relevant to such fish, but the chemical instability of some waters brought about by the seepage of fertilisers from adjacent land and the insufficiency of water purification systems has caused problems to certain brown trout fisheries, most notably Loch Leven

---

[119] 1951 Act, s. 3.
[120] See the 1951 Act, s. 19.
[121] See the 1951 Act, s. 9 as amended.
[122] As noted above, fish farms are not included within the scope of this chapter.
[123] See discussion above in relation to salmon fishing.
[124] 1976 Act, s. 1.
[125] Ibid.

in Fife. Pollution control in relation to water generally is discussed further in Chapter 4, to which further reference should be made.

The adequacy or otherwise of fish stocks in fresh water has a knock on effect on other endangered species such as the osprey which has been successfully reintroduced in Scotland in recent years and which feeds on wild fish. Reintroduction of other scarce and locally extinct species such as otter, sea eagles and beavers has also recently been considered.

CHAPTER 10

THE PROTECTION OF SPECIES

Kathryn Last

Introduction

Protection for species has evolved over a considerable period of time.[1] Its origins are in the game laws which provide close seasons and restrictions on the persons who can take species that are considered to be valuable.[2] Modern UK species protection is founded on the nineteenth-century legislation which was designed to prevent cruelty and excessive collecting.[3] Domestic animals received protection from cruelty as early as 1822,[4] however the first protection for wild-life was the Sea Birds Preservation Act 1869.[5] Birds were the first wild creatures to be protected, primarily due to public outrage at the slaughter of birds at Flamborough Head. Statutory protection was only extended to wild animals[6]

---

[1] For general discussions of the history of protection see: Sheail, *Nature In Trust: The History of Nature Conservation in Great Britain* (London, 1976); Evans, *A History of Nature Conservation in Britain* (London, 1992); and Lowe, "Values and Institutions in the History of British Nature Conservation", Chap. 19 in Warren and Goldsmith (eds), *Conservation in Perspective* (London, 1983).

[2] Some examples of 15th-century measures are discussed in Reid, *Nature Conservation Law* (Edinburgh, 1994), p. 3. These laws were, however, designed to protect the position of the landowner rather than the species.

[3] See Turner, *Reckoning With the Beast: Animals, Pain and Humanity in the Victorian Mind* (London, 1980); and Allen, *The Victorian Fern Craze: A History of Pteridomania* (London, 1969). Some collecting was considered acceptable: "much foolish clamour and senseless abuse is often directed against ornithologists, whose greatest ambition is to add some new bird to the British list, for shooting the rarest birds as soon as they see them. The charge may be true, but the offence is, on the whole, excusable. If a vulture is foolish enough to perch on the rocks in Cork Harbour, as one did in 1843, it must expect to be shot and placed in a museum" (Russell, "The Protection of Wild Birds" (1897) 42 *The Nineteenth Century*, p. 616).

[4] An Act to Prevent the Cruel and Improper Treatment of Cattle, 1822.

[5] For a discussion of this and subsequent legislation to protect wild birds see Russell, op. cit., n. 3, pp. 614–622.

[6] Seals were protected earlier than all other animals. The Grey Seals (Protection) Act 1914 introduced a close season to prevent over-exploitation.

and plants[7] in the Conservation of Wild Creatures and Wild Plants Act 1975, when the ecological importance of protecting them came to be recognised.[8] The approach taken more recently has been influenced by developments at the European and international level, particularly the Bonn Convention,[9] the Berne Convention,[10] the EC Birds Directive[11] and the EC Habitats Directive.[12] It is such developments that are increasingly providing the impetus for change.

Due to their rather piecemeal development, the current provisions for the law on species protection have no unifying objective. Some are designed to prevent cruelty, some to restrict collecting, while others focus on the maintenance of biodiversity. The focus of this chapter is to consider the laws relating to species protection in Scotland. It is, however, important to recognise that species protection alone cannot guarantee the maintenance of biodiversity. Valuable as the provisions for species protection undoubtedly are, the ultimate protection for species, and in turn biodiversity, lies in the protection of habitat.[13] The integration of species and habitat protection is an essential component of the UK Biodiversity Action Plan 1994.[14] Scottish Natural Heritage (SNH) is responsible for promoting biodiversity in Scotland in accordance with this plan, and the Biodiversity Steering Group, of which SNH is a member,[15] has now developed a number of species action programmes to ensure the long-term survival of certain native

---

[7] See Allen, *The Early History of Plant Conservation in Britain* (1980) 34, Proceedings of Leicester Literary and Philosophical Society; and Horwood, "The State Protection of Wild Plants" (1913) 7 *Science Progress*, pp. 629–637.

[8] See Royal Society, *The Scientific Aspects of Nature Conservation in Great Britain* (London, 1977); and *Hansard*, HC, Vol. 884, January 24, 1975, col. 2123.

[9] Convention on the Conservation of Migratory Species of Wild Animals 1979, HMSO Treaty Series No. 87, Cm. 1332 (1990). The Bonn Convention arose from Recommendation 32 of the Action Plan from the United Nations Conference on the Human Environment 1972. The recommendation was that governments should consider the need to enact conventions and treaties to protect migratory species or those inhabiting international waters. This recommendation was based on the recognition that migratory species needed protection throughout every stage of their migration. Thus, the objectives of the Bonn Convention were to provide strict protection for migratory species in danger of extinction throughout all or a significant portion of their range and to persuade range states to conclude agreements for the conservation and management of migratory species with an unfavourable conservation status which would significantly benefit from international co-operation. For a detailed discussion of the Convention see Lyster, *International Wildlife Law* (Cambridge, 1985), Chap. 13.

[10] Convention on the Conservation of European Wildlife and Natural Habitats 1979, HMSO Treaty Series No. 56, Cmnd. 8783 (1982). The Bonn Convention was followed by the Berne Convention, agreed under the auspices of the Council of Europe. It aimed to conserve European wild flora and fauna and their natural habitats, extending similar protection to that under the Bonn Convention to non-migratory species. The Berne Convention has been of great importance because of its clear obligations on parties and by inspiring the European Community Directives on birds and habitats. For a detailed discussion of the Convention see Lyster, *International Wildlife Law* (Cambridge, 1985), Chap. 8.

[11] EC Directive on the Conservation of Wild Birds (79/409, OJ L130, April 25, 1979, p. 1).

[12] EC Directive on the Conservation of Natural Habitats and of Wild Fauna and Flora (92/43, OJ L206, July 22, 1992, p. 7).

[13] See Chap. 11.

[14] *Biodiversity: The UK Action Plan*, Cm. 2428 (1994). This policy was formulated as part of the UK's commitments under the Convention on Biological Diversity, 1992, HMSO miscellaneous series no. 3, Cm. 2127 (1993). For details of the convention see Glowka *et al.*, *A Guide to the Convention on Biological Diversity*, IUCN Environmental Policy and Law Paper No. 30 (Gland, Switzerland, 1994).

[15] Department of the Environment, 1995, *Biodiversity: The UK Steering Group Report*, Vol. II.

species.[16] Red squirrels, otters, dolphins, corncrakes and capercaillie are among the priority species for which such plans exist.

The approach to species protection

The legislative approach to species protection in Scotland involves the establishment of criminal offences for certain actions involving specified wildlife. This is accompanied by a list of exceptions and defences for acceptable activities, which vary for different species, many of which require permission or a licence from an official body.

However, this approach suffers from a number of problems. First, there are problems experienced generally with the use of criminal sanctions: discovering that offences have occurred, problems in the drafting of offences and defences[17] and problems of enforcement. It is often difficult to prove the intent necessary for some of the offences. The Royal Society for the Protection of Birds has also expressed concern that "the government have put time, effort and money into the passing of legislation and its general administration yet has not seriously tackled the problem of enforcement".[18] However, the establishment of the Partnership for Action Against Wildlife Crime may go some way towards alleviating this problem. The partnership's objective is to co-ordinate the statutory and non-statutory organisations involved in combating wildlife crime in the UK, and to provide a strategic overview of wildlife law enforcement activity.[19] It supports a national network of Police Wildlife Liaison Officers and Customs and Excise CITES[20] officers and there is a working group specifically for Scotland.

There is also the problem that protection is only afforded to those species listed in the Schedules to the provisions.[21] As Reid points out, "by requiring the express prohibition of the undesired conduct, there is a risk that some forms of harm, or some species in need of protection, will be omitted, or will come to be appreciated only after the law is in place".[22] The use of schedules listing protected species partly circumvents this problem as the schedules can easily be amended.[23] However, there is a problem with the hybridisation of plants whereby the legislation will apply only to the named species and not to the hybrids.

Finally, there is a problem of identification: whether people are able to identify particular protected species so as to avoid harmful actions. As de Klemm and

---

[16] See Scottish Natural Heritage, *Annual Report 1996–1997*, p. 8.

[17] Proposals 26, 28 and 32 in *The EC Fauna, Flora and Habitats Directive: SSSIs and the Wildlife and Countryside Act—Proposals for New/Amended Legislation From the RSPB* (Royal Society for the Protection of Birds internal documents, 1992) highlight this problem.

[18] *Evidence to the House of Commons Environment Committee: The Wildlife and Countryside Act* (Royal Society for the Protection of Birds internal documents, 1984), p. 41.

[19] Partnership for Action Against Wildlife Crime, *PAW Bulletin*, No. 1, October 1998, Department of the Environment, Transport and the Regions.

[20] See n. 170 below and associated text.

[21] Except for birds which all receive some degree of protection: see n. 29 below and associated text.

[22] Reid, *Nature Conservation Law* (Edinburgh, 1994), p. 80.

[23] They can be amended by the Minister by statutory instrument under s. 22 of the Wildlife and Countryside Act 1981. The conservancy councils, acting jointly through the Joint Nature Conservation Committee, review the schedules of protected animals and plants every five years: s. 24(1) of the Wildlife and Countryside Act 1981.

Shine point out, "long lists of species are of relatively little use if few people can recognise the species concerned".[24] The solution is to educate the general public and Scottish Natural Heritage, together with the Royal Society for the Protection of Birds and other conservation groups, are committed to increasing public awareness of endangered or protected species and biodiversity more generally.[25]

Birds

In Scotland wild animals and birds are *res nullius*.[26] Unlike plants,[27] as wild birds and animals belong to no one, they do not benefit from protection through property law. Much of the protection that is provided for birds is contained in the Wildlife and Countryside Act 1981 ("the 1981 Act").[28] All wild birds[29] and their nests and eggs are protected. However, the level of protection varies and depends on the rarity of the species. Birds are grouped into four schedules under the 1981 Act. Schedule 1 birds are rare, declining or vulnerable species which receive a higher degree of protection than other wild birds. Part I of Schedule 1, which lists those species receiving this higher protection at all times, includes *inter alia* osprey, corncrake and golden eagles. Part II, which lists those species receiving this higher protection only during the close season, includes only goldeneye, greylag goose and pintail. Schedule 2 birds are those that can be killed or taken. Part I of Schedule 2 lists species that can be killed or taken outside the close season and includes a number of wildfowl. There are now no birds listed in Part II of Schedule 2.[30] Part I of Schedule 3 lists birds that may be sold alive if they have been ringed and bred in captivity. Part II of Schedule 3 lists

---

[24] De Klemm and Shine, *Biological Diversity Conservation and the Law: Legal Mechanisms for Conserving Species and Ecosystems,* IUCN Environmental Policy and Law Paper No. 29 (Gland, Switzerland, 1993), p. 121.

[25] SNH spent £2.9 million on environmental education in the year 1996–97: Scottish Natural Heritage, *Annual Report 1996–1997.* The Royal Society for the Protection of Birds is working with government advising on environmental education in primary schools and has produced a Gaelic/English textbook on corncrakes for 11–14 year olds: Royal Society for the Protection of Birds, *Annual Review 1996/97.* SNH, in conjunction with the Scottish Office and the Partnership for Action Against Wildlife Crime, is trying also to raise awareness of the offences that may be committed in relation to wildlife. SNH has published a booklet describing the offences: Scottish Natural Heritage, *Wildlife, the Law and You* (1998), and a poster campaign to draw attention to wildlife crime was launched in October 1997 by the Scottish Office and Scottish police forces.

[26] Carey Miller, *Corporeal Moveables in Scots Law* (Edinburgh, 1991), pp. 18–24.

[27] See n. 151 below and associated text.

[28] Which implemented the EC Directive on the Conservation of Wild Birds, 79/409, OJ L130, April 25, 1979, p. 1.

[29] s. 27(1) of the 1981 Act defines wild bird as "any bird of a kind which is ordinarily resident in or is a visitor to Great Britain in a wild state but does not include poultry". Poultry means domestic fowls, geese, ducks, guinea-fowls, pigeons, quails and turkeys. Also excluded from the definition of wild bird (except for the purposes of ss 5 and 16 of the 1981 Act) are game birds, which are defined as pheasant, partridge, black grouse, red grouse or ptarmigan. In addition, under s. 1(6) of the 1981 Act, any bird shown to have been bred in captivity is not a wild bird. A bird will only be treated as bred in captivity if its parents were lawfully in captivity when the egg was laid.

[30] This originally listed 13 common birds considered to be pests which often need controlling to protect crops, game, livestock and trees. They were removed from the Schedule by the Wildlife and Countryside Act 1981 (Variation of Schedules 2 and 3) Order 1992 (SI 1992/3010) to comply with the EC Directive on the Conservation of Wild Birds, 79/409, OJ L130, April 25, 1979, p. 1.

those birds that may be sold dead at all times.[31] Part III of Schedule 3 lists those birds that may be sold dead from September 1 to February 28. These include a number of wildfowl that are also listed in Schedule 2, Part I. Schedule 4 lists birds which must be registered and ringed if kept in captivity: primarily birds of prey.

Provisions applicable to all birds

The killing, injuring or taking of birds and the taking, damaging or destroying of eggs and nests: The basic protection for all wild birds is provided by section 1 of the 1981 Act. This creates an offence of intentionally killing, injuring or taking any wild bird or taking, damaging or destroying a nest while it is in use or being built.[32] It is also an offence to take or destroy[33] the eggs of any wild bird.[34] However, there are a number of exceptions for which the burden of proof is on the accused.

No offence is committed if the action is taken by an authorised person[35] in relation to a bird formerly listed in Schedule 2 (Pt II).[36] To allow action to be taken to control or prevent disease, the following are exempt[37] from these offences: anything done in respect of an order under sections 21 or 22 of the Animal Health Act 1981; and actions taken under section 39 of the Agriculture (Scotland) Act 1948 in pursuance of a requirement by the appropriate Minister.[38] General exceptions are provided for anything done in accordance with the terms of a licence issued under section 16(1) of the 1981 Act,[39] or for actions which are the incidental result of a lawful operation and which could not reasonably have

---

[31] The only bird currently listed on Pt II of Sched. 3 is the woodpigeon.

[32] s. 1(1) of the 1981 Act.

[33] s. 27(1) of the 1981 Act defines "destroy" as doing anything to the egg which is calculated to prevent it from hatching.

[34] s. 1(1)(c) of the 1981 Act. Section 19A of the 1981 Act provides for the accused to be convicted of this offence on the evidence of one witness. It is lawful to remove eggs from nestboxes from August to January: Scottish Office Licence SOGEN/15. It is also permissible for an authorised person to take the eggs of Mallard Ducks for the purpose of incubation before March 31: Scottish Office Licence SOGEN/16.

[35] s. 2(2) of the 1981 Act. Section 27(1) of the Act defines "authorised persons" as the owner/occupier of the land on which the action is taken or any person authorised by them; any person authorised by the local authority, Scottish Natural Heritage, a district fishery board, a local fisheries committee, a water authority or any other statutory water undertakers. "Occupier" includes any person having the right of hunting, shooting or fishing, on any land other than the foreshore.

[36] Scottish Office Licence PS/1998. There are now no birds listed in Pt II; however, this licence permits these species to be taken and killed and their nests and eggs to be taken, damaged and destroyed by an authorised person, by any method not prohibited by s. 5 of the 1981 Act, for the purpose of preventing the spread of disease or preventing serious damage to livestock, foodstuffs for livestock, crops, vegetables, fruit, growing timber, fisheries and inland water. Licence SOGEN/10 allows the same activities for the purposes of protecting any collection of wild birds or for preserving public health or air safety. Licence SOGEN/09 permits these activities in respect of nine of these species for the purpose of conserving wild birds.

[37] s. 4(1) of the 1981 Act.

[38] s. 53 of the Scotland Act 1998.

[39] An example of this is Scottish Office Licence SOGEN/13 issued under s. 16(1)(i) which allows the killing and taking of certain birds and the taking and destruction of their nests and eggs for the purpose of preserving air safety. For full details of licensing see n. 203 and associated text.

been avoided.[40] This will include such things as road accidents and the destruction of skylark nests when harvesting hay. As Garner and Jones point out: "the Act does not require the court to ask whether it would have been reasonable to have avoided doing the lawful operation in the circumstances; it simply requires consideration of whether, in performing that lawful operation the consequence was or was not one which could reasonably have been avoided".[41]

It is permissible to take a disabled[42] bird for the purpose of tending it and later releasing it, or to kill a disabled bird where there was no reasonable chance of its recovery.[43] However, if the bird is one of those listed in Schedule 4 the finder must either hand the bird over to a licensed person[44] or register it with the Minister. The killing or injuring of a wild bird is permissible when the action is necessary for the protection of public health and safety, disease prevention or preventing serious damage to livestock, foodstuffs for livestock, crops, vegetables, fruit, growing timber, fisheries or inland waters.[45]

Possession of birds or eggs: The continuing possession of birds or eggs taken from the wild constitutes a further offence.[46] Because of the difficulties associated with proving the deliberate killing or taking of birds and eggs, the offence of possession is one of strict liability. Thus, the prosecution merely has to prove possession.[47] However, there is an additional exception to those listed above: if the bird or egg had not been killed or taken, or had been killed or taken or sold without contravening the provisions of the Act.[48] Thus, possession of the remains of your pet cat's latest kill will not constitute an offence.

Sale of birds or eggs: It is an offence if a person sells,[49] offers or exposes for sale, or has in his possession or transports for the purpose of sale, any live wild bird,

---

[40] s. 4(2)(c) of the 1981 Act. The action must be incidental and not a direct result of the operation: *Robinson* v *Everett and W & FC Bonham & Son Ltd* [1988] Crim LR 699.

[41] Garner and Jones, *Countryside Law* (3rd edn, Crayford, 1997), p. 229.

[42] If it can be shown that the bird was disabled otherwise than by his unlawful act.

[43] s. 4(2) of the 1981 Act.

[44] Who is authorised under the general licence WLF 100099 issued by the Department of the Environment, Transport and the Regions.

[45] s. 4(3) of the 1981 Act. The defence in s. 4(3)(c) for livestock and crop protection will only apply where it can be shown that there was no other satisfactory solution: s. 4(4) of the 1981 Act. Furthermore, the defence cannot be relied upon where it has become apparent that the action would be necessary and a licence under s. 16 of the 1981 Act has not been applied for, or an application for such a licence has been determined, or where the agriculture Minister has not been notified as soon as reasonably practicable after the time that he has taken the action: ss 4(5) and 4(6) of the 1981 Act.

[46] s. 1(2) of the 1981 Act. Scottish Office Licence SOGEN/16 permits the possession by an authorised person of eggs of Mallard Ducks taken for the purposes of incubation and any bird hatched from such an egg (until July 31 in the year the egg was hatched) to assist in the successful rearing of birds which otherwise would have been unlikely to withstand adverse weather conditions.

[47] Thus it is no defence that the accused did not know that the bird was wild. In *Kirkland* v *Robinson* [1987] Crim LR 643 the appellant was convicted of possessing live wild goshawks which he honestly believed to have been bred in captivity. The justification given by the court was that those who chose to possess wild birds must ensure that their possession is a lawful possession.

[48] s. 1(3) of the 1981 Act. This includes the provisions of the Protection of Birds Acts 1954–67. Thus if it had been taken prior to 1954 or was a product of lawful activity, no offence will have been committed.

[49] This includes any offer to exchange or trade for other birds or goods in kind: s. 27(1) of the 1981 Act.

other than a bird included in Part I of Schedule 3,[50] or an egg of a wild bird or any part of such egg.[51] It is also an offence to advertise such buying or selling.[52] There are similar limitations in respect of dead birds or anything derived from them, except those that are included in Part II or III[53] of Schedule 3, if the person is not registered in accordance with regulations made by the Minister.[54] The competition showing of any live wild bird not in Schedule 3, Part I or any live bird with a parent who was a wild bird is also prohibited.[55] These offences attract a harsher penalty if they occur in respect of a Schedule 1 bird.[56]

The importance of these offences relates to the willingness of collectors to pay high prices for the rarer birds and their eggs which can pose a very real threat to such species. Garner and Jones consider that "the mere existence of the offences may hinder this trade to some extent, but to be really effective there is a clear need for a degree of zeal in relation both to the detection of offences and the prosecution of those caught".[57]

Methods of killing and taking: It is an offence to set in position articles of such nature and so placed as to be calculated to cause bodily injury to any wild bird coming into contact with them.[58] However, it is a defence to show that the article was set in position for the purpose of killing or taking, in the interests of public health, agriculture, forestry, fisheries, or nature conservation, any wild animals which could be lawfully killed or taken by those means and that all reasonable precautions were taken to prevent injury thereby to wild birds.[59] It is also an

---

[50] These are birds bred in captivity which have been ringed or marked in accordance with the Wildlife and Countryside (Ringing of Certain Birds) Regulations 1982 (SI 1982/1220).

[51] s. 6(1)(a) of the 1981 Act. The sale of a number of species is permitted by Scottish Office Licences SOGEN/08, SOGEN/02, SOGEN/18 and SOGEN/11.

[52] s. 6(1)(b) of the 1981 Act.

[53] Scottish Office Licence SOGEN/06 allows the sale of feathers and parts of these species, with the exception of the barn owl, during the period February 29 to August 31 if the sale is of small numbers of dead birds, or any part or product of dead birds that were bred in captivity or removed from the natural state within Great Britain under legal provisions in force in Great Britain.

[54] s. 6(2) of the 1981 Act. The relevant regulations are the Wildlife and Countryside (Registration to Sell etc. Certain Dead Wild Birds) Regulations 1982 (SI 1982/1219), as amended by SI 1991/ 479. Scottish Office Licence SOGEN/07 authorises acts which would be prohibited under s. 6(2) of the 1981 Act, for any dead wild bird included in Sched. 2 (Pt I), barnacle geese and the Greenland race of white fronted geese. The licence only applies to the sale of small numbers of dead birds, or any part or product of dead birds that were bred in captivity or originated from a Member State of the European Community which were removed from the natural state under legal provisions in force in that Member State.

[55] s. 6(3) of the 1981 Act. Scottish Office licences SOGEN/03, SOGEN/04 and SOGEN/17 permit competitive showing for certain captive-bred species.

[56] s. 6(4) of the 1981 Act. Ordinarily offences in relation to birds attract a level 3 fine; however, if the offence occurs in relation to a bird listed in Sched. 1 of the 1981 Act this increases to a level 5 fine.

[57] Garner and Jones, *Countryside Law* (3rd edn, Crayford, 1997), p. 231.

[58] s. 5(1)(a) of the 1981 Act. This restriction applies to any spring, trap, gin, snare, hook and line, any electrical device for killing, stunning or frightening or any poisonous, poisoned or stupefying substance. According to *Robinson v Hughes* [1987] Crim LR 644, the section distinguishes a substance that is poisonous *per se*, a substance with which poison has been mixed (so that it becomes a poisoned substance) and a substance with the effect of stupefying and the three are thus separate offences.

[59] s. 5(4) of the 1981 Act.

offence to use a number of articles[60] for the purpose of killing or taking a wild bird, or to knowingly cause or permit to be done any of the offences.[61] These offences carry the "special penalty" on conviction.[62]

Some success in the measures against illegal poisoning can be seen in the Scottish Office publication *Counting the Cost*.[63] Successful prosecutions coupled with an anti-poisoning campaign led to an increase in the number of buzzards in Scotland. However, other types of persecution, particularly of birds of prey, still occur most noticeably in areas where game birds are reared for shooting and on grouse moors.

Nest sites: In addition to protection for specific species, the Minister has the power to issue orders to create "areas of special protection" for wild birds.[64] These are designed to control the activities of parties entering these areas. The order can create additional offences for all or part of the area. It can extend the protection given to all or specified wild birds in the area so that the disturbance of such a bird while it is building a nest, or on or near a nest containing eggs or young, or the disturbance of the young, is also an offence.[65] Furthermore, the order can make it an offence to enter the area or any part of it at any time or at specified times[66] and can provide for these additional offences to be subject to the "special penalty".[67]

The order can only be made with the consent of the owners/occupiers. To encourage the consent the order "shall not affect the exercise by any person of

---

[60] It is prohibited to use any spring, trap, gin, snare, hook and line, any electrical device for killing, stunning or frightening or any poisonous, poisoned or stupefying substance, net, baited board, bird-lime or similar substance, any bow or crossbow, any explosive other than ammunition for a firearm, any automatic or semi-automatic weapon, any shot-gun having a muzzle more than one-and-three-quarter inches in diameter, any device for illuminating a target, or any sighting device for night shooting, any form of artificial lighting or any mirror or other dazzling device, any gas or smoke or any chemical wetting agent, the use as a decoy of any sound recording or any live bird or other animal whatever which is tethered, or which is secured by means of braces or other similar appliances or which is blind, maimed or injured, or to use any mechanically propelled vehicle in immediate pursuit of a wild bird: ss 5(1)(b)–(e) of the 1981 Act. Section 5(5) permits the use of nets for the purpose of taking wild duck in a duck decoy that is shown to have been in use immediately before the passing of the Protection of Birds Act 1954 or the use of a cage-trap or net for the purposes of taking any game bird if the taking of the bird is solely for the purpose of breeding.

[61] s. 5(1)(f) of the 1981 Act. A Scottish Office Licence permits the use of semi-automatic weapons by authorised persons to kill or take certain birds (those formerly listed in Sched. 2, Pt II, to the 1981 Act) for the purposes of preserving public health or air safety, or the prevention of the spread of disease or serious damage to livestock, foodstuffs for livestock, crops, vegetables, fruit, growing timber or fisheries. Scottish Office Licence SOGEN/05 permits the use by an authorised person for the same purposes of any device for illuminating a target, or any sighting device for night shooting, any form of artificial lighting or any mirror or other dazzling device, to kill feral pigeons, house sparrows and starlings when roosting on buildings or other man-made structures. Scottish Office Licence SOGEN/01 permits the keeping of certain birds in cage-traps as decoys for the purpose of conserving wild birds, protecting any collection of wild birds and preventing serious damage to livestock, crops, vegetables, fruit, growing timbers or fisheries.

[62] See n. 70 below and associated text.

[63] Scottish Office, *Counting the Cost—The Continuing Persecution of Birds of Prey in Scotland* (1998).

[64] s. 3 of the 1981 Act.

[65] s. 3(1)(a) of the 1981 Act.

[66] s. 3(1)(b) of the 1981 Act.

[67] s. 3(1)(c) of the 1981 Act. The special penalty is level 5: s. 21 of the 1981 Act.

any right vested in him, whether as owner, lessee or occupier of any land in that area or by virtue of a licence or agreement".[68] Garner and Jones note that designations are rare but that they "may be useful when it is felt necessary to keep people well away from a particular location, such as one where a rare species may nest".[69]

Provisions applicable to specified birds

Birds listed in Schedule 1 to the 1981 Act: Higher protection is afforded to those species listed in Schedule 1 to the 1981 Act. If any of the aforementioned offences is committed in respect of such a bird, then the "special penalty" is incurred,[70] the maximum penalty increasing from level 3 to level 5 of the standard scale.[71] Furthermore, there is an offence of intentionally disturbing a Schedule 1 bird whilst it is building a nest or is in, on or near a nest containing eggs or young, or disturbing its dependent young.[72] This offence also incurs the higher penalty. The exceptions to liability under section 1 of the 1981 Act for preserving public health and safety or preventing disease or protection of crops and livestock do not apply where Schedule 1 birds are concerned.

Birds listed in Schedule 4 to the 1981 Act: The rules on registration and ringing are important in helping to identify birds that have been taken from the wild rather than bred in captivity because "in some areas, persecution rather than lack of suitable habitat is the main reason why birds of prey are scarce or non-existent".[73] If any person keeps or has in their possession or control any bird included in Schedule 4 which has not been registered[74] and ringed or marked in accordance with the regulations made by the Minister[75] they shall be guilty of an offence and liable to a special penalty.[76] If the bird is wild an offence of possession will also have been committed.[77] It has been submitted that the theft of young birds of

---

[68] s. 3(3) of the 1981 Act.

[69] Garner and Jones, *Countryside Law* (3rd edn, Crayford, 1997), p. 228.

[70] s. 1(4) of the 1981 Act.

[71] s. 21 of the 1981 Act. Schedule 1 is divided into two parts: the birds in Pt I are protected by the special penalty at all times, those in Pt II are only protected by the special penalty during the close season that is defined in s. 2(4) of the 1981 Act. Outside the close season, the ordinary offences under s. 1 apply but the special penalty will not arise.

[72] s. 1(5) of the 1981 Act.

[73] Scottish Office, *Counting the Cost—The Continuing Persecution of Birds of Prey in Scotland* (1998), foreword.

[74] A period of seven days is allowed after hatching before the bird has to be registered: SOGEN/ 20. The registration provisions apply to the keeper of the bird and the address at which it is normally kept. This is not necessarily the same as the owner of the bird and the owner's address.

[75] Wildlife and Countryside (Registration and Ringing of Certain Captive Birds) Regulations 1982 (SI 1982/1221) amended by the Wildlife and Countryside (Registration and Ringing of Certain Birds) (Amendment) Regulations 1991 (SI 1991/478), the Wildlife and Countryside Act (Variation of Schedule 4) Order 1994 (SI 1994/1151), and the Wildlife and Countryside (Registration and Ringing of Certain Captive Birds) (Amendment) Regulations 1994 (SI 1994/1152).

[76] s. 7(1) of the 1981 Act. The special penalty is a level 5 fine: s. 21(1)(a) of the 1981 Act. There are a number of persons such as Scottish Society for the Prevention of Cruelty to Animals inspectors, veterinary surgeons and reserve wardens of the Royal Society for the Protection of Birds who may not be guilty of an offence because of authorisation by licence: Scottish Office Licence SOGEN/19, DETR Licence WLF 100099, Scottish Office Licence SOGEN/12 and DETR Licence WLF 100074.

[77] s. 1(2) of the 1981 Act.

prey seems to have waned recently[78] perhaps indicating some degree of success for this measure. This may have been assisted by the development of DNA profiling which has made it relatively straightforward to prove the heredity of individual birds. The Wildlife and Countryside Act 1981 does not provide a power to obtain samples for DNA analysis[79]; however, as Taylor points out, "where a person is being charged with an offence under section 1(2) of the Wildlife and Countryside Act 1981 of being in possession of a wild bird, the onus is on that person to prove that the bird had been acquired lawfully".[80]

To deter persistent offenders, following a conviction in respect of a Schedule 4 bird that is the subject of a special penalty, a further offence is committed if within five years of the conviction the offender keeps or has in their possession or under their control a Schedule 4 bird.[81] If the original conviction does not carry a special penalty then the period is three years.[82] Following a conviction in respect of one of these offences there is a further period during which restrictions apply. A further offence is committed if they knowingly dispose, or offer to dispose, of a Schedule 4 bird within five years of a conviction under section 7(3)(a) or within three years of an offence under section 7(3)(b).[83]

Animals/invertebrates

The offences which apply to wild animals under the 1981 Act are similar to those for wild birds; however, unlike birds, only selected species enjoy protection.

Species listed in Schedule 5 to the 1981 Act
Schedule 5 includes all bats and certain reptiles and amphibians, but only the rarest mammals, fish, butterflies and other creatures. Examples include wild cats, dolphins, porpoises, pine martens, otters and red squirrels.

Killing, injuring, taking and possessing: It is an offence for any person intentionally to kill, injure or take wild animals listed in Schedule 5.[84] However, no offence will be committed if the action has been taken in accordance with a licence issued under section 16 of the 1981 Act,[85] in pursuance of a requirement by the Minister under section 39 of the Agriculture (Scotland) Act 1948, in pursuance of an order under the Animal Health Act 1981,[86] or where the act was an incidental result of a lawful operation and could not reasonably have been avoided.[87] It is also permissible to take animals where the animal was injured and the purpose was

---

[78] Scottish Office, *Counting the Cost—The Continuing Persecution of Birds of Prey in Scotland* (1998).
[79] There is such a power in regs 9(3) and 9(5) of the Control of Trade in Endangered Species (Enforcement) Regulations 1997: below, n. 174 and associated text.
[80] Taylor, *Wildlife Crime: A Guide to Wildlife Law Enforcement in the United Kingdom* (London, 1998), p. 28.
[81] s. 7(3)(a) of the 1981 Act.
[82] s. 7(3)(b) of the 1981 Act.
[83] s. 7(4) of the 1981 Act.
[84] s. 9(1) of the 1981 Act. Offences under s. 9 give rise to a fine not exceeding level 5: s. 21(2) of the 1981 Act.
[85] See n. 217 below and associated text.
[86] s. 10(1) of the 1981 Act.
[87] s. 10(3)(c) of the 1981 Act.

to tend and release it, provided that the animal had not been disabled by that person's unlawful act, and to kill animals where the animal is so seriously injured that it would not recover.[88] In addition, the killing and injuring of an animal included in Schedule 5 is permissible if the action was by an authorised person and was necessary for the prevention of serious damage to livestock, feedstuffs for livestock, crops, fruit, growing timber or any other form of property or fisheries.[89] However, this defence will not apply where it had become apparent before the action was undertaken that it would be necessary and a licence under section 16 of the 1981 Act had not been applied for as soon as reasonably practicable after that fact became apparent, or an application for such a licence had been determined.[90]

It is also an offence to have in one's possession or control any live or dead Schedule 5 animal or any part thereof.[91] No offence is committed if the possessor can prove: the animal has not been killed or taken, or has been killed or taken without contravening the relevant provisions[92]; or a licence has been issued under section 16 of the 1981 Act. In proceedings for these offences the animal in question is presumed to have been a wild animal unless the contrary is shown.[93]

Sale: It is an offence to sell, offer or expose for sale, or have possession of or transport for sale or advertise any live or dead wild animal listed in Schedule 5.[94] It is also an offence for any person to publish or cause to be published any advert likely to be understood as conveying that they buy or sell or intend to buy or sell any live or dead wild animal listed in Schedule 5 or anything derived from such an animal. Twenty-one species of butterfly[95] are protected in this way; however, they are not protected from being taken from the wild in the first place.[96] According to Taylor, "this apparent anomaly is to protect the rarer, but not threatened, butterfly species from excessive collecting by dealers, whilst not deterring scientists, responsible collectors or children from catching butterflies".[97]

Nests/roosts: It is an offence intentionally to damage, destroy or obstruct access to places of shelter or protection of a Schedule 5 animal[98] or intentionally to disturb a Schedule 5 animal while occupying such a place.[99] For these offences,

---

[88] ss 10(3)(a) and (b) of the 1981 Act.
[89] s. 10(4) of the 1981 Act.
[90] s. 10(6) of the 1981 Act.
[91] s. 9(2) of the 1981 Act.
[92] s. 9(3) of the 1981 Act. This includes provisions of the superseded Conservation of Wild Creatures and Wild Plants Act 1975.
[93] s. 9(6) of the 1981 Act.
[94] s. 9(5) of the 1981 Act.
[95] Which were added to Sched. 5 of the 1981 Act by SI 1989/906.
[96] A similar restriction applies to the sale of adult specimens of common frogs, common toads, smooth newts and palmate newts. However, by a general licence, sale is permitted outwith their breeding seasons.
[97] Taylor, *Wildlife Crime: A Guide to Wildlife Law Enforcement in the United Kingdom* (London, 1998), p. 54.
[98] With the exception of the Atlantic stream crayfish, the pearl mussel and the pink sea-fan to allow for accidental damage during legitimate fishing.
[99] s. 9(4) of the 1981 Act.

the animal is presumed to be wild unless the contrary is shown. This offence does not include anything done within a dwelling-house[100] and no offence is committed if the action is taken in accordance with a licence issued under section 16 of the 1981 Act.

All wild animals

It is an offence to set in position any self-locking snare[101] which is so placed as to be calculated to cause bodily injury to any wild animal or to use such a snare for the purpose of killing or taking any wild animal.[102] It is an offence if any snare which is so placed as to be calculated to cause bodily injury to any wild animal is not inspected at least once every day.[103] In addition, certain other methods of killing or taking wild[104] animals are prohibited.[105]

Species listed in Schedule 6 to the 1981 Act

Schedule 6 lists a number of species including badgers, wild cats, otters, hedge-hogs and red squirrels. Additional methods of killing and taking are prohibited in respect of these species.[106] However, a defence is provided to the offence of setting in position traps, snares, electrical devices for killing or stunning or any poisonous, poisoned or stupefying substance calculated to cause bodily injury to an animal listed in Schedule 6 to the 1981 Act, where the article was set in position for the purpose of killing or taking, in the interests of public health, agriculture, forestry, fisheries or nature conservation, any wild animals which could be lawfully killed or taken by those means and that all reasonable steps to prevent injury to wild animals included in Schedule 6 were taken.[107]

There are gaps in the protection that is provided by the 1981 Act for mammals. This was highlighted by a case involving the use of a hedgehog as a football[108] which is not an offence under the Act. Proceedings were taken for breach of the peace; however, this would now constitute an offence under the Wild Mammals (Protection) Act 1996 which makes it an offence cruelly to ill-treat any wild mammal.[109]

---

[100] s. 10(2) of the 1981 Act.

[101] Self-locking snares are banned for use against any wild animal; other types of snares are banned only for animals listed in Sched. 6 of the 1981 Act.

[102] ss 11(1)(a) and (b) of the 1981 Act. Offences under ss 11(1) and (2) give rise to a fine not exceeding level 5: s. 21(2) of the Act.

[103] s. 11(3) of the 1981 Act. The maximum fine for this offence is level 4: s. 21(3) of the Act.

[104] The animal in question is presumed to be wild unless the contrary is shown: s. 11(5) of the 1981 Act.

[105] Bows, crossbows, any explosive other than ammunition for a firearm and any live mammal or bird used as a decoy are prohibited: s. 11(1) of the 1981 Act.

[106] Traps, snares, electrical devices for killing or stunning or any poisonous, poisoned or stupefying substance, nets, automatic or semi-automatic weapons, devices for illuminating a target or night sighting devices, artificial light or mirrors or other dazzling devices, gas or smoke, sound recordings used as decoys and any mechanically propelled vehicle in immediate pursuit of the animal for the purpose of driving, killing or taking that animal: s. 11(2)(a) of the 1981 Act.

[107] s. 11(6) of the 1981 Act. For all offences the maximum penalty is level 5: s. 21(2) of the Act.

[108] *The Scotsman*, October 22, 1993.

[109] s. 1 of the Wild Mammals (Protection) Act 1996. This offence gives rise to a level 5 fine or six months' imprisonment: s. 5(1) of the Wild Mammals (Protection) Act 1996.

European protected species

Under the Conservation (Natural Habitats etc.) Regulations 1994 ("the 1994 Regulations")[110] there are provisions for the protection of "European protected species".[111] For those animals that qualify as European protected species, protection is provided which is almost identical to that which they already receive by virtue of their listing in Schedule 5 to the 1981 Act.[112] The majority of differences are semantic, for example, for some equivalent offences the 1981 Act uses "intentionally" and "take", whereas the 1994 Regulations use "deliberately" and "capture".

There are, however, some other differences in the protection. The 1994 Regulations do not provide an offence for injury to a European protected species or for obstruction of its place of shelter or protection. The offence of damaging or destroying such a place does not have to be intentional under these regulations and the definition of such a place is wider than in the 1981 Act.[113] There is an additional offence of disturbing a European protected species which is not limited to disturbance at its breeding site or resting place.[114] Furthermore the offences in the 1994 Regulations apply to all stages of the life of the species.[115] The exceptions to liability in the regulations are identical to those in the 1981 Act and they use the language of that Act.

The prohibitions in the 1994 Regulations on methods of killing and taking wild animals[116] are also very similar to those in the 1981 Act. However, in the 1994 Regulations, the prohibition on decoys is limited to blind or mutilated animals, and only tape recorders rather than sound recordings are prohibited. There is also no mention of snares as a prohibited method and nets and traps are only prohibited if they are non-selective according to their principle or their conditions of use.[117] Fish, which are not included in Schedule 6 to the 1981 Act, are protected from poisoning and explosives under the 1994 Regulations.[118]

Bats

All British bats are European protected species. They are also listed in Schedules 5 and 6 to the 1981 Act and are thus protected by sections 9 and 11 of that

---

[110] SI 1994/2716, implementing EC Directive on the Conservation of Natural Habitats and of Wild Fauna and Flora, 92/43, OJ L206, July 22, 1992, p. 7.

[111] These are listed in Sched. 2 to the 1994 Regulations, and include *inter alia* dolphins, porpoises, wild cats and otters.

[112] To avoid having to enact new primary legislation, many of the provisions of the Directive are copied out. For a discussion of the problems associated with such copying out, see Ramsey, "The Copy Out Technique: More of a 'Cop Out' Than a Solution" (1996) 17 *Statute Law Review*, pp. 218–228.

[113] reg. 39(1)(d), of the 1994 Regulations, provides protection for a breeding site or resting place whereas s. 9(4)(a) of the 1981 Act provides protection for a structure or place used for shelter or protection.

[114] reg. 39(1)(b) of the 1994 Regulations.

[115] reg. 39(3) of the 1994 Regulations. The offences give rise to fines not exceeding level 5 for animals: reg. 39(6) and reg. 41(6); and not exceeding level 4 for plants: reg. 43(7); the same as for the equivalent offences under the 1981 Act. However there are differences where the offence concerns more than one animal: see n. 195 below and associated text.

[116] reg. 41 of the 1994 Regulations.

[117] reg. 41(3)(i) and (j) of the 1994 Regulations.

[118] reg. 41(4) of the 1994 Regulations.

Act.[119] However, bats are further protected by a restriction to the provision which permits interference to the nests or roosts of species listed in Schedule 5 if it is within a dwelling-house. For bats, interference with their nests or roosts is only permissible in the living area of a dwelling-house. Interference in other areas is not permitted unless SNH has been notified and been allowed a reasonable time to advise on whether the operation should be carried out and, if so, which method should be used.[120] Householders "must simply liaise with the relevant Country Conservation Agency, to obtain the correct advice as to how any exclusion should be carried out and to the timing of such an operation".[121] However, this provision "does not require compliance with the advice given; it simply requires that the conservation agency be given an opportunity to give that advice before any disturbing action can lawfully take place".[122]

Badgers

In addition to the protection afforded by virtue of listing in Schedule 6 to the 1981 Act, badgers are also protected by the provisions of the Protection of Badgers Act 1992 ("the 1992 Act"): an unusual degree of protection for an animal which is not endangered. Under the 1992 Act, it is an offence wilfully to kill, injure or take a badger or attempt to do so.[123] In order to assist the prosecution of this offence, section 1(2) of the 1992 Act provides that if "there is evidence from which it could reasonably be concluded that at the material time the accused was attempting to kill, injure or take a badger, he shall be presumed to have been attempting to kill, injure or take a badger unless the contrary is shown". Section 1(2) means that the burden of proof is shifted to the defence to disprove the statutory presumption.

The most important additional protection is the creation of an offence of interfering[124] with a badger sett.[125] The offence is committed if the interference is intentional or if the person is reckless as to whether their actions would constitute such interference. With the exception of destroying the sett, no offence will be committed if it is shown that the action was the incidental result of a lawful operation and could not reasonably have been avoided.[126] There are also specific exemptions for the purpose of fox-hunting which allow for certain forms of obstruction.[127]

---

[119] The protection afforded by these provisions is considered sufficient for the implementation of the Agreement on the Conservation of Bats in Europe 1991, HMSO Treaty Series No. 9, Cm. 2472 (1994) concluded under the Convention on the Conservation of Migratory Species of Wild Animals 1979 ("the Bonn convention"), HMSO Treaty Series No. 87, Cm. 1332 (1990) .

[120] s. 10(5) of the 1981 Act.

[121] Taylor, *Wildlife Crime: A Guide to Wildlife Law Enforcement in the United Kingdom* (London, 1998), p. 38.

[122] Garner and Jones, *Countryside Law* (3rd edn, Crayford, 1997), p. 247.

[123] s. 1(1) of the 1992 Act.

[124] This is defined as damaging, destroying, obstructing access to or any entrance of, causing a dog to enter or disturbing a badger when it is occupying a badger sett, intending to do any of those things or being reckless as to whether one's actions would have any of those consequences: s. 3 of the 1992 Act.

[125] The definition of a sett is "any structure or place which displays signs indicating current use by a badger": s. 14 of the 1992 Act.

[126] s. 8(3) of the 1992 Act.

[127] s. 8(4)–(9) of the 1992 Act.

A person will not be guilty of the aforementioned offences if they show that their action was necessary for the purpose of preventing serious damage to land, crops, poultry or any other form of property.[128] However, this will not apply where it had become apparent before the action was undertaken that it would be necessary and a licence under section 10 of the 1992 Act[129] had not been applied for as soon as reasonably practicable after that fact became apparent, or an application for such a licence had been determined.[130]

It is an offence cruelly to ill-treat a badger, to use tongs in the course of killing, taking or attempting to kill or take a badger and to dig for a badger.[131] If there is evidence from which it could reasonably be concluded that at the material time the accused was digging for a badger they shall be presumed to have been digging for a badger unless the contrary is shown.[132] This provision is designed to help "when proceeding against persons who had been apprehended whilst digging, but without having actually taken or injured a badger, because such persons would claim to have been digging, quite lawfully, for a fox".[133] It is also an offence to kill or take a badger by use of any firearm other than a shotgun of greater than 20 bore or a rifle using ammunition of muzzle energy not less than 160 footpounds and bullet greater than 38 grains.

It is an offence to have possession or control of a live badger, to sell or offer a live badger for sale,[134] and to possess any dead badger or part thereof.[135] However, if the badger has not been killed in contravention of the provisions of the Act or if the person has purchased the badger and has no reason to believe that it has been killed in contravention of the provisions of the Act, then no offence has been committed.[136] It is also an offence to mark or attach a ring, a tag or any other device to any badger if not authorised by licence.[137]

The general exceptions to the offences are similar to those provided under the 1981 Act for birds and animals. Thus, no offence is committed if the person has taken or attempted to take a badger which has been disabled otherwise than by their act and the badger is taken or to be taken solely for the purpose of tending it,[138] or if the person has killed or attempted to kill a badger which appears to be so seriously injured or in such a condition that to kill it would be an act of mercy.[139] In addition there is a general defence of unavoidably killing or injuring a badger as an incidental result of a lawful action.[140]

---

[128] ss 7(1) and 8(1) of the 1992 Act.
[129] Licences may be granted for a number of purposes by SNH or the Minister. See n. 235 below and associated text.
[130] ss 7(2) and 8(2) of the 1992 Act.
[131] s. 2 of the 1992 Act.
[132] s. 2(2) of the 1992 Act.
[133] Garner and Jones, *Countryside Law* (3rd edn, Crayford, 1997), p. 242.
[134] s. 4 of the 1992 Act.
[135] s. 1(3) of the 1992 Act. Apart from the offence of possession or sale of a live badger which attracts a penalty of a level 5 fine, the offences under the 1992 Act attract a penalty of up to six months' imprisonment and/or a level 5 fine: s. 12(1) of the Act.
[136] s. 1(4) of the 1992 Act.
[137] s. 5 of the 1992 Act.
[138] s. 6(a) of the 1992 Act.
[139] s. 6(b) of the 1992 Act.
[140] s. 6(c) of the 1992 Act.

Seals

Two species of seal can be found in Britain's coastal waters: the grey seal and the common seal. Both are European protected species and there are specific offences in the Conservation of Seals Act 1970 ("the 1970 Act"). It is an offence to use poisonous substances for the purpose of killing or taking any seal[141] and to use firearms with less than 600 footpounds muzzle energy and bullets less than 45 grains for the purpose of killing, taking or injuring any seal.[142] The possession of any of these items for the purpose of committing an offence under the 1970 Act is also prohibited, as is any attempt to commit an offence.[143] The 1970 Act also provides a close season during which it is an offence wilfully to kill, injure or take a seal.[144] The effect of the close season can be extended by the Minister where it appears necessary for the proper conservation of seals.[145] This extension has been applied to common seals in the Shetland Islands and their adjacent territorial waters.[146]

There are general exemptions for killing a seal which has been so seriously disabled[147] that there was no chance of its recovering[148] or where a licence has been granted by the Minister.[149] There are also exemptions from prohibited actions during the close season for taking disabled seals for the purpose of tending and releasing them, the killing or injuring of a seal as an incidental result of a lawful action, and the killing or attempted killing of a seal to prevent it from causing damage to a fishing net or tackle or to any fish in the net, providing the seal is in the vicinity of the net or tackle at the time.[150]

Plants

Growing plants belong to the owner of the soil upon which they are growing[151] and are thus subject to property laws as well as specific conservation laws. Any unauthorised interference with a plant will therefore constitute a civil wrong and the owner can sue any person who damages or takes his plants. However, as Reid points out, any action faces the problem that wild plants are "not generally recognised as having any monetary value, so that the pursuer may be unable to demonstrate that any loss has been suffered by the harm done. This will pose a major practical problem in assessing the value of damage done, and may even lead the courts to say that in fact no actionable wrong has occurred".[152] The

---

[141] s. 1(1)(a), Conservation of Seals Act 1970. The offences give rise to a fine not exceeding level 4: s. 5(2) of the 1970 Act.

[142] s. 1(1) of the 1970 Act.

[143] s. 8 of the 1970 Act.

[144] s. 2(2) of the 1970 Act. The close season is from September 1 to December 31 inclusive for grey seals and from June 1 to August 31 inclusive for common seals: s. 2(1) of the Act. These close seasons coincide with the puppy seasons when the seals are at their most vulnerable.

[145] s. 3 of the 1970 Act.

[146] The Conservation of Seals (Common Seals) (Shetland Islands Area) Order 1991 (SI 1991/2638).

[147] Otherwise than by his act.

[148] s. 9(2) of the 1970 Act.

[149] These may be granted under s. 10 of the 1970 Act for a variety of purposes. See n. 247 below and associated text.

[150] s. 9(1) of the 1970 Act.

[151] See, eg, *Burns* v *Fleming* (1880) 8 R 226 and *Stewart* v *Stewart's Exrs* (1761) Mor 5436.

[152] Reid, *Nature Conservation Law* (Edinburgh, 1994), p. 198.

"protection" provided by property law is not, however, limited to actions for damages once harm has occurred. An owner could obtain an interdict to prevent harm that may be threatened.

As plants are private property they are also protected by the general criminal law. The offences of theft, malicious mischief, vandalism and fire-raising are all therefore potential offences that may apply to the damage of plants.[153] However, it may be difficult to establish the necessary *mens rea* in some cases.[154] Tree preservation orders made pursuant to planning legislation offer added protection.[155] The unlawful felling of a tree subject to a tree preservation order is a criminal offence.[156]

The 1981 Act makes it an offence for anyone except an authorised person[157] intentionally to uproot any wild plant.[158] There is increased protection for those wild plants listed in Schedule 8 to the 1981 Act. These are plants which are very rare or are in danger of becoming extinct, such as alpine gentians. For these species it is an offence for anyone intentionally to pick,[159] uproot or destroy them.[160] Thus, owners and occupiers of land may take any action in respect of a plant not included in Schedule 8 and persons who are not owners and occupiers of the land will only commit an offence in respect of such a plant if they uproot it without the owner's consent. A defence is provided where the act is an incidental result of a lawful operation and could not reasonably have been avoided.[161] In order to restrict trade in plants listed in Schedule 8 to the 1981 Act, it is also an offence to sell, offer or expose them for sale, or to have possession of or transport them for sale, live or dead, or to advertise to this effect.[162] Bluebells have been recently added to Schedule 8 so as to benefit from this protection.[163]

The 1994 Regulations[164] provide protection for those plants which qualify as European protected species.[165] For these species of plants, as with protection for animals, the protection provided is almost identical to that which they already receive by virtue of the 1981 Act. However, it is also an offence to collect and cut

---

[153] Reid, op. cit., p. 199.

[154] See, eg, *Ward* v *Robertson* 1938 JC 32.

[155] See the Town and Country Planning (The Preservation Order and Trees in Conservation Areas) (Scotland) Regulations (SI 1975/1204).

[156] s. 171, Town and Country Planning (Scotland) Act 1997. A conviction for such an offence can give rise to a fine in summary proceedings of up to £20,000.

[157] The same definition applies as for birds and animals: above, n. 35.

[158] s. 13(1)(b) of the 1981 Act. Wild plant is defined in s. 27(1) of that Act as any plant which is or (before it was picked, uprooted or destroyed) was growing wild and is of a kind which ordinarily grows in Great Britain in a wild state. Under s. 13(4) of the Act, the plant will be presumed to be wild unless the contrary is shown. Any offences under s. 13 attract fines not exceeding level 4: s. 21(3) of the Act.

[159] This is defined to include the gathering or plucking of any part of a plant without uprooting it, which includes the collection of seeds.

[160] s. 13(1)(a) of the 1981 Act.

[161] s. 13(3) of the 1981 Act.

[162] s. 13(2) of the 1981 Act.

[163] Wildlife and Countryside Act 1981 (Variation of Schedules 5 and 8) Order 1998 (SI 1998/878). Bluebells do not, however, benefit from the full protection afforded to most plants listed on Sched. 8 to the 1981 Act, they only receive protection from s. 13(2) of the Act.

[164] SI 1994/2716, implementing EC Directive on the Conservation of Natural Habitats and of Wild Fauna and Flora, 92/43, OJ L206, July 22, 1992, p. 7.

[165] These are listed in Sched. 4 to the 1994 Regulations, which currently lists only nine species.

such a plant[166] and the offence of transport is not limited to transport for the purpose of sale. In addition, all offences apply to all stages of the biological cycle of the plants.[167] However, there is no offence of advertising the buying and selling of these plants and there is an additional defence to the offence of sale, etc., where the plant or other thing in question had been lawfully[168] sold. The other differences are again of wording: the 1981 Act uses "intentionally" and "possession" whereas the 1994 Regulations use "deliberately" and "keep". The offences do not apply where a licence has been granted by SNH or the Minister.[169]

Trade in endangered species

The Convention on International Trade in Endangered Species of Wild Fauna and Flora (CITES)[170] provides for the regulation of international trade in certain species of animals and plants.[171] Three appendices list the plants and animals subject to CITES. Appendix I species are those threatened with extinction and they include a number of whale species. Appendix II species are those which may be threatened with extinction if trade in them is not controlled. Wild cats, golden eagles, porpoises and a number of dolphin species are listed in Appendix II. Appendix III is for protected species in a signatory country for which international co-operation is sought to control trade. Otters and bats are included in Appendix III.

CITES is implemented within the European Union by EC Regulations 338[172] and 939[173] of 1997. Offences in the UK are provided in the Control of Trade in Endangered Species (Enforcement) Regulations 1997.[174] These operate alongside the Endangered Species (Import and Export) Act 1976[175] which applies the same controls in respect of non-CITES parties. Regulation 338 has four annexes. Annex A includes all Appendix I species, together with almost 200 Appendix II and III species, and some non-CITES species. Annex B includes all the Appendix II species not in Annex A, over 50 Appendix III and a number of non-CITES species. Annex C includes approximately 200 Appendix III species. Annex D contains non-CITES species that are imported into the community in such numbers as to warrant monitoring.

Permits must be obtained before any Annex A or B species can be imported,[176] exported or re-exported,[177] or any Annex C species can be exported or re-

---

[166] reg. 43(1) of the 1994 Regulations. Thus Sched. 4 plants are protected from the collecting of seed which does not harm the plant itself.

[167] reg. 43(3) of the 1994 Regulations.

[168] Without any contravention of the Regulations or Pt I of the 1981 Act.

[169] See n. 231 below and associated text.

[170] HMSO Treaty Series No. 101, Cmd. 6647 (1976).

[171] For details of the convention see de Klemm, *Guidelines For Legislation to Implement CITES*, IUCN Environmental Policy and Law Paper No. 26 (Gland, Switzerland, 1993).

[172] OJ L061, March 3, 1997, p. 1.

[173] OJ L140, May 30, 1997, p. 9. As amended by EC Regulations 767 of 1998: OJ L109, April 8, 1998, p. 7 and 1006 of 1998: OJ L145, May 15, 1998, p. 3.

[174] SI 1997/1372.

[175] As amended by Sched. 10 to the 1981 Act, and Statutory Instruments 2677 and 2684 of 1996.

[176] Art. 4(1) and (2), EC Regulation 338/97.

[177] Art. 5(1) and (4), EC Regulation 338/97.

exported.[178] Import of Annex C and D species needs only an import notification.[179] There are specific derogations for scientific institutions[180] and captive-bred or artificially propagated specimens.[181] The restrictions apply to living and dead animals and plants, their parts and any derivatives obtained from them. It is not an offence to be in possession of a CITES item, but commercial activities[182] are restricted.[183]

Restrictions on the introduction of non-native species

"Alien species introduced, deliberately or accidentally, by man may threaten the native flora and fauna, as predators or as competitors for the same limited resources."[184] Thus the 1981 Act prohibits the release into the wild or the allowing to escape into the wild of any animal which is of a kind not ordinarily resident in or a regular visitor to Great Britain in a wild state or which is included in Part I of Schedule 9 to the 1981 Act.[185] Part I of Schedule 9 lists animals already in the wild but whose further release is undesirable. It includes sika deer, American mink, grey squirrels and the New Zealand flatworm. It also includes the barn owl, a native species. This is to prevent captive-bred birds being released into the wild, which often results in their starving to death.[186]

It is also an offence for a person to plant or otherwise cause to grow in the wild any plant listed in Part II of Schedule 9 to the 1981 Act.[187] The list includes giant hogweed and Japanese knotweed. The restriction for plants applies only to plants listed in the schedule and not to non-native plants generally. As Taylor notes, "the latter would be impossible as virtually every garden in the country is stocked with mainly non-native plants".[188]

It is a defence to these offences that all reasonable steps were taken and all due diligence exercised to avoid committing the offence[189] or that a licence has been issued and all the conditions have been complied with. To assist the investigation of offences there is a power of entry to land[190] and the intentional obstruction of a person acting in the exercise of this power is also an offence.[191]

---

[178] Art. 5(4), EC Regulation 338/97.
[179] Art. 4(3) and (4), EC Regulation 338/97.
[180] Art. 7(4), EC Regulation 338/97.
[181] Art. 7(1), EC Regulation 338/97.
[182] This includes: the purchase, offer to purchase, acquisition for commercial purposes, display for commercial purposes, use for commercial gain and sale, keeping for sale, offering for sale or transporting for sale: Art. 8(1), EC Regulation 338/97.
[183] Art. 8, EC Regulation 338/97.
[184] Reid, *Nature Conservation Law* (Edinburgh, 1994), p. 231.
[185] s. 14(1) of the 1981 Act. Offences under s. 14 give rise to a fine not exceeding the statutory maximum on summary conviction and to a fine on conviction on indictment: s. 21(4) of the Act.
[186] Barn owls can be released so long as a licence has been issued: see n. 229 below and associated text.
[187] s. 14(2) of the 1981 Act.
[188] Taylor, *Wildlife Crime: A Guide to Wildlife Law Enforcement in the United Kingdom* (London, 1998), p. 93.
[189] s. 14(3) of the 1981 Act.
[190] For those authorised in writing by the Minister: s. 14(5) of the 1981 Act.
[191] s. 14(6) of the 1981 Act.

General provisions

Under the 1981 Act, the 1994 Regulations and the 1970 Act, any person who attempts to commit any of the offences under these provisions will be guilty of an offence.[192] Under the 1992 Act it is an offence to attempt to kill, injure or take a badger[193] but it is not an offence to attempt to commit any of the other offences under the 1992 Act.

Any person who has in their possession anything capable of being used for committing an offence, for the purposes of committing an offence under the 1981 Act, the 1994 Regulations or the 1970 Act, will be guilty of an offence and punishable on the same basis as if the offence had been committed.[194] There is no such provision in the 1992 Act.

Where an offence has been committed in respect of more than one bird, nest, egg, other animal, plant or other thing under the 1981 Act, or more than one badger under the 1992 Act, the maximum fine which may be imposed should be determined as if the person convicted had been convicted of a separate offence in respect of each.[195] There is no equivalent provision in the 1994 Regulations, although the levels of fines are commensurate between the 1981 Act and 1994 Regulations. Thus, if an offender has committed an offence is respect of more than one bird, etc., proceedings should be taken under the 1981 Act, where possible, because this gives the opportunity to impose fines in respect of each. There is also no such provision in the 1970 Act.

For offences under the 1981 Act and the 1994 Regulations, the court must order the forfeiture of any bird, nest, egg, other animal, plant or other thing in respect of which the offence was committed and may also order the forfeiture of any vehicle, animal, weapon or other thing which was used to commit the offence.[196] For offences under the 1970 Act, the court may order the forfeiture of any seal or seal skin in respect of which the offence was committed or of any seal, the skin of any seal, firearm, ammunition or poisonous substance in the offender's possession at the time of the offence.[197] For offences under the 1992 Act, the court shall order the forfeiture of any badger or the skin of any badger in respect of which the offence was committed and may, if they think fit, order the forfeiture of any weapon or article in respect of or by means of which the offence was committed.[198] Where a dog has been used in, or was present at, the commission of an offence of taking, injuring, killing or being cruel to a badger, the court may, in addition to or instead of any other punishment, order the destruction of, or disposal of, the dog and order that the accused be disqualified from having custody of a dog.[199]

---

[192] s. 18(1) of the 1981 Act, reg. 100(1) of the 1994 Regulations, s. 8(1) of the 1970 Act.
[193] s. 1(1) of the 1992 Act.
[194] s. 18(2) of the 1981 Act, reg. 100(2) of the 1994 Regulations and s. 8(2) of the 1970 Act.
[195] s. 21(5) of the 1981 Act and s. 12(2) of the 1992 Act.
[196] s. 21(6) of the 1981 Act and reg. 103(1) of the 1994 Regulations.
[197] s. 6 of the 1970 Act.
[198] s. 12(4) of the 1992 Act.
[199] s. 13 of the 1992 Act.

Licences

General or specific licences may be granted to allow almost every action that would otherwise constitute an offence.[200] The Royal Society for the Protection of Birds has criticised "the unsatisfactory way in which provisions for licensing various otherwise illegal activities have been interpreted and put into effect by a variety of Government departments and agencies".[201] Of particular concern are: the rather opaque criteria for issuing licences; the complete lack of any regulation once licences are issued; and in some cases a lack of scientific evidence to justify the issuing of licences. In relation to the latter point, licences for the shooting of goosanders[202] on the River Tweed have caused some concern to the Royal Society for the Protection of Birds. With general licences, some problems arise because of a lack of easily accessible information which can lead to confusion as to exactly which activities are permitted.

Licences under the 1981 Act

Licences may be granted[203] which permit: the killing, injuring and taking of wild birds and the taking, damaging and destruction of nests and eggs; possession of birds and eggs; the disturbance of birds listed in Schedule 1 to the 1981 Act[204]; the use of prohibited methods of killing and taking wild birds[205]; the competitive showing of birds[206]; the possession of a bird listed in Schedule 4 to the 1981 Act without registration and ringing[207]; and actions in areas of special protection.[208] Licences authorising these actions may not be granted unless the authority granting them is satisfied that there is no other satisfactory solution.[209] They may be granted by the Minister[210] or SNH[211] for: scientific, research or educational purposes; ringing or marking, or examining any ring or mark on, wild birds; conserving wild birds; the repopulation of an area with, or the reintroduction into an area of, wild birds, including any breeding necessary for those purposes; and conserving flora or fauna.[212] The Minister[213] may grant

---

[200] Only the offences under s. 6(8) and s. 11(3) of the 1981 Act cannot be exempted by licence.

[201] Royal Society for the Protection of Birds, *Evidence to the House of Commons Environment Committee: The Wildlife and Countryside Act* (Royal Society for the Protection of Birds internal documents, 1984), p. 29.

[202] Wild birds that receive protection under s. 1 of the 1981 Act.

[203] s. 16 of the 1981 Act.

[204] Actions that may constitute an offence under s. 1 of the 1981 Act.

[205] Actions that may constitute an offence under s. 5 of the 1981 Act.

[206] Actions that may constitute an offence under s. 6(3) of the 1981 Act.

[207] Actions that may constitute an offence under s. 7 of the 1981 Act.

[208] Actions that may constitute an offence under s. 3 of the 1981 Act. These licences may be granted under s. 16(1) of the Act. If the licence authorises action in respect of wild birds the licence must specify the species, the circumstances and the conditions subject to which the action may be taken and the methods, means or arrangements for taking the action: s. 5A of the Act.

[209] s. 1A(a) of the 1981 Act. This provision was added in the Wildlife and Countryside Act 1981 (Amendment) Regulations 1995 (SI 1995/2825) after the Royal Society for the Protection of Birds brought an action for judicial review against the Ministry of Agriculture, Fisheries and Food.

[210] In consultation with SNH: s. 16(9)(a) of the 1981 Act.

[211] Details of the number of licences issued by SNH are given in Scottish Natural Heritage, *Facts and Figures 1996–1997*, p. 1.

[212] s. 16(1)(a)–(cb) of the 1981 Act.

[213] In consultation with SNH: s. 16(9)(b) of the 1981 Act.

them for: protecting any collection of wild birds; falconry or aviculture; public exhibition or competition; taxidermy[214]; preserving public health or public or air safety; preventing the spread of disease; and preventing serious damage to livestock, foodstuffs for livestock, crops, vegetables, fruit, growing timber, fisheries or inland waters.[215] Licences may be granted by SNH for photographic purposes.[216]

Licences may also be granted[217] to allow the killing, injuring and taking of a wild animal[218]; possession and control of a wild animal[219]; the damage, destruction or obstruction of nests or roosts and the disturbance of a wild animal in its nest or roost[220]; the use of prohibited methods of killing and taking,[221] the picking, uprooting and destruction of a plant listed in Schedule 8 to the 1981 Act or the uprooting of any other plant.[222] They may be granted by SNH for: scientific or educational purposes; ringing or marking, or examining any ring or mark on, wild animals; conserving wild animals or wild plants or introducing them to particular areas; protecting any zoological or botanical collection; and photography.[223] The Minister may grant licences for: preserving public health or air safety; preventing the spread of disease; and preventing serious damage to livestock, foodstuffs for livestock, crops, vegetables, fruit, growing timber or any other form of property, or fisheries.[224] In consultation with SNH, the Minister may grant licences[225] to allow the sale and advertisement of birds, eggs,[226] animals[227] and plants,[228] and the introduction of new species.[229]

Licences for European protected species

For European protected species, actions may be licensed under the 1981 Act or under the 1994 Regulations. All of the actions that may constitute offences[230] under the 1994 Regulations can be permitted by licence. Licences under the 1994 Regulations will only be granted when two criteria are satisfied: there is no satisfactory alternative; and the action authorised will not be detrimental to the maintenance of the population of the species concerned at a favourable conser-

---

[214] s. 16(1)(d)–(g) of the 1981 Act.

[215] s. 16(1)(i)–(k) of the 1981 Act.

[216] s. 16(1)(h) of the 1981 Act. Licences may only be granted for those purposes in paras (e) to (h) on a selective basis and in respect of a small number of birds: s. 1A(b) of the 1981 Act.

[217] s. 16(3) of the 1981 Act. Any licence which authorises the killing of wild animals or wild birds must specify the area within which and the methods by which they may be killed: s. 16(6) of the 1981 Act.

[218] Actions that may constitute an offence under s. 9(1) of the 1981 Act.

[219] Actions that may constitute an offence under s. 9(2) of the 1981 Act.

[220] Actions that may constitute an offence under s. 9(4) of the 1981 Act.

[221] Actions that may constitute an offence under s. 11 of the 1981 Act. The use of snares which are prohibited under s. 11(3) of the 1981 Act cannot be licensed under s. 16(3) of the Act.

[222] Actions that may constitute an offence under s. 13(1) of the 1981 Act.

[223] s. 16(3)(a)–(e) of the 1981 Act.

[224] s. 16(3)(f)–(h) of the 1981 Act.

[225] Under s. 16(4) of the 1981 Act.

[226] Actions that would otherwise constitute an offence under s. 6(1) and (2) of the 1981 Act.

[227] Actions that would otherwise constitute an offence under s. 9(5) of the 1981 Act.

[228] Actions that would otherwise constitute an offence under s. 13(2) of the 1981 Act.

[229] Actions that would otherwise constitute an offence under s. 14 of the 1981 Act.

[230] Those restrictions in regs 39, 41 and 43.

vation status in their natural range.[231] As the second criterion is not applicable to licences under the 1981 Act, better protection is seemingly afforded under the 1994 Regulations. However, this is offset by the provision for licences to be granted by the Minister for imperative reasons of overriding public interest including those of a social or economic nature.[232]

As under the 1981 Act, licences can be granted by SNH for: scientific or educational purposes; ringing or marking, or examining any ring or mark on, wild animals; conserving wild animals or wild plants or introducing them to particular areas; and protecting any zoological or botanical collection.[233] The Minister may grant licences for: preserving public health or public safety; preventing the spread of disease; or preventing serious damage to livestock, foodstuffs for livestock, crops, vegetables, fruit, growing timber or any other form of property, or fisheries.[234]

Licences under the Protection of Badgers Act 1992

The killing and taking of badgers may be permitted by licences[235] granted by SNH for scientific and educational purposes or for the conservation of badgers[236]; and by the Minister for preventing the spread of disease and preventing serious damage to land, crops, poultry or any other form of property.[237] Licences may also be granted by SNH to take badgers for zoological gardens or specified collections or for ringing and marking them[238] and to permit the possession and sale of badgers for scientific and educational purposes or for the conservation of badgers, or for zoological gardens or specified collections.[239]

SNH may also grant licences to permit interference with a sett for: scientific and educational purposes or for the conservation of badgers[240]; development[241]; the preservation or archaeological investigation of a Scheduled Ancient Monument[242]; and investigating whether any offence has been committed or gathering evidence in connection with any court proceedings.[243] The Minister may grant such licences for: preventing the spread of disease; preventing serious damage to land, crops, poultry or any other form of property; any agricultural or forestry operation[244]; and operations to maintain or improve existing watercourses or drainage works and the construction of new works required for the drainage of

---

[231] reg. 44(3) of the 1994 Regulations.

[232] reg. 44(1)(e) of the 1994 Regulations.

[233] reg. 44(2)(a)–(d) of the 1994 Regulations.

[234] reg. 44(2)(e)–(g) of the 1994 Regulations.

[235] The licences will generally specify the number of badgers, the area within which the licence applies and the means by which the actions can be carried out. However, those granted by the Minister for the purposes associated with n. 244 are not subject to any limit on the number of badgers.

[236] s. 10(1)(a) of the 1992 Act.

[237] s. 10(2)(a) and (b) of the 1992 Act.

[238] s. 10(1)(b) and (c) of the 1992 Act.

[239] s. 10(1)(a) and (b) of the 1992 Act.

[240] s. 10(1)(a) of the 1992 Act.

[241] As defined in s. 26 of the Town and Country Planning (Scotland) Act 1997: s. 10(1)(d) of the 1992 Act.

[242] s. 10(1)(e) of the 1992 Act. As to the law relating to ancient monuments see Chap. 16.

[243] s. 10(1)(f) of the 1992 Act.

[244] s. 10(2)(a)–(c) of the 1992 Act.

land.[245] Licences may also be granted by either the Minister or SNH to permit interference with a sett for the purpose of controlling foxes to protect livestock, game or wildlife.[246]

Licences under the Conservation of Seals Act 1970

These licences are granted by the Minister[247] and they can permit the killing or taking of seals within a specified area by any means other than use of strychnine for: scientific or educational purposes[248]; the prevention of damage to fisheries; the reduction of a population of seals for management purposes; the use of a population surplus of seals as a resource; and the protection of flora or fauna in a nature reserve, Site of Special Scientific Interest, or marine nature reserve.[249] The taking of a specified number of seals can also be permitted for the purposes of zoological gardens or a specified collection.[250]

Conclusions

The majority of problems with species protection relate to the enforcement of offences. Some of these, such as discovering who has shot a protected species whose corpse has been found in a remote location, are very difficult to solve. However, the Partnership for Action Against Wildlife Crime has made a number of recommendations to the Government to enhance enforcement. These include an express power to require tissue samples to be taken for DNA analysis and specific powers of arrest. It is also recommended that the offences in the 1981 Act of intentionally disturbing nests be brought into line with the provisions of the 1992 Act. Intent to disturb is very difficult to prove: "people found near nests have claimed that they were going about their legitimate business, or that the disturbance was accidental rather than intentional".[251] If the concept of recklessness was introduced the prosecution would not have to prove that the accused had "a subjective appreciation of the risk . . . but only that he failed to consider an obvious risk".[252]

Furthermore, it is recommended that the penalties applicable to offences under the 1981 Act be amended. Under the Control of Trade in Endangered Species (Enforcement) Regulations 1997, the 1992 Act and the Wild Mammals (Protection) Act 1996, people convicted of offences can be imprisoned. However, the 1981 Act does not provide for the imposition of custodial sentences. The Partnership for Action Against Wildlife Crime highlight a number of anomalies

---

[245] Including sea defences: s. 10(2)(d) of the 1992 Act.

[246] s. 10(3) of the 1992 Act.

[247] In consultation with Natural Environment Research Council. However, if the licence is for the killing or taking of seals (otherwise than for the prevention of damage to fisheries) in a nature reserve, Site of Special Scientific Interest or marine nature reserve, then the consent of SNH must be obtained.

[248] s. 10(1)(a) of the 1970 Act.

[249] s. 10(1)(c) of the 1970 Act.

[250] s. 10(1)(b) of the 1970 Act. The area and the methods of taking will be specified in the licence.

[251] Partnership for Action Against Wildlife Crime, *Proposals For Legislative Changes*.

[252] Ibid. Clause 5 of the Wildlife Bill, sponsored by Wildlife and Countryside Link, which was presented to the House of Commons on November 3, 1998, provides for the insertion of the words "or recklessly" in every offence that currently uses the word "intentionally".

that are a consequence of this. Under the Wild Mammals (Protection) Act 1996, a person who kicks a hedgehog can be imprisoned for up to six months, but a person who kills an endangered British bird can only be fined. A person who robs a nest or kills a bird can only be fined under the 1981 Act, but if he sold the same bird (depending on the species) he could be imprisoned under the Control of Trade in Endangered Species (Enforcement) Regulations 1997. It is therefore recommended that custodial sentences be available for offences under Part I of the 1981 Act.[253]

---

[253] Ibid.

CHAPTER 11

THE PROTECTION OF HABITATS

Jeremy Rowan-Robinson
Christina Philp
Maria de la Torre

Introduction

In Chapter 10 reference was made to the long history of legislative intervention to protect species. However, it was not until the middle of the twentieth century that legislation intervened to protect the habitats of species and other habitats of nature conservation importance. Unlike the protection of species, where reliance has been placed on systems of regulation, intervention to protect habitats has, until recently, relied heavily on the "voluntary approach". The significance of this is explored below. A hierarchy of designated sites of nature conservation importance has evolved and provision has been made for influencing land management practices through the negotiation of agreements or, in some cases, through land acquisition.

The first legislation to deal with the protection of habitats was the National Parks and Access to the Countryside Act 1949 ("the 1949 Act"). Part III of the Act made provision for what was then the Nature Conservancy and for local authorities to arrange, through land acquisition,[1] leasing or the negotiation of agreements,[2] for the management of land as Nature Reserves. Nature Reserves are areas of land managed primarily for their nature conservation interest. The provision reflected the recommendations of the Huxley[3] and Ritchie[4] Committees which reported in 1947. Part III still survives although the powers of the Nature Conservancy are now exercised by Scottish Natural Heritage (SNH).

In addition, section 23 of the 1949 Act required the Nature Conservancy to notify the local planning authority of any land which in the opinion of the Conservancy was of special interest by reason of its flora, fauna, or geological or physiographical features. These became known as Sites of Special Scientific

---

[1] 1949 Act, ss 17 and 18.
[2] 1949 Act, s. 16.
[3] *Conservation of Nature in England and Wales*, Cmd. 7122 (1947).
[4] *Nature Reserves in Scotland*, Cmd. 7184 (1947).

Interest (SSSIs). SSSIs differ from Nature Reserves in that the nature conservation interest generally has to co-exist with other land uses. The Scott Committee, in its report in 1942, had identified development as a major threat to important habitats.[5] Agriculture and forestry were perceived to be environmentally benign. The objective of the notification requirement was to ensure that the nature conservation interest was at least taken into account by the planning authority when considering proposals for development. Although SSSIs still survive in the hierarchy of designated sites, the legislative arrangements are now to be found in Part II of the Wildlife and Countryside Act 1981 (see below). The Countryside Act 1968 subsequently mirrored the power in the 1949 Act to negotiate nature reserve agreements by making provision for the negotiation of agreements restricting land use in SSSIs.[6]

In 1965 the Natural Environment Research Council (NERC) was established as successor to the Nature Conservancy,[7] although its nature conservation functions were discharged through a committee referred to as the Nature Conservancy. Subsequently, the nature conservation functions of the NERC were transferred to the Nature Conservancy Council established by the Nature Conservancy Council Act 1973. The Council operated throughout Great Britain, although advisory committees were established for the constituent countries.[8]

In 1981, Part II of the Wildlife and Countryside Act 1981 ("the 1981 Act") made a fresh start with regard to SSSIs. The legislation was a manifestation of the breakdown in the rural consensus which had prevailed in the countryside since the Second World War. The growth of the conservation movement, combined with a realisation that measures designed to safeguard the countryside were proving inadequate in the face of agricultural intensification and afforestation, fuelled demands for reform.[9] This coincided with the advent of the Council of Europe Convention on the Conservation of European Wildlife and Habitats 1979 ("the Berne Convention") and of Directive 79/409 on the Conservation of Wild Birds ("the Birds Directive"). Both reflected public disquiet at the annual slaughter of migratory birds which was customary in southern Europe and northern Africa. The latter obliged Member States to designate special protection areas for the conservation of rare species of birds and migratory species. As a first step towards meeting its obligations under the Convention and the Directive and in response to the demand for reform, the Government introduced legislation to strengthen the arrangements for protecting SSSIs. The present law on SSSIs is explained below. As we shall see, the reforms rely heavily on the voluntary approach and experience has revealed a number of weaknesses in the arrangements which are now the subject of further proposals for reform[10] (see below).

---

[5] *Report of the Committee on Land Utilisation in Rural Areas,* Cmnd. 6378 (1942).

[6] s. 15.

[7] Science and Technology Act 1965, s. 3(3).

[8] 1973 Act, s. 2(2).

[9] For an interesting study of the genesis of the Wildlife and Countryside Bill see P. Lowe, G. Cox, M. MacEwen, T. O'Riordan and M. Winter, *Countryside Conflicts* (Gower/Maurice Temple Smith, 1986).

[10] *People and Nature: A New Approach to SSSI Designation in Scotland* (Scottish Office Consultation Paper, 1998).

The Environmental Protection Act 1990 ("the 1990 Act") brought an end to the unified approach to the discharge of nature conservation functions in Great Britain.[11] The background to this was discussed in Chapter 2. The Government felt that conservation issues were being determined for Scotland and Wales with too little regard to the particular requirements of these countries. The unpopularity of the NCC in Scotland seems to have been a prime motivation for the reform.[12] Part VII of the 1990 Act provided for the establishment of a separate Nature Conservancy Council for Scotland (NCCS). Concern about the potential break up of the NCC's "science base"[13] led to the establishment of a Joint Nature Conservation Committee (JNCC).[14] The Joint Committee provides advice to Government on nature conservation issues having a GB-wide dimension and has an important role in developing common standards for designation, monitoring and data analysis.[15]

However, the establishment of NCCS proved to be only the first step in the reform of the arrangements for discharging nature conservation functions in Scotland. NCCS, itself, was short-lived. The Natural Heritage (Scotland) Act 1991 replaced NCCS and the Countryside Commission for Scotland with Scottish Natural Heritage (SNH) with effect from April 1, 1992. The objective was to integrate the discharge of countryside and conservation functions.[16]

More recently, moves to strengthen the arrangements for habitat protection have come from the EC Directive 92/43 on the Conservation of Natural Habitats and of Wild Fauna and Flora ("the Habitats Directive"). This builds on the principles established in the Berne Convention. The Directive requires Member States to designate special areas of conservation which, together with the special protection areas designated under the Birds Directive, will make up a European network of habitats to be known as European sites or Natura 2000. The Habitats Directive has been implemented through the Conservation (Natural Habitats etc.) Regulations 1994.[17] As will be explained below, these Regulations mark a significant move away from the voluntary approach towards a more prescriptive regime for the protection of certain habitats.

In this introduction we have traced the changing administrative arrangements for the promotion of habitat protection in Scotland from the Nature Conservancy in 1949 through to the establishment of SNH in 1991. We have also introduced the principal components of the hierarchy of designated sites: SSSIs, Nature Reserves and European sites. These are examined in more detail below. In a recent consultation paper the Government reaffirmed its commitment to the use of designated sites, what it referred to as protected areas, to meet the continuing need to give special attention to safeguarding the most precious parts of our natural heritage:

---

[11] See generally F. Reynolds and W. Sheate, "Reorganization of the Conservation Authorities" in *Agriculture, Conservation and Land Use* (W. Howarth and C. Rodgers (eds), University of Wales Press, 1993).

[12] Ibid, p. 74. See, too, C.T. Reid, *Nature Conservation Law* (W. Green/Sweet & Maxwell, 1994), para. 2.5.3.

[13] Ibid, p. 77.

[14] 1990 Act, s. 128(4).

[15] 1990 Act, s. 133.

[16] See Scottish Development Department consultation paper, *Scotland's Natural Heritage: The Way Ahead* (1990).

[17] SI 1994/2716.

"Protected area status enables the most important and vulnerable parts of our natural heritage to be recognised as a focal point for conservation measures and for educational and demonstration activities which generate complementary conservation effort in the wider countryside."[18]

However, these are not the only measures in place to safeguard habitats and a number of other provisions are examined at the end of the chapter. It has been estimated that some 11 per cent of Scotland's land surface is subject to some form of nature conservation protection.[19]

Sites of Special Scientific Interest[20]

The most commonly employed means of safeguarding habitats is through their designation as an SSSI. The designation is important, not only in itself, but because it underpins the network of national Nature Reserves and the Natura 2000 programme. For this reason it is appropriate to consider it before the other designations. As at March 31, 1999, there were 1,448 SSSIs in Scotland, covering 919,597 hectares.[21]

Reciprocal notification

The provisions governing SSSIs are set out in Part II of the 1981 Act, as amended by the Wildlife and Countryside (Amendment) Act 1985. Section 28(1) imposes a duty on SNH to notify the planning authority, the owner and occupier of land and the Minister of any area of land which in its opinion is of special interest by reason of any of its flora, fauna or geological or physiographical features. The notice takes effect at once.[22] A public register of notifications must be maintained for each planning authority area (s. 28(12) and (12B)). The consequences of notification are explained below. The requirement under the 1981 Act to notify the owner and occupier and the Minister was new and one effect of this provision was that all SSSIs in Scotland at that time had to be renotified. This tied up an enormous amount of the then NCC and NCCS budget during the early and mid-1980s and the crash renotification programme generated considerable hostility on the part of the farming and landowning community who saw themselves as being subjected to additional controls.[23] However, the appropriate conservation body has no discretion with regard to notification (or renotification); where the scientific criteria are fulfilled, the site must be designated.[24] The scientific criteria are set out in guidelines[25]; these vary according to the type of habitat.

---

[18] *People and Nature: A New Approach to SSSI Designations in Scotland* (Scottish Office, 1998), para. 19.

[19] R. Crofts, "Protected areas in Scotland—Where are we going?", unpublished lecture, Department of Geography (Aberdeen University, March 1998).

[20] See generally B. Denyer-Green, *Wildlife and Countryside Act 1981* (Royal Institution of Chartered Surveyors, 1983).

[21] *Facts and Figures 1998–99* (SNH, 1999).

[22] 1981 Act, s. 28(5), as amended by the Wildlife and Countryside (Amendment) Act 1985, s. 2(5)(a).

[23] L. Livingstone, J. Rowan-Robinson and R. Cunningham, *Management Agreements for Nature Conservation*, Department of Land Economy Occasional Paper (Aberdeen University, 1990).

[24] *R v Nature Conservancy Council, ex p. London Brick Property Ltd* [1995] ELM 95.

[25] Guidelines for the Selection of Biological SSSIs were published by the former NCC in 1989. Separate criteria are provided for the selection of geological and physiographical SSSIs with reliance being placed on the Geological Conservation Review.

The notification will specify the special scientific interest and will list any operations which appear to SNH to be likely to damage[26] that interest (s. 28(4)). SNH has developed standardised lists for the different types of habitat, for example geological SSSIs or raised bogs. The list of potentially damaging operations (PDOs) tends to be fairly lengthy because this is a once and for all notification; SNH has no opportunity to review and upgrade the list in the light of changing circumstances. The lengthy list of PDOs also generated hostility during the renotification programme.[27]

The notification will specify a period (minimum three months) within which any objections or representations may be made to SNH. Such objections or representations may be directed only at the scientific basis of the notification.[28] Any such objections or representations, if not withdrawn, must be referred by SNH to the Advisory Committee on SSSIs which provides an independent review of the scientific case for notification.[29] No equivalent provision operates south of the border. SNH may not confirm the notification without having regard to any objections or representations (s. 28(2)) and without having received and considered the advice of the Committee.[30] Only 10 cases have been referred to the Advisory Committee since 1991.[31] In the light of the objections and representations and of the advice of the Committee, SNH will, within nine months of the original notification, either withdraw the notification or confirm it with or without modification (s. 28(4A)).

The effect of the notification process is to activate two distinct forms of control. First of all, planning authorities must consult SNH about planning applications for "development"[32] within an SSSI. This control is explained in Chapter 3. Second, section 28(5) provides that the owner or occupier of land subject to notification must not carry out, or cause or permit to be carried out, any PDO without first notifying this intention to SNH. This control is now explained in more detail.

The effect of section 28(1) and (5) is to create a regime for protecting habitats which revolves around a process of reciprocal notification. SNH notifies sites of special interest to owners and occupiers and provides a list of PDOs; owners and occupiers intending to carry on a PDO must first notify SNH. The PDO may not be carried out unless either SNH consents to the operation,[33] the operation is carried out in accordance with the terms of a management agreement concluded under either section 16 of the 1949 Act or section 15 of the 1968 Act, or four months[34] have elapsed from the giving of notice without any response from SNH (s. 28(5) and (6)).

---

[26] In *North Uist Fisheries Ltd* v *Secretary of State for Scotland* 1992 SLT 333 the court considered that the phrase "likely to damage" referred to operations which would probably cause damage, not to operations which might possibly do so.

[27] L. Livingstone *et al.*, op. cit., n. 23.

[28] Natural Heritage (Scotland) Act 1991, s. 12(5).

[29] Ibid. The Committee will also consider cases where an owner or occupier makes representations to the effect that the original grounds for designating an SSSI are no longer valid (s. 12(6)).

[30] Ibid, s. 12(7).

[31] *People and Nature* (Scottish Office, 1998), para. 36.

[32] As defined in the Town and Country Planning (Scotland) Act 1997.

[33] To avoid undue bureaucracy, SNH has granted a general consent to certain PDOs in certain circumstances.

[34] Four months was substituted by the Wildlife and Countryside (Amendment) Act 1985, s. 2(6). The period may be extended by agreement between the parties (s. 28(6A)).

It should be noted that section 28(5) does not prohibit the carrying out of a PDO; it subjects the owner or occupier to a period of delay to allow SNH to consider the impact of what is proposed and, where appropriate, to try to negotiate a management agreement. There is no obligation on an owner or occupier to fall in with SNH's wishes and after four months he or she may simply proceed with the operation. It is a system of voluntary protection. This has been the subject of criticism. In *Southern Water Authority* v *Nature Conservancy Council*[35] Lord Mustill observed:

> "it needs only a moment to see that this regime is toothless, for it demands no more from an owner or occupier of an SSSI than a little patience . . . In truth the Act does no more in the great majority of cases than give the Council a breathing space within which to apply moral pressure, with a view to persuading the owner or occupier to make a voluntary agreement".

Nonetheless, research published in 1990 showed that NCC and NCCS were generally successful in Scotland in securing their nature conservation objectives under the voluntary approach.[36] This was no doubt assisted by the arrangements for payment to owners and occupiers for entering into a management agreement (see below). It is clear, however, that statistics show a continuing picture of loss of or damage to SSSIs.[37]

A contravention of the provisions of section 28(5) is a criminal offence (s. 28(7)).[38] It is, however, a defence to proceedings to show that the PDO was authorised by a planning permission granted on an application under the 1997 Act (see Chapter 3)[39] or that it was an emergency operation and particulars were notified to SNH as soon as reasonably practicable (s. 28(8)).

Management agreements[40]

Although the regime introduced by section 28 is essentially voluntary, there is a clear incentive for owners and occupiers to fall in with SNH's wishes and to enter into a management agreement where this is offered. Where SNH, in

---

[35] [1992] 1 WLR 775.

[36] L. Livingstone *et al.*, op. cit., n. 23.

[37] *Protecting and Managing Sites of Special Scientific Interest* (National Audit Office, 1994); and see generally *Facts and Figures* published annually by SNH.

[38] For action taken in response to recent cases of damage to SSSIs, see *Facts and Figures 1998–99* (SNH, 1999), pp. 55–56. For a discussion of enforcement in England and Wales see D. Withrington and W. Jones, "The Enforcement of Conservation Legislation: Protecting Sites of Special Scientific Interest" in *Agriculture, Conservation and Land Use* (W. Howarth and C. Rodgers (eds), University of Wales Press, 1993). It should be noted that s. 28(5) applies to the owner and occupier of land. In *Southern Water Authority* v *Nature Conservancy Council* [1992] 1 WLR 775 it was held that an "occupier" referred to someone with a legal interest in the land and not, in that case, to the water authority carrying out work on the land.

[39] It should be noted that a general grant of planning permission under the Town and Country Planning (General Permitted Development) (Scotland) Order 1992 will not suffice. The defence for operations granted planning permission is regarded by some as a weakness in the regime because the nature conservation interest will only be one among a number of factors in the decision whether or not to grant permission. In other words, the nature conservation interest may, for example, be traded by the planning authority for local economic development.

[40] See generally C. Rodgers and J. Bishop, *Management Agreements for Nature Conservation* (RICS, 1998); also Country Landowners' Association, National Farmers Union and the Royal Institution of Chartered Surveyors, *Management Agreements in the Countryside* (Surveyors Publications, 1984).

response to a notice of intention to carry out a PDO, is of the view that, for the purposes of conserving the special scientific interest of the site, the PDO should not go ahead or should only go ahead in a certain way, it may offer to enter into a management agreement under section 16 of the 1949 Act or section 15 of the 1968 Act. Section 16 of the 1949 Act makes provision for agreements relating to Nature Reserves and these are considered below. Section 15 of the 1968 Act makes provision for agreements relating to SSSIs. It empowers SNH to enter into an agreement with the owners, lessees and occupiers of all or part of an SSSI or of any adjacent land[41] with a view to imposing restrictions on the exercise of rights over the land. The agreement may provide for the carrying out of work on the land and for the doing of anything that may be considered expedient for the purposes of the agreement; and provision may be made for defraying the cost of such works (s. 15(3)(b)). It may also contain such other provision with regard to the making of payments as may be specified (s. 15(3)(c)). The agreement may be recorded in the Register of Sasines or the Land Register of Scotland and may be enforced by SNH, with minor exceptions, against singular successors (s. 15(6)).

The level of payment to be made in an agreement entered into under section 15 of the 1968 Act is governed by section 50 of the 1981 Act. This provides that the payment shall be of such amount as may be determined by SNH in accordance with guidance given by the Minister (s. 50(2)). In the event of disagreement between the parties over the amount, the matter is to be referred to an arbiter (s. 50(3)).[42] The necessary guidance is contained in *Financial Guidelines for Management Agreements* issued in 1983.[43] These provide either for annual payments based on the net profit forgone because of the agreement or, for owners, the option of an annual payment calculated on the restricted and unrestricted capital values of the property. For woodland, an alternative basis calculated on the capitalised value of net profits forgone is permitted. As at March 31, 1999, there were in operation in Scotland 626 section 15 agreements covering some 126,484 hectares of land and for which £2,024,094 had been paid out.[44]

The arrangement whereby payments are made to owners and occupiers who threaten to damage a site of nature conservation interest while those who voluntarily manage their sites in accordance with that interest receive nothing, has been strongly criticised.[45] Further criticism has come from the Environment Committee of the House of Commons. In a report in 1985 the Committee commented on the negative and preventive character of most section 15 agreements and recommended that the legislation should be amended to allow for positive conservation measures to be included in agreements.[46] The Government in its

---

[41] The power to enter into an agreement with those having an interest in land adjacent to an SSSI was added by the Environmental Protection Act 1990, s. 132(1)(a) and Sched. 9, para. 4(2)(a).

[42] See *Cameron* v *Nature Conservancy Council* 1991 SLT (Lands Tr) 85; *Nature Conservancy Council for England* v *Deller* (1992) 43 EG 137; *Thomas* v *The Countryside Council for Wales* [1994] 4 All ER 853.

[43] The Guidelines were reviewed in 1985—see Laurence Gould Consultants Ltd, *Wildlife and Countryside Act 1981, Financial Guidelines for Management Agreements: Final Report*—but no changes were made.

[44] *Facts and Figures 1998–99* (SNH, 1999), p. 77.

[45] See L. Livingstone *et al.*, op. cit., n. 23.

[46] First Report from the Environment Committee, *Operation and Effectiveness of Part II of the Wildlife and Countryside Act*, Session 1984–85 (HMSO, 1985), para. 44.

response observed that it was a misreading of the Act to construe it in a way which discourages the possibility of positive conservation operations.[47] Provided the overall purpose of a section 15 agreement is to impose restrictions on the exercise of rights over the land by owners and occupiers, it is probably correct that the individual obligations may be either positive or negative. In the event of doubt, section 49A of the Countryside (Scotland) Act 1967[48] confers wide powers to do whatever may be necessary to secure the conservation and enhancement or to foster the understanding and enjoyment of the natural heritage of Scotland.[49] The criticism seems to have had an effect. Rodgers and Bishop note in a recent and comprehensive review of the use of management agreements to promote nature conservation in England and Wales that the trend over the last 15 years has been towards the adoption of proactive conservation measures.[50] The same is true of Scotland as well.[51]

Nature conservation orders

Where SNH encounters difficulties in securing a management agreement for an SSSI, it may, in certain cases, ask the Minister to make a nature conservation order (NCO). As at March 31, 1999, 12 NCOs were in force in Scotland.[52] Provision for such an order is made in section 29 of the 1981 Act. A nature conservation order may be made where it appears to the Minister expedient to do so for the purpose of securing the survival of any kind of animal or plant, of complying with an international obligation or for the purpose of conserving the flora, fauna, or geological or physiographical features of a site of national importance (s. 29(1) and (2)). The requirement to demonstrate national importance appears to be a limitation on the use of section 29; it seems that not all SSSIs are of national importance.[53] NCOs are used in practice to supplement the normal regime for controlling activity in an SSSI.

The procedure for making and confirming such an order is set out in Schedule 11 to the 1981 Act. An NCO takes effect when it is made; but it will lapse after nine months unless the Minister has given notice that he does, or does not, propose to amend or revoke it (para. 1) having gone through the following procedure. Public notice must be given of the making of the order and a copy must be served on the owner and occupier of the land affected and on the relevant local authority (para. 2). This provides an opportunity for representations or objections. Where any representations or objections are made, the Minister will convene a local inquiry or will afford any person who has responded the opportunity of being heard (para. 4). Public notice and notice to the owner and

---

[47] Department of the Environment, *The Government's Reply to the First Report from the Environment Committee*, Cmnd. 9522 (1985).

[48] Added by the Countryside (Scotland) Act 1981, s. 9.

[49] For details of the purposes for which s. 49A agreements have been employed see *Facts and Figures 1998–99* (SNH, 1999)).

[50] C. Rodgers and J. Bishop, *Management Agreements for Promoting Nature Conservation* (RICS, 1998).

[51] *People and Nature: A New Approach to SSSI Designation in Scotland* (Scottish Office), p. 29.

[52] SNH, *Annual Report 1996–97* (1997).

[53] D. Withrington and W. Jones, "The Enforcement of Conservation Legislation: Protecting Sites of Special Scientific Interest" in *Agriculture, Conservation and Land Use* (W. Howarth and C. Rodgers (eds), University of Wales Press, 1993), pp. 94 and 95; and see *Sweet v Secretary of State for the Environment* [1989] 2 PLR 14.

occupier must be given of the outcome of the Minister's consideration of the order and the response to it (para. 6). An NCO is to be registered in the Register of Sasines or in the Land Register of Scotland (s. 29(10)).

The effect of an NCO is to prohibit the carrying out by anyone of any operation specified in the order which is likely to destroy or damage the flora, fauna, or geological or physiographical features by reason of which the order was made (s. 29(3)). It is an offence, without reasonable excuse, for anyone[54] to carry out such an operation (s. 29(8)) and, in addition to a fine, a court may order restoration of the land (s. 31). In the event of default, SNH may restore the land and recover the cost (s. 31(6)). It is a "reasonable excuse" if the operation has the benefit of a planning permission under the Town and Country Planning (Scotland) Act 1997 or if it was an emergency operation the particulars of which were notified to SNH as soon as practicable after commencement (s. 29(9)).

The prohibition in section 29(3) will not apply where notice of a proposal to carry out the operation has been given to SNH and SNH have either consented to the operation, the operation is to be carried out in accordance with the terms of a management agreement or three months have elapsed from the giving of the notice (s. 29(4) and (5)).[55] If, before the expiry of the period of three months from the giving of notice, SNH offer to enter into a management agreement or offer to acquire that person's interest in the land, the period is extended from three to twelve months or to three months from the rejection or withdrawal of the offer, whichever is the later (s. 29(6)). If within the extended period SNH is unsuccessful in securing agreement, it may promote a compulsory purchase order and the making of the order has the effect of further postponing the commencement of the operation (s. 29(7)). Compulsory purchase powers have not yet been exercised by SNH or its predecessors, so that the practical effect of an NCO is generally to extend the period for negotiation from three to 12 months. It has been suggested that NCOs have been generally effective south of the border in getting owners and occupiers to negotiate management agreements.[56]

Where an NCO has been made, notice of a proposal to carry out a prohibited operation has been given and the extended period for negotiating an agreement applies, an entitlement to compensation may arise (s. 30(1)). Where the NCO relates to land comprising an agricultural unit,[57] a person having an interest in that land who can show that the value of his interest is less than it would have been if the order had not been made will be entitled to compensation from SNH (s. 30(2)). Compensation may also be payable by SNH to any person having an interest in land to which an NCO relates who can show that he has incurred abortive expenditure or has incurred other loss or damage (other than a reduction in the value of the interest in land) as a direct result of the extended period for negotiation. The procedure for making claims is set out in the Wildlife and Countryside (Claims for Compensation under Section 30) Regulations 1982[58]

---

[54] This may be contrasted with s. 28(7) where the offence may only be committed by an owner or occupier (*Southern Water Authority* v *Nature Conservancy Council* [1992] 1 WLR 775).

[55] See, with regard to the operation of the time period, *North Uist Fisheries Ltd* v *Secretary of State for Scotland* 1992 SLT 333.

[56] D. Withrington and W. Jones, op. cit., n. 53, p. 96.

[57] Defined in s. 30(11).

[58] SI 1982/1346.

and disputes are referred to the Lands Tribunal for Scotland for determination (s. 30(8)).

Farm capital grants and SSSIs

There is a further situation in which a management agreement will be offered by SNH and payment made to prevent damage to an SSSI. It arises where an application is made to the appropriate Minister for a farm capital grant[59] to fund expenditure in carrying out activity, such as agricultural improvements, within an SSSI. SNH will be consulted about the application and its response must be taken into account by the Minister in determining the application (s. 32(1)). So far as may be consistent with the purposes of the grant provisions, the Minister is required to exercise grant-awarding functions so as to further the nature conservation interest of an SSSI (1981 Act, s. 32(1)(a)). Where, in consequence of an objection by SNH, an application for grant aid is refused because of the damage or potential damage to the nature conservation interest of the site, SNH must within three months of receiving notice of the Minister's decision offer to enter into a management agreement restricting such activity and providing for payment to the applicant (s. 32(2)).

The Government is reviewing the question whether the loss of agricultural grant should be taken into account as a factor in assessing payments for management agreements.[60]

Proposals for reform

In a consultation paper issued in September 1998, the Scottish Office expressed the view that the identification of protected areas through the SSSI regime enabled important and vulnerable parts of our natural heritage to be identified and protected but that there are a number of features of the system where change might be considered.[61] For example, should the designation focus simply on the "jewels in Scotland's nature conservation crown" or should it encompass sites of local significance as well as those of national or international importance? Is there a role for a strengthened regime of local designations? Is reciprocal notification the best arrangement or would there be some advantage in negotiating a binding conservation contract at the time of designation for the positive management of an SSSI? Could the list of PDOs be reduced if subsequent amendment was allowed for? Is there a case for bringing the SSSI regime into line with planning control by removing the compensation entitlement? If so, should a right of appeal against a refusal of consent to carry out a PDO be introduced? Would it be appropriate to introduce an order-making power to tackle problems of inappropriate or insufficient land management?

Following the consultation exercise, the then Secretary of State for Scotland, in a speech in February 1999, set out a number of principles which should guide further consideration of these issues. These included clearer integration with the

---

[59] As defined in the 1981 Act, s. 32(3).

[60] *People and Nature* (Scottish Office, 1998), para. 70. The paper notes that removing the loss of woodland grant from the assessment of compensation in forestry cases in 1989 effectively ended the threat to SSSIs from commercial forestry operations.

[61] Ibid. A separate consultation paper, *Sites of Special Scientific Interest: Better Protection and Management*, was issued by the DETR for England and Wales.

objective of sustainable development, the denotification of sites which do not meet clear criteria of national importance, the incorporation of social and economic dimensions into the management of SSSIs with a stronger voice for local authorities and local communities, an end to large compensatory payments for not damaging the environment, the introduction of an appeals mechanism where people are prevented from undertaking activity within an SSSI, and an emphasis on the funding of positive management of sites rather than simply on protection. At the time of writing, a more detailed statement on proposed reforms to the SSSI regime is awaited from the Scottish Executive

Nature Reserves

The National Parks and Access to the Countryside Act 1949 makes provision for Nature Reserves. The expression applies to land managed for either or both of the following purposes:

(1) providing special opportunities for the study of and research into matters relating to the fauna and flora of Great Britain and the physical conditions in which they live and for the study of geological and physiographical features of special interest in the area;

(2) preserving flora, fauna or geological or physiographical features of special interest in the area (s. 15).

As Reid notes[62]:

"The study and conservation of nature are thus the prime objectives in the management of the land, in marked contrast to the other designations where nature conservation is either accommodated within the landowner's own use of the land or is balanced with or subordinate to other aims such as the provision of recreation or the protection of landscape."

A Nature Reserve may be declared on land held or leased by SNH. In addition, section 16 of the 1949 Act provides that SNH may enter into an agreement with the owner, lessee and occupier of any land which SNH considers should, in the national interest, be managed as a Nature Reserve with a view to securing that it will be managed as such.[63] Such agreements may impose restrictions on the exercise of rights over the land by the persons bound by the agreement (s. 16(2)) and may provide for the management of the land as a Nature Reserve and the carrying out of work and the doing of such other things as may be expedient for the purposes of the agreement (s. 16(3)). The agreement may also provide for the distribution of the cost of any of the matters mentioned in the agreement and may include provision for the payment by SNH of compensation for the effect of the restrictions on the exercise of rights (s. 16(3)). Section 17 provides that, failing agreement, SNH may compulsorily acquire land for the

---

[62] C.T. Reid, *Nature Conservation Law* (W. Green/Sweet & Maxwell, 1994), p. 147.

[63] Such agreements must be registered in the Register of Sasines or the Land Register for Scotland (1949 Act, s. 16(5)(c)).

establishment of Nature Reserves.[64] Section 19 provides that the declaration by SNH or its predecessors that land (whether acquired or the subject of agreement) is being managed as a Nature Reserve is to be conclusive. A Nature Reserve may also be declared by SNH on land held and managed by an "approved body".[65]

Reserves declared by SNH and its predecessors have generally been referred to as "National Nature Reserves" (NNRs). The 1981 Act subsequently made express provision for the declaration by SNH that Nature Reserves of national importance, held or managed by them under agreement or held by an approved body, are "National Nature Reserves" (s. 35(1)).[66] As at March 31, 1999 there were 71 National Nature Reserves in Scotland covering a total area of 114,277 hectares.[67] Some 34,071 hectares are owned by SNH, 3,572 hectares are leased and 75,517 hectares are the subject of an NNR agreement.[68] All NNRs are also SSSIs although the consequences of that regime will be modified in practice by the control which SNH exercises over an NNR through ownership, leasing or agreement. SNH may promote byelaws for NNRs, including NNRs held and managed by an approved body, restricting activity that would be incompatible in a Nature Reserve, including restriction on the entry of people (s. 20).

Planning authorities also have power to provide, or to secure the provision of, Nature Reserves on any land in their area where it appears expedient to the authority that it should be so managed in the interests of the locality (1949 Act, s. 21). Such reserves are generally known as "Local Nature Reserves". As at March 31, 1999, 29 Local Nature Reserves had been established in Scotland.[69] The provisions applying to NNRs apply also to Local Nature Reserves (s. 21(4)). The planning authority must consult with SNH over the exercise of this power (s. 21(6)).

European sites

Directive 92/43 on the conservation of natural habitats and of wild fauna and flora ("the Habitats Directive") provides that "[a] coherent European ecological network of special areas of conservation shall be set up under the title Natura 2000" (Art. 3(1)). Article 3 continues by stating that the network will include the special protection areas classified by Member States under Directive 79/409 on the conservation of wild birds ("the Birds Directive"). The objective of the network, states Article 3, is to enable the natural habitat types and the species' habitats concerned to be maintained or, where appropriate, restored at a favourable conservation status in their natural range. In this section of the chapter

---

[64] Compulsory powers may also be invoked in certain circumstances where there has been a breach of an agreement entered into under s. 16 (s. 18).

[65] An "approved body" is a body approved by SNH for the purposes of the section (s. 35(5)). Such bodies include NGOs such as the National Trust for Scotland, the Royal Society for the Protection of Birds and the Scottish Wildlife Trust.

[66] Reid suggests that the express provision in s. 35 of the 1981 Act has given rise to potential for confusion given the earlier quite widespread use of the term "National Nature Reserve" (C.T. Reid, *Nature Conservation Law* (W. Green/Sweet & Maxwell, 1994), p. 150).

[67] *Facts and Figures 1998–99* (SNH, 1999).

[68] Ibid.

[69] Ibid.

we describe the steps taken to implement the Birds and Habitats Directives in Scotland with a view to contributing to the establishment of this network of European sites.

Chronologically, the Birds Directive came first. As mentioned earlier, it stemmed from disquiet about the annual slaughter of migratory birds that was customary in southern Europe and northern Africa.[70] It provides for the protection, management and control of all naturally occurring species of wild birds in the territory of Member States. Reference has already been made to some of the provisions of the Directive and their consequences for domestic law in Chapter 10 dealing with the "Protection of Species". This chapter is concerned with the requirement on Member States to take special measures to conserve the habitats of certain particularly rare species (mentioned in Annex I to the Directive) and of regularly occurring migratory species (not listed in Annex I). As part of these special measures, they must classify the most suitable areas for these species as special protection areas (SPAs). SPAs are classified by the Minister following consultations by SNH with owners and occupiers and other local interests.

The obligations under the Birds Directive with regard to the classification of sites have given rise to some difficulties. In particular, it was initially unclear how far economic and other considerations could be taken into account in deciding the suitability of a site for classification. The matter was resolved in *Commission* v *Spain*[71] where the European Court of Justice (ECJ) held that by failing to designate an important wetland area as an SPA, the Spanish Government was in breach of the Directive. Member States had a duty to designate an area as an SPA if it fulfilled the objective ornithological criteria provided for in the text of Article 4(1) of the Directive. A similar view was taken by the ECJ in *R* v *Secretary of State for the Environment, ex p. RSPB*.[72] The RSPB challenged the failure by the UK Government to designate part of Lappel Bank as an SPA. The point in issue was how far economic considerations (the need to expand the port of Sheerness) could be taken into account in deciding what area to designate as an SPA. Following the earlier decision against Spain, the ECJ ruled that only ornithological considerations were relevant. In the same case, Advocate General Fenelly indicated that the criteria for the selection of SACs were also entirely conservation-related.

The Directive initially provided that within SPAs Member States should take appropriate steps to avoid pollution or deterioration of habitats or any disturbances affecting the birds, in so far as these would be significant (Art. 4(4)). To achieve this, SNH will first notify and confirm a proposed landward SPA as an SSSI so that it can receive the protection of Part II of the 1981 Act (see above). Part II of the 1981 Act was in fact introduced in part to meet the Government's obligations under the Birds Directive. The effect of the obligation in Article 4(4) was to impose a strong presumption against activity in an SPA. In *Commission* v

---

[70] N. Haigh, *EEC Environmental Policy and Britain* (Longman, 2nd edn, 1987), p. 292.

[71] Case C–355/90; [1993] ECR I–4221.

[72] Case C–44/55; [1997] JEL 245. See too *Commission* v *Kingdom of the Netherlands* Case C–3/96; *Commission* v *Federal Republic of Germany* [1991] ECR 1–883. In *WWF-UK and Others* v *Secretary of State for Scotland and Others*, Outer House, October 27, 1998, unreported, Lord Nimmo Smith held that the Government had some discretion in defining the boundaries of European sites, which discretion must, however, be exercised on scientific criteria.

Federal Republic of Germany[73] the ECJ held that reduction of an SPA was only justifiable on very limited grounds such as public health or public safety (in that case the latter) and that works could not be permitted for economic or recreational reasons.[74] It should be noted that activities within an SPA which fall within the definition of "development" in the Town and Country Planning (Scotland) Act 1997 are governed by that Act (see Chapter 3).

The obligations in Article 4(4) of the Birds Directive were subsequently replaced by Article 6(2), (3) and (4) of the Habitats Directive. The Habitats Directive transposes the Bern Convention on European Wildlife and Natural Habitats into community law. Its objective is to promote biodiversity. It has been described as probably the most important piece of wildlife legislation in Europe.[75] Amongst other things, it imposes on Member States the requirement referred to above to contribute towards establishing a coherent community-wide network of special areas of conservation (SACs) under the title Natura 2000. This network is to comprise sites hosting the natural habitat types listed in Annex I and habitats of species listed in Annex II. Certain natural habitat types and certain habitats of species are identified in the Annexes as "priority" habitats; the significance of this is explained below. The objective is to maintain or, where appropriate, restore the habitats at a favourable conservation status in their natural range (Art. 3(1)). (There is current debate as to whether the objective should be achieved through the designation of sites or through use of the wider mechanisms available to Member States.) The network also includes SPAs classified under the Birds Directive. The timetable (which has slipped) is that Member States were to send the Commission a list of candidate SACs by June 5, 1995. Candidate sites were to be selected having regard to the criteria in Annex III of the Directive and to other relevant scientific information.[76] The Government consulted with owners and occupiers and other interests prior to the inclusion of a site on the list. From these proposed sites the Commission would then draw up a draft list of sites of "Community Importance" by June 1998. The implication would seem to be that not all the sites submitted will necessarily be listed by the Commission, although it appears that all priority sites will automatically be considered to be sites of Community Importance. Once this list is finally adopted, Member States will have a duty to designate the sites as SACs as soon as possible and within a further period of six years at the most (by June 2004). The Minister must maintain a public register of European sites in Scotland and a copy will also be maintained by SNH.[77] SNH must give notice of registration to all owners and occupiers of land within a European site, to the relevant planning authority and to such other persons as the Minister may direct.[78] Planning authorities must also maintain a public register of all registered European sites about which they have been notified.[79]

[73] Case C–57/89; [1991] ECR 1–883.

[74] The point was reinforced subsequently in *Commission* v *Spain*, above, n. 71.

[75] *The impact of the EU on the UK Planning System* (DETR, 1998).

[76] The JNCC has produced *Approach to the selection of a UK list of possible SACs* to assist the process. See too JNCC (1997) The Habitats Directive: Selection of Special Areas of Conservation in the UK, Report No. 270.

[77] The Conservation (Natural Habitats etc.) Regulations 1994 (SI 1994/2716), regs 11–15.

[78] Ibid, reg. 13(1).

[79] Ibid, reg. 15(1).

The Habitats Directive has been given effect in the UK through the Conservation (Natural Habitats etc.) Regulations 1994.[80] These were made under section 2(2) of the European Communities Act 1972. Helpful guidance on the Regulations is given in SOEnvD Circular 6/1995. This states that potential SPAs and candidate SACs should be treated in the same way as classified SPAs for the purpose of considering development proposals or other uses of land affecting them (para. 14). In other words, the Regulations are effectively being applied to potential as well as actual European sites.

Article 6(2) imposes a general requirement on Member States to take appropriate steps to avoid, in both SPAs and SACs, significant deterioration of natural habitats and of the habitats of species as well as disturbance of the species for which the sites have been designated, in so far as such disturbance could be significant in relation to the objectives of the Directive. Under regulation 20 of the 1994 Regulations SNH has power to make byelaws for the protection of European sites.[81]

As with SPAs, SNH will first notify and confirm a proposed landward SAC as an SSSI so that it receives the protection of Part II of the 1981 Act.[82] Indeed, many proposed SPAs or candidate SACs will already be SSSIs and, in some cases, also national Nature Reserves and will already be subject to a measure of protection. This is recognised in the Regulations which provide that any management agreements previously entered into under section 16 of the 1949 Act, section 49A of the 1967 Act or section 15 of the 1968 Act are to continue in effect in European sites as if entered into under regulation 16 of the 1994 Regulations (reg. 17(1)).

However, the Directive and the Regulations go somewhat further than Part II of the 1981 Act in conferring protection on a European site. The procedure is complex and it may be helpful to set it out sequentially:

- An owner or occupier wanting to carry out a PDO in a European site must notify SNH in the normal way (1981 Act, s. 28(5); 1994 Regulations, regs 18 and 19(1)).[83]

- The operation may not proceed in the absence of consent[84] or unless it is carried out in accordance with the terms of a management agreement[85] or four months have elapsed from notification (1981 Act, s. 28(6); reg. 19(2)).

- It is an offence, without reasonable excuse, to breach these provisions (1981 Act, s. 28(7); reg. 19(3)). It is a reasonable excuse that the operation

---

[80] See n. 77 above.

[81] The regulation invokes the power in s. 20 of the National Parks and Access to the Countryside Act 1949 to make byelaws for the protection of Nature Reserves.

[82] Exceptionally, the River Spey candidate SAC was submitted to the Commission for consideration without the underpinning SSSI having been confirmed. This was also the case with the candidate SAC and SPAs on the Island of Lewis and the SPAs classified for the protection of corncrakes.

[83] SNH may alter the PDO list for a European site at any time (1994 Regulations, reg. 18(2)).

[84] Existing consents must be reviewed having regard to their compatibility with the conservation objectives of the site (reg. 21(2)). The modification or withdrawal of a consent will not, however, affect anything already done in reliance on the consent (reg. 21(4)).

[85] Specific powers to enter into a management agreement relating to land in or adjacent to a European site are contained in reg. 16.

was an emergency operation the particulars of which were notified to SNH as soon as practicable after commencement or that the operation was authorised by planning permission granted on an application under Part III of the Town and Country Planning (Scotland) Act 1997 (1981 Act, s. 28(8); reg. 19(4)). The effect of the Habitats Directive on planning control is discussed in Chapter 3.

- Where notice of an intention to carry out a PDO has been given and it appears to SNH that the operation is, or forms part of, a plan or project which is not directly connected with or necessary for the management of the site and which is likely to have a significant effect on the site,[86] SNH must make an assessment of its implications for the conservation objectives of the site (Habitats Directive, Art. 6(3); reg. 20(1)).

- Consent may only be given to the operation if SNH conclude, having regard to the assessment, that it will not adversely affect the integrity of the site (Art. 6(3); reg. 20(1) and (2)).

- It is important to bear in mind that, up to this point, the regime is voluntary. There is nothing so far to compel an owner or occupier to fall in with SNH's wishes. If SNH considers that, notwithstanding the absence of consent, there is a risk that the operation may nevertheless be carried out, it must notify the Minister at least one month before the expiry of the consultation period (reg. 20(4)).

- Where negotiations to prevent a PDO have failed, the Minister may make a special nature conservation order with regard to the site (SCNO) (reg. 22).[87] This will list the operations which appear likely to destroy or damage the nature conservation interest of the site.

- No person may carry out any operation specified in the SCNO unless notice has first been given to SNH and SNH has consented to it or it is carried out in accordance with the terms of a management agreement (reg. 23(1) and (2)).

- A person who, without reasonable excuse, breaches this requirement will be guilty of an offence (reg. 22(3)). "Reasonable excuse" is defined as before. If convicted of carrying out a PDO without consent, a person may be required to take such steps as may be necessary to restore the land to its former condition (reg. 26).

- An SNCO is modelled on the nature conservation order for SSSIs but differs in one important respect. SNH is not constrained by any time-limit. Its effect is to impose an absolute obligation not to proceed with the operation in the absence of consent.

- Where it appears to SNH that an operation, the subject of notice under regulation 23(1), is or forms part of a plan or project which is not directly connected with or necessary to the management of the site and is likely to have a significant effect on the site,[88] it must make an appropriate

---

[86] Either alone or in combination with other plans or projects.

[87] The procedure for making, objecting to, determining and bringing into operation such an order is set out in Sched. 1 to the Regulations.

[88] Either alone or in combination with other plans or projects.

assessment of the implications for the site (Habitats Directive, Art. 3; reg. 24(1)).

- SNH may only consent to the operation having ascertained, in the light of the assessment, that it will not adversely affect the integrity of the site (Art. 6(3); reg. 24(2)).

- SNH must give reasons for refusing consent. The owner or occupier may within two months of receipt of notice of refusal (or within three months of notification of the operation if no determination has been made) request that the matter be referred to the Minister (reg. 24(3) and (4)).

- If the Minister is satisfied that, there being no alternative solutions, the plan or project must be carried out for imperative reasons of overriding public interest, SNH may be directed to issue consent (Art. 6(4); reg. 24(5)). It is specifically stated that "reasons of overriding public interest" may be reasons of a social or economic nature.[89] Exceptionally, where the site concerned hosts a priority natural habitat type or priority species (above), reasons of overriding public interest must be either reasons relating to health, public safety or beneficial consequences of primary importance to the environment or other reasons, which in the opinion of the Commission, are imperative reasons of overriding public interest (Art. 6(4); reg. 24(6)).

- Where the Minister directs SNH to give consent under regulation 24(5), such compensatory measures as are necessary to ensure that the overall coherence of Natura 2000 is protected, must be provided for (Art. 6(4); reg. 24(7)).[90]

- SNH must compensate any person having an interest in land comprised in an agricultural unit to which the SNCO relates who can show that the value of the interest is less than it would have been if the order had not been made (reg. 25(1)). This entitlement is modelled on that for nature conservation orders under section 30 of the 1981 Act. As SNH will have offered a management agreement in response to a PDO notice to which it cannot consent, it is thought that the compensation entitlement under regulation 25(1) will seldom be invoked.

Where SNH is unable to secure a management agreement for a European site or such an agreement has been breached in a way which prevents or impairs the satisfactory management of the site, it may promote a compulsory purchase order (reg. 32(1)). Circular 6/1995 puts this provision more strongly and states that "SNH will in extreme circumstances be obliged to initiate compulsory purchase procedures" (para. 17). No authority is given for that statement but it is likely to be a reference to the overriding requirement in Article 6(2) of the Habitats Directive (which applies to both SACs and SPAs) to take appropriate steps to

---

[89] This exception for reasons of overriding public interest appears to water down the protection formerly given to SPAs under the Birds Directive (see *Commission* v *Federal Republic of Germany* Case C–57/89; [1991] ECR 1–883).

[90] Regulation 24 does not apply to a site which is a European site by reason only of reg. 10(1)(c).

avoid the deterioration of habitats and disturbance to species and to regulation 3(2) of the 1994 Regulations which requires SNH to exercise its functions "under the enactments relating to nature conservation so as to secure compliance with the requirements of the Habitats Directive".

At March 31, 1999, the Government had classified 103 SPAs in Scotland covering 372,261 hectares and a further 14 sites had been proposed. By the same date a list of 128 candidate SACs had been forwarded to the Commission covering some 643,484 hectares and a further 20 possible sites were under consideration by the Government.[91] There is, not surprisingly, considerable geographic overlap between SPAs and SACs; nonetheless, the designations will clearly cover a significant amount of Scotland's rural area.

Other measures for protecting habitats

In addition to what might reasonably be described as the principal habitat protection designations (SSSIs, Nature Reserves and European sites) discussed above, there are a number of other policy initiatives and designations which have, or could have, a role to play in habitat protection. These include the following:

Biodiversity action plans

"Biodiversity" is a term which is growing in importance. It encompasses "the whole rich variety of life that surrounds and sustains us".[92] It includes all kinds of animals, plants and microbes, the air, land- and water-scapes in which they live, their interaction with each other and with their surroundings and the differences between them. At the UN Conference on Environment and Development in Rio in 1992 the Government signed the Biodiversity Convention. Broadly, the Convention seeks to promote action to secure the future of the Earth's resources. In the UK this led to the publication in 1994 of *Biodiversity: the UK Action Plan*[93] and 1995 of *Biodiversity: the UK Steering Group Report*.[94] These stressed the need for all parts of the UK and all sectors of society to recognise the dangers and to play their part in conserving biodiversity. A Scottish Biodiversity Group was set up in 1996 to oversee action as part of a co-ordinated UK strategy. It brings together a wide range of interests, both public and private. The Group has been promoting action plans for species and habitats of importance in Scotland, preparing guidance to encourage the preparation and implementation of local biodiversity action plans, and generally raising public awareness.[95] The first local biodiversity action plans are beginning to emerge.

No new legislation has been introduced to implement obligations under the Convention. Instead, the focus is very much on improving the information base, preparing action plans for conserving species and habitats and co-ordinating and developing existing plans and resources from various sources and sectors so as to achieve a more effective employment of existing mechanisms (such as planning

---

[91] SNH, *Facts and Figures 1998–99* (1999).
[92] *Biodiversity in Scotland: The Way Forward* (Scottish Biodiversity Group, 1997), p. 1.
[93] Cm. 2428.
[94] (HMSO).
[95] Op. cit., n. 92.

control and the principal habitat protection mechanisms described above) to achieve biodiversity goals.

Environmentally Sensitive Areas

Reid observes that "[m]uch of the landscape and habitat in Great Britain has been shaped by agricultural practices, but is threatened by the pressure on farmers to change to more intensive and more efficient, but environmentally more harmful, methods if they are to make a living in the current agricultural markets".[96] The Agriculture Act 1986, s. 18 made provision for the introduction of Environmentally Sensitive Areas (ESAs). ESAs are areas where farming practices have contributed to the creation of distinctive landscapes and to the maintenance of wildlife and historic features. The designation of an ESA by the Minister, after consultation with SNH, allows farmers and crofters access to payments to support the adoption or continuation of environmentally friendly land management practices. The arrangement, which is entirely voluntary, is achieved through an agreement. Between 1987 and 1997 10 ESAs were designated in Scotland. ESAs are examined in more detail in Chapter 4.

The Countryside Premium Scheme introduced by the Government under the Agri-Environment Programme in 1997 enables assistance to be given to environmentally friendly farming practices outwith ESAs. This too is examined in more detail in Chapter 4. Plans to merge the schemes were announced in June 1998.

National heritage property

"National heritage property" is a term applied, amongst other things, to land of outstanding scenic, scientific or historic interest and buildings of outstanding architectural or historic interest. The maintenance of such interest clearly makes an important contribution to the state of the environment.

One mechanism which is employed to secure this is the use of conditional exemption from taxation. The normal position is that, subject to a threshold, inheritance tax, introduced by the Finance Act 1986, is charged when property changes ownership as a result of a bequest. Certain lifetime gifts may also be chargeable if the donor dies within seven years of the gift.

A claim for exemption may be made in connection with national heritage property after a charge to tax has arisen.[97] The owner may apply to the Capital Taxes Office for conditional exemption. The Capital Taxes Office will ask SNH, for land of scenic or scientific interest, to assess whether the property qualifies as national heritage property. If it does, the owner, in order to secure exemption, will be required to undertake to manage the land so as to preserve its national heritage interest, to refrain from doing anything that will detract from that interest, and to promote reasonable public access. The undertaking may be in the form of a statement of conditions or a management plan. In the event of such an undertaking, the Capital Taxes Office will confirm that the transfer is conditionally exempt. SNH will monitor the arrangement, in so far as it applies to land of scenic or scientific interest, to ensure compliance with the undertaking. The transfer is conditionally exempt in the sense that the tax is deferred until the undertaking ceases to apply.

---

[96] C.T. Reid, *Nature Conservation Law* (W. Green/Sweet & Maxwell, 1994), p. 173.
[97] See generally *Capital Taxation and National Heritage* (Board of the Inland Revenue, 1986).

It is difficult to obtain information about the operation and impact of this exemption in terms of habitat protection. The problem is the confidential nature of tax arrangements. Although the Inland Revenue will publish global information about inheritance tax relief (for example, in 1997 some 48,000 hectares of land in Scotland benefited from the exemption)[98], it is impossible to find out which particular bits of the countryside are safeguarded through such undertakings. The Inland Revenue Statistics for 1996[99] show, for example, that the estimated cost of inheritance tax relief for heritage property and maintenance funds for 1995–96 was £75 million and, for 1996–97, £100 million. However, it seems that, of the global figure, the amount attributable to heritage land and buildings is actually quite small—no more than £5 million for 1995–96.[100]

Nitrate-Sensitive Areas and Nitrate-Vulnerable Zones

Concern at European level about the concentration of nitrates in water led to the Nitrate's Directive (91/676). This has been implemented in Scotland through section 31B of the Control of Pollution Act 1974 which provides for the designation by the Minister of Nitrate-Sensitive Areas where the level of nitrates in water supplies is in danger of exceeding a target threshold. Within such areas nitrates from agricultural sources can be addressed through payments to farmers for voluntarily making changes to farming methods. A second type of designation, the Nitrate-Vulnerable Zone, adopts a regulatory approach. Within such zones farmers are required to follow certain farming methods which broadly equate with good agricultural practice. These arrangements are discussed in more detail in Chapter 4.

Natural Heritage Areas

Section 6 of the Natural Heritage (Scotland) Act 1991 provides for the designation by the Minister on the recommendation of SNH of an area as a "Natural Heritage Area". This will be an area of such outstanding value to the natural heritage that special protection measures are appropriate. NPPG 14, *Natural Heritage*, states that the designation shares many of the objectives of National Parks and that, as the Government now supports the introduction of National Parks into Scotland, it is unlikely that this designation will ever be employed.[101]

Ramsar Sites

Ramsar Sites are designated by the Minister to satisfy obligations arising from the *Convention on Conservation of Wetlands of International Importance, especially as Waterfowl Habitat.*[102] The Convention recognises that birds are ecologically dependent on wetlands and that these must be protected.[103] Countries bound

---

[98] Parliamentary Debates, Vol. 274, No. 80, col. 777, 1997.
[99] HMSO.
[100] Parliamentary Debates, Vol. 289, No. 52, col. 234, 1997.
[101] para. 34.
[102] Cm. 6464 (1971). See generally C.T. Reid, *Nature Conservation Law* (W. Green/Sweet & Maxwell, 1994), pp. 265–266.
[103] Wetlands are defined in Art. 1(1) to include areas of marsh, fen, peatland or water, whether natural or artificial, permanent or temporary, with water that is static or flowing, fresh, brackish or salt, and including areas of marine water the depth of which at low tide does not exceed six metres.

by the Convention must designate suitable wetlands for inclusion in the "List of Wetlands of International Importance".[104] The designation does not invoke any statutory protection but in practice all listed sites are also SSSIs and may be Nature Reserves. Most will also fulfil the criteria for designation as a special protection area under the Birds Directive. Planning policies must be formulated and implemented so as to promote the conservation of such sites.[105]

As at March 31, 1999, 48 Ramsar Sites had been classified in Scotland and a further four potential sites had been identified.[106]

World Heritage Sites

A World Heritage Site is a site which appears on the World Heritage List of sites of "Outstanding Universal Value" from a scientific, aesthetic or nature conservation standpoint. The list is compiled by the World Heritage Committee set up under the *Convention Concerning the Protection of the World Cultural and Natural Heritage* (1972). The objective of the Convention is to give international recognition and assistance for the protection of monuments, buildings and sites which are the natural and man-made treasures of the world.[107] Reid, quoting Article 4 of the Convention, notes that a state has a duty to secure the "protection, conservation, preservation, presentation and transmission to future generations" of the natural heritage in its territory and "to do all it can to this end, to the utmost of its own resources". What this amounts to is that a high standard of management is required before listing will be considered.

No new protective measures have been introduced to implement the Convention within Great Britain. Instead reliance is being placed on existing mechanisms such as designation as a national Nature Reserve. The only site in Scotland currently on the list is St Kilda in the Western Isles (853 hectares), designated because of its natural heritage. The Cairngorms and the Flow Country are being submitted to the Committee for consideration as natural sites and the Forth Rail Bridge and New Lanark as man-made "treasures".[108]

Limestone Pavement Orders

Limestone pavements are a landscape formation of both biological and geological importance. The habitat is extremely fragile and is recognised at a European level as vulnerable to disappearance.[109]

Section 34 of the 1981 Act provides that where SNH is of the opinion that a limestone pavement is of special nature conservation interest it must notify that fact to the appropriate planning authority. The intention presumably is that the planning authority can act to prevent anyone from carrying on a business of removing and selling the pavement, for example for garden rockeries. If additional protection is considered necessary, the Minister or the planning authority may prohibit the removal of the pavement, or its disturbance, by making a Limestone Pavement Order. Breach of an order is an offence. The

---

[104] Art. 4(1).
[105] Art. 3(1).
[106] *Facts and Figures 1998–1999* (SNH, 1999).
[107] See C.T. Reid, op. cit., n. 101, pp. 194–195 and 263–265.
[108] *Scottish Environment News*, April 1999, p. 1.
[109] See the Habitats Directive, Annex 1.

number of limestone pavements in Scotland is limited and no such order has yet been made.

NGOs

The contribution of voluntary bodies (often referred to as "non-governmental organisations" or "NGOs") to habitat protection has always been important; indeed, Bell comments that for a long time "the weight of conservation fell on voluntary organisations".[110] Even before the 1949 Act, voluntary bodies such as the National Trust for Scotland had taken an interest in the purchase of land as a means of protecting the countryside. Wightman notes that this was the beginning of a process of increased involvement in landownership by voluntary bodies as a means of securing wildlife and wild land conservation.[111] Between them, the National Trust for Scotland, the Royal Society for the Protection of Birds, the John Muir Trust, the Scottish Wildlife Trust and the Woodland Trust now own some 333,000 acres of the Scottish countryside managed very largely for the purposes of conservation.[112]

---

[110] S. Bell, *Ball and Bell on Environmental Law* (Blackstone Press, 4th edn, 1997), p. 491; and see generally J.C. Dwyer and I.D. Hodge, *Countryside in Trust* (John Wiley & Sons, 1996).

[111] A. Wightman, *Who Owns Scotland* (Canongate, 1996), p. 182.

[112] Ibid, p. 186.

CHAPTER 12

ACCESS: GENERAL CONSIDERATIONS

Donna McKenzie Skene
Jeremy Rowan-Robinson

Introduction

An increasing demand for access to the countryside for the purposes of recreation has given rise recently to wide-ranging and high-profile debate on the issue. The starting-point for any consideration of the issues relating to access to the countryside in Scotland is the basic principle of Scots law that an owner of land is entitled to the exclusive use of that land.[1] The right to the exclusive use of land and the interlinked right to use and enjoy the land, which includes the right to grant its use and enjoyment to others, are the main incidents of ownership of land in Scotland.[2] These rights may be qualified in certain circumstances, for example, by statute. Subject to any such qualifications, however, the corollary of the right of exclusive use is that no-one may use or enter land without permission or some other right. Anyone who does enter land without such permission or right commits a trespass, for which the law provides a number of remedies.[3] This obviously has serious implications for those seeking to exercise access to the countryside.

Permission to enter or use land may be express or implied, but may be withdrawn at any time unless there is a binding agreement to the contrary.[4] A right to enter land may arise in a number of ways: in the context of access to the countryside, it is most likely to take the form of a public right of way *or* a right arising as a result of the creation of linear or area access under various statutory provisions.[5] Even rights of access created under the relevant statutory provisions, however, will usually have been created by agreement. There are provisions for the creation of both linear and area access without agreement, but these are rarely utilised.

Access to the countryside for the purposes of recreation is, therefore, largely dependent at the time of writing on the consent and co-operation of those to

---

[1] Erskine, *Inst*, II.i.1.
[2] Gordon, *Land Law*, para. 13–06.
[3] See further below.
[4] *Love-Lee v Cameron of Lochiel* 1991 SCLR 61.
[5] See further Chaps 13 and 14, which deal with linear and area access respectively.

whose land access is sought, but this is currently under review as part of the wider debate on land reform. In January 1999, Scottish Natural Heritage (hereafter "SNH") published its advice to government on access.[6] That advice took account of the work and conclusions of the Access Forum[7] and essentially endorsed, subject to some further recommendations, the Access Forum's recommendation for "a right of access to land and water for informal recreation and passage, subject to responsible exercise of that right, to protection of the privacy of individuals, to safeguards for the operational needs of land managers, and subject to any necessary restraints for conservation needs".[8] The proposed right of access would extend to enclosed as well as open and hill ground. The Government indicated its acceptance of that advice as a starting point for developing detailed legislative proposals to be placed before the Scottish Parliament.[9] It is probable, therefore, that a statutory right of access, subject to certain qualifications, will become a reality in the near future.

One issue of increasing importance in relation to access is the possibility of liability arising from recreational access to the countryside. Possible liability may be a factor in a landowner's decision whether, or to what extent, to permit access under the current arrangements and will need to be addressed if and when a statutory right of access is introduced. The principal concern here is with potential liability *to* those taking access to the countryside for any injury, loss or damage resulting from such access, but there is also concern over damage caused *by* those taking access. These concerns increase with the numbers of persons taking access.

This chapter examines the role of the law of trespass in the context of access to the countryside under the existing system, with particular reference to the issue of self-help as a remedy for trespass, and the current law relating to civil liability for injury and damage arising from recreational access to the countryside.

Trespass

As noted above, the corollary of a landowner's right of exclusive use of his land is that no one may use or enter that land without permission or some other right, and anyone who does so commits a trespass. Trespass has been defined as a "temporary or transient intrusion into land owned or otherwise lawfully possessed[10] by someone else".[11] The intrusion may be by persons, by animals or by things, and even a slight intrusion amounts to trespass.[12] If a statutory right of access is enacted, then any "intrusion" into land within the terms of that right would not amount to a trespass, but any intrusion into land falling outwith the

---

[6] *Access to the Countryside for Open-air Recreation: Scottish Natural Heritage's Advice to Government* (Scottish Natural Heritage, 1999).

[7] Established in 1994 and consisting of the Access Forum and the Access Forum (Inland Water). Rights of access to water are dealt with in Chap. 15.

[8] See op. cit., n. 6. As noted above, rights of access to water are dealt with in Chap. 15.

[9] See speech by the Secretary of State for Scotland at Balmaha Visitor Centre by Loch Lomond, February 2, 1999 and the Scottish Executive White Paper *Land Reform: Proposals for Legislation,* SE/1999/1 (Stationery Office, July 1999).

[10] Possession in this context means natural possession: see (para. 175, n. 1) *Stair Memorial Encyclopaedia,* Vol. 18.

[11] *Stair Memorial Encyclopaedia,* Vol. 18, para. 180.

[12] Ibid.

terms of that right would amount to a trespass, and trespass will therefore continue to be relevant in the context of access even if such a right is enacted.[13]

Remedies for trespass

There are a number of different remedies available against trespass. Interdict may be available to prevent anticipated or repeated trespass, damages may be recovered for actual loss resulting from a trespass and self-help may be utilised to prevent a trespass or bring an existing trespass to an end and each of these remedies raises particular issues in the context of access. There are also certain additional remedies where the trespass is committed by straying animals. Trespass by straying animals raises special issues and is therefore considered separately below.

Interdict

In principle, interdict is available to prevent anticipated or future acts of trespass, but in practice, it may be difficult to obtain an interdict. Interdict is a discretionary remedy and each case will turn on its own particular facts. However, interdict will not generally be granted in trivial cases: there must be an "appreciable wrong" to the pursuer.[14] It has been pointed out that since, by definition, trespass is always temporary, it may be vulnerable to arguments based on triviality, but these may be negatived where continuance of the wrong renders it sufficiently serious to justify an interdict.[15] Furthermore, it must generally be shown that there is a sufficient likelihood of trespass or further trespass. In *Inverurie Magistrates v Sorrie*,[16] interdict was refused where there had been no past acts of trespass and no threat of future acts of trespass, even although the defender was asserting a right to enter the petitioner's land, and in *Hay's Trs v Young*,[17] interdict was also refused in circumstances where there was no likelihood of a trespass being repeated. A related point is that the court may refuse interdict unless the trespasser has been warned and the effect of the warning has been monitored[18]; conversely, where a warning has been given and ignored, the case for interdict will be strengthened.

There are also purely practical considerations which may make it difficult or inappropriate to obtain an interdict. It may be difficult to sufficiently identify a trespasser in order to bring proceedings for interdict against him or her. This would be a particular difficulty where trespass is being committed by ordinary members of the public, who will generally be unknown to the landowner and who cannot be compelled to identify themselves to him. Furthermore, interdict is only effective against the person or persons named therein. It is not possible to obtain an interdict against the world at large, and an interdict against a named person or persons will not offer any protection against trespass by other persons. Again, this is likely to be a particular issue where trespass is being routinely

---

[13] Although depending on the terms of the right, there may be practical and legal difficulties in determining when the intrusion is lawful and when it amounts to a trespass.

[14] *Winans v Macrae* (1885) 12 R 1051, which involved trespass by a straying lamb.

[15] *Stair Memorial Encyclopaedia*, Vol. 18, para. 183, referring in turn to Burn-Murdoch, *Interdict in the Law of Scotland* (1933), para. 96.

[16] 1956 SC 175.

[17] (1877) 4 R 398.

[18] *Paterson v McPherson* (1916) 33 Sh Ct Rep 237.

committed by members of the public taking access to the land for the purposes of recreation. Quite apart from the practical considerations of raising proceedings against every single trespasser individually, each person will generally be trespassing only on a one-off basis, so that even if they could be identified, there would be a lack of that sufficient likelihood of repetition necessary to justify an interdict in the first place.

Interdict will not, therefore, generally be a practical remedy for trespass committed in the course of taking access to the countryside for recreation.

Damages

In contrast to the position in England and Wales, where nominal damages may be recovered for trespass even where there is no loss,[19] damages may only be recovered for trespass in Scotland where actual loss has been caused.[20] A landowner has no remedy in damages against a trespasser for the mere act of trespass, which it is thought will be the usual case: most trespasses committed in the course of taking access to the countryside for recreation will not result in any damage or loss.

Self-help[21]

Self-help may be utilised to prevent a trespass or to bring an existing trespass to an end, but must be exercised with caution in order to avoid potential criminal and/or civil liability. Self-help in this context may conveniently be dealt with in three parts: defensive measures designed to prevent a trespass from occurring, the use of force in self-defence against violence offered by a trespasser and the use of force to bring a trespass to an end.

Defensive measures designed to deter trespassers may take a variety of forms, for example, erecting walls, fences or gates, installing security lights, alarms or cameras, posting warning notices, operating security patrols, etc.[22] Any form of defensive measure which may, or actually does, cause injury to trespassers, however, may result in criminal and/or civil liability. There are a number of potentially relevant criminal offences in this context. In the case of *Craw*,[23] it was held that a gamekeeper who had set a spring gun which was triggered by a poacher who died of the injuries received as a result was relevantly charged with murder, although it is perhaps doubtful whether this case would be followed today.[24] The most relevant criminal offences today are likely to be reckless injury, reckless endangerment and causing real injury. The main authority on reckless injury is *H.M. Advocate* v *Harris*,[25] where the court held that the conduct which

---

[19] See 45 *Halisbury's Laws of England* (4th edn), para. 1403.

[20] *Stair Memorial Encyclopaedia*, Vol. 18, para. 185.

[21] This particular issue in this context is discussed in detail in a recent article by the authors: see "Self Help and Access to the Countryside", 1998 JR 299.

[22] The use of dogs as a defensive measure raises special issues, a detailed discussion of which is beyond the scope of this chapter, but the position with respect to liability for injury caused by animals generally, including dogs, is discussed below.

[23] 1827 Syme 188 at 210.

[24] See Rowan-Robinson and McKenzie Skene, "Self Help and Access to the Countryside", op. cit., n. 21. The use of firearms generally raises special issues because of the detailed laws relating to their use: a detailed examination of these is beyond the scope of this chapter, but some aspects are discussed in Chap. 8.

[25] 1993 SCCR 559.

could give rise to a charge of reckless injury was not confined to conduct of a particular class or classes, that the offence could be committed even where there was no intention to cause injury and that the offence could be committed even where the injury resulted from a lawful act if that act was carried out recklessly, recklessly in this context meaning without due regard for foreseeable dangerous consequences or with culpable disregard for the consequences.[26] It is easy to see that some types of defensive measure designed to deter trespassers, such as hidden traps, may potentially give rise to criminal liability in this way. With respect to reckless endangerment, reckless conduct which causes danger to the public may be an offence even if no actual injury results.[27] As with reckless injury, the offence may be committed even where the danger results from a lawful act if that act is carried out recklessly.[28] Again, it is easy to see that some defensive measures which are potentially dangerous, such as glass cemented into the top of a wall, may give rise to criminal liability in this way even where no injury has actually been caused. Finally, with respect to causing real injury, the basis of this offence is to be found in a passage from Hume,[29] from which the court in the case of *Khaliq* v *H.M. Advocate*[30] concluded that "within the category of conduct identified as criminal are acts, whatever their nature may be, which cause real injury to the person".[31] That formulation is very broad and, once again, it is easy to see that defensive measures which actually cause injury may give rise to criminal liability in this way. Furthermore, it seems that this will be so even where the injury has resulted from a voluntary act of the injured party, such as climbing onto a wall with broken glass cemented into the top of it, where it was known that the conduct complained of would or could cause real injury and it actually does so.[32]

In relation to civil liability arising from the use of defensive measures, this is most likely to arise under the Occupiers' Liability (Scotland) Act 1960 (hereafter "the 1960 Act"), which provides that a person occupying or having control of land or premises must take such care as is reasonable in all the circumstances to see that persons entering thereon will not suffer injury or damage as a result of the state of the premises or anything done or omitted to be done on them.[33] The placing of defensive measures will amount to something done on the premises, or such measures may affect the state of the premises. The occupier's duty under the 1960 Act extends to trespassers, although the fact that a person who sustains injury or damage is a trespasser is a factor to be taken into account in deciding whether the occupier has fulfilled his duty of reasonable care or not.[34] Where defensive measures are utilised, the occupier's duty of care should be fulfilled if

---

[26] For these two slightly different formulations of recklessness, see Lord Prosser at 547E–F and Lord Morrison at 572D respectively.

[27] *H.M. Advocate* v *Harris* 1993 SCCR 559.

[28] See *McPhail* v *Clark* 1983 SLT (Sh Ct) 37, which involved a farmer failing to take any steps to prevent danger to motorists from smoke obscuring visibility on the road adjacent to his field where he was burning stubble, an activity otherwise perfectly lawful in itself.

[29] (3rd edn), Vol. 1, p. 327.

[30] 1983 SCCR 483.

[31] Ibid, at 492.

[32] *Khaliq* v *H.M. Advocate*, above, n. 30; see also *Ulhaq* v *H.M. Advocate* 1990 SCCR 593.

[33] s. 2(1).

[34] See further below.

the measures are obvious and/or adequate warning of them is given, and a trespasser who is injured after voluntarily choosing to run the gauntlet of such measures in the face of obvious danger or adequate warnings will generally be successfully met with the statutory form of the defence of *volenti non fit injuria* contained in section 2(3) of the 1960 Act. Liability may also arise under the normal principles of delict at common law. The 1960 Act and the common law are discussed fully below in the context of civil liability to those taking access to the countryside generally, and reference should be made to that discussion.

Self-help in the form of defensive measures designed to prevent trespass from taking place may be contrasted with self-help designed to bring a current trespass to an end. The main issue in relation to self-help designed to bring a trespass to an end is the extent to which force can be used. A distinction may be drawn here between the use of force in response to violence offered by a trespasser, and the use of force to remove a trespasser where no violence is offered. There is no doubt that a person may use force in response to an unjustified attack on his own person or that of another,[35] and it will be a defence to any subsequent criminal charge, for example assault, to show that the force so offered was offered in self-defence. There are, however, limits to this defence: there must be imminent danger to life or limb, any (reasonable) means of escape or retreat, where available, must be taken in preference to using force and the retaliation must not be excessive in comparison with the force used by the assailant, although it need not necessarily be in exact proportion, some allowance being made for the heat of the moment.[36] If any of these conditions is not satisfied, for example, reasonable means of escape were not utilised, or excessive force was used, there may be criminal liability for that use of force. The use of reasonable force in self-defence will also be a defence to a civil action, for example for assault, provided again that the use of force is not excessive.[37]

The most difficult aspect of the use of force is where it is utilised to remove a trespasser where no violence is offered by the trespasser but he or she simply refuses to leave the property on request. The position has been summarised thus:

> "The precise rules are in some doubt. On the one hand, it is lawful to persuade a trespasser to leave, even, in some circumstances, by means of force. But, on the other hand, the use of force may sometimes be a civil or a criminal wrong or indeed both."[38]

With respect to criminal wrongs, the use of force where no violence is offered by the trespasser may amount to assault. A victim need not sustain actual injury for there to be an assault, and therefore even a minor use of force with no resulting injury may amount to assault. Assault need not even involve physical contact: it is assault, for example, to aim a blow at someone even although it misses, or to use threatening gestures of a kind which would induce fear in a reasonable

---

[35] G.H. Gordon, *The Criminal Law of Scotland* (2nd edn with Second Cumulative Supplement), Chap. 24 and paras 24.11–24.14.

[36] See Lord Keith in *H.M. Advocate v Docherty* 1954 SLT 169. The qualification stated here that a person is only bound to utilise means of escape which are reasonable is not specifically stated in the judgment, but is a logical qualification: see Gordon, op. cit., n. 35 at para. 24.12.

[37] See, eg, *Aitchison v Thorburn* (1869) 7 SLR 604.

[38] *Stair Memorial Encyclopaedia*, Vol. 18, para. 184.

person, although it is thought that purely verbal abuse would probably not amount to assault. It is also an assault to set a dog on someone.[39] Assault does, however, require intention. It is arguable that the necessary intention would be lacking where a landowner used force only in exercise of his recognised legal right to remove trespassers from his land. Even then, however, the use of force might still be criminal. In *H.M. Advocate* v *Harris*,[40] it was stated that while it was recognised that some persons may have to seize and push people in the course of their employment, and no criminal intent could be imputed to such behaviour, such lawful handling could readily spill over into assault or might, even if reasonable force was not exceeded, amount to a crime if carried out recklessly in the face of danger to the victim or to his actual injury.[41] By analogy, the same would seem to apply to a landowner exercising his legal right to remove a trespasser from his land: he has a right to do what he does, therefore there may not be the criminal intent necessary for assault, but if there is the necessary recklessness, he may commit the offence of reckless injury or reckless endangerment. Similarly, if the use of force does result in injury, the landowner may be guilty of the offence of causing real injury.[42] At the very least, conduct involving the physical manhandling of others may amount to a breach of the peace.[43]

With respect to civil wrongs, the use of force in exercise of the landowner's right to remove trespassers will not give rise to a civil claim provided the force is no more than necessary to achieve this or, to put it another way, is not excessive. As in the context of criminal wrongs, what is reasonable and what is excessive will depend on the facts. In *Bell* v *Shand*,[44] for example, it was held that there was no liability in delict for taking a poacher who had a gun hidden under his coat by the scruff of the neck and marching him 200 yards off the land on which he had been trespassing, while in *MacDonald* v *Robertson*,[45] it was held that there was liability in delict in circumstances where the defender had discharged a loaded shotgun at a poacher who had been attempting to run away and injured him.[46] Where persons are trespassing only for the purpose of taking access to land for recreation, peacefully and causing no damage, it is thought that only minimal force would be justified in removing them.

Trespass committed by straying animals

In principle, interdict may be granted to prevent trespass which is being committed by straying animals, but the courts may be reluctant to grant interdict in such circumstances, at least partly because of the practical difficulties of preventing certain types of animals from straying.[47]

---

[39] See *Kay* v *Allan* (1970) SCCR Supp. 188.

[40] 1993 SCCR 559.

[41] See in particular Lord Morrison at 566.

[42] This offence is discussed above in connection with defensive measures.

[43] *H.M. Advocate* v *Harris* 1993 SCCR 559, per Lord McCluskey at 570.

[44] (1870) 7 SLR 267.

[45] (1910) 27 Sh Ct Rep 103.

[46] See also *Wood* v *North British Ry Co.* (1899) 2 F 1; *Highland Railways* v *Menzies* (1875) 5 R 887; *Althorpe* v *Edinburgh Tramways* (1882) 10 R 344; *Scott* v *Great Northern Ry* (1895) 22 R 287; *Cook* v *Paxton* (1910) 48 SLR 7.

[47] *Stair Memorial Encyclopaedia*, Vol. 18, para. 187 and cases there cited. Other remedies for trespass by straying animals are discussed separately below.

Where straying animals cause actual damage, damages may be recovered for the resultant loss. In certain circumstances, liability for such damage will be strict. This is discussed further below in the context of civil liability arising out of access to the countryside generally, and further reference should be made to that discussion.

Self-help may also be utilised in relation to trespass by straying animals. The Animals (Scotland) Act 1987 provides that an occupier of land may detain any animal which strays onto the land, and which is not under the control of any person, for the purpose of preventing injury or damage by the animal.[48] Where the use of self-help has given rise to injury to, or the death of, an animal, there may be civil or criminal liability for such injury or death. The Animals (Scotland) Act 1987 provides a defence to civil proceedings for injury to, or the death of, an animal in certain defined circumstances. In order for the defence to apply, the person causing the injury or death of the animal must have been acting in self-defence, for the protection of any other person or for the protection of livestock and, where he was acting for the protection of livestock, he must have been the keeper of the livestock, the occupier of the land where the livestock was present or a person authorised to act for the protection of the livestock by the keeper or occupier.[49] In all cases, the person causing the injury or death must also have given notice of the killing or injury of the animal to the police within 48 hours of the event.[50] A person will only be regarded as acting in self-defence or for the protection of another or of livestock if the animal was *either* attacking him, the other person or the livestock and he had reasonable grounds for believing that there was no other practicable means of ending the attack *or* he had reasonable grounds for believing either that the animal was about to attack and there was no other practicable means of preventing the attack or that the animal had been attacking a person or livestock, was still in the vicinity of the attack, was not under the control of anyone and there was no other practicable means of preventing a further attack.[51] It is thought that it would similarly be a defence to any criminal charge resulting from injury to, or the death of, an animal that the injury or death was caused in self-defence or in the defence of another person or animal.[52]

Trespass as a criminal offence

It has been said that "[t]respassers, despite the familiar notice to the contrary, are very rarely 'prosecuted'".[53] In certain circumstances, however, trespass and certain other activities associated with it may be a criminal offence. For example,

---

[48] Animals (Scotland) Act 1987, s. 3(1). Where an animal is so detained, the provisions of Pt VI of the Civic Government (Scotland) Act 1982, which deal with lost and abandoned property, apply to the disposal of an animal other than a stray dog, subject to certain specified and any other necessary modifications; disposal of a stray dog is governed by the Dogs Act 1906 subject to any necessary modifications: Animals (Scotland) Act 1987, s. 3(2).

[49] Animals (Scotland) Act 1987, s. 4(1)(a), (3). "Livestock" is widely defined for this purpose to include all domestic animals, including in particular sheep, cattle and horses, and any other animal in captivity: s. 4(6).

[50] Animals (Scotland) Act 1987, s. 4(1)(b).

[51] Ibid, s. 4(4).

[52] See *Stair Memorial Encyclopaedia*, Vol. 18, para. 189.

[53] *Stair Memorial Encyclopaedia*, Vol. 18, para. 182.

the Trespass (Scotland) Act 1856 makes it an offence to lodge or encamp on private property; the Night Poaching Act 1828 and the Game (Scotland) Act 1832 create various offences associated with trespass in pursuit of game or rabbits (ie poaching) at night and during the day respectively[54]; and the Criminal Justice and Public Order Act 1994 creates a number of offences relating to trespasses which give rise to what might be loosely described as problems of public order in the countryside. Trespass other than in contravention of such statutory provisions is not, however, a crime, and most trespass occurring as a result of taking access to the countryside for recreation is therefore unlikely to amount to crime.

Liability for injury or damage[55]

As noted above, possible liability for injury or damage may be a factor in a landowner's decision whether, or to what extent, to permit access to his land under the current arrangements and is an issue which will need to be addressed if and when a statutory right of access is introduced. The principal concern here is with potential liability *to* those taking access to the countryside for any resulting injury, loss or damage and this section accordingly concentrates on such liability, but there is also concern over damage caused *by* those taking access and this is specifically referred to where appropriate: the principles to be applied in determining liability are generally the same in both cases. The concerns in both cases increase with the numbers of persons taking access.

People seek access to the countryside for a wide range of activities, from picnicking to potholing and all things in between. There is therefore an almost infinite variety of circumstances in which a claim might arise, and potential liability may accordingly stem from a number of different sources. The first is contract. There may be a contract between the parties, for example, where a charge is made for access itself, or for related facilities, such as parking. Liability for injury or damage may arise under any such contract, but only where the injury or damage complained of was caused by a breach of the contract, liability for which has not been validly excluded.[56] The second is the criminal law. There are a variety of circumstances in which criminal liability might arise: for example, where the landowner is conducting forestry or farming operations, criminal liability for injury or damage sustained as a result of those operations by a person taking access to land might arise under the Health and Safety at Work etc. Act 1974 or the regulations made thereunder, or there may be criminal liability for damage caused by a person taking access to the landowner's property or as a result of the taking of things from the land without permission. The third is delict. The law of delict is concerned with compensating a person who has suffered loss as a result of the wrongful actions of another and is the most likely basis for any claim for injury or damage sustained in the context of access to the countryside. The remainder of this section therefore concentrates on delictual liability.

---

[54] See generally the discussion in Chap. 8. See also the Salmon Fisheries (Scotland) Act 1868 and the Deer (Scotland) Act 1996.

[55] See also McKenzie, Rowan-Robinson and Saunders, "Civil Liability for Injury and Damage Arising from Access to the Scottish Countryside" 1997 SLPQ 214 at 274.

[56] Any such exclusion may, however, be subject to statutory control: see the Unfair Contract Terms Act 1977 and the Unfair Terms in Consumer Contracts Regulations 1994.

Delictual liability generally

Delictual liability arises *ex lege* and independently of the will of the parties. In general, delictual liability is based on *culpa*, that is fault, although in some circumstances liability may arise without fault (strict liability). *Culpa* encompasses both intentional and unintentional conduct, but in the context of access to the countryside, claims resulting from deliberate conduct, such as assault or vandalism, are likely to be rare. Claims arising from circumstances where liability is strict are similarly likely to be rare. Most claims will be based on unintentional conduct which amounts, in law, to negligence or breach of statutory duty. In such cases, the pursuer alleges that the defender owed him or her a duty of care, that there was a breach of that duty of care and that that breach of the duty of care caused the loss, injury and damage sustained by the pursuer.

Duty of care

The circumstances in which a duty of care arises at common law are set out in Lord Atkin's famous dictum in the celebrated case of *Donoghue* v *Stevenson*[57]:

> "The rule that you are to love your neighbour becomes in law, you must not injure your neighbour; and the lawyer's question, Who is my neighbour? receives a restricted reply. You must take reasonable care to avoid acts or omissions which you can reasonably foresee would be likely to injure your neighbour. Who, then, in law is my neighbour? The answer seems to be— persons who are so closely and directly affected by my act that I ought reasonably to have them in contemplation as being so affected when I am directing my mind to the acts or omissions which are called into question."[58]

In other words, a duty of care is owed to a person whom the defender can reasonably foresee as being potentially affected by his actions or, to put it another way, there must be sufficient proximity between the parties, which does not necessarily mean physical proximity, although in some cases this may be important.[59] It is likely that a common law duty of care will be owed by a landowner to a person taking access to land, since a landowner could reasonably be expected to foresee that a person taking access to the land would be affected by his acts or omissions and there will therefore be a sufficient degree of proximity between the parties for a duty of care to arise.[60] In *McCluskey* v *Lord Advocate*,[61]

---

[57] 1932 SC (HL) 31.

[58] Ibid at 44. It should be noted that although the concept of "neighbourhood" invoked here may suggest an affinity with the law of nuisance, with its roots in the law of neighbourhood, there is in fact no connection between the two.

[59] See, eg, the well known case of *Bourhill* v *Young* 1942 SC (HL) 78, where a pursuer who suffered nervous shock as a result of seeing the aftermath of an accident was held not to be owed a duty of care by the motorcyclist involved as she was outwith the area in which she could have been at risk of physical injury and could not therefore have been within his contemplation as being potentially affected by his actions.

[60] It is thought that this would be the case under the current arrangements, at least where access is permitted or encouraged, and would certainly be the case if and when a new statutory right of access is enacted, at least to the extent that persons were on land in exercise of that right. More difficult issues might arise if persons were on land, but not within the terms of the statutory right of access.

[61] 1994 SLT 452.

for example, it was held that the Forestry Commission owed a duty of care at common law to a visitor to Rogie Falls in Ross-shire where the Commission managed a network of forest walks on land owned by private individuals. Similarly, it is also likely that a common law duty of care will be owed to landowners and their employees, and also to fellow recreational users, by those taking access to the land, since they could reasonably be expected to foresee that these other persons would be affected by their acts or omissions.

Quite apart from any duty of care arising at common law, a person "occupying or having control of" land or other premises (hereafter referred to as "an occupier") owes a duty of care to all persons entering thereon by virtue of the 1960 Act. Occupiers' liability, as this type of liability is generally known, is "a special subhead of the general doctrine of negligence".[62] The question of who qualifies as an occupier for the purposes of the 1960 Act, and therefore owes the occupier's duty of care to those entering onto land or premises, is regulated by the common law,[63] which looks to possession and control of the land or premises, rather than ownership, to determine the matter. In *Murdoch* v *A. & R. Scott*,[64] it was stated that a person who was in a position to allow or forbid others to enter the land or premises in question would be sufficiently in control of the premises to be an occupier for this purpose. In the English case of *Wheat* v *Lacon*,[65] in which the court was considering the corresponding English statute (the Occupiers' Liability Act 1957), the court went further and stated that this definition was too narrow: while a person who could permit or forbid entry would undoubtedly be an occupier, others could be occupiers even although they did not have such power, any degree of control of the premises in question being sufficient. In *McCluskey* v *Lord Advocate*,[66] however, the court seemed to prefer the narrower view: it held that although the Forestry Commission were occupiers of the forest walks man-aged by them for the purposes of the 1960 Act, they could not be regarded as occupiers of the surrounding land, which included another path which formed the subject of the dispute.

Standard of care

At common law, the standard of care is usually expressed as being that of a reasonable person in the position of the defender: if, therefore, the defender has acted as a reasonable person would have acted, then he will have fulfilled his duty of care. A person may attempt to restrict or exclude liability for his failure to meet this standard of care, but any such attempt may be subject to statutory control.[67] The standard of care owed by an occupier under the 1960 Act is set out in section 2(1) of that Act, which provides that the occupier must show to persons entering the premises "such care as in all the circumstances of the case is reasonable" to see that they do not suffer any injury or damage as a result of dangers which are due to the state of the premises or anything done or omitted

---

[62] Lord Wright in *Muir* v *Glasgow Corporation* 1943 SC (HL) 3 at 13.
[63] 1960 Act, s. 1(2).
[64] 1956 SC 309.
[65] [1966] AC 552.
[66] 1994 SLT 452.
[67] See the Unfair Contract Terms Act 1977 and the Unfair Terms in Consumer Contracts Regulations 1994.

to be done on the premises and for which the occupier is in law responsible. Again, the occupier may extend, restrict, modify or exclude by agreement his obligations under the 1960 Act in so far as he is entitled to do so,[68] but any such attempt may be subject to statutory control.[69] The standard of care in both cases may for all practical purposes be regarded as the same: in *McCluskey* v *Lord Advocate*,[70] it was argued that the principles to be applied at common law and under the 1960 Act were effectively the same, and this approach was not disputed.

What is reasonable in any given situation depends on the circumstances of the individual case, and of course these may vary widely. What is reasonable in a countryside setting, for example, may differ from what is reasonable in an urban setting, or even in a different countryside setting. Each case will involve a balancing process: "[t]he relevant factors to be considered include the probability of injury, the seriousness of the injury, the practicability of precautions, the cost of the precautions and the utility of the defender's activities".[71]

In the context of occupiers' liability in particular, a number of specific factors have been identified by the courts as relevant to the question of reasonableness. One such factor is the extent of the entrant's right to be on the premises. Prior to the 1960 Act, entrants onto premises were divided into three categories, invitees, licencees and trespassers, and the degree of care owed to each category varied accordingly, a high degree of care being owed to invitees, a lesser degree of care being owed to licencees and no duty of care at all being owed to trespassers except a duty not to harm them maliciously.[72] The 1960 Act effectively abolished these categories by providing for a similar standard of care, ie reasonable care, to be owed to all entrants onto premises, but nonetheless, the extent of a person's right to be on the premises may be a factor in determining whether the occupier has acted reasonably. It has been said that it may be the case that an occupier must do more to protect someone he permits to be on his premises than he need do to protect someone who enters his property without permission,[73] and this obviously has implications for access because the degree of care will therefore generally be higher where access is permitted than where it is not, and may be higher still where it is positively encouraged, for example, where land is managed specifically for recreation. It has been held, however, that where access is taken by virtue of a public right of way, although the proprietor of the land over which the way passes owes those using the way a duty of care under the 1960 Act, this does not extend to maintaining the way or making it safe and there would only be liability for a failure to take reasonable care in respect of any danger created by the landowner or any failure which went beyond a mere failure to maintain, and, further, that the proprietor of the land over which the public right of way passed did not owe the users any duty of care at all at common law. This raises the question of whether the same would apply if access was being

---

[68] 1960 Act, s. 2(1).
[69] See the Unfair Contract Terms Act 1977 and the Unfair Terms in Consumer Contracts Regulations 1994.
[70] 1994 SLT 452.
[71] Thomson, *Delictual Liability* at p. 103.
[72] *Dumbreck* v *Robert Addie and Sons (Collieries) Ltd* 1929 SC (HL) 51.
[73] *McGlone* v *British Railways Board* 1966 SC (HL) 1, per Lord Reid at 11.

exercised in terms of a statutory right, such a right perhaps being regarded as analogous to a public right of way, and this is something which will need to be clarified by any access legislation.

Another factor to be taken into account in determining reasonableness is the characteristics of the entrants onto the land where these are known or should be anticipated by the landowner. Characteristics such as age and infirmity may affect what is reasonable: usually, more would need to be done to protect the very young and the very old,[74] and the same reasoning would apply to those who are infirm or disabled in some way. Again, this has obvious implications for access: paths may need to be maintained to a higher standard if it is known that persons other than fit adults may use them; dangers which are obvious to adults may need to be fenced if they would be less obvious, or even an attraction, to children.

Another factor in determining reasonableness is the nature of the dangers themselves. The courts have drawn a distinction between physical features of land, whether natural (eg a precipice) or artificial (eg an artificial pond), and mechanical or similar contrivances (eg a haulage system), the former representing obvious dangers against which all persons, adult or child, are expected to protect themselves, the latter requiring more care on the part of the landowner.[75] As a general rule, therefore, leaving land in its natural state or creating features which represent obvious dangers will not generally amount to a breach of the duty of care.[76] However, where there are hidden dangers, even if these are natural, more may require to be done. In *McCluskey* v *Lord Advocate*,[77] for example, the court specifically commented on the fact that the path in question was not attended by any hidden or unusual dangers: this implies that if there had been hidden or unusual dangers, it would not have been reasonable to take no steps to deal with them.[78] Man-made features close to a public road appear to form a distinct category of case where failure to take appropriate steps will amount to a breach of the duty of care.[79] By analogy, it may be unreasonable not to take appropriate steps where such features are to be found near paths or areas where access is taken.

Causation

In order to succeed in his claim, the pursuer must prove that the defender's breach of duty has caused, in both a factual and a legal sense, the loss, injury and damage sustained by the pursuer. This may be particularly problematic in cases involving access: for example, in *McCluskey* v *Lord Advocate*,[80] the pursuer was not able to say exactly how she had come to fall and therefore failed to establish that it was the dangerous condition of the path which had caused her accident.

Defences to claims at common law or under the 1960 Act

A defender may be able to show that he did not owe the pursuer any duty of care, that he did not fall short of the appropriate standard of care or that any

---

[74] *Titchner* v *British Railways Board* 1984 SLT 192.
[75] See *Dumbreck* v *Robert Addie and Sons (Collieries) Ltd* 1929 SC(HL) 51.
[76] See, eg, *Cotton* v *Derbyshire Dales District Council* [1994] TLR 335.
[77] 1994 SLT 452.
[78] See also *Nagle* v *Rottnest Island Authority* (1993) 112 ALR 393.
[79] See, eg, *Black* v *Cadell* 1804 M 13905: which involved a pit close to the road.
[80] 1994 SLT 452.

breach of the duty of care on his part did not cause the pursuer's loss, injury and damage, but there are also a number of specific defences available.

First, the defender may prove that the pursuer accepted the risk of loss, injury and damage. This defence is encapsulated in the maxim *volenti non fit injuria* and in the context of occupiers' liability is given statutory form in section 2(3) of the 1960 Act, which provides that nothing in the Act will be held to impose on an occupier any obligation to a person entering on the premises in respect of risks which that person has willingly accepted as his. The same principles apply to this statutory form of the defence as apply at common law. Acceptance of risk is a difficult concept. It can be seen as negating the existence of a duty of care to the pursuer, so that where the pursuer has accepted the risk, no duty of care is owed to him by the defender at all (primary assumption of risk) or it can be seen as a defence to an established duty of care (secondary assumption of risk). It is thought that the first approach is more logical, but there is a lack of judicial analysis of the concept in Scots law and the discussion of the concept in *Winnick* v *Dick*[81] tends to support a secondary assumption of risk approach. In order to establish that the pursuer accepted the risk, the defender must show that the pursuer not only knew, but had a proper appreciation, of the risks involved, and decided to proceed regardless.[82] He must also show that the kind of risk which materialised was the type of risk which the pursuer had accepted. In *Titchner* v *British Railways Board*,[83] it was said that a pursuer who was injured by a train while crossing a railway line could be said to have accepted the risk of being injured by a train being driven in a normal and accepted fashion, as it was in that case, but that if the train had been driven negligently, that was not a risk which the pursuer could have been said to have accepted. The doctrine obviously has great significance in the context of access, since it will generally be obvious what the risks are in taking access and if these are accepted, there will be no liability on the landowner for such obvious risks.[84] SNH suggested in its advice to government[85] that it should be clarified that people do engage in open-air recreation at their own risk, but any such legislation would need to be carefully considered and framed.[86]

Another defence is that of contributory negligence. Everyone is expected to take reasonable care for his or her own safety, and where the pursuer's failure to do so has contributed to his loss, injury and damage, any award of damages may be reduced accordingly.[87] Again, this doctrine has great significance in the

---

[81] 1984 SC 48.

[82] See, eg, *McGlone* v *British Railways Board* 1966 SC(HL) 1; *Titchner* v *British Railways Board* 1984 SLT 192; *McCluskey* v *Lord Advocate* 1994 SLT 452.

[83] 1984 SLT 192.

[84] See in particular *McCluskey* v *Lord Advocate* 1994 SLT 452.

[85] *Access to the Countryside for Open-air Recreation: Scottish Natural Heritage's Advice to Government*, op. cit., n. 6.

[86] A number of countries have legislation specifically designed to regulate issues of liability in recreational situations, most notably the United States of America. Such legislation is not, however, free from problems, hence the cautionary note sounded here concerning the careful consideration which would need to be given to the type of provision to be enacted and the drafting of it. For a discussion of the relevant US legislation, see McKenzie, Rowan-Robinson and Saunders, "Civil Liability for Injury and Damage Arising from Access to the Scottish Countryside", op. cit., n. 55, pp. 284–285 and references there cited.

[87] Law Reform (Contributory Negligence) Act 1945.

context of access: for example, persons taking access who are not properly equipped or who persist in the face of obvious danger may be held to have contributed to their own loss and so reduced any liability on the part of the landowner accordingly.[88]

Finally, as noted above, a defender may have attempted to restrict or exclude liability for negligence at common law or under the 1960 Act, and a valid restriction or exclusion of liability will act as a defence to a claim by a pursuer. Liability under the 1960 Act may only be restricted or excluded by contract,[89] but it may be possible to validly restrict or exclude liability at common law even where there is no contract. Attempts to restrict or exclude liability may, however, be subject to statutory control.[90]

Particular types of claim

Some types of claim arising in an access context may prove particularly problematic. One example is claims against local and public authorities, which may manage, for public access, their own land or land which is leased from, or the subject of a formal agreement with, the owner. If the authority satisfies the relevant test, it may be an occupier for the purposes of the 1960 Act[91] and, irrespective of whether it is an occupier for the purposes of the 1960 Act or not, it will generally owe a duty of care at common law to those entering the land for access. Local authorities also have certain statutory powers and obligations which are relevant in this context, such as the power under section 46 of the Countryside (Scotland) Act 1967 to repair and maintain any public right of way and the obligation created under section 33 of that Act to bring paths created under public path creation agreements and orders into a fit state for use by the public and to maintain them thereafter. These provisions may raise complex questions such as whether there would be a breach of statutory duty on the part of the local authority if it failed, for example, to fulfil its obligation to maintain a public path created under a public path creation agreement and someone was injured as a result.

Another example is claims arising from reliance on misleading literature. Many public authorities and private estates provide literature describing access opportunities, routes, facilities, etc. If such information is misleading, it is possible that a person may suffer injury, damage and consequential economic loss as a result of relying on that information.[92] A number of issues may arise here, perhaps most notably whether there is a duty of care owed by the providers of the literature to the users. It is thought that the providers of literature and probably also its authors, if different, would owe a duty of care to the users of the literature,

---

[88] See in particular *McCluskey* v *Lord Advocate* 1994 SLT 452, where there was some question about the suitability of the pursuer's footwear; the court also commented on the fact that the pursuer had chosen to continue on the path despite its obvious condition and despite the fact that she knew of an alternative route. The court said that in the light of these factors, it would have held her two-thirds to blame for the accident, although in fact it was unnecessary to decide the point.

[89] This is implicit from the fact that s. 2(1) of the 1960 Act uses the phrase *by agreement*: see above.

[90] See the Unfair Contract Terms Act 1977 and the Unfair Contract Terms in Consumer Contracts Regulations 1994.

[91] The test is possession and control: see above.

[92] It is thought that pure economic loss—eg, a lost hotel deposit—could also be recoverable under the principles set out in *Hedley Byrne & Co* v *Heller & Partners* [1964] AC 465.

particularly where the literature is specific to a particular estate or area, rather than a general guide. It is reasonably foreseeable that if information is incorrect, loss may result. Even if a duty of care is established, however, there may be other issues. Reasonable care may have been taken to ensure the information was correct. Causation may also be problematic, and there may be questions of *volenti non fit injuria* and contributory negligence.

Another example is claims against organisers of recreational activities. In Scotland, there are commercial providers of recreational opportunities, organisations such as the British Horse Society which organise access on behalf of its members and a variety of clubs and other organisations which organise recreational activities and may or may not make charges for membership, transport, use of equipment, etc. Where the organisers of the activity in question are occupiers, within the meaning of the 1960 Act, of the land or premises on which it takes place, liability may arise under that Act and, irrespective of whether they are occupiers for the purposes of the 1960 Act or not, liability may also arise at common law under the normal principles of contract or delict. Delictual claims against the organisers of recreational activities raise difficult questions, however, because of the nature of such activities and the different types of relationships between organisers and recreational users. In general, the organisers of recreational activities owe a duty of care to participants, spectators and third parties,[93] and it is thought that, quite apart from any contract, a duty of care will certainly be owed to participants where the organiser is providing a commercial service. In the case of clubs, however, there may be some doubt about whether, and by whom, a duty of care is owed, and the less formal the organisation, the more problematic this issue becomes, because whether the requisite degree of proximity can be established will depend on the nature of the relationship between the parties. Acceptance of risk may also be a particular issue. Generally, it is thought that a participant would be held to have accepted risks inherent in the activity, so long as he was aware of and appreciated those risks,[94] but there might be liability if the organisers failed to warn of risks which, to their knowledge, the participants were too inexperienced to know of or understand, or if the risk which materialised was one which was not inherent in the activity, for example, an injury resulting from a defective ski tow. Claims may also arise from the provision of equipment by the organisers of an activity, as a result of the provision of unsuitable or incorrect equipment, the failure to ensure that the user was able to operate the equipment correctly or the provision of defective equipment. In the first two cases, the main issue is likely to be whether there was a duty of care in the first place, which will depend on factors such as the relative experience of the parties and whether the participant relied on the organisers' knowledge and experience; in the third case, liability is more likely to depend on whether the defect, whether inherent or caused by damage or normal wear and tear, was discoverable by reasonable inspection.

Another example is claims arising from the supply of equipment generally, particularly where the equipment is purchased on the advice of another, whether the seller or not. The primary issue here is likely to be the existence of a duty of

---

[93] *Stair Memorial Encyclopaedia*, Vol. 19, para. 1241.
[94] See above.

care, which will depend on factors such as the degree of reliance placed on the advice and whether that reliance was reasonable and known to the adviser. Where equipment is inherently defective, the purchaser may have an action in contract against the seller, and anyone injured by it will have an action in delict against the manufacturer or anyone else responsible for the defect. The latter type of claim requires that the product be intended to reach the consumer in substantially the same form as it left the manufacturer, with no opportunity for intermediate inspection,[95] and any warnings or instructions are relevant. These requirements, together with the need to identify what may be a very technical fault in the product and to prove causation, make a successful claim in delict difficult. In certain circumstances, there may be strict liability for defective products under Part I of the Consumer Protection Act 1987.

Damage caused by animals

Injury or damage by animals may occur in a variety of circumstances: animals kept on land may cause injury or damage to those taking access to the land or to their property; animals brought onto land, usually dogs, may cause injury or damage to the landowner, his employees or his animals or other property or to other recreational users or their property.

Liability may result from deliberate conduct, such as riding a horse at a pedestrian[96] or setting a dog on another,[97] or from unintentional conduct which amounts to negligence. The courts have recognised a number of specific duties in relation to animals, such as a duty not to pasture potentially dangerous animals on land over which there is a right of way,[98] and a duty to control dogs so that they will not cause harm to others in the vicinity.[99] In addition, there may be strict liability for injury or damage caused by animals in the circumstances provided for in the Animals (Scotland) Act 1987.[100] The animals to which the strict liability provisions of that Act apply are animals "of a species whose members are generally by virtue of their physical attributes or habits likely, unless controlled or restrained; to injure severely or kill persons or animals, or damage property to a material extent".[101] Certain animals are deemed to fall within that definition[102]; in other cases, it will be a matter for the court to decide whether they do fall within that

---

[95] Although simply taking the product out of its wrapping for display does not count for this purpose: see *Grant* v *Australian Knitting Mills Ltd* [1935] 2 All ER 209.

[96] *Ewing* v *Earl of Mar* (1851) 14 D 314.

[97] This may also amount to the criminal offence of assault.

[98] s. 59 of the Wildlife and Countryside Act 1981 also specifically prohibits the pasturing of bulls on land over which there is a right of way.

[99] *Brogan* v *Wharton* (1891) 7 Sh Ct Rep 89.

[100] The Act replaces the previous common law rules on strict liability for injury or damage caused by animals, but specifically preserves the right to pursue an action based on negligence where strict liability does not apply. See, however, s. 1(8).

[101] s. 1(1)(b).

[102] All dogs and dangerous wild animals within the meaning of the Dangerous Wild Animals Act 1976 are deemed to be likely, unless controlled or restrained, to injure severely or kill persons or animals by biting or otherwise savaging, attacking or harrying them (s. 1(3)(b)), although it is perhaps unlikely that many of the latter category will be encountered in taking recreational access in Scotland; similarly, all cattle, horses, asses, mules, hinnies, sheep, pigs, goats and deer in the course of foraging are deemed likely (unless controlled or restrained) to damage to a material extent land or the produce of land, whether harvested or not (s. 1(3)(b)).

definition or not. In order for there to be strict liability, the damage complained of must be directly attributable to the attributes or habits of the animal which bring it within the Act: for example, a dog is deemed to be within the Act because of its attribute or habit of biting, savaging, attacking or harrying, so if the damage is caused by such means, there will be strict liability, whereas if it was caused by the dog knocking something over, there will not, because that damage is not attributable to the habits which bring it within the Act. The person who is strictly liable for the damage is the animal's keeper, that is, the owner or possessor of the animal or the person who has actual care and control of a child under 16 who is the owner or possessor of the animal.[103] There are, however, a number of defences: it is a defence to show that the injury or damage was wholly the fault of the person who sustained it, that the person who sustained the injury or damage willingly accepted the risk or that the animal was on its own territory and the person sustaining the injury or damage was not authorised to be on the keeper's property (in other words, was a trespasser).[104] The provisions of the Act relating to self-help in the case of trespassing animals have already been discussed.[105]

Rescues

The taking of access may result in a situation where a rescue becomes necessary. There is little Scottish authority on rescue situations, but it is possible to draw some reasoned conclusions from general principles. It is a basic principle of Scots law that there is no liability for pure omissions, and so there is no obligation to go to the rescue of another person *in the absence of a duty of care being owed to that person*.[106] Thomson suggests that the emergency services would have a duty to act in such a situation,[107] but there is English authority that the emergency services do not owe a duty of care to individual citizens, except where they have created the situation of danger.[108] Where a person does go to the rescue of another in distress, it is suggested that they will normally have put themselves in sufficient proximity to that person to create a duty of care even if there was no duty to give assistance in the first place, and so will be liable for any failure to take reasonable care in carrying out the rescue.[109] The "rescued", and any other person who has

---

[103] s. 5(1).

[104] The last defence does not apply where the animal was kept for the purpose of protecting persons or property unless that was reasonable, the use made of the animal was reasonable and, where the animal is a guard dog, the keeper has also complied with the provisions of the Guard Dogs Act 1975.

[105] See above.

[106] The requirements for establishing a duty of care are discussed above. In rescue situations, if a duty of care is owed, it will generally be either because there is a pre-existing relationship between the parties or because the rescuer has created the situation of danger in the first place.

[107] *Delictual Liability*, p. 61.

[108] See *Capital and Counties plc v Hampshire County Council; John Munroe (Acrylics) Ltd v London Fire and Civil Defence Authority*; and *Church of Jesus Christ and Latter-Day Saints (Great Britain) v West Yorkshire Fire and Civil Defence Authority* [1997] TLR 141. See also *Skinner v Secretary of State for Transport* [1995] TLR 2.

[109] See *Capital and Counties plc v Hampshire County Council* [1997] TLR 141 and *Duff v Highland and Islands Fire Board* 1995 SLT 1362. Cf *John Munroe (Acrylics) Ltd v London Fire and Civil Defence Authority* [1997] TLR 141, where it was held that there was no sufficient proximity to create a duty of care in the particular circumstances of that case.

created the situation of peril, may also be liable for any injury or damage sustained by the rescuer in coming to the rescue.[110]

Path furniture

Bridges and other path furniture, such as stiles, and buildings such as bothies, may be erected on land by the owner or others such as the Scottish Rights of Way Society. Such structures become part of the land and belong to the person who owns the land irrespective of who built them, by virtue of the principle of accession. If such structures are carelessly erected or maintained, liability in negligence may result for the persons responsible for the careless erection or maintenance, but there does not appear to be any duty on the erector to maintain such a structure after erection. The principles of occupiers' liability will also apply, however, which may impose further duties on the occupier, and specific duties may apply, for example where a bridge is part of a path created by a public path creation order, where the local authority has a statutory duty to maintain the path.[111] There is no obligation to provide path furniture in the first place.[112]

Conclusion

From the foregoing discussion, it can be seen that there are many important and complex issues surrounding access to the countryside for recreational purposes both under the current system and in the event of a statutory right of access being created. This chapter has attempted to set these issues in context as a background for the following chapters which deal specifically with the current law relating to linear and area access.

---

[110] See *Baker* v *T. E. Hopkins Ltd* [1958] 3 All ER 147; *Harrison* v *British Railways Board* [1981] 3 All ER 679; *Videan* v *British Transport Commission* [1963] 2 All ER 860. This applies to the emergency services also: see *Ogwo* v *Taylor* [1988] AC 431 and *Bermingham* v *Sher Brothers* 1980 SC (HL) 67.

[111] See above.

[112] See *Johnstone* v *Sweeney* 1985 SLT (Sh Ct) 2.

CHAPTER 13

LINEAR ACCESS

Douglas Cusine

Members of the public in Scotland have been accustomed for a long time, certainly for well over two centuries, to taking access to the countryside and the hills. In most instances, they do this without having first obtained the permission of the landowner, but equally, their enjoyment of the countryside is not usually objected to, provided the public do not cause damage, or otherwise conduct themselves in a manner which does not find favour with the owner.

In Chapter 14 reference is made to the current proposals to enshrine in legislation a "right to roam". At the time of writing there is no such right, but there are various regimes which give the public an entitlement to make use of the countryside. This chapter will consider public rights of way, public path creation agreements and orders, long-distance footpaths, permissive paths, various problems which arise and proposals for reform.

Public rights of way

Most rights of way in Scotland, of which there are approximately 7,000, are created by prescriptive use and while servitudes can also be constituted in this way, some methods by which servitudes may be created, for example by implication, by acquiescence and *rebus ipsis et factis*, are not competent in relation to rights of way. The remaining two methods by which servitudes may be created, namely express grant and Act of Parliament, can apply also to rights of way. Although it is competent to create a right of way by express grant, it is uncommon and, for that reason, this chapter deals only with constitution by prescription and the various types of route which may be created by an Act of Parliament.

Prescription

The Prescription and Limitation (Scotland) Act 1973, which came into force on July 25, 1976, provides in section 3(3):

> "If a public right of way over land has been possessed by the public for a continuous period of twenty years, openly, peaceably, and without judicial

247

interruption, then as from the expiration of that period, the existence of the right of way as so possessed shall be exempt from challenge."

The basis for the constitution of a right of way in Scotland by the operation of prescription was described by Lord Watson in *Mann* v *Brodie* as follows:

"According to the law of Scotland, the constitution of such a right does not depend upon any legal fiction, but upon the fact of user by the public, as a matter of right, continuously and without interruption, for the full period of the long prescription . . . But with the exception of one ingenious author,[1] who says that the possession of the public ought to be ascribed to the *jus coronae*, no one has suggested that any title is required as the foundation of a prescriptive right of public way. I am aware that there are *dicta* to be found, in which the prescriptive acquisition of a right of way by the public is attributed to implied grant, acquiescence by the owner of the soil, and so forth; but these appear to me to be mere speculations as to the origin of the rule, and their tendency is to obscure rather than elucidate its due application to a case like the present."[2]

While the 1973 Act is the starting-point for any discussion of the constitution of rights of way by prescription, the Act does not set out anything other than the period of possession and the nature of that possession, leaving the other requirements to be provided by the common law. In order to constitute a right of way, a number of conditions must be fulfilled. The route (1) must lead from one public place to another, (2) be by a defined route, which is (3) used by the public, (4) openly, peaceably and without judicial interruption, (5) for a continuous period of 20 years, (6) as of right, (7) after which the existence of the right of way as so possessed is exempt from challenge. These criteria will be dealt with in more detail in the following paragraphs. Court proceedings regarding a right of way may be raised or defended by any member of the public,[3] other bodies having an interest in such matters, for example the Scottish Rights of Way Society,[4] and local authorities.[5]

The termini must be public: It is worth saying at this point that in Scotland the fact that something is shown on an Ordnance Survey map as a public footpath is not evidence that it is a right of way and one could not therefore assume that the *termini* are public places. If either or both of the *termini* is not a public place, then there cannot be a right of way.[6]

Public place: The issue of what is a public place has been the subject of a considerable amount of litigation, but it is not possible to ask the abstract question whether a particular place, for example the foreshore, is a public place. Whether it is a public place will depend upon proof that the public have resort to it. What

---

[1] Napier, p. 370

[2] (1885) 12 R (HL) 52 at 57; see also *Davidson* v *Earl of Fife* (1863) 1 M 874 at 884.

[3] eg *Duke of Athol* v *Torrie* (1852) 1 Macq 65.

[4] *Macfie* v *Scottish Rights of Way and Recreation Society (Ltd)* (1884) 11 R 1094.

[5] Countryside (Scotland) Act 1967, s. 46.

[6] *Burt* v *Barclay* (1861) 24 D 218; *Jenkins* v *Murray* (1866) 4 M 1046, per Lord President McNeill at 1047; *Campbell* v *Laing* (1853) 1 Macq 451, per Lord Chancellor Cranworth at 453.

the public do when they get there is irrelevant so long as the purpose is a lawful one.[7] Once the right is created, it can be used for all lawful purposes, and so if a public right of way is constituted for the purposes of visiting shops, there is nothing to prevent the public using it for the purpose of visiting some other public place.

There are a number of cases dealing with whether particular places are public places for the purposes of the law on rights of way. A public road is probably the most obvious example of a public place.[8] Likewise a town or a village,[9] a public harbour[10] and, on the analogy of a harbour, a public port is a public place. One of the issues which has been litigated quite frequently is whether the foreshore is a public place, but it will not be so considered without further specification because, for example, the foreshore might be inaccessible.[11] If there are other reasons why the public resort to the foreshore or a part of the foreshore, then it could qualify as a public place. In *Richardson* v *Cromarty Petroleum*,[12] there was evidence that the beach was regularly used for recreational purposes and it was held to be a public place, and a similar decision was reached in *Lauder* v *MacColl*.[13] A church-yard might also be a public place.[14] The existence of a lane which is used to obtain access to a public place from a garage situated in the lane will not make the lane into a right of way. In *Strathclyde (Hyndland) Housing Society Ltd* v *Cowie*[15] it was argued by the pursuers that there was a right of way for people on foot and also for vehicles between Lorraine Road and Westbourne Gardens in Glasgow. In a careful judgment, the sheriff was of the opinion that since the subjects were urban, a substantial amount of possession of the correct type would have to be established. While there was evidence that some proprietors had used the lane to drive vehicles to and from garages, that had occurred only over a four-year period and the use had not been from end to end. The sheriff there-fore, correctly it is submitted, dismissed the action. The existence of garages in lanes is a common feature of urban properties and the lane may in some instances have been taken over by the local authority, but if it is not, the land will not become a right of way unless it is used to go from one public place, ie a street, to another.

One might have thought that it would have been decided whether a railway station or a bus station or an airport is a public place, but there are no authorities directly on the point. There is, however, authority for the proposition that if a statutory purpose for which land was acquired is inconsistent with the existence of a servitude or right of way then such a right cannot be acquired.[16] The fact that some railway stations and bus stations are closed for part of the day might

---

[7] *Marquis of Bute* v *McKirdy & McMillan* 1937 SC 93, per Lord Moncreiff at 132.

[8] *Jenkins* v *Murray* (1866) 4 M 1046; *Darrie* v *Drummond* (1865) 3 M 496.

[9] *Duncan* v *Lees* (1870) 9 M 855, per Lord President Inglis at 856.

[10] *Moncreiffe* v *Lord Provost of Perth* (1842) 5 D 298; *Cuthbertson* v *Young* (1851) 14 D 300, per Lord Cockburn at 309.

[11] *Darrie* v *Drummond* (1864) 3 M 496.

[12] 1982 SLT 237.

[13] 1993 SCLR 753.

[14] *Smith* v *Saxon* 1927 SN 98 at 142.

[15] 1983 SLT (Sh Ct) 61; see also *Cowie* v *Strathclyde Regional Council* 1985 SLT 333.

[16] *Magistrates of Edinburgh* v *N.B.Ry* (1904) 6 F 620, per Lord Kinnear at 637; *Ayr Harbour Trustees* v *Oswald* (1883) 10 R (HL) 85; *Ellice's Trs* v *Caledonian Canal Commissioners* (1904) 6 F 325.

indicate that these are not public places, but even if they are not it might be difficult to argue that the public are there as of right.[17] For example, it has been held that a market is not a public place if it is closed on some days.[18] So far as the summit of a hill or mountain is concerned, in the absence of other factors that cannot be a public place.[19] It has not been decided whether a right of way can exist if it goes from one public place to the same public place. In *Cuthbertson* v *Young*[20] Lord Medwyn was of the view that a circular road could be a right of way, but that seemed to be doubted by Lord Sands in *Rhins District Committee of Wigtonshire* v *Cuninghame*.[21] Certainly in England and Wales, a right of way can exist on a circular route which leads from a public place back to the same one.[22]

The route between the two public places must be used by the public from end to end on a continuous journey.[23] Thus, if a route was used by postmen, the emergency services and cleansing services, it would not be used by members of the public as such, and accordingly would not constitute a right of way. It is also essential that the public use the route from end to end on a continuous journey. In other words this requirement is to distinguish those who use the route to get from one end to the other from those who use only part of the route or who enter from one of the *termini*, stroll around and exit from the same point or another one, but not the other public *terminus*.[24] It is also important to emphasise that the use must be substantial, but the use which can reasonably be expected will depend upon the location of the alleged right of way. For example in *Ayr Burgh Council* v *British Transport Commission*[25] it was not enough in an urban context to establish that access was taken to a market on four out of seven days. By contrast, however, the fact that a drove road was used once per year to get to a fair was held to be sufficient.[26] In *Scottish Rights of Way and Recreation Society Ltd* v *Macpherson*[27] the Lord Ordinary, Lord Kinnear, recognised that very little use might be made during winter months of a route traversing some very high ground and suitable only for walkers or sheep but not for cattle. That did not, however, prevent the route from Braemar through Glen Doll to Clova from being a right of way.

In *Cumbernauld & Kilsyth District Council* v *Dollar Land (Cumbernauld) Ltd*[28] involving a walkway through the town centre, the evidence to establish public use (although that was not the central issue) consisted of the following activities all of which involved going from one end of the walkway to the other: (i) people going to church; (ii) people going to and from the railway station; (iii)

[17] *Wood* v *N.B.Ry* (1899) 2 F 1.
[18] *Ayr Burgh Council* v *British Transport Commission* 1955 SLT 219.
[19] *Jenkins* v *Murray* (1866) 4 M 1046, per Lord Deas at 1054.
[20] (1851) 14 D 304, affd (1854) 1 Macq 455.
[21] 1917 2 SLT 169 at 169.
[22] *Dyfed County Council* v *Secretary of State for Wales* (1990) 59 P&CR 275.
[23] *Norrie* v *Mags of Kirriemuir* 1945 SC 302, per Lord Moncrieff at 315–316.
[24] *Cuthbertson* v *Young* (1850) 12 D 521; (1851) 13 D 1308; (1851) 14 D 300, 375, 465; (1854) 1 Macq 455; *Jenkins* v *Murray* (1866) 4 M 1046; *McRobert* v *Reid* 1914 SC 623; *Rhins District Committee of Wigtonshire* v *Cuninghame* 1917 2 SLT 169; *Strathclyde (Hyndland) Housing Society* v *Cowie* 1983 SLT (Sh Ct) 61.
[25] 1955 SLT 219.
[26] *Porteous* v *Allan* (1769) 5 Bro Supp 598; M 14512.
[27] (1887) 14 R 875, per Lord Kinnear (Ordinary) at 881.
[28] 1993 SC (HL) 44.

people going to and from the town hall; (iv) children going to and from school and students going to and from the technical college; (v) residents in one estate going to and from local facilities, such as the health centre and the swimming pool; (vi) people going to and from entertainment centres; (vii) people going to and from banks and cash dispensers; and (viii) mothers and young children crossing the town for social purposes.

By a definite route: It is important to note that the requirement is not that there be a definite path or track, but merely a definite route and the reason for that is that one has to have in mind the possibility of obstructions or obstacles of either a temporary or a permanent nature. If, for example, a large tree fell over a track then the public would be entitled to go round the tree in order to get to the other public place. The route would be identifiable, but if the requirement was to use a definite track then the public would not be allowed to deviate as indicated. That said, however, it has been pointed out in a number of cases that if the public stroll about or roam indiscriminately, that activity will not constitute the assertion of a right of way since they will not be using a definite route between two public places.[29]

Even if the route is definite, it is possible for another route to be substituted during the running of prescription, provided it is clear that the new route is a substitute for the old one and not a completely new route. If it is proved that it is a new route, the original one will not become a right of way because it will not have been used for the prescriptive period. As Professor Gordon states, "The essential question is whether it is a case of substitution with continued use as of right, or discontinuance of the old right of way and use of a new one either by tolerance, which will not constitute a right, or by right, which requires a new period of prescription."[30]

That is the position at common law, but that has been alleviated by the provisions of the Countryside (Scotland) Act 1967, s. 35(1), which permit an owner, tenant or occupier of land crossed by a public right of way to apply to the planning authority for an alteration or diversion of the route on the ground that the alteration or diversion will secure, "the efficient use of the land" which is crossed "or other land held with it or provide a shorter or more convenient path". If the local authority agrees, this is done by way of a "path diversion order" and in granting the order the local authority may impose conditions and may also extinguish a right of way in whole or in part. The new route is, however, declared to be a right of way. Before the order is granted, the matter must be referred to the Minister,[31] who must be satisfied that the diversion is expedient and that the proposed new route will not be substantially less convenient to the public.[32] The Minister must take various factors into consideration, namely what effect a diversion would have on the public enjoyment of the path as a whole, what effect the proposed new route would have on other land served by the existing route and what effect the new route would have on the land over which it will go and land held with that land.

---

[29] *Jenkins* v *Murray* (1866) 4 M 1046.

[30] *Land Law*, para. 24–123; *Hozier* v *Hawthorn* (1884) 11 R 766; *Kinloch* v *Young* 1911 SC (HL) 1.

[31] s. 35(1)–(3) and (5). The procedure for applying for such an order is laid down in the Countryside (Scotland) Regulations 1982 (SI 1982/1467).

[32] s. 35(5).

Continuous: The 1973 Act requires possession which is "continuous", but in determining whether the possession is continuous, a number of factors must be looked at, including the location of the route and any interruptions which there might have been. As has already been pointed out, if the route is in a remote area, the amount of use which can be expected before the use could be regarded as "continuous" would be less than the use expected of a route in an urban area.

So far as interruptions are concerned the 1973 Act mentions only "judicial interruption", but it is thought that other forms of interruption are still relevant in that they may demonstrate, for example, that a right of way has never existed. If, for example, the route was blocked off or rendered unusable, say by the removal of a bridge, the result would be that no right of way existed. In *Mann v Brodie*,[33] Brodie and others raised an action for declarator that there was a right of way through the defender's property. However, it was established that for 47 years, the public had been excluded from the route and the House of Lords held that no right of way existed. At that time, the prescriptive period was 40 years.

It is important to observe at this stage that it is not essential that there is evidence of use up to the date of raising the action; it is sufficient if there is evidence of use which ends at a point not less than 20 years prior to the raising of the action.[34] There are a number of cases which clearly indicate two things. The first is that the longer the period of interruption, the more likely it is that the court will hold that a right of way has not been established because the use was not continuous, and the second is that if there is evidence of use prior to interruption the court will probably assume that the use prior to the interruption was of the same type and quality as the use after the interruption and so the period before the interruption may be added to the period after, in order to establish whether a right of way has been established or not.[35]

Openly, peaceably and without judicial interruption: The Latin tag *nec vi nec clam nec precario* is sometimes used in this connection in cases prior to the 1973 Act, but while *nec vi* (without force) is the same as peaceable and *nec clam* (without stealth) is the same as openness, *nec precario* means that the possession must be as of right which is not related to the requirement that there should not be judicial interruption, although there is no doubt that the use must be as of right.

With respect to the requirement of openness there are very few cases on the question of openness, but in *McInroy's v Duke of Athole*,[36] it was held that clandestine use of a shortcut by deer stalkers did not create a servitude right and accordingly, by analogy, could not create a right of way.

With respect to the requirement of peaceableness, again there are very few cases on this point but in one, *McKerran v Gordon*,[37] a case involving alleged public use of a footpath in Aberdeenshire, there was evidence of a meeting of the District Road Trustees indicating that the public use was not regarded as being lawful and that was accepted by the court because there was evidence that the proprietor

---

[33] (1885) 11 R 52.
[34] *Harvie v Rodgers* (1828) 3 W&S 251, per Lord Chancellor Lyndhurst at 260.
[35] Ibid; *Young v Robertson* (1854) 1 Macq 455; *Mags of Elgin v Robertson* (1862) 24 D 301; *Mags of Edinburgh v N.B.Ry* (1904) 6 F 620.
[36] (1891) 18 R (HL) 46.
[37] (1878) 3 R 429.

had dug up the *solum* of the route, planted trees across it and put up notices to the effect that trespassers would be prosecuted. It was held in these circumstances that the public were not entitled to a possessory judgment based on seven years' possession.

With respect to the requirement of without judicial interruption, so far as the 1973 Act is concerned, judicial interruption means taking "appropriate proceedings" to challenge the possession and appropriate proceedings are usually court proceedings but may be an arbitration.

Continuous period of 20 years: What is meant by "continuous" has already been discussed. So far as the period is concerned, since the coming into force of the 1973 Act, the period of prescription is now 20 years rather than 40. The 1973 Act states that "a public right of way" shall be exempt from challenge if it has been possessed for the prescriptive period. An argument has been advanced that the right must exist before it can be possessed and so either the public right of way must be created by other means in order to be exempt from challenge or the public right of way may be constituted by prescriptive possession which must be followed by a further period of 20 years to be exempt from challenge. That argument has, however, been rejected by the courts.[38] The 1973 Act applies retrospectively to allow any period after July 25, 1956 to be taken into account. Mention was made above of a presumption about the nature of use prior to interruption, but that may be of less significance because of the shortening of the period of prescription from 40 years to 20.

As of right: That is *nec precario*. This distinguishes use which is with the permission of the owner and that which is not. The onus is on the person seeking to establish a right of way to prove that there has been possession "as of right".[39] Before possession can be "as of right", it must be proved that it was known to the owner, or that he ought to have known about it. In *Cumbernauld & Kilsyth District Council v Dollar Land (Cumbernauld) Ltd*,[40] it was argued that unless the public user was adverse to the interests of the proprietor, the use had to be ascribed to tolerance, but this argument was rejected by the House of Lords, in other words, the owner could not stand by and have his inaction attributed to tolerance. The possession should be with the intention of establishing an adverse right, rather than exercising a right with the agreement of the servient owner. This point was well put by Lord Watson in *McInroy's Trs v Duke of Athole*[41] and his comment was approved in *McGregor v Crieff Co-operative Society Ltd*.[42] In *McGregor*, Lord Sumner said,

> "There is much enjoyment of access, without leave ever asked or given, which on both sides is truly tolerance. He who uses, knows and accepts that his enjoyment is none the less permission . . . It would be strange if, long afterwards, in a question of the acquisition of a prescriptive servitude

---

[38] *Richardson* v *Cromarty Petroleum* 1982 SLT 237.
[39] *McInroy's Trs*, per Lord Justice-Clerk Macdonald at 463.
[40] 1993 SC (HL) 44.
[41] (1891) 18 R (HL) 46 at 48.
[42] 1915 SC (HL) 93.

right, this friendly commerce should be treated as an assertion and inchoate establishment of a right, merely because to the question 'Where was the permission?', the only answer must be that no proof of any is forthcoming. Open unqualified user in ordinary course may be deemed to be in fact user as of right, when no more appears; but if the evidence suggests that it was after all due to tacit permission, the question must be whether the user does, upon the whole case, establish the growing acquisition of a servitude right."[43]

The existence of the right of way as so possessed is exempt from challenge: In this context the use, or possession, over the prescriptive period will determine the nature of the right which has been acquired. As it has been put by Bell[44] possession here is not only the badge but also the measure of the right—*tantum praescriptum quantum possessum*. To take one example, there may be a route from one public place to another but a question might arise whether the route can be used only by those on foot, or those on foot and, say, those on horseback, or whether the route can be used for vehicles. The phrase in the 1973 Act "as so possessed" means that one would have to demonstrate that the use of the prescriptive period had been by, say, vehicles in order to establish that there was a right of access for vehicular purposes. That said, however, it may be that the rule *tantum praescriptum quantum possessum* is not applied as strictly in connection with rights of way as it is in relation to servitudes. That point is certainly made both by Professor Gordon[45] and by Rankine.[46] In support of his view Rankine cites *Forbes* v *Forbes*.[47] In that case, the pursuer brought an action of declarator that there was no right of way across his land for carts or carriages. He accepted that the road had been used as a horse and foot road and he also conceded that it had been used for carts and carriages for 30 years which was the period during which carts and carriages had been in operation in the area. The court held that the road was a cart and carriage road. In *Mackenzie* v *Bankes*,[48] the issue was whether a road was a public road for carts and carriages which, according to the evidence, had only recently been introduced into the district. The First Division held that the road could not be used for carts and carriages, because in order to accommodate these vehicles the road would have to be widened. The earlier case of *Forbes* was distinguished on the basis that in *Forbes* the road was already suitable for carts and carriages whereas in *Mackenzie* it was not.

At common law, if a right of way is established for vehicular purposes, it may be used both for pedestrian use and by those on horseback.[49] That is based on the view that the greater includes the lesser. That said, if a right of way is established for all purposes, it may subsequently be restricted to certain uses if for the prescriptive period these are the only uses made of the route. Thus, in

---

[43] 1915 SC(HL) 93 at 107–108.

[44] *Prin.*, s. 993.

[45] *Land Law*, para. 24–121.

[46] *Landownership*, p. 328.

[47] (1829) 4 Fac Dec 563. The case is also reported in *Shaw* (1829) 7 S 441 but the report in *Faculty Decisions* is better.

[48] (1868) 6 M 936.

[49] *Hope Vere* v *Young* (1877) 14 R 425, per Lord Young at 435.

Macfarlane v *Morrison*,[50] a jury found that prior to 1806 a road was a public road for all purposes, but since then, it had been used only by those on foot. The court held that the road was public, but that it could only be used as a foot road and was not a vehicular route.

By Act of Parliament

The Countryside (Scotland) Act 1967 provides[51]:

> "It shall be the duty of a planning authority to assert, protect and keep open and free from obstruction or encroachment any public right of way which is wholly or partly within their area, and they may for these purposes institute and defend legal proceedings and generally take such steps as they may deem expedient."

That section replaced section 42 of the Local Government (Scotland) Act 1894 and the intention of the 1894 Act was to allow local authorities the right to institute legal proceedings in order to have something declared to be a right of way.[52] The new statement by a local authority that something is a right of way would not suffice, but if the landowner(s) did not challenge that, the practical result might be the creation of such a right. Members of the public may be uncertain about the status of a particular route or for other reasons may not wish to be involved in what could be lengthy and expensive litigation and in these circumstances might look to local authorities to "assert" rights of way. Obviously, some local authorities are more active than others, but a great deal may depend upon the resources available to them. Local authorities tend, however, to try to negotiate with local landowners rather than use their statutory powers. There are, however, certain statutory methods by which public paths can be created.

Public path creation agreements and orders

In terms of sections 30 and 31 of the Countryside (Scotland) Act 1967, local authorities have powers to create "public paths" by agreement under section 30 or by order under section 31. A "public path" is defined in section 30(3) as a "way" which is a footpath or bridle way or a combination of those, and a "foot-path" is a "way over which the public have the following, but no other, rights of way, that is to say a right on foot with or without a right of way on pedal cycles", and a "bridle way" is a "way over which the public have the following, but no other, rights of way, that is to say, a right of way on foot and a right of way on horseback or leading a horse, with or without a right to drive animals of any description along that way".

Agreements: In terms of section 30, the local authority may enter into an agreement "with any person having the necessary power in that behalf for the creation by that person of a public path over land in their area". It is not clear who, apart from the owner of the land, has such a power and it would probably be unsafe to

---

[50] (1865) 4 M 257.
[51] s. 46.
[52] *Hope* v *Landward Committee of the Parish Council of Inveresk* (1906) 8 F 896, particularly Lord McLaren at 900.

enter into an arrangement with anyone other than the owner. The agreement entered into may be unconditional or conditional in the sense that it may restrict times for access or access of particular types. The agreement must contain either a particular description of the lands or a statutory description by reference[53] and it may be recorded in the Register of Sasines or registered in the Land Register, the effect of which is to make the agreement enforceable by the local authority against singular successors of the original party unless the singular successor acquired the land in good faith and for value in ignorance of the agreement.[54] Once the agreement is entered into, the local authority may carry out work to bring the path into a fit condition for use by the public and it is required to maintain it thereafter.[55]

Orders: The provisions just noted apply equally to public path creation orders, but there are other provisions which apply to orders but do not apply to agreements. Before an order is made, the local authority must be satisfied that it is expedient to create a path and impracticable for an agreement to be entered into. It must have regard to the extent to which the creation of the path would add to the convenience or enjoyment of a substantial section of the public or to persons resident in the area and also the effect which the creation of the path would have on persons interested in the land which would be affected by the creation of the path.[56] As with an agreement, the order may be unconditional or subject to conditions. The procedures to be followed for the making of such an order are found in Schedule 3 to the 1967 Act and in the Countryside (Scotland) Regulations 1982.[57] In certain circumstances, the order has to be confirmed by the Minister (ie where there are objections or representations) and if that is so the Minister may add conditions.[58]

It would seem that local authorities make much less use of public path creation orders than they do of agreements. That is understandable since if the local authority cannot persuade a landowner to enter into an agreement, they would be faced with an unco-operative owner on whom they may be reluctant to impose such an order.

Long-distance routes

These routes are the West Highland Way, the Southern Upland Way and the Speyside Way. They were created following upon a report by the former Countryside Commission for Scotland. Scottish Natural Heritage (SNH) is required to consult every local authority through whose area the proposed route will pass.[59] If SNH considers that the public should be able to make what the Act calls "extensive journeys" along such a route on foot, on pedal cycle or on horseback, it may make a proposal for a long-distance route and submit it to the Minister. The report must have (1) a map showing the route and identifying those

---

[53] Countryside (Scotland) Act 1967, s. 38(4).
[54] Countryside (Scotland) Act 1967, s. 38(5).
[55] Countryside (Scotland) Act 1967, s. 33(1).
[56] Countryside (Scotland) Act 1967, s. 31(1).
[57] SI 1982/1467, regs 9–17.
[58] Countryside (Scotland) Act 1967, s. 31(2).
[59] Countryside (Scotland) Act 1967, s. 39.

parts which are already rights of way, (2) proposals for the provision, maintenance and enjoyment of the route, (3) an estimate of the capital outlay and annual expenditure, and (4) details of any representations made by the local authorities who have been consulted.[60] The report may also contain recommendations about traffic restrictions on existing roads along which the route will go.[61]

The Minister may approve or reject the proposal or approve it with modifications and if he does that, he must consult further with SNH and with local authorities and other persons as he sees fit. The Act also provides for alteration of the route if it becomes impracticable to implement the original scheme.[62]

Town and Country Planning (Scotland) Act 1997

The Minister may exercise a power to stop up or divert a road to enable some form of development to be carried out and that may require the stopping-up or diversion of some existing route which may be permitted subject to the creation of another route which may become a right of way.[63] The planning authority may also create alternative footpaths and bridleways where any contemplated development would have the effect of closing one of these off.[64] This requires to be confirmed by the Minister.[65] The local authority may also apply to the Minister for an order to convert a road into a footpath or bridleway or other track and/or to restrict or extinguish the right to use the route for vehicular purposes.[66]

Permissive paths

Despite the fact that a public right of way may not exist over a person's land, there is nothing to stop a landowner voluntarily permitting the public to take access perhaps along identified routes and he or she may respond to a suggestion from the local authority and agree to an informal arrangement. Sections 2 and 3 of the Local Government (Development and Finance) (Scotland) Act 1964 enables the local authority to arrange with a landowner for the provisions of footpaths on any land to enable members of the public to enjoy the countryside which can include the provision of gates, stiles, steps, bridges, signposts and other ancillary works. The agreement may, in appropriate cases, be recorded in the Register of Sasines or in the Land Register, in which event it will be enforceable against singular successors of the original landowner. It will be obvious that the public will be entitled to use the path in line with the agreement and not otherwise and the disadvantage is that unless the agreement is recorded in the Register of Sasines or registered in the Land Register, the arrangement does not offer any security to the public.

Problems

There are a number of problems which surround rights of way in Scotland and if some rights of way are not vindicated, they may disappear.

---

[60] Countryside (Scotland) Act 1967, s. 39(5).
[61] Countryside (Scotland) Act 1967, s. 39(2), (3).
[62] Countryside (Scotland) Act 1967, s. 42.
[63] Town and Country Planning (Scotland) Act 1997, s. 202(1).
[64] Town and Country Planning (Scotland) Act 1997, s. 208.
[65] Town and Country Planning (Scotland) Act 1997 Sched. 16, paras 4 and 5.
[66] Town and Country Planning (Scotland) Act 1997, s. 203(1).

Proof: The onus of proof of a right of way lies with the person asserting it[67] but that is not a peculiarity of rights of way. If the defender does not accept the pursuer's position witnesses have to be produced and some of them might be unwilling to appear in court and give evidence despite their willingness to co-operate at an earlier stage.

Cost: The preparation for litigation and the litigation itself may be costly and that expense is one which members of the public and local authorities may be unwilling to incur if they do not have adequate resources. Even the availability of legal aid may not be much of an incentive against, say, a landowner who may have the resources to take a case to the House of Lords. The Scottish Rights of Way Society has limited resources and for these reasons any doubtful case may not be vigorously pursued.

The law itself: Certain aspects of the law are unclear. For example, there has been a great deal of litigation about what is a "public place" but there is still doubt about whether some places are "public". Another problem is that the use has to be continuous and "as of right" rather than attributable to tolerance. There may be some doubt about whether the evidence can demonstrate "continuous" possession and whether what perhaps began as tolerance became possession as of right.

Even if use is established it is not clear whether a footpath, or a horse road, can be used by pedal cyclists,[68] or whether someone walking can wheel a pram on a footpath. One might have assumed that a walker could be accompanied by a dog but some doubt is cast on this by a paper produced by the Scottish Landowners' Federation.[69]

The law on obstructions is not clear because the cases have dealt with physical obstructions and even then there is some doubt about the type of gate which might be permitted on a right of way. The whole issue of displaying misleading notices on rights of way has not been explored in the case law nor has the effect of allowing animals to graze (apart from bulls),[70] and so the public might be cautious about being on the right of way in their presence. Even if the animals themselves present no threat, their feeding habits might render parts of a right of way impassable, and that would also be a disincentive to using the route.

One final problem relates to maintenance. There is no obligation on the proprietor of the ground to maintain a right of way. In the context of servitudes, the proprietor of the dominant tenement is entitled to carry out repairs and so one assumes that members of the public are entitled to carry out repairs to a right of way. However repairs, for example in relation to bridges or the removal of fallen trees, might require vehicles to be brought on to, say, a footpath and there is doubt about whether that is permissible.

---

[67] *Bates & Baring* v *McQuean* (1853) 15 D 455.

[68] *GlenTannar Rights of Way Case* 1931 (unreported), judgment of Lord Mackay. The case was ultimately settled before the Inner House had an opportunity to consider Lord Mackay's views.

[69] Paper of September 1990, p. 7, para. 20(e).

[70] Countryside (Scotland) Act 1967, s. 44(2) makes it an offence if the owner permits a bull to be at large on a right of way unless the bull is not more than 10 months' old and is not one of the recognised dairy breeds and is with cows or heifers.

Law reform

The Scottish Rights of Way Society published proposals in September 1990 (which were updated in March 1998), about reform of the law in relation to rights of way. There are a large number of these but among the more important ones are the following:

1. If it can be shown that a public right of way existed at some time in the past there should be a presumption that there remains a right of way unless the contrary is proved.

2. Nothing should be regarded as a right of way if it leads from a public place to a place of public resort such as the top of a frequently visited hill or a geological site of interest.

3. In order to avoid the difficulties arising from use "as of right" rather than use as a matter of tolerance, it is suggested that the use "openly, peaceably and without judicial interruption" (ie the words which appear in section 3(3) of the 1973 Act) should be sufficient.

4. Because of the difficulties which local authorities face in relation to their obligations under section 46(1) of the 1967 Act, it is suggested that the Government should carefully consider what options are available for securing rights of way. In England and Wales there is power in county councils to make an order following upon notice to the public and to landowners that something is a right of way and it is suggested that that should be introduced into Scotland.

5. The law in relation to obstructions and in particular misleading notices requires to be considered.

6. The entitlement to maintain rights of way requires also to be clarified.

7. The Society also suggested that an index of rights of way and Public Path Agreements or Orders should be created and that the inclusion of something within that index should be conclusive.

The Scottish Office Land Reform Policy Group produced a paper in February 1998 entitled "Identifying the Problems" and while the topics under consideration by the LRPG are wider than merely access, the paper and the subsequent report "Recommendations for Action" published in January 1999 do recognise that, at present, control of land in every aspect is largely in the hands of landowners and land managers and that the interests of others in using the land, for example, for recreational purposes, rests almost entirely on tolerance by these landowners. It is that last aspect on which the Government has committed itself to reform. If something along the lines of a general right of access is introduced (see Chapter 14), consideration will need to be given to the position of public rights of way.

CHAPTER 14

AREA ACCESS

Jeremy Rowan-Robinson
Donna McKenzie Skene

Introduction

In Chapter 13 the arrangements for linear access to the countryside were discussed. This chapter is devoted to a discussion of the arrangements for area access, ie access to land otherwise than along a more or less defined route. As we mentioned in Chapter 12, the starting point for any consideration of the issues relating to access is the basic principle of Scots law that an owner of land is entitled to the exclusive use of that land.[1] It follows from this that no one may enter land without permission of the landowner or without some other right to do so. If he does, he commits a trespass. The remedies for trespass are discussed in Chapter 12. In this chapter we consider the circumstances in which permission for area access may arise, the statutory provisions for creating a right to area access and a number of other statutory provisions which contribute in one way or another to the provision of public access to the countryside or to its enjoyment.

It should be said at the outset that much of the discussion in this chapter is likely to become redundant in due course. Scottish Natural Heritage (SNH) has recommended to the Government the introduction of a general right of access to land and water for informal recreation and passage.[2] The recommendation, which is subject to a number of qualifications, reflects the consensus on access achieved by the Access Forum (below) about the best way forward to provide the public with greater freedoms to enjoy Scotland's countryside.[3] In a speech at Balmaha on February 2, 1999, the then Secretary of State for Scotland stated that the Government had accepted SNH's recommendation as a starting point for developing detailed legislative proposals which it would be for the Scottish Parliament to consider and implement. Subsequently, the White Paper *Land*

---

[1] Erskine, *Inst,* II.1.

[2] *Access to the Countryside for Open-air Recreation: Scottish Natural Heritage's Advice to Government* (January 1999).

[3] *Access to the Countryside: The Access Forum's Advice* (October 1998).

Reform: Proposals for Legislation,[4] issued by the new Scottish Executive in July 1999, contained a commitment by the Scottish Ministers to early legislation on the matter. If the recommendation is implemented as proposed, then the basic principle of Scots law which we referred to above will be subject to an important qualification. The right of the landowner to the exclusive use of the land will be subject to the general right of access. The details of the recommendation are examined below. However, until such a right is introduced, the present arrangements continue and these are now explained.

Permission for access[5]

A person who enters land with the permission of the landowner is not a trespasser.[6] Such permission may be express or implied.[7] No difficulty arises from express permission. For example, user groups from time to time secure the express permission of a landowner to enter land for the purposes of a particular event or to pursue particular recreational activities. Access is subject to the terms of the permission; and, subject to those terms, the permission may be withdrawn by the landowner at any time.

However, for many years, members of the public have enjoyed freedom of access to the Scottish countryside, particularly the hills and mountains, without any express permission. This has often been referred to as "the freedom to roam". This freedom was endorsed by the Scottish Landowners Federation as signatories to the Concordat on Access (1996) which states that, subject to reasonable constraints, the public should continue to enjoy access to hill land in Scotland.[8] In a policy paper issued in 1994 SNH observed that some legal opinion suggests that the tradition of customary access to land may be based on implied or *de facto* consent to the visitor.[9] In other words, there is some question whether it is right to regard members of the public exercising customary access as trespassers or whether there may be said to be an implied permission in such cases from the landowner.

There seems little doubt that permission can be implied. In *Duke of Buccleuch* v *Edinburgh Magistrates*[10] it was held that implied consent was a complete defence to an action for encroachment. Encroachment differs from trespass only in that the intrusion on to land is permanent rather than temporary. The case involved a building, the pillars of which extended on to a pavement owned by the magistrates. No objection had been taken by the magistrates at the time of construction of the building; indeed, it was not until the owner of the building proposed further works involving the pillars some 30 years later that objection was taken. It was held that, although there was no express consent, the circumstances showed implied consent. Lord Justice-Clerk Inglis said:

---

⁴ SE/1999/1 (Stationery Office, July 1999).
⁵ See generally J. Rowan-Robinson and A. Ross, "The Freedom to Roam and Implied Permission" (1998) 2 *Edinburgh Law Review* 225.
⁶ *Steuart* v *Stephen* (1877) 4 R 873.
⁷ *Duke of Buccleuch* v *Edinburgh Magistrates* (1866) 3 M 528.
⁸ *Scotland's Hills and Mountains: a Concordat on Access.*
⁹ SNH, "Enjoying the Outdoors: A Programme for Action" (1994).
¹⁰ (1866) 3 M 528.

"If a building is erected with the consent of the owner of the ground, he cannot be heard to complain of that which has been done with his consent; and that consent may be inferred from facts and circumstances."[11]

Walker applies the concept of implied consent to cases of trespass. "A person prima facie a trespasser may be deemed a licensee if trespass in such circumstances has been so repeatedly tolerated as to imply acquiescence by the occupier in his presence."[12] The decisions in *Dumbreck* v *Addie & Sons Collieries Ltd*[13] and *Breslin* v *London and North Eastern Railway Co.*[14] are cited as authority for this proposition. Both cases involved claims for damages for personal injury suffered by someone (a child) entering the land of another in the absence of a right or express permission. In both cases, it was accepted that the conduct of an owner could sometimes amount to implied permission for access. The *Dumbreck* and *Breslin* cases are part of a long line of cases involving personal injury to children, an analysis of which[15] shows that the judges were prepared to go to considerable lengths to avoid the harsh application of the law resulting from the very limited duty of care owed, at that time, by occupiers of land to trespassers. The law in this area has since changed. The Occupiers' Liability (Scotland) Act 1960 subsequently enlarged the duty of care owed by occupiers of land to trespassers (see Chapter 12). Nonetheless, the cases recognise the concept of implied permission. The question is: in what circumstances will implied permission be held to exist?

This is not an easy question to answer. It seems, however, that implied permission will not be inferred lightly. In *Buccleuch* Lord Justice-Clerk Inglis observed that the doctrine of acquiescence "must be carefully guarded, especially when it affects heritable rights. The facts from which acquiescence is to be inferred must be such as to leave no reasonable doubt as to what was the intention of the parties"[16]; and in *Breslin* Lord Justice-Clerk Aitchison referred to the "clearly implied consent of the owner" being a necessary prerequisite.

Although the courts have stressed that a great deal will turn on the particular circumstances of each case,[17] an attempt to answer the question[18] suggests that there are three factors which may help to determine the existence of implied consent. First of all, the landowner must be aware that access is being taken before any question of implied consent can arise,[19] although actual knowledge on the part of the landowner may not be necessary; awareness on the part of an employee of the landowner whose duties encompass permitting access could be sufficient. It is unlikely that awareness of every instance in which access is taken is required. It will be enough that the owner is aware that the public are in the habit of taking access. It seems that awareness may be presumed; but the presumption will only arise if the practice of frequenting a particular place

---

[11] (1866) 3 M 528 at 531.
[12] D.M. Walker, *Principles of Scottish Private Law* (Scottish Universities Law Institute, 4th edn, 1989), Vol. 3, p. 207.
[13] 1929 SC (HL) 51.
[14] 1936 SC 816.
[15] See J. Rowan-Robinson and A. Ross, op. cit., n. 5.
[16] (1865) 3 M 528 at 531.
[17] See, eg, *Dumbreck*, op. cit., n. 13, per Viscount Dunedin at 60.
[18] See J. Rowan-Robinson and A. Ross, op. cit., n. 5.
[19] *Breslin*, op. cit., n. 14, per Lord Justice-Clerk Aitchison at 822.

extends over such a period of time as to warrant the inference that it was known to and acquiesced in by the owner.[20] As Viscount Dunedin observed in *Dumbreck* "[i]t is permission that must be proved, not tolerance, though tolerance in some circumstances may be so pronounced as to lead to a conclusion that it was really tantamount to a permission".[21]

Second, if a landowner takes appropriate steps to prevent people taking access, that may be enough to rebut the presumption of implied permission.[22] Just what steps are required to be taken is not clear. In *Dumbreck*, for example, the practice of warning people off the land was held to be sufficient even though the defenders were aware that the warnings were sometimes ineffectual. The Lord Chancellor, Lord Hailsham, said

> "I cannot regard the fact that the appellants [the defenders] did not effectively fence their field, or the fact that their warnings were frequently disregarded, as sufficient to justify an inference that they permitted the children to be on the field and, in the absence of such permission, it is clear that the respondent's child was merely a trespasser."[23]

On the other hand, it has been suggested that a half-hearted attempt to resist access, such as simply putting up a warning notice, might be regarded as the equivalent of doing nothing.[24]

Third, the state of knowledge of the person taking access may be relevant to the question of implied consent. In other words, implied consent will not arise if the person taking access is in no doubt that he or she is a trespasser.[25] In the English case *Edwards* v *Railway Executive*[26] Lord Oaksey in the House of Lords said:

> "[I]n my opinion, in considering the question whether a licence can be inferred, the state of mind of the suggested licensee must be considered. The circumstances must be such that the suggested licensee could have thought and did think that he was not trespassing but was on the property in question by the leave and licence of its owner."

It is likely to be easier to establish this state of knowledge for an adult, having regard to the actions of the landowner, than for a child.

Access taken in reliance on implied permission may be said to be precarious in the sense that it is open to the landowner expressly to withdraw the consent at any time. As observed in the *Stair Memorial Encyclopaedia*,[27] "possession on the basis of a licence revocable at will is sometimes referred to as 'possession

---

[20] *Breslin*, op. cit., n. 14 at 823.

[21] 1929 SC (HL) 51 at 60.

[22] Conversely a failure to take any steps may suggest implied permission: *Boyd* v *The Glasgow Iron and Steel Co. Ltd* 1923 SC 758; *Lowery* v *Walker* [1911] AC 10; but see *Devlin* v *Jaffray's Trs* (1902) 5 F 130.

[23] 1929 SC (HL) 51 at 58.

[24] Ibid, per Viscount Dunedin at 60; and see *Cooke* v *Midland and Great Western Railway of Ireland* [1909] AC 229.

[25] *Breslin*, op. cit., n. 14, per Lords Mackay and Wark.

[26] [1952] AC 737 at 748. See too *Hardy* v *Central London Ry* [1920] 3 KB 459 (CA).

[27] Vol. 18, para. 128.

precario'". Even express permission may be withdrawn unless there is an agreement not to, or only to do so on certain conditions.

Access as of right

At the present time, the only circumstances in which the public, generally, will have a *right* to enjoy area access to the countryside is where such a right has been created by statute. With linear access it is possible, subject to satisfying certain requirements, to create a right by continuous use for a period of 20 years (see Chapter 13). This is not possible with area access; the law has not developed in the same way.[28] Habitual access to the open countryside over a period of 20 years confers no right to roam.[29] In *Dyce* v *Hay*,[30] for example, the Second Division rejected a claim that a servitude right existed on behalf of the public at large from time immemorial of walking and recreation on land by the River Don in Old Aberdeen. This was not a servitude recognised by the law of Scotland and such a right could not be acquired by use. Lord Justice-Clerk Hope observed: "[t]here is no case whatever in which a right to wander over, to rest or to lounge upon the ground of a private proprietor, under the name of recreation, has ever been sustained".[31] In *Harvey* v *Lindsay*[32] the First Division held that a right to curl, skate, etc., though exercised on a loch from time immemorial, could not be acquired as a servitude by feuars and inhabitants of the neighbouring village or by the public generally. The court agreed with the Lord Ordinary at first instance who viewed it as amounting to nothing more than tolerance.

There are, however, several statutory provisions which can be employed to create a right to area access.[33] Of these, the provisions of the Countryside (Scotland) Act 1967 ("the 1967 Act"), as amended,[34] relating to access agreements and access orders are the most significant.[35]

Access agreements

The provisions for promoting access agreements and access orders are contained in Part II of the 1967 Act.[36] They confer powers on planning authorities and SNH to be exercised for the purpose of enabling the public to have access for open-air recreation to the open country (1967 Act, s. 10(1)). "Open country" is defined as "any land appearing to SNH or to the authority with whom an access agreement

---

[28] See generally F. Lyall, "Recreation, Landownership and the Countryside" (1970) 3 JR 203.

[29] *Dyce* v *Hay* (1849) 11 D 1266; (1852) 1 Macq 305 (HL); *Harvey* v *Lindsay* (1853) 15 D 768.

[30] Ibid.

[31] Ibid at 1275. Earlier case law dealing with servitude rights claimed on behalf of communities and with presumed dedication was distinguished. The requirement that a servitude must be appurtenant to a dominant tenement has been an impediment to the development of the law in this area (see Lyall, op. cit., n. 27).

[32] (1853) 15 D 768.

[33] See generally J. Rowan-Robinson, W.M. Gordon and C.T. Reid, *Public Access to the Countryside: A Guide to the Law, Practice and Procedure in Scotland* (SNH and COSLA, 1993).

[34] By the Natural Heritage (Scotland) Act 1991.

[35] For the background to the legislation see F. Lyall, op. cit., n. 27.

[36] For a detailed description of the provisions see J. Rowan-Robinson, W.M. Gordon and C.T. Reid, op. cit., n. 32; and F. Lyall, "Access to the Countryside", 1969 SLT (News) 197. Provision is also made for the acquisition by SNH or a planning authority of land for public access (s. 24). Acquisition may be by agreement or by compulsory purchase.

is made or to the authority by whom an access order is made . . . as the case may be, to consist wholly or predominantly of mountain, moor, heath, hill, woodland, cliff or foreshore, and any waterway."[37]

Section 13(1) provides that SNH or a planning authority may make an access agreement with any person having an interest in land. A model form of agreement was prepared by the former Countryside Commission for Scotland. There is no set procedure. An agreement may contain provision for the making of payments by SNH or the authority (s. 13(2)). These payments may be made as consideration for the making of the agreement[38] and by way of defraying or contributing towards expenditure incurred by the person making the agreement.

Where an access agreement is in force in respect of any land, a person who enters that land for the purpose of open-air recreation is not to be treated as a trespasser (s. 11(1)).[39] This provision does not, however, apply to anyone who commits an offence on the land or who, without lawful authority, carries out any of the activities listed in Schedule 2 to the Act (s. 11(4)). These activities include driving or riding any vehicle, lighting a fire or doing anything likely to cause a fire, allowing a dog to be on the land which is not under proper control, leaving litter, wilfully damaging the land or anything on it, wantonly disturbing, annoying or obstructing any person engaged in any lawful occupation and wilfully taking any animal, bird or fish or taking or injuring any eggs or nest. Furthermore, the agreement itself may make specific provision for restrictions on the right of access (s. 11(3)); and the agreement must exclude any land where this is necessary to avoid danger to members of the public (s. 27(1)).

The right of access conferred by an access agreement does not extend to excepted land (s. 11(1)). "Excepted land" is defined as:

- land used for agricultural purposes other than livestock rearing;
- land comprising a Nature Reserve designated by SNH or by a planning authority in so far as byelaws for the reserve prohibit entry;
- buildings and their curtilage;
- land used for the purpose of a park, garden or pleasure ground;
- land used for the surface working of minerals;
- land used for the purposes of a railway or an airport;
- land used as a golf course, sports ground, playing field or racecourse;
- land used for the purposes of a statutory undertaker or telecommunications operator;
- land where development, having the benefit of planning permission, is underway which will bring it within one of the above categories (s. 11(5)).

---

[37] s. 10(2). "Waterway" and "foreshore" are to include any bank, barrier, dune, beach, flat or other land adjacent to the waterway or foreshore.

[38] In which case they are to be made on the basis of an assessment of the capital value of the land arrived at in accordance with the provisions of Sched. 4 (s. 13(11), added by the Countryside (Scotland) Act 1981, s. 3(1)).

[39] Whether it is correct to refer to such a cautiously worded provision as conferring a "right" of access is debatable; but the term is used in this chapter for the sake of convenience.

In addition, where an access agreement is in existence and representations are made to the Minister that the use or impending use of land for agriculture or forestry comprised within an area covered by the agreement would be prejudiced by the right of access and the Minister is satisfied of this and is of the view that this prejudice would outweigh the benefits arising from increased public access, the access agreement must be varied to exclude the land (s. 15). SNH or the planning authority may erect and maintain notices indicating the boundaries of agreement land and excepted land (s. 28).

A person interested in land comprised in an access agreement (other than excepted land) is prohibited from carrying out work on the land which would have the effect of substantially reducing the area to which the public have access (s. 16(1)). In the event of default, SNH or the planning authority, as appropriate, may serve a notice on the person responsible requiring the matter to be remedied (s. 18(1)) and may take direct action in the event of non-compliance (s. 18(2)). There is a right of appeal to the sheriff against such a notice (s. 18(3)).

The agreement may make such provision as appears to be expedient for the purpose of securing safe and sufficient access for the public (s. 17(1)). This may include provision for repairing or improving any means of access,[40] the construction of a new access, carrying out works to safeguard the public from injury due to the state of the land or anything done or omitted to be done on it, restrictions on the destruction, removal, alteration or closure of any such access or works[41] and the maintenance of such access or works (s. 17(2)). SNH or the planning authority, as appropriate, will decide with the owner and occupier of the land who will do any work required to give effect to these provisions and how the cost is to be defrayed. Where SNH or the planning authority are unable to reach agreement on these matters or the owner or occupier fails to carry out what has been agreed, SNH or the planning authority, as appropriate, may take all necessary steps and recover any cost beyond their own agreed contribution (s. 17(5)).

An agreement must be recorded in the Register of Sasines or the Land Register for Scotland, as appropriate (s. 16(5)). A recorded agreement may be enforced, subject to limited exceptions, by SNH or the planning authority against singular successors.

A planning authority whose area comprises any land which is subject to an access agreement must prepare and keep up to date a map of such land and the map must be available for inspection by the public (s. 26).

Access orders

Where it appears to SNH or a planning authority that it is impracticable to secure an access agreement, for example because of the intransigence of the landowner, it may promote an access order (s. 14). An access order is of no effect unless and until it is confirmed by the Minister. The procedure to be followed is set out in Schedule 3 to the 1967 Act. An access order must contain a map defining the land comprised in the order and any excepted land. Notice in the prescribed form

---

[40] As defined in s. 17(6).

[41] Non-compliance with any such restriction may trigger the notice of default procedure in s. 18(1) of the 1967 Act.

must be published in a local newspaper and served on the owner and any occupiers, stating the general effect of the order that is about to be made and naming a place where a draft may be inspected and specifying the time within which any objections are to be made. If no representations or objections are made, the Minister may confirm the order with or without modifications or conditions. In the event of representations or objections, the Minister must cause a local inquiry to be held or afford an opportunity for the person making the representations or objections to be heard by a person appointed for the purpose. The Minister may then confirm the order with or without modifications or conditions. It should be noted that the Minister may not confirm an order before byelaws have been made and confirmed under section 54 or made under section 55 of the Act (s. 14(5)). Notice of confirmation of an order must be published in a local paper and served on the owner and any occupier. The order will become operative on the date on which the notice is published or on such later date as may be specified in the order.

An access order has the same effect as an access agreement. A person who enters land which is the subject of an order for the purposes of open-air recreation is not to be treated as a trespasser (s. 11(1)). Most of the provisions described above with regard to access agreements apply also to access orders.

Where the value of an interest of any person in land is depreciated as a result of the coming into operation of an access order or a person suffers damage through disturbance as a result of the order, that person is entitled to compensation from SNH or the planning authority, as appropriate, equal to the depreciation or damage (s. 20(1)). In assessing depreciation, Rules (2)–(4) set out in section 12 of the Land Compensation (Scotland) Act 1963 are applied. Generally, the position is that the compensation cannot be claimed, nor will it be payable, until five years from the date on which the order took effect. This will ensure that the compensation is calculated having regard to the actual effect on the land of the order (s. 21(1)). Provision is made, however, for payment on account (s. 23). Any dispute over the amount is to be determined by the Lands Tribunal for Scotland (s. 70).

Comment

A questionnaire survey conducted by the former Countryside Commission for Scotland (CCS) in 1990 showed that 63 access agreements had been concluded since the legislation came into force but that no access orders had been made. The non-use of the access order provisions is not surprising. It has been suggested that such an order is likely to provoke resentment on the part of the landowner and the task of managing an access area in the face of hostility from the landowner would be difficult. "[I]t is the antithesis of the sort of partnership approach upon which so much of the arrangements for public access to the countryside depends."[42]

The questionnaire survey showed that the access agreements were for varying periods of time: 5, 10, 15, 20 and 21 years, with some entered into for an indefinite period. The CCS Annual Reports showed a very slow take-up of agreements during the 1970s. Although there had been some activity during the 1980s, part

---

[42] J. Rowan-Robinson, W.M. Gordon and C.T. Reid, op. cit., n. 32 at para. 8.4.7.

of it was associated with the programme of long-distance routes. Nineteen of the access agreements were linked to that programme. Others were linked to the provision of country parks (see below). Others still had been negotiated as "linear access agreements" prior to the improvement in the legislative provisions for public paths. Few were employed to create discrete opportunities for area access to the countryside. CCS in successive Annual Reports expressed disappointment about the slow take-up in the use of the powers.

Research published by SNH in 1994 suggested that there were three reasons for the slow take-up.[43] First of all, there was a feeling on the part of landowners that the disadvantages of statutory agreements outweighed their advantages. Although the support of a ranger service and, to a lesser extent, the prospect of payment, were attractions, these were outweighed by the loss of control which an agreement involved. The level of payment, based on the loss to the landowner rather than the gain to the community, was regarded as no more than a limited attraction. Second, planning authorities, faced with continuing severe restrictions on public expenditure, were understandably reluctant to commit themselves to continuing obligations in terms of maintenance, repair and ranger support. The time and expense involved in negotiating agreements was also a disincentive. The CCS Annual Report for 1979 noted that between 6 and 18 months was the norm and that some agreements had taken several years to settle. Third, there was a discernible feeling on the part of some local authority officers that statutory agreements operate to restrict and regulate rather than extend access for the public and they could see no reason why authorities should pay for something which the public had hitherto enjoyed by tradition. Agreements had, however, been found to make a useful contribution where a local authority was implementing a positive programme of access, such as the long-distance routes, or in resolving management problems in "honeypot" areas.

Other statutory provisions

This section examines a number of other provisions in the 1967 Act and in other legislation which have an impact on the opportunities available to the public to take access to the countryside otherwise than along a more or less defined route. Some of these, such as the powers of the Forestry Commission and the provisions relating to recreational access to water, are considered more fully in other chapters and are mentioned here simply for completeness.

Acquisition of land

Where it appears to SNH or a planning authority, as respects any land in their area comprising open country or access to it, that the public should have access to the land for open-air recreation, they may acquire land, either by agreement or compulsorily, if they consider it expedient to do so (s. 24(1)). They may carry out on any land so acquired such work as may be necessary for providing convenient means of access to the land (s. 24(2)). The land must be managed so as to give the public access for open-air recreation to so much of it as may be practicable (s. 24(3)). Any such land must be shown on the map of land subject to certain forms of public access maintained by the planning authority (s. 26(1)).

---

[43] J. Rowan-Robinson, *Review of rights of way procedure* (SNH Review No. 9, 1994).

Country parks

Section 48 of the 1967 Act makes provision for country parks. A country park is a relatively small area of countryside which by reason of its proximity to major areas of population affords convenient opportunities to the public for enjoyment of the countryside or for open-air recreation (s. 48(1)). Every planning authority is required to assess the need for country parks in its area, having regard to the existence and adequacy of opportunities for enjoying the countryside and for open-air recreation, and must keep the need under review (s. 48(2)). Authorities have power to acquire land and to provide, lay out, improve, maintain and manage country parks. In discharge of this duty they may also provide such buildings, facilities, equipment and other services and works as are required. There are now 36 country parks in Scotland, mainly but not wholly in the central belt. Byelaws or management rules may be applied in the parks and a ranger service provided to facilitate visitor enjoyment. Most of these parks are owned or managed by local authorities with support from SNH. However, an authority may arrange for the exercise of these powers by someone on its behalf (s. 48(7)). Typically, facilities are provided in country parks for informal recreation such as picnicking, walking and water sports.

Regional parks

Section 48A of the 1967 Act[44] makes provision for the designation by local authorities of regional parks. The concept of regional parks was defined in the report of the CCS *A Park System for Scotland* (1974). They were to be extensive areas, perhaps covering land in the jurisdiction of more than one local authority, located in attractive countryside and conveniently situated near to large population centres. Unlike country parks (see above), they are to be areas of mixed land use. The idea was that designation would enable local authorities to manage the area as a single administrative unit and thereby integrate informal recreation more effectively with the predominant land uses such as agriculture and forestry. It was hoped this would lead to a more co-ordinated approach to the management of the different uses.

The procedure for designation is set out in the Regional Parks (Scotland) Regulations 1981.[45] A designation is to be by way of order; the order will not take effect until it is confirmed by the Minister (s. 48A(3)). A regional park is defined as an extensive area of land, part of which is devoted to the recreational needs of the public (s. 48A(1)). The legislation provides for the making of byelaws relating to access; this in turn will allow the extension of the ranger service to some of the more popular areas of the countryside. Four regional parks were designated by the former regional councils and their management has been transferred to the new local authorities established under the Local Government etc. (Scotland) Act 1994. These are Clyde Muirshiel (26,425 hectares), Pentland Hills (9,000 hectares), Fife (6,500 hectares) and Loch Lomond (44,200 hectares). The Loch Lomond area, by way of example, has been managed as a collaborative venture between the constituent local authorities acting in concert as the Loch Lomond Park Authority.

---

[44] Added by the Countryside (Scotland) Act 1981, s. 8.
[45] SI 1981/1613.

Management agreements

Section 49A of the 1967 Act[46] enables SNH or a planning authority to enter into a management agreement with any person having an interest in land. SNH may employ such an agreement to secure the conservation and enhancement of, or to foster the understanding and enjoyment of, the natural heritage of Scotland (s. 49A(1)). A planning authority may use such an agreement to preserve or enhance the natural beauty of the countryside or to promote its enjoyment by the public (s. 49A(2)). Such agreements may contain financial provisions. If recorded in the Register of Sasines or the Land Register of Scotland the agreement may be enforced, subject to limited exceptions, by SNH or the planning authority, as appropriate, against singular successors (s. 49A(9)).

The terms of section 49A are broad enough for agreements to be used to provide or to enhance opportunities for access to the countryside. What limited information is available on the use of these agreements suggests that they are beginning to be used for this sort of role.[47] It seems the terminology is important and that the word "management" has more pleasing connotations for landowners and perhaps also for planning authorities than "access".

Planning agreements

Section 75 of the Town and Country Planning (Scotland) Act 1997 provides that a planning authority may enter into an agreement with any person interested in land for the purpose of restricting or regulating the development or use of that land (see Chapter 3). Such agreements may contain incidental financial provisions. If recorded in the Register of Sasines or the Land Register for Scotland, the agreement may be enforced, subject to limited exceptions, by a planning authority against singular successors.

Research shows that such agreements are almost always triggered by and linked to an application for planning permission.[48] This is not the place for an examination of the legitimate scope of these agreements (see Chapter 3); but they deserve mention in the context of this chapter because they have been employed on occasion to promote public access to the countryside. For example, in one case planning permission for residential development in part of a woodland area was linked to an agreement which provided for the preparation of a management plan for the rest of the woodland and for public access to the woodland; in several instances in West Lothian planning permission has been granted for a cluster of new houses in the countryside in return for certain public benefits including access to the countryside; and there have been a number of cases where planning permission has been granted for residential development near Loch Lomond in return for the provision of public access to the loch side.

Facilitating access

There are a number of provisions in the 1967 Act and elsewhere which may be used, not so much for the provision of access, but for the provision of facilities to

---

[46] Added by the Countryside (Scotland) Act 1981, s. 9.

[47] J. Rowan-Robinson, *Review of rights of way procedure* (SNH Review No. 9, 1994), paras 3.2.7–3.2.9.

[48] Scottish Office, *Section 50 Agreements*, consultants' report by J. Rowan-Robinson and R. Durman (1992).

enable the public to enjoy the countryside and to engage in open-air recreation. Sections 3 and 4 of the Local Government (Development and Finance) (Scotland) Act 1964 enable a planning authority to enter into negotiations with a landowner with a view to the authority or the landowner providing facilities such as picnic places, footpaths, gates, stiles, steps, bridges, seats, shelters, public conveniences, viewpoints and indicators of one sort or another. Such agreements may be recorded in the Register of Sasines or the Land Register of Scotland. If recorded, an agreement may be enforced, with limited exceptions, by the planning authority against singular successors.

The 1967 Act empowers a local authority to acquire land by agreement or, with the approval of the Minister, compulsorily for the provision of camping sites for holiday or recreational purposes and to lay out and manage such sites (s. 49). A local authority may also make arrangements for the provision in the countryside of accommodation, meals and refreshments, in so far as the existing provision is inadequate or unsatisfactory, and may acquire land, erect buildings and carry out such works as seem to them expedient for this purpose (s. 50). The power to provide parking places includes power to provide such places so as to facilitate the enjoyment of the countryside by members of the public (s. 51).

Local authorities have a general duty under section 14 of the Local Government and Planning (Scotland) Act 1982 to ensure the adequate provision of facilities for the inhabitants of their area for recreational and sporting activities. Amongst other things, an authority may enter into an agreement with the owner of any park or with any other person to secure or enhance public access to the park or to provide for its management. "Park" is defined to include public open space and public walk.

Forestry Commission

Section 58 of the 1967 Act confers extensive powers on the Forestry Commission to promote the recreational use of its woodlands. The way in which the Commission has exercised these powers are examined in Chapter 7.[49] It is sufficient here to say that the effect of section 58 has been that visitors have been welcomed on foot throughout the Commission's woodlands in Scotland.

Water authorities

Section 65(2)(c) of the Local Government etc. (Scotland) Act 1994 imposes a duty on the Minister and the three water authorities to have regard, when exercising their functions, to the desirability of preserving for the public any freedom of access (including access for recreational purposes) to areas of forest, woodland, mountains, moor, bog, cliff, foreshore, loch or reservoir and to other places of natural beauty.

Under section 63 of the 1967 Act, the water authorities may, if it appears reasonable to do so, permit the use by members of the public, for the purposes of any form of recreation, of any waterway or land in which the authority have an interest. Furthermore, the authorities may provide, or otherwise make available, facilities for use by people resorting to such waterways or land for the purposes of any such form of recreation. The authorities have the power, having regard to

---

[49] See too J. Rowan-Robinson, W.M. Gordon and C.T. Reid, op. cit., n. 32, paras 8.10.2–8.10.11.

the need to avoid pollution and to avoid conflict between recreational users, to make byelaws restricting or regulating the recreational use of such waterway or land (s. 63(7)). They may also employ rangers to oversee compliance with the byelaws. The law relating to recreational access to water is considered more fully in Chapter 15.

Proposals for reform

At the beginning of this chapter we pointed out that much of what we have said so far may become redundant if the proposals for reform currently under consideration become law.

In October 1997 the Government, in pursuit of its manifesto commitment to create greater freedom for the public to enjoy the open countryside, asked SNH to review the legal arrangements for access to land and inland water. The review was to be completed by November 1998. SNH was asked to convene a working party of the main interests to progress the review. SNH invited the Access Forum to fulfil this role. The Forum had been established in 1994 to debate and resolve access issues at a national level. Its initial membership reflected the different interests involved in access to the open hills. It was successful in negotiating a concordat[50] between the parties relating to access to upland areas which was published in 1996. A separate group called the Access Forum (Inland Water) was set up in 1996 to explore access issues relating to water-based recreation on inland water. Both groups were involved by SNH in the review commissioned by the Government. However, in the light of the wide-ranging nature of the review, the membership of the hill-based forum was enlarged to include lowland interests. The Forum (both groups) reported to SNH in October 1998.[51]

The Forum's conclusion was that the existing law does not provide a sensible or workable foundation for providing people with greater freedoms to enjoy the countryside. A distinctive new approach was needed. Their key proposal, reflecting a consensus view of the individual members, was that:

> "The Scottish Parliament should introduce a right of access to land and water, exercised responsibly, for informal recreation and passage. This right should be one part of a balanced package which includes codes of behaviour, a major programme of education, obligations on local authorities and land managers, better mechanisms for facilitating and managing access, and a co-operative approach in which the needs of all interests are respected."

The proposal was welcomed and endorsed by SNH. In its advice to government SNH emphasised the global nature of the package.[52] The proposal was a package built on four pillars:

- a right for responsible non-motorised access;
- responsible behaviour on the part of people exercising that right;

---

[50] *Scotland's Hills and Mountains: a Concordat on Access* (1996).
[51] *Access to the Countryside: The Access Forum's Advice* (October 1998).
[52] *Access to the Countryside for Open-air Recreation: Scottish Natural Heritage's Advice to Government* (January 1999).

- safeguards to protect the privacy of those who live in the countryside, legitimate land management operations and conservation interests; and
- the provision of additional resources to support the inescapable costs which will fall on the public bodies whose duty is to assist the provision of access, and on owners and land managers.

In a speech at Balmaha on February 2, 1999, the then Secretary of State for Scotland indicated that the Government had accepted SNH's recommendation as a starting point for developing detailed legislative proposals which it would be for the Scottish Parliament to consider and implement. Following devolution, the White Paper *Land Reform: Proposals for Legislation* included a commitment from the Scottish Ministers to early legislation.

The degree of consensus achieved so far is remarkable. Nonetheless, a great deal still remains to be worked out. As the Access Forum report notes, the detail of the measures accompanying the new right of access will be crucially important. What, for example, is to happen to the network of public rights of way? How will privacy be safeguarded? Should the landowners' public liability (see Chapter 12) be reviewed? How will normal land management practices such as crop spraying, tree felling, deer management and conservation co-exist with the new right? What will be the role of the proposed local access fora? What is to be the position of cyclists and horse-riders? Are those carrying on open-air businesses to be treated differently to those taking access for informal recreation? Will new and more streamlined path creation procedures be developed? What arrangements will be put in place for monitoring and enforcement? How will disputes be resolved? What is to go in legislation and what is to go in the new countryside code? What status will the code have? Above all, will the additional resources necessary to educate people about their responsibilities, to enhance access opportunities, to maintain an enlarged path network, to manage, monitor and enforce the new arrangements, and to resolve disputes, be made available? SNH has asked the Forum to continue with its work with a view to filling out the detail.

CHAPTER 15

WATER

Sharon Fitzgerald

Introduction

"The fresh waters of Scotland are a valuable economic, recreational and environmental resource: for commercial and recreational fisheries—for fish farming; for the supply of potable, agricultural and industrial water; as a source of energy for hydro-electric power; for the dilution of industrial and sewage effluent discharges; for recreational activities, both on and around the water; and as a tourist attraction."[1]

Scotland is famous for its water: Loch Ness; Loch Lomond; the River Clyde; the River Forth; the River Tay; the Crinan Canal; and the Caledonian Canal. According to Scottish Natural Heritage, Scotland has more than 90 per cent of the volume and 70 per cent of the total surface area of fresh water in the United Kingdom.[2] There are 316 major Scottish lochs and reservoirs, and approximately 50,000 kilometres of rivers and burns.[3]

In Scotland, the total average demand on the public water supply by domestic and commercial users has been calculated to be 2,312 megalitres per day.[4] The West of Scotland Water Authority (WOSWA) has calculated that its domestic customers use an average of 148 litres per person per day as follows: flushing toilets—43 litres; dishwashing and cleaning—12 litres; showering and bathing—50 litres; washing clothes—37 litres; drinking and cooking—five litres; and gardening and car washing—one litre.[5] Other sources suggest that the average daily water consumption per person is as high as 463 litres.[6]

---

[1] Quote taken from Scottish Natural Heritage website: www.snh.org.uk.
[2] Ibid.
[3] Information taken from the Scottish Environmental Protection Agency website: www.sepa.org.uk.
[4] 1 megalitre = 1000m³/d: Scottish Office, *The Scottish Environment Statistics—1998* (Edinburgh, 1998).
[5] Information taken from educational material provided by WOSWA.
[6] Scottish Office, *The Scottish Environment Statistics*, op. cit., n. 4.

Given the prevalence and importance of water in Scotland, it is not surprising that water has been the subject of extensive legislative control and judicial intervention throughout the history of Scotland.[7] This control and intervention has covered matters such as the supply of water, water pollution, navigation rights, canals, the quality of drinking water, and the addition of fluoride to the water supply.

The law relating to water covers issues common to both urban and rural areas. The aims of this chapter are to:

- provide a general introduction to the legislative framework which controls various aspects of the use of water;
- give an overview of who is responsible for Scotland's water;
- explain in detail the legislative controls relating to the public supply of water, water quality and regulation of private water supplies (which are often relied upon in rural areas). The role of the water authorities, the Scottish Executive acting through the appropriate Minister (referred to hereafter as the "Minister"), the Scottish Water and Sewerage Customers Council and the Scottish Environment Protection Agency will also be discussed;
- discuss the recreational use of water in the countryside including a general discussion of the role of the water authorities, local authorities, British Waterways Board and the Scottish Sports Council. The issues of the management of conflict between water-users and public rights of navigation will also be examined.

Further water-related issues are discussed in other chapters of this book, for example, water pollution (Chapter 4), fishing (Chapter 9) and the coastal zone including foreshore, bathing water quality, coast protection and flood prevention (Chapter 17).

The legal framework

"Water is of fundamental importance to life. The problems of its use and equitable regulation have, therefore, accumulated a considerable body of law."[8]

In Scotland, the legal framework controlling water and water rights is complex and is derived from two sources: common law and statute. Lyall explains that the control of water and water rights developed as "an important segment of the law relating to landownership" and that a great deal of common law was formed.[9] Common law refers to law which has not originated from a statute but has instead

---

[7] For a detailed consideration of the historical development of the law relating to water and water rights see J. Ferguson, *The Law of Water and Water Rights in Scotland* (Edinburgh, 1907), F. Lyall, "Water and Water Rights" in *The Laws of Scotland: Stair Memorial Encyclopaedia* (Edinburgh, 1988) and E. Bain, "Water Supply" in *The Laws of Scotland: Stair Memorial Encyclopaedia* (Edinburgh, 1988), Vol. 25.

[8] C.T. Reid (ed.), *Environmental Law in Scotland* (W. Green/Sweet & Maxwell, 2nd edn, Edinburgh, 1997) at p. 52.

[9] F. Lyall, op. cit., n. 7 at p. 72.

been derived from judicial decisions, authoritative writings including Roman, canon and feudal law, and custom. For example, common law provisions have been derived with respect to the ownership of water, water servitudes and public rights of navigation.[10]

In addition to the control of water and water rights under the common law, a diverse range of water-related activities are controlled by statute. A selection of the main statutes are as follows:

- **Water supply**   Water (Scotland) Act 1980, as amended
                         Water Act 1989, as amended
                         Local Government (Scotland) Act 1994, as
                         amended

- **Water pollution**   Control of Pollution Act 1974, as amended

- **Water byelaws**   Civic Government (Scotland) Act 1982, as amended
                         Countryside (Scotland) Act 1967, as amended

- **Canals**   Transport Acts 1962 and 1968, as amended
                         British Waterways Act 1995

- **Hydro-Electric**
  Power Generation   Electricity Act 1989, as amended

- **Reservoirs**   Reservoirs Act 1975, as amended

- **Sewerage**   Sewerage (Scotland) Act 1968, as amended

- **Irrigation**   Natural Heritage (Scotland) Act 1991

- **Drought**   Natural Heritage (Scotland) Act 1991

- **Fluoridation**   Water Industry Act 1991, as amended

There are also statutory provisions relating to coast protection, flood prevention, land drainage, territorial waters, fishing, bathing waters, mineral water, drinking water in containers and recreational craft. In addition, many European legislative provisions relating to water have been implemented in Scotland. For example, the Water Supply (Water Quality) (Scotland) Regulations 1990[11] implemented certain provisions of Directive 80/778 (which relates to the quality of water intended for human consumption) and Directive 75/440 (which relates to the quality required of surface water intended for the abstraction of drinking water).

It is important to note that the regulation and set-up of the water industry in Scotland is completely different from England and Wales. In England and Wales, there are 10 private companies which provide both water and sewerage services and 18 companies which supply water only. There are three main regulators: the Office of Water Services (OFWAT), the Environment Agency and the Drinking Water Inspectorate of the Department of the Environment, Transport and the Regions.[12]

---

[10] See J. Ferguson, op. cit., n. 7; F. Lyall, op. cit., n. 7 and W.M. Gordon, *Land Law* (Scottish Universities Law Institute, Edinburgh, 1989) for further information.

[11] SI 1990/119.

[12] The websites of these English regulatory agencies are as follows: OFWAT (www.open. gov.uk/ofwat); the Environment Agency (www.environment-agency.uk); the Drinking Water Inspectorate (www.dwi.detr.gov.uk).

It is not proposed that the entire Scottish legal framework relating to water will be examined in this chapter: as already mentioned, segments of this framework are discussed in Chapters 4, 9 and 17. In this chapter, the legal framework relating to ownership, public rights of navigation, water supply, water quality, and water byelaws will be discussed.

Who is responsible for Scotland's water?

The ownership and management of water in Scotland has been described as "extremely complex" and involves a diverse range of individuals and organisations.[13] In particular, the common law principles of ownership of water are complicated and are dependant on the "type" of water or water body involved. The ownership of water itself is treated separately from the ownership of the *alveus* (channel or bed on which water lies).[14] The position can be summarised as follows:

- **Running water**—following Roman law principles, running water is treated as ownerless because of "the evident impracticality of attributing ownership of individual molecules in a fast-running stream and partly because water, like air and light, is regarded as a natural resource which should not be the property of any one person".[15]

- **Standing water**—it can be appropriated as it is "capable of bounds".[16]

- **Tidal waters**—these include tidal rivers, sea lochs, estuaries and the sea. The *alveus* is presumed to belong to the Crown.[17]

- **Non-tidal lochs**—the *alveus* belongs to the proprietor(s) of the land which surrounds it (referred to as riparian proprietors). If a loch is bordered by the land of more than one proprietor, the loch is presumed to be divided up equally among each proprietor. However, any division is subject to rebuttal by the titles of the lands concerned.[18]

- **Non-tidal rivers**—the *alveus* is owned by the riparian proprietors of the land through which the river runs. The *alveus* may be wholly owned by one riparian proprietor, or by a succession of consecutive owners each owning a section (the River Tay has over 110 riparian owners)[19] or the river may be on the boundary of two estates and may therefore be split on the *medium filum* (middle line) subject always to the titles of the properties involved.[20]

The activities of riparian proprietors are always subject to:

---

[13] Scottish Sports Council, *Calmer Waters* (Edinburgh, 1997) at p. 8.
[14] K.G.C. Reid, *The Law of Property in Scotland* (Butterworths/The Law Society of Scotland, Edinburgh, 1996) at p. 217. See also F. Lyall, op. cit., n. 7 and W.M. Gordon, op. cit., n. 7 for further information on this area.
[15] K.G.C. Reid, op. cit., n. 14 at p. 217.
[16] Ibid.
[17] Ibid at pp. 236–238.
[18] F. Lyall , op. cit., n. 7 at pp. 86–87.
[19] Scottish Sports Council, op. cit., n. 13 at p. 8.
[20] K.G.C. Reid, op. cit., n. 14 at p. 219.

- the common interest of any other proprietors, for example the diversion of the flow of a river would not be allowed if it affected the rights of any proprietor downstream;
- any water servitudes, for example *aquaehaustus* which is the right to draw water;
- the law of nuisance;
- any public right of navigation; and
- any statutory restrictions.[21]

In addition to riparian proprietors and the Crown, there are a number of other organisations which are responsible for Scotland's water. The main organisations (together with their area of responsibility) include:

- **Water authorities**—water supply and water quality.
- **The appropriate Minister**—water supply and water quality.
- **Water Services Unit** (Scottish Executive)—water supply and water quality.
- **Local authorities**—environmental health, planning, structural safety of reservoirs and recreation.
- **Health boards**—fluoridation of water supplies and general health of the community (assessment of threat from contaminated water).
- **Scottish Water and Sewerage Customers Council**—represents interests of the customers of the water authorities.
- **British Waterways**—canals.
- **Scottish Sports Council**—promotion of water sports.
- **Electricity companies**—use of water for hydro-electric power generation.
- **Scottish Natural Heritage**—conservation, enhancement and promotion of enjoyment of the natural heritage.
- **Scottish Environmental Protection Agency**—water pollution and conservation.
- **Marine and Coastguard Agency**—marine safety and pollution.
- **Loch Lomond Park Authority**—management of Loch Lomond.[22]

The responsibilities of the Minister, the Water Services Unit, the water authorities, the Scottish Water and Sewerage Customers Council, SEPA, British Waterways Board, local authorities and the Scottish Sports Council will be discussed later in this chapter.

---

[21] K.G.C. Reid, op. cit., n. 14 at p. 219.

[22] Other organisations which also have interests in the regulation of water include: Scottish Enterprise; Scottish Tourist Board; Forest Enterprise; the Scottish Landowners Federation; the National Farmers Union of Scotland; community councils and associations; residents' groups; sports governing bodies; watersports operators; the Royal Society for the Protection of Birds; the Scottish Wildlife Trust; and the National Trust for Scotland. See Scottish Sports Council, n. 13 at pp. 8–9 and 29.

Water supply and quality

"All water supply is essentially derived from rain. On reaching the ground, some of the rain flows into burns, rivers, lochs and man-made impounding reservoirs. These are the main sources of surface water. Some of the rain soaks into the ground until it reaches impervious rocks where it remains as an aquifer. Boreholes may be drilled in the ground to collect this water, or it may come out on hillsides in the form of springs. These are the principal sources of groundwater. Groundwater is intrinsically purer than surface water, as many pollutants are naturally filtered out as it passes through the ground. As a result, water taken from surface sources generally requires more extensive treatment, and the most rigorously treated water is that abstracted from lowland rivers (where more pollutants are likely to be present)."[23]

The issues of water supply and water quality are of enormous importance to everyone living in Scotland. However, for those living in rural areas, these issues are of particular importance because there may be no public water supply available in certain areas and private supplies may have to be relied upon. Also, in a recent review of drinking water quality by the Scottish Office, it was stated that the poorest performing public water supplies tended to be "small rural supplies where treatment facilities are deficient".[24]

Legislative framework

Section 6 of the Water (Scotland) Act 1980 ("the 1980 Act") states that:

"(1) It shall be the duty of every water authority to provide a supply of wholesome water to every part of their limits of supply where a supply of water is required for domestic purposes and can be provided at a reasonable cost;

(2) but a water authority is not required to do anything which is not practicable at a reasonable cost".[25]

Consequently, many people have to resort to using private supplies of water and there are about 20,000 private water supplies in use in Scotland which supply about 129,000 people.[26] The 1980 Act also contains provisions relating to the

---

[23] EOSWA, *Water Treatment* (1998). This leaflet explains that various processes can be utilised to treat water including: storage; screening; aeration; coagulation and flocculation; sedimentation; dissolved air flotation; filtration; slow sand filtration; granular activated carbon; pH adjustment; and disinfection.

[24] Scottish Office, *Drinking Water Quality Report in Scotland 1997* (Edinburgh, 1998). This is a very detailed report on the quality of drinking water in Scotland and it reports on the performance of each water authority. It gives details on the microbiological quality of water leaving treatment works, water in service reservoirs, etc. Undertakings given by the water authorities regarding improvements in standards, details of any relaxations, incidents, comments from local councils and action by the water services unit are also mentioned.

[25] The section also states that in the event of any dispute, individuals can contact the Minister who will then discuss the matter with the water authority concerned. Section 7 of the Act defines the supply of water for domestic purposes as being "a sufficient supply for drinking, washing, cooking, central heating and sanitary purposes".

[26] Scottish Office, op. cit., n. 24.

powers and duties of water authorities in respect of the supply of water including the acquisition of water rights, powers to carry out works and compensation powers.

As well as provisions relating to supply, the 1980 Act also includes provisions relating to the quality of water. These provisions were added to the 1980 Act by Schedule 22 to the Water Act 1989 in order to implement provisions of European Directive 80/778 relating to the quality of water intended for human consumption. Section 76A of the 1980 Act specifies that water authorities must supply wholesome water for domestic purposes. The Act gives the Minister powers to take enforcement action against any water authority that fails to supply wholesome water[27] and it is a criminal offence to supply water unfit for human consumption.[28] The Act also sets out the duties of local authorities and specifies that they are required to keep themselves informed about the wholesomeness and sufficiency of both private and public water supplies in their area and inform the water authorities of any problems.[29]

In addition to provisions under the 1980 Act, there are a number of statutory instruments which regulate issues of water quality. These include:

- **The Surface Waters (Abstraction for Drinking Water) (Classification) (Scotland) Regulations 1996,**[30] which prescribe a system for classifying the quality of inland waters according to their suitability for abstraction for supply as drinking water in implementation of Directive 75/440 relating to surface water.

- **The Water Supply (Water Quality) (Scotland) Regulations 1990,**[31] which are concerned with the quality of water supplied in Scotland for drinking, washing and cooking and prescribe standards of "wholesomeness" of water. There are also provisions regarding relaxation of these Regulations in specified circumstances, publication of information about water quality, monitoring, frequency of water sampling and water treatment. In addition, the Regulations also set out in detail the levels or parameters of the elements, substances and properties which are permitted in drinking water. Examples of these parameters relate to: taste; odour and colour; pH; turbidity; coliforms; iron; chlorine compounds; lead; aluminium; nitrates; pesticides; manganese; polycyclic aromatic hydrocarbons (PAHs); chlorinated solvents; and ammonia.

- **The Private Water Supplies (Scotland) Regulations 1992,**[32] which classify private water supplies into category one and category two supplies. Category one relates to all supplies used for supplying water for domestic purposes[33] and category two relates to supplies used for food production purposes or for supplying water for domestic purposes

---

[27] 1980 Act, s. 76E.
[28] 1980 Act, s. 76C.
[29] 1980 Act, s. 76F. Section 76G also gives remedial powers to local authorities with regard to private supplies.
[30] SI 1996/3047.
[31] SI 1990/119 as amended by SI 1991/1333 and SI 1992/575.
[32] SI 1992/575 as amended by SI 1998/1856.
[33] reg. 10.

used in (a) staff canteens or for the purposes of a business of preparing food or drink for consumption on the premises, (b) hospitals, nursing homes, residential homes, hostels and boarding schools or similar institutions, or (c) campsites or touring caravan sites or places providing holiday or short-term accommodation.[34] These Regulations prescribe standards of "wholesomeness"[35] and also set out the requirements for obtaining and analysing samples of water and the parameters which are to be analysed.

Local authorities should have procedures in place for ensuring that they are meeting the requirements of the 1992 Regulations, and it has been commented that these Regulations place a considerable workload on those local authorities serving the more rural areas.[36] It is the responsibility of local authorities to identify, classify and monitor private supplies. In 1997, about 3,500 private supplies tested by local authorities failed to meet the regulatory requirements.[37]

Regulatory bodies

The current legislative framework relating to water supply and quality is overseen by the Minister, the Water Services Unit in the Scottish Executive, the three water authorities, the Scottish Water and Sewerage Customers Council and SEPA. Changes are proposed by the Water Industry Bill which was published on November 25, 1998.[38] This Bill was prepared following a review of the Scottish water industry in 1997 which "identified a consensus that the current division between price regulation by the Customers Council and efficiency regulation by the Secretary of State had proved untenable".[39] The Bill proposes to:

- dissolve the Scottish Water and Sewerage Customers Council;
- establish the Water Industry Commissioner for Scotland to promote the interests of customers of the water and sewerage authorities. The Commissioner will assume most of the existing duties of the Council and will have new advisory functions in relation to the fixing of water and sewerage charges. In fixing these charges, it is proposed that he will take into account information relevant to the performance and service standards which the water and sewerage authorities have to meet in consequence of statutory requirements and government policies, the investment programmes necessary to deliver those standards and the scope for the authorities to secure efficiency savings; and
- establish Water Industry Consultative Committees for each of the water and sewerage authorities. These Committees will advise the Commissioner on the promotion of the interests of customers.[40]

---

[34] Category one and two supplies are further divided into "classes" for monitoring purposes.
[35] reg. 3(3).
[36] Scottish Office, op. cit., n. 24.
[37] Ibid.
[38] The Bill is available from the House of Commons website and has very useful explanatory notes attached to it.
[39] Ibid. See also Scottish Office, *Scottish Water Industry Review* (Edinburgh, 1997).
[40] Ibid.

It has been stated that the purpose of these changes is to:

> "assist the water and sewerage authorities to meet the needs of their customers as efficiently as possible by providing a stable business framework within which to make plans for future delivery of service".[41]

Water authorities and the Minister

On April 1, 1996, following a review of local government in Scotland, responsibility for the provision of water and sewerage services was transferred from the former regional and islands councils to three new water authorities: North of Scotland Water Authority (NOSWA), West of Scotland Water Authority (WOSWA) and East of Scotland Water Authority (EOSWA). These water authorities are public corporations of a trading nature.[42]

The local authority areas (see Map 3 in Chapter 2) for which NOSWA is responsible are Dundee City, Aberdeen City, Perth and Kinross, Angus, Aberdeenshire, Moray, Highland, Western Isles, Orkney and Shetland. EOSWA is responsible for the local authority areas of Borders, Midlothian, East Lothian, City of Edinburgh, West Lothian, Falkirk, East Dunbartonshire (water only), Stirling, Clackmannanshire and Fife. WOSWA is responsible for the local authority areas of Dumfries and Galloway, South Ayrshire, East Ayrshire, South Lanarkshire, North Ayrshire, Renfrewshire, East Renfrewshire, City of Glasgow, North Lanarkshire, East Dunbartonshire (sewage only), West Dunbartonshire, Inverclyde, and Argyll and Bute.[43] Each water authority has a Board appointed by the Minister, consisting of a chairperson and between six and 10 members.[44]

The Minister is responsible for the water authorities and section 1 of the Water (Scotland) Act 1980 as amended sets out the general duties of the Minister and of the water authorities as being:

> "(a) to promote the conservation and effective use of the water resources of, and the provision of adequate water supplies throughout, Scotland; and
>
> (b) to secure the collection, preparation, publication and dissemination of information and statistics relating to such resources and supplies".[45]

This section also states that when exercising their functions or powers, the Minister and the water authorities are required:

> "(a) to have regard to the interests of every person who is a customer or potential customer of any such authority and especially of such of those persons as—

---

[41] Ibid.

[42] Scottish Affairs Committee, *The Work of the Scottish Water Authorities. Minutes of Evidence and Appendices* (HMSO, 1998) at p. 5. This Report contains much useful background information on the set-up of the water industry in Scotland.

[43] Information on the work of water authorities can be found in their annual reports, environmental statements and leaflets. For example, water quality failures, expenditure, compliance with regulations, response to customers' complaints, charges, geographical area covered, new projects and new plant.

[44] Details of the members of the various Boards can be found in each water authority's annual report.

[45] 1980 Act, s. 1(1) as amended by s. 65 of the Local Government (Scotland) Act 1994.

(i) are likely, by reason of some persistent medical condition or of family circumstances, to require to have a much greater supply of water, or to make much greater use of facilities for the disposal of sewage, than might ordinarily have been expected; or

(ii) are ordinarily resident in some rural part of Scotland;

(b) to further, so far as may be consistent with the purposes of any enactment:

    (i) the conservation and enhancement of natural beauty and the conservation of flora and fauna;

    (ii) the conservation of geological or physiological features of special interest;

(c) to have regard to the desirability of preserving for the public any freedom of access (including access for recreational purposes) to areas of forest, woodland, mountains, moor, bog, cliff, foreshore, loch or reservoir and to other places of natural beauty; and

(d) to have regard to the desirability of protecting and conserving—

    (i) buildings;

    (ii) sites; and

    (iii) objects,

of archaeological, architectural or historic interest and of maintaining the availability to the public of any facility for visiting or inspecting any such building, site or object".[46]

WOSWA has summarised its responsibilities and states that it:

- promotes the conservation and effective use of its water resources and manages the safe recreational use of its reservoirs;
- provides a water supply which is reliable, sufficient in pressure and meets the requisite quality standards;
- drains premises of sewage and surface water from roofs and paved areas;
- extends water and sewerage services to new customers wherever this is possible at reasonable cost;
- safeguards the quality of the water supply and prevents contamination, waste or misuse of water by means of byelaws which set standards for plumbing installations;
- provides effective treatment of sewage received, accepts and deals with trade effluent from industrial and commercial premises and maintains the quality of effluent discharges into the aquatic environment within the standards set;
- empties private septic tanks on request for a payment; and
- sets charges for its services and recovers payment either directly or through local authorities.[47]

---

[46] 1980 Act, s. 1(2) as amended by s. 65 of the Local Government (Scotland) Act 1994.

[47] WOSWA, *Introducing West of Scotland Water* (1998).

The specific duties of the Minister are as follows:

- responsibility to the Scottish Parliament for the activities of the water authorities;
- responsibility for the economic regulation of the three water authorities, specifying the financial regime within which the water authorities will have to operate;
- to consider the Scheme of Charges and the Code of Practice if the Customers Council and the water authority are unable to agree;
- to consider statutory appeals related to water and sewerage services;
- to ensure that the water authorities carry out their functions effectively and at the same time increase efficiency;
- to appoint and remove Members of the Boards of the three water authorities;
- to determine Members' remuneration and allowances, with the consent of H.M. Treasury; and
- to approve the general terms and conditions of employment of the Authorities' staff including Chief Executives.[48]

The Water Services Unit is part of the Environment Group within the Scottish Executive. The Unit is responsible for: "sponsorship and economic and financial regulation of the three Scottish Water and Sewerage Authorities and sponsorship of the Scottish Water and Sewerage Customers Council; policy and legislation on water and sewerage including EC Directives; regulation of drinking water quality".[49] The Unit also carries out the administration of the 1990 Regulations. This includes:

- checking compliance with monitoring requirements and water quality standards;
- authorisation of the relaxation of standards;
- accepting undertakings for carrying out improvement work on behalf of the Minister;
- checking that authorities are complying with their undertakings and taking appropriate action if they are not; and
- recording and assessing incidents affecting water quality.[50]

Scottish Environmental Protection Agency (SEPA)

SEPA is responsible for the environmental aspects of water regulation. The role of SEPA is discussed in Chapters 2 and 4. In general terms, SEPA has described its functions and duties in relation to water as follows:

- to control discharges to surface waters including tidal waters out to a three-mile limit;

---

[48] Ibid and Scottish Office, op. cit., n. 24.
[49] Information taken from the Scottish Executive's website.
[50] Scottish Office, op. cit., n. 24.

- to conserve water resources as far as possible and gauge river flows;
- to remove potentially polluting material from controlled waters, serve remedial notices for silage, slurry and agricultural fuel installations, sample the water environment, measure rainfall, seek irrigation abstraction controls and implement flood warning schemes;
- to test bathing water quality;
- to classify controlled waters in anticipation of proposed Water Framework (to be discussed later in this chapter);
- to advise planning authorities of any information regarding potential flooding and assess the risk of flooding in any area; and
- to promote the conservation and enhancement of the natural beauty and amenity of controlled waters and the associated land as well as the conservation of related flora and fauna.[51]

Scottish Water and Sewerage Customers Council (SWSCC)

Section 67 of the Local Government (Scotland) Act 1994 ("the 1994 Act") established the Scottish Water and Sewerage Customers Council as an independent body responsible for representing the interests of customers and potential or former customers of the three water authorities. As discussed above, it is proposed in the Water Industry Bill, introduced in November 1998, that the SWSCC will be abolished. However, its current functions are to:

- keep under review all matters appearing to it to affect the interests of customers of the water and sewerage authorities;
- consult each authority about such of those matters as appear to affect the interests of the customers;
- make such representations as it considers appropriate to those authorities about any such matter;
- investigate any complaint made to it by a customer as respects a function of that authority, unless it appears to the Council that the complaint is vexatious or frivolous;
- make representations on behalf of the complainer to the authority;
- approve the Scheme of Charges and Code of Practice prepared by the water authority; and
- give advice to the Minister on the standards of service provided by the water authorities.[52]

Recreational use of water

"Water sports are a diverse group of activities but taken as a whole they are the fastest growing recreational activity. Scotland's lochs, inshore waters,

---

[51] Information taken from SEPA's website. See also s. 34 of the Environment Act 1995, as amended.
[52] The Local Government (Scotland) Act 1994, ss 66 and 68.
[53] Scottish Office, *Sport, Physical Recreation and Open Space* (NPPG 11) (Edinburgh, 1996).

rivers and canals are under increasing pressure to provide venues suited to all types of water sport as well as angling/fishing."[53]

Water sports include: sailing; yachting; powerboating; windsurfing; surfing; water skiing; swimming; fishing; jet skiing; diving; canoeing; rowing; and rafting. Lyall has commented that "recreation is an important feature of modern life" and explained that since the Second World War, "the wish to provide the public with recreational access to land and water has resulted in statutory provision, sometimes to require access and sometimes to authorise agencies either to provide or to negotiate such access".[54] For example, section 10 of the Countryside (Scotland) Act 1967 provides for access to the open country which includes access to waterways.[55]

Various organisations are involved in the regulation, promotion or encouragement of water-based recreation. These organisations include the water authorities, local authorities, British Waterways Board and the Scottish Sports Council.

Water authorities

Under section 63 of the Countryside (Scotland) Act 1967 ("the 1967 Act"),[56] water authorities have discretionary powers to permit recreational use of their waterways and land, and to provide or make available facilities for such use. Under section 54 of the 1967 Act, byelaws can be enacted to regulate recreational use of these waterways and under section 56 use of pleasure boats can be regulated in respect of matters including speed, silencers, safe navigation or confining use to an area or time.[57]

In "Conservation, Access and Recreation", a code of practice for water authorities, the Scottish Office commented that wherever compatible with the aims of good water management, the water authorities should aim to:

- preserve public access to their holdings and, in particular, to places of natural beauty and archaeological and historic sites; and

- promote responsible recreational use of, and access to, water and associated land.[58]

The Report also commented that past concerns regarding the effects of access and recreation on drinking water can often be largely overcome, but where "there are difficulties which might prejudice the quality of the public water supply or impose unreasonable costs then the water supply must take priority".[59] Examples

---

[54] F. Lyall, op. cit., n. 7 at p. 94.

[55] As amended by the Natural Heritage (Scotland) Act 1991.

[56] As amended by the Water (Scotland) Act 1980 and Local Government (Scotland) Act 1994.

[57] s. 78 of the 1967 Act defines waterways to include any loch, lake, river, reservoir, canal or other water, being (in any case) water suitable or which can reasonably be rendered suitable for sailing, boating, bathing, fishing or other water sport or recreation.

[58] Scottish Office, *Conservation, Access and Recreation—Code of Practice for Water and Sewerage Authorities and River Purification Authorities* (HMSO, 1993) at p. 20. This report was published prior to local government reorganisation. However, the Scottish Minister responsible at the time, Sir Hector Monro, commented that this Report would be "equally relevant" to the work of the new water authorities.

[59] Ibid.

of recreational use provided by water authorities include the following: country park and visitor centre at Gartmorn Dam; sailing facilities on Whiteadder Reservoir; viewing areas, car park, boathouse, access paths and landscaping at Megget Reservoir; car park, toilets and picnic area at Backwater Reservoir; and, cruising on the SS *Sir Walter Scott* on Loch Katrine.[60]

Local authorities

In planning for water sports, it is suggested in National Planning Policy Guideline (NPPG) 11 that the following should be taken into account by local authorities:

- the need for access across land to inland or coastal water should be recognised when considering land uses adjacent to these waters;
- a strategic approach should be adopted to identifying and protecting water resources, taking account of the need to avoid overcrowding and for access across land;
- sites or general locations for additional mooring facilities should be identified systematically through local plans;
- proposals for new moorings must demonstrate that they do not damage the wider aquatic environment;
- landward facilities for watersports should take account of traffic congestion, environmental features and the long-term impact on the visual quality of the shore; and
- the wider environmental impacts, for example noise, shoreline erosion and loss of amenity for other users, should be considered.

It is also suggested in NPPG 11 that local authorities should consult with SEPA, or the Scottish Sports Council or an appropriate sports governing body when planning for water-based recreation.

British Waterways Board

The British Waterways Board was established by section 10 of the Transport Act 1962 and is a publicly owned body accountable to the Department of the Environment, Transport and the Regions. It is responsible for a 2,000-mile, 200-year-old network of canals and rivers.[61] In Scotland, there are five canals: Caledonian Canal, Crinan Canal, Forth & Clyde Canal, Union Canal and Monkland Canal. The legal framework relating to canals consists of the Transport Act 1962, the Transport Act 1968, the British Waterways Act 1971, the British Waterways Act 1983 and the British Waterways Act 1995.

British Waterways states that it maintains canals and rivers for a wide range of leisure and business uses. Its work includes:

- making sure canals and rivers are safe places for people to enjoy;
- maintaining structures such as locks, aqueducts and towing paths as well as the waterways themselves for boating, angling and other purposes;

---

[60] Ibid, p. 24.
[61] British Waterways, *Caring for Britain's Waterways* (Website, 1998).

- looking after the whole environment that is associated with canals and rivers (ie buildings, wildlife and traditions); and
- earning income from a wide range of waterway-related businesses to invest in the future of the waterways.[62]

British Waterways has prepared guides on how to enjoy canals safely and without spoiling the enjoyment of others. Examples include different Waterways Codes for cyclists, anglers, users of unpowered craft and boaters. British Waterways may make byelaws preventing or regulating bathing in its canals and for prohibiting or controlling water skiing or any similar activity, either generally or during specified periods.[63]

Scottish Sports Council (SSC)

The SSC has stated that it wishes to ensure that:

- opportunities for watersports and recreational activities on inland water are safeguarded and enhanced for the benefit of current users and future generations; and
- watersports and recreational pursuits take place in harmony with each other, with the natural environment and with local amenity and economic interests.[64]

The SSC has a number of policies in relation to the recreational use of water:

- motor based water sports: "the Council will defend the continued use of powered boating at sites of traditional use. It is recognised that power boats may be excluded from some areas of particular waters where these are favoured locations for activities such as fishing and canoeing";
- water sports and the redevelopment of former mineral workings;
- environmentally acceptable craft for water sports;
- water sports in the sea (better access and facilities);
- support and safety facilities for marine sports (new safe moorings, slip-ways and harbours should be developed);
- use of water: "the Council generally encourages the use of privately and publicly-owned bodies of water for recreational purposes, and recommends that in most instances adequate powered safety boat provision should be available wherever water activities take place";
- safety of onshore facilities (banks and jetties should be maintained in safe order); and
- water quality: "sewage discharges into waters used substantially for recreation should be given effective treatment to the prescribed European standard."[65]

---

[62] Ibid.
[63] For further information on canals see S. Scott Robinson, "Railways, Canals and Tramways" in *The Law of Scotland: Stair Memorial Encyclopaedia* (Edinburgh, 1990), Vol. 19.
[64] Scottish Sports Council, op. cit., n. 13 at p. 2.
[65] See Scottish Sports Council, *Earth, Wind and Water* (Edinburgh, 1996) for further details.

The management of conflict caused by recreational use of water

> "Recreation can result in both positive and negative impacts. The positive benefits to society include the promotion of public health and well-being, and a contribution to the local economy. Negative impacts may all be managed to a greater or lesser extent through water treatment, careful siting of facilities, strict adherence to the management plan, water zoning and the encouragement of mutual respect between various users."[66]

The SSC has recently published a major report which sets out guidelines for planning and managing watersports on inland waters in Scotland. The SSC identified that the following conflicts can be encountered during recreational use of water:

- disturbance of angling by other recreational users;
- dangers to swimmers from watersports;
- conflicts between watercraft;
- disturbance of residents and visitors by watersports;
- impact on commercial activities;
- environmental impacts;
- noise and pollution from powered watercraft;
- wildlife disturbance; and
- impact on shoreline vegetation.[67]

However, it was concluded in the Report that:

- there are relatively few environmental impacts of significance and limited recreational conflicts on Scotland's inland waters;
- any impacts resulting from recreation tend to be occasional, site specific and for a short duration;
- any problems are usually attributable to irresponsible or unknowing behaviour by a small minority of users; and
- non-recreational causes (eg storms, water extraction) can be more damaging to shores, vegetation, birds and other wildlife than most recreational activities.[68]

The Report explains that the mechanisms for managing watersports and recreational activities can be either advisory/voluntary or statutory. Examples of advisory/voluntary mechanisms include: codes of conduct and conditions of use; voluntary agreements and self-regulation; permit and ticket schemes; area zoning; speed restrictions; registration and licensing schemes; and water user and other information. Examples of statutory mechanisms include: access agreements, access orders and management agreements; access restrictions; byelaws;

---

[66] Scottish Office, op. cit., n. 58.
[67] Scottish Sports Council, op. cit., n. 13 at pp. 11–12.
[68] Ibid, p. 11.

management rules; fisheries protection orders; and other legislation.[69] The Report gives a number of examples of how various organisations have managed conflict by planning for watersports at sites including: Loch Ken; Harperrig Reservoir; Loch Ore; and Fairnilee, River Tweed.

Section 121 of the Civic Government (Scotland) Act 1982 as amended by section 141 of the Local Government (Scotland) Act 1994 gives local authorities the power to make byelaws for the purpose of "preventing nuisance or danger at, or preserving or improving the amenity of, or conserving the natural beauty of, the seashore, adjacent waters and inland waters.[70] In relation to inland waters, these byelaws could relate to:

- regulating or promoting any activity by way of trade or business with, or in expectation of personal reward from, members of the public;
- regulating the use of vehicles;
- regulating the exercise of sporting and recreational activities;
- speed of pleasure boats;
- use of pleasure boats so as to prevent their navigation in a dangerous manner or without due care and attention or reasonable consideration for other persons;
- the use of effective silencers on pleasure boats; or
- the activities of divers, surfers, water skiers and persons engaged in similar recreational pursuits.

An example of byelaws made under section 121 are the Loch Lomond Registration and Navigation Byelaws 1995 which came into force on February 1, 1996. These byelaws contain provisions relating to the registration of power-driven boats, the use of lights, conduct in restricted visibility, speed limits, reckless navigation, drunken navigation, water skiing, wakeboards, kneeboards, parascending, steering and sailing, noise and silencers, accidents, the shore and age restrictions.[71] Poustie has examined the various legal mechanisms used on Loch Lomond to minimise and manage the conflicts between various water-based recreational users and concluded that the existence of byelaws has had a positive impact on behaviour on the loch.[72]

Public rights of navigation

"Recreational use of water is only possible if access can be obtained from adjacent land. . . . The public right of navigation does not include as one of its incidents a right of access to water. . . . Access to water and the foreshore

---

[69] Ibid, p. 47.

[70] s. 123 of the Civic Government (Scotland) Act 1982 defines "adjacent waters" as waters within a distance from low water mark of ordinary spring tides not exceeding 1,000 metres and "inland waters" as any inland loch or non-tidal river, or lake or reservoir whether natural or artificial and including the bed and the shores or banks thereof.

[71] On January 12, 1998, the first person was found guilty of speeding on the Loch. He was fined £200. Reported in *The Herald*, January 13, 1998.

[72] M. Poustie, "Bonny Banks no more? Water-based Recreational Conflict Management on Loch Lomond" (1997) *Water Law*, pp. 137–148.

may be exercised from a public place such as a harbour, public slipway or public road. However, the banks of navigable rivers and lochs are often in private ownership. In such cases, access to water may only be obtained if there is a public right of way, a servitude right of access, a statutory right of access, a voluntary agreement with the landowner, or consent or tolerance on the part of the landowner. If access is taken in the absence of any of these then it is trespass."[73]

The question of access is discussed separately in Chapters 12, 13 and 14 of this book. Public rights of navigation are another complicated area of the law relating to water. These navigation rights are dependent on the body of water involved and can be summarised as follows:

- **The sea**—the right of navigation gives the right of passage on the sea and the right to moor, and to load and unload goods on the shore, but it gives no permanent right to stay at a particular place. It may be regulated or protected by statute.[74]

- **Tidal rivers**—the *alveus* and the foreshore are owned by the Crown and there is a public right of navigation in all tidal rivers provided only that the waters are navigable.[75] A tidal river is presumed to be navigable but the character of the river and its size and nature may displace that presumption.[76] The Crown cannot deprive members of the public of their rights of navigation but the Crown in Parliament can and does regulate these rights.[77]

- **Non-tidal waters** are in private ownership. Public rights in non-tidal waters are correspondingly less extensive than in tidal waters.[78] In *Will's Trustees* v *Cairngorm Canoeing and Sailing School Limited*,[79] it was held that the River Spey was a public navigable river. This case involved a sailing school which regularly canoed down a section of the River Spey and the owners of a section of the river and salmon fishings who alleged that the canoeing had adversely affected the fishings. This case set out that the fundamental requirements for a public right of navigation in a non-tidal river are as follows:
  - it must be navigable, defined as being capable for the means of passage of vessels or rafts so as to provide a means of communication;
  - it must be proved that there has been regular habitual use from time immemorial (at least 40 years);
  - it is not strictly analogous to a right of way on land and does not require to exist between two public places; and
  - the question of public interest or benefit is irrelevant.[80]

---

[73] Brodies W.S., *Recreational Access to Scotland's Water* (unpublished paper commissioned by SNH) (1996) at p. 22.
[74] W.M. Gordon, op. cit., n. 10 at p. 152.
[75] K.G.C. Reid, op. cit., n. 14 at p. 420.
[76] F. Lyall, op. cit., n. 7 at p. 75.
[77] W.M. Gordon, op. cit., n. 10 at p. 152.
[78] K.G.C. Reid, op. cit., n. 14 at p. 423.
[79] 1976 SLT (HL) 162.
[80] Ibid, p. 162.

The best advice to anyone planning to participate in water-based recreation is to contact the SSC or one of the governing bodies for individual sports for guidance. For example, the Scottish Canoe Association (SCA) has produced a detailed guide to Scottish rivers which includes details relating to the Clyde, the Tweed, the Spey, the Tay and the Leven among many others.[81] This Guide not only gives detailed canoeing information on the grades of the rivers and hazards but also gives specific information on access and egress points, rights of navigation and any local access agreements which are in effect. Also, the SCA has a network of river advisors who can be contacted for information about likely flows, any access difficulties or considerations and new hazards.

Future proposals

There are two proposals for reform which deserve mention.

Framework convention for water policy

> "Much progress has been made in water protection in Europe, in individual Member States, but also in tackling significant problems at European level. But Europe's waters are still in need of increased efforts to get them clean or to keep them clean. After 25 years of European water legislation, this demand is expressed, not only by the scientific community and other experts but to an ever increasing extent by citizens and environmental organisations. We should take up the challenge of water protection, one of the great challenges for the European Union, as it approaches the new millennium."[82]

In 1996, a Proposal for a Council Directive establishing a framework for community action in the field of water policy was published.[83] Article 1 of this proposed Directive states that the overall purpose of this proposal is to:

> "establish for the protection of surface fresh water , estuaries, coastal waters and groundwater in the Community, a framework which:
>
> (a) prevents further deterioration and protects and enhances the status of aquatic ecosystems and, with regard to their water needs, terrestrial ecosystems; and
>
> (b) promotes sustainable water consumption based on long-term protection of available water resources;
>
> and thereby contributes to the provision of a supply of water of the qualities and in the quantities needed for sustainable use of these resources".[84]

It was anticipated that this proposed Directive would have become a Directive by the end of 1998. However, at the time of writing, this Directive has not yet been issued. When it is issued, changes will be required to the current legislative framework. It has been stated that:

---

[81] Scottish Canoe Association, *A Guide to Scottish Rivers* (1994).
[82] Quote taken from Europa website.
[83] OJ C184/20, dated June 17, 1997.
[84] The House of Lords Select Committee on the European Communities has prepared a detailed report on the terms of the proposed Directive. For further details, see its Eighth Report, "Community Water Policy", dated November 18, 1997, available from its website.

"The regulatory pressures on water quality, and on the effects of discharges on the environment can be expected to strengthen. These pressures will continue to place a heavy burden of investment on the water and sewerage industry."[85]

To meet the demands of the future, it has been suggested that £5 billion will have to be invested over the next 10 to 15 years in order to meet European water quality standards and reduce contamination of Scottish rivers and coasts.[86]

A general right of access to water

In Chapter 14 reference was made to the request by the Government to Scottish Natural Heritage in 1997 to review the legal arrangements for access to land and inland water. The Access Forum (Inland Water), which had been set up in 1996 to look at access issues relating to water-based recreation on inland water, was involved by SNH in the review and contributed to the report on *Access to the Countryside* for SNH in October 1998.[87] The report advocated that the Scottish Parliament should introduce a right of access to land and water, exercised responsibly, for informal recreation and passage. That recommendation was endorsed by SNH in its advice to government.[88] The White Paper *Land Reform: Proposals for Legislation*[89] published by the Scottish Executive in July 1999 promised early legislation.

---

[85] Scottish Office, op. cit., n. 24.

[86] Ibid.

[87] *Access to the Countryside: The Access Forum's Advice* (October 1998).

[88] *Access to the Countryside for Open-air Recreation: Scottish Natural Heritage Advice to Government* (January 1999).

[89] *Land Reform: Proposals for Legislation*, SE/1999/1 (Stationery Office, July 1999).

CHAPTER 16

THE PROTECTION OF ARCHAEOLOGICAL SITES AND MONUMENTS

Carolyn Shelbourn

Summary

Scotland is rich in sites and monuments of archaeological interest, and the remains may either be readily visible above ground, or consist only of features under the surface, and which may not be apparent. These remains may be damaged by development, or by many agricultural and forestry activities which disturb the soil. The law seeks to provide a framework within which the most important of these archaeological sites and monuments may be identified and protected, by limiting activities on land through the planning system and by the scheduling and control of monuments. This framework is supplemented by government policy guidance and codes of practice which seek to minimise the threat to the varied remains of Scotland's history.

Why protect sites of archaeological interest?

The reasons given for protecting sites of archaeological or historic importance are many and varied. They are an obvious source of information and study for experts in the field, and are a valuable teaching resource for students in universities and schools, but the value of such sites goes beyond the educational. The history of a people contributes largely to its sense of national identity and historic remains form an important part of cultural heritage. The last 30 years have seen a dramatic increase in public interest in historical and archaeological matters, something which is reflected in the number of television series and popular books on the subject. Public pressure on the Government to "do something" to preserve historic sites has been added to the demands of the professional historian and archaeologist, and has resulted in the growth of legal controls and the development of government policy on the protection of the historic heritage.

In practice, however, one of the most important reasons for protecting such sites is the recognition that they are a finite resource which, as with so many of the Earth's natural resources, require careful management in the interests of sustainable development. Despite increasing knowledge about such sites, many are destroyed or damaged each year. Some sites are threatened by natural forces such as wind, frost, or encroaching coastal erosion, but the greatest potential for damage to archaeological sites in rural areas comes from activities such as mineral and peat extraction, drainage, and modern deep ploughing, with perhaps the greatest threat being posed by afforestation (both in the form of commercial forestry and the planting of amenity forests) where damage may be caused by deep ploughing, driving heavy machinery over sites and root penetration, as well as through the actual planting process.

The principal legislative controls over archaeological sites are contained in the Ancient Monuments and Archaeological Areas Act 1979, although a number of other statutes require consideration to be given to the protection of archaeological and historic features.[1] The 1979 Act requires "scheduled monument consent" to be obtained before certain operations which might damage a scheduled monument or its immediate vicinity are carried out, and makes it an offence to do so without consent. The Act also provides for the management of scheduled monuments, and imposes restrictions on the use of metal detectors and the removal of objects discovered by their use. Archaeological sites are also afforded a degree of protection by the development control process under the Town and Country Planning (Scotland) Act 1997. Guidance on the implementation of legislation to protect historic sites is given in government policy statements[2] and in various codes of practice.[3] The protection of historic sites is currently under review, following the publication of a Green Paper, *Protecting the Built Heritage*,[4] by the then Secretary of State of Scotland and Historic Scotland in May 1996. Some changes reflecting proposals in this Green Paper have already been implemented and other changes seem likely in the near future. Under the Scotland Act 1998 the implementation of the legal controls over archaeological sites and monuments is a devolved matter and responsibility now lies with the Scottish Executive acting through the appropriate Minister (referred to hereafter as the "Minister") and the Executive Agency, Historic Scotland.[5]

Identifying the location of archaeological sites

It is clearly important that landowners and land managers make themselves aware of the presence of any historic or archaeological features on land before

---

[1] eg, the Forestry Act 1967, s. 1(3A); the Coal Industry Act 1994, s. 3(7); the Coal Mining Subsidence Act 1991, s. 19 and the Environment Act 1995.

[2] Principally National Planning Policy Guideline 5 (NPPG 5) and Planning Advice Note 42 (PAN 42) published by the Scottish Office Environment Department in January 1994.

[3] eg, "Forestry and Archaeology Guidelines" used by the Forestry Commission; the British Archaeologists' and Developers' Liaison Group Code of Practice on Archaeology and Development; and the Confederation of British Industry has published a Code of Practice for Minerals Operators: *Archaeological Investigations Code of Practice for Minerals Operators in Scotland*. These codes of practice do not have the force of law and this can mean that the protection and good management of many sites is heavily dependent on the good will of the landowner and those carrying out activities on the land.

[4] Historic Scotland: *Protecting the built heritage: A Green Paper*, Cm. 3267 (May 1996).

[5] At the time of writing, the impact of the new Scottish Executive on Executive Agencies like Historic Scotland is unclear, but it is anticipated that Historic Scotland will continue to discharge the legal controls under the Ancient Monuments and Archaeological Areas Act 1979, in the immediate future.

carrying out activities which might prove damaging to them. Often the presence of historic sites and monuments is obvious—a castle, standing stone, Celtic cross or remains of industrial buildings are difficult to miss. In many cases, however, all that remains is below ground or is not immediately apparent, such as sites of Roman forts, hut circles or remains of ancient field systems. Although many such sites have been identified over the last 30 years through systematic surveys by archaeologists, through surveys linked to particular development projects such as roads, and through the increasing use of aerial photography and new technology in archaeology, recognising the presence of such remains may not be easy for the layman.

There are two main sources from which information on the location of known archaeological sites may be determined, the schedule of protected monuments and Sites and Monuments Records. These are considered in turn.

Scheduled monuments

The Minister is under a duty to compile and maintain a list of monuments in Scotland to be afforded statutory protection[6] and a list of scheduled monuments may be obtained from Historic Scotland. Owners and occupiers of the land on which a monument is located, and the local authority for the area where it is situated, are notified of scheduling,[7] and a copy of the entry in the Schedule relating to any heritable monument is to be recorded in the Register of Sasines or the Land Register.[8] In addition, all owners and occupiers of scheduled monuments are now contacted, and monuments are inspected on a regular (three- to five-year) basis by a Monument Warden from Historic Scotland.

Sites and Monuments Records

Useful information on the location of known archaeological sites may be gathered from the National Monuments Record of Scotland[9] or the local Sites and Monuments Records maintained by local authorities. These contain a list and description of all known archaeological sites and monuments, supported by a map giving details of their location. This information will be relevant to local authorities drafting policies on the protection of historic sites or determining planning applications relating to such sites and may prove helpful to developers and others planning operations which may affect archaeological sites. Unfortunately not all local authorities maintain a Sites and Monuments Record at the present time, a fact which can cause problems when attempts are being made to determine whether or not a proposed activity will affect any known archaeological remains.

Development control and archaeological sites

Planning permission is required for "development" (see Chapter 3), which includes not only building operations, but also civil engineering operations[10] and

---

[6] Ancient Monuments and Archaeological Areas Act 1979, s. 1. The Minister must publish a list of scheduled monuments under s. 1(7).

[7] s. 1(6).

[8] s. 1(10).

[9] Which is maintained by the Royal Commission on the Ancient and Historical Monuments of Scotland.

[10] Which could include the laying out of golf courses.

mineral extraction[11] on land, although it is not required for most agricultural or forestry activities[12] and many operations undertaken by statutory undertakers.[13] Guidance for local authorities and developers on the consideration to be given to archaeological remains in planning matters is given in National Planning Policy Guideline 5 (NPPG 5) *Archaeology and Planning* and Planning Advice Note 42 (PAN 42) *Archaeology—the Planning Process and Scheduled Monument Procedures*[14] which were issued in 1994.

Development plans and archaeology

It is clear from NPPG 5 that the development plan for the area should take full account of the potential impact of land use on archaeological remains and should state the planning authority's policy for the protection, enhancement, excavation and recording of nationally important sites and their settings.[15] The importance of development plan policies is revealed by section 25 of the Town and Country Planning (Scotland) Act 1997 which requires planning decisions to be "in accordance with the plan unless material considerations indicate otherwise". Development plan policies can thus be a useful indicator to a prospective developer of how the planning authority may react to a development proposal and will play an important role in shaping the local authority's decision on a planning application.

Development proposals affecting archaeological sites

NPPG 5 also makes it clear that the preservation of ancient monuments and their setting is "a material consideration in determining planning applications and appeals, whether a monument is scheduled or not"[16] and both NPPG 5 and PAN 42 urge planning authorities to encourage prospective developers to enter into discussions with the authority at an early stage of formulating the development proposal.[17] Early consultation is in the developer's interest as it is much cheaper to change plans (where this proves necessary) at the "design stage".

Where appropriate, the local authority will require a prospective developer to carry out an archaeological assessment and, if necessary, a field evaluation of the site as part of the pre-application process. Additionally, under the Environmental Assessment (Scotland) Regulations 1999,[18] the developer may be required by the planning authority to prepare an environmental statement giving an assessment of the environmental impact on the environment (including "material assets and the cultural heritage")[19] of certain development proposals (including holiday

---

[11] Town and Country Planning (Scotland) Act 1997, s. 26.
[12] Town and Country Planning (Scotland) Act 1997, s. 26(2)(e), and Pts 6 and 7; Town and Country Planning (General Permitted Development) (Scotland) Order 1992 (SI 1992/223), although permitted development rights may be restricted where the land in question comprises a scheduled monument.
[13] Ibid.
[14] And see n. 3 above.
[15] See paras 21 and 22 of NPPG 5.
[16] para. 25.
[17] See para. 18 of PAN 42.
[18] Scottish SI 1999/1. These regulations implement EC Directive 85/337 on Environmental Impact Assessment, as amended by Directive 97/11.
[19] Ibid, Sched. 2.

villages, hotel complexes and ski lifts and cable cars), where the authority consider that the development is likely to have a "significant effect" on the environment.

While it is government policy that nationally important archaeological sites (and their settings), whether scheduled or not, should be physically preserved wherever possible, it is also accepted that in practice it is not feasible to preserve all archaeological remains *in situ*.[20] Following consultation with the Council Archaeologist[21] (where there is one in post), the local authority may decide that physical preservation of the remains is not merited and may grant planning permission for development provided it is satisfied that suitable arrangements will be made by the developer, at his expense,[22] to ensure the excavation, recording, analysis and publication of the remains prior to development work going ahead. Where the nature or value of the archaeological remains is uncertain, the planning authority may require that a nominated archaeologist hold a "watching brief" during the carrying out of the work and that this person be allowed access to the site at any time.

These requirements may be enforced through the use of planning conditions[23] or an agreement between the developer and the planning authority under section 75 of the Town and Country Planning (Scotland) Act 1997; but, wherever possible, the Government favours the use of voluntary agreements between the developer and the authority to secure the preservation (or at least the archaeological investigation) of the site.[24] Where an archaeological site is threatened by the exercise of permitted development rights, the local authority may consider withdrawing such rights through a Direction made under Article 4 of the Town and Country (General Permitted Development) (Scotland) Order 1992 although the requirement to pay compensation may inhibit the use of this power.

Scheduled monument controls

The Ancient Monuments and Archaeological Areas Act 1979 grants powers to the Minister and local authorities in relation to monuments, although in Scotland most of these powers are in practice exercised by Historic Scotland, which is responsible for implementing legislation and policy on the protection of historic buildings, monuments and archaeological sites.

What is a "monument"?

Monuments: For the purposes of the 1979 Act, a "monument" may be a building or other structure above or below the surface of the land, or a cave or excavation; the remains of a building, structure or cave or excavation; and a site comprising,

---

[20] NPPG 5, paras 17 and 26.

[21] It is suggested that the decision as to whether the remains merit physical preservation should be made in consultation with the Council Archaeologist (a professional archaeologist employed by the local authority). In Orkney and Shetland the Council Archaeologist is called the Island Archaeologist.

[22] PAN 42, paras 26 and 29, and NPPG 5, para. 26.

[23] Suggested model conditions are given in paras 33–35 of PAN 42. Conditions will typically be of the condition precedent or "Grampian" variety, see *Grampian Regional Council* v *Aberdeen District Council* (1984) SLT 197.

[24] These agreements to be based on agreed codes of practice: see n. 3 above.

or comprising the remains of, any vehicle, vessel, or aircraft (provided the protection of the latter is of public interest and the site is not that of a wreck protected under the Protection of Wrecks Act 1973).[25] The scheduling of a monument will include the land on which it is situated and any machinery attached to the monument, if that machinery "could not be detached without being dismantled".[26]

Ancient monuments: Interestingly, the statutory definition of an "ancient" monument does not make any stipulation that it should be of great antiquity but simply states that an "ancient monument" is any scheduled monument *and* any other monument which in the opinion of the Minister is of public interest by reason of the historic, architectural, traditional, artistic, or archaeological interest attaching to it.[27] Ancient monument status is thus wider than scheduled monument status and is of importance in relation to arrangements for guardianship and management of monuments.

The schedule of monuments

Today there are over 6,500 scheduled monuments in Scotland but it is generally accepted that the list is inadequate and a truly representative list might include double or treble the current number. As an interim measure, Historic Scotland and the Council Archaeologists are undertaking the compilation of a non-statutory register of sites which seeks to identify those sites and monuments which meet the criteria for scheduling and which should be put forward for consideration by the Minister should they come under threat.[28] Clearly, the fact that archaeological remains are not currently scheduled is no guarantee that they will not be so in the future, especially where the threat to them is immediate.

Exclusions from scheduling: Buildings and structures which are occupied as a dwelling-house (other than by a caretaker) may not be scheduled[29]; nor may ecclesiastical buildings currently in use as such.[30] A monument situated on Crown land may be scheduled but the controls are restricted: in particular, there are limits on powers of entry and no such land may be the subject of compulsory purchase.[31]

Monuments of "national importance": Section 1(3) of the 1979 Act gives the only statutory criterion for scheduling a monument—that the Minister considers it to be "of national importance". Guidance on what is to be considered of national importance is given in paragraphs 45–48 of PAN 42. The general criteria are

---

[25] s. 61(7)–(9).
[26] s. 61(7).
[27] s. 61(12).
[28] See PAN 42, para. 43. Inclusion of a building or structure on this non-statutory register may also be taken into account as a material consideration in the case of planning applications affecting the site.
[29] s. 1(4).
[30] s. 61(8).
[31] s. 50.

that the monument should have acknowledged importance for archaeology, architectural history or history, such that it can be "recognised as part of the national consciousness", that it retains structural, decorative or field characteristics to a "marked degree", or is likely to provide a "significant" archaeological resource. In determining whether a monument meets these criteria, regard is to be had to the state of the monument (bearing in mind that some monument categories are now so very rare that *all* surviving examples will be scheduled even if in poor condition), to the need to ensure that the schedule is representative of monuments of all types and periods and to the fragility or vulnerability of the monument in question.

Challenging the decision to schedule: If the Minister decides to schedule a monument (or if he refuses to do so), the decision can only be challenged by judicial review. The Minister has wide discretion: for example in *R* v *Secretary of State for the Environment, ex p. Rose Theatre Trust Company*[32] Schiemann J. considered that the Secretary of State could legitimately take into account the fact that a decision to schedule the remains would result in the payment of a large sum in compensation to the developers, who already had planning permission to develop the site, and that scheduling might jeopardise a voluntary agreement with the developers to allow excavation and to protect the remains *in situ*.

Restrictions on works to scheduled monuments

Once a monument has been scheduled, it becomes an offence to carry out certain works without consent from the Minister. The restriction applies to *any* works which will result in the demolition or destruction of or damage to a scheduled monument; *any* works for the purpose of removing, repairing, altering or making additions to a scheduled monument (or any part of it), and *any* flooding or tipping operations on land in or under which there is a scheduled monument.[33]

As a result of the proposals included in the 1996 Green Paper, *Protecting the Built Heritage*,[34] it seems likely that further restrictions on works to scheduled monuments may be imposed in the future. Section 2 of the 1979 Act currently restricts works which may damage or demolish the monument but makes no specific reference to operations which disturb the ground (other than mining or flooding operations). The Green Paper remarked that the courts have proved reluctant to convict under section 2 unless there has been clear damage to the exposed parts of a monument[35] and therefore proposed that the category of works for which scheduled monument consent is required should be extended to include any operations which disturb the ground in the vicinity of a scheduled monument.

---

[32] [1990] 1 QB 504.

[33] s. 2(2). The controls over scheduled monuments are thus stricter than those which apply to listed buildings, where only those works which would affect the character of the building as a building of architectural or historic interest are restricted.

[34] See n. 4 above.

[35] Pt II, para. 3.

Scheduled monument consent

Applications for consent: Applications for scheduled monument consent should be made to Historic Scotland, which acts for the Minister in these matters.[36] Historic Scotland recommend that prospective applicants contact them to discuss their proposals before submitting the formal application form, so as to allow the identification of any likely problems and means by which they may be avoided or limited.[37] Before determining the application, the applicant, the owner of the monument, and "any other person to whom it appears expedient to afford it",[38] will be given the opportunity to comment on the application. Although applications are not usually advertised, Historic Scotland may do so if the application appears to be controversial; and where objections are received, Historic Scotland or the Minister have the power to call a public local inquiry.

Decision on the application: An application may be granted unconditionally, but will almost invariably be subject to conditions,[39] which may stipulate both the manner in which the works are to be carried out and who is to be allowed to carry them out. Conditions may also require archaeological investigation of the site prior to the works being carried out.[40]

It is usual for Historic Scotland to advise an applicant of the provisional decision on the application, usually within six weeks of the date of the application. If this reveals that the application is to be refused or if it contains conditions unacceptable to the applicant, the applicant may informally ask Historic Scotland to reconsider the matter or may ask the Minister to hold a public local inquiry (if this has not already been done), thereby giving the applicant an opportunity to put the case for the application. If after this the decision remains unchanged, the applicant or any person "aggrieved by" the decision may, within six weeks of the decision, ask the Court of Session to review the decision, but only on the grounds that the decision was based on some procedural defect or was *ultra vires*.[41] This means that the merits of a decision to refuse scheduled monument consent, or the merits of any conditions attached, cannot be challenged.

Compensation: If any person with an interest in the monument can show that he has incurred expenditure or suffered loss as a result of the refusal of scheduled monument consent, he may be able to claim compensation from the Minister under section 7. The rules on compensation are complex but, briefly, compensation is payable for refusal of two general classes of works: development permitted under planning law and works reasonably necessary for the continuation of the use to which the monument was being put immediately before the date of the application for scheduled monument consent. Where the works would

---

[36] Procedure for applications is governed by Sched. 1 of the Ancient Monuments and Archaeological Areas Act 1979 and the Ancient Monument and Archaeological Areas (Applications for Scheduled Monument Consent) (Scotland) Regulations 1981 (SI 1981/1467).

[37] At present no fee is charged for advice given by Historic Scotland, or for an application for scheduled monument consent.

[38] Sched. 1, para. 3.

[39] s. 2(4).

[40] s. 2(4) and (5).

[41] s. 55.

involve the total or partial demolition of the monument, compensation will not be granted (unless the demolition is incidental to the purposes of agriculture or forestry); and where scheduled monument consent is granted conditionally, compensation will only be payable if the conditions make it impossible to continue a current use. Compensation will also be payable if scheduled monument consent is subsequently revoked, varied, or modified by the Minister[42] and expense is incurred because works have to be aborted or other loss or damage is sustained as a result of the change.

In *Currie* v *Secretary of State for Scotland*[43] it was held that the amount of compensation payable is to be based on the value of the land at the time of the refusal of scheduled monument consent, not the date on which the monument was scheduled. Compensation will also be based on what the Lands Tribunal for Scotland considers to be the *actual* value of the land at that time, not some putative value it might have were the refused works to have taken place. In *Currie* the owners of the land applied for scheduled monument consent to plough land and plant young trees on the site of the Torr Righ Mor monument, a complex of Bronze Age hut circles on the Isle of Arran which had been scheduled in June 1987. When this was refused, an application for £66,600 compensation was made, based on the alleged diminution in the market value of the land, given that forestry operations could not now be carried out. The application had been made in line with plans for the use of the land formulated prior to the land being scheduled, but in the interim the value of forestry land had fallen as a result of the removal of tax concessions in the 1988 Budget. Evidence was also brought that the Forestry Commission had adopted a policy of refusing grants for planting on sites of scheduled monuments. In the light of this the Lands Tribunal for Scotland held that the planned afforestation would have been unlikely to have been carried out in practice as it would no longer have been commercially viable. As the land was not "forestry land", there had been no diminution in value occasioned by the refusal of scheduled monument consent and no compensation was payable.

Class consents

In the case of nine classes of operations which might affect a scheduled monument, it is not necessary to obtain scheduled monument consent because they are authorised by the Ancient Monuments (Class Consents) (Scotland) Order 1996.[44] As with the development control system, some agricultural and forestry operations are allowed without consent, but in the case of scheduled monuments these activities are more restricted than within the planning regime.

Class I. Agricultural, horticultural and forestry works: Class I generally allows the continuation of routine ploughing and some other minor agricultural or forestry activities, provided they are of the same nature and carried out in the same place as works lawfully carried out during the six years (or, in the case of ploughed

---

[42] s. 9. Powers to revoke or modify scheduled monument consent are given by s. 4 of the 1979 Act and may be exercised where the Minister considers it "expedient" to do so.

[43] [1993] 2 EGLR 221 .

[44] SI 1996/1507 made under powers granted to the then Secretary of State for Scotland by s. 3 of the 1979 Act.

land, 10 years) immediately preceding the date on which the current works begin. Nevertheless, the potentially damaging nature of some agricultural and forestry operations on underground features, stratigraphical features and contextual material connected with monuments is recognised by the fact that the Order does *not* extend consent to operations which involve disturbance of the soil at deeper levels than those normally associated with agricultural activity. Scheduled monument consent is required for six types of agricultural or forestry operations: deeper ploughing than has been customary and other works on unploughed land which involve disturbance of the soil below the depth of 300 millimetres; works which will affect or involve the removal of top-soil[45]; the demolition, removal, alteration or disturbance of any building or structure, or its remains; the erection of new buildings or structures; the laying of paths, hardstandings or foundations for buildings; and the erection of fences and other barriers.[46]

Class II and Class III: Classes II and III provide for consent for certain activities carried out by the Coal Authority or their licensees[47] and by British Waterways.

Class IV. Works for the repair or maintenance of machinery: Under Class IV works of repair or maintenance are given consent provided they do not involve material alteration or reconstruction of a scheduled monument.

Class V. Works urgently necessary for health or safety: Here there are three qualifying provisions: to be granted consent under the terms of the 1996 Order the works must be "urgently necessary", they must be limited to the "minimum measures immediately necessary", and notice in writing justifying in detail the need for the works should be given to the Minister as soon as practicable. The requirement that health and safety works be limited to the minimum measures which are urgently necessary is a new provision, implementing proposals in the Green Paper, *Protecting the Built Environment.*

Classes VI to IX: These Classes also enlarge the categories of works given class consent, and authorise works carried out under various provisions of the Ancient Monuments and Archaeological Areas Act 1979, including works of archaeological evaluation (Class VI), works for the maintenance or preservation of a scheduled monument or its amenities under a section 17 agreement (Class VII); works for the preservation, maintenance or management of a scheduled monument grant-aided, in whole or part, by the Minister under section 24 (Class VIII); and some survey work carried out by the Royal Commission on the Ancient and Historical Monuments of Scotland (Class IX).

Scheduled monument offences

Under section 2 of the 1979 Act it is an offence to execute, or to cause or to permit the execution of, restricted works without scheduled monument consent, or to

---

[45] This will include operations such as drainage works, planting or uprooting of trees and shrubs, removal of top soil or commercial cutting and removal of turf.
[46] Except in the case of operations carried out in a domestic garden.
[47] Works carried out 10 metres below ground level are granted consent by the Order.

fail to comply with any conditions imposed in a scheduled monument consent.[48] The owner or occupier of a scheduled monument should therefore ensure that all contractors and others carrying out works on the land are aware of the scheduling. In addition to the offence under section 2, it is also an offence under section 28 of the 1979 Act to cause damage to a "protected" monument, provided the accused was aware of the monument's protected status and intended to cause the damage, or was reckless as to whether the damage was caused, to the monument. A "protected monument" is a scheduled monument which is in the ownership or guardianship of the Minister under section 12 of the 1979 Act. This provision is usually used to deal with acts of vandalism by trespassers, but may also be used against an owner who causes damage to a monument.[49]

Defences: It is a defence in both cases to show that all reasonable precautions were taken and due diligence was exercised to avoid or prevent damage to the monument. Second, it is currently a defence in relation to works of demolition or destruction of a scheduled monument, or flooding or tipping on the site, to show that the accused did not know and had no reason to believe that a scheduled monument was within the area affected by the works. This position may change in the future: the 1996 Green Paper, *Protecting the Built Heritage*, proposed the abolition of this defence in view of the wide ranging procedures now in place by which scheduled monument status is made public.[50] Third, it is a defence[51] for the accused to show that the works were urgently necessary in the interests of safety or health and that written notice of the works was given to the Minister as soon as practicable. Again, in the 1996 Green Paper, *Protecting the Built Heritage*, it was proposed that works under section 2(9) be limited to the minimum measures necessary and a change in the law can be expected, given the fact that where the works *are* restricted to the minimum works urgently necessary in the interests of public health or safety they will already have consent under Class V of the Ancient Monuments (Class Consents) (Scotland) Order 1996, provided a detailed explanation of the need for the works was given to the Minister as soon as practicable.

PAN 42 advises that "well publicised, successful prosecutions . . . can provide a valuable deterrent to wilful damage or destruction of monuments"[52] and where there is good evidence to back up a prosecution, the matter will be referred to the procurator fiscal, at whose discretion the decision whether to prosecute lies. Successful recent prosecutions under these provisions include a fine of £1,000 imposed in 1990 where ploughing for tree planting by the Economic Forestry Group damaged the Ashkirkshiel earthwork in the Borders, a fine of £2,000 imposed in 1993 on a coal company for operations damaging Blackbraes Coke

---

[48] s. 2(6).

[49] Where a monument has been damaged by someone other than the owner, a prosecution may also be brought for criminal damage under the normal provisions of the criminal law.

[50] This would also bring ancient monument protection into line with listed buildings law where ignorance of listing is no defence.

[51] s. 2(9).

[52] PAN 42, para. 54.

Ovens in Falkirk and a fine of £250 imposed in 1995 for repair work to Dairsie Castle in Fife which did not have scheduled monument consent.[53] A case referred to the procurator fiscal in 1993 following serious breach of conditions in a scheduled monument consent relating to work to a castle in Aberdeenshire only escaped prosecution because of the poor health of the owner.

To protect monuments from possible damage by "treasure hunters" and others, it is also an offence under section 42 of the 1979 Act to use a metal detector in a "protected place" without written permission of the Minister. A "protected place" is defined in section 42(2) as the site of a scheduled monument or of any monument under the guardianship of the Minister or a local authority or which is a designated area of archaeological importance.[54] In 1991 three men found guilty of using metal detectors on Newstead Roman Fort in the Borders were each fined £750 and subsequently two others were fined £100; but other prosecutions have been dropped by the procurator fiscal because of the difficulties in identifying the culprits.[55]

Enforcement of scheduled monument controls is thus currently effected only through the use of criminal prosecutions and there are at present no administrative enforcement powers comparable with those relating to listed buildings. In the 1996 Green Paper, *Protecting the Built Heritage,* the Government recommended the introduction of a power whereby the owner of a monument which has been subjected to damage by unauthorised operations, or by failure to comply with conditions in a scheduled monument consent, might be served with a notice requiring remedial works to be carried out. It further recommended that a local authority be empowered to carry out remedial works themselves in default of action by the owner and to recover the costs from the owner.

The management of monuments

Scheduling a monument currently imposes no obligation on the owner or occupier of the land on which it stands to maintain or protect it, although Historic Scotland encourages landowners and land managers to play a positive role in the management of land on which monuments are located.[56] The Ancient Monuments and Archaeological Areas Act 1979 therefore gives a range of powers to public authorities to ensure the maintenance of monuments and it is here that the distinction between "monuments" and "ancient monuments" becomes important.

---

[53] The fine imposed in this case was little more than a token, as the sheriff professed himself impressed by photographs of the repair work. The procurator fiscal has suggested using a civil action of interdict in similar cases in future (information supplied by Historic Scotland).

[54] There are no designated areas of archaeological importance in Scotland.

[55] In England the courts have proved willing to impose more substantial fines for these offences. In an unreported case, *R v J.O. Sims Ltd* in 1992, the defendant, who had already pleaded guilty to a previous charge of damaging the site of a scheduled monument, was fined £75,000 with £1,000 costs for removing stone and chalk walls from the site; and in *R v Seymour* [1988] 1 PLR 19 the defendant was fined £3,000 (reduced on appeal from an initial fine of £10,000) for ploughing a field containing Roman remains, causing them serious damage.

[56] See, eg, the leaflet *Managing Scotland's Archaeological Heritage: A Guide to the Management of Archaeological Sites for Owners, Land Managers and Others,* produced by Historic Scotland.

Management agreements

Under section 17 of the 1979 Act the Minister, acting through Historic Scotland, or a local authority, may enter into an agreement with any person who has an interest in an ancient monument or adjoining land. A management agreement may impose limits on the activities which may be undertaken on the land, may require works of preservation and maintenance, and may require public access. Such agreements are particularly useful where a monument is situated on agricultural land, and payment may be made to the occupier for carrying out fencing, pest and weed control, or in respect of agreements to limit stock levels on such land—although the possibility that the public be admitted may deter some landowners and their land managers from entering into such agreements.

Where the owner of the monument or a local authority is prepared to undertake maintenance of a monument, grant aid (usually up to a maximum of 75 per cent of the cost) may be available for the upkeep or protection of a monument from the Minister, through the Ancient Monuments Grant system,[57] which is administered by Historic Scotland. Any application for grant aid must be made in advance of the works or operations for which financial assistance is sought and a grant will almost invariably be subject to rigorous conditions on how the works are to be carried out. Works which are grant-aided by the Ancient Monuments Grants programme do not require separate scheduled monument consent, but no works should be undertaken before receipt of the formal, written offer of the grant and all conditions must be strictly adhered to.

Acquisition of ancient monuments

Where the preservation of the monument cannot be achieved by agreement, the Minister has the power to acquire an ancient monument by compulsory purchase under section 10, or to acquire an ancient monument by agreement or gift under section 11. In practice these powers will only be exercised where the protection of the monument cannot be achieved by other means and where it can be justified in the national interest.

Guardianship of ancient monuments

Section 12 allows the guardianship of the monument[58] to be passed to the Minister or a local authority, subject to their agreement to act as guardians. Ownership of a monument in guardianship is not affected, but the guardian assumes full control and management of the monument and is under a duty to maintain it. The guardian of the monument may carry out works of maintenance and archaeological examination, or may remove all or part of the monument for the purpose of preserving it. Section 19 requires that public access be allowed to all ancient monuments in the ownership or under the guardianship of the Minister or a local authority, although access may be limited (for example, in relation to times when access is permitted) and a fee may be charged for entry. The Minister or the

---

[57] Established under s. 24 of the 1979 Act. Monuments need not be scheduled to receive assistance, but in a time of scarce resources, funds will obviously be directed to those monuments which are regarded as being the most important.

[58] Ancient monuments which are occupied as a dwelling-house (other than by a caretaker) may not be subject to a guardianship scheme—s. 12(10).

local authority also has the power to exclude the public from all or part of a monument where this is deemed necessary in the interests of safety or for the preservation of the monument.[59]

An agreement establishing guardianship of a monument must be by way of a deed, and may be recorded in the Register of Sasines or the Land Register under section 12(8). Where the owner is not the occupier, the latter must also be joined as a party to the deed by which the public authority is constituted guardian of the monument[60] and the deed of guardianship is binding on every person subsequently deriving title from a party to it.[61] Guardianship ends if the monument is subsequently acquired by the guardian[62] and it may also be unilaterally terminated by any occupier who was not a party to the guardianship deed but who has an interest in the monument. It is therefore essential to ensure that all those who have an interest in the monument are made parties to the guardianship deed.

Finally, although there is at the moment no positive obligation on landowners to maintain a monument situated on their land, they should be aware that where a scheduled monument is falling into a state of disrepair, section 5 empowers the Minister to enter land to carry out those works which are "urgently necessary for the preservation of a scheduled monument", after giving the owner and the occupier seven days' written notice.

Areas of archaeological importance

Section 33 of the Ancient Monuments and Archaeological Areas Act 1979 also gives the Minister power to designate as an area of archaeological importance any area which appears "to merit treatment as such". These provisions have not been brought into force in Scotland. It is highly unlikely that any such areas will be designated in the future as the Government considers that the same effects can now be produced through application of planning powers exercised in accordance with the guidance in NPPG 5 and PAN 42. Repeal of the relevant provisions has now been recommended.[63]

Objects and human remains discovered during works

As valuable information may be available from the context in which an object is found, anything uncovered during works or operations on land should, wherever possible, be left in place for removal by an archaeologist. Under common law, where the original or rightful heir to it cannot be ascertained, the object is treasure trove[64] and belongs to the Crown and its discovery should be reported to the

---

[59] s. 19(2). This may, for example, be necessary in times of drought to protect field monuments against possible damage by fire.

[60] s. 12(4).

[61] s. 12(9)(b).

[62] s. 14.

[63] See Pt II, para. 17 of the 1996 Green Paper, *Protecting the Built Heritage*.

[64] On treasure trove see D.L. Carey Miller and A. Sheridan, *Treasure Trove in Scots Law* [1996] *Art, Antiquity and the Law* 393. The leading case on Scottish treasure trove is *Lord Advocate* v *University of Aberdeen* 1963 SC 533.

Archaeology Department of the National Museums of Scotland or to a local museum acting on their behalf. In order to ensure the prompt reporting of such finds, it is usual where the Crown takes the object (for example, for display in a museum), for the finder to be given a reward based on the market value of the object in question. In addition the Civic Government (Scotland) Act 1982 states that no person who finds any property appearing to have been lost or abandoned; or who is the employer of a finder of such property; or who owns or occupies the land or premises on which such property is found, shall have any right to claim ownership of the property by reason of having found it.[65] This Act further provides that the finder must take "reasonable care" of it and deliver it, or report the finding of it, to the police or other persons specified in the Act "without unreasonable delay". As at common law non-owned property belongs to the Crown; the importance of these statutory provisions relates mainly to the duty to report and care for such finds. In addition to these provisions relating to the finding of objects during works, it is important to remember that any discovery of human remains must also be reported to the police.

Landowners and occupiers should note that it is also an offence under section 42 of the 1979 Act to remove any object of archaeological or historic interest located by the unauthorised use of a metal detector in a protected place.[66] Prosecution may also be brought for theft in appropriate cases. For example, in a case heard by Knightsbridge Crown Court in 1995, two men in breach of a written undertaking not to enter a site did so and discovered a hoard of some 500 pieces which they sold to a dealer for £10,000. They were successfully prosecuted for theft. In the 1996 Green Paper, *Protecting the Built Heritage,* the introduction of a new offence of removing an object (whether located with a metal detector or otherwise) from a scheduled monument without the consent of the Secretary of State was proposed, but has not as yet been implemented.

Conclusion

It is clear that those proposing works which may affect archaeological features must exercise caution. It is essential to identify at an early stage whether a scheduled monument or any other known archaeological feature lies on the site and, where the proposed works constitute development or works restricted under the Ancient Monuments and Archaeological Areas Act 1979, the necessary consents should be obtained. Although the procurator fiscal has exercised his discretion and has not prosecuted in several cases referred to him by Historic Scotland, local authorities and the police, convictions have been obtained in a number of cases, with attendant bad publicity for those concerned. At a time when the concept of sustainable development is very much to the fore, a responsible attitude should be adopted by all those whose activities may damage or destroy Scotland's finite archaeological heritage.

---

[65] Civic Government (Scotland) Act 1982, ss 67 and 73.

[66] As defined in s. 42(2).

CHAPTER 17

THE COASTAL ZONE

Jack Robertson

Introduction

Scotland has over 10,000 kilometres of coastline, of which over 6,000 kilometres is island coastline, and nowhere in Scotland is further than 65 kilometres from the coast.[1] Coastal issues are, therefore, of particular significance. In 1992, the House of Commons Environment Select Committee (hereafter "the Environment Committee") examined the issues surrounding coastal zone protection and planning and highlighted the often-conflicting demands affecting the coast, the fragmentation of responsibility for coastal issues and the resulting problems.[2] It stated that:

> "we firmly believe that coastal protection, planning and management in the United Kingdom suffer from centuries of unco-ordinated decisions and actions at both the national and local levels. We found that there are inadequacies in legislation, anomalies in the planning system, a lack of central guidance, and overlapping policies and responsibilities (and in some cases a lack of action) among a host of bodies, with poor co-ordination between them".[3]

It recommended, *inter alia*, the adoption of an integrated approach to management of the coastal zone. In its response to the Environment Committee Report, the Government emphasised its commitment to effective protection and planning

---

[1] See NPPG 13 (Coastal Planning).
[2] House of Commons Environment Committee Second Report, *Coastal Zone Protection and Planning* (1992) (hereafter "the Environment Committee Report"). The Report was concerned primarily with England and Wales, but its conclusions and recommendations are equally relevant to Scotland: see the Environment Committee Report itself, para. 8 and *Review of Scottish Coastal Issues*, a consultants' report to the Scottish Office by Drs Peter and Veronica Burbridge (Scottish Office, 1994), para. 2.0.
[3] Environment Committee Report, op. cit., n. 2, para. 3.

of the coast and recognised the particular need for the strategic management of coastal issues,[4] but many of the problems identified by the Environment Committee remain today. This is at least partly due to the nature of the coastal zone itself and the diverse activities affecting it, and the Environment Committee itself accepted that there was no panacea for resolving all the problems experienced in the coastal zone.[5] This area therefore remains a complex and somewhat fragmented one. This chapter outlines the principal issues affecting the coastal zone and the legal framework within which management of the coastal zone takes place and then goes on to consider the current initiatives designed to achieve integrated management and sustainable development of the coastal zone.

Definition of the coastal zone

It is necessary first of all to consider what is meant by "the coastal zone". The Environment Committee noted that there was no universally accepted definition of the coastal zone, but that there was widespread support for including within it elements of coastal land, the inter-tidal zone and the adjacent sea.[6] Accordingly, they recommended that the coastline should not be seen as a physical or administrative boundary, but treated as one integrated unit embracing inshore waters, inter-tidal areas and maritime land,[7] while at the same time concluding that definitions of the coastal zone might vary from area to area and from issue to issue and that a pragmatic approach must therefore be taken at the appropriate national, regional or local level.[8] This approach was accepted by the Government in its response to the Environment Committee Report,[9] and this definition of the coastal zone is adopted, for example, in National Planning Policy Guideline 13 on Coastal Planning (hereafter "NPPG 13").[10] For the purposes of this chapter, therefore, the coastal zone will be treated as including coastal land, the inter-tidal zone and the adjacent sea.

Issues affecting the coastal zone

The principal, and most important, issue affecting the coastal zone is the often-competing demands made on it. The Environment Committee found that "[t]he coast is subject to all manner of valid demands by maritime communities, maritime-based industries and conservation and recreation bodies".[11] As a result:

---

[4] Department of the Environment, The Government's Response to the Second Report from the House of Commons Select Committee on the Environment, *Coastal Zone Protection and Planning*, Cmnd. 2011 (1992), paras 1 and 7 respectively.

[5] Environment Committee Report, op. cit., n. 2, para. 5.

[6] Environment Committee Report, op. cit., n. 2, para. 17. Inter-tidal land, as noted by the Environment Committee, is the land between high- and low-water marks: see n. 1 to para. 17.

[7] Environment Committee Report, op. cit., n. 2, para. 17.

[8] Environment Committee Report, op. cit., n. 2, para. 18.

[9] Department of the Environment, The Government's Response to the Second Report from the House of Commons Select Committee on the Environment, *Coastal Zone Protection and Planning*, op. cit., n. 4, para. 14.

[10] NPPG 13, para. 11.

[11] Environment Committee Report, op. cit., n. 2, para. 4.

"[t]he coastal zone is subject to increasing pressure of all kinds. The natural resources of the coastal zone support the livelihood of many people. Many more use the coast for recreation, while the coast offers attractive locations for commercial, housing and leisure developments. By virtue of its natural resources, then, the coastal zone has to bear the competing pressures of fishing, fish farming, shell fishing, ports and harbours, navigation, sport and recreation, coastal settlements, sand dredging, marine aggregate extraction, oil and gas extraction, land claim and coastal engineering, conventional and renewable energy installations, waste disposal from land- and sea-based sources, landscape and wildlife conservation".[12]

The principal issue for management of the coastal zone is therefore to balance the competing demands made upon the coast, including that of the need to preserve its resources for present and future generations. To date, economic benefits derived from activities at or affecting the coast often seem to have taken precedence in determining the treatment of its resources, to the detriment of other interests, including, most importantly, food for mankind. Food chains as high as the human palate are now affected by pollution[13] and noticeable effects have been observed on the biology of the habitat and species at the coast.[14] Leaching of land chemicals to the coast and ultimately to the whole marine environment water system have caused eutrophication with its attendant negative and unnatural effects on flora and fauna.[15] The continuing search for and extraction of hydrocarbons from the sea floor continues to present difficult planning and pollution issues. In addition to such human activities, "the coastal zone is subject to the shifting dynamics of physical processes and change",[16] for example sea level rise,[17] which must also be taken into account.

Related to this issue are two other important issues. First, there is the fragmentation of responsibility for coastal issues. There is a large number of organisations with varying responsibilities for, or interests in, activities affecting the coast, including governmental departments and agencies, non-governmental bodies and others.[18] As highlighted by the Environment Com-

---

[12] Environment Committee Report, op. cit., n. 2, para. 15.

[13] See B.J. Howard *et al.*, "A review of radionuclides in tide-washed pastures on the Irish Sea coast in England and Wales and their transfer to food products" (1996) 39 *Environmental Pollution* 63. See also R.B. Clark, *Marine Pollution* (Clarendon Press, Oxford, 1989).

[14] A. Morris, "The Implications of Marine and Coastal Contamination by Radiological Discharges from UK Nuclear Sites" in J. Taussik and J. Mitchell, *Partnership in Coastal Zone Management* (Samara Publishing Ltd, 1986). For details of the effects of several polluting substances, see C. Plasman, "The State of the Marine Environment of the North Sea and of the Baltic Sea: A Comparison in Relation to Dangerous Substances" (1998) 13 *International Journal of Marine and Coastal Law* 325. See also J. Hughes and B. Goodall, "Marine Pollution" in A. Mannion and S. Bowlby (eds), *Environmental Issues in the 1990s* (Wiley, 1992) for a general discussion on the effects of pollution.

[15] P.W. Balls, "Nutrient inputs to estuaries from nine Scottish east coast rivers: influence of estuarine processes on inputs to the North Sea" (1994) 39 *Estuarine, Coastal and Shelf Science* 329.

[16] Environment Committee Report, op. cit., n. 2, para. 16.

[17] For a useful discussion of this problem in a Scottish context, see G. Jones, "Identifying sites for flood protection—a case study from the River Clyde" to be published in D.R. Green and S.D. King (eds), *GIS and the coastal environment: Information management in the coastal zone*.

[18] For a review of the relevant organisations, see Environment Committee Report, op. cit., n. 2, para. 28; *Review of Scottish Coastal Issues*, op. cit., n. 2, Chap. 5 and Scottish Natural Heritage, *A review of legislation relating to the coastal and marine environment in Scotland* (1995). The last of these is the

mittee,[19] this can lead to an unco-ordinated approach, which can in turn lead to conflicting actions, a lack of any action or wasteful duplication of effort. In its response to the Environment Committee Report, the Government did not accept that there was widespread duplication of effort or poor co-ordination in relation to coastal zone issues,[20] but in view of the many organisations involved, ensuring that such difficulties are avoided remains an issue.

Second, there is the range of legislation affecting the coastal zone. This includes international conventions and agreements, European Union legislation, domestic primary and secondary legislation and local legislation. The Environment Committee considered that the legislation affecting the coastal zone was too diffuse to provide an integrated or efficient framework for coastal protection and planning.[21] In its response to the Environment Committee Report, however, the Government noted that certain measures had been or were being taken to consolidate legislation, but felt that an attempt to consolidate the whole range of legislation affecting the coastal zone would not be feasible.[22] While this is probably true, the diversity of the provisions relating to the coastal zone remains a difficult issue.

Management of the coastal zone—the legal framework

The starting point for consideration of the legal framework within which the management of the coastal zone takes place is its ownership. The territorial sea adjacent to the United Kingdom extends to 12 nautical miles,[23] and within that limit the seabed, and the bed of other tidal waters, for example tidal rivers, belongs to the Crown.[24] The foreshore, that is, that part of the shore wholly covered by the sea at high tide and wholly uncovered by the sea at low tide,[25] may be in either Crown or private ownership,[26] as may the land adjacent to the coast itself. The owner of land (including the seabed and river beds) generally has the right to exclusive use of that land and the right to the use and enjoyment

---

most up to date, but it should be noted that: district and regional councils have been replaced with unitary authorities; matters formerly dealt with by Departments of the Scottish Office are now dealt with by the relevant Minister, where appropriate, following devolution; and H.M. Industrial Pollution Inspectorate and the River Purification Authorities have been replaced by the Scottish Environmental Protection Agency (hereafter "SEPA").

[19] See above.

[20] Department of the Environment, The Government's Response to the Second Report from the House of Commons Select Committee on the Environment, *Coastal Zone Protection and Planning*, op. cit., n. 4, para. 29.

[21] Environment Committee Report, op. cit., n. 2, para. 19.

[22] Department of the Environment, The Government's Response to the Second Report from the House of Commons Select Committee on the Environment, *Coastal Zone Protection and Planning*, op. cit., n. 4, para. 26.

[23] Territorial Sea Act 1987. For the development of territorial seas in general, see S.J. Buck, *The Global Commons: An Introduction* (Earthscan, 1998).

[24] *Crown Estate Commissioners v Fairlie Yacht Slip Ltd* 1979 SC 156 at 169; see also *Stair Memorial Encyclopaedia of the Laws of Scotland*, Vol. 18, para. 309.

[25] *Bowie v Marquis of Ailsa* (1887) 14 R 649, per Lord Trayner at 660; *Fisherrow Harbour Commissioners v Musselburgh Real Estate Co. Ltd* (1903) 5 F 387.

[26] The Crown owns approximately half of the foreshore in Scotland, the remaining half being in private ownership.

of the land,[27] and therefore has the right to determine how the land is managed. These rights are, however, subject to any other legal or conventional rights and any statutory restrictions or controls, and there are a number of these which are relevant in the context of the coastal zone. It is impossible in the space available to give a detailed description of all of these, but the most important are outlined in the remainder of this section under the following headings: legal and conventional rights; planning and development; environmental impact assessment; fisheries and aquaculture; conservation and landscape designations; harbours and ports; oil and gas; marine aggregates; waste disposal and pollution; and coast protection.

Legal and conventional rights

The right of an owner of land to the exclusive use of that land and to the use and enjoyment of the land may be circumscribed by other legal or conventional rights affecting the land, for example a public right of way or a lease of the land. Of particular importance in the context of the coastal zone, the rights of an owner may be circumscribed by a number of public rights. Reid states that:

> "Members of the public at large have certain rights in respect of the sea, rivers and other waters, and also in respect of the foreshore and other adjacent land. The public rights include the right of navigation, the right of fishing for white fish and shellfish, and the right of recreation. In addition, there may also be public rights of way over any piece of (dry) land, provided that the rules of constitution for such rights have been satisfied."[28]

Public rights of way are considered in detail in Chapter 13, to which further reference should be made. The other public rights mentioned are rights which are held by the Crown in trust for the public,[29] although they are directly enforceable by members of the public as well as by the Crown on their behalf.[30] Most of these rights are tacit rights, that is, they arise by operation of law, but some, most importantly the right of navigation in non-tidal rivers, are acquired rights, that is, they fall to be acquired by public use over a number of years.[31] This is discussed further below. These rights may now be considered in more detail.

Navigation: There is a public right of navigation in the sea and all tidal waters provided only that they are "navigable", that is, physically capable of being navigated.[32] The right of navigation is primarily one of passage, but includes activities such as recreational sailing and fishing; it also extends to activities ancillary to the right of navigation itself and reasonably necessary for its exercise, such as mooring,[33] although it has been held that the laying of fixed moorings on the seabed is not a right ancillary to navigation.[34] The right of navigation in tidal

---

[27] Gordon, *Land Law*, para. 13–06.
[28] K.G.C. Reid, *The Law of Property in Scotland*, para. 494.
[29] Ibid, para. 514.
[30] Ibid, para. 515.
[31] Ibid, para. 516.
[32] Ibid, para. 519.
[33] Ibid, para. 520.
[34] *Crown Estate Commissioners* v *Fairlie Yacht Slip Ltd* 1979 SC 156.

waters is a tacit right.[35] There is also a public right of navigation in non-tidal waters, but it is an acquired, not a tacit, right: it depends not only on the waters in question being navigable in the physical sense, but on there having been use since "time immemorial", normally 40 years.[36] The public may exercise the right of navigation in and from the foreshore, and again this includes the right to carry out any necessary activities ancillary to the exercise of that right.[37] It does not, however, carry with it a right of access to the foreshore,[38] and access to the foreshore may only lawfully be gained by a public road, public right of way or other lawful means of access,[39] although there is a public right of passage along and through the foreshore itself.[40] The exercise of the public right of navigation can be, and is, regulated by statute.

Fishing: There is a public right of fishing for white fish and shellfish in the sea and all tidal waters and in and from the foreshore.[41] In this context, white fish means all fish except salmon,[42] and shellfish means all shellfish except mussels and oysters and, possibly, lobsters.[43] The right includes the right to perform any ancillary activities reasonably necessary to the exercise of the right to fish, such as beaching a boat, landing fish and nets and drying nets, but not erecting permanent structures.[44] These ancillary rights have in some cases been enhanced by statute.[45] As noted in relation to navigation, however, the public rights do not carry with them a right of access to the foreshore, and such access may only lawfully be gained by a public road, public right of way or other lawful means of access or, of course, by sea in exercise of the right of navigation.[46] Like navigation, the public right of fishing can be, and is, regulated: this is discussed further below. It should be noted that the public right of navigation has preference, although not an absolute preference, over the public right of fishing.[47]

Recreation: The nature and scope of the public right to recreation is somewhat uncertain. Reid states in relation to tidal waters that in addition to the well-understood public rights of navigation and fishing, "it might be thought that a third, a right of swimming for recreation, should be added to satisfy reasonable public expectation"[48] and Gordon states that "[i]n so far as the public have a right

---

[35] See above.

[36] *Will's Trs v Cairngorm Canoeing and Sailing School Ltd* 1976 SC (HL) 30.

[37] K.G.C. Reid, *The Law of Property in Scotland*, para. 525.

[38] Ibid, para. 524.

[39] Access is discussed in Chaps 12–15; Chap. 13 in particular deals with linear rights of access. The foreshore could also, of course, be approached from the sea itself.

[40] See further below.

[41] K.G.C. Reid, *The Law of Property in Scotland*, paras 521 and 525.

[42] Ibid, para. 521.

[43] In tidal waters, mussels and oysters are part of the *regalia minora* of the Crown, and in non-tidal waters, they belong to the proprietors of the banks or bed of the waters in question; as such, they are not available to be taken by the public: see Gordon, *Land Law*, para. 8–26. The issue of whether lobsters also fall outwith the right of public fishing has been raised but not decided, hence the possible further exception mentioned: see K.G.C. Reid, op. cit., para. 521 and n. 2.

[44] See Gordon, *Land Law*, para. 8–07 and cases there cited.

[45] See, for example, the Fisheries Act 1705 and the White Herring Fisheries Act 1771.

[46] Access is discussed in Chaps 12–15; Chap. 13 in particular deals with linear rights of access.

[47] *Walfor v Crown Estate Commissioners* 1988 SLT 377.

[48] K.G.C. Reid, *The Law of Property in Scotland*, para. 518.

of recreation on the shore, they would seem to have a right to exercise it in the sea also".[49] So far as the public right to recreation on the foreshore is concerned, Reid states that the balance of authority suggests that, whatever its extent, the right is a tacit right as opposed to an acquired right[50]: this is important since, if tacit, such a right, whatever its extent, would exist throughout the coastline of Scotland, and would not depend on proof that it had been exercised at a particular location since time immemorial. It would seem to be settled that the right to recreation includes the right to shoot[51]; beyond this, as Reid notes,[52] it is easier to say what it does not include rather than what it does include: it does not include, for example, the right to gather sea-ware.[53] In addition to the right of recreation, there is a right of passage along and through the foreshore.[54] As noted above in relation to navigation and fishing, the public rights do not carry with them a right of access to the foreshore, and access to the foreshore may only lawfully be gained by a public road, public right of way or other lawful means of access or, of course, by sea in exercise of the public right of navigation.

It should be noted that under the Civic Government (Scotland) Act 1982, local authorities may make byelaws restricting or regulating trade or business activity, the use of vehicles and leisure activities at the sea shore and in the adjacent waters in order to prevent nuisance or danger *or* to preserve or improve the amenity, or conserve the beauty, of the shore.[55] They may also execute any works on the seashore or in or on the adjacent waters or seabed for the purpose of preserving, improving or restoring amenity.[56] The Act sets out detailed procedures to be followed in each case.

Planning and development

Development at the coast, as elsewhere, is subject to the controls imposed by planning law. The operation of these controls is described fully in Chapter 3, to which reference should be made. Coastal planning is specifically dealt with in NPPG 13 (Coastal Planning) and Planning Advice Note (PAN) 53 (Classifying the Coast for Planning Purposes). NPPG 13 divides the coast into three categories, namely developed, undeveloped and isolated, and gives guidance on planning policy in relation to each category, while PAN 53 sets out the criteria to be applied in determining into which category a particular stretch of coast falls. Many other NPPGs and PANs are also relevant to coastal planning, however, for example NPPG 7 on Planning and Flooding and PAN 36 on Siting and Design of New Housing in the Countryside.

It should be noted, however, that planning control extends seawards only as far as the mean low-water mark of ordinary spring tides,[57] and development

---

[49] Gordon, *Land Law*, para. 7–04.
[50] K.G.C. Reid, *The Law of Property in Scotland*, para. 526.
[51] *Hope* v *Bennewith* (1904) 6 F 1004; *Burnet* v *Barclay* 1955 JC 34; *McLeod* v *McLeod* 1982 SCCR 130.
[52] K.G.C. Reid, op. cit., para. 526.
[53] See, eg, *Paterson* v *Marquis of Ailsa* (1846) 8 D 752.
[54] *Officers of State* v *Smith* (1846) 8 D 711, affd *sub nom Smith* v *Officers of State* (1849) 6 Bell App 487; *Marquis of Bute* v *McKirdy and McMillan* 1937 SC 93.
[55] Civic Government (Scotland) Act 1982, s. 121.
[56] Civic Government (Scotland) Act 1982, s. 122(1).
[57] *Argyll and Bute District Council* v *Secretary of State for Scotland* 1977 SLT 33.

beyond this is not therefore affected by planning control as such. It is, however, subject to a form of planning control in practice, as a result of the requirement to obtain a lease of the seabed or other appropriate agreement for any such development from the Crown Estate Commissioners. The Crown Estate Commissioners manage the Crown estate,[58] which includes the seabed.[59] Persons wishing to carry out development or other operations below the low-water mark therefore require a lease of the seabed or other appropriate agreement from the Crown Estate Commissioners in order to do so.[60] Where an application is made to the Crown Estate Commissioners for such a lease or other agreement, they may grant or refuse it in the normal way. In reaching a decision, they may take into account factors which are essentially of a planning nature and may decide to grant the lease or other agreement only on certain terms and conditions, which may include conditions of an essentially planning nature; in practice, therefore, they exercise a quasi-planning function. In doing so, however, they consult with other interested persons where appropriate: for example, where applications are made for licences for the extraction of marine aggregates, there is a recognised procedure known as Government View whereby wide consultation is undertaken before a licence is granted[61]; similarly, where applications are made for leases for the purposes of fish farming, the Crown Estate Commissioners consult with a wide range of bodies in accordance with agreed consultation procedures.[62]

Even where the planning regime does not apply, any development may be subject to the requirement for an environmental impact assessment. Environmental impact assessments are discussed further below. Furthermore, construction below the level of mean high water springs requires the consent of the Minister under section 34 of the Coast Protection Act 1949, as amended, and such consent may be refused, or granted subject to conditions, where the construction causes or is likely to result in obstruction or danger to navigation.[63]

The Environment Committee saw the division between the planning control system at sea and on land as the root of many of the problems with coastal protection and planning policies.[64] The quasi-planning role of the Crown Estate Commissioners has been criticised,[65] and they themselves have expressed reservations about this role.[66] The Environment Committee recommended that the quasi-planning functions exercised by the Crown Estate Commissioners be transferred to a more appropriate authority[67] and that the issue of harmonisation of the planning regimes on land and at sea as far as the 12 nautical mile limit of

---

[58] Crown Estate Act 1961.

[59] See above.

[60] They will, of course, also require such a lease or other agreement to carry out development or other operations on Crown land above the low-water mark, but in that case the normal planning procedures will operate in addition.

[61] Marine aggregate extraction is discussed further below.

[62] Fish farming generally is discussed further below.

[63] Coast Protection Act 1949, s. 34.

[64] Environment Committee Report, op. cit., n. 2, para. 49.

[65] See, eg, the evidence given to the Environment Committee, referred to in Environment Committee Report, op. cit., n. 2, para. 54.

[66] See, eg, Environment Committee Report, op. cit., n. 2, para. 58.

[67] Environment Committee Report, op. cit., n. 2, para. 54.

territorial waters should be addressed.[68] One option considered by the Environment Committee was an extension of planning control to the marine environment, either as a blanket extension or by the extension of certain planning control powers where needed.[69] However, in its response to the report, the Government did not accept that this would necessarily be the most effective approach and proposed that further investigation into the matter should be undertaken.[70] At present, however, the system remains as described above.

Environmental impact assessments

Certain projects, irrespective of whether or not they are also subject to planning control, are, or may be, subject to a requirement to have an environmental impact assessment (hereafter "EIA") carried out to assess their impact on the environment. The requirement for EIAs stems from Directive 85/337 on the assessment of the effects of certain public and private projects on the environment (hereafter "the Environmental Assessment Directive"), which requires EIAs to be carried out in relation to projects which are likely to have significant effects on the environment due to their size, location or the nature of the project, and which lists in Annex I a relatively small number of major projects for which such an EIA is mandatory and in Annex II a larger number of projects in relation to which the requirement for such an EIA is at the discretion of Member States. The Environmental Assessment Directive came into force in July 1988 and was duly implemented in the UK by a series of Regulations; it was subsequently amended by Directive 97/11, which extended the range of projects to which it applied, and the relevant UK legislation has for the most part now also been duly amended to take account of these changes.[71] EIA as a process is discussed in more detail in Chapter 3, to which further reference should be made. EIAs are of particular significance in the context of the coastal zone, since many projects within the coastal zone will in practice require an EIA even although, as in a number of important cases, they are not subject to planning control.[72]

Fisheries and aquaculture

Fishing has long been one of the primary uses of the coastal zone in Scotland, while aquaculture, in the form of fish and shellfish farming, has more recently become a significant industry, particularly in the Highlands and Islands. Fishing

---

[68] Environment Committee Report, op. cit., n. 2, para. 52.

[69] Environment Committee Report, op. cit., n. 2, para. 51.

[70] Department of the Environment, The Government's Response to the Second Report from the House of Commons Select Committee on the Environment, *Coastal Zone Protection and Planning*, op. cit., n. 4, para. 38.

[71] See now the Environmental Impact Assessment (Scotland) Regulations 1999 (Scottish SI 1999/1); the Harbour Works (Assessment of Environmental Effects) (No. 2) Regulations 1989 (SI 1989/424), as amended and the Harbour Works (Assessment of Environmental Effects) (Amendment) Regulations 1996 (SI 1996/1946); the Electricity and Pipe-line Works (Assessment of Environmental Effects) Regulations 1990 (SI 1990/442), as amended; the Environmental Assessment (Forestry) Regulations 1998 (SI 1998/1731); the Offshore Petroleum Production and Pipe-lines (Assessment of Environmental Effects) Regulations 1999 (SI 1999/360); the Environmental Impact Assessment (Fish Farming in Marine Waters) Regulations 1999 (SI 1999/367) and the Public Gas Transporter Pipe-Line Works (Environmental Impact Assessment) Regulations 1999 (SI 1999/1672).

[72] See further above.

and, increasingly, aquaculture play an important role in the Scottish economy; at the same time, they have a significant effect on the coastal zone. As noted above, there is a public right of fishing for white fish (being all fish except salmon) and shellfish (being all shellfish except mussels and oysters and, possibly, lobsters) in the sea and other tidal waters and in and from the foreshore, but this right can be, and is, regulated. Aquaculture raises slightly different issues. This section outlines the main provisions relevant to the regulation of sea fisheries and to aquaculture; salmon and freshwater fisheries are described separately in Chapter 9.[73]

Sea fisheries: Much of the law relating to sea fisheries is very specialised and involves consideration of questions of international law and EU law as well as domestic law. What follows is therefore only a brief outline of the main areas of importance. There are two main issues which are of concern in relation to sea fisheries in modern times: access to fisheries, and regulation of fisheries, particularly for the purpose of conservation of fish stocks. The question of access to fisheries, in particular, involves consideration of international law. In this context, it is necessary first to consider briefly the various zones of jurisdiction affecting the seas off Scotland, namely the territorial sea, the exclusive fisheries zone, the continental shelf and the high seas.[74] As noted above, the territorial sea surrounding the UK extends to 12 nautical miles.[75] The sea up to 200 nautical miles is designated as an exclusive fisheries zone.[76] The Continental Shelf Act 1964 makes provision for the exercise of the UK's rights in relation to the continental shelf,[77] but the law relating to the continental shelf is of limited relevance in the context of sea fisheries, since the resources affected by it only include living resources to the extent that they fall within the rather restricted definition of sedentary species, which does not include the species generally the subject of fisheries activity.[78] The high seas are all seas outwith territorial seas

---

[73] Considerations of space preclude a detailed examination of this complex area, but for a detailed description of the law relating to sea fisheries, see *Stair Memorial Encyclopaedia*, Vol. 11, paras 65 *et seq.*, and for that relating to fish farming, *Stair Memorial Encyclopaedia*, Vol. 11, paras 57 *et seq.*

[74] For a detailed description, including a narrative of the history of the current position, see *Stair Memorial Encyclopaedia*, Vol. 11, paras 65 *et seq.*

[75] Territorial Sea Act 1987. This limit was consistent with the Convention on the Territorial Sea and Contiguous Zone (Geneva, April 29, 1958), one of the four Geneva Conventions on the Law of the Sea adopted following the first United Nations Conference on the Law of the Sea in 1958, to which the UK was a party, and is consistent with the United Nations Convention on the Law of the Sea (1982) (hereafter "UNCLOS 1982"), which superseded the Convention on the Territorial Sea and Contiguous Zone and to which the UK acceded on July 25, 1997.

[76] The 200-mile limit was first enacted in the Fishery Limits Act 1976, following agreement within the EC to extend the fisheries limits of Member States bordering the Atlantic Ocean. It is consistent with UNCLOS 1982, which provides for a 200-mile "Exclusive Economic Zone", and to which the UK acceded on July 25, 1997: see the Fishery Limits Order 1997 (SI 1997/1750), which brings the fisheries limits into conformity with UNCLOS 1982.

[77] For a detailed discussion of the international and domestic law relating to the continental shelf, see *Stair Memorial Encyclopaedia*, Vol. 21.

[78] Sedentary species are defined in both the Convention on the Continental Shelf (Geneva, April 29, 1958), to which the UK is a party, and UNCLOS 1982 as "organisms which, at the harvestable stage, are either immobile on or under the seabed or are unable to move except in constant physical contact" therewith.

and the exclusive fisheries zone[79]: they are open to be fished by all states. Since this chapter is concerned with the coastal zone, the main concern is fisheries activity within the 200-mile limit. Access by foreign fishing boats to the seas within that limit is governed by the Fishery Limits Act 1976, under which the countries whose registered boats may fish therein, the specific areas within which they may fish and the species for which they may fish may be designated by statutory instrument. The UK as a whole is, of course, subject to the Common Fisheries Policy of the EU (hereafter "the CFP"), and the relevant designations will therefore change from time to time to take account of changes in the CFP and any agreements concluded by the EU with non-Member States, as well as to take account of any other changes in fisheries policy unconnected with the implementation of the CFP. Fishing boats allowed to fish under these provisions must strictly observe the limits of the rights accorded to them and, subject to some exceptions, no other foreign fishing boats may enter the 200-mile limit except for purposes recognised in international law (for example, as being in distress) or in accordance with any treaty between the UK and its flag state.[80]

With respect to the regulation of fisheries, there are many reasons why this is seen as necessary: these include preventing or minimising conflicts within the fishing industry itself, for example by controlling competition for increasingly scarce resources and regulating the use of different fishing methods which may not be compatible with each other; preventing or minimising both physical damage caused by some types of fishing gear and other environmental damage; the requirement to ensure that fish stocks are exploited only in a sustainable way; and preventing or minimising conflicts between fishing and other legitimate uses of the coastal zone. The Environment Committee was particularly concerned about the environmental effects of fishing methods and noted, for example, that trawling in the North Sea had essentially changed the nature of the benthic communities there, which were losing diversity.[81] They recognised that a balance required to be struck between protecting the richness and diversity of the marine environment and protecting the livelihoods of fishermen and related industries, and recommended that the Government "seek to achieve a balance between the exploitation of fish and shellfish in the coastal zone and marine habitat and wildlife conservation", zoning of coastal fishing waters according to sensitivity being one option.[82] In its response to the Environment Committee Report, the Government stated that it was firmly committed to conservation objectives in fisheries management, and that it recognised that special measures might be appropriate in sensitive areas, which was reflected in the arrangements for Marine Nature Reserves, the proposals for Marine Consultation Areas and the provisions

---

[79] The Convention on the High Seas (Geneva, April 29, 1958), to which the UK is a party, provides that the high seas comprise all seas which are not part of the territorial or inland waters of a state, but this must now be read subject to the provision for the 200-mile exclusive economic zones contained in UNCLOS 1982.

[80] Fishery Limits Act 1976, s. 2.

[81] Environment Committee Report, op. cit., n. 2, paras 111 and 112. Benthic communities are those on the seabed.

[82] Environment Committee Report, op. cit., n. 2, para. 113.

for Special Areas of Conservation under the Habitats Directive.[83] Whether an appropriate balance has yet been struck, however, remains a matter of debate.

In broad terms, regulation can be split into two types: national controls, which affect only the UK fishing fleet, and EU controls, which affect the entire EU fishing fleet. The principal regulatory measures are as follows:

(a) The Inshore Fishing (Scotland) Act 1984, as amended ("the 1984 Act"). This Act regulates fishing within Scottish inshore waters, that is, waters between the mean high-water mark of spring tides and a six nautical mile-limit offshore.[84] It was introduced partly to implement the CFP and partly to deal with conflict between vessels using static and mobile fishing gear respectively, and provides for the making of orders by statutory instrument to regulate various aspects of inshore fishing. In particular, orders may be made regulating fishing for sea fish[85] in any specified area within inshore waters: such orders may prohibit all fishing within the specified area or may prohibit fishing for particular species within that area and/or fishing by a specified method and/or fishing from a specified type of boat or other vehicle and/or fishing by means of a specified description of equipment; an order may also specify particular periods within which a prohibition is effective and any exceptions.[86] A new section 2A was inserted into the 1984 Act by the Environment Act 1995 providing for the making of orders to restrict fishing or prohibit the carriage of specified types of net for marine environmental purposes.[87] The 1984 Act also gives extensive powers to British sea-fishery officers in relation to British fishing boats within British fishery limits.

(b) The Sea Fisheries (Shellfish) Act 1967, as amended. This provides, *inter alia*, for the regulation of fisheries for shellfish, which are defined as including crustaceans and molluscs of any kind.[88] In particular, it provides for the granting of orders for the establishment or improvement, and for the maintainance or regulation, of a fishery for specified

---

[83] The Government's Response to the Second Report from the House of Commons Select Committee on the Environment, op. cit., n. 4, paras 140 and 141. Marine Nature Reserves, Marine Consultation Areas and Special Areas of Conservation and the Habitats Directive are discussed further below. At the time of the Report, Marine Consultation Areas were being proposed in England and Wales, but already existed in Scotland.

[84] 1984 Act, s. 9(1).

[85] Defined as fish of any kind found in the sea, including shellfish, salmon and migratory trout: 1984 Act, s. 9(1).

[86] 1984 Act, s. 1(2). See, eg, the Inshore Fishing (Prohibition of Fishing and Fishing Methods) (Scotland) Order 1989 (SI 1989/2307), as amended; the Inshore Fishing (Salmon and Migratory Trout) (Prohibition of Gill Nets) (Scotland) Order 1986 (SI 1986/59); the Inshore Fishing (Prohibition of Fishing for Cockles) (Scotland) Order 1995 (SI 1995/1373); the Inshore Fishing (Monofilament Gill Nets) (Scotland) Order 1996 (SI 1996/1907).

[87] "Marine environmental purposes" are defined as the purposes of "conserving or enhancing the natural beauty or amenity of marine or coastal areas (including their geological or physiographical features) or of any features of archaeological or historic interest in such areas" and "conserving flora and fauna which are dependent on, or associated with, a marine or coastal environment": see 1984 Act, s. 2A(3)(a) and (b) respectively.

[88] Sea Fisheries (Shellfish) Act 1967, s. 22(2).

kinds of shellfish.[89] Such orders may confer on a person a right of several fishery in respect of the whole fishery (a several order) or a right of regulating a whole fishery (a regulating order) or a right of several fishery in respect of part of a fishery and the right of regulating the remainder.[90] Such orders may be granted in relation to shellfish fisheries in waters up to six nautical miles offshore[91] and the particular area involved will be delineated, and the shellfish species involved specified, in the relevant order. Orders are for a fixed period which may be up to 60 years.[92] Several orders confer on the grantee exclusive rights to the shellfish fishery concerned, including the right to carry out specific operations relating to it,[93] and therefore effectively allow the grantee to stop others from using the seabed for any other reason. Regulating orders confer more limited rights, which may include the right to require others to obtain a licence or to pay tolls or royalties to obtain access to the regulated area to take specific species in accordance with the order.[94] This Act also makes provision for the control of diseases or pests in relation to shellfish fisheries.

(c) The Sea Fisheries (Conservation) Act 1967, as amended. This makes provision for a number of important matters relating to sea fish,[95] including the prescription of size limits for such fish, minimum net sizes, licensing of fishing boats, the trans-shipment of fish from vessel to vessel, restrictions on fishing in certain areas, for specific periods or at certain times of the year, and restrictions on the length of time that a fishing vessel may spend at sea. British sea-fishery officers are given extensive powers of enforcement under this Act. The Act was amended by the Environment Act 1995 to allow the power to restrict fishing to be exercised for marine environmental purposes.[96]

(d) The Sea Fisheries Act 1968, as amended. This is the principal piece of legislation regulating sea fishing operations. British sea-fishery officers are given extensive powers of enforcement under this Act.

(e) The CFP of the EU.[97] The CFP regulates commercial fishing for a variety of species: those of most relevance to Scottish fishermen include cod,

---

[89] Sea Fisheries (Shellfish) Act 1967, s. 1.

[90] Ibid.

[91] Ibid.

[92] Ibid.

[93] Sea Fisheries (Shellfish) Act 1967, s. 2. For an example of a Several Order, see the Camus an Lighe, Loch Ceann Traigh, Argyll, Oysters and Scallops Several Fishery Order 1997 (SI 1997/2711).

[94] Sea Fisheries (Shellfish) Act 1967, s. 2.

[95] This means fish, whether fresh or cured, of any kind found in the sea, including shellfish, but not, except in relation to certain provisions, salmon or migratory trout: Sea Fish (Conservation) Act 1967, s. 22(1).

[96] See Sea Fish (Conservation) Act 1967, s. 5A. The definition of marine environmental purposes, set out in s. 5A, is the same as that contained in s. 2A(3) of the 1984 Act: see n. 87 above.

[97] See, in particular, EC Council Regulation 3760/92, OJ L389, 31/12/92, pp. 1–14, which establishes a Community system for fisheries and aquaculture. For a detailed discussion of the CFP, see M. Holden, *The Common Fisheries Policy* (Fishing News Books, 1994).

haddock, whiting, Nephrops and herring. There are three principal elements of the CFP. The first is the setting of quotas on fish caught: each year, Total Allowable Catches (TACs) are set for each species and split between Member States' fishing fleets. The second is what might be described as technical conservation: regulation of matters such as the type of fishing gear which may be used (for example, the prescription of minimum mesh sizes for nets) and minimum landing sizes. The third is fleet structure: a variety of measures are in place to try to achieve a closer correspondence between fleet capacity and the available catch as limited by the relevant quotas.

In addition, it should be noted that the Sea Fisheries (Wildlife Conservation) Act 1992 requires appropriate Ministers and other specified bodies to have regard to the conservation of marine flora and fauna and to endeavour to achieve a reasonable balance between such conservation and any other considerations to which they are required to have regard when discharging any functions under the Sea Fisheries Acts.[98]

Aquaculture: Fish farming (used here to include shellfish farming unless otherwise stated) may be carried on in inland or marine waters, and different considerations apply in each case. In the case of fish farming in inland waters, the site of the fish farm may be owned by the operator or leased by him from the owner. In either case, planning permission will require to be obtained for the fish farm.[99] In the case of fish farming in marine waters, however, as noted above, the seabed within the limit of territorial waters belongs to the Crown, and the operator will therefore require a lease of the seabed from the Crown Estate Commissioners in so far as the fish farm involves its use; this is so even where the foreshore and/or adjacent land on which the land-based parts of the fish farm will be sited are owned by the operator or leased by him from another.[100] In so far as planning control for marine fish farms is concerned, as noted above, the planning regime extends only so far as the low-water mark. Planning permission for those parts of the fish farm above the low-water mark will therefore be required in the normal way, but those parts of the fish farm below the low-water mark are not subject to planning control. They are subject to a form of planning control in practice, however, because in considering applications for leases for fish-farming, the Crown Estate Commissioners may take into account what are essentially planning and/or environmental factors,[101] and may decide to grant leases only on conditions including conditions which are essentially of a planning and/or environmental nature, thereby exercising a quasi-planning function. Prior to any decision on an application for a lease, however, a non-statutory consul-

---

[98] Sea Fisheries (Wildlife Conservation) Act 1992, s. 1.

[99] Planning law is discussed in detail in Chap. 3. Formerly, certain fish farms would have been permitted development by virtue of the fact that development affecting certain operations on agricultural land is permitted development and the definition of agricultural land formerly extended to certain fish farms, but this is no longer the case.

[100] Ownership of the foreshore is discussed above. Of course, if the foreshore also remains in Crown ownership, a lease of the foreshore will also be required.

[101] See above in the context of the discussion on planning and development.

tation procedure takes place. The application is advertised in the local newspaper and post office and notified to other interested parties such as the local authority, SEPA, SNH, the Royal Yachting Association, the Royal Society for the Protection of Birds, etc. Any comments are then collated. Until recently, the Crown Estate Commissioners would simply have made a decision on the application at that stage, having taken any comments into account and, if appropriate, referred any formal objections made by consultees to the applicant in order to try to resolve the issues giving rise to the objections. As noted above, however, the quasi-planning role of the Crown Estate Commissioners in general has been criticised,[102] they themselves have expressed reservations about this role[103] and the Environment Committee recommended that the quasi-planning functions exercised by the Crown Estate Commissioners be transferred to a more appropriate authority.[104] In relation to fish farming in particular, the Environment Committee recommended that the Government consider bringing fish farming within direct control of the planning authorities as part of the recommended wider review of extending planning controls below the low-water mark.[105] In its response to the Environment Committee Report, the Government stated that it was committed to an evolutionary approach to the relevant arrangements,[106] and at the time of writing, an interim procedure has been adopted whereby the Crown Estate Commissioners, on receipt of the comments of consultees, refer the application and comments to the relevant local authority for a decision. The Crown Estate Commissioners then implement that decision by granting or refusing the lease or granting it subject to conditions as appropriate. It is understood, that the primary legislation necessary to fully transfer control to planning authorities is not likely to be forthcoming in the near future.

There are a number of other matters which affect marine fish farms in particular. Consent for marine fish farms will require to be obtained from the relevant Minister under the provisions of section 34 of the Coast Protection Act 1949, as amended, and such consent may be refused, or granted subject to conditions, where the operation in question causes or is likely to result in obstruction or danger to navigation. Where a marine fish farm is within the jurisdiction of any harbour authority, the consent of the harbour authority may also be required.[107] Marine fish farms in the coastal waters off the Orkney and Shetland Islands require a licence from Orkney or Shetland Islands Council, as appropriate.[108]

Both inland and marine fish farms are also regulated in a number of important ways. The Environmental Assessment (Fish Farming in Marine Waters) Regu-

---

[102] See, eg, the evidence given to the Environment Committee, referred to in Environment Committee Report, op. cit., n. 2, para. 54.

[103] See, eg, Environment Committee Report, supra, n. 2, para. 58.

[104] Environment Committee Report, op. cit., n. 2, para. 54.

[105] Environment Committee Report, op. cit., n. 2, para. 114.

[106] The Government's Response to the Second Report from the House of Commons Select Committee on the Environment, op. cit., n. 4, para. 143.

[107] Harbour authorities are discussed further below. In some cases, such consent may supersede the need for consent under the Coast Protection Act 1949 discussed above: see the Merchant Shipping Act 1988, s. 37.

[108] Orkney County Council Act 1974 and Zetland County Council Act 1974 respectively.

lations 1999[109] make provision for the carrying out of EIAs in relation to fish farms in marine waters in certain circumstances, and consent for the discharge of effluent from fish farms into controlled waters is required from SEPA under the Control of Pollution Act 1974.[110] Furthermore, fish farming businesses must be registered,[111] and there are important statutory provisions for the control of fish diseases.[112]

With regard to shellfish farming in particular, the provisions of the Sea Fisheries (Shellfish) Act 1967 have already been discussed above. It was noted in the Discussion Paper *Scotland's Coasts*[113] that several orders under that Act may be of particular use to the shellfish farming industry in the light of research showing the benefits of growing shellfish on the seabed rather than on suspended ropes. Such orders are not always welcomed, however, by local fishermen, who feel that their own legitimate activities are unfairly restricted by them. A discussion paper on the use of several and regulating orders in Scotland was issued in December 1994 and a public meeting on the issue was held in Inverness in the same year. As a result, a requirement for more detailed information to accompany applications for such orders was introduced, and some legislative changes were also recommended. Two private members bills seeking to implement the recommendations for legislative change were unsuccessfully introduced at Westminster, but it is understood that the necessary legislation is likely to be introduced in the Scottish Parliament in due course.

Conservation, landscape and other designations

There are a number of conservation, landscape and other designations which are relevant to the coastal zone. Many of these are discussed more fully in other chapters: accordingly, the main designations relevant to the coastal zone are considered only briefly here. This is followed by a brief assessment of the overall effect of the various designations.

Sites of Special Scientific Interest: Sites of Special Scientific Interest (hereafter "SSSIs") are areas designated as such under section 28 of the Wildlife and Countryside Act 1981 to protect areas of important flora or fauna or geological or physiographical features. Designation is done by SNH. SSSIs enjoy considerable statutory protections: these are discussed in detail in Chapter 11, to which reference should be made. SSSIs also form the foundation of a number of other conservation designations, discussed further below. However, the designation only affects land above the low-water mark, and consequently, although long stretches of coastline have been designated as SSSIs,[114] and the designation can

---

[109] SI 1999/367.

[110] Control of Pollution Act 1974, s. 34, as amended.

[111] See the Registration of Fish Farming and Shellfish Farming Businesses Order 1985 (SI 1985/1391), as amended.

[112] See the Diseases of Fish Act 1937; the Diseases of Fish Act 1983; the Diseases of Fish (Control) Regulations 1994 (SI 1994/1447) and the Fish Health Regulations 1997 (SI 1997/1881).

[113] *Scotland's Coasts* (Scottish Office, 1996).

[114] See Fig. 1 of the Annex to *Scotland's Coasts*, op. cit., n. 113, which shows, *inter alia*, designated SSSIs in coastal areas.

cover inter-tidal areas,[115] SSSIs have often been seen as of limited use in relation to conservation in coastal areas in particular.[116]

National Nature Reserves: National Nature Reserves (hereafter "NNRs") are areas which are owned or leased by SNH or are subject to a management agreement between SNH and the owner for the purposes of protecting and enhancing nature conservation in the area while allowing public access. NNRs are designated as such by SNH under section 16 of the National Parks and Access to the Countryside Act 1949 and are discussed in detail in Chapter 11, to which reference should be made. All are based on SSSIs and so have the statutory protections applicable to SSSIs,[117] but the limitations in terms of the areas open to designation as SSSIs already discussed apply.[118] Many NNRs do, however, have coastal frontages or are offshore islands.[119]

Local Nature Reserves: Local Nature Reserves (hereafter "LNRs") may be established by local authorities in conjunction with SNH under section 21 of the National Parks and Access to the Countryside Act 1949. They are established for their conservation and amenity value and for public enjoyment of the countryside and are discussed in more detail in Chapter 11, to which reference should be made. Some coastal LNRs have been established.[120]

Marine Nature Reserves: Marine Nature Reserves (hereafter "MNRs") are marine areas designated as such under sections 36 and 37 of the Wildlife and Countryside Act 1981 to protect their marine flora and fauna. The designation extends from the high-tide mark to three miles off the coast[121] and is the only statutory designation which specifically relates to marine areas below the low-water mark, a matter which was of concern to the Environment Committee.[122] MNRs may be protected by byelaws[123] which may, *inter alia*, prohibit or restrict access to the MNR,[124] but byelaws may not, broadly speaking, interfere with rights of navigation.[125] No MNRs have been designated in Scotland, although Loch Sween is currently under consideration for designation. The designation procedure involves a wide range of bodies and extensive consultation and consequently seems to mitigate against the timely and appropriate establishment of MNRs. The Environment Committee felt that MNRs, *inter alia*, had proved to be "unsatisfactory and unworkable"[126] and recommended that the Government consider

---

[115] The inter-tidal mudflats of the Forth and Clyde estuaries, eg, are designated SSSIs: see para. 94 of, and Fig. 1 of the Annex to, *Scotland's Coasts*, op. cit., n. 113.

[116] See, eg, the Environment Committee Report, op. cit., n. 2, para. 102. The problems in relation to SSSIs generally are discussed further in Chap. 11; the problems in relation to the existing conservation and landscape designations in the coastal context in particular are discussed further below.

[117] See above and Chap. 11.

[118] See above.

[119] See para. 96 of, and Figure 1 of the Annex to, *Scotland's Coasts*, op. cit., n. 113.

[120] See Annex to *Scotland's Coasts*, op. cit., n. 113.

[121] Wildlife and Countryside Act 1981, s. 36(1) as amended.

[122] Environment Committee Report, op. cit., n. 2, para. 100.

[123] Wildlife and Countryside Act 1981, s. 37.

[124] Wildlife and Countryside Act 1981, s. 37(2).

[125] Wildlife and Countryside Act 1981, s. 37(3). Rights of navigation are discussed above.

[126] Environment Committee Report, op. cit., n. 2, para. 101.

other options in reviewing marine conservation legislation generally, but this recommendation has not been implemented to date.[127]

Special Protection Areas: Special Protection Areas (hereafter "SPAs") are areas designated as such under Directive 79/409 on the Conservation of Wild Birds ("the Birds Directive") to safeguard the habitats of regularly occurring migrating species of birds and certain other specified rare species of birds. Designation is by the Minister following consultation with SNH and other relevant interests. SPAs are also designated as SSSIs and therefore have the statutory protections applicable to SSSIs,[128] but the limitations in terms of the areas open to designation as SSSIs already discussed apply.[129] SPAs are discussed more fully in Chapter 11, to which reference should be made.

Special Areas of Conservation and Marine Special Areas of Conservation: Special Areas of Conservation (hereafter "SACs") are areas designated as such under Directive 92/43 on the Conservation of Natural Habitats and of Wild Fauna and Flora ("the Habitats Directive"). The Directive requires an international network of SACs to be introduced to conserve various habitats and species that are threatened or rare which, together with the SPAs established under the Birds Directive,[130] will form a European-wide network of sites known as Natura 2000. The designation can be used in the marine environment and marine sites will be known as Marine Special Areas of Conservation (hereafter "MSACs"). The Habitats Directive has been given effect in the UK by the Conservation (Natural Habitats etc.) Regulations 1994[131] and the procedure for designating SACs and MSACs is now underway. A number of areas have been proposed for MSAC status[132] and three such sites are now in the process of setting up at Loch Maddy, Papa Stour and The Vadills. Proposed SACs will generally also be SSSIs, and therefore have the statutory protections applicable to SSSIs,[133] but the limitations in terms of the areas open to designation as SSSIs already discussed apply,[134] so that MSACs will not be protected in this way. SACs generally are discussed more fully in Chapter 11, to which reference should be made.

Ramsar Sites: Ramsar sites are sites designated under the Convention on Wetlands of International Importance Especially as Waterfowl Habitat (the Ramsar Convention) and are discussed in more detail in Chapter 11, to which reference should be made. The designation does not confer any statutory protection, but in practice all Ramsar sites are SSSIs and so have the statutory protections applicable to SSSIs,[135] and they may also be Nature Reserves. It should be noted that under the Convention, designated sites may extend seawards to a depth of six metres,

---

[127] See further below.
[128] See above and Chap. 11.
[129] See discussion of SSSIs above.
[130] See above.
[131] SI 1994/2716.
[132] See *Scotland's Seas and Habitats Directive: Proposed Special Areas of Conservation in the Marine Environment* (Scottish Office, June 1996).
[133] See above and Chap. 11.
[134] See discussion of SSSIs above.
[135] See above and Chap. 11.

but since in practice current Ramsar sites are SSSIs, which do not extend below the low-water mark, they do not in fact extend below the low-water mark.[136]

Areas of Special Conservation: Areas of Special Conservation (hereafter "ASCs") are areas originally designated as bird sanctuaries and now protected under section 3 of the Wildlife and Countryside Act 1981; some are also SSSIs and therefore have the statutory protections applicable to SSSIs.[137] Several small islands are ASCs.[138]

National Scenic Areas: National Scenic Areas (hereafter "NSAs") are areas of outstanding landscape importance as identified by SNH. Appropriate policies for protecting NSAs are set out in development plans and SNH must be consulted on specific categories of development in NSAs. A number of NSAs incorporate part of the coast.[139] NSAs are discussed in more detail in Chapter 3, to which reference should be made.

National Heritage Areas: National Heritage Areas (hereafter "NHAs") are areas designated by the Minister under section 6 of the National Heritage (Scotland) Act 1991 as areas of such outstanding value to the national heritage that special protection measures are justified, and are discussed further in Chapter 3, to which reference should be made. NHAs may include coastal areas, but none have actually been designated to date.

Areas of Great Landscape Value: Areas of Great Landscape Value (hereafter "AGLVs") are areas identified by local authorities in development plans to which appropriate policies apply for the protection of regional or local landscape importance. They may include coastal areas. AGLVs are discussed further in Chapter 3, to which reference should be made.

Marine Consultation Areas: Marine Consultation Areas (hereafter "MCAs") are a non-statutory designation introduced in 1986 to allow consultation on developments likely to have an impact on the marine environment. The Environment Committee felt that MCAs, *inter alia*, had proved to be "unsatisfactory and unworkable"[140] and recommended that the Government consider other options in reviewing marine conservation legislation generally. This recommendation has not been implemented to date.[141]

Environmentally Sensitive Areas: Environmentally Sensitive Areas (hereafter "ESAs") are areas designated by the Minister under section 18 of the Agriculture Act 1986 and in respect of which grants are available to encourage landowners to manage the land in a way which will protect and enhance nature conservation, the landscape and the cultural interest of the land. Some ESAs cover coastal areas.[142]

---

[136] See discussion of SSSIs above.
[137] See discussion of SSSIs above.
[138] See Annex to *Scotland's Coasts*, op. cit., n. 113.
[139] Ibid.
[140] Environment Committee Report, op. cit., n. 2, para. 101.
[141] See further below.
[142] See para. 102 of, and Annex to, *Scotland's Coasts*, op. cit., n. 113.

ESAs are discussed in more detail in Chapters 4 and 11, to which reference should be made.

Regional and Country Parks: Regional and Country Parks are parks established by local authorities under the provisions of section 48 of the Countryside (Scotland) Act 1967 to provide informal outdoor recreation for, and to protect local landscape and amenity for the enjoyment of, the public. Some of these parks incorporate coastal areas. They are discussed in more detail in Chapter 4, to which further reference should be made.

The overall effect of conservation, landscape and other designations: Despite the numerous designations available, there is still concern over whether the coastal zone, particularly the marine element of it, is adequately protected in conservation terms. The Environment Committee noted that there were numerous designations available for the landward side of the coastal zone, but that conservationists were still not satisfied with the degree of protection afforded to the areas concerned; and that the main cause for concern was that there was only one type of statutory designation applicable in marine areas, the MNR, which had been heavily criticised.[143] As noted above, the Environment Committee ultimately concluded that both MNRs and MCAs were unsatisfactory and unworkable and recommended that the Government, in reviewing marine protection legislation generally, explore other approaches, including the concept of integrated Marine Protection Areas.[144] It was concerned that "the conservation of areas below the low-water mark is hampered by the inability of landward designations to straddle the land/sea divide"[145] and recommended that the Government "address the issue of how to link the conservation of land and sea areas, how to protect sites of marine conservation importance and consider as an option extending SSSI-type mechanisms below the low-water mark".[146] Although the introduction of MSACs will go some way to meeting the criticism of the lack of marine-based designations, other criticisms remain and there seems little doubt that a major review of the various designations as they apply to the coastal zone and appropriate action to ensure that it is adequately protected is still required.

Harbours and ports

There are a large number of harbours and ports (the terms may generally be used interchangeably)[147] around Scotland and they vary considerably in size and in the volume and nature of their activities. Almost all are now managed by harbour authorities established under statute (commonly private legislation) and exercising statutory powers.[148] Harbour authorities therefore have an important role

---

[143] Environment Committee Report, op. cit., n. 2, para. 100.

[144] Environment Committee Report, op. cit., n. 2, para. 101.

[145] Environment Committee Report, op. cit., n. 2, para. 102.

[146] Ibid.

[147] For a discussion of the meanings of the respective terms, see *Stair Memorial Encyclopaedia*, Vol. 11, para. 1303.

[148] The common law may remain relevant in some cases, however: see *Stair Memorial Encyclopaedia*, Vol. 11, para. 1301 and paras 1304 *et seq.* for a description of the relevant common law.

to play in management of the coastal zone, although the nature, functions and powers of individual harbour authorities may in fact vary widely. These will now be considered briefly.

Nature of harbour authorities: Harbour authorities are defined by the Merchant Shipping Act 1995 for the purposes of that Act as including "all persons entrusted with the function of constructing, improving, managing, regulating, maintaining or lighting a harbour".[149] They may take a variety of forms, for example, boards, commissioners, trustees, depending on the legislation under which they are established. Provision was made for the privatisation of harbours and ports in the Ports Act 1991, and a number of Scottish ports have now been privatised, for example Forth Ports and Clydeport.

Functions of harbour authorities: The functions of each harbour authority are generally set out in the legislation by which it is established, or may be conferred on it by other legislation.

Powers of harbour authorities: The powers of each harbour authority are also generally set out in the legislation by which it is established, and that legislation must be consulted in every case in order to ascertain the precise powers of the particular harbour authority. It may also be necessary, however, to refer to other legislation. The Harbours, Docks and Piers Clauses Act 1847 ("the 1847 Act"), much of which remains in force, contains a basic set of powers of harbour authorities, and where the statute regulating a harbour expressly incorporates the 1847 Act within it, the harbour authority will have the powers set out therein except to the extent that they are excluded or modified by the incorporating legislation.[150] The Harbours, Piers and Ferries (Scotland) Act 1937 also contains provisions applying to many harbours and piers, although with a number of important exceptions,[151] and the Harbours Act 1964 and the Docks and Harbours Act 1966 contain important provisions relating to a variety of aspects of harbour management. The powers of harbour authorities are generally extensive; they usually include wide powers to make byelaws,[152] by which means a wide variety of activities within the harbour area may be regulated, and where the 1847 Act applies, they include certain compulsory purchase powers. Harbour authorities may not, however, act beyond their express or implied statutory powers.[153] The appropriate Minister has powers under the Harbours

---

[149] s. 313(1).

[150] 1847 Act, s. 1.

[151] Namely the principal ports of the Clyde, the Forth, Aberdeen and Dundee: see Harbours, Piers and Ferries (Scotland) Act 1937, Sched. 3, as amended.

[152] Such powers will generally be conferred in the legislation establishing the harbour authority either directly or through the incorporation of the relevant provisions of the 1847 Act, which contains wide powers relating to the making of byelaws. See also the Harbours, Piers and Ferries (Scotland) Act 1937 where applicable.

[153] *D. and J. Nicol* v *Dundee Harbour Trustees* 1915 SC (HL) 7; see also *Piggins and Rix Ltd* v *Montrose Port Authority* 1995 SLT 418, where it was held that although the powers of a statutory corporation included those which were reasonably incidental to or consequential upon its main purposes, that did not entail an implied power to do whatever appeared to be sensible, convenient and profitable or whatever was consistent with or conducive to the achievement of those purposes.

Development (Scotland) Act 1972 to develop, maintain and manage harbours or to authorise others to do so.

Harbour works may have a significant impact on the coastal zone and as such may be a matter of concern. Where such works occur above the low-water mark, most harbour authorities will be subject to the planning regime in the normal way,[154] but even where the planning regime applies, certain developments are permitted developments[155] and, as noted above, development below the low-water mark falls outwith the planning regime; this has given rise to concern over the apparent lack of external control over harbour works.[156] It should be noted, however, that harbour works may require an EIA even where planning control is not applicable,[157] and consent under section 34 of the Coast Protection Act 1949, as amended and/or a licence under Part II of the Food and Environment Protection Act 1985 may be required. Furthermore, where it is necessary to obtain appropriate powers to carry out any proposed works, the procedures for doing so allow a measure of control to be exercised over the proposed development.[158]

The day-to-day activities carried on in harbours may raise particular environmental concerns, and some of these activities are now specifically regulated. For example, the Dangerous Substances in Harbour Areas Regulations 1987[159] provide for the control of the carriage, loading, unloading and storage of dangerous substances in harbours and harbour areas, and the Merchant Shipping (Port Waste Reception Facilities) Regulations 1997[160] require port authorities to provide adequate reception facilities for ships' waste to which garbage, waste oil and other noxious liquid substances can be offloaded for a charge and also introduce a new requirement for harbour authorities to prepare waste management plans.

Oil and gas

The development of the oil and gas industry has had a major impact on the economy in Scotland and in the UK as a whole. With respect to its impact on the coastal zone in Scotland in particular, it has been said that:

> "[d]espite the huge scale of the operation the effect on the coast of Scotland has been concentrated in relatively few locations. Most of the coastal developments have taken place in the Northern Isles and North East Scotland . . . [s]ome of these developments have been controversial, with

---

[154] Harbour authorities who are Crown bodies, for example, are not subject to the planning regime, although they do in practice follow a procedure which is equivalent to the normal procedure for obtaining planning permission under the planning legislation.

[155] See the Town and Country Planning (General Permitted Development) (Scotland) Order 1992 (SI 1992/223).

[156] Permitted development rights in particular were criticised by a number of those giving evidence to the Environment Committee: see Environment Committee Report, op. cit., n. 2, para. 66.

[157] EIAs are discussed above.

[158] A detailed discussion of these is beyond the scope of this work, but see *Stair Memorial Encyclopaedia*, Vol. 11, paras 1311 *et seq.*

[159] SI 1987/37, as amended.

[160] SI 1997/3018

the main concerns being visible impact and loss of important habitats, and the influx of incomers into existing communities".[161]

Once again, the main issue is one of balancing competing interests, principally those of the economy and the environment, but also those of the oil industry and others using the sea.

The law relating to the exploration for and exploitation of oil and gas is complex, and a detailed description is beyond the scope of this work.[162] In essence, the rights to oil and gas in Great Britain and the territorial sea, and the exclusive right to search and bore for it and to get it are vested in the Crown[163]; with respect to oil and gas situated outwith those areas, the UK has the exclusive right to exploit the natural resources of the UK continental shelf, which include oil and gas.[164] Licences for exploration and production are issued to persons allowing them to explore for and exploit these resources. Licences are applied for in licensing rounds, and relate to particular areas known as blocks. There are different procedures and licensing rounds for estuarine and inland waters on the one hand and offshore waters on the other hand. The licences take the form of bilateral contracts, but in reality are not negotiable, and strict conditions may be imposed, breach of which may lead to revocation of the licence. Any developments resulting from the award of a licence are the subject of a separate consent procedure and in certain cases, an EIA may be required.[165] Developments above the low-water mark will be subject to planning control in the normal way, while those outwith planning control are generally controlled by the imposition of appropriate conditions on the consents necessary for the development to proceed.[166]

One of the main concerns arising from oil and gas exploration and production is that of pollution. Pollution generally is discussed further below. Another concern is the decommissioning of installations when they are no longer required. Detailed provisions on the abandonment of offshore installations are now to be found in Part III of the Petroleum Act 1998.

Marine aggregates

Marine aggregate dredging in the coastal zone may have a significant effect on the coastal environment. At present, such activity is not subject to normal planning control but, like other forms of development involving the seabed, is subject to a form of planning control in practice since it requires permission, in the form of a licence, from the Crown Estate Commissioners as owners of the seabed.[167] Where

---

[161] *Scotland's Coasts*, op. cit., n. 113, para. 34.

[162] For a more detailed description, see *Stair Memorial Encyclopaedia*, Vol. 9, paras 724 *et seq.* and Daintith and Willoughby, *United Kingdom Oil and Gas Law*.

[163] See originally the Petroleum (Production) Act 1934 and now the Petroleum Act 1998.

[164] Continental Shelf Act 1964. This Act gave effect to the Convention on the Continental Shelf (Geneva, April 29, 1958) to which the UK is a party; see now also UNCLOS 1982, to which the UK acceded on July 25, 1997. For a detailed description of the law on the continental shelf, see *Stair Memorial Encyclopaedia*, Vol. 21.

[165] See the Offshore Petroleum Production and Pipe-lines (Assessment of Environmental Effects) Regulations 1999.

[166] In relation to the construction of pipelines, see the Petroleum Act 1998, s. 14.

[167] See further above.

an application is made to the Crown Estate Commissioners for such a licence, they may grant or refuse it in the normal way and, in reaching their decision, may take into account what are essentially planning and/or environmental factors,[168] thereby exercising a quasi-planning function. Prior to any decision on an application for a licence, however, a non-statutory consultation procedure known as Government View takes place. This is a two-stage procedure. The first stage involves the Crown Estate Commissioners consulting informally with those potentially affected by the proposals and instructing the preparation of a professional consultants' report on the potential effects of the proposals on coastal protection issues. The second stage involves the preparation of a report by the Crown Estate Commissioners, which includes a summary of the comments received as a result of the informal consultation and the professional consultants' report and assesses the need for an EIA.[169] A formal application for a licence is then made, accompanied, if appropriate, by an Environmental Statement, and this is passed to government for a Government view. Formal consultation within government then takes place. Following this, the Crown Estate Commissioners make a formal decision on the application in accordance with the Government View.[170] As noted above, the quasi-planning role of the Crown Estate Commissioners in general has been criticised,[171] they themselves have expressed reservations about this role[172] and the Environment Committee recommended that the quasi-planning functions exercised by the Crown Estate Commissioners be transferred to a more appropriate authority.[173] The method of dealing with applications for licences for marine aggregate dredging is, therefore, to be replaced in the near future with a statutory procedure. In 1998, the Government issued for consultation draft Environmental Assessment and Habitats (Extraction of Minerals by Marine Dredging) Regulations which set out a new statutory procedure for licensing marine aggregate dredging and which were designed to implement its obligations under the Environmental Assessment and Habitats Directives in so far as they affected that activity. The Regulations were not, however, brought into force before devolution, and it will now therefore fall to the Scottish Parliament to enact the appropriate legislation for Scotland in due course.

Waste disposal and pollution

Water quality at the coast, as elsewhere, is a matter of major concern, and the disposal of waste at sea and pollution have a considerable impact on this. Concern over water quality generally is not new, but the influence of the EU in particular has led to major changes in the law in this respect. Of particular relevance to the

---

[168] See above in the context of the discussion on planning and development.

[169] EIAs are discussed above.

[170] It was noted in the Environment Committee Report, op. cit., n. 2, that the Crown Estate does not issue a licence if there is a negative Government View, and accepts in every case any conditions contained in a favourable View by incorporating them into the licence: Environment Committee Report, para. 56.

[171] See, eg, the evidence given to the Environment Committee, referred to in the Environment Committee Report, op. cit., n. 2, para. 54.

[172] See, eg, Environment Committee Report, op. cit., n. 2, para. 58.

[173] Environment Committee Report, op. cit., n. 2, para. 54.

coast in this context are Directive 76/160 on the quality of bathing water (hereafter "the Bathing Water Directive"), which sets quality standards for bathing waters and requires improvements where these are not met, and Directive 91/271 on urban waste water treatment (hereafter "the Urban Waste Water Directive"), which sets requirements for the provision of treatment of urban waste water according to the size of the discharge and the nature and type of the receiving waters in relation to the period to 2005. This section outlines the main provisions relating to the control of disposal of waste at sea and of pollution; reference should also be made to Chapter 4, which discusses in detail water pollution generally.

The common law: A common law action for nuisance or negligence may be available in respect of pollution or the effects of pollution in appropriate circumstances. The utility of such actions in controlling pollution, however, is probably minimal,[174] particularly in the coastal zone.

The Control of Pollution Act 1974: This Act is the principal means of controlling water pollution generally; it controls the discharge of pollutants into "controlled waters", which are defined as relevant territorial waters, coastal waters, inland fresh water and groundwater.[175] Discharges into controlled waters are discussed in detail in Chapter 4, to which reference should be made.

The Water (Scotland) Act 1980: This Act makes provision for water authorities to make byelaws, *inter alia*, for preventing contamination of water supplied to them and for prevention of pollution of any surface or underground water which belongs to it or which it is authorised to take.

The Food and Environment Protection Act 1985: This Act replaced the Dumping at Sea Act 1974 and extended the controls imposed by the latter over dumping of waste at sea. In terms of the Act, a licence is required for a wide range of activities connected with the dumping of waste at sea. The dumping of sewage sludge at sea caused particular concerns, and was prohibited from December 31, 1998. The Act also makes provision for regulating the use of pesticides: this is discussed further in Chapter 4, to which reference should be made.

The Environment Protection Act 1990: This Act introduced new, stringent controls on waste production, management and disposal generally. These are discussed further in Chapter 4, to which reference should be made.

The Radioactive Substances Act 1993: Together with licence conditions imposed under the Nuclear Installations Act 1965, this Act provides for the control of disposal of radioactive waste. At an OSPAR meeting in July 1998, Ministers agreed on progressive and substantial reductions of radioactive discharges to the coastal seas by 2020 to close to zero for artificial radioactive substances: such

---

[174] For a discussion of the role of the common law in environmental protection generally, see McKenzie Skene and Rowan-Robinson, "Environmental Protection and the Role of the Common Law: A Scottish Perspective" in J.P. Lowry and R. Edmunds (eds), *Environmental Protection and the Common Law* (Hart Publishing, 1999).

[175] The Control of Pollution Act 1974, s. 30A.

action will help to clean the environment and reduce detrimental effects on flora and fauna, although the accumulated effects of past discharges will continue for many years.

The Urban Waste Water Treatment (Scotland) Regulations 1994[176]: These Regulations implement the Urban Waste Water Treatment Directive, discussed above, in Scotland.

The Merchant Shipping Act 1995: Part VI of the Merchant Shipping Act 1995 consolidates a number of enactments concerning both civil and criminal aspects of marine pollution law. Together with a number of orders and regulations, it makes provision for various aspects of marine pollution and the implementation of a number of international Conventions dealing with oil and other marine pollution.[177] The main orders and regulations dealing with marine pollution are: the Merchant Shipping (Prevention of Oil Pollution) Order 1983[178]; the Merchant Shipping (Prevention and Control of Pollution) Order 1987[179]; the Merchant Shipping (Prevention of Pollution by Garbage) Order 1988[180]; the Merchant Shipping (Prevention and Control of Pollution) Order 1990[181]; the Merchant Shipping (Prevention of Pollution) (Law of the Sea Convention) Order 1996[182]; the Merchant Shipping (Prevention of Pollution: Substances Other than Oil) (Intervention) Order 1997[183]; the Merchant Shipping (Oil Pollution Prepared-ness, Response and Co-operation Convention) Order 1997[184]; the Merchant Shipping (Prevention of Pollution) (Intervention) (Foreign Ships) Order 1997[185]; the Merchant Shipping (Control of Pollution) (SOLAS) Order 1998[186]; the Merchant Shipping (Reporting Requirements for Ships Carrying Dangerous or Polluting Goods) Regulations 1995[187]; the Merchant Shipping (Prevention of Pollution) (Limits) Regulations 1996[188]; the Merchant Shipping (Prevention of Oil Pollution) Regulations 1996[189]; the Merchant Shipping (Dangerous or Noxious Liquid Substances in Bulk) Regulations 1996[190]; the Merchant Shipping (Dan-

---

[176] SI 1994/2842.

[177] These include the International Convention for the Prevention of Pollution of the Sea by Oil (1954), the International Convention relating to Intervention on the High Seas in Cases of Oil Pollution Casualties (1969), the International Convention on Civil Liability for Oil Pollution Damage (1969), the International Convention on the Establishment of an International Fund for Compensation for Oil Pollution Damage (1971), the International Convention for Prevention of Pollution from Ships (1973), the Convention on Civil Liability for Oil Pollution Damage from Offshore Operations (1976), the UN Convention on the Law of the Sea (1982) and the International Convention on Oil Pollution Preparedness, Response and Co-operation (1990).

[178] SI 1983/1106.
[179] SI 1987/470.
[180] SI 1988/2252.
[181] SI 1990/2595.
[182] SI 1996/282.
[183] SI 1997/1869.
[184] SI 1997/2567.
[185] SI 1997/2568.
[186] SI 1998/1500.
[187] SI 1995/2498.
[188] SI 1996/2128.
[189] SI 1996/2154.
[190] SI 1996/3010.

gerous Goods and Marine Pollutants) Regulations 1997[191]; the Merchant Shipping
(Oil Pollution Preparedness, Response and Co-operation Convention) Regulations 1998[192]; and the Merchant Shipping (Prevention of Pollution by Garbage)
Regulations 1998.[193] There are also a series of orders extending specified provisions of Part VI of the Merchant Shipping Act 1995 to certain other countries
and territories.[194]

*The Protection of Water Against Agricultural Nitrate Pollution (Scotland) Regulations
1996*[195]: These Regulations provide for the designation of Nitrate Vulnerable
Zones (hereafter "NVZs") as required by Directive 91/676 concerning the protection of waters against pollution caused by nitrates from agricultural sources.
The only NVZ in Scotland at Balmacolm in Fife has little bearing on the coast,
and although the Ythan Estuary in Aberdeenshire has been suggested by SEPA
as an NVZ, it has not so far been so designated.[196] NVZs are discussed further in
Chapter 4, to which reference should be made.

Coast protection

In general, coastal erosion is not a significant problem in Scotland, and while
there are some areas where it is of concern, the need for coast protection works
is likely to be less, and on a smaller scale, than, for example, in England.[197]
Government policy on coastal protection is "to reduce the risk to life and to the
built and natural environment by encouraging the provision of defences against
flooding, erosion and encroachment by the sea which are technically, environmentally and economically sound and sustainable".[198] The primary role in
protecting land lies with the landowner, but local authorities also have extensive
powers to take appropriate measures for coastal defence. In particular, the Coast
Protection Act 1949 makes special provision for protection of the coast against
erosion and encroachment by the sea. Local authorities any part of whose area
adjoins the sea are designated by the Coast Protection Act 1949 as coast protection
authorities for that area[199] and have a number of powers and duties relating to
protection of the coast. A detailed description of the legislation is beyond the
scope of this text, but a brief outline of the main powers of coast protection
authorities is given here.[200] Briefly, a coast protection authority is empowered to
carry out, either within or outwith its area, coast protection work which is
necessary or expedient for the protection of land in its area, and to enter into

---

[191] SI 1997/2367.
[192] SI 1998/1056.
[193] SI 1998/1377.
[194] eg, the Merchant Shipping (Oil Pollution) (Montserrat) Order 1998 (SI 1998/1262).
[195] SI 1996/1564.
[196] The problems at the Ythan were identified some time ago: see, eg, D. Raffaelli *et al.*, "Long-
term changes in nutrients, weed mats and shorebirds in an estuarine system" (1989) 30 *Cahiers de
Biologie Marine* 259.
[197] See *Scotland's Coasts*, op. cit., n. 113, para. 81.
[198] See *Scotland's Coasts*, op. cit., n. 113, para. 157.
[199] Coast Protection Act 1949, s. 1, as amended by the Local Government (Scotland) Act 1994,
s. 180(1) and Sched. 13, para. 32.
[200] For a more detailed description, see *Stair Memorial Encyclopaedia*, Vol. 25, paras 380 *et seq.* and
Vol. 14, paras 470 *et seq.*

agreements with other persons and to acquire land for these purposes.[201] Compulsory purchase powers are available in respect of land which the coast protection authority has power to acquire for the purposes of coast protection work.[202] Where coast protection work is work other than maintenance or repair work and *either* involves the use of compulsory powers *or* the coast protection authority wishes to recover charges (called coast protection charges) from those benefited by the work, the work must be carried out under a coast protection works scheme, which is subject to confirmation by the appropriate Minister.[203] Otherwise, a coast protection authority may carry out such works after following the procedure specified in the Coast Protection Act 1949.[204] The Coast Protection Act 1949 also contains provisions relating to the repair and maintenance of coast defence works, including provisions relating to the recovery of charges for such works. The carrying out of coast protection works other than maintenance or repair without the consent of the appropriate coast protection authority or in contravention of any condition of any such consent is, with certain exceptions, an offence, and the unauthorised works may be removed by the coast protection authority at the offender's expense.[205] Coast protection authorities also have certain powers to regulate the extraction or excavation of certain materials at the seashore.[206]

Local authorities also have various powers to take action in relation to flooding, principally under the Flood Prevention (Scotland) Act 1961, which may be relevant in the context of coast protection.[207]

Current initiatives relating to management of the coastal zone

In its response to the Environment Committee's Report, the Government stated that it was firmly committed to the effective protection and planning of the coast and was already undertaking a substantial programme of work to achieve this.[208] In the Discussion Paper *Scotland's Coasts* issued in 1996, which also forms part of the Government's response to the Environment Committee's Report, it was stated that the time had come "to take stock" and that it was hoped, *inter alia*, that the paper would lead "to the widest possible consensus on how to formulate sound and sustainable coastal development strategies".[209] Although there may still be some way to go in achieving this, there are a number of current initiatives relating to management of the coastal zone, and this section considers the most important of these.

---

[201] Coast Protection Act 1949, s. 4.

[202] Coast Protection Act 1949, ss 4 and 14.

[203] Coast Protection Act 1949, s. 6. A detailed description of the procedure is beyond the scope of this text, but see *Stair Memorial Encyclopaedia*, Vol. 25, para. 383.

[204] A detailed description of the procedure is beyond the scope of this text, but see *Stair Memorial Encyclopaedia*, Vol. 14, para. 472.

[205] Coast Protection Act 1949, s. 16.

[206] Coast Protection Act 1949, s. 18.

[207] A detailed description of the provisions of this Act is beyond the scope of this text, but see *Stair Memorial Encyclopaedia*, Vol. 25, paras 375 *et seq.* and Vol. 14, paras 459 *et seq.*

[208] The Government's Response to the Second Report from the House of Commons Select Committee on the Environment, op. cit., n. 4, para. 1.

[209] *Scotland's Coasts*, op. cit., n. 113, para. 2.

The Scottish Coastal Forum

The concept of a Scottish Coastal Forum to develop and encourage debate on coastal issues was discussed in *Scotland's Coasts* and such a forum has now been established. Its members represent the broad range of users of the coast and marine environment and it has set in place a workplan to review current coastal planning powers, investigate inshore fisheries management, contribute to the Advisory Group on Sustainable Development, commission an audit of coastal plans, establish a best practise guide for local coastal fora and prepare a Scottish Coastal Strategy. In addition, it will consider marine national parks, local biodiversity action plans and the 2002 review of the Common Fisheries Policy, seek to influence the final arrangements for transfer of planning control of fish farming to local authorities from the Crown Estate and monitor near-shore developments in the oil and gas industry. It is intended to have a significant influence on planning regulation at the coast.

The Firths Initiative

This is an initiative by Scottish Natural Heritage to put in place management strategies for the various firths around the Scottish coast. The plans for each firth are developed through a partnership, or Firth Forum, which includes all the statutory, economic and other interest groups connected with the firth. A number of active partnerships are now in place, including partnerships relating to the Firth of Forth, the Firth of Clyde, the Solway Firth, the Moray Firth and the Cromarty Firth.

The way ahead

There are essentially two types of approach which have consistently been proposed for management of the coast and resolution, so far as possible, of the conflicting pressures affecting it, namely that based on an extension of planning control, and that based on a system of integrated coastal zone management. The wholesale adoption of either of these types of approach has effectively been rejected by the Government.[210] *Scotland's Coasts* proposed instead a more diffuse approach involving, along with specific changes to legislation and procedures seen as necessary from time to time, the establishment of local coastal fora along the lines of the Firths Fora, the establishment of a Scottish Coastal Forum, which has now been done as discussed above, and the publication of further national guidance and advice on key issues. Whether this proves to be a satisfactory approach to the problems of the coastal zone remains to be seen.

---

[210] See, in particular, *Scotland's Coasts*, op. cit., n. 113, paras 186 *et seq.* and 198 *et seq.*

CHAPTER 18

WAYLEAVES[1]

Douglas Cusine
Jeremy Rowan-Robinson

Introduction

Utility wayleaves for such things as pipe-lines and overhead cables impose restrictions on land use. This is particularly the case in the countryside where pipe-lines and cables run for many miles and affect the land through which they run. The utilities having most impact on the Scottish countryside are the bodies engaged in the supply of electricity and water, the transportation of gas and oil, the disposal of sewage and the establishment of a telecommunications network. Their powers are considered in more detail below. There are, however, many other situations in which a right of entry to private land in the countryside to carry out works is conferred by statute on a body exercising public functions. These include land drainage, coast protection, flood prevention, the construction of roads and paths and the haulage of timber.

Rural activity such as agriculture and forestry may have to be adjusted to accommodate utility infrastructure, and although these are the land uses most affected, the impact of utility wayleaves goes wider than that. Gas pipe-lines, for example, have a safety zone which effectively precludes development of the land, not just on top of the pipe-line, but on either side up to a certain distance.

The term "wayleave" is employed loosely here to cover the range of rights obtainable under statutory powers to install pipe-lines, cables and associated works. The precise nature of these rights is examined in more detail below. Utility wayleaves are created under, or under the shadow of, statutory powers. There is a strong public interest dimension in the adequate and efficient supply of gas, electricity, water and in sewage disposal and so on. The utilities are given powers which enable them to ensure that through the creation of wayleaves and other rights they are able to discharge their public duty.

Many of the bodies exercising these statutory powers have been privatised in recent years and the question has been raised whether they should continue to

---

[1] See generally H.W. Wilkinson, *Pipes, Mains, Cables and Sewers* (FT Law & Tax, 6th edn, 1995) for a detailed discussion of this area of the law in England and Wales.

have the benefit of the statutory powers which they enjoyed as public bodies.[2] As companies incorporated under the Companies Act 1985 they will have the power to negotiate whatever arrangements may be necessary to discharge their functions. However, it is recognised that negotiations may not always succeed and that, in the absence of statutory rights, the public interest in the discharge of the service may be frustrated.

The term "wayleave" has been imported into Scots law from England where its original connotation was a money payment in exchange for the use of land for the extraction of minerals.[3] Now it is used loosely in connection with statutory rights which resemble servitudes in that they allow access in general terms to another person's land. They are, however, different in that they are creatures of statute; they do not have both a dominant and servient tenement—only the latter; they permit the statutory operator to do things on the land which, in general, the holder of a servitude right could not do, for example, to construct things on the land; and because the right to enforce them lies with the body and not with the land itself.

Although we have used the term "wayleave" generally to describe these statutory rights, they come in two quite different forms and the terminology can be confusing. First, utilities will commonly be given compulsory purchase powers, including the power to acquire a right in land through the creation of a new right. This power to create a new right is commonly but inaccurately referred to in practice as a "servitude". The exercise of the power in any particular case will be subject to authorisation or confirmation by the Minister. Second, utilities will commonly be given a less formal power simply to install and maintain their infrastructure on, over or under private land, whether this be a cable, pipe or pylon. Provision is generally made in such cases for dispute resolution. This less formal right is commonly referred to in practice as a "wayleave" or "licence" in contra-distinction to the more formal right. Both statutory rights may be employed for the same purpose, for example to secure the installation and use of a pipe-line. The factors determining which right will be employed will vary. Wilkinson notes that a wayleave tends to be personal to the parties and precarious and will not, therefore, run with the land so as to bind successors in title,[4] but as we shall see, this is not always so. There are also differences of procedure and in the measure of compensation which may influence the choice of mechanism. Furthermore, utilities may prefer the comfort of a more formal "servitude" where the arrangement is to be of considerable duration.

The rights described below to instal and use apparatus on private land may be supplemented in statute by other rights, such as powers of entry to inspect, maintain, repair and replace the infrastructure and powers to construct things on land (see below). One preliminary issue is whether, if something is constructed on, or more likely, through the lands of another, there is a right of support. The general position is that if something is constructed on the basis of rights conferred by

---

[2] See B. Denyer-Green, "Specific Purposes, Specific Powers: The Powers of Privatised Utilities" in *Proceedings of the National Symposium, Compulsory Purchase: An Appropriate Power for the 21st Century* (Department of the Environment, Transport and the Regions, 1999).

[3] See *Halsbury's Laws of England*, Vol. 31, "Mines, Minerals and Quarries", para. 228.

[4] H.W. Wilkinson, op. cit., n. 1, Chap. 2.

Parliament and the thing requires support, a right of support will be implied, especially where the construction is for the public benefit.[5]

Although this chapter is given over to a description of these statutory rights, it should be noted that, in practice, most of the utilities operate where possible through the voluntary approach. Arrangements for the installation and use of apparatus are generally concluded through negotiation and the terms will be incorporated into a contract. However, there is no doubt that these negotiations are conducted in the shadow of the statutory rights and that the terms agreed reflect to a large extent what statute would have provided.

The statutory rights available to the principal utilities operating in the countryside are now considered in turn.

Electricity

The Electricity Act 1989 (hereafter "the 1989 Act") privatised the electricity industry. It makes provision for the licensing of public electricity suppliers. There is a duty on such suppliers to develop and maintain an efficient, co-ordinated and economical system of electricity supply.[6]

To assist in the discharge of this duty, the 1989 Act makes provision for the compulsory purchase of rights in land, including the acquisition of a right by the creation of a new right.[7] The standard compulsory purchase procedure set out in the Acquisition of Land (Authorisation Procedure) (Scotland) Act 1947 is applied, with minor modifications, to the acquisition of such a right.[8] This involves:

- preparation of the order;
- notice to owners, lessees and occupiers of the making of the order;
- public advertisement of the making of the order;
- submission of the order for authorisation of the Minister;
- the opportunity for objection;
- a right to be heard in support of the objection;
- notice to owners, lessees and occupiers of the confirmation of the order (if confirmed);
- public notice of confirmation of the order (if confirmed).[9]

The 1989 Act makes provision for compensation for the creation of a new right.[10] It applies section 61 of the Lands Clauses Consolidation (Scotland) Act 1845, as amended, in this respect.[11] In its amended form this reads:

---

[5] *London & North Western Ry* v *Evans* [1893] 1 Ch 16; approved in *Edinburgh & District Water Trs* v *Clippens Oil Co.* (1903) 6 F (HL) 7 and followed in *Midlothian C.C.* v *National Coal Board* 1960 SC 308.

[6] 1989 Act, s. 9(1).

[7] Ibid, s. 10 and Sched. 3, para. 1(2).

[8] Ibid, s. 10, Sched. 3, Pt III, para. 16.

[9] 1947 Act, First Schedule.

[10] See the 1989 Act, Sched. 3, Pt III, paras 25 and 29. See too N. Hutchison, A. Cameron and J. Rowan-Robinson, "Assessing the compensation for electricity wayleaves" (1999) 17 *Journal of Property Investment and Finance* 2, p. 176.

[11] As substituted by the 1989 Act, Sched. 3, Pt III, para. 24.

"In estimating the purchase money or compensation to be paid by the licence holder under the special Act, in any of the cases aforesaid, regard shall be had not only to the extent (if any) to which the value of the land over which the right is to be acquired is depreciated by the acquisition of the right, but also to the damage (if any) to be sustained by the owner of the land by reason of its severance from other land of his, or injuriously affecting that other land by the exercise of the powers conferred by this or the special Act."

This identifies two heads of claim: depreciation in the value of the land in, on or over which the apparatus is to be laid, including any lost development potential; and severance and other injurious affection. Any value attributable to the scheme of the electricity supplier would be ignored on the basis of the rule in *Pointe Gourde*.[12] Disturbance would seem to be payable, if incurred, on the basis that disturbance is part of the value of the land to the owner.[13]

In addition to the power for the compulsory creation of a new right in land, the 1989 Act also makes provision for an application to the Minister for the grant of a wayleave where this cannot be secured by agreement.[14] The procedural steps are as follows:

- the electricity supplier must be satisfied that it is necessary or expedient to install and keep installed an electric line on, over, etc., land;
- the owner or occupier of the land must be given notice requesting the grant of a wayleave in appropriate terms within a specified period (minimum of 21 days);
- the owner or occupier must fail to grant the wayleave or must grant it subject to terms and conditions which are not acceptable to the electricity supplier;
- the electricity supplier applies to the Minister for the grant of the necessary wayleave on acceptable terms and conditions;
- the Minister will afford the owner and occupier an opportunity of being heard in connection with the application;
- the Minister will make a decision on the application;
- if granted, the wayleave will run for whatever period is stipulated.

Such a wayleave may be for the installation of a line and for the inspection, maintenance, adjustment, repair, alteration, replacement and removal of a line. The right to instal a line includes the incidental right to place support for such a line.[15] A wayleave granted by the Minister will, for its duration, bind any person who is at any time the owner or occupier of the land over which it is granted.

The 1989 Act makes provision for compensation for the grant by the Minister of a wayleave (the Act expressly uses that term).[16] It provides that the occupier

---

[12] *Pointe Gourde Quarrying and Transport Co.* v *Sub-Intendent of Crown Lands* [1947] AC 565.
[13] *Commissioners of Inland Revenue* v *Glasgow and South-Western Ry* (1887) 14 R (HL) 33.
[14] 1989 Act, s. 10 and Sched. 4, para. 6.
[15] 1989 Act, s. 64(1).
[16] 1989 Act, Sched. 4, para. 7.

and the owner (if the occupier is not the owner) may recover compensation from the electricity supplier in respect of the grant. The owner or occupier may also recover for any damage caused to land or moveables arising from the exercise of the right granted and for disturbance. The normal rules for assessing compensation for compulsory purchase set out in section 12(1) of the Land Compensation (Scotland) Act 1963 are not applied. The compensation may be paid as a lump sum or as a periodical payment or partly one way and partly the other. Disputes over compensation are to be determined by the Lands Tribunal for Scotland.

The electricity suppliers have negotiated rates of payment for wayleaves with the Scottish Landowners Federation and the National Farmers Union for Scotland, representing the people most affected by the installation of electricity apparatus.

Gas

Three bodies are involved in the supply of gas: the public gas transporter (PGT) who is responsible for providing and operating the pipe-line system through which gas is delivered, the public gas shipper who arranges with the transporter for gas to be moved through a pipe-line system, and the public gas supplier who sells piped gas to the customer. This note focuses on the PGT as the body most affecting the countryside. The principal PGT at the time of writing is Transco.

The Gas Act 1995 imposes a duty on a PGT to develop and maintain an efficient and economical pipe-line system for the conveyance of gas.[17] To assist in the discharge of this duty, a PGT is given power to acquire land compulsorily, including the acquisition of a right by the creation of a new right.[18] The exercise of the right requires the authorisation of the Minister. The procedure for exercising the right is set out in the Acquisition of Land (Authorisation Procedure) (Scotland) Act 1947.[19] The procedure for the compulsory purchase of land is slightly, but not significantly, modified for the compulsory creation of a new right.[20] The procedure is described above in the context of the section on "Electricity". Where a pipe is laid through someone else's ground, there may be an entitlement to support,[21] and if so, there will be liability for wrongful withdrawal of that support[22] and an entitlement to compensation.[23]

The compensation arrangements for the creation of a new right on, over or under land are also the same as for "Electricity" with the principal measure of compensation being set out in a slightly modified version of section 61 of the Lands Clauses Consolidation (Scotland) Act 1845.[24]

---

[17] Gas Act 1986, s. 9, as substituted by the Gas Act 1995, Sched. 3, para. 3.

[18] s. 9(3) and Sched. 3, Pt III, para. 1 to the Gas Act 1986, as amended by the Gas Act 1995, Sched. 3, para. 56.

[19] 1986 Act, Sched. 3, Pt III, paras 14–27, as amended by the 1995 Act, Sched. 3, para. 56.

[20] Acquisition of Land (Authorisation Procedure) (Scotland) Act 1947 and the 1986 Act, Sched. 3, Pt III.

[21] W.M. Gordon, *Scottish Land Law* (Scottish Universities Law Institute, 1989), paras 7–64 to 7–66; *Stair Memorial Encyclopaedia*, Vol. 18, paras 281 and 341.

[22] *Mid & East Calder Gas Light Co.* v *Oakbank Oil Co. Ltd* (1891) 18 R 788.

[23] For coal workings this is governed by the Coal Mining Subsidence Act 1991.

[24] Gas Act 1986, Sched. 3, para. 24.

Unlike electricity, there is no separate provision in the Gas Acts of 1986 and 1995 for the compulsory creation of wayleaves, although there is provision for the installation by the PGT of pipes in streets.[25]

Water supply and sewage disposal

Unlike the position in England and Wales, water supply and sewage disposal are services which in Scotland remain in the public sector. However, they were taken out of the hands of local government by the Local Government etc. (Scotland) Act 1994 (hereafter "the 1994 Act") and given to three appointed water authorities. Section 1 of the Sewerage (Scotland) Act 1968 (hereafter "the 1968 Act") imposes a general duty on the authorities to provide such public sewers as may be necessary for effectively draining their area of domestic sewage, surface water and trade effluent. Section 6 of the Water (Scotland) Act 1980 (hereafter "the 1980 Act") requires the authorities to provide a supply of wholesome water to every part of their limits of supply where a supply of water is required for domestic purposes and can be provided at a reasonable cost. Section 9 of the 1980 Act deals with the supply for non-domestic purposes.

To discharge these duties, water authorities are given power in section 98 of the 1994 Act to acquire land by agreement. Provision for the compulsory purchase of land is made in section 99 of that Act although no mention is made of acquiring a right by the creation of a new right.[26] The procedure set out in the Acquisition of Land (Authorisation Procedure) (Scotland) Act 1947 is applied to the exercise of compulsory purchase powers[27] and an entitlement to compensation arises.[28]

Water authorities are also given specific powers to lay pipes. Section 3 of the 1968 Act gives an authority power to lay a public sewer in private land, but subject to the prior service of a notice on the owner and occupier of the land. Section 3A of that Act allows an authority to authorise some other person to exercise the same power. There is an opportunity for objection within two months of the notice to the laying of the pipe and the authority must obtain the consent of the sheriff before proceeding. Section 20 of the 1968 Act makes provision for compensation for any loss, injury or damage sustained by any person by reason of the exercise of this power. Any disputes are to be settled by arbitration.[29]

Similarly, under the section 23 of the 1980 Act, water authorities are given power to lay a main in private land after first giving reasonable notice to the owner and occupier. Until the 1994 Act came into force, there was no provision for objection and for the resolution of disputes. That is still the position in England and Wales.[30] However, section 23(1A) of the 1980 Act[31] provides that, if within two months of the giving of notice, the owner or occupier objects, the authority cannot proceed but must refer the matter by summary application to the sheriff

---

[25] 1986 Act, Sched. 4, para. 1.
[26] See too s. 19 of the Sewerage (Scotland) Act 1968.
[27] See "Electricity" above.
[28] 1947 Act, s. 1(3), as amended.
[29] See the long-running litigation *Edinburgh & District Water Trustees* v *Clippens Oil Co. Ltd* (1898) 25 R 370; (1900) 3 F 156; (1903) 6 F (HL) 7.
[30] Water Industry Act 1991, s. 159.
[31] Introduced by s. 109 of the 1994 Act.

whose decision on the matter will be final. In *Central Regional Council v Ferns*[32] Lord Kincraig described the rights to lay a water main and maintain it as "similar to, if not identical with, those of a servitude of *aquaeductus* in which the Board is the dominant owner and the proprietors of the land the owners of the servient tenement".[33] Again, if there is a right to support, removal of this will entitle the relevant authority to damages. Section 23(2) makes provision for compensation for any damage done to or injurious affection of the land resulting from the laying of the main. Disputes are to be settled by arbitration.

Telecommunications

The Telecommunications Act 1984 (hereafter "the 1984 Act") privatised the operation of telecommunications systems. It provides for the operation of such systems by licensed public telecommunications operators (PTOs). The 1984 Act imposes no direct specific public duties on PTOs. There is, nonetheless, a public interest dimension in the provision of telecommunication services; indeed, the Telecommunications Code (below) refers to the "principle" that no person should be unreasonably denied access to a telecommunications system.[34]

The 1984 Act provides for the compulsory acquisition of land by PTOs for telecommunications purposes, including the acquisition of a right by the creation of a new right.[35] The procedure in the Acquisition of Land (Authorisation Procedure) (Scotland) Act 1947 is applied and an entitlement to compensation arises.[36]

Section 10 of and Schedule 2 to the 1984 Act sets out a "Telecommunications Code". Amongst other things, the Code deals with the arrangements for the execution of works on private land. Paragraph 2 of the Code provides that the agreement in writing of the occupier of the land must be obtained to confer on a PTO a right (in effect a wayleave) to carry out works for telecommunications purposes on that land. The right includes the installation of lines to connect to the telecommunications apparatus.[37] Paragraph 2 also deals with the extent to which an owner is bound by such agreement if the owner is not the occupier. Anything done by a PTO in exercise of such a right is deemed to be done in exercise of statutory powers.[38]

Normally, the PTO will give notice to the occupier of what is required. If after 28 days the required agreement in writing has not been given by the occupier, the PTO may apply to the sheriff for an order conferring the proposed right and dispensing with the need for the agreement of the person.[39] The sheriff is to make an order only if he is satisfied that any prejudice caused by such an order is (a) capable of being "adequately" compensated for by money (below); or (b) the prejudice is outweighed by the benefit accruing from the order to the persons

---

[32] 1979 SC 136.
[33] Ibid, at 139.
[34] 1984 Act, Sched. 2, para. 5(3). It should be noted that public duties will be imposed on PTOs through the licence.
[35] 1984 Act, s. 35.
[36] 1947 Act, s. 1(3), as amended.
[37] para. 10.
[38] para. 4(1).
[39] para. 5.

whose access to a telecommunication system will be secured by the order. The Code provides that, in determining the extent of prejudice, the sheriff is to have regard to all the circumstances and to the principle that no person should unreasonably be denied access to a telecommunication system. The order may include such terms and conditions as appear to the court appropriate for ensuring that the least possible damage is caused by the exercise of the right.

The compensation provisions for the wayleave granted under the Code are unusual. For wayleaves granted by agreement, paragraph 4(4) of the Code provides that where the right causes depreciation in the value of an interest in land, compensation equal to the amount of the depreciation is to be paid. Any dispute is to be determined by the Lands Tribunal for Scotland. Rules (2)–(4) of section 12 of the Land Compensation (Scotland) Act 1963 are applied in determining the extent depreciation. However, where an agreement is dispensed with, the court will fix the terms and conditions governing the right, including the financial terms. The financial terms will include such payment, reflecting consideration for the "agreement" or the exercise of rights, as appears to the court would have been fair and reasonable if the agreement had been given willingly.[40]

The compensation will also include recompense for any loss or damage sustained in consequence of the exercise of the right.[41] In addition, regard is to be had to the prejudicial effect, if any, of the order or the exercise of the right on the claimant's enjoyment of land other than that in relation to which the right is conferred.[42]

Oil

It will be clear from what has been said so far in this chapter that public and private bodies exercising public functions have the benefit of statutory powers to instal the infrastructure necessary for the discharge of these functions. Private bodies carrying on their day-to-day activities enjoy no such benefit and must rely on negotiation with owners and occupiers or must attempt to promote private legislation. However, these activities may sometimes have a public interest dimension. For example, the efficient distribution of oil by pipe-line throughout the UK could be regarded as just as much in the public interest as the distribution of gas (see above). This was recognised with the introduction of the Pipe-lines Act 1962 (hereafter "the 1962 Act"). This provides a means by which private industry, including the oil industry, can secure authorisation for the installation of a commercial pipe-line. It empowers the Minister in response to a request from industry to make a compulsory purchase order or a compulsory rights order to enable pipe-line works to proceed. The oil industry has relied quite extensively on the powers in the 1962 Act to instal a network of pipe-lines in the UK.

The 1962 Act applies to pipes on land. This includes the landfall section of an offshore pipe-line. The 1962 Act distinguishes "cross country pipe-lines" (those

---

[40] As to the implications of this see *Mercury Communications Ltd* v *London and India Dock Investments Ltd* [1994] 1 EGLR 229.

[41] para. 7(1).

[42] para. 7(2).

exceeding or intending to exceed 10 miles in length)[43] from "local pipe-lines" (those up to 10 miles in length). Section 1 of the Act provides that a cross-country pipe-line is not to be constructed without a pipe-line authorisation from the Minister. The purpose of the authorisation procedure is to establish the case for the pipe-line, the route to be followed and the specification; it does not confer any rights in, over or under the land. The negotiation of the necessary wayleave is a separate matter (see below). A local pipe-line is subject to planning control in the normal way (see Chapter 3). Again, the grant of planning permission confers no right with regard to the land; the negotiation of the wayleave is a separate matter (see below).

The statutory procedure for obtaining an authorisation involves consultation with appropriate bodies, public notice, an opportunity for objections and the holding of a public inquiry into unresolved objections.[44] An environmental statement will be required where the proposed development is considered likely to have a significant effect on the environment by virtue of factors such as its nature, size and location.[45] Publicity must be given to any such statement and no authorisation may be granted unless the Minister has first taken the environmental information into consideration.[46] The planning authority will generally be consulted about appropriate conditions to attach to an authorisation. The Minister may regulate the size of the pipe-line and may require that it be offered for use by others in order to avoid unnecessary duplication. Planning permission will generally be deemed to be granted for any works covered by an authorisation.

Negotiations for the necessary wayleave(s) for the pipe-line will proceed separately to the authorisation or planning permission processes. If negotiations fail, a person wishing to instal a pipe-line may apply to the Minister for a compulsory purchase order[47] or a compulsory rights order[48] to enable installation to take place and the use of the pipe-line to commence. The Acquisition of Land (Authorisation Procedure) (Scotland) Act 1947 is applied to a compulsory purchase order promoted under the 1962 Act. In the event of unresolved objection to a proposal to make a compulsory purchase order or a compulsory rights order, a public inquiry will be held.[49] A compulsory rights order may be granted subject to conditions.[50]

The normal Land Compensation Act Rules apply to the assessment of compensation arising from a compulsory purchase order under the 1962 Act. Section

---

[43] 1962 Act, s. 66(1). The Pipe-lines (Metrication) Regulations 1992 (SI 1992/449) substitutes 16.093 kilometres for 10 miles.

[44] See generally DTI, "Guidance Notes for Applications and Notifications for Onshore Pipe-lines" (HMSO, 1993). As regards public inquiries see the Pipe-lines (Inquiries Procedure) Rules 1995 (SI 1995/1239), as amended by the Electricity Generating Stations and Overhead Lines and Pipe-lines (Inquiries Procedure) (Amendment) Rules 1997 (SI 1997/712).

[45] Electricity and Pipe-lines Works (Assessment of Environmental Effects) Regulations 1990 (SI 1990 442), as amended by the Electricity and Pipe-lines Works (Assessment of Environmental Effects) (Amendment) Regulations 1996 (SI 1996/422).

[46] Ibid, reg. 7.

[47] 1962 Act, s. 11.

[48] Ibid, s. 12.

[49] The inquiry will be conducted under the Pipe-lines (Inquiries Procedure) Rules 1995 (SI 1995/1239), as amended, op. cit., n. 45.

[50] 1962 Act, s. 13.

14 of the 1962 Act makes provision for compensation for a compulsory rights order. The compensation will equal the amount of any depreciation in the value of an interest in land in consequence of the making of the order.[51] Compensation must also be paid for any damage or disturbance arising from the exercise of any right conferred by such an order.[52]

In practice, resort to compulsory powers to obtain the necessary right is rarely required. No doubt the existence of such powers in the background facilitates the negotiation process.

Supplementary rights

Implied powers

There are English[53] and Scottish[54] cases on the issue of the extent of the rights acquired under compulsory powers. The general rule in both countries is that additional rights, such as a right of access, will not readily be implied, because the rights to the land are being compulsorily acquired. However, in one case, additional rights were implied where land was so acquired because both parties knew that it was to be made into a railway depot. A road had been formed in respect of which adjoining feuars had been given servitude rights. A jury had awarded compensation on the basis of the existence of a right of access and it was held that the right of access over the road was implied.[55] It has, however, been held that where land is acquired compulsorily, and there are additional rights which are necessary for the operation of the original right, such as a right to maintain, the person whose land is being acquired cannot be compelled to grant a servitude in respect of these additional rights,[56] because the statute had dealt with the matter in great detail and had not contemplated that an express servitude would be granted.

Powers of construction

Many of the statutes considered above give bodies power to construct works on, over or under a person's land. In earlier times, one of the most significant powers was that given to the railway companies in the middle of the nineteenth century to construct railway lines.[57] Although the construction of a new railway line is unlikely today, the powers associated with the initial construction will still remain, for example, the power to inspect and to carry out repairs and reconstruction. It has been held that the installation of iron pipes alongside existing clay pipes was a repair and not something to which the landowner could object as being beyond the statutory powers.[58] In England, it has been held that where a

---

[51] Ibid, s. 14(1).

[52] Ibid, s. 14(2).

[53] *Central Electricity Generating Board* v *Jennaway* [1959] 1 WLR 937; *Sovmots Investments* v *Secretary of State for the Environment* [1979] AC 144.

[54] *Maule* v *Moncrieffe* (1846) 5 Bell 333; *Baxter* v *North British Ry Co.* (1846) 8 D 1212; *Scott* v *Edinburgh, Leith & Granton Ry Co.* (1848) 11 D 91; *Mercer* v *Esk Valley Ry Co.* (1867) 5 M 1024.

[55] *Scott* v *Edinburgh, Leith & Granton Ry Co.*, op. cit., n. 51.

[56] *Mackenzie* v *Gillanders* (1870) 7 SLR 333.

[57] See the Railways Clauses Consolidation (Scotland) Act 1845 and the private legislation modelled on that Act.

[58] *Bridges* v *Police Commissioners of Fraserburgh* (1887) 25 SLR 151.

wayleave is obtained under statutory powers, that implies authority to construct such ancillary works as are required to make the initial right effectual[59]; and that should be the position in Scotland also. The fact that a right is conferred by statute does not, however, entitle the acquirer to a written deed of servitude.[60]

---

[59] *Central Electricity Generating Board* v *Jennaway* [1959] 1 WLR 937.
[60] Cf. *Mackenzie* v *Gillanders* (1870) 7 SLR 333.

BIBLIOGRAPHY

Chapter 1 : Introduction

Callender, R., *How Scotland is Owned* (Canongate, 1998)

Gordon, W.M., *Scottish Land Law* (Scottish Universities Law Institute, 1989)

Lloyd, M.G. and Shucksmith, D.M., "Economic development and land policies in the Highlands and Islands of Scotland", 1985 2 *Land Use Policy* 114

Land Reform Policy Group, *Identifying the Problems* (Scottish Office, 1998)

Land Reform Policy Group, *Identifying the Solutions* (Scottish Office, 1998)

Land Reform Policy Group, *Recommendations for Action* (Scottish Office, 1999)

Mackay, D., *Scotland's Rural Land Use Agencies* (Scottish Cultural Press, 1995)

McKenzie Skene, D., Rowan-Robinson, J., Paisley, R. and Cusine, D., "Stewardship: From Rhetoric to Reality", 1999 *Edinburgh Law Review* 151

Pearce, D., Turner, R., O'Riordan, T., Adger, N., Brisson, I., Brown, K., Durborg, R., Frank-Hauser, S., Jordan, A., Maddison, D., Moran, D. and Powell, J., *Blue Print 3* (Earthscan, 1993)

Rodgers, C. and Bishop, J., *Management Agreements for Promoting Nature Conservation* (RICS, 1998)

Ross, A., and Rowan-Robinson, J., "Behind Closed Doors: The Use of Agreements in the UK to Protect the Environment", 1999 1(2) *Environmental Law Review* 82

Scottish Executive, *Land Reform: Proposals for Legislation* (Stationery Office, 1999)

Scottish Law Commission, *Discussion Paper on Real Burdens*, No. 106, 1998

Scottish Law Commission, *Discussion Paper on Real Burdens*, No. 106, 1998

Scottish Law Commission, *Report on the Abolition of the Feudal System*, No. 168, 1999

Scottish Natural Heritage, *Access to the Countryside for Open-air Recreation*, 1999

Scottish Natural Heritage, *National Parks for Scotland*, 1999

Scottish Office, *Towards a Development Strategy for Rural Scotland: The Framework*, 1998

Scottish Office, *Natural Heritage Designations in Scotland* (Scottish Office, 1998)

Scottish Office, *People and Nature*, 1998

Select Committee on Scottish Affairs, *Land Resource Use in Scotland*, Session 1971–72 (HMSO, 1972)

Wightman, A., *Who Owns Scotland* (Canongate, 1996)

Chapter 2 : The Institutional Framework

Harlow, C., and Rawlings, R., *Law and Administration* (Butterworths, 2nd edn, 1997)

HMSO, *A Better Quality of Life—a strategy for sustainable development in the UK*, Cm. 4345, 1999

Kramer, L., "The Implementation of Community Environmental Directives with Member States: Some Implications of the Direct Effect Doctrine" [1991] 3 *JEL* 39

Mackay, D., *Scotland's Rural Land Use Agencies* (Scottish Cultural Press, 1995)

Rodgers, C., "Environmental Gain, Set-aside and the Implementation of EU Agricultural Policy in the United Kingdom" in *Nature Conservation and Countryside Law* (C. Rodgers, ed., University of Wales Press, 1996), Chap. 5

Rowan-Robinson, J., "Heads I win, tails you lose: Cameron v Nature Conservancy Council" (1994) 34 *Scottish Planning Law and Practice* 10–13

Select Committee on Scottish Affairs, *Land Resource Use in Scotland*, Session 1971–72 (HMSO, 1972)

Chapter 3 : Development in the Countryside

Carnwath, R., *Enforcing Planning Control* (HMSO, 1989)

Collar, N., *Planning* (W. Green/Sweet & Maxwell, 2nd edn, 1999)

McAllister, A. and McMaster, R., *Scottish Planning Law* (Butterworths, 2nd edn, 1999)

The Hon. Lord Osborne, "Planning Conditions" in the *Scottish Planning Encyclopedia* (the Hon. Lord Gill, ed., W. Green/Sweet & Maxwell)

The Hon. Lord Reid, "Judicial Review" in the *Scottish Planning Encyclopedia* (the Hon. Lord Gill, ed., W. Green/Sweet & Maxwell)

Reid, C.T., "Failure to Exhaust Statutory Remedies", 1984 *Juridical Review* 185

Rowan-Robinson, J. and Durman, R., *Section 50 Agreements* (Scottish Office, 1992)

Rowan-Robinson, J. and Young, E., "Enforcement—The Weakest Link in the Scottish Planning Control System", 1987 8 *Urban Law and Policy* 255

Scottish Natural Heritage, *National Scenic Areas: A Consultation Paper*, 1999

Scottish Planning Encyclopedia (the Hon. Lord Gill, ed., W. Green/Sweet & Maxwell)

Select Committee on Scottish Affairs, *Land Resource Use in Scotland*, Session 1971–72 (HMSO, 1972)

Young, E. and Rowan-Robinson, J., *Scottish Planning Law and Procedure* (W. Hodge, 1985)

Chapter 4 : Environmental Controls

Agenda 2000 for a Stronger and Wider Union, Com. (97) 2000 final, July 15th, 1997

Blackhurst, J. and Payne, M., *Agricultural Pollution* (Sweet & Maxwell, 1997)

Hawke, N. and Kovaleva, N., *Agri-Environmental Law and Policy* (Cavendish Publishing Ltd, 1998)

Lennon, A., "Set-aside of Agricultural Land: Policy, Practice and Problems" in *Agriculture, Conservation and Land Use* (W. Howarth and C. Rodgers, eds, University of Wales Press, 1993)

Reid, C.T. (ed.), *Environmental Law in Scotland* (W. Green/Sweet & Maxwell, 2nd edn, 1997)

Rodgers, C., *Agricultural Law* (Butterworths, 2nd edn, 1998)

Rodgers, C., "Environmental Gain, Set-aside and the Implementation of EU Agricultural Reform in the United Kingdom" in *Nature Conservation and Countryside Law* (C. Rodgers, ed., University of Wales Press, 1996)

Scottish Office Agriculture, Environment and Fisheries Department, *Countryside Premium Scheme*, 1998

Smith, C., Collar, N. and Poustie, M., *Pollution Control: The Law in Scotland* (T & T Clark, 1997)

Chapter 5 : Agriculture

Sir Crispin Agnew of Lochnaw, *Agricultural Law in Scotland* (Butterworths, 1996)

The Hon. Lord Gill, *The Law of Agricultural Holdings in Scotland* (W. Green, 3rd edn, 1997)

Land Reform Policy Group, *Recommendations for Action*, 1999

Murray, J., Scott Robinson, S. and Usher, J.A., "Agriculture" in *Stair Memorial Encyclopaedia*, Vol. 1

The Scottish Office, *The Integrated Administration and Control System*, 1998

Chapter 6 : Crofting

Cameron, E.A., *Land for the People* (Tuckwell Press, 1996)

Day, J.P., *Public Administration in the Highlands and Islands of Scotland* (LUP, 1918)

Grassie, J., *Highland Experiment* (AUP, 1983)

Graham, K.H.R., *Scottish Land Court—Practice and Procedure* (Butterworths, 1993)

Hunter, J., *The Making of the Crofting Community* (John Donald, 1976)

Hunter. J., *The Claim of Crofting —The Scottish Highlands and Islands, 1930–1990* (Mainstream, 1991)

HMSO, *Report of the Commission of Enquiry into Crofting Conditions*, Cmnd. 9091, 1954

Land Reform Policy Group, *Recommendations for Action*, 1999

MacCuish, D.J., "The Case for Converting Crofting Tenure to Ownership", 1969–70 *TGSI* 89

MacCuish, D.J. and Flyn, D., *Crofting Law* (Butterworths/Law Society of Scotland, 1990)

Macphail, I.M., *The Crofters War* (Acair, 1989)

Scott Robinson, S., "Crofting and Smallholdings" in *Stair Memorial Encyclopaedia*, Vol. 1

Chapter 7 : Forestry

Sustainable Forestry: The UK Programme (Cm. 2429, 1994)

The UK Forestry Standard: The Government's Approach to Sustainable Forestry, Forestry Commission (Edinburgh, 1998)

Reid, C., *Nature Conservation Law* (W. Green/Sweet & Maxwell, Edinburgh, 1994), Chap. 6

Reid, C., "Forestry, the Law and the Environment" in *Nature Conservation and Countryside Law* (C. Rodgers, ed., University of Wales Press, 1996)

Reid, C., "The Changing Pattern of Environmental Regulation: British Forestry and the Environmental Agenda" (1997) 9 *Journal of Environmental Law* 23

Chapter 8 : Hunting and Shooting

Clifford, S., "Animals" in *Stair Memorial Encyclopaedia*, Vol. 2

Murdoch, J.L., "Firearms" in *Stair Memorial Encyclopaedia*, Vol. 10

Parkes, C. and Thornley, J., *Fair Game—The Law of Country Sports and the Protection of Wildlife* (Pelham Books, new revised edition, 1994)

Satterley, G., *The Highland Game—Life on Scottish Sporting Estates* (Swan Hill Press, 1992)

Scott Robinson, S., *The Law of Game, Salmon and Freshwater Fishing in Scotland* (Butterworths, 1989)

Scott Robinson, S. and Barry, G.W.S., "Game" in *Stair Memorial Encylopaedia*, Vol. 11

Whitehead, G.K., *Half a Century of Scottish Deer Stalking* (Swan Hill Press, 1996)

Wigan, M., *The Scottish Highland Estate* (Swan Hill Press, 1991)

Chapter 9 : Fishing

Barry, G.S., "Salmon and Freshwater Fisheries" in *Stair Memorial Encyclopaedia*, Vol. 11

Gordon, W.M., *Scottish Land Law* (Scottish Universities Law Institute, 1989)

MacLeod, D., "The Unseasonable Salmon" 1995 *JLSS* 106

Rankine, J., *Law of Land-ownership in Scotland* (W. Green & Son, 4th edn, 1909)

Reid, K.G.C. *et al*, "Property" in *Stair Memorial Encyclopaedia*, Vol. 18

Scott Robinson, S., *The Law of Game, Salmon and Freshwater Fishing* (Butterworths, 1989)

Chapter 10 : The Protection of Species

Garner, J.F. and Jones, B.L., *Countryside Law* (Shaw & Sons, 3rd edn, 1997)

Lyster, S., *International Wildlife Law* (Grotius, 1985)

Reid, C.T., *Nature Conservation Law* (W. Green/Sweet & Maxwell, 1994)

Scottish Natural Heritage, *Wildlife, the Law and You*, 1998

Scottish Office, *Counting the Cost—The Continuing Persecution of Birds of Prey in Scotland*, 1998

Taylor, *Wildlife Crime: A Guide to Wildlife Law Enforcement in the United Kingdom*, 1998

Chapter 11 : Protection of Habitats

Ball, S., "Reforming the Law of Habitat Protection" in *Nature Conservation and Countryside Law* (C. Rodgers, ed., University of Wales Press, 1996)

Board of the Inland Revenue, *Capital Taxation and National Heritage*, 1986

Denyer-Green, B., *Wildlife and Countryside Act 1981* (Royal Institution of Chartered Surveyors, 1983)

Department of the Environment, *The Government's Reply to the First Report from the Environment Committee*, Cmnd. 9522, HMSO, 1985

Environment Committee, First Report, *Operation and Effectiveness of Part II of the Wildlife and Countryside Act*, Session 1984–85, HMSO, 1985

Haigh, N., *EEC Environmental Policy and Britain* (Longman, 2nd edn, 1987)

Lawrence Gould Consultants Ltd, *Wildlife and Countryside Act, Financial Guidelines for Management Agreements: Final Report*, 1985

Livingstone, L., Rowan-Robinson, J. and Cunningham, R., *Management Agreements for Nature Conservation* (Department of Land Economy Occasional Paper, Aberdeen University, 1990)

Lowe, P., Cox, G., MacEwen, M., O'Riordan, T. and Winter, M., *Countryside Conflicts* (Gower/Maurice Temple Smith, 1986)

National Audit Office, *Protecting and Managing Sites of Special Scientific Interest*, 1994

Reid, C.T., *Nature Conservation Law* (W. Green/Sweet & Maxwell, 1994)

Reynolds, F. and Sheate, W., "Reorganisation of the Conservation Authorities" in *Agriculture, Conservation and Land Use* (W. Howarth and C. Rodgers, eds, University of Wales Press, 1993)

Rodgers, C. and Bishop, J., *Management Agreements for Nature Conservation* (Royal Institution of Chartered Surveyors, 1998)

Scottish Biodiversity Group, *Biodiversity in Scotland: The Way Forward*, 1997

Scottish Office, *People and Nature: A New Approach to SSSI Designation in Scotland*, Consultation Paper, 1998

Scottish Office, *National Heritage Designations in Scotland*, 1998

Wightman, A., *Who Owns Scotland* (Canongate, 1996)

Withrington, D. and Jones, W., "The Enforcement of Conservation Legislation: Protecting Sites of Special Scientific Interest" in *Agriculture, Conservation and Land Use* (W. Howarth and C. Rodgers, eds, University of Wales Press, 1993)

Chapter 12 : Access: General Considerations

Gordon, G.H., *The Criminal Law of Scotland* (Scottish Universities Law Institute, 2nd edn, 1978)

McKenzie Skene, D., Rowan-Robinson, J. and Saunders, A.M., "Civil Liability for Injury and Damage Arising from Access to the Scottish Countryside", 1997 SLPQ 214, 274

Reid, K.C.G. *et al*, "Property" in *Stair Memorial Encyclopaedia*, Vol. 18

Rowan-Robinson, J. and McKenzie Skene, D., "Self Help and Access to the Countryside", 1998 *Juridical Review* 299

Scottish Executive, *Land Reform: Proposals for Reform*, White Paper, 1999

Scottish Natural Heritage, *Access to the Countryside for Open-air Recreation: Scottish Natural Heritage's Advice to Government*, 1999

Thomson, J.M., *Delictual Liability* (Butterworths, 1994)

Chapter 13 : Linear Access

Cusine, D. and Paisley, R., *Servitudes and Rights of Way* (Scottish Universities Law Institute, 1998)

Gordon, W.M., *Scottish Land Law* (Scottish Universities Law Institute, 1989), Chap. 24

Rowan-Robinson, J., Gordon, W.M. and Reid, C.T., *Public Access to the Countryside: A Guide to Law, Practice and Procedure in Scotland* (COSLA/Scottish Natural Heritage, 1993)

Rowan-Robinson, J., "Public Access to the Scottish Countryside" in *Nature Conservation and Countryside Law* (C. Rodgers, ed., University of Wales Press, 1996)

Scottish Rights of Way Society Ltd, *Rights of Way: A Guide to the Law in Scotland*, 1986

Scottish Rights of Way Society Ltd, "Proposals for the reform of the law relating to public rights of way in Scotland", 1990

Chapter 14 : Area Access

The Access Forum, *Scotland's Hills and Mountains: A Concordat on Access*, 1996

The Access Forum, *Access to the Countryside: The Access Forum's Advice to Scottish Natural Heritage*, 1998

Lyall, F., "Access to the Countryside", 1969 SLT (News) 197

Lyall, F., "Recreation, Landownership and the Countryside", 1970 3 *Juridical Review* 203

Rowan-Robinson, J., Gordon, W.M. and Reid, C.T., *Public Access to the Countryside: A Guide to Law, Practice and Procedure in Scotland* (COSLA/Scottish Natural Heritage, 1993)

Rowan-Robinson, J., *Review of Rights of Way Procedure* (SNH Review No. 9, 1994)

Rowan-Robinson, J. and Ross, A., "The Freedom to Roam and Implied Permission", 1998 *Edinburgh Law Review* (2) 225

Scottish Natural Heritage, *Enjoying the Outdoors: A Programme for Action*, 1994

Scottish Natural Heritage, *Access to the Countryside for Open-air Recreation: Scottish Natural Heritage's Advice to Government*, 1999

Chapter 15 : Water

Bain, E., "Water Supply" in *Stair Memorial Encyclopaedia*, Vol. 25, 1998

Ferguson, J., *The Law of Water and Water Rights in Scotland* (W. Green & Son, Edinburgh, 1907)

Gordon, W.M., *Scottish Land Law* (Scottish Universities Law Institute, Edinburgh, 1989), Chap. 7

Lyall, F., "Water and Water Rights" in *Stair Memorial Encyclopaedia*, Vol. 25

Lyall, F., "Water Pollution" in *Environmental Law in Scotland* (C. Reid, ed., W Green/Sweet & Maxwell, 2nd edn, 1997), Chap. 3

Poustie, M., "Bonny Banks no more? Water-based Recreational Conflict Management on Loch Lomond" (1997) *Water Law* 137

Reid, K., *The Law of Property in Scotland* (Butterworths, Edinburgh, 1996), Chap. 6

Scott Robinson, S., "Railways, Canals and Tramways" in *Stair Memorial Encyclopaedia*, Vol. 19

Scottish Affairs Committee, *The Work of the Scottish Water Authorities*, Session 1997–98, HMSO, 1998

Scottish Office Environment Department, National Planning Policy Guideline 11, "Sport, Physical Recreation and Open Space", 1996

Scottish Office, *Scottish Water Industry Review*, 1997

Scottish Sports Council, *Earth, Wind and Water*, 1996

Scottish Sports Council, *Calmer Waters*, 1997

Smith, C., Collar, N. and Poustie, M., *Pollution Control: The Law in Scotland* (T & T Clark, Edinburgh, 1997), Chap. 8

Stewart, J.B., "Recreation" in *Stair Memorial Encyclopaedia*, Vol. 19

Chapter 16 : Archaeological Sites

Barclay, G.J., "Forestry and Archaeology in Scotland, 1992 46(1) *Scottish Forestry* 27

Macinnes, L., "Archaeology as Land Use" in *Archaeological resource management in the UK: an introduction and handbook* (Hunter, J. and Ralston, I.B.M., Stroud, eds., 1993), p. 243

Miller, D.L.C. and Sheridan, A., "Treasure Trove in Scots Law" [1996] *Art and Antiquity* 393

Mynors, C., *Listed Buildings, Conservation Areas and Monuments* (Sweet & Maxwell, London, 3rd edn, 1999)

Pugh-Smith, J. and Samuels, J., *Archaeology in Law* (Sweet & Maxwell, London, 1996)

Scottish Office Environment Department, National Planning Policy Guideline 5, "Archaeology and Planning", 1994

Scottish Office Environment Department, Planning Advice Note 42, "Archaeology—The Planning Process and Scheduled Monument Protection", 1994

Secretary of State for Scotland and Historic Scotland, *Protecting the built heritage: a Green Paper,* Cm. 3267, HMSO, 1996

Shelbourn, C., "Protecting the Archaeological Heritage—a Step Forward?" [1982] JPL 686

Chapter 17 : Coastal Zone

Barry, G.W.S. and Birnie, P., "Fisheries" in *Stair Memorial Encylopaedia,* Vol. 11

Burbage, P. and Burbage, V., *Review of Scottish Coastal Issues,* consultant's report to the Scottish Office, 1994

Department of the Environment, *The Government's Response to the Second Report from the House of Commons Select Committee on the Environment, Coastal Zone Protection and Planning,* 1992

Environment Committee Second Report, *Coastal Zone Protection and Planning,* Session 1991–92, 1992

Gilmore, W.C., "Sea and Continental Shelf" in *Stair Memorial Encyclopaedia,* Vol. 21

Gordon, W.M., *Scottish Land Law* (Scottish Universities Law Institute, 1989)

Lyall, F., "Water Rights" in *Stair Memorial Encyclopaedia,* Vol. 25

Reid, K., *The Law of Property in Scotland* (Butterworths, 1996)

Scottish Natural Heritage, *A review of legislation relating to the coastal and marine environment in Scotland,* 1995

Scottish Office, *Scotland's Coasts,* 1996

Chapter 18 : Wayleaves

Cusine, D. and Paisley, R., *Servitudes and Rights of Way* (Scottish Universities Law Institute, Edinburgh, 1998), Chap. 26

Denyer-Green, B., "Specific Purposes, Specific Powers: The Powers of Privatised Utilities" in *Proceedings of the National Symposium, Compulsory Purchase: An Appropriate Power for the 21st Century* (DETR, 1999)

Hutchison, N., Cameron, A. and Rowan-Robinson, J., "Assessing the compensation for electricity wayleaves" (1999) 17 (2) *Journal of Property Investment and Finance* 176

Wilkinson, H.W., *Pipes, Mains, Cables and Sewers* (FT Law & Tax, 6th edn, 1995)

INDEX

COUNTRYSIDE LAW IN SCOTLAND